A+ Certification Bible

A+ Certification Bible

Ed Tetz, Glen E. Clarke, Joseph Phillips,
Angshuman Chakraborti, Meeta Gupta,
Mridula Parihar, Rashim Mogha

Hungry Minds™

Hungry Minds, Inc.

Best-Selling Books • Digital Downloads • e-Books • Answer Networks • e-Newsletters • Branded Web Sites • e-Learning

New York, NY ✦ Indianapolis, IN ✦ Cleveland, OH

A+ Certification Bible

Published by
Hungry Minds, Inc.
909 Third Avenue
New York, NY 10022
www.hungryminds.com

Library of Congress Catalog Card No.: 2001090749

ISBN: 0-7645-4810-7

Printed in the United States of America

10 9 8 7 6 5 4 3 2 1

1P/RS/QX/QR/IN

Distributed in the United States by Hungry Minds, Inc.

Distributed by CDG Books Canada Inc. for Canada; by Transworld Publishers Limited in the United Kingdom; by IDG Norge Books for Norway; by IDG Sweden Books for Sweden; by IDG Books Australia Publishing Corporation Pty. Ltd. for Australia and New Zealand; by TransQuest Publishers Pte Ltd. for Singapore, Malaysia, Thailand, Indonesia, and Hong Kong; by Gotop Information Inc. for Taiwan; by ICG Muse, Inc. for Japan; by Intersoft for South Africa; by Eyrolles for France; by International Thomson Publishing for Germany, Austria, and Switzerland; by Distribuidora Cuspide for Argentina; by LR International for Brazil; by Galileo Libros for Chile; by Ediciones ZETA S.C.R. Ltda. for Peru; by WS Computer Publishing Corporation, Inc., for the Philippines; by Contemporanea de Ediciones for Venezuela; by Express Computer Distributors for the Caribbean and West Indies; by Micronesia Media Distributor, Inc. for Micronesia; by Chips Computadoras S.A. de C.V. for Mexico; by Editorial Norma de Panama S.A. for Panama; by American Bookshops for Finland.

For general information on Hungry Minds' products and services please contact our Customer Care department within the U.S. at 800-762-2974, outside the U.S. at 317-572-3993 or fax 317-572-4002.

For sales inquiries and reseller information, including discounts, premium and bulk quantity sales, and foreign-language translations, please contact our Customer Care department at 800-434-3422, fax 317-572-4002 or write to Hungry Minds, Inc., Attn: Customer Care Department, 10475 Crosspoint Boulevard, Indianapolis, IN 46256.

For information on licensing foreign or domestic rights, please contact our Sub-Rights Customer Care department at 212-884-5000.

For information on using Hungry Minds' products and services in the classroom or for ordering examination copies, please contact our Educational Sales department at 800-434-2086 or fax 317-572-4005.

For press review copies, author interviews, or other publicity information, please contact our Public Relations department at 317-572-3168 or fax 317-572-4168.

For authorization to photocopy items for corporate, personal, or educational use, please contact Copyright Clearance Center, 222 Rosewood Drive, Danvers, MA 01923, or fax 978-750-4470.

About the Authors

Edward Tetz graduated from Saint Lawrence College in Cornwall, Ontario with a degree in Business Administration in 1990. He spent a short time in computer sales, which eventually led to a computer support position. He has spent the last eight years performing system and LAN support for small and large organizations. In 1994 he added training to his repertoire. He holds the following certifications: A+, Microsoft Certified Trainer (MCT), Microsoft Certified Systems Engineer (MCSE), and Chauncey Group's Certified Technical Trainer (CTT). Over his years of work experience, he has supported Apple Macintosh, IBM OS/2, Linux, Novell NetWare, and all Microsoft operating systems from MS-DOS to Windows 2000. He is currently an Information Technology Coordinator and an Instructor for PBSC, a national training company in Canada. Most of the training that he delivers is Microsoft-certified, but he also delivers technical training outside of that product line. He welcomes comments from his readers and can be contacted at ed_tetz@hotmail.com.

Glen E. Clarke is a Microsoft Certified Systems Engineer (MCSE), Microsoft Certified Solution Developer (MCSD), and Microsoft Certified Trainer (MCT). Glen is also an A+ certified technician and holds Prosoft's Certified Internet Webmaster-Certified Instructor certification (CIWCI). Glen currently works as a technical trainer for PBSC, one of Canada's largest technical training centers, where he delivers the A+ courses and Microsoft Certified Curriculum for the MCSE and MCSD programs. When he's not working, Glen loves to spend quality time with his wife, Tanya, and their two children, Sara and Brendon. He is an active member of the martial arts community, where he currently holds his first-degree black belt in Tae Kwon Do. You can contact Glen at gleneclarke@hotmail.com.

Joseph Phillips is an MCSE, MCT, and CTT, as well as a CompTIA A+ and Network+ Certified Technician. Joseph has taught, consulted on, and written about computer technologies since 1993. When he's not working with computers, you can find Joseph on the golf course, behind a camera, or on the working end of a fly rod. Sometimes you can catch him at www.josephphillips.com.

Angshuman Chakraborti is an MCSD and an MCSE. He is currently employed with NIIT Ltd. as a consultant. He has been with NIIT for the last 4 years. He spent the first two years training career students and professionals in technologies, including C, C++, Visual C++, Windows NT, TCP/IP, SQL, Sybase, HTML, JAVA, Visual Basic, and JavaScript. The second two years has been spent leading teams to create instructor-led training material for various clients. During this period, he has also worked as a subject matter expert in various technologies, including Linux, Mac OS, Cisco Networking (CCNA), Windows 2000, JavaScript, and DHTML, among others. His responsibilities also include training development executives, managing projects, and instructionally and technically reviewing training material.

Meeta Gupta is certified in C++, JAVA, JFC/Swing, Java Script, Visual Basic 5.0–6.0, VBA, HTML, DHTML, SQL, Sybase, MS Access, UML, Windows NT 4.0, Novell NetWare 4.x, UNIX SCO, and MAC OS 9. She is presently employed as a development executive with NIIT Ltd., with one year of experience in planning, organizing, writing, and maintaining technical documentation. Meeta also possesses 1½ years of experience as a trainer at NIIT Ltd., where she was responsible for conducting interactive training modules for varied audiences and maintaining hardware and software including LAN (Novell NetWare).

Mridula Parihar is a Microsoft Certified Solution Developer (MCSD). She has worked with NIIT Ltd. for two years. In her first year, she worked as a technical instructor in the Career Education Group (CEG) division of NIIT Ltd. She has been working with the Knowledge Solutions Business (KSB) group for the last 12 months. Here, Mridula has had the opportunity to work on many technical projects. Her work involves design, development, testing, and implementation of instructor-led training courses. Also, she handles the additional responsibility of ensuring ISO compliance.

Rashim Mogha is a Microsoft Certified Solution Developer (MCSD). She has worked for two years at NIIT Ltd. Her first year was spent in the Career Education Group (CEG), where she taught NIIT students, handled computer installation and maintenance, and managed resources. For the past year, she has been working in the Knowledge Solutions Business (KSB) division of NIIT. In the KSB division, Rashim has had the opportunity to work on varied technical assignments. Her work involves design, development, testing, and implementation of instructor-led training courses. Her primary responsibilities include training development executives, project management, instructional review, technical review, and ensuring ISO compliance.

Credits

Acquisitions Editors
Nancy Maragioglio
Katie Feltman

Project Editors
Amanda Munz
Keith Cline

Technical Editors
Brian McCann
Trevor Kay

Question Writer
Joseph Phillips

Copy Editors
Gabrielle Chosney
Maryann Steinhart
Kyle Looper
Pat O'Brien
James Russell
Barry Childs-Helton
Rebekah Mancilla

Editorial Managers
Ami Frank Sullivan
Kyle Looper

Project Coordinators
Regina Snyder
Emily Wichlinski
Joe Shines

Graphics and Production Specialists
Amy Adrian
LeAndra Johnson
Heather Pope
Kendra Span
Brian Torwelle
Jeremey Unger
Erin Zeltner

Quality Control Technicians
Laura Albert
John Greenough
Andy Hollandbeck
David Faust
Susan Moritz
Luisa Perez
Carl Pierce
Nancy Price
Marianne Santy
Charles Spencer

Permissions Editor
Laura Moss

Media Development Specialist
Brock Bigard

Media Development Coordinator
Marisa Pearman

Proofreading and Indexing
TECHBOOKS Production Services, Inc.

I would like to dedicate this book to my wife, Sharon, and my children, Emily and Mackenzie. They have put up with a lot during the writing of this book, especially the loss of my time, which is now gone forever. — Ed

This book is dedicated to my beautiful wife, Tanya, who has shown amazing support throughout the long nights and early mornings of this book. If it were not for your love and understanding, I would not have had the inspiration to write. — Glen

This book is dedicated to my many friends: Mary Jane, Don, Mick, Linda Linda, Mark and Antonietta of Il Gargona, Kenny, Greg, Stacey, Mary, Nancy, Derek, Jason, Lila, and so many others. Thank you all for your friendship. — Joe

Preface

Welcome to the A+ Certification Bible. This book is intended to help people who are interested in pursuing their A+ Certification. It covers material that will be found on both of the required A+ Certification Exams (A+ Core Hardware Exam and A+ OS Technologies Exam). The layout of this book has been designed to make the material easy to digest and navigate. We hope that you enjoy your experience with this book.

Once you have attained your A+ Certification, you may want to pursue another major industry certification, such as CompTIA's Network+, CompTIA's Server+, CompTIA's Linux+, Microsoft's MCSE, Novell's CNE, or Cisco's CCNA. Any of these certifications will make you more valuable to your current employer or future employers. Good luck on your path to certification.

Who Should Read this Book?

This book is designed as a study aid for people who plan to write their A+ certification exams from CompTIA. If you are interested in the A+ certification, this book is the only study guide that you will need. And because it provides more detailed information than is required for the exam, it can be used as a reference at a later date.

What is CompTIA?

CompTIA (Computer Technology Industry Association) is an association whose members come from all areas of the computing industry. It has corporate memberships, which include more than 10,000 companies; the IT professionals in its membership come from more than 50 countries. Its main goal is to act as a unifying force to create vendor neutral certifications. You can find more information about CompTIA at http://www.comptia.org.

What is A+?

From 1999 to 2000, CompTIA saw a 40 percent increase in the number of people taking the A+ certification exam. Over 116,000 people passed this certification in 2000, bringing the number of certified professionals to over 260,000. The A+ certification is clearly one of the fastest growing certifications in the industry.

Structure of this Book

This book is broken down into eight parts. Each part focuses on a different set of components from either the A+ Core Hardware exam or the A+ OS Technologies exam. The only exception to this rule is Part VII, which covers the networking components from both exams.

Part I: A+ Core Hardware Exam — Hardware Basics

Part I covers the basics of all the hardware components that make up your computer. The first chapter provides an overview of some of the basic components that will then be examined in subsequent chapters. Components that will be examined include: CPUs, motherboards, RAM, CMOS, ports, cables, and printers. Part I concludes with a review of major system resources, such as IRQs, that are used by the major types of devices.

Part II: A+ Core Hardware Exam — Installing and Configuring Hardware

Part II focuses on installation of various devices. It includes an examination of internal hard drives, modems, USB peripherals, FireWire, and components that are included in portable devices.

Part III: A+ Core Hardware Exam — Maintenance and Troubleshooting

Part III provides information about maintaining computer devices, including preventive maintenance and safety procedures, how to handle and care for computer components, and maintenance specifically related to printers. Part III ends with a chapter that covers basic troubleshooting of each of the major components that make up your computer.

Part IV: A+ Operating System (OS) Technologies Exam — Operating System Basics

Part IV introduces the different operating systems, providing a comparison of Windows 9x systems and Windows 2000, a description of different commands that can be used from command prompt, and a discussion of graphical operating systems that carry out major system functions. These system functions include routing disk maintenance procedures. Part IV also discusses memory management and configuration for MS-DOS and Windows 9x.

Part V: A+ Operating System (OS) Technologies Exam — Installing and Configuring Operating Systems

Part V of the book discusses how to get the OS going. It includes chapters on installing and upgrading Windows, how to control the boot process, and how to work with devices and applications. When working with applications, the differences between 16-bit, 32-bit and MS-DOS based applications are discussed.

Part VI: A+ Operating System (OS) Technologies Exam — Troubleshooting Operating Systems

The focus of Part VI is how to troubleshoot problems from the OS perspective. This part examines different tools that can be used to troubleshoot aspects of your operating system and common problems that may arise in day-to-day use of the operating system. Since many computer problems arise from viruses, there is a section that deals with defining and dealing with viruses.

Part VII: A+ Exams — Networking

Part VII deals with networking. An overview of underlying network hardware — including cabling, network cards, and protocols — is provided, as well as a discussion about networking from the OS level and Internet access methods.

Appendixes

This book has four appendixes. The appendixes include a description of what is found on the accompanying CD-ROM, an objective mapping table to let you know which chapters cover which exam objectives, a sample exam, and some exam-taking tips.

Chapter Structure

Each chapter in this book follows a common structure:

+ **Objectives:** A bulleted list that states the specific exam objectives that will be covered in the chapter.

+ **Pre-Test:** A short test that assesses your knowledge of the material in the chapter. The pre-test questions will help you identify areas to focus on.

+ **The body of the chapter** follows the Pre-Test.

+ **Key Point Summary:** A summary of the crucial facts in the chapter.

✦ **Study Guide:** The study guide in each chapter contains some or all of the following elements.

   • **Assessment Questions:** Multiple-choice questions, similar to the ones you will see on the exam, that test your knowledge of material presented in the chapter.

   • **Scenarios:** Exercises that require you to apply your critical thinking skills and understanding of the chapter material to solve a hypothetical problem.

   • **Labs:** Hands-on or paper-based exercises that follow a step-by-step approach. Labs are designed to help you solidify the material that is in the chapter.

   • **Answers** to Pre-Test questions, Assessment Questions, Scenarios, and Labs.

Icons Used in this Book

In order to draw attention to content in the chapter, a number of icons are used. These icons and their uses include the following:

 This icon is used when there is something that is discussed or being done in a lab that could have serious consequences to you or your computer.

 This icon is used to reference information that is found elsewhere in the book.

 This icon is used to provide tips that may help you in the exam. It may also be used to stress points that are important to the exam.

 This icon is used to deliver material that discusses practices that are opposite to those presented in the study material and the exam.

 This icon denotes test objectives that are to be covered in a section.

 This icon is used for tips or facts that are worth noting, but are not related specifically to the exam.

Exam Components

The A+ Certification exams can be scheduled at Vue or Prometric testing centers. For more information about scheduling your exam, check the Testing Locations page on CompTIA's Web site at `http://www.comptia.org/certification/ test_locations.htm`.

Pricing

As of January 1, 2001, the cost of taking the A+ exams is $82 US per exam for corporate members and $132 US per exam for non-members.

What's on the exam?

The objectives for the A+ Core Hardware exam are found in Table 1, and the objectives for the A+ OS Technologies exam are found in Table 2.

Table 1 A+ Core Hardware Exam (220-201)	
Domain	**% of Examination**
1.0 Installation, Configuration and Upgrading	30%
2.0 Diagnosing and Troubleshooting	30%
3.0 Preventive Maintenance	5%
4.0 Motherboard/Processors/Memory	15%
5.0 Printers	10%
6.0 Basic Networking	10%
Total	100%

Table 2
A+ OS Technologies Exam (220-202)

Domain	% of Examination
1.0 OS Fundamentals	30%
2.0 Installation, Configuration and Upgrading	15%
3.0 Diagnosing and Troubleshooting	40%
4.0 Networks	15%
Total	100%

Passing scores

CompTIA uses a scale score to determine the total number of points that each question on the exam will be calculated out of. This scale score is between 100 and 900. In any case, the passing score (not a percentage due to the scale) is 683 or 76% for the A+ Core Hardware exam and 614 or 68% for the A+ OS Technologies exam. The scale score system allows the number of points assigned to questions to vary between each copy of the exam, which makes it harder for test candidates to compare scores across exams.

The revised exams for A+ were released January 31, 2001. Each exam contains 70 questions, and you will have 90 minutes to complete each exam. In the third quarter of 2001, the exams are scheduled to become adaptive. Adaptive exams ask a minimal number of questions (usually about 15), and then will ask additional questions based on any incorrect answers. Appendix D provides additional information about the differences between standard and adaptive exams.

Acknowledgments

I would like to thank Hungry Minds, Inc., especially Nancy Maragioglio, the acquisitions editor who got me involved with this project. It has always been great to work with her. That feeling of thanks also goes out to Amanda Munz, the project editor with whom I worked very closely. Both Nancy and Amanda made this process fulfilling. Not least, I want to thank the technical editors, copy editors, and other staff at Hungry Minds who helped bring this book to print. — Ed

First, I would like to thank Ed Tetz for getting me involved in this project. I would also like to thank the staff at Hungry Minds, Inc., especially Nancy Maragioglio, Acquisitions Editor, and Amanda Munz, Project Editor. You all have made this experience one of the most enjoyable of my career. — Glen

Many thanks to Nancy Maragioglio for asking me to write this book and for her guidance and support. Thanks also to Amanda Munz for her incredible patience and leadership, and to Ed Tetz and Glen Clarke for their hard work and late nights invested in this book. Many thanks to the technical editors, copy editors, and countless other individuals who've made this book a success — Joe

Contents at a Glance

Contents

Chapter 7: Printer Operations and Components 169

Chapter 8: System Resources Used By Devices 193

Part II Installing and Configuring Hardware   227

Part III: Maintenance and Troubleshooting   333

Chapter 12: Preventive Maintenance and Safety Procedures 335

Chapter 13: Managing Replaceable Components 363

Part IV: Operating System Basics   463

Part V: Installing and Configuring Operating Systems   663

Hardware Basics

As an A+ Certified Technician, not only do you have to understand how to troubleshoot and fix hardware-related problems, you also have to understand an entire new dictionary of terms. These terms are ones used in the computer industry describing a number of different hardware technologies.

In Part I, you will explore the common components that are found in a computer system. Then you will be walked through the wonderful world of different hardware technologies, from motherboards, CPUs, and RAM technologies to different types of ports and connectors, as well as printer operations.

At the end of this part, Chapter 8 will cover how to troubleshoot hardware resources. It will discuss some of the common problems that occur when installing devices in a system that deals with conflicting I/O addresses or IRQs.

Basic Terms, Concepts, and Functions of System Modules

EXAM OBJECTIVES

Exam 220-201 ✦ **A+ Core Hardware**

✦ **1.1** Identify basic terms, concepts, and functions of system modules, including how each module should work during normal operation and during the boot process. Examples of concepts and modules are:

- System board
- Power supply
- Processor/CPU
- Memory
- Storage devices
- Monitor
- Modem
- Firmware
- BIOS
- CMOS
- LCD (portable systems)
- Ports
- PDA (Personal Digital Assistant)

CHAPTER PRE-TEST

1. What computer component stores settings about devices such as hard drives?

2. What are the two major technologies that are used for hard drives in today's computers?

3. What is the difference between firmware and software?

4. The BIOS of your computer contains settings for the types of hard drives that are installed and for the current time. True or False?

5. All devices receive their power from the system board. True or False?

6. What is the first step in the boot process?

7. Modems perform what type of signal conversion?

8. Name at least two technologies that are generally associated with portable computers.

✦ Answers to these questions can be found at the end of the chapter. ✦

This chapter defines basic terms and provides a brief overview of many topics that will be covered in this book. By the time you finish reading this chapter, you should have a good understanding of the major components of the personal computer, from the motherboard to the monitor.

System Board

Objective

1.1 Identify basic terms, concepts, and functions of system modules, including how each module should work during normal operation and during the boot process. Content may include the following: System board

The term *system board* can be used to describe any number of circuit boards that make up the internals of your computer, but it is used most often to describe the *motherboard*. The motherboard is the main board in your computer that contains the BIOS chips, RAM, I/O ports, and CPU. This board maintains the electrical pathways that enable all other components to communicate with each other.

In some computers, you will hear the term *daughter board* used. A daughter board is a board that contains some of the chips that should have been put on the motherboard, but were not — perhaps due to space limitations or other reasons.

Cross-Reference   More information about motherboards is provided in Chapter 3.

Power supply

Objective

1.1 Identify basic terms, concepts, and functions of system modules, including how each module should work during normal operation and during the boot process. Content may include the following: Power supply.

The power supply does exactly what its name suggests: supplies power to the rest of the components in the computer. The power supply takes 120 volts or 240 volts (depending on the country you are in) from your building and converts it to output ranging from 5 volts down to 1.5 volts. It contains a number of leads that supply different voltages for different types of devices (such as floppy drives and hard drives).

Cross-Reference   More information about power supplies is provided in Chapter 12.

Processor/CPU

1.1 Identify basic terms, concepts, and functions of system modules, including how each module should work during normal operation and during the boot process. Content may include the following: Processor/CPU

The processor is the "brains of the organization," so to speak. It has been designed to do very few things, but do them extremely fast. The processor performs a limited set of calculations based on requests from the operating system and controls access to system memory. Processor speed is measured in several different ways, including clock cycles, Megahertz (MHz), or millions of instructions per second (MIPS). Either of these measures will give you an estimate of the processor's power.

The speed of early processors ranged from 4–8MHz, while today's processors have broken the Gigahertz (GHz) mark.

Cross-Reference   More information about processors is provided in Chapter 2.

Memory

1.1 Identify basic terms, concepts, and functions of system modules, including how each module should work during normal operation and during the boot process. Content may include the following: Memory

RAM *(Random Access Memory)* is the computer's primary working memory. The OS *(Operating System)* controls the computer's functions. When the OS loads, it loads into RAM; when applications load, they load into RAM; when you open documents, they load into RAM; and when you need to send output to your monitor, the output is loaded into RAM before it hits your monitor.

RAM is used in many areas of your computer, and in many different forms. It is used by the base OS in one big chunk that most people think of as RAM, but it is also implemented as processor cache (L1 and L2), video RAM for your video card, and any number of components that claim to have caching.

RAM speeds are usually measured in nanoseconds. One nanosecond is a billionth of a second.

There are many delivery forms for RAM. These include DIMM and SIMM packaging.

Cross-Reference   More information about memory is provided in Chapter 4.

Firmware

 Objective **1.1** Identify basic terms, concepts, and functions of system modules, including how each module should work during normal operation and during the boot process. Content may include the following: Firmware

It is human nature to want to classify everything we see or work with into categories. Many of these categories seem very distinct until something comes along to challenge our opinions, and then the waters become murky. Take the subject of hardware and software, for example, which at one time were thought to be distinct and separate entities. *Software* is programming code that is stored on your disk, or some other form of media. *Hardware* refers to the physical components — boards, peripherals, and other equipment — that make up your computer. Firmware fills in a middle ground between these two, where the distinct line begins to disappear.

Firmware is programming code (software) that is contained in or stored on the IC (Integrated Circuit) chips (hardware) on your computer. This combination of hardware and software makes up the BIOS on several different devices, with potential settings stored in CMOS.

BIOS

 Objective **1.1** Identify basic terms, concepts, and functions of system modules, including how each module should work during normal operation and during the boot process. Content may include the following: BIOS

BIOS is short for *Basic Input Output System*. The BIOS is actually software that is stored in a ROM (Read Only Memory*)* chip on your motherboard. Most systems today use a Flash EPROM (Erasable Programmable ROM) so that the user can update them.

The BIOS is responsible for controlling or managing the POST (Power On Self Test), the boot process, and the interaction of components on the motherboard. These are all low-level processes that the BIOS is responsible for, but still extremely important to your system.

 Cross-Reference More information about BIOS is provided in Chapter 3.

CMOS

 Objective **1.1** Identify basic terms, concepts, and functions of system modules, including how each module should work during normal operation and during the boot process. Content may include the following: CMOS

CMOS is short for *Complementary Metal-Oxide Semiconductor*, which is the type of manufacturing process that creates most integrated circuits. This development process is used to create the following:

- ✦ High-density DRAM (Dynamic Random Access Memory)
- ✦ High-speed processors
- ✦ Low-power devices for mobile use

The term *complementary* refers to the fact that these chips use negatively and positively charged transistors (which complement each other) to store information. Most RAM chips rely on CMOS technology to store information, but when discussing CMOS, you will probably be referring to the hardware configuration settings that are saved between reboots of your computer. These settings include:

- ✦ Hard drives and floppy drives
- ✦ Memory
- ✦ Keyboard
- ✦ Mouse
- ✦ Reserved resources (such as IRQ, I/O addresses, and DMA channels)
- ✦ Power on password
- ✦ Date
- ✦ Time
- ✦ ACPI (Advance Configuration Power Interface)

    More information about CMOS is provided in Chapter 5.

Storage Devices

 1.1 Identify basic terms, concepts, and functions of system modules, including how each module should work during normal operation and during the boot process. Content may include the following: Storage devices

Storage devices on your computer are responsible for storing data, such as the operating system, applications, and actual output of applications or user data. Depending on the amount and type of data, there are three basic types of devices to work with:

- ✦ Floppy drives, including some of the high-capacity formats such as 120MB Superdisks
- ✦ Hard drives, including some of the removable cartridge drives such as SyQuest drives
- ✦ Optical drives, including CD-ROM and DVD drives

Any one of these formats will enable you to read data into your computer, and some can be used for storing data as well.

When dealing with hard drives, there are two major attachment interfaces: IDE (Integrated Device Electronics) or ATA (AT Attachment), and SCSI (Small Computer System Interface). ATA opens up the IDE interface to accept a wider variety of devices. There has been a long ongoing battle for speed and performance between IDE and SCSI, but in general, SCSI provides faster and more reliable transportation.

IEEE-1394 or FireWire provides a fast enough bus to enable hard drives to be attached to a computer by this method. There are also PCMCIA or PC Card hard drives that can be used with your computer.

The type of drives that you will be attaching to your computer will depend on the types that are supported by your motherboard or I/O cards.

 More information about hard drives and storage devices is supplied in Chapter 9.

Monitor

 1.1 Identify basic terms, concepts, and functions of system modules, including how each module should work during normal operation and during the boot process. Content may include the following: Monitor

The different types of buses that can be used to provide video services include:

✦ ISA, which runs at a speed of 8 MHz

✦ PCI, which runs at a speed of 33 MHz

✦ AGP, which runs at a speed of 66 MHz

You have probably already guessed that the faster the bus speed, the faster your video card is likely to function. The AGP bus was designed specifically for video. In addition to a fast bus speed, video performance and color depth is provided by RAM or Video RAM. This RAM is found on the video card itself. Some high-end video cards will also have a small processor to handle some of the work of displaying information on your monitor.

Video cards traditionally allow for color depths that include:

✦ 4 bit or 16 colors

✦ 8 bit or 256 colors

✦ 16 bit or 65 thousand colors

✦ 24 bit or 16 million colors

✦ 32 bit or 4 billion colors

Screen resolutions usually include:

✦ 640 x 480

✦ 800 x 600

✦ 1024 x 768

✦ 1152 x 864

✦ 1280 x 1024

✦ 1600 x 1200

Modern video cards follow the SVGA (Super Video Graphics Array) standard, but support at least VGA as well. The VGA standard is output in 16 colors at 640 x 480.

 Cross-Reference More information about monitors and video is supplied in Chapter 10.

Modem

 Objective **1.1** Identify basic terms, concepts, and functions of system modules, including how each module should work during normal operation and during the boot process. Content may include the following: Modem

Modem is short for *Modulator Demodulator*. Modulation refers to the conversion of a digital signal to an analog signal, and demodulation reverses this process. Your computer is digital, while the phone lines that you want to communicate over are analog. In order to allow the digital signal to be passed over the analog lines, you must use a modem.

The speeds at which modems operate have been increasing since their use with computers. They started with transfer rates of 300 bps (bits per second) and have moved up to 115 Kbps.

Today, there are more and more cases where modems have been replaced with other remote connectivity options, such as ADSL, ISDN, and Broadband Cable.

Modems may be connected to your computer through the serial port, the ISA bus, or the PCI bus. Modems may support synchronous or asynchronous communication. Most modems that are purchased for a computer are asynchronous.

 Cross-Reference More information about modems is provided in Chapter 10.

LCD and Portable Systems

 1.1 Identify basic terms, concepts, and functions of system modules, including how each module should work during normal operation and during the boot process. Content may include the following: LCD (portable systems)

Portable, or laptop, systems have a special place in the hardware technology side of computing. Portable systems make use of technologies that are not normally used by desktop or stationary computers.

In addition to standard desktop components such as hard drives, floppy drives, and CD-ROMs, you can expect to find many of the following components in use with your portable system:

✦ LCD (Liquid Crystal Display) panels

✦ PCMCIA (Personal Computer Memory Card International Association) or PC Card slot

✦ Battery

✦ Low-power CPU

✦ Port Replicator or Docking Station

LCD panels provide a low-power, flat, thin display solution that is required by laptop systems. This technology is actually making its way into the desktop market. There are a few standard types of LCD displays — active matrix, passive matrix, and dual scan — that differ in the way power is supplied to the diodes that make up the display and in the quality of the output.

PC Card slots offer an easy expansion slot for laptop computers. PCI and ISA slots are not suited to portable device use due to their size and lack of hot swapping. Enter PC Card technology. The cards fit the size requirements for portable use since they are about the size of credit cards. They support hot swapping and Plug-and-Play for easy insertion and removal. Most systems come with support for Type I, II, or III cards. One of the differences in the type specification is the height of the cards. PC Cards offer a simple and expandable bus for portable device users, but may be succeeded by USB (Universal Serial Bus) devices for a number of components. The most used PC Cards have been network cards and modems, which are often integrated onto the motherboard of most new laptops.

Since most portable devices are used remotely, batteries are another technology component that play a big role in the development. Batteries come in three basic flavors:

✦ Nickel-Cadmium (NiCad)

✦ Nickel-Metal Hydride (NiMH)

✦ Lithium-Ion (LiIon)

Nickel-Metal Hydride batteries replaced Nickel-Cadmium batteries, since they seemed to be less susceptible to developing a charging memory. The charging memory is developed when the battery is regularly charged, and then only used a small amount before recharging. After repeating this usage pattern over several charges, the battery would only last for a short period of time. Lithium-Ion batteries are even more memory-free and do a better job of holding their charge when not in use, and their charge lasts longer when in use.

Battery life in your portable device depends on use, power management, and the battery itself.

In order to extend the battery life of your portable device as much as possible, manufacturers developed low-power versions of their CPUs. These low-power versions were then combined with motherboards that offered enhanced power management. This allowed the speed of the processor to be reduced when not in use, further reducing power consumption.

Since the space inside a portable device is so precious, port replicators and docking stations were created, which allows for a minimum of resources built into the unit. For example, you can purchase an ultra-light portable computer that comes with only one external port, a CD-ROM, and no floppy drive. Such a computer is great when you want to carry it around, but lousy when it comes to getting data in and out of the unit. Enter the port replicator or docking station that connects to the one external (usually proprietary) connector on the back of the unit. The port replicator is usually a smaller unit than the docking station, and usually only provides additional ports such as video, serial, parallel, and additional PCMCIA slots; however, it could also provide networking, floppy disk, and additional battery. The docking station is a larger unit that can provide additional hard drives, PCI and ISA slots, and other components that would normally be included in desktop computer.

More information about portable systems is provided in Chapter 11.

Boot Process

1.1 Identify basic terms, concepts, and functions of system modules, including how each module should work during normal operation and during the boot process. Content may include the following: Boot process

The boot process begins with the application of electricity to your computer, which starts the POST (Power On Self Test) and moves through a procedure that locates a bootable device and loads an operating system.

The POST starts the procedure and performs the following tasks:

✦ Testing RAM

✦ Locating devices, such as hard drives and floppy drives

✦ Searching drives for bootable devices

✦ Loading the boot sector from a bootable device

✦ Transferring control of computer to operating system

Bootable devices are scanned for in the order of preference that is specified in the computer's CMOS — usually the A: drive, C: drive, CD-ROM, and network. For each device, the boot sector is examined for a program to load an OS. For hard drives, the boot sector will be on the partition that is marked as active.

The program that is searched for in the boot sector is the boot loader — `io.sys` on Windows 9x computers and `ntldr` on Windows NT and Windows 2000 computers. The boot loader takes control of the computer from the POST process. It is also responsible for locating the files that make up the rest of the OS and loading them, or reporting the errors.

Cross-Reference   More information about the boot process is provided in Chapter 22.

Ports

Sailing ports provide a location for ships to load and unload goods that are being transferred from one location to another. On your computer, ports act as connection points for cables, enabling the transfer of data between your computer and another device. There are several different types of connectors and cables that are used to join devices together. The list of devices that can be communicated with through the different types of ports is limitless. Some of the basic types of ports and their uses are listed in Table 1-1.

Table 1-1 Basic Types of Ports	
Port	**Use**
Serial	Connects serial devices, such as modems, to your computer.
Parallel	Connects parallel devices, such as printers, to your computer.
Video	Connects a monitor to your computer.
USB	Connects various types of devices to your computer. This port is being used to connect new versions of devices that would have used other ports in the past. Devices that use this port include: printers, modems, mice, keyboards, and scanners.
Keyboard	Connects a keyboard to your computer.
Mouse	Connects a mouse to your computer.

Cross-Reference More information about the ports on your computer is provided in Chapter 6.

PDA (Personal Digital Assistant)

It was less than twenty years ago when standard computers came with 4K of memory and you loaded programs from audiotape. Ten years ago, you were able to buy a Sharp Electronic Organizer with 256K of memory. The Sharp device was about the size of a bundle of dollar bills (when closed) with a small qwerty keyboard and an eight-line by forty-character display. These devices were capable of storing schedules, addresses, and a small database. I used to keep our corporate price list in mine. At the time, I thought that this device was absolutely amazing.

Today, there are two main types of PDA devices on the market: the devices that run the Palm OS and those that run Windows for Pocket PC. Windows for Pocket PC is the evolved cousin of Microsoft's Windows CE (Consumer Electronics). Both types of devices come with cradles that act as battery charges and allow a connection to a desktop computer through a USB connection. This connection to the computer allows you to synchronize your schedule and e-mail with your office scheduling and e-mail systems.

Current versions of the Palm PDA from Palm Inc. are about half the size of a CD-ROM jewel case. They sport a 65,000 color display, 8MB of RAM, and a proprietary expansion card slot that allows you to add storage space and applications to your Palm PDA.

Current versions of Pocket PC PDAs — such as the Compaq iPAQ — come with a scaled-back version of Microsoft office (Word and Excel), Internet Explorer, and Microsoft Reader (which supports a new electronic book format). This PDA includes a 206 MHz Intel processor, 64MB of RAM and 16MB of Flash ROM memory. The screen on the PDA supports 4,096 colors, and it supports a PC card (PCMCIA card) and CF card (Compact Flash, which is a storage medium) expansion.

These new PDAs are capable of functioning as mini-extensions of your desktop computer.

Key Point Summary

This chapter provides an overview of the major components found in a computer system, including:

✦ The system board, which contains most of the computer circuitry.

✦ The power supply, which converts building AC to useable DC for the computer.

✦ The processor/CPU, which efficiently executes instructions for the OS.

✦ The memory, which is used to hold working data and application code.

✦ The storage devices, which are long term storage areas.

✦ The monitor, which is used to display data from the computer.

✦ The modem, which is used to communicate with other devices.

✦ The firmware, which is a crossbreed between hardware and software.

✦ The BIOS, which are low-level internal communication routines.

✦ The CMOS, which is a storage area for configuration settings.

✦ The LCD and portable systems, which contain unique hardware to support portability.

✦ The ports, which are used as connection points for other devices.

✦ The PDA (Personal Digital Assistant), which is used to place some computing power in your shirt pocket.

✦　　✦　　✦

STUDY GUIDE

This Study Guide will test your knowledge of the hardware components found in your computer. Unlike the study guides found in other chapters, this study guide will assess your knowledge of concepts and terminology discussed in future chapters — in much the same way as a Chapter Pre-Test. The study guides found in other chapters will deal with many of the same areas discussed here, but will cover that material in greater detail. This Study Guide consists of 15 assessment questions.

Assessment Questions

1. Which of the following components is not usually found on a motherboard?

   A. Hard drive controller

   B. DVD drive controller

   C. Memory

   D. Video adapter

2. What type of memory is not usually found on a motherboard?

   A. CMOS memory

   B. L1 Cache

   C. L2 Cache

   D. DIMM

3. The power supply converts 110 volt AC current to which of the following?

   A. 3.3 volts and 5 volts

   B. 3.3 volts

   C. 6 volts

   D. 12 volts

4. What is the primary purpose of the processor?

   A. To convert digital signals into analog signals

   B. To process signals so that they can be displayed on your monitor

   C. To carry out instructions from the operating system

   D. To convert 16-bit data into 8- or 32-bit data

5. What unit is used to measure RAM speed?

    A. Milliseconds

    B. Gigaseconds

    C. Picoseconds

    D. Nanoseconds

6. Which of the following bus types is the hard drive usually attached to? (Select two)

    A. ADE

    B. IDE

    C. PCA

    D. SCSI

7. What standard do most current monitors follow?

    A. VGA

    B. SVGA

    C. CGA

    D. FLAT

8. Modems are usually attached to a computer through the _____ port.

    A. Serial

    B. Sequential

    C. Parallel

    D. Modem

9. Firmware is composed of which of the following? (Choose two)

    A. Software

    B. Middleware

    C. Hardware

    D. Componentware

10. Which of the following is part of the POST process?

    A. Loading of device drivers

    B. Scanning the hard drive for errors

    C. Processes in `config.sys`

    D. Locating a bootable device

11. The programs that allow the POST to take place are stored in
_____.

    A. BIOS

    B. CMOS

    C. RAM

    D. POSTOS

12. What is the purpose of a "port replicator"?

    A. It enables you to double the number of COM ports on your computer.

    B. It routes data from one computer to another.

    C. It provides additional ports for a laptop computer.

    D. It provides a communication path between serial and parallel ports.

13. CPU stands for _____.

    A. Core Predetermination Utility

    B. Complementary Provider Unit

    C. Central Processing Unit

    D. Co-Primary Uniprocessor

14. CMOS stands for _____.

    A. Complementary Metal-Oxide Semiconductor

    B. Co-Management of Operating System

    C. Configuration Management and Option Semiconductor

    D. Configuration Memory Option System

15. SCSI stands for _____.

    A. Serial Component System Interface

    B. Small Component Serial Interface

    C. Serial Computing Storage Interface

    D. Small Computer System Interface

Answers to Chapter Questions

Chapter Pre-Test

1. **CMOS RAM** stores settings about devices such as hard drives.

2. **IDE (Integrated Drive Electronics)** or **ATA (AT Attachment)**, and **SCSI (Small Computer System Interface)** are used for hard drives in today's computers.

3. **Firmware consists of software (or programming code) that is embedded in a piece of hardware**, such as the BIOS routines that are embedded in the ROM chips that help to boot your computer. **Software is programming code that is found on some type of magnetic media**, such as a hard drive.

4. **False.** These settings are stored in the CMOS. The BIOS are the boot routines that are stored in ROM.

5. **False.** Some devices receive their power from the system board, while others get their power from the power supply.

6. **POST (Power On Self Test)** is the first step in the boot process.

7. Modems are modulators and demodulators. **They convert digital signals from the computer into analog signals that are used by the phone lines, and then reverse the process at the destination.**

8. **PCMCIA** or **PC slots**, **LCD displays**, **lower-power CPUs**, **batteries**, **docking stations**, and **port replicators** are all technologies that are generally associated with portable computing.

Assessment Questions

1. **B.** DVD drives will use either the ATA or SCSI bus to attach to a computer, so they are not likely to require a controller. Thus, a controller will not be found on the motherboard. For more information, see the section labeled "Storage Devices."

2. **B.** L1 Cache is integrated into the CPU, so it is not found on the motherboard. For more information, see the section labeled "Memory."

3. **A.** Most power supplies have leads that supply either 3.3 volts or 5 volts. For more information, see the section labeled "Power Supply."

4. **C.** Modems are responsible for converting signals between analog and digital. For more information, see the section labeled "Modem."

5. **D.** The normal measurement for RAM is nanoseconds. For more information, see the section labeled "Memory."

6. **B, D.** Hard drives are usually attached to IDE and SCSI buses. The IDE bus is now usually referred to as ATA. Many laptops also support PCMCIA, or PC card drives as well. For more information, see the section labeled "Storage Devices."

7. **B.** SVGA is the current graphic standard that monitors follow. For more information, see the section labeled "Monitor."

8. **A.** Modems are serial devices, and as such, are attached to the serial port. For more information, see the section labeled "Modem."

9. **A, B.** Firmware consists of programming code or software that is contained within a hardware component, such as a ROM chip. For more information, see the section labeled "Firmware."

10. **D.** Locating a bootable device is part of the POST. Once the device is found, `config.sys` is processed by the boot loader. For more information, see the section labeled "Boot Process."

11. **A.** BIOS contains the programs that allow the POST to take place. The BIOS is stored on a ROM or an EPROM. For more information, see the section labeled "BIOS."

12. **C.** A port replicator provides additional ports for some laptop computers. Some laptops do not have external serial, parallel, video, or other ports. The port replicator provides these ports so that additional devices can be connected to the laptop. For more information, see the section labeled "LCD and Portable Systems."

13. **C.** Central Processing Unit. For more information, see the section labeled "Processor/CPU."

14. **A.** Complementary Metal-Oxide Semiconductor. For more information, see the section labeled "CMOS."

15. **D.** Small Computer System Interface. For more information, see the section labeled "Storage Devices."

Popular CPU Chips and their Characteristics

CHAPTER 2

EXAM OBJECTIVES

Exam 220-201 ✦ A+ Core Hardware

✦ **4.1** Distinguish between the popular CPU chips in terms of their basic characteristics. Content may include the following:

- Popular CPU chips (Intel, AMD, Cyrix)
- Characteristics
- Physical size
- Voltage
- Speeds
- On board cache or not
- Sockets
- SEC (Single Edge Contact)

CHAPTER PRE-TEST

1. How many instruction pipelines does a Pentium processor have?

2. What is the major difference between an 80486DX and an 80486SX?

3. What is the major difference between the Pentium II processor and the Celeron processor?

4. How much memory can a Pentium II processor access?

5. Processors that have MMX technology built-in have how much L1 cache?

6. What type of socket does a Pentium II sit in on the system board?

7. What is the major difference between an 80386DX and an 80386SX?

8. What types of cache does the Pentium Pro have built-in?

9. How many new instructions does the MMX technology add to the processor?

10. The processor's data bus enables the processor to transfer information to _____.

✦ Answers to these questions can be found at the end of the chapter. ✦

Although all components of the computer function together as a team, every team needs a leader—someone who gives out instructions and keeps everyone working toward the same goal. If any PC component were to be considered the team leader, it would probably be the CPU, or central processing unit. The key word here is "central," which implies "center" or "focus." The CPU can be considered the focus of the computer because it controls a large number of the computer system's capabilities, such as the type of software that can run, the amount of total memory that the computer can physically see, and the speed at which the system will run. This chapter will look at some of the features of the CPU that are responsible for setting the capabilities of the computer system. It will also discuss the importance of the CPU and its role as a PC component, as well as identify some of the main characteristics that make one CPU better than another.

Processor Terminology

4.1 Distinguish between the popular CPU chips in terms of their basic characteristics. Content may include the following: Characteristics, Speeds

In this section, you will learn some basic terms that are used to describe characteristics of different processors—past and present. The exam may not ask for the specific definition of each term, but understanding the terms will help you answer the related questions in this topic area.

Processor speed

Processor speed is the speed at which the processor executes its instructions or commands. This speed is measured in millions of cycles per second, or megahertz (MHz). Original CPUs had a speed of 4.77 MHz, while systems at the time of this writing are running around 1.5 GHz. Although processor speed is not the only factor affecting performance, in general, the larger the MHz the faster the system.

Data bus

A city bus is responsible for transferring people from one location to another. In the world of computers, a *data bus* is responsible for delivering data from one location on the PC to another (for example, from the processor to memory).

What would happen if 50 people needed to go from one location to another, but a city bus only had 25 available seats? The answer is simple: the bus would make two trips. But wouldn't it be more efficient to upgrade the bus? If you upgraded the bus to 50 seats, the bus would only have to make one trip to transfer the 50 people from one location to another, which increases the efficiency of our public transit system.

The data bus works the same way, only it transfers data in the form of bits (ones or zeros). All data processed by the computer is in the form of bits. The data bus has a "full capacity" point where it cannot handle any more bits of data, just as the bus system in your city has a "full capacity" point (50, measured in "seats").

If a processor has a 16-bit data bus, it means that it can deliver 16 bits at any given time. If the same processor needs to deliver 32 bits of information, it will have to take two trips. Taking that same 32 bits of information and processing it on a 32-bit processor means that the information will get delivered in one trip as opposed to two, which increases the overall efficiency of the system. It is as if you had two pieces of paper to put in the garbage can, and instead of walking one piece of paper over to the garbage can, walking back, and then walking the second piece over, it would be more efficient to walk both pieces of paper over to the garbage can at the same time.

Data bus in terms of processors means the pathway to memory. The processor uses the data bus solely for delivering data back and forth from system memory and the processor. Because the processor accesses information from memory so often, an entire bus — the data bus — is dedicated to this action.

Address bus

Figure 2-1 shows that your system memory is organized like a spreadsheet, in rows and columns. These rows and columns make up blocks that can be written to or read from. If you want to store information in one of the blocks, you have to reference the location by address (by specifying "B2," for example).

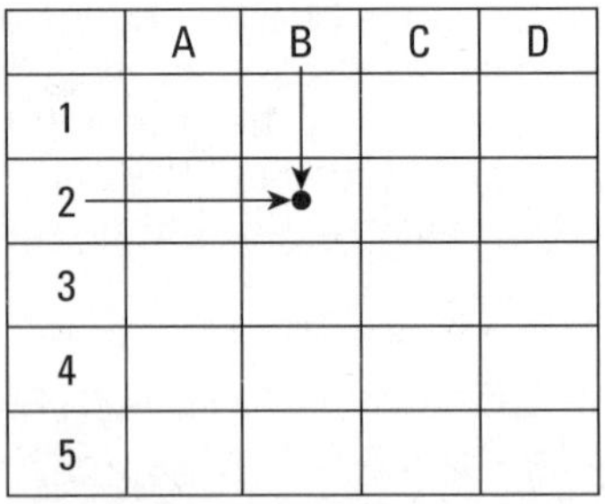

Figure 2-1: How system memory is organized

To store information into system memory, your processor would have to give an address that points to a particular storage location. Only the address does not look like "B2." It looks something like "1-0," or maybe "1-1," which are two completely different memory locations.

Your processor accesses memory locations through the *address bus*. If, for example, the address bus is 2-bit, the processor has two *address lines* from the processor to system memory. The address lines are just tunnels to locations in memory, each with an on/off state (1 representing on and 0 representing off). The combination of the on/off states of both address lines at any given time is how a reference to an area in memory is made. Figure 2-2, Side A, illustrates a processor making a reference, or call, to Address 1-0, while Side B shows a reference to Address 1-1 being made. These two address calls are referencing completely different locations in memory.

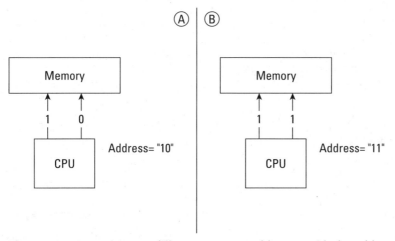

Figure 2-2: Accessing two different memory addresses with the address bus

If you add another address line to the address bus, there are even more possible addresses that the processor can access because the processor has more variations with three bits than with two. A two-bit address bus can make a reference to four possible memory addresses (2×2), while a three-bit address bus can make a reference to eight possible memory addresses ($2 \times 2 \times 2$).

Therefore, the address bus dictates how much physical memory the processor can access. For example, an 80286 processor has a 24-bit address bus, which means that it can access 16,777,216 memory addresses, or 16MB of system memory.

Registers

Registers are storage areas within the processor. They are used to store and process data, and perhaps write back the result of the processed data. It is as if information to be processed was in your pocket, rather than across a room, where you would have to walk all the way over and pick it up. Having information in your pocket means it can be accessed much more quickly, saving time to increase performance. Registers give a processor quicker access to data, and the more registers a processor has, the more data it can get to.

Registers are measured in bits. A processor with 16-bit registers would have 16 containers to store information used by the system. A processor with 32-bit registers would have double the amount of containers that it would use to store information.

Cache memory

The processor accesses information that resides in system memory, which is a slower process than if the information was stored in the processor's own "memory." When the information is sitting in system memory and the processor sends a request for that information, the request goes to the memory controller (which manages data in memory). The memory controller finds the data in memory, retrieves it, and delivers it to the processor. Throughout this entire process, the processor is simply "waiting around" for the information. Thus, many of the newer processors include their own memory within the processor's chip (called *cache*). Cache can be thought of as a "bucket" that holds information accessed by the processor on a regular basis. This cache bucket is integrated right into the processor's chip and is made up of SRAM. (*SRAM* is an acronym for static RAM; it is very expensive, because it is much quicker than regular system memory.) As a result of this extra memory being integrated into the chip, the processor becomes more costly.

 Cross-Reference   For more information on SRAM and other types of memory, see Chapter 4.

There are two types of cache memory: Level 1 (L1) cache and Level 2 (L2) cache. *L1 cache* is cache that is built into the processor, whereas *L2 cache* usually resides on the main system board and is considered external cache memory because it is outside of the CPU. When you upgrade the cache memory on your computer, you are adding L2 cache. Because L1 cache is built into the chip, it will never be upgraded without upgrading to a processor that has more L1 cache.

How does the processor use the cache memory? The first time the processor has to access the information it needs, it grabs the information from system memory. As we mentioned earlier in this section, system memory is very slow; thus, when the processor is finished with the information, it stores the information in its cache. Think of the processor's L1 cache as a little bucket to store information that it believes it will need again in the future. If the processor is right — and it needs the information again — it will retrieve it from its bucket of cache instead of making the "day-long" trip over to system memory to retrieve it. As a result, the entire system appears to perform more quickly when accessing frequently used data.

The integration of cache memory into processor chips didn't come to market until the 80486 chips were developed in 1989. Generally, 80486 chips had 8K of L1 cache, and the Pentium chip increased that amount to 16K. In fact, many of the newer processors have increased the L1 cache to over 16K and have also included some L2 cache. These chips will be more expensive because the type of memory (SRAM) that cache memory is made of is expensive.

Math co-processor

The math co-processor (also known as the NPU, or Numeric Processing Unit) is the processor's sidekick. Systems that have math co-processors can well outperform systems that do not have math co-processors, because the math co-processor takes some of the workload off the CPU. For example, it performs many of the large calculations that applications may require, such as floating point arithmetic. Overall system performance increases, because the CPU can focus on logic functions while the math co-processor executes complicated mathematical functions.

If you have large spreadsheets, or use large graphics applications, you may find that applications run very poorly or not at all on systems without a math co-processor. If you are running a system that does not have a math co-processor integrated into the CPU, then you can add one to the system board — or perhaps upgrade the main processor.

In earlier computers, the processor was one chip and the math co-processor was a separate chip on the system board. In newer systems, the processor chip includes a built-in math co-processor. All CPU chips, starting with the 80486DX, have a built-in math co-processor.

Chip types

There are two major chip types that processors have used. The first is the Dual In-line Package (DIP) chip, a rectangular chip with two rows of 20 pins. Pin 1 is located at the end of the chip that has a square notch carved into it. It is important to identify Pin 1, because when adding the chip to the system board, you will have to match Pin 1 on the chip with Pin 1 in the chip socket.

Older processors such as the 8088 and many math co-processor chips used the DIP chip style. Although they are no longer used for CPUs, DIP chips are still used for cache memory, or BIOS chips on system boards. They are also found on memory modules. When you purchase RAM from a store, you will receive a card (called a memory module) with many memory chips (DIP chips) on it. You will then install the memory module into your system to perform a memory upgrade.

The second major chip type is the Pin Grid Array (PGA), one of the most popular processor chip types in use today. The PGA chip is a square chip that has an array of pins filling up its shape. In general, the PGA chip uses hundreds of pins. Pin 1 is identified in one of the corners by the little notch carved into it. Figure 2-3 compares a DIP (right side) with a PGA (left side) chip type.

Figure 2-3: Identifying popular chip types

Many times, the PGA chip fits into a ZIF (Zero Insertion Force) socket. The ZIF socket is ideal for upgrading processors because it has a lever that you pull up on, which raises the chip out of the socket. Once it is raised, you can replace the old chip with a new one. Not all boards use ZIF sockets, so you may need to get some special extractors to pull the chip out (carefully!). Figure 2-4 shows a ZIF socket.

Figure 2-4: Identifying a ZIF socket

Early Intel Processors

4.1 Distinguish between the popular CPU chips in terms of their basic characteristics. Content may include the following: Characteristics, On board cache or not, Speeds

This section will discuss some of the processors of the past and how they have evolved, starting with the 8086 and working forward to the 80486 processors. Along the way, the characteristics — data bus, address bus, and speed — of each processor will be identified.

I will also identify any new architecture changes that are introduced with a specific processor (for example, a built-in math co-processor). Once a change like this is implemented, all subsequent processors follow.

When preparing for the exam, concentrate on the Pentium class processors and above. The information on the older processors has been provided primarily to give you background information about the changes in the processor technology and to explain some of the early concepts.

8086

In 1978, Intel introduced the first major processor for personal computers — the 8086 — which had a 16-bit data bus, 16-bit registers, and a 20-bit address bus. A 20-bit address bus meant that the 8086 could access 1MB of RAM. The speed of the 8086 ranged from 4.77 MHz to around 10 MHz, which is extremely slow considering today's standards (approximately 1.5 GHz).

8088

The 8086 chip was too expensive for PC manufacturers to use in their systems and still sell the system at a reasonable price to their customers. So Intel introduced the cheaper 8088 chip a year after the 8086. Like the 8086, the 8088 processor had 16-bit registers and a 20-bit address bus (which meant it could access 1MB of RAM). However, the data bus was decreased from 16-bits to 8-bits. The 8088 ran at the same speed as the 8086, keeping its speeds at 4.77 MHz and 8 MHz.

The 8086/8088 did not include a built-in cache, nor did it have a built-in math co-processor. If you wanted to add a math co-processor to your system, you would purchase an 8087 chip to sit on the system board beside the CPU. The 8087 chip was specifically designed as the math co-processor for the 8086 and 8088 processors.

80286

In 1982, Intel produced the 80286 chip, which had 16-bit registers and a 16-bit data bus, and ran at speeds ranging between 6 MHz and 20 MHz. Other than the speed increase, these characteristics matched that of the 8086 — this time, however, the market was there.

The 80286 also increased the size of the address bus to 24-bits, which meant that it could access up to 16MB of RAM. Like the 8086/8088, the 80286 processor did not contain its own internal cache, nor did it include a math co-processor. Processors prior to the 80286 chip ran in *real mode*, while the 80286 processor introduced what is known as *protected mode*. The following sections compare real mode with protected mode.

Real mode

Real mode meant that the processor accessed memory as a whole and dealt with it as a single entity. In other words, real-mode processors did not have any *multitasking* capabilities — the capacity to divide memory up into multiple parts and run a different application (or task) in each part, switching back and forth between them.

Protected mode

Protected-mode processors support the dividing up of system memory into different parts and assigning a different application to each part of memory. Therefore, protected-mode processors support multitasking and multitasking operating systems, such as Windows 95/98, Windows NT, and Windows 2000.

Protected-mode processors also support virtual memory, which is the process of using hard disk space as emulated memory. This means you could have 2MB of RAM while the system is also using 10MB of hard disk space as "pretend" RAM. In this case—as far as the applications that are running are concerned—there is 12MB of RAM.

80386DX

In 1985, Intel released its first 32-bit processor, the 80386DX, which had a 32-bit data bus, a 32-bit address bus, and 32-bit registers. The 32-bit address bus meant that the 80386DX processor could access 4 gigabytes (GB) of RAM, which is an amazing improvement over previous processors (unfortunately, most people can't afford to purchase 4 GB of RAM).

The speed of the 80386DX processor ranged between 16 MHz and 40 MHz. The 80386DX contains no built-in cache, and the math co-processor (the 80387 chip) has to be purchased separately. Once again, the math co-processor would be inserted on the system board in the math co-processor socket.

80386SX

Three years after the 80386DX chip was out, Intel released the 80386SX, which was a lower-end 386 chip. The 80386SX was a 16-bit processor, meaning it had a 16-bit data bus. It could also only access 16MB of RAM, so the address bus had been reduced to 24-bit. The speed of the 80386SX processor ranged from 16 MHz to 33 MHz. The registers were maintained as 32-bit registers.

Although both flavors of the 80386 chips support real and protected mode, they have taken this support to the next level. These chips enable on-the-fly switching between the two modes, whereas the 80286 processor had to be reset before it could switch from one mode to another.

The major difference between the 80386DX processor and the 80386SX processor is that the DX flavor is a 32-bit processor, while the SX flavor is a 16-bit processor. When you compare the characteristics of the 80286 and the 80386SX chip, you realize that the 80286 chip is competitive with the 80386SX chip. In reality, an 80386SX chip is nothing more than a glorified 80286 chip with a bigger price tag.

80486DX

In 1989, major advancements were made in the performance of the computer system when Intel released the 80486DX chip. This chip had a 32-bit data bus, a 32-bit address bus (4GB of RAM), and 32-bit registers.

The 80486DX chip introduced two major advancements in CPU technology. The first was the idea of integrating cache directly into the chip. The 80486DX had 8 kilobytes (K) of built-in cache, or what is called L1 cache. The second major advancement was that the math co-processor was integrated inside the 80486DX chip. Now, instead of buying a math co-processor chip and inserting it onto the system board, the chip was integrated and working as long as it was enabled in the system BIOS.

The speed of the 80486DX ranged from 20 MHz to 50 MHz (20 MHz, 25 MHz, and 33 MHz were the most popular speeds). After the original 486s, a second generation of the 80486DX arrived that were marketed as 80486DX2-50, 80486DX2-66, and 80486DX4-100. The following sections discuss the DX2 and DX4 model processors.

DX2

The "80486DX" portion of "80486DX2-50" means that the processor is the DX flavor of the 80486. The "2" after the "DX" implies "clock double," a term indicating that the CPU is working at twice the speed of the system board. In our example, the CPU works at a speed of 50 MHz, while the system board runs at 25 MHz. So, as information travels out of the CPU and hits the system board, the data slows down to half the speed. The same could be said for the 80486DX2-66. The CPU works at a speed of 66 MHz, while the system board runs at 33 MHz.

DX4

The DX4 model works exactly the same way as the clock double, only the clock double is actually a clock triple. In other words, the CPU works at three times the speed of the system board. So, why call it a "DX4" if it's really a clock triple? Because one extra enhancement, other than the clock triple, was added to the DX4: 8K more of L1 cache to the chip. The idea is that our clock triple plus the extra 8K of cache memory gives us a DX4 chip: *(clock)*3 plus 8*(K)* equals *(DX)*4.

Tip All 80486 chips — except the DX4 chips, which have 16K of L1 cache — have 8K of L1 cache. Also, all processors created after the 80486 chip use L1 cache, though they may differ in the actual amount. This becomes one of the selling points of the different processors.

80486SX

Two years after the success of the 80486DX chip, Intel decided to market a lower-end 80486 chip. This new chip, released in 1991, was called the 80486SX.

What did the 80486SX chip have that made it so special? Or maybe a better question to ask is: What didn't it have? The 80486SX chip was a full-blown 80486DX with the integrated math co-processor disabled. This time, Intel was trying to attract customers who could not justify the price of the more functional chip, so Intel simply downgraded the 80486DX, marketing it as a different chip and selling it at a lower price.

Because the 80486SX chip did not have an integrated and functioning math co-processor, there was a place on the system board to add a math co-processor chip (the 80487SX).

Suppose the 80486DX chip sold for $900 and the 80486SX chip sold for $700. Assume also that I'm not using the computer for a lot of large mathematical calculations or graphics applications. In this case, I don't really need a math co-processor integrated into my CPU. I could save myself $200 by buying the system with the 80486SX chip. However, as time goes on, I may start using the computer more and more, playing with a lot of graphics applications. My best friend (let's call him Dan), tells me that I would get a performance increase by purchasing a math co-processor for my system. It just so happens that the math co-processor that I have to purchase, the 80487SX, is on sale for $400. I purchase the 80487SX chip and place it in the empty socket by my CPU on the system board

When I place the 80487SX chip on the system board in the math co-processor socket, it disables the 80486SX entirely so that my system is just using the 80487SX chip. So, I spent $700 on an 80486SX chip (that gets disabled) and $400 on an 80487SX (which is really the 80486DX) chip — a total of $1100 — when I could have made the original purchase of $900 and obtained the same system in the long run.

Popular Intel Processors

 4.1 Distinguish between the popular CPU chips in terms of their basic characteristics. Content may include the following: Popular CPU chips (Intel, AMD, Cyrix), Characteristics, Voltage

In this section, we will provide an overview of some new terms, such as voltage, transistors, and sockets. We will also discuss the Pentium class processors and their characteristics, including data bus, address bus, registers, and any new technologies.

CPU voltage and transistor integration

One important CPU characteristic that you have to watch for when upgrading your processor is the voltage the processor requires. The *voltage* is the power the processor draws from the main system board, which it receives originally from the power supply.

A processor is designed to run at a certain voltage. You need to ensure that the system board you are placing the processor into is providing that voltage. If a system board supports more than one voltage, you can change a jumper on the system board — which will then control the voltage used by the processor.

Processors are made up of thousands, even millions, of transistors. A *transistor* acts as a switch, either permitting or prohibiting the flow of current. If current is allowed to flow through the transistor, then some form of result is generated. If the current is not allowed to flow through the transistor, a different result is generated. How does the switch get turned on to allow the flow of current? The answer is from an input device, such as the keyboard. The action of pressing keys on a keyboard sends a positive charge to the transistor to turn on the switch.

Table 2-1 lists some of the popular processors, their required voltage, and the number of transistors used to build the logic of that particular CPU.

Table 2-1 CPU Voltages/Transistors		
Processor	*Voltage*	*Transistors*
8088	5	29,000
80286	5	134,000
80386DX	5	275,000
80386SX	5	275,000
80486DX	5	1.2 million
80486SX	5	1.2 million
80486DX-2	3.3 or 5	2 million
80486DX-4	3.3 or 5	2.5 million
Pentium	3.3 or 5	3.3 million
Pentium Pro	3.1	5.5 million
Pentium II	2.8	7.5 million

Socket

4.1 Distinguish between the popular CPU chips in terms of their basic characteristics. Content may include the following: Sockets

Intel decided to develop a new standard for upgrading a processor on system boards, beginning with the 80486 chips and continuing with the Pentium class processors. This standard was processor sockets. A *processor socket* is a socket designed to hold a specific processor chip with the appropriate number of pins. This enabled Intel to develop new chips with compatibility in mind. They could design a new chip for an old socket so that customers could update their computers by dropping the new processor in the compatible socket.

Popular Pentium processors supported mainly Socket 5 with 320 pins or Socket 7 with 321 pins. Thus, to add a Pentium processor to a system board, you would have to find out what socket existed on that board, then purchase a CPU that would fit in that socket. You would also have to remember to match the voltage of the board to the voltage required by the CPU. Figure 2-5 will help you identify a CPU socket in your system.

Figure 2-5: Identifying a processor socket

Table 2-2 lists the different types of sockets and the processors that support them. It also shows the number of pins associated with the different types of sockets.

Table 2-2		
Processor Sockets		
Socket	**Processor**	**Number of Pins**
Socket 1	80486, 80486DX2, 80486DX4	169
Socket 2	80486, 80486DX2, 80486DX4	238
Socket 3	80486, 80486DX2, 80486DX4	237
Socket 4	Pentium 60/66	273
Socket 5	Pentium 75-133	320
Socket 6	Not Used	235
Socket 7	Pentium 75-200	321
Socket 8	Pentium Pro	387
Slot 1	Pentium II	242

Exam Tip   Although it is not necessary to memorize the entire list of sockets and their supported processors, it is important to be able to identify the popular sockets, such as Socket 5, Socket 7 and Slot 1.

Pentium

The original Pentium processor was released in 1993. Intel had not been able to copyright this brand of processor for legal reasons using the label "586." Thus, they created a new name for their next generation of processors: Pentium.

The Pentium processor was originally developed at speeds of 60 MHz and 66 MHz. Soon after, Intel marketed 75MHz, 90MHz, 100 MHz, 120 MHz, 133 MHz, 150 MHz, 166 MHz, and 200 MHz flavors, which were really just multipliers of the original 60 MHz or 66 MHz systems.

As with clock double and clock triple in the case of the 80486s, we now have the same marketing technique in the case of the Pentium, the only difference being that the Pentium motherboards ran at either 60 MHz or 66 MHz. For example, a 120 MHz computer has a processor running at 120 MHz while the system board runs at 60 MHz, which meant that the processor runs twice as fast as the rest of the system.

From a consumer's point of view, clock multipliers become important when you take a look at computers such as the Pentium 133 or the Pentium 150. Which is faster? The obvious answer is the system with the higher megahertz speed. But is it really? The Pentium 133 is a clock double of the 66 MHz board, while the Pentium 150 is a clock double and a half of the 60 MHz board. Table 2-3 compares the speed of the motherboard and processor for the different Pentium systems.

Table 2-3 Pentium Clock Multipliers			
Processor	**Motherboard Speed (MHz)**	**Multiplier**	**Processor Speed (MHz)**
Pentium 90	60	1.5	90
Pentium 100	66	1.5	99
Pentium 120	60	2	120
Pentium 133	66	2	132
Pentium 150	60	2.5	150
Pentium 180	60	3	180
Pentium 200	66	3	198

By looking at the system board speeds of the Pentium 133 and the Pentium 150, you could assume that the computer running the Pentium 133 may be able to keep up with, if not outperform, the one running the Pentium 150.

The Pentium processor had a 32-bit address bus, 32-bit registers, and a 64-bit data bus. The Pentium took the 8K of L1 cache that was found on the 80486 and doubled it to 16K — two 8K channels. One channel was for data cache and the other for application code cache.

Heat sinks and CPU fans

Due to the size of the Pentium processor and the number of transistors passing current, the chip reached undesirable levels of heat, which caused it to become unstable. Thus, many of the Pentium processors came with either a cooling fan or heat sinks.

Heat sinks are a group of metal-like pins that are placed on the chip to draw heat away from it. A *cooling fan* is a small fan placed on top of the processor. The function of the cooling fan is to pull the hot air away from the processor, helping to keep the processor cool. Some processors may get so hot that a heat sink may not be enough of a cooling device; in this case, the manufacturer may place a fan on top of the heat sink. Figure 2-6 shows you what a heat sink looks like.

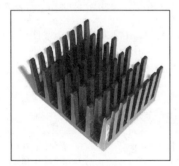

Figure 2-6: Looking at a heat sink

Superscalar design

Before the Pentium came along, processors used one instruction pipeline. This meant that when an application executed, it would run each stage of the application job one step after the other. For example, if an application has three lines of code, as seen in Figure 2-7, each line of code can only be processed after the previous line of code is fully completed. This creates a delay, or wait time, that slows performance.

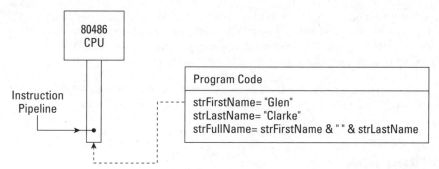

Figure 2-7: Single instruction pipelined processor executing application code

The Pentium processor has two instruction pipelines, named U and V. Having two instruction pipelines enables the processor to execute two instructions at the same time. Thus, the three lines of program code, shown in Figure 2-8, can be quickly executed on a Pentium processor because Lines 1 and 2 are processed at the same time, causing Line 3 to be processed that much faster. Notice that Lines 1 and 2 execute parallel to one another; therefore, "parallel processing" is taking place.

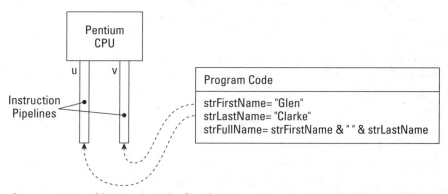

Figure 2-8: Dual instruction pipelined processor processing application code

An application would have to be designed to take advantage of two instruction pipelines. These applications could be labeled something like "Pentium Aware" or "Pentium Ready."

MMX

After the Pentium was developed, Intel introduced MMX (multimedia extensions) technology. MMX comprised 57 new instructions that were built into the processor and told the system how to work with audio, video, and graphics. If these instructions were not built-in, the processor would have to retrieve them from somewhere else. Since both the home and business user seemed to be heading towards the world of multimedia, it made sense to enhance the processor and make it "multimedia-aware." Running any kind of multimedia application on a processor that supports MMX will give you a major performance increase.

MMX also increases the L1 cache by 16K, so any processors that support MMX have their L1 cache increased by 16K, on top of the 16K that the original Pentiums had.

Pentium Pro

In 1995, Intel released the Pentium Pro chip, which added a new level of performance to the Pentium processor. The Pentium Pro had all the characteristics of the Pentium processor — such as a 64-bit data bus and 32-bit registers — but it increased the address bus to 36-bit, which meant that the Pentium Pro could access 64GB of RAM. The speed of the Pentium Pro ranged from 120 MHz to around 200 MHz.

The Pentium Pro added two additional features to its chip that helped it outperform the original Pentiums. First, the Pentium Pro chip was really a two-chip team. One chip (the actual processor) had 16K of L1 cache like the Pentium chip, but the other chip held an extra 256K (or 512K, 1MB, 2MB) of cache memory. Since this cache memory was physically outside of the CPU, it was considered L2 cache.

The second feature, which led to the performance gain of the Pentium Pro, is what is known as dynamic execution. *Dynamic execution* has three stages: multiple branch prediction, dataflow analysis, and speculative execution.

Multiple branch prediction is the idea that the processor will look ahead and predict a number of instructions that may be needed in the very near future. *Dataflow analysis* occurs when the processor looks at the instructions it has predicted will be needed next and then assigns them a logical order of execution. *Speculative execution* is the actual executing of a given instruction based on the prediction and the order of execution assigned.

Pentium II

4.1 Distinguish between the popular CPU chips in terms of their basic characteristics. Content may include the following: SEC (Single Edge Contact)

In 1997, Intel produced the Pentium II, which was really just an enhanced Pentium Pro with speeds ranging from 233 MHz to 450 MHz. The Pentium II had a 64-bit data bus, a 36-bit address bus (64GB of RAM), and 64-bit registers.

The Pentium II increased the amount of L1 cache that was integrated into the CPU to 32K, as opposed to 16K. The 32K of L1 cache was still divided into two equal channels: one 16K channel for data and one 16K channel for application code.

Intel has packaged the Pentium II in the Single Edge Contact Connector (SECC) that fits into Slot 1 on the system board. The Single Edge Connector is a module enclosed in a casing or shell with two chips inside, one chip being the processor and the other chip being the 512K of L2 cache. Figure 2-9 shows a Pentium II processor and Slot 1.

Figure 2-9: The Pentium II (SEC) located alongside the 486, Pentium and AMD processors

SIMD

Another enhancement that accompanied the Pentium II was SIMD (Single Instruction Multiple Data). When I think of SIMD, I like to think of a playroom full of toddlers. Suppose there are five toddlers in the playroom and that these toddlers are at the entertaining age of two — the age, of course, when the toddlers are preparing for their teen years and they answer "no" to everything you say. You walk into the playroom and see that the five toddlers have found your box of darts and are throwing them at the walls. You are faced with a choice: you can either walk around to each child and explain why throwing darts at your walls is not a good thing (which means you will have to explain the same thing five different times) or you can have a good scream at the top of your lungs, which means that all the children will stop immediately and listen. SIMD works on the same basic principle. Suppose, for example, that you have a system running multiple processes at any given time and each process has data that it's working with. If the processor has to give out instructions to modify a certain type of data, instead of explaining these instructions to each individual process one after the other (which takes a lot of time), the processor yells, or broadcasts, the instructions to everyone. Thus, the processor saves time and creates a much more efficient way to communicate information.

Celeron

The Pentium II processor performs very well (and with all that cache memory, it should). Unfortunately, performance comes with a price. If you are not willing to pay that price, Intel has created a chip for you: the Celeron.

The Celeron chip is nothing more than a Pentium II processor with the built-in L2 cache either removed or reduced and then sold at a cheaper price. The first-generation Celeron chip was code-named the Covington. It had no L2 cache memory on it. The second-generation Celeron was code-named the Mendocino. It contained 128K of L2 integrated into the processor itself. This L2 cache was not another chip sitting beside the processor, like the Pentium II.

Pentium III

The Pentium III processor shares many of the Pentium II's characteristics. It supports dynamic execution, MMX technology, and has either 256K or 512K of L2 cache. The Pentium III runs at a speed of 450 MHz to 1,000 MHz, or 1 GHz.

The Pentium III chip offers 70 additional instructions that are integrated into the chip, enhancing the user's experience with 3D graphic applications. The Pentium III chip also supports a number of low power states to help conserve power when the system is not in use. This processor is designed to run on either a 100 MHz or 133 MHz system board.

Physical size

4.1 Distinguish between the popular CPU chips in terms of their basic characteristics. Content may include the following: Physical size

As the processors increase in functionality, they also increase in size. Table 2-4 lists the dimensions of some of the popular processors. For the exam, you will want to make sure that you take a look at these dimensions.

Table 2-4 Processor Size			
Processor	**Width (Inches)**	**Height (Inches)**	**Depth (Inches)**
Pentium	1.95	1.95	
Pentium Pro	2.46	2.66	

Processor	**Width (Inches)**	**Height (Inches)**	**Depth (Inches)**
Pentium II	5.505	2.473	0.647
Celeron	5.0	2.275	0.208

Non-Intel Chips

 4.1 Distinguish between the popular CPU chips in terms of their basic characteristics. Content may include the following: Popular CPU chips (Intel, AMD, Cyrix), Characteristics

One of Intel's major competitors is AMD. AMD has developed a family of processors that compete with the Pentium class processors. In this section, we will provide an overview of some of the characteristics of the AMD processors.

 Exam Tip It is important to focus on the Intel processors for the exam. The AMD processors have been identified here because they may be encountered in the real world.

K6

The AMD K6 processor is designed to compete with the Intel Pentium. The K6 has 64K of L1 cache, supports MMX technology, and has built-in branch prediction techniques. This processor has 321 pins, which means that it will fit into a Socket 7–supported system board.

K6-2

The K6-2 processor is designed to compete with the Pentium II chip. It has 64K of L1 cache and 256K of L2 cache. The K6 also supports dynamic execution, MMX technology, and superscalar design.

The K6-2 has added 3DNow! Technology — a number of additional instructions integrated into the chip to improve 3D graphic applications. The K6-2 chip also uses a 100 MHz system board speed. This is a big improvement over the 60/66 MHz system board speed that the original Pentiums were using.

The K6-2 has 321 pins, which means that it will fit into a Socket 7–supported system board.

K6-III

The K6-III processor is designed to compete with the Pentium III chip. This chip shares many of the features of the K6-2, including a system bus of 100 MHz. One of its new features is a Tri-Level cache. Not only can it take advantage of an L1 and L2 cache, but an L3 cache as well that can be included on the system board.

Athlon

The Athlon chip is probably one of the fastest processors that exists today. The Athlon chip has 128K of L1 cache, and 256K of L2 cache. It supports improved dynamic execution, MMX technology, and 3Dnow! Technology. The Athlon chip runs at speeds of up to 1.2 GHz and is designed to run on a 200 MHz system bus speed!

Unlike the K6-2 and K6-III, the Athlon is not a PGA-packaged chip that supports Socket 7. It uses its own socket type, called *Slot A*. The Slot A socket is not compatible with Intel's Slot 1, which means users will have to purchase a system board designed for the Athlon chip.

Increasing Performance

When it comes to processors, there are a number of different ways to increase the performance of your system. A first and obvious way is to buy the faster processor when upgrading; for example, upgrade a PII 300 MHz to a P II 450 MHz. Also, get a processor that is designed to run on the faster motherboard. For example, the Pentium III chip runs on a 133 MHz system board, compared to a Pentium chip, which still runs on 60/66 MHz system boards.

You will have to look at other features of the processor, such as the L1 cache and L2 cache that resides either on or around the processor. Acquiring a processor with more cache memory can dramatically increase system performance.

Key Point Summary

This chapter provided an overview of the key terms that are used to identify the popular processors and their capabilities. Some of the major milestones in the Intel processor history include the following:

✦ The clocking of the chip

✦ The inclusion of the math co-processor

✦ The involvement of internal cache memory

Today's processors have a number of features that help the performance of applications that run on these systems. These features include the following:

✦ Superscalar design

✦ Dynamic execution

✦ MMX and 3DNow! Technology

✦   ✦   ✦

STUDY GUIDE

In this chapter, we discussed the characteristics of the popular types of processors. In the next section, you will be presented with 20 assessment questions to test your knowledge of the exam objectives. There won't be any labs or scenarios for this chapter.

Assessment Questions

1. Which of the following best describes superscalar design?

   A. The processor is designed using only 3.1 transistors

   B. The processor predicts the next few instructions to be executed, and then determines the optimal order for the execution of these instructions.

   C. The processor has two instruction pipelines, which enables multiple instructions to execute at the same time

   D. The processor works twice as fast as the system board

2. Which of the following sockets would you find a Pentium II processor in:

   A. Socket 5

   B. Socket 1

   C. Socket 7

   D. Slot 1

3. Which of the following processors have a 64-bit data bus?

   A. 80486SX

   B. Pentium

   C. 80386DX

   D. 80286

   E. 80486DX

   F. 80386SX

4. What chip type was the Pentium processor packaged in?

   A. Slot 1

   B. PGA

   C. DIP

   D. Socket 5

5. Which of the following is a characteristic of protected mode processors?

    A. Heat sink support

    B. Virtual memory

    C. Run only one application

    D. Encased in protective shell

6. How much L1 cache does a Pentium processor have built-in?

    A. 32K

    B. 64K

    C. 8K

    D. 16K

7. Which of the following acts as a storage container for information that will be processed by the processor?

    A. Data bus

    B. Address bus

    C. Registers

    D. Math co-processor

8. How much memory can a Pentium Pro address?

    A. 128MB

    B. 4GB

    C. 64GB

    D. 512MB

9. Which statement best describes the purpose of a math co-processor?

    A. The math co-processor performs all of the logic functions on behalf of the processor.

    B. The math co-processor performs floating point calculations on behalf of the processor.

    C. The math co-processor runs all applications, while a processor runs the operating system in a multitasking environment.

    D. The math co-processor allows for communication between devices.

10. Which sockets do Pentium chips typically fit into? (Choose two)

    A. Socket 1

    B. Socket 5

    C. Slot 1

    D. Socket 7

11. How much L1 cache memory does a Pentium II have built-in?

    A. 32K

    B. 64K

    C. 8K

    D. 16K

12. Which of the following is a voltage supported by the Pentium processor?

    A. 3.3 volts

    B. 3.5 volts

    C. 3.1 volts

    D. 5.5 volts

13. What is the major difference between a Celeron processor and a Pentium II chip?

    A. The Celeron has more L1 cache memory

    B. The Celeron has less L1 cache memory

    C. The Celeron has more L2 cache memory

    D. The Celeron has less L2 cache memory

14. Which of the following CPU characteristics determines how much total memory the system can access?

    A. Data bus

    B. Address bus

    C. Registers

    D. Math co-processor

15. What chip type was the 8088 processor packaged in?

    A. Slot 1

    B. PGA

    C. DIP

    D. Socket 5

16. How many instruction pipelines does a Pentium processor have?

    A. 1

    B. 2

    C. 3

    D. 4

17. What chip type uses a ZIF socket?

    A. Slot 1

    B. PGA

    C. DIP

    D. Socket 5

18. Which processor runs on a 133 MHz system board?

    A. Pentium

    B. Pentium III

    C. Pentium II

    D. AMD K6

19. A Pentium 133 runs on what speed system board?

    A. 60 MHz

    B. 66 MHz

    C. 100 MHz

    D. 133 MHz

20. What type of cache is integrated into the Pentium processor's chip?

    A. L1 cache

    B. L2 cache

    C. Integrated cache

    D. DRAM cache

Answers to Chapter Questions

Chapter Pre-Test

1. A Pentium processor has **two** instruction pipelines.

2. The difference between the 80486DX and the 80486SX is that **the 80486DX processor includes a built-in math co-processor.**

3. The major difference between the Pentium II processor and the Celeron processor is that **the Celeron processor either reduced the amount of L2 cache to 128K or totally removed it, depending on the version of the Celeron processor.**

4. A Pentium II processor can access **64GB** of system memory.

5. MMX technology raises the L1 cache on the processor to **32K.**

6. The Pentium II rests inside **a Slot 1 socket.**

7. The major difference between an 80386DX and an 80386SX is that **the 80386DX processor has a 32-bit data bus, while the 80386SX chip has a 16-bit data bus.**

8. The Pentium Pro has **16K of L1 cache** and **either 256K of L2 cache** or **512K of L2 cache.**

9. MMX technology adds **57** new multimedia type instructions to the processor to enhance performance when dealing with audio, video, and graphics.

10. The processor's data bus enables the processor to transfer information to **system memory.**

Assessment Questions

1. **C.** Superscalar design is the idea that the processor has more than one instruction pipeline to process application code. Choice B is describing a feature called dynamic execution, and choice D is describing a clock double chip. For more information, see the section labeled "Popular Intel Processors."

2. **D.** The Pentium II chip comes in a new package called the Single Edge Connector (SEC), which fits into Slot 1. Sockets 5 and 7 are used by original Pentiums, and Socket 1 is used by some 80486 chips. For more information, see the section labeled "Popular Intel Processors."

3. **B.** The Pentium processor was the first Intel processor to have a 64-bit data bus. 386DX and all 486 chips had a 32-bit data bus. The 286 and 386SX had a 16-bit data bus. For more information, see the section labeled "Popular Intel Processors."

4. **B.** The Pentium processor was packaged in the Pin Grid Array (PGA) chip type, which fits into either Socket 5 or Socket 7. Socket 5 and Socket 7 are incorrect choices because they are not chip types; they are the names of sockets. Dual In-Line Package (DIP) is an older type of packaging for processor chips. For more information, see the section labeled "Popular Intel Processors."

5. **B.** Virtual Memory is one of the features of protected mode processors. Choice C is the opposite of one of the benefits of protected-mode processors (being able to run multiple applications at the same time). For more information, see the section labeled "Early Intel Processors."

6. **D.** All 486 chips had 8K of L1 cache except for the DX4 model, which had 16K of L1 cache. The Pentium chip had 16K, and the Pentium II had 32K of L1 cache. For more information, see the section labeled "Early Intel Processors."

7. **C.** The data bus is the pathway to system memory, the address bus controls how much memory can be physically seen by the processor, and the math co-processor performs many of the complicated mathematical operations. Registers are storage areas for information to be processed by the processor. For more information, see the section labeled "Processor Terminology."

8. C. The Pentium Pro has a 36-bit address bus, which enables it to access 64GB of system memory. The Pentium processor could address up to 4GB of system memory. For more information, see the section labeled "Popular Intel Processors."

9. B. The math co-processor performs many of the complicated math operations on behalf of the CPU, while the CPU itself performs the logic functions. For more information, see the section labeled "Processor Terminology."

10. B, D. The Pentium processor is placed into either Socket 5 or 7. Pentium II uses Slot 1, and some 486 chips use Socket 1. For more information, see the section labeled "Popular Intel Processors."

11. A. The Pentium II chip has increased the L1 cache to 32K, which is broken into two 16-KB channels. One channel is used for application code and one for data. 486 chips originally used 8K, and Pentium chips originally used 16K. For more information, see the section labeled "Popular Intel Processors."

12. A. Pentium chips supported voltages of either 3.3 volts or 5 volts — not 5.5 volts. The Pentium Pro chip used 3.1 volts. For more information, see the section labeled "Popular Intel Processors."

13. D. The Celeron chip is a cut-price Pentium II chip. The L2 cache is decreased to save on cost. Celeron chips either have no L2 cache or 128K cache, while the Pentium II chip has 512K of L2 cache. For more information, see the section labeled "Popular Intel Processors."

14. B. The address bus dictates how much memory the CPU can address. The data bus is the pathway to system memory, and registers are storage areas for data being processed. For more information, see the section labeled "Processor Terminology."

15. C. There are two major chip types in use today: the DIP chip and the PGA. The PGA was used for 486 chips and Pentium class processors, while the DIP was used for older processor chips, such as the 8088. Socket 5 and Slot 1 are not chip types — they are socket types. For more information, see the section labeled "Processor Terminology."

16. B. The Pentium processor has two instruction pipelines named U and V. For more information, see the section labeled "Popular Intel Processors."

17. B. The PGA packaged chips could be placed in a ZIF socket. These sockets had a lever; when the lever was pulled, the processor chip would pop out of the socket. For more information, see the section labeled "Processor Terminology."

18. B. The Pentium III processor runs on 133 MHz system boards. The Pentium and the K6 run on either 60 or 66 MHz system boards, while the Pentium II can run on 100 MHz system boards. For more information, see the section labeled "Popular Intel Processors."

19. B. The Pentium 133 is a clock double processor. It runs twice as fast as the system board. Therefore, the system board speed is 66 MHz. For more information, see the section labeled "Popular Intel Processors."

20. A. L1 cache is integrated into the processor, while L2 cache typically has always resided outside the CPU, usually on the system board. DRAM is a type of memory used for RAM. It is not used for cache memory. For more information, see the section labeled "Processor Terminology."

Motherboards: Components and Architecture

◆   ◆   ◆   ◆

CHAPTER 3

EXAM OBJECTIVES

Exam 220-201 ◆ A+ Core Hardware

◆ **4.3** Identify the most popular types of motherboards, their components, and their architecture (bus structures and power supplies). Content may include the following:

- **Types of motherboards:** AT (Full and Baby), ATX
- **Components:** Communication ports, SIMM and DIMM, Processor sockets, External cache memory (Level 2)
- **Bus Architectures:** ISA, PCI, AGP, USB (Universal Serial Bus), VESA Local Bus (VL-Bus)
- **Basic compatibility guidelines:** IDE (ATA, ATAPI, ULTRA-DMA, EIDE), SCSI (Wide, Fast, Ultra, LVD (Low Voltage Differential))

CHAPTER PRE-TEST

1. Which system board form factor incorporates AGP?

2. Which socket type is used to hold classic Pentium processors?

3. Which bus architectures have a 32-bit data path?

4. An ISA card can fit into which other bus architecture's slot?

5. What is the purpose of bus mastering?

6. PCI cards come in two flavors, _____ bit and _____ bit.

7. What bus architecture is typically found on Pentium systems?

8. ISA cards come in two flavors, _____ bit and _____ bit.

9. What is the transfer rate of USB devices?

10. PCI devices run at _____ MHz.

✦ Answers to these questions can be found at the end of the chapter. ✦

One of the major replaceable components in your computer is the system board, also known as the motherboard. The *system board* is the big green board (that may not be a technical description, but I think that looking inside your system will demonstrate that it is an accurate one) connected to the computer case holding your RAM, processor, and a number of other components.

This system board is the glue that connects all the other PC components. For example, following the IDE ribbon cable from your hard disk demonstrates that it connects to the system board. If you do the same with the IDE cable that connects to the floppy drive, you can see that it also connects to the system board. The memory sockets and the processor socket are likewise located on the system board.

All the components that work together to make the computer functional connect to the motherboard. If you take a close look at the system board, you can see that there are wires embedded on the board that form little pathways that span the system. Think of these wires as the highway system that data signals use to travel from one location to another. This connection allows information to travel from one component to another component.

In this chapter we introduce you to the different types of components you find on a motherboard. Then we take a look at the different types of motherboards. Finally, we explore what an expansion bus is and discuss the different bus architectures.

Exam Tip For the exam, remember that the terms *system board* and *motherboard* are interchangeable.

Motherboard Components

4.3 Identify the most popular types of motherboards, their components, and their architecture (bus structures and power supplies).

When you look at the motherboard inside your computer, you notice that there are a number of different items connected to this board. The memory sockets are installed on this board; the CPU socket is located on the motherboard, and the BIOS chip is also located on the motherboard. In this section, we will identify the different system board components.

Processor

One of the easiest items to recognize on the motherboard is the processor. The processor is usually the largest chip on the system board and can be identified generally because it often has a heat sink or fan located on top of it.

Classic Pentium motherboards typically have a socket 7 slot that the processor is inserted into. This socket is implemented as a ZIF (zero insertion force) socket, which means that the processor chip can be removed or added to the socket with very little effort. ZIF sockets (shown in Figure 3-1) typically have a lever that you pull to pop the processor out of the socket.

Socket 7 Zif Socket

Figure 3-1: Looking at a ZIF socket

Pentium II system boards had to implement a different socket for the Pentium II chip because the Pentium II chip was designed with a single edge connector and was inserted into the board standing up. The processor socket for Pentium II chips is called slot 1. For more information on processors, refer to Chapter 2.

Exam Tip   Remember for the exam that classic Pentium chips are inserted into socket 7, whereas Pentium II chips are inserted into slot 1.

SIMM/DIMM sockets

When you look at a system board, one of the first items that should stand out is the processor or its socket; the next thing that you will usually take notice of are the memory slots that are used to install RAM.

There are typically two types of sockets to install memory: SIMM (Single InLine Memory Module) sockets and DIMM (Dual Inline Memory Module) sockets. Original Pentium systems typically have either four 72-pin SIMM sockets, or two 168-pin DIMM sockets to install memory. Figure 3-2 shows a motherboard with four 72-pin SIMM sockets and two DIMM sockets.

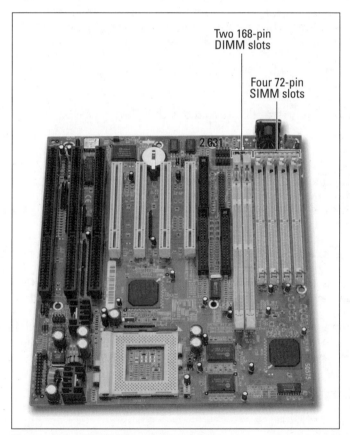

Figure 3-2: Identifying memory slots

When installing SIMMs in Pentium motherboards, you have to install them in pairs, but when installing DIMMs, you can install them individually. The reason for the difference in the installation process is that when installing memory, you must fill a memory bank, which is the size of the processor's data path. That is, if you install 72-pin (32-bit) SIMMs onto a Pentium (64-bit) motherboard, then you have to install two modules to fill the 64-bit data path of the processor. DIMMs are 64-bit memory modules, which is why you only have to install one at a time.

Cache memory

In Chapter 2, we explained how cache memory increases performance by storing frequently used program code or data. Because cache memory is faster than RAM, the system can store information accessed from RAM in cache memory when the data is accessed the first time. The processor can then retrieve the information from the faster cache memory for subsequent calls.

All the processors today have integrated cache memory, which is known as level-1 cache. The types of cache are as follows:

✦ **L1 (level-1) cache:** Cache that is integrated within the processor.

✦ **L2 (level-2) cache:** Cache that is located outside the processor, like on the motherboard.

Older motherboards implemented cache memory as rows of DIP chips placed directly on the motherboard. This area was sometimes even labeled "cache." Labels on a motherboard seem to be something that you cannot always rely on though — if they are there, consider it an added bonus!

Newer systems have implemented the cache as a memory module, so you may see an empty slot on the motherboard that looks like a place where you would install a SIMM, but it will really hold a cache module. A lot of times this will be labeled as *cache* on the system board. Figure 3-3 shows L2 cache on the system board.

Exam Tip   Remember for the exam that the L2 cache is usually located on the motherboard in close proximity to the processor. That way, data travels over a shorter distance from cache to processor — increasing overall system performance.

Figure 3-3: Looking at L2 cache on the system board

Expansion slot

Most motherboards have one or more *expansion slots*, which serve the purpose of adding functionality to the computer. Even if, for example, your computer doesn't have sound capability right now, you can install a sound card into the expansion slot to add that capability.

Expansion slots come in different varieties on systems today, and it is extremely important to understand the benefits of each type. We discuss these issues later in the chapter, in the section titled "Bus Architectures."

If you look at the system board, you can see a number of expansion slots. There are probably some white narrow slots on the board, which are the PCI slots. You may also see some larger black slots; these are ISA slots.

Note   Most newer systems coming out today no longer include ISA slots.

In Figure 3-4, you can see the PCI slots (the white slots) along with the ISA slots (the larger black slots). You can also see that there are three PCI slots and four ISA slots.

PCI Slots   ISA Slots

Figure 3-4: Looking at ISA and PCI expansion slots

Communication ports

Newer system boards have communication ports integrated directly into the board. The communication ports are also known as the COM ports. Typically, there are two COM ports on each system, COM1 and COM2.

 Exam Tip   Remember for the exam that the official standard that governs serial communication is known as RS-232, and you may see serial ports referred to as RS-232
ports.

COM ports are also known as serial ports. The reason that they are called serial ports is because they send data in a series—a single bit at a time. If eight bits of data are being delivered to a device connected to the COM ports, then the system is sending the eight bits of data, one at a time.

You usually connect an external modem, or a serial mouse, to these ports. Each of these devices is used for communication; a modem is used to allow your computer to talk to another computer across phone lines, while a serial mouse is a communication device that allows you to communicate with the system. Figure 3-5 shows two serial ports connected to a motherboard.

Serial ports on the back of the system board are one of two types:

✦ **DB9-male** is a male serial port with 9 pins.

✦ **DB25-male** is a male serial port with 25 pins.

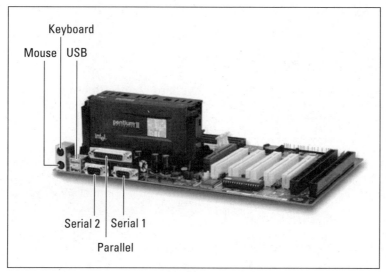

Figure 3-5: Looking at integrated ports

Parallel port

Another type of connector that you will have on the back of the motherboard is the parallel port. The parallel port is also known as the printer port, or LPT1. The parallel port gets its name by being able to send information eight bits at a time. Whereas serial ports only send one bit at a time in single file, parallel ports send can send eight bits in one operation — side-by-side rather than single file.

The parallel port is a female port located on the back of the system board with 25 pins, which is known as DB25-female. Looking back at Figure 3-5, you can see the parallel port located above the two serial ports.

It is important not to confuse the serial port with the parallel port. The serial port is a male port, and the parallel port is a female port.

You connect the parallel port to a printer by using a parallel cable that has a different type of connector at each end. On one end of the cable is a DB25 connector that attaches to the parallel port on the back of the computer (that makes sense—a female DB25 port has a cable with a DB25 male connector on it). On the other end of the cable (the end that connects to the printer) you will have a 36-pin Centronics connector. For more information on the Centronics connector, refer to Chapter 6.

Remember for the exam that a standard printer cable has two different types of connectors on it, one at either end of the cable. On one end there is a DB25 connector with 25 pins, while on the other end there is a 36-pin Centronics connector.

Keyboard/mouse connector

Most motherboards today have mouse and keyboard connectors that are most likely PS2 style connectors. In Figure 3-5 you can see the keyboard and mouse connector on the left side of the diagram.

Older motherboards may have an older DIN keyboard connector, which you can see on baby AT motherboards. These systems may or may not have a mouse port on the system board. If not, the mouse connector was located on the case that the system board was inserted into; the mouse connector would connect by wires to the system board.

Power connector

Located on the system board, you should see a type of connector that you can use to connect the power supply to the motherboard. All of these devices connected to the motherboard need to get power from somewhere, so the power supply is connected to the motherboard, which supplies power to the board and its components.

Figure 3-6 shows the power connectors on the motherboard. There are power cables coming from the power supply to connect to the motherboard with very unique connectors on the end, these may be labeled as P1 and P2, or on some systems, P8 and P9.

Motherboard Power Connector

Figure 3-6: Looking at power connectors located on the motherboard

You have to be extremely careful to make sure that these connectors are inserted properly, or you could damage the motherboard. Often, the connectors are keyed (meaning that they can only go in one way) so that you cannot put both of the connectors in the wrong way.

Video adapter

Many motherboards today come with a built-in video adapter, sometimes called a video card or video controller. Figure 3-7 shows how information flows from the system to the monitor. The following steps refer to the numbers in Figure 3-7.

1. The video adapter is responsible for receiving digital data from the processor, which instructs the video adapter on how the images are to be drawn on the screen.

2. The video adapter stores the information about drawing the images in its memory and starts converting the information into analog data that the monitor can understand.

3. The data is sent in analog format from the video adapter to the monitor.

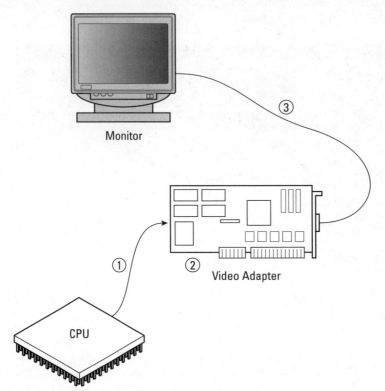

Figure 3-7: Looking at the flow of information being processed by a video adapter

Tip   The video adapter does not have to be a separate card; it may be integrated into the motherboard. The purpose of the video adapter is the same whether it is integrated into the motherboard or is a separate card.

Hard disk controller

A *controller* is a device that is responsible for controlling data flow, so a *hard drive controller* is responsible for both of the following:

✦ Receiving information from the processor and converting or interpreting the information into signals that the hard disk can understand

✦ Sending information back to the processor and converting the information into signals that the processor can understand

Older drives implemented the controller as an expansion card installed into the system that connected to the hard disk via a cable connection. Today, however, hard disk controllers are integrated into the hard disks.

You can also find either one or two hard disk controllers on newer motherboards (for more information, see the section titled "EIDE/ATA-2"). The controller on the motherboard has 40 pins and connects to the drive using a 40-wire ribbon cable.

IDE/ATA

A number of hard drive standards have been developed over the last number of years — the first major standard being the *IDE standard*. The IDE (Integrated Drive Electronics) standard calls for an integrated controller on the drive to manage information entering and leaving the hard disk.

IDE has been around since 1989. IDE drives attach to the motherboard by means of a 40-wire ribbon cable. The IDE standard also allows two drives to connect in a daisy-chain fashion, creating a master/slave relationship between devices. The master drive is responsible for sending and receiving information in the chain.

The IDE standard is also known as the ATA (Advanced Technology Attachment) standard, which is sometimes known as the ATA-1 standard.

EIDE/ATA-2

The EIDE (Enhanced IDE) standard followed shortly after the IDE standard. The EIDE standard is a specification that allows four drives to be connected to a dual-channel controller. This is usually implemented as a motherboard having two controllers, one being the primary controller and the other being the secondary controller. You would then connect two drives off of each controller, making a master/slave chain off each controller; Figure 3-8 shows a primary controller and a secondary controller on the motherboard. EIDE also supports larger hard disks; the typical size of an IDE drive was about 504 MB. The EIDE standard is also known as ATA-2.

ATAPI

Typically, IDE devices are implemented as hard drives, but there has been a new ATA specification that has allowed other types of devices to exist on an ATA (or IDE) chain. This specification is known as the ATA Packet Interface, which allows devices like CD-ROMs and tape drives to exist on an ATA chain. Other types of ATAPI devices are CD writers, DVD devices, and zip drives.

ULTRA DMA

Ultra DMA drives have two major benefits over ATA drives:

✦ **Speed:** Ultra DMA devices function at double the speed of regular IDE devices. IDE devices execute commands at 16.6MB per second, whereas ultra DMA devices execute commands at 33.3MB per second.

✦ **Reliability:** Ultra DMA devices implement error correction, which provides for increased data reliability compared with IDE, which does not implement error correction.

Primary Controller

Floppy Controller

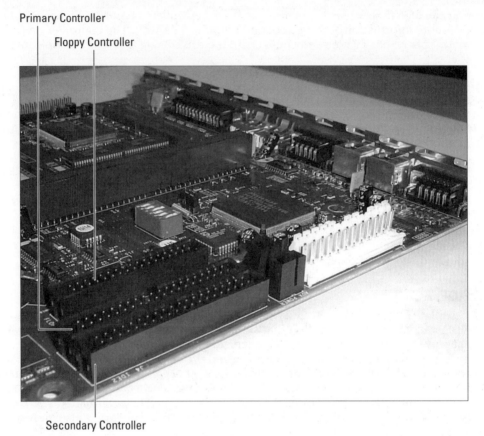

Secondary Controller

Figure 3-8: Looking at primary and secondary controllers along with the floppy controller

To take advantage of ultra DMA technology, you need an ultra DMA drive and an ultra DMA compatible BIOS. In addition, you need an ultra DMA compatible driver loaded in the operating system that uses the device.

It is important to note that ultra DMA technology is backward compatible with IDE and EIDE. For example, if you have a motherboard with ultra DMA support, you can still plug an IDE or EIDE device into the controllers on the motherboard. You can also take a ultra DMA drive and install it on an EIDE board.

Floppy disk controller

Located very close to the hard disk controllers, you should see a smaller *floppy drive controller* that connects the floppy drive to the motherboard. This controller supports a 33-wire ribbon cable, which connects the floppy drive to the motherboard. Figure 3-8 shows the floppy controller on the system board.

When connecting the floppy drive to the system, you will notice that the ribbon cable for the floppy drive has one end where the wires are twisted. This is the end of the ribbon cable that must be connected to the floppy drive. The opposite end is connected to the controller on the motherboard.

Exam Tip Remember for the exam that the twist in the ribbon cable for the floppy drive is the end that connects to the floppy drive. The opposite end connects to the system board.

SCSI controller

Some high-end machines, particularly those designed for use as servers, may have a controller on the motherboard with 50 pins on it. This is the footprint of a SCSI (Small Computer System Interface) controller on the motherboard. Because SCSI devices outperform IDE devices, SCSI controllers are extremely popular for use in servers (which have greater hard-disk access and storage needs than regular desktop computers).

Exam Tip Remember for the exam that an internal SCSI connector has 50 pins that connect to a 50-wire ribbon cable.

The following list compares the various flavors of SCSI. Know them for the exam:

✦ **SCSI:** SCSI is an example of a technology that has been out for many years and has progressed within those years. The original version of SCSI, also known as SCSI-1 was an 8-bit technology with a transfer rate of 5 Mbps. One of the major benefits of SCSI is that you are not limited to two devices in a chain like you are with IDE SCSI-1 allows you to have eight devices in the chain, with the controller counting as one.

✦ **Fast SCSI-2:** Fast SCSI-2 increases the performance of SCSI by doubling the transfer rate. Fast SCSI-2 devices transfer information at 10 Mbps, as opposed to 5 MBPS (SCSI-1). Fast SCSI-2 is still an 8-bit technology and supports eight devices in the chain.

✦ **Wide SCSI-2:** Wide SCSI-2 takes the data path of SCSI (8-bit) and doubles it to 16 bits; because the width of Wide SCSI-2 has been doubled the transfer rate is also 10 Mbps. The number of devices in a Wide SCSI-2 chain is 16.

Exam Tip When trying to remember the difference between SCSI-1, Fast SCSI-2, and Wide SCSI-2, think of it this way: *fast* implies speed, so the transfer rate is increased. *Wide* implies "wider" or bigger, which is the data path that has been increased; as a result, you will also get a larger transfer rate.

✦ **Fast Wide SCSI-2:** Fast Wide SCSI-2 is the combination of Fast SCSI-2 and Wide SCSI-2. The data path of Fast Wide SCSI-2 is 16 bits, the transfer rate is 20 Mbps, and the number of devices that is supported in the chain is 16.

✦ **Ultra SCSI:** Ultra SCSI takes the transfer rate of 10 Mbps and doubles it again to 20 Mbps! With Ultra SCSI, the bus width is only eight bits, and the number of devices that exist in the chain is eight.

✦ **Ultra Wide SCSI:** Ultra Wide SCSI is Ultra SCSI with the bus width increased to 16 bits and the number of devices in the chain is increased to 16! The transfer rate of Ultra Wide SCSI has been increased to 40 Mbps.

✦ **LVD (Ultra2):** Low Voltage Differential, also known as Ultra2 SCSI, has a bus width of 16 bits and supports up to 16 devices. LVD gets its reputation from having a transfer rate of 80 Mbps. For more detailed information on SCSI devices and configuring them, see Chapter 9, "Internal drives."

BIOS chip

Locating the BIOS chip on the system board is easy; it is usually rectangular in shape and generally features the manufacturer's name as a label on the chip. Some of the popular manufacturers are AMI, AWARD, and IBM.

The *Basic Input Output System* (*BIOS*) is the low-level program code that allows all the system devices to communicate with one another. This low-level program code is stored in the BIOS chip on the motherboard.

The BIOS chip is a ROM (read only memory) chip, which means that you can read information from the chip, but you cannot write to the chip under normal circumstances. Today's implementation of BIOS chips is EEPROM (Electrically Erasable Programmable ROM), which means that you can get special software from the manufacturer of the BIOS to write to the chip.

Why would you want to erase the BIOS? Suppose, for example, that your BIOS is programmed to support a hard disk up to 2GB in size, but that you want to install a new, larger hard disk instead. What can you do about it? You can contact the BIOS manufacturer and get an update for your BIOS chip, which is usually a software program today (in the past, you generally had to install a new chip). Running the software program writes new instructions to the BIOS to make it aware that there are hard disks bigger than 2GB and provides instructions for dealing with them. But before new instructions can be written, the old instructions need to be erased.

The BIOS chip also contains code that controls the boot process for your system. It contains code that will perform a power on self test (POST), which means that the computer goes through a number of tests, checking itself out and making sure that it is okay. Once it has made it past the POST, the BIOS then locates a bootable partition and calls on the master boot record, which will load an operating system. Figure 3-9 shows a BIOS chip on a motherboard.

ROM BIOS Chip

Figure 3-9: Looking at a BIOS chip located on a motherboard

Battery

The computer keeps track of its inventory in what is known as *Complementary Metal Oxide Semiconductor* (*CMOS*). CMOS is a listing of system components, such as the size of the hard disk that is installed in the computer, the amount of RAM, and the resources (IRQs and IO addresses) used by the serial and parallel ports.

This inventory list is stored in what is known as CMOS RAM, which is a bit of a problem because RAM loses its content when the power is shut off. You don't want the computer to forget that it has a hard disk or forget how much RAM it has installed. To prevent this sort of problem, a small watch-like battery on the system board maintains enough energy so that CMOS RAM does not lose its charge. If CMOS RAM loses its charge, it results in the CMOS content being lost. Figure 3-10 identifies a battery on the system board.

CMOS Battery

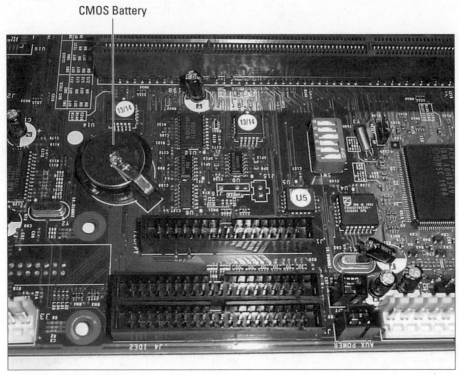

Figure 3-10: Looking at the CMOS battery on the system board

Types Of Motherboards

 4.3 Identify the most popular types of motherboards, their components, and their architecture (bus structures and power supplies). Content may include the following: Types of motherboards—AT (Full and Baby); ATX

Now that you understand some of the major components of the system board, it is important to mention the different motherboard form factors. A *motherboard form factor* just describes the dimensions or size of the motherboard and what the layout of the motherboard components are.

It is important to understand the different motherboard form factors, because you cannot take any motherboard and place it in a computer case. You must put an ATX board in an ATX case. Figure 3-11 shows the three major types of motherboards, which gives you an idea of size and shape differences between the three types.

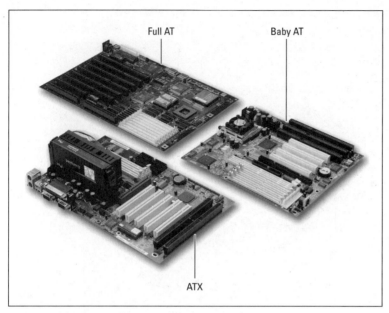

Figure 3-11: Looking at motherboard form factors

Full AT

The first type of motherboard that we want to talk about is the full AT motherboard. The full AT motherboard is 12 inches wide and 11 inches long. The full AT suffered from a problem with accessing some of the items on the motherboard because the drive bays hung over the motherboard. This situation made installation and troubleshooting of the components on the motherboard very difficult.

Another problem with the layout of the full AT board is that the expansion cards, once inserted into the systems, would cover the processor. This situation led to cooling problems due to the fact that ventilation was insufficient to keep the chip from overheating. Figure 3-12 displays a full AT system board being installed in a full AT case.

Baby AT

The baby AT system board form factor has been one of the most popular motherboard types until recent years. The baby AT board is 8.5 inches wide and 10 inches long. This motherboard can be easily recognized because it usually has a DIN keyboard connector in the top-right corner of the board.

Figure 3-12: Looking at a full AT system board

The baby AT board was about two-thirds the size of the full AT board and incorporated a socket 7 ZIF slot for classic Pentium processors. The baby AT board usually had a mixture of ISA/EISA and PCI slots located on the system board and included a plug and play BIOS. Figure 3-13 shows a baby AT system board and identifies the popular components.

Take a minute to consider some of the key components on the baby AT motherboard shown in Figure 3-13. You can see the socket 7 ZIF slot at the bottom of the motherboard where the processor is to be installed. Also notice the SIMM and DIMM sockets on the right side of the motherboard, which are used to house RAM memory. To the left of the SIMM and DIMM slots, you can see the primary and secondary EIDE controllers for connecting the hard drives to the board. To the left of the EIDE controllers, notice the types of expansion slots that are used: There are four PCI slots and three EISA slots. Above the PCI slots, you can also see a silver circle, which is the CMOS battery.

ATX

In 1995, Intel wanted a system board that would be used to support the Pentium II processor and the new AGP slot, so the ATX form factor was built (shown in Figure 3-14). The ATX board is 7.5 inches wide and 12 inches long and has all the IO ports integrated directly into the board, including USB ports.

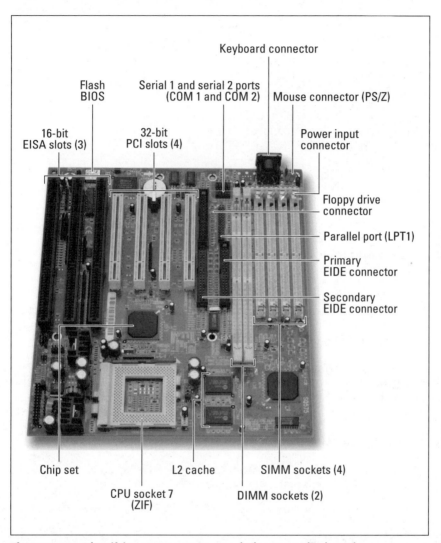

Keyboard connector

Flash BIOS

Serial 1 and serial 2 ports (COM 1 and COM 2)

Mouse connector (PS/Z)

16-bit EISA slots (3)

32-bit PCI slots (4)

Power input connector

Floppy drive connector

Parallel port (LPT1)

Primary EIDE connector

Secondary EIDE connector

Chip set

L2 cache

SIMM sockets (4)

CPU socket 7 (ZIF)

DIMM sockets (2)

Figure 3-13: Identifying components on a baby AT motherboard

Exam Tip   Remember for the exam that the ATX motherboard incorporated slot 1 for the Pentium II chip and added an AGP slot for high performance video cards.

The ATX board introduced a 100 MHz system bus, whereas older Pentium boards ran at 60/66 MHz and had one AGP slot for video cards. The ATX board also had soft power support, which meant that the system could be shut down by the operating system.

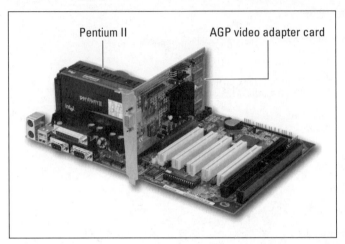

Pentium II   AGP video adapter card

Figure 3-14: Looking at an ATX board with a Pentium processor and an AGP video card

The ATX form factor rotated the baby AT components by 90 degrees so that any cards inserted into the bus architectures would not cover the processor and prevent proper cooling. Figure 3-15 shows an ATX motherboard.

Figure 3-15 highlights some of the common components on the ATX board. Notice, for instance, slot 1, where a Pentium II chip can be inserted. Notice also, in the top-right corner, the BIOS chip with a white label on top of it. At the top of the figure you can identify the EISA and PCI slots, and located in the center of the board is an AGP slot. The hard drive controllers are located on the left side beside the three slots that hold the DIMM memory.

Note   AMD has designed some processors — specifically the K6-2 line of processors — that can take advantage of the ATX form factor.

Bus Architectures

Objective   **4.3** Identify the most popular types of motherboards, their components, and their architecture (bus structures and power supplies). Content may include the following: Bus Architectures — ISA; PCI; AGP; USB (Universal Serial Bus); VESA local bus (VL-Bus)

On the system board are a number of expansion slots that are used to expand on the computer's capabilities. When it is first purchased, a computer only has so many capabilities — the nice thing is that you can expand on those capabilities.

In the Real World   When I first purchased my old 486 computer, it came without sound, but when I went out and purchased a sound card and installed it into the expansion slot — voila! — I had sound.

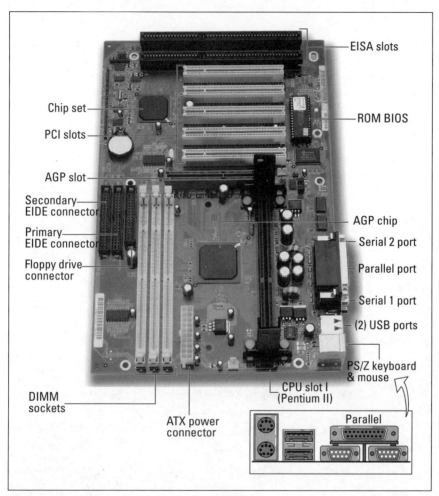

Figure 3-15: Layout of an ATX motherboard

Expansion slots expand on what the computer can do. The problem is that there are different types of expansion slots in the system, so when you go to purchase that sound card or network card, you have to make sure that you purchase the right type. In the following sections, we will look at the different type of expansion slots and compare their characteristics.

It is important to mention that another term for the expansion slots is bus architectures. There are a number of different bus architectures (or expansion slots) that have been developed over time. It is important to identify the differences between each of these architectures and also mention which ones are a little more popular today.

ISA

The *Industry Standard Architecture* (ISA) was the first major expansion bus architecture that was originally developed as an 8-bit architecture and then a 16-bit architecture. The ISA bus architecture had a speed of 8 MHz, which is extremely slow when looking at the speed of processors and other system components today. Figure 3-16 shows 16-bit ISA slots.

Figure 3-16: Looking at 16 bit ISA slots

 Exam Tip   Remember for the exam that ISA is an 8-bit or 16-bit technology that runs at 8 MHz.

One of the reasons why you still see 16-bit ISA slots in systems today is because ISA was the popular bus architecture for many years. This means that companies who have been buying ISA network cards for many years and are upgrading to a new system can use their old network card if they want to, thereby avoiding the additional cost of a new network card to go with the new system. Figure 3-17 shows a 16-bit ISA network card.

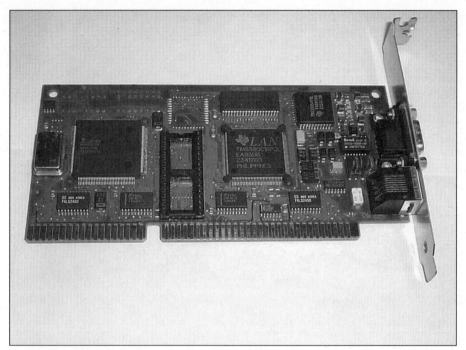

Figure 3-17: Looking at a 16-bit ISA network card

MCA

The expansion card concept was a big hit, and there was a lot of money to be made in manufacturing components that could be added to a computer to give the system more functionality, so everyone wanted a piece of this market. One of the major downfalls of the ISA bus architecture is its performance. It runs at only 8 MHz, and it is only a 16-bit architecture—that was fine years ago, but everything evolves, and new and improved standards arise.

The *Micro Channel Architecture* (MCA), which was developed by IBM, was a 32-bit architecture. The MCA architecture ran at 10 MHz and was not compatible with ISA. You would usually find the MCA slots in high-end IBM machines, such as those that might be used as a server.

Exam Tip   Remember for the exam that MCA transfers information in 32-bit chunks and runs at 10 MHz.

With the MCA, IBM came up with a feature called bus mastering. *Bus mastering* works like this: devices in the bus don't have to send information through the CPU if they want to talk to one another; they just send the information directly. This takes some of the workload off the processor and allows it to perform other tasks. Bus mastering became an important feature in future bus architectures. Figure 3-18 shows an MCA card.

Figure 3-18: Looking at an MCA network card

EISA

In 1988 the industry standard for expansion cards was still ISA, but bus architectures had already been created that performed better. So a number of companies got together with the goal of extending ISA, while maintaining backward compatibility so that companies could use their existing ISA cards.

As a result, the *Extended Industry Standard Architecture* (EISA) was developed as a 16- and 32-bit architecture. The big advantage to EISA is that it maintained support for the ISA cards that companies already had in large quantities, and it also supported 32-bit EISA cards. EISA also included the major advancement in expansion bus technology that MCA created, known as bus mastering. Because both types of cards fit into the same slot, they had to keep the speed of 8 MHz.

Exam Tip   Remember for the exam that EISA is an extension on ISA and is a 16-bit or 32-bit technology. For backward compatibility, EISA runs at 8 MHz.

The bus architecture holds both 16- and 32-bit cards because the EISA slots have two levels. The EISA cards have very deep edge connectors that fill the two levels (32-bit) of the slot, but ISA cards only filled the top level (16-bit). Figure 3-19 shows an EISA slot and shows two different levels in the slot; one level for the ISA card to fill and the other level for the EISA card to fill.

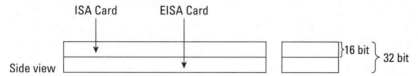

Figure 3-19: Looking at an EISA slot

VESA

In 1992 *Video Electronics Standard Association* (VESA) developed a bus architecture that outperformed ISA. VESA was a 32-bit architecture, supported bus mastering, and ran at the same speed as the processor, which back then was around 25 to 33 MHz. Because the bus ran at the speed of the processor, they called this the VESA local bus. VESA slots were typically used for video cards because the bus ran at the speed of the local system.

 Exam Tip   Remember for the exam that VESA is a 32-bit architecture that ran at the processor's speed. It is generally used for video adapters.

VESA slots are extremely easy to identify because they are tan in color and act as an extension to the ISA slot. You will notice the black ISA slots and then right beside them may be a tan slot. The VESA card fills the entire ISA slot and the additional extension to make the full 32-bit path for VESA. This allows an ISA card to be inserted into the slot for backward compatibility or, with the extension slot, it can hold a VESA card. Figure 3-20 shows a VESA slot.

PCI

Peripheral Component Interconnect (PCI) is one of the newer bus architectures that has hit the market. PCI has two flavors: 32-bit cards and 64-bit cards. When Pentium systems hit the market, they had motherboards shipped with them that featured both ISA/EISA slots and PCI slots. If you want to buy a new card today, you would most likely buy a PCI device for one of the PCI slots in your system.

The PCI bus has a speed of 33 MHz and also supports bus mastering. One of the other major benefits of PCI is that it is a plug and play architecture. If you are running a plug and play operating system like Windows 95/98/2000 (Windows NT is not a plug and play operating system) and you have a plug and play BIOS, then the system resources like IRQs and IO addresses can be dynamically assigned for PCI components.

 Exam Tip   Remember for the exam that PCI is a 32- or 64-bit technology, runs at 33 MHz, and supports plug-and-play.

PCI slots are easily identified on the system board as the small white slots on the motherboard, usually alongside the ISA or EISA slots. Figure 3-21 identifies PCI slots on a motherboard.

ISA Slots   VESA Slot

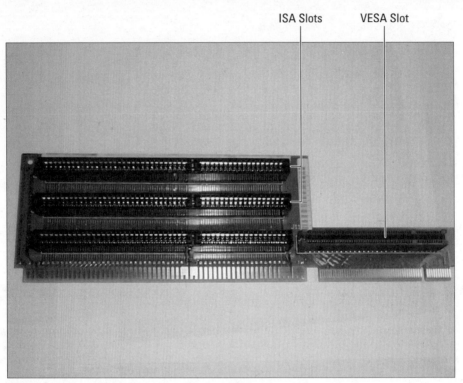

Figure 3-20: Looking at a VESA slot on a system board

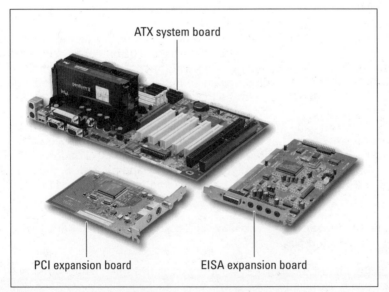

Figure 3-21: Identifying PCI slots on a system board

PCMCIA

Personal Computer Memory Card Industry Association (PCMCIA) is a unique type of expansion bus architecture because of its small size. PCMCIA is popular in laptop computers.How are you going to get a big network card like the one that is used in a desktop computer into a little laptop to add network support to the laptop? The answer is that you can't; you have to purchase a PCMCIA network card for the laptop to add network support. PCMCIA cards, also known as *PC Cards*, are a little bit larger than a credit card and can fit into your back pocket. Figure 3-22 shows a PCMCIA network card.

A Canadian Quarter

PCMCIA Network Card

Figure 3-22: Looking at a PCMCIA network card

PCMCIA (say that five times fast!) is a 16-bit architecture that runs at 33 MHz and has three different types of slots named type 1, type 2, and type 3.

Exam Tip It's too bad that you will not be asked on the exam what the three types of PCMCIA slots are. But you may get asked, "What type of devices does a type 2 PCMCIA slot hold?"

Table 3-1 shows you the different PCMCIA slot types and the types of devices you can find in the different type of slots.

Table 3-1 **Types Of PCMCIA Slots**		
Slot Name	*Thickness*	*Types of Devices*
Type 1	3.3 mm	Memory cards
Type 2	5.0 mm	Modems/Network cards
Type 3	10.5 mm	Removable drives

Type 1 cards were originally used to add memory to laptop computers or personal computers. This is where the "personal computer memory card" part of the PCM-CIA name comes from. Type 1 cards are 3.3 millimeters thick, and type 2 cards are 5 millimeters thick. Type 2 cards are used for everyday devices like modems and network cards. Type 3 cards are 10.5 mm thick and are used for removable drives.

AGP

Advanced Graphics Port (AGP) has been around since the Pentium II processor in 1997 and runs at 66 MHz, which is double the speed of the PCI bus. Today's motherboards have one AGP slot to insert an AGP video card. The performance gain from the AGP port not only comes from the increase in speed, but also the fact that the AGP bus has a direct path to the processor so that information travels quickly from the processor to the AGP card. Figure 3-23 shows an AGP slot beside a PCI slot and an EISA slot.

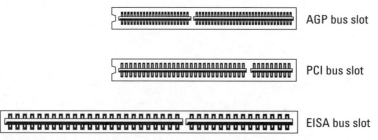

Figure 3-23: Comparing AGP slot with PCI and EISA

USB

Universal Serial Bus (USB) is a high-speed serial technology that transfers data at 12 Mbps. One of the major benefits of USB is the fact that USB devices use a similar type of connector so that with USB you will not have to guess what port on the back of the computer the mouse, keyboard, or monitor is to connect to. If they are all USB devices, they connect to the same type of port.

Tip There is a new USB standard called USB 2.0 that has a transfer rate of 480 Mbps.

USB devices also support daisy chaining. For example, you can connect device A to the back of the computer and then connect device B to device A, and so on. You can connect up to 127 devices in a USB chain. Figure 3-24 shows an example of a USB chain.

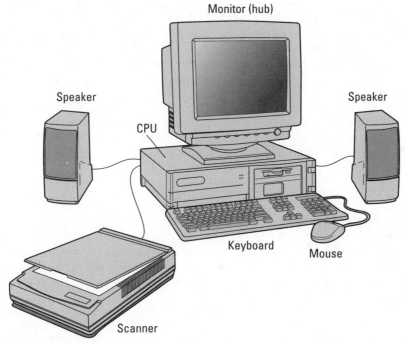

Figure 3-24: Looking at a USB chain

A USB device that connects to the computer and then has other devices connected to it is considered a hub device. In Figure 3-24, you can see that the monitor is acting as the hub device. If you don't have a USB device that can act as a hub device, then you can purchase a specific USB hub device that will allow you to chain other devices off of it.

As far as the "real world" is concerned, or from an exam perspective, you need to be extremely strong in the area of bus architectures. A big part of servicing computers is installing network cards, sound cards, or video cards — these components come as ISA, PCI, or AGP cards. You will have to know how to look at a system and say, "We are going to buy a PCI network card for this system."

Performance Considerations

When looking at improving system performance with motherboards, one of the first things you can do is check to see what the speed of the motherboard is. For example, some systems today have 100 MHz system boards, and some have 133 MHz system boards. You can get a performance increase from a faster system board.

Another performance consideration occurs when you add expansion cards to the system. You should first evaluate what expansion slots are free, and then purchase a card that will give you the best performance. For example, if you need to buy a network card for your computer, you start by looking at what expansion slots are free. If only two slots are free, an ISA slot and a PCI slot, then your choices are limited to an ISA network card or a PCI network card. Because PCI outperforms ISA, however, you would be better off purchasing a PCI network card.

You can also get a performance increase from system boards that have more cache memory. Look at the system board to see if there is a place to install some level 2 (L2) cache. L2 cache can dramatically increase performance because it is generally closer to the processor than the system memory (RAM) and is a faster type of memory than the system memory. Bottom line: the more cache memory you install, the better the system board's performance.

Key Point Summary

This chapter has introduced you to a number of key components of the system board and different system board form factors. The following is a list of the key points to remember when dealing with system boards:

✦ The motherboard is the computer component that interconnects all other components.

✦ Serial (COM) ports come in two flavors: DB9-male, or DB25-male. Parallel ports come in only a DB25-female port.

✦ There are two main types of cache memory: L1 and L2 cache. L1 cache memory is integrated into the processor, while L2 cache is contained outside the processor (typically on the motherboard).

✦ IDE supports two devices in the IDE chain, whereas EIDE has two channels with two devices in each channel (a total of four devices).

✦ There are three major motherboard form factors; Full AT, baby AT, and the ATX motherboard form factor. Motherboard form factors differ in the size of the board and the layout of the components stored on the board.

✦ You may add components, such as a sound card or network card, to the computer by inserting an expansion card into one of the expansion slots in the system.

✦ ISA was the popular bus architecture for years, but because of its limitations (16-bit bus width and a speed of 8 MHz) it has been replaced by the PCI bus architecture. PCI has a bus width of 32/64 bit and a speed of 33 MHz.

✦ You may increase the performance of the system by using a motherboard with a faster speed, or by purchasing better performing expansion cards.

✦   ✦   ✦

STUDY GUIDE

This study guide presents 20 assessment questions, one scenario, and two lab exercises to test your knowledge of this exam area topic.

Assessment Questions

1. What was the original system board speed of the ATX board?

    A. 33 MHz

    B. 60 MHz

    C. 66 MHz

    D. 100 MHz

2. Which bus architecture supports 32-bit / 64-bit cards and transfers information at 33 MHz?

    A. ISA

    B. EISA

    C. AGP

    D. PCI

3. Which motherboard component is responsible for charging the CMOS RAM so that CMOS can maintain its CMOS data?

    A. Battery

    B. BIOS chip

    C. CMOS chip

    D. Power supply

4. How many pins does a standard IDE controller have?

    A. 33 pins

    B. 40 pins

    C. 50 pins

    D. 20 pins

5. Which of the following best describes a baby AT system board?

    A. Uses Slot 1

    B. Runs at 100 MHz

    C. Uses a socket 7 ZIF socket

    D. Incorporates AGP

6. How many devices are supported in a USB chain?

    A. 10

    B. 27

    C. 127

    D. 32

7. How many pins does a standard floppy drive controller have?

    A. 33 pins

    B. 40 pins

    C. 50 pins

    D. 20 pins

8. Which bus architecture might be found in older IBM servers?

    A. ISA

    B. MCA

    C. VESA

    D. EISA

9. What type of cache memory will you find on system boards?

    A. L1

    B. L2

    C. SDRAM

    D. SRAM

10. Which type of memory module supports 32-bit data chunks?

    A. DIMM

    B. Cache

    C. SIMM

    D. Video

11. Which bus architecture runs at 8 MHz and has support for 16-bit ISA cards?

    A. MCA

    B. AGP

    C. PCI

    D. EISA

12. What is the bus architecture used in laptop computers?

    A. PCI

    B. PCMCIA

    C. EISA

    D. ISA

13. Which of the following best describes AGP?

    A. AGP slots have a direct path to the processor to help increase performance of AGP devices.

    B. AGP cards run at 33 MHz.

    C. AGP runs at 66 MHz and gets access to the processor through the PCI bus.

    D. AGP stands for Advanced Graphics Port and is used to install additional video memory.

14. Which PCMCIA card type is used for modems?

    A. Type I

    B. Type II

    C. Type III

    D. Type IV

15. Which port is typically used for a modem?

    A. USB

    B. LPT1

    C. COM1

    D. LPT2

16. Which of the following best describes EIDE devices?

    A. EIDE supports four devices in the chain.

    B. EIDE only supports 504 MB hard disk.

    C. EIDE devices have a 50-wire ribbon cable connected to them.

    D. EIDE supports up to eight devices in the chain, with the controller counting as one of the devices.

17. When connecting a floppy drive to the system, which end of the ribbon cable will get connected to the floppy drive?

    A. The end with a red stripe

    B. The end with a twist

    C. The end with a blue stripe

    D. The end without a twist

18. What are the labels given to the power connectors that supply power to the motherboard?

    A. P1 and P2

    B. P22 and P2

    C. PT1 and PT2

    D. PS1 and PS2

19. How many pins are in a parallel cable connector that connects to the computer?

    A. 36

    B. 40

    C. 25

    D. 33

20. Which port sends information 8 bits at a time side-by-side?

    A. COM1

    B. LPT1

    C. COM2

    D. USB

Scenarios

This chapter has discussed the components of the system board, as well as some of its performance considerations. The following scenario is designed to help you apply what you have learned in this chapter to a real-life situation.

1. Your manager wants to increase the performance of a computer that will be used for storing and processing mission-critical information. What methods would you recommend to increase system performance?

Lab Exercises

Lab 3.1 Identifying motherboard components

1. In the following diagram, identify the major system board components by placing the letter alongside the component.

___ Processor

___ 8-bit ISA slots

___ 16-bit ISA slots

___ VESA slots

___ ROM BIOS chip

___ 72-pin SIMMs

___ 30-pin SIMMs

___ CMOS battery

___ L2 cache

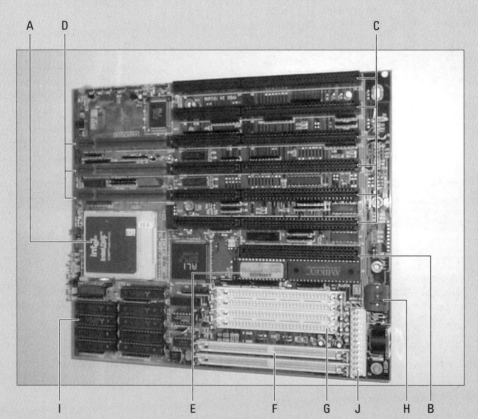

Figure 3-25: Lab 3.1: Identifying motherboard components

Lab 3.2 Identifying performance characteristics of bus architectures

1. In the following table, fill in the blanks identifying the different performance characteristics of each of the standard bus architectures.

Bus Architecture Characteristics

Bus Architecture	Speed	Data Path	Bus Mastering Support
ISA		8 /16 bit	No
EISA	8 MHz		
MCA			
VESA		32 bit	
PCI			

Answers to Chapter Questions

Chapter Pre-Test

1. The **ATX** motherboards incorporate the AGP slot.

2. Classic Pentium processors use **socket 7**.

3. **VESA, MCA, EISA, and PCI** all have the potential to use 32-bit data paths.

4. An ISA card can fit into **EISA slots**.

5. Bus mastering allows **devices in the bus to communicate directly with one another**; they don't have to bother the CPU for internal communication.

6. PCI cards come in two flavors, **32-bit** and **64-bit**.

7. Typically you will find the **PCI** bus architecture on Pentium systems.

8. ISA cards came in **8-bit** and **16-bit**.

9. USB devices transfer information at **12 Mbps**, but USB 2.0 transfers information at 480 Mbps.

10. PCI devices run at **33 MHz**.

Assessment Questions

1. **D.** The ATX board had an original system board speed of **100 MHz**. Older boards, such as the baby AT, had motherboard speeds of 60 and 66 MHz. For more information, see the section titled "Types Of Motherboards."

2. D. The **PCI** bus architecture is a 32-bit and 64-bit architecture that runs at 33 MHz. AGP runs at 66 MHz, while both ISA and EISA run at 8 MHz. For more information, see the section titled "Bus Architectures."

3. A. The **battery** is responsible for maintaining a charge so that the CMOS RAM does not forget its information. The BIOS chip stores the core system code that allows all of the devices to communicate. For more information, see the section titled "Motherboard Components."

4. B. An IDE controller has **40 pins** to allow a 40-wire ribbon cable to connect a hard disk or CD-ROM to it. A floppy controller uses 33 pins, and 50 pins are used by internal SCSI devices. For more information, see the section titled "Motherboard Components."

5. C. The baby AT motherboard uses a **socket 7 ZIF socket to insert a Pentium processor**. Both slot 1, which is the processor slot for Pentium II processors, and the AGP slot that is used by video cards exists on the ATX board. For more information, see the section titled "Types Of Motherboards."

6. C. There are **127 USB devices** supported in a USB chain. For more information, see the section titled "Bus Architectures."

7. A. A floppy drive controller has **33 pins** while an IDE controller has 40 pins, and an internal SCSI devices has 50 pins. For more information, see the section titled "Motherboard Components."

8. B. In the past you were likely to see **MCA** in older IBM servers because IBM developed the MCA bus architecture. For more information, see the section titled "Bus Architectures."

9. B. Level 2 (L2) cache is the type of cache memory that is found on system boards, whereas level 1 (L1) cache is found in the processor. Choices C and D are not types of cache memory. For more information, see the section titled "Motherboard Components."

10. C. 72-pin SIMM modules are 32-bit modules, whereas a DIMM is a 64-bit memory module. Choices B and D have no purpose to the question. For more information, see the section titled "Motherboard Components."

11. D. The **EISA** bus architecture runs at 8 MHz and supports ISA cards. Choice A is incorrect because MCA does not support ISA, choice C is incorrect because PCI runs at 33 MHz, while AGP runs at 66 MHz. For more information, see the section titled "Bus Architectures."

12. B. The bus architecture used in laptop computers is called **PCMCIA** (Personal Computer Memory Card Industry Association). The other three choices are bus architectures available to desktop computers. For more information, see the section titled "Bus Architectures."

13. A. The AGP slot **runs at 66 MHz and has a direct path between the slot and the processor** so that information will not have to travel through one of the slower buses. For more information, see the section titled "Bus Architectures."

14. **B. Type II cards** are used for network cards and modems. Type I cards were used for memory upgrades, while type III cards were used as removable drives. For more information, see the section titled "Bus Architectures."

15. **C. COM1** is a serial port on the back of the system that is typically used for modems or serial mice. LPT ports are parallel ports that are generally used to connect to printers. For more information, see the section titled "Motherboard Components."

16. **A.** EIDE **supports 4 devices** in an EIDE chain. EIDE drives also have exceeded the typical 504 MB barrier of IDE devices. Choice B is wrong because it is IDE that only supports 504 MB drives. Choice C and D are describing SCSI technology, not EIDE. For more information, see the section titled "Motherboard Components."

17. **B.** The floppy ribbon cable has one **end that is twisted**, it is that end that must be connected to the A: drive. No matter what end of the cable is connecting to the drive or the controller on the motherboard, you will have to make sure that the colored wire is connected to pin 1. For more information, see the section titled "Motherboard Components."

18. **A. P1 and P2** are the typical labels given to power connectors that are connecting to the motherboard. For more information, see the section titled "Motherboard Components."

19. **C.** The parallel cable has two different style connectors at either end of the cable. The **end that connects to the computer has 25 pins**, while the end that connects to the printer has 36 pins. For more information, see the section titled "Motherboard Components."

20. **B. Parallel ports send information in 8-bit chunks**, side-by-side; LPT1 is the only parallel port listed. The other three ports are serial ports that send information 1 bit at a time. For more information, see the section titled "Motherboard Components."

Scenarios

1. One of the first things you can do to help increase overall system performance on this system is to take the highest performance network card and install it in that computer. You could use a 64 PCI network adapter for this, which runs at 33 MHz.

   You could also install more RAM or a faster hard disk (maybe a fast wide SCSI 3) on the machine, which will increase performance of the system. You could also look at installing more L2 cache memory on the motherboard.

Lab Exercises

Lab 3.1

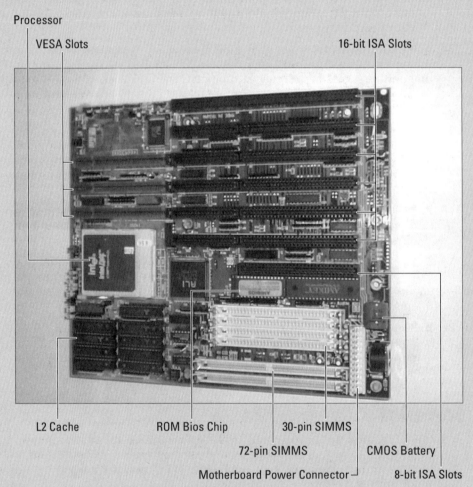

Figure 3-26: Lab 3.1: Identifying motherboard components

Lab 3.2

Bus Architecture Characteristics

Bus Architecture	Speed	Data Path	Bus Mastering Support
ISA	8 MHz	8 /16-bit	No
EISA	8 MHz	16/32-bit	Yes
MCA	10 MHz	32-bit	Yes
VESA	Processor Speed	32-bit	Yes
PCI	33 MHz	32/64-bit	Yes

RAM Terminology

EXAM OBJECTIVES

Exam 220-201 ✦ A+ Core Hardware

✦ **4.2** Identify the categories of RAM (Random Access Memory) terminology, their locations, and physical characteristics. Content may include the following:

- **Terminology:** EDO RAM (Extended Data Output RAM); DRAM (Dynamic Random Access Memory); SRAM (Static RAM); RIMM (Rambus Inline Memory Module 184 Pin); VRAM (Video RAM); SDRAM (Synchronous Dynamic RAM); WRAM (Windows Accelerator Card RAM)

- **Locations and physical characteristics:** Memory bank; Memory chips (8-bit, 16-bit, and 32-bit); SIMMs (Single In-line Memory Modules); DIMMs (Dual In-line Memory Modules); Parity chips versus non-parity chips

CHAPTER PRE-TEST

1. The type of DRAM that the CPU can access at the system speed is

   _____.

2. Memory that contains data that cannot be changed is called _____.

3. A 72-pin memory module is called a _____.

4. Cache memory stored on the motherboard is what type of cache memory?

5. Memory that must be constantly refreshed is what type of memory?

6. What is the average speed of DRAM?

7. The time it takes the CPU to access data in memory is measured in

   _____.

8. Cache memory is made up of what type of memory?

9. What is the average speed of SRAM?

10. Cache memory integrated into the CPU is what type of cache memory?

✦ Answers to these questions can be found at the end of the chapter. ✦

Finding out how much memory a computer has is one popular way to measure the computer's power and capabilities. Think about it: If someone asked you what kind of computer you had, what would you say? Probably something like, "I have a Pentium 600 with 128MB of RAM." But why do we measure the power of a computer based on the amount of memory it has?

In this chapter, you will learn the purpose of memory and some of the different types of memory that you will find in a computer. This chapter also discusses issues that affect the installation of memory in personal computer systems.

Memory Use

The term *memory* refers to anything that stores information either permanently or temporarily. Computers have two different flavors of memory, RAM and ROM, and probably the most fundamental of these flavors is RAM, or *random access memory*. As the computer's primary working memory, RAM only stores information on a temporary basis. If you were looking for permanent storage, you would need to save information to the hard disk. When the computer is powered off, all the contents of RAM are flushed out.

Whether sitting at your home or office desk (working on a proposal or preparing for your A+ Certification exam), chances are your desk is covered with documents, books, and papers. This desk is your work area, and its size dictates how many documents you can work on at any given time.

System memory works the same way. You have documents and applications stored on the hard disk. When you want to work on these documents, you open them and place them in the computer's work area. The work area (or desk space) for a computer is system memory. When you want to work with any application or document, the computer must move that information from the hard disk and execute it from memory.

Assume, for instance, that your computer has 16MB of memory (not a lot in this day and age). You start up your system, which is running Windows 98, and decide to run Microsoft Word and Microsoft Excel at the same time. Assume further that you are using 10MB of precious memory at this point — a few MBs for the operating system to load, and a few for each running application. As you can see, your memory usage adds up quickly.

In this scenario, you have already used 10MB of memory before your real work has even started. You only have 6MB left to perhaps open up some documents and copy and paste information from one spot to another. To put it simply: you are running out of desk space. You can solve the problem in one of two ways. You can either do less work (in other words, work on one application at a time — although this solution would not serve business users very well, since they often need to run multiple applications simultaneously.) Or you can get a bigger desk, which in computer terminology means "buying more RAM." When you install more RAM, you have a bigger desk to work on.

Types of Memory

4.2 Identify the categories of RAM (Random Access Memory) terminology, their locations, and physical characteristics. Content may include the following: Terminology—DRAM (Dynamic Random Access Memory); SRAM (Static RAM); RIMM (Rambus Inline Memory Module 184 Pin); VRAM (Video RAM); WRAM (Windows Accelerator Card RAM)

This section outlines different types of computer system memory. From an exam perspective, make sure you fully understand the different types of memory and their uses.

Read-only memory

Read-only memory (ROM) is a type of memory that cannot be written to. Information is written to ROM chips by the manufacturer, and this information cannot be changed. In the past, if ROM information needed to be updated, you had to remove the original chip and replace it with an updated ROM chip.

Tip   Software written to ROM chips is called *firmware*.

One of the major uses for ROM is to store the system BIOS, which contains Power-On Self-Test (POST) routines and other routines that initiate the loading of the operating system. The BIOS also contains the low-level code that makes communication possible between the central processing unit (CPU) and the hardware devices. Because the system BIOS is stored in ROM, you must remove and replace the ROM chip to update the BIOS software.

Exam Tip   For the exam, you need to know that the POST is part of the system BIOS code stored in ROM. The POST contains routines that initiate the loading of the operating system, and routines that make possible the communication between hardware devices.

EPROM

Erasable Programmable Read-Only Memory (EPROM) is a type of memory that normally cannot be written to because it is a variation of ROM. An EPROM chip is a special ROM chip on which the manufacturer can rewrite information with a special programming device that uses ultraviolet light to erase all the data.

EEPROM

A new implementation of ROM is called Electrically Erasable Programmable ROM (EEPROM), or flash ROM. The manufacturer writes the software instructions into the ROM chip, but you can update these instructions by running special software provided by the manufacturer. The special software is usually provided on a disk or can be downloaded from the manufacturer's Web site.

Exam Tip For the exam, know that EEPROM, better known as flash ROM, is a ROM chip that can be rewritten with special EEPROM update software provided by the manufacturer of the chip.

EEPROM has become the typical way to update your system BIOS. When my 486SX25 was designed, for example, it was not "aware" of my brand-new 6GB hard disk that I had purchased and planned to install in that computer. The manufacturer of the BIOS chip that's installed in my 486SX is well aware of current devices. Therefore, the manufacturer places BIOS updates on its Web site for computer users running those BIOSs. I just have to download the update to a floppy disk and then run the BIOS update. The update rewrites the BIOS instructions, making the computer "more aware" of today's hardware.

Random access memory

ROM is permanent memory, or permanent storage of information. RAM, or random access memory, is information stored temporarily. RAM is volatile, meaning that it needs constant current to maintain the information that resides in its chips. If current is lost, the contents of RAM will be erased.

This section will discuss the different flavors of RAM. On the exam, you can expect a few questions on the different types of memory.

DRAM

Dynamic RAM (DRAM) is probably the most popular type of memory today and the one that you are most often going to upgrade. When someone says to you, "I have 128MB of RAM!" they are talking about DRAM.

Dynamic RAM gets its name from the fact that the information stored in DRAM needs to be constantly refreshed. Refreshing involves reading the bits of data stored in DRAM and then rewriting the same information back.

Because the CPU accesses data in memory, we measure the memory's performance based on the time it takes the CPU to access that data. The measurement used to determine the speed of memory is nanoseconds (ns). One *nanosecond* equals a billionth of a second. If I have memory that is 50ns and my best friend has memory that is 70ns, we can assume that my memory is faster. My CPU receives the information from memory after waiting only 50 billionths of a second, whereas my best friend's CPU waits 70 billionths of a second.

The speed of DRAM ranges from 60ns to 80ns. The lower the number of nanoseconds, the better the performance.

CMOS RAM

The Complementary Metal-Oxide Semiconductor (CMOS) is the area where the computer stores its configuration information, such as whether or not it has a floppy drive, the date and time for the system, and the number and size of the hard drives that are installed. Think of the CMOS information as an inventory list for the majority of components that are installed on the computer. For more information on CMOS, see Chapter 5.

Exam Tip CMOS is the computer's inventory list. It tells the computer which devices reside in the system. For example, the CMOS information lists your hard drive, floppy drive, and other information — such as the date and time.

Is the CMOS information stored in the BIOS chip, or perhaps another ROM chip? The answer is no. In fact, if the information were stored in a ROM chip, you wouldn't be able to go into the CMOS Setup program and change the configuration. The CMOS configuration information is stored in a type of RAM called CMOS RAM.

CMOS RAM is a special volatile RAM chip that stores the CMOS information. Volatile means that if power is lost, the information is wiped out. This could present a problem with regard to CMOS configuration, since if the CMOS RAM is wiped out, the computer forgets its inventory information and has to relearn it. Thus, the computer has a small battery on the motherboard that maintains enough of a charge to avoid CMOS RAM erasure.

Exam Tip For the exam, know that CMOS information is stored in CMOS RAM, which is volatile memory maintaining its information by a battery stored on the system board.

Shadow RAM

Part of the boot process involves copying some of the BIOS instructions from ROM up to RAM and then executing those instructions from RAM rather than from the ROM chip. Why? Because ROM is much slower than RAM, you will get a performance increase because you are executing the instructions from (faster) RAM, as opposed to (slower) ROM. This entire process is called *shadowing*, in which a copy of the BIOS instructions are shadowed, or copied, to an area of memory called *shadow RAM*.

SRAM

Static RAM (SRAM) — so-called because the information held in its memory cells doesn't need to be refreshed — requires less overhead to maintain the information stored in memory.

With speeds running at 10ns to 20ns, SRAM is much faster than DRAM. This speed increase comes with a price, however, which is why people add DRAM to their systems more often than they add SRAM.

SRAM is typically used for cache memory. Cache memory is used to store frequently used data and program code from slower DRAM. Think of cache memory as a bucket that sits beside the CPU and stores frequently used information. After the system has searched through DRAM once for specific information, it can store that information in the bucket for easy access later.

Because cache memory is much faster than DRAM, the CPU retrieves information from cache rather than from DRAM; thus, system performance is increased due to the reduced wait time.

Exam Tip Cache memory is used to store frequently used data and program code. Because cache memory is faster than DRAM, retrieving information from cache means that the processor does not have to wait for the slower DRAM, thus enhancing system performance.

VRAM

Video RAM (VRAM) is dual-ported memory, meaning it can be read from and written to at the same time. DRAM is single-ported (which means that the memory can be written to and read from, but not simultaneously; it has to go one way at a time).

VRAM is most commonly used on video accelerator cards and is used to store the values of the pixels on the screen for refresh purposes. VRAM is the favored memory for video purposes because it outperforms the other memory types by being dual ported.

WRAM

Windows RAM (WRAM), also known as *Windows Accelerator Card RAM*, is a modification of VRAM and is also used for video display purposes. Like VRAM, WRAM is dual-ported memory, but runs about 25 percent faster. In general, WRAM offers better performance than VRAM (and at a cheaper price).

RIMM

There is a new high-speed flavor of DRAM on the market called *Rambus DRAM* (RDRAM), which runs at speeds around 800 MHz! The RDRAM chips have a 16-bit internal bus width and are packaged together in a 184-pin (gold plated) memory module called a Rambus Inline Memory Module (RIMM). In order to take advantage of this type of memory, you will need a motherboard and chipset that support RDRAM.

Types of DRAM

4.2 Identify the categories of RAM (Random Access Memory) terminology, their locations, and physical characteristics. Content may include the following: Terminology — EDO RAM (Extended Data Output RAM); SDRAM (Synchronous Dynamic RAM)

DRAM is the most popular type of memory used in systems today. It is also the most popular type of memory that computer users are adding to their computers for the purpose of upgrading memory. Therefore, you must understand the different types of DRAM and what types of DRAM outperform others.

Standard DRAM

Memory is organized into rows and columns like a spreadsheet. The information is stored in the different cells or blocks that make up these rows and columns. With standard RAM, the CPU requests data by sending the address of the row and the address of the column for every block of data that needs to be read. The memory controller then fetches the information from that memory location. Figure 4-1 shows two memory cells with data the CPU wants to have.

	0	1	2	3	4	5
0						
1			▓		▓	
2						
3						
4						

Figure 4-1: How data is accessed in memory

To access the information shown in Figure 4-1, the CPU follows these steps:

✦ In the first clock tick, it sends the row address (1).

✦ In the second clock tick, it sends the column address (2).

✦ On the third clock tick, the memory controller is ready to retrieve the information (Address 1-2).

✦ In the fourth clock tick, the row address is given again (1).

✦ In the fifth clock tick, the column address is given (4).

✦ In the sixth clock tick, the second cell address is read (Address 1-4).

Fast Page Mode

Fast Page Mode (FPM) improves on the performance of standard DRAM by not requiring a row address for each request to memory, assuming that the next block of data is on the same row (which in most cases will be true). The following list outlines the steps to access the same two blocks of data, shown in Figure 4-1, via Fast Page Mode.

- ✦ In the first clock tick, the CPU sends the row address (1).
- ✦ In the second clock tick, it sends the column address (2).
- ✦ On the third clock tick, the memory controller is ready to retrieve the information (Address 1-2).
- ✦ In the fourth clock tick, the column address is given (4).
- ✦ In the fifth clock tick, the second cell address is read (Address 1-4).

You can see in this example that it has taken less time to read both blocks of data from memory with Fast Page Mode DRAM.

Extended Data Output

Extended Data Output (EDO) memory is about 10 to 15 percent faster than FPM memory and is usually found on 66 MHz motherboards. With EDO memory, the memory controller can read data from a memory block while listening for the next instruction. This capability increases performance, because the memory controller does not have to wait for the next instruction after reading a block of memory; while it is reading one block of memory, it is receiving the next instruction. With FPM RAM, the reading of one memory block and listening for the next instruction would be done in multiple steps.

Burst Extended Data Output

Burst Extended Data Output (BEDO) is a bursting-type technology. The word *burst* refers to the fact that when one memory address is requested and that address is retrieved, the system bursts into the next couple of blocks and reads those as well. The theory behind BEDO is that the system has already gone through the trouble of locating that block, and chances are that the next request will be for the next block, so why not take it while we are there? If that extra block is the next requested block from the CPU, the memory controller already has the data and can pass it to the CPU immediately.

BEDO is 50 percent faster than EDO. Because of lack of support from computer manufacturers, however, BEDO has not been used in many systems. It seems that PC manufacturers are using SDRAM instead.

Synchronous DRAM

Synchronous DRAM (SDRAM) is memory synchronized at system speed. This synchronized speed means that the data stored in memory is refreshed at the system speed and data is accessed in memory at the system speed.

SDRAM is the popular RAM in systems today. Because you are running at the system speed, however, you must match the RAM with the motherboard speed. Thus, if you have a 100 MHz motherboard, you need 100 MHz SDRAM. If you have a 133 MHz motherboard, you need 133 MHz SDRAM.

DRAM Packaging

 4.2 Identify the categories of RAM (Random Access Memory) terminology, their locations, and physical characteristics. Content may include the following: Locations and physical characteristics — Memory bank; Memory chips (8-bit, 16-bit, and 32-bit); SIMMs (Single In-line Memory Modules); DIMMs (Dual In-line Memory Modules); Parity chips versus non-parity chips

Whether you are purchasing or installing RAM, it is important to understand the different types of memory packages available. This section identifies different memory packages and distinguishes between parity and non-parity memory.

SIMMs

Single in-line memory modules (SIMMs) have been one of the most popular types of memory modules for the past few years. A SIMM is a card with a number of memory chips installed on it and an edge connector containing a number of pins that make contact with the motherboard. This design makes it quite a bit easier to install memory than it was years ago. In the past, you had to take a dual in-line package (DIP) chip out of the system board and reinsert a new chip. Today, you purchase a card of chips (a SIMM) and install the SIMM into one of the SIMM sockets.

 For more information on chip types such as DIP, refer to Chapter 2.

SIMMs come in two flavors, 30-pin or 72-pin, which describes the number of connectors that make contact with the motherboard. Before purchasing a SIMM to install in a computer, review the documentation for the computer or look at the system board to determine what size SIMM module you need. Figure 4-2 shows a 30-pin SIMM, a 72-pin SIMM, and a dual in-line memory module (DIMM).

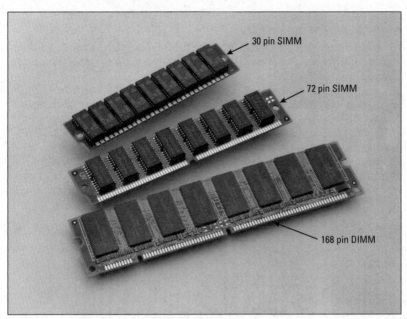

30 pin SIMM

72 pin SIMM

168 pin DIMM

Figure 4-2: Looking at memory modules

The 30-pin SIMMs have an 8-bit data path, meaning they supply information in 8-bit blocks. When installing memory into a system, you *must* install enough SIMMs to fill a memory bank. A *memory bank* is the number of SIMMs it takes to fill the data path of the processor. If you have a system with a 486 processor, for example, the processor is a 32-bit processor. Therefore, the processor wants to deal with information in 32-bit chunks. If you are using 30-pin SIMMs, you need to install four of them at a time to fill a bank (8 bits × 4 SIMMs = 32-bit chunks).

The 72-pin SIMMs supply information in 32-bit chunks. Therefore, if you are installing 72-pin SIMMs in a 486 chip, you need just one SIMM to fill a memory bank. If you are installing 72-pin SIMMs in a Pentium system, you must put the SIMMs in pairs because the Pentium data path is 64-bit; to fill a bank on these systems, you need two 32-bit modules (72-pin SIMMs).

Exam Tip   For the exam, know the data path of the SIMM modules. You should also know how many SIMMs it takes to fill a memory bank on 486 and Pentium processors.

In this day and age, SIMMs usually conform to the 72-pin format. If you support some 486 systems or below, however, you may bump into 30-pin SIMMs.

Tip   You can easily distinguish what size SIMM a system uses, even if you do not have the documentation for that system. The 72-pin SIMMs have a notch close to the center of the module. If the SIMMs are installed in the system already, you can take them out and examine them. They usually have a label with a 1 or a 72 at either end of the module representing the pin numbers — so if you see a number 72, you know you have a 72-pin SIMM.

DIMMs

Dual in-line memory modules (DIMMs) are like SIMMs, only they supply information in 64-bit chunks. DIMMs are found with 168 pins on the module and are a little larger than the 72-pin SIMMs.

Exam Tip   For the exam, know that SIMMs come in 30-pin and 72-pin flavors, whereas DIMMs have 168 pins.

Consider the memory bank issue again. Because the DIMM supplies data in 64-bit chunks, and the data path of a Pentium processor is 64-bit, you can install DIMMs singly in a Pentium system. On the other hand, you must install SIMMs in pairs in a Pentium system. Figure 4-3 shows what 72-pin SIMM and DIMM sockets look like.

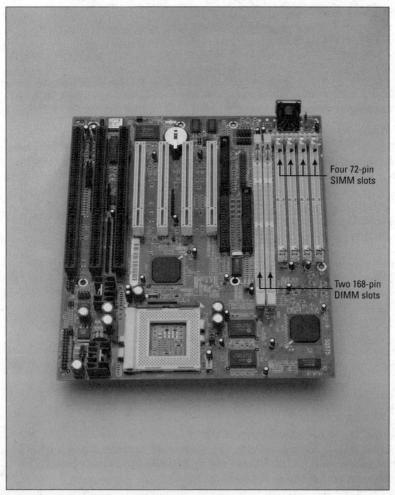

Four 72-pin
SIMM slots

Two 168-pin
DIMM slots

Figure 4-3: Looking at memory sockets

Parity versus non-parity

When upgrading memory, know whether the system you are working with uses parity memory. Once again, the best way to determine this is to look at the documentation.

There are two types of parity: odd parity and even parity. Both parity methods function the same way. This discussion uses odd parity as the example.

For every byte of data (8 bits), there is a parity bit. The number of the enabled data bits (bits set to 1) are added up, and if an even value results, the parity bit is set to 1 (enabled). If the result of all the enabled data bits is odd, the parity bit is set to 0 (disabled). After the parity bit has been set, the byte of data and the parity bit are written to memory. Note that even parity works the same way, only you are looking for an even number of enabled bits; if there is not, then the parity bit is enabled.

Exam Tip   For the exam, know that parity memory has an extra bit (the parity bit) for every 8 bits of data. SIMMs with parity come in 9-bit (30-pin SIMM) or 36-bit (72-pin SIMM) flavors.

When the CPU requests data from memory, the data byte is retrieved along with the parity bit that had been generated when the byte of information was stored in memory. The system looks at the data byte and calculates whether the parity bit is set to 1 or 0. It then compares the answer it has just generated with the value of the parity bit stored in memory. If the two match, the integrity of the information in memory is considered okay, the parity bit is stripped from the data byte, and the data is delivered to the CPU. If the two differ, you have a *parity error*, meaning that there is a problem with the integrity of the data stored in memory. Note that parity memory cannot correct the error; it just reports that an error exists.

Exam Tip   For the exam, know that a parity error indicates that there's something wrong with the integrity of data stored in memory.

Types of Cache Memory

Cache memory is memory made up of SRAM, which is much faster than DRAM. The average speed of DRAM is 60ns, whereas the average speed of SRAM is 20ns. If at all possible, you want the CPU's request for information to be serviced by cache memory for a quicker response. To help service these responses, the system has two levels of cache memory: L1 and L2 cache.

L1 cache

Another name for L1 cache is "internal cache," *internal* meaning that the memory exists within the CPU. This memory is SRAM-integrated into the processor's chip, giving the processor instant access to this memory with no wait time. *Wait time* is the amount of time it takes for the processor to request information stored in memory to actually receive the information.

Every processor since the 80486 has L1 cache integrated into the processor chip, but the amount of L1 cache can vary. For example, the 80486 chips had 8K of L1 cache, whereas the Pentium chips had 16K of L1 cache. Newer processors have doubled that amount to 32K of L1 cache.

L2 cache

L2 cache exists outside the CPU, usually on the motherboard or just outside the processor but in the processor casing. Therefore, some delay occurs with the processor accessing the information in L2 cache due to the distance to the memory chips and the bus speed.

 Exam Tip   For the exam, know that L1 cache is SRAM integrated into the processor's chip, whereas L2 cache is SRAM located outside the CPU, usually on the system board.

One of the selling points of different processors is the amount of cache memory that comes with the system. Many processors today typically have at least 32K of L1 cache and either 256K or 512K of L2 cache inside the casing of the processor. The more cache memory a system has, the bigger the bucket to store more frequently used information.

When the processor retrieves information, it first checks to see whether the information it needs is stored in L1 cache (because L1 cache has no wait time). If the processor does not find the information in L1 cache, it checks the L2 cache. If the information cannot be found in either L1 or L2 cache, the processor finally retrieves the information from RAM. Figure 4-4 shows the steps the processor takes to retrieve information.

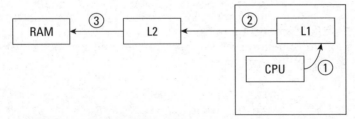

Figure 4-4: CPU information retrieval

Installation of Memory

Moving on from the different types of memory, the discussion in this section focuses on issues related to memory upgrades. In general, upgrading memory is a simple task — assuming you purchase the proper type of memory for the upgrade. Factors that affect the proper type of memory are:

✦ The speed of the memory

✦ Pin connector type

✦ Parity versus non-parity

The following sections discuss each of the factors that affect the purchase of memory for your system.

Speed

When purchasing memory, you need to first take into account the speed of the memory, which is typically measured in nanoseconds (ns). SIMMs usually run between 60ns and 80ns. Make sure you don't mix and match these speeds. The speed of the module is usually indicated on the chips themselves (by displaying either a numeric value or a simple minus sign with a number). For example, a memory module running at 70ns would show either a "70" or a "–7" on the chips.

Connectors

Another important issue with regard to memory installation is that you need to purchase the proper metal used for the pins on the memory modules. The metal used is either silver or gold. If the SIMM socket uses silver-plated connectors, the memory module you purchase must use silver-plated pins.

Parity/non-parity

The final issue with regard to memory upgrades is whether the system uses parity or non-parity memory. This information can be determined by checking the documentation that came with the system, or by trying to find the information on the Internet at the vendor's Web site.

Installing memory

Now that you have purchased either parity or non-parity memory at the correct speed and with the proper metal-plated pins, you are ready to install the memory.

After taking off the computer's cover, you should see either SIMM banks or DIMM banks — maybe even both types. Look at the sockets and determine whether the memory modules will sit diagonally or vertically. This step is very important. I have seen many people struggle to install memory because they didn't understand how to correctly place the modules in the bank.

If the bank is on a diagonal, lightly place the memory module vertically and then lay it back diagonally; it should just snap in. If the bank is a vertical socket, place the memory module at a 45-degree angle and lightly lay it back to the vertical position; it should snap in. Figure 4-5 shows the installation of memory modules.

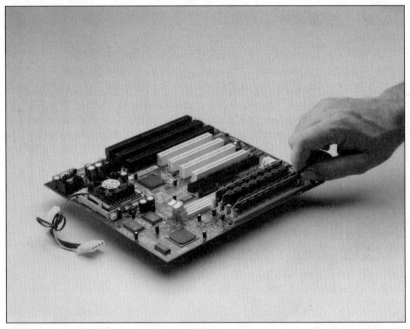

Figure 4-5: Installing memory modules

When you install the memory module, make sure you install Pin 1 on the memory module with Pin 1 in the SIMM bank. To locate Pin 1 on the memory module, look for the cut-out on the memory module (shown in Figure 4-6) and place it over the shoulder of the SIMM bank.

Figure 4-6: Locating Pin 1 on a memory module

Performance Issues

Evaluating the type(s) of memory supported on your system is something you can do to increase its performance.

First, make sure you're using the fastest type of memory possible for your system. For example, although I have a Pentium 100 that will use either FPM or EDO memory, I should populate the memory banks with EDO memory because it is the faster of the two types.

You can also make sure the system has as much cache memory as possible. Remember that cache memory is high-speed memory used to store information that will be accessed again and again. The more cache memory, the better. Thus, when considering a processor upgrade, look for a processor that has the most built-in cache memory — you find this information in the documentation. The cache gives you more bang for your dollar because it means you really optimize two portions of the system: the processor and the memory.

Another way to maximize system performance is to make sure that shadowing is enabled in CMOS. Remember that shadowing is the copying of the BIOS instructions from ROM to RAM. Although it should already be enabled on your system, someone may have disabled shadowing due to software compatibility issues. Some software may not like the fact that the area of memory that the BIOS routines are written to is being used up. When you hit problems with an application, as a last resort you may try disabling shadowing and see if the problem passes.

Key Point Summary

This chapter provided an overview of the different types of memory and installation of memory. The following points were touched on:

✦ Read-only memory (ROM) is memory that can be read from but not written to, and the information stored there is permanent.

✦ Random-access memory (RAM) is volatile memory that can be written to and read from; information stored there is flushed out when power is lost.

✦ DRAM is memory that needs constant refreshing of its memory cells; it is also the type of memory that is typically upgraded on systems.

✦ SRAM is static memory, meaning that it does not need refreshing as often as DRAM does. SRAM is also faster than DRAM. SRAM is typically used for cache memory.

✦ L1 cache is cache memory integrated into the processor, whereas L2 cache is cache memory that exists outside the processor's chip.

✦   ✦   ✦

STUDY GUIDE

This study guide presents 20 multiple-choice questions to test your knowledge of this exam topic area. It provides a scenario to help you apply critical thinking skills to the solution of a real-life problem. Finally, 2 labs provide hands-on experience, in a step-by-step format, in the area of memory installation.

Assessment Questions

1. Which of the following types of memory is used for cache memory?

   A. SRAM

   B. DRAM

   C. EDO RAM

   D. SDRAM

2. How many bits make up the data path of a 30-pin SIMM?

   A. 12

   B. 8

   C. 32

   D. 64

3. What type of cache memory resides on the system board?

   A. L1 cache

   B. SRAM

   C. L2 cache

   D. SDRAM

4. What type of memory must be constantly refreshed?

   A. DRAM

   B. SRAM

   C. VRAM

   D. L1 cache

5. What type of memory is dual-ported and can be read from and written to at the same time?

    A. VRAM

    B. DRAM

    C. SRAM

    D. L1 cache

6. Which of the following is a faster-speed memory?

    A. 30ns

    B. 10ns

    C. 120ns

    D. 70ns

7. How many 72-pin SIMMs make up a memory bank on Pentium systems?

    A. 3

    B. 1

    C. 2

    D. 4

8. Which of the following indicates the number of pins found on a DIMM?

    A. 64

    B. 128

    C. 168

    D. 32

9. How many bits of parity information are found in a 72-pin SIMM?

    A. 1

    B. 2

    C. 3

    D. 4

10. When a data corruption problem is found in memory, what error type typically displays onscreen?

    A. File access error

    B. Parity error

    C. Data corruption error

    D. DRAM error

11. When installing memory, how can you identify Pin 1 on the memory module?

    A. Square solders

    B. Red ribbon wire

    C. Blue ribbon wire

    D. SIMM cutout

12. Which of the following best describes VRAM?

    A. VRAM is memory that has video instructions burned into it by the manufacturer and cannot be changed.

    B. VRAM is dual-ported memory usually found on video accelerator cards.

    C. VRAM is memory stored in the CPU and is used for storing frequently used instructions.

    D. VRAM is memory that has video instructions burned into it by the manufacturer and can be reprogrammed only by special software.

13. What type of memory is typically used for storing computer BIOS code?

    A. DRAM

    B. SRAM

    C. RAM

    D. ROM

14. Which of the following best describes shadow RAM?

    A. Shadow RAM is an area of system memory where some of the BIOS functions are copied during the boot process.

    B. Shadow RAM is an area of system memory that stores the information twice so that if the system crashes, there will be a backup copy.

    C. Shadow RAM is the process of having frequently used data stored in cache for quicker access.

    D. Shadow RAM is another term for SRAM.

15. How many 30-pin SIMMs are required to fill a memory bank on an 80486?

    A. 1

    B. 2

    C. 3

    D. 4

16. What type of DRAM is synchronized with the system clock?

    A. EDO

    B. BEDO

    C. FPM

    D. SDRAM

17. How many DIMMs are used to fill a memory bank in a Pentium system?

    A. 1

    B. 2

    C. 3

    D. 4

18. When a CPU needs to access data, where will it look for this data first?

    A. L2 cache

    B. RAM

    C. L1 cache

    D. ROM

19. Which of the following best describes odd-parity memory?

    A. When a byte of data is stored, the value of all the bits in the byte are added up; if the number is an even number, the parity bit is enabled to create an odd number. If all the bits in the data byte add up to an odd number, the parity bit is turned off, leaving the total an odd number.

    B. All the data stored in memory is added up, and the answer is then stored in the parity bit.

    C. When a byte of data is stored, the value of all the bits in the byte are added up; if the number is an odd number, the parity bit is enabled to create an even number. If all the bits in the data byte add up to an even number, the parity bit is turned off, leaving the total an even number.

    D. Every 8 bits of data are added up, and the total is stored in the parity bit for that particular 8 bits of data.

20. What is the purpose of CMOS RAM?

    A. On system boot, the content of the BIOS is copied to faster RAM.

    B. Memory used to store the CMOS information. CMOS RAM maintains its information by a battery found on the motherboard.

    C. CMOS RAM is the amount of memory registered into CMOS.

    D. CMOS RAM is read-only memory that stores the CMOS information.

Scenario

This chapter has introduced a number of issues related to memory installation. The following scenario tests your knowledge of these issues.

1. Your co-worker has installed some memory received from his best friend, but the system does not seem to recognize the memory. What are some possible reasons for this?

Lab Exercises

Lab 4.1 Identifying RAM Requirements

1. Look at the documentation for your system and fill out the following table showing the RAM requirements for your system:

Memory Type (EDO, SDRAM):	
Memory Speed (60ns, 100 MHz):	
Gold or Silver Pins:	
SIMM or DIMM:	

Lab 4.2 Installing Memory

1. Remove the computer case.

2. Locate the SIMM or DIMM socket.

3. Identify whether the SIMMs will be seated either vertically or diagonally.

4. Install the memory into its socket.

5. Restart the system and save the changes to CMOS.

Answers to Chapter Questions

Chapter Pre-Test

1. The type of DRAM that the CPU can access at the system speed is **SDRAM**.

2. Memory that contains data that cannot be changed is called **read-only memory (ROM)**.

3. A 72-pin memory module is called a **single in-line memory module (SIMM)**.

4. Cache memory stored on the motherboard is **L2 cache memory**.

5. Memory that must be constantly refreshed is **random-access memory (RAM)**.

6. The average speed of DRAM is anywhere between **50ns and 80ns**.

7. The time it takes the CPU to access data in memory is measured in **nanoseconds (ns)**, for billionths of a second.

8. Cache memory is made up of **static RAM (SRAM)**.

9. The average speed of SRAM is **10ns to 20 ns**.

10. Cache memory integrated into the CPU is called **L1 cache memory**.

Assessment Questions

1. **A.** SRAM is the type of memory used for cache memory. DRAM is what is known as system memory and is what stores data and program code that is currently running. EDO and SDRAM are a type of DRAM. For more information, see the section titled "Types of Memory."

2. **B.** A 30-pin SIMM has an 8-bit data path. 72-pin SIMMs have a 32-bit data path, and a DIMM has a 64-bit data path. For more information, see the section titled "DRAM Packaging."

3. **C.** L2 cache memory is external to the CPU. Unlike L1 cache memory, which is integrated into the CPU, L2 cache memory is inserted onto the system board as additional cache memory. For more information, see the section titled "Types of Cache Memory."

4. **A.** DRAM must be constantly refreshed. The other types of memory do have to be refreshed, but not as often as DRAM. For more information, see the section titled "Types of Memory."

5. **A.** VRAM, or video RAM, is dual-ported memory that can read and write at the same time. Because of the performance increase with this type of memory, it is the desired memory for video accelerator cards. The other types of memory are single-ported, which means that you have to read and write through the same port and can go only one way at a time. As a result, the memory is slower. For more information, see the section titled "Types of Memory."

6. **B.** The general rule when working in nanoseconds is: the lower the number, the faster. Because memory speed is measured in billionths of a second and determines how long it takes the system to access the information stored in memory, 10ns is faster than them all. For more information, see the section titled "Installing Memory."

7. **C.** 72-pin SIMMs are 32-bit modules. Therefore, to fill a bank, the answer is two modules, because Pentium processors have a 64-bit data path. For more information, see the section titled "DRAM Packaging."

8. C. There are 168 pins on a DIMM. The other answers in this question are just common numbers used in the computer field. As far as number of pins, no memory modules use those numbers. For more information, see the section titled "DRAM Packaging."

9. D. There is always one parity bit for every eight bits of data. Because a 72-pin SIMM is a 32-bit module made up of four 8-bit chunks, there will be four parity bits. For more information, see the section titled "text."

10. B. Parity errors are the type of errors that display on-screen if there are any problems with data stored in memory. For more information, see the section titled "DRAM Packaging."

11. D. When looking at the memory module, you will notice that one end of the module is cut out. This indicates where Pin 1 is located on the module. A memory module has no ribbon wires. For more information, see the section titled "Installing Memory."

12. B. VRAM, or video RAM, is dual-ported memory that is usually found on video accelerator cards. *Dual-ported* means that the memory can be written to one port and read from another port. For more information, see the section titled "Types of Memory."

13. D. Read-only memory is typically used for storage of the computer manufacturer's BIOS code. Today's version of the BIOS chip can be reprogrammed by special software to update the BIOS. For more information, see the section titled "Types of Memory."

14. A. The term *shadowing* implies "making a copy." More specifically, it means making a copy of the BIOS instructions and copying them to system memory so that the functions can be executed more quickly. For more information, see the section titled "Types of Memory."

15. D. It would take four 30-pin SIMMs to fill a bank in a 486 processor, because 30-pin SIMMs are only eight bits wide and the processor's data path is 32-bit. A memory bank's data path is the equivalent of a processor's data path. If the SIMMs were 72-pin, you would need only one, because the 72-pin SIMMs have a 32-bit data path and the 486 chip has a 32-bit data path. For more information, see the section titled "DRAM Packaging."

16. D. SDRAM is the type of memory synchronized with the system clock speed. If the board runs at 100 MHz, you must buy the same speed memory for the board. For more information, see the section titled "Types of DRAM."

17. A. Pentiums have 64-bit data paths, and a DIMM has a 64-bit data path as well. Therefore, it would take only one DIMM chip to fill a bank in a Pentium system. For more information, see the section titled "DRAM Packaging."

18. C. The CPU will check in L1 cache first, because it is SRAM memory integrated into the chip and has no wait time. If the data is not in L1 cache, the system checks in L2 cache, which is cache memory outside of the chip (usually found on the motherboard). If the data is still not found, the CPU finally checks in RAM. For more information, see the section titled "Types of Cache Memory."

19. **A.** Odd-parity memory stores a parity bit for every byte of data. The parity bit is enabled (set to 1) if the data bits equal an even number, and disabled (set to 0) if the data bits equal an odd number. Thus, with odd-parity every byte of data must have an odd numeric value calculated. For more information, see the section titled "DRAM Packaging."

20. **B.** CMOS RAM is a small amount of memory that maintains the CMOS configuration information. Because this information is stored in a type of RAM, the memory needs constant power. This power comes from the battery found on the system board. Choice A describes shadow RAM. For more information, see the section titled "Types of Memory."

Scenarios

1. A system may not accept the RAM that has been added to it for a number of reasons. For one, you may not have added the right type of memory (for example, maybe you added FPM memory, and the system required EDO memory). Or perhaps you installed non-parity memory, when what the system really required was parity memory. Inserting the wrong speed memory modules could also have been a factor in the system's rejection of the memory. If at all possible, you will want to review any documentation before installing the memory.

CMOS Basic Parameters

Exam 220-201 ✦ A+ Core Hardware

- ✦ **4.4** Identify the purpose of CMOS (Complementary Metal-Oxide Semiconductor), what it contains, and how to change its basic parameters. Example of basic CMOS settings:

  - Printer parallel port — Uni, bi-directional, disable/enable, ECP, EPP

  - COM/serial port — memory address, interrupt request, disable

  - Floppy drive — enable/disable drive or boot, speed, density

  - Hard drive — size and drive type

  - Memory — parity, non-parity

  - Boot sequence

  - Date/Time

  - Passwords

  - Plug-and-Play BIOS

CHAPTER PRE-TEST

1. CMOS stands for Complementary Metal-_____ Semiconductor.

2. What are some typical keystrokes that are used to enter CMOS?

3. What LPT mode is typically used for scanners?

4. Which hard drive type is user-definable?

5. What is the IRQ associated with LPT1?

6. What is the IRQ associated with COM2?

7. What is the IRQ associated with COM1?

8. What is the purpose of Enhanced Parallel Printer mode?

9. What is the IO address associated with COM1?

10. What is the IO address associated with LPT1?

✦ Answers to these questions can be found at the end of the chapter. ✦

A wonderful talent to have as a service technician is the ability to understand CMOS and its functionality. Although CMOS doesn't seem like a place where you'd need to go every day, there are many PC-related problems that can be solved in CMOS.

This chapter will introduce you to some of the common CMOS options that are found in modern systems. Keep in mind that these options are system-based, which means that the options you see on one system are not necessarily present on the next system. You can rely on the fact that systems of the same model from the same manufacturer will be consistent, but even different models made by the same manufacturer can vary in terms of available CMOS options.

Complementary Metal-Oxide Semiconductor

Complementary Metal-Oxide Semiconductor (CMOS) is the computer's inventory list and advanced setup options. It can be considered an inventory list because it contains a record of all the devices connected to the system, such as the floppy drive, the hard drive, and so on. Not only does CMOS list the devices, it dictates their capacity — for example, whether the system has a 2GB or a 6GB hard disk.

During the boot up process, the system compares its inventory list to what it has detected during boot up. If there are any discrepancies, the system takes you into CMOS right away. For example, assume your system has 32MB of RAM and you add another 8MB of RAM to it. When you power the system up, it compares what it had in inventory (32MB) the last time it booted with what it sees now (40MB). Because there is a difference, CMOS will report a memory size error. CMOS doesn't know that the difference is for the better; if it sees a difference, it reports an error. Because CMOS has detected the new memory, all you have to do is save the changes to the inventory list and reboot.

Before discussing the different CMOS settings, it's important to know how to enter the CMOS setup program. Figuring this out is difficult on some systems, but extremely easy on others. Some systems display a message on bootup that indicates what keystroke is used to enter into the "setup" program (oftentimes, Del or F1). IBM systems typically use F1.

F10 is another important keystroke. In many Compaq systems, pressing the F10 key when you see a squared cursor in the top right-hand corner will enable you to enter the CMOS program.

In some systems, you enter CMOS by holding down multiple keys at the same time — Ctrl+Alt+S or Ctrl+Alt+INS, for example. Entering into these systems is a little trickier, so reviewing your documentation is helpful.

Caution In some systems, the CMOS setup program is located on a small 2MB or 4MB partition. Removing these partitions prevents you from entering CMOS — although the setup disk for the system will usually help you restore the partition. CMOS information is held in CMOS RAM, which is volatile memory maintaining its information from a small battery located on the motherboard. Thus, if battery power is lost, the CMOS data is also lost.

Cross-Reference For more information on RAM, consult Chapter 4.

Basic CMOS Settings

Objective **4.4** Identify the purpose of CMOS (Complementary Metal-Oxide Semiconductor), what it contains, and how to change its basic parameters. Example of basic CMOS settings: Printer parallel port — Uni, bi-directional, disable/enable, ECP, EPP; COM/serial port — memory address, interrupt, disable; Floppy drive — enable/disable drive or boot, speed and density; Hard drive — size and drive type; Memory — parity, non-parity; Boot sequence; Date/Time; Passwords; Plug-and-Play BIOS

This section will introduce to you some common setup options — consistent with all systems — once you have entered CMOS.

Hard disk drive type

In CMOS, you will see an option that specifies your hard drive type, which indicates the size of the hard disk. For example, a Type 2 drive may be 1.2GB in size, while a Type 10 drive may be 1.5GB in size (the actual values of hard drive types may vary from system to system). There is also a custom type, usually Type 47, which enables you to specify the dimensions of the drive (sectors, cylinders, heads); it will calculate the size in megabytes.

Some older CMOS programs only display the size of the hard drive and do not allow you to change the type; in this example, the hard disk size is based on what was detected at startup.

Floppy disk drive type

There is an entry in CMOS to enable or disable the floppy disk drive. When the floppy disk drive is enabled, its size is also specified. Many systems still have multiple entries for floppy disk drives — a popular setup years ago, when we had the 5¼ inch and 3½ inch floppy disk drives.

Memory

CMOS has an entry indicating the total amount of memory installed on the system. Typically, this entry is not modified unless you add or remove more RAM, but if you do, the system will detect the change and make the modification for you. All you need to do is save the modification. Some systems today will inform you that the system has saved the change for you and not require you to enter into the CMOS setup program.

Some systems will not only tell you in CMOS how much memory you have installed, but will also allow you to change the type of memory (FPM, EDO) or specify whether it is parity or non-parity memory.

 For more information on types of memory, see Chapter 4.

Parallel ports

There is an entry in CMOS for the configuration of your parallel port. This configuration allows you to either disable the port or change the mode the port is running in. Disabling the parallel port involves entering your CMOS program and switching the parallel port to disabled. Although you may assume that there's not a lot of configuration required for a parallel port, think about this: Have you ever had problems with a scanner plugged into your parallel port? Or more specifically, have you ever had problems with your scanner plugging into your computer and the printer then connecting to your scanner? The problems may derive from the parallel port mode configured on the system. The *parallel port mode* dictates the capabilities of the parallel port. Table 5-1 lists the three parallel port modes that can be configured for your system.

Table 5-1 Parallel Port Mode	
Mode	**Description**
Standard Parallel Port (SPP)	Standard parallel port mode only supports communication in one direction — from the computer to the device. This mode also has a transfer rate of 150Kbps.
Enhanced Parallel Port (EPP)	Enhanced parallel port mode is a bi-directional port mode that enables communication in either direction — from the computer to the device and the device to the computer. This mode has a transfer rate of 2Mbps and also supports the daisychaining feature (where one device can be connected to another device that is then connected to the computer).
Extended Capabilities Port (ECP)	Extended capabilities port enables communications over 2Mbps and supports bi-directional devices.

Service technicians need to understand the characteristics and capabilities of these three port modes. For example, if a customer calls because he's having trouble daisy chaining the scanner and printer off the computer, the technician would check to make sure that the proper port mode is selected in the CMOS setup program. The resources of the parallel port may also need to be configured if there are conflicts with another device. The default IRQ for LPT1 is 7, while the default IO address is 378-37F.

Cross-Reference   For more information on default resource settings, see Chapter 8.

Serial ports

A typical system includes two serial ports, and CMOS should have an entry for each of them — entries that enable you to change the resources, such as the IRQ and IO address, used by the serial ports. For more information on IRQs and IO addresses, see Chapter 8.

Exam Tip   The default IRQ for COM1 is 4, and the default IRQ for COM2 is 3. The default IO address for COM1 is 3F8-3FF, and the default IO address for COM2 is 2F8-2FF.

In CMOS, you will not only find an option to change the resources for the serial ports, but you will also be able to disable them. Disabling the serial ports involves entering your CMOS program and switching the Serial port to disabled.

Date/time

The date and time has an entry in CMOS as well, which is where the operating system time is being read. You know your CMOS battery is dying when, during startup, the system constantly asks you the date and time. During the startup after a battery failure, all of the other settings are detected again — which is why you don't specify the hard disk or the floppy disk. However, the date and time must be specified again.

Boot sequence

Take special note of the CMOS entry for boot sequence; it determines what drives the system will try to load the operating system off of and the order in which it checks each of those drives. Most systems are set up to boot off a floppy disk if a bootable floppy diskette is present, and if not, to boot off the hard disk.

Newer systems enable you to boot off a CD-ROM device, or even off the network, which makes installing an operating system extremely easy if the operating system installation supports these methods. For example, you can boot off the Windows NT or Windows 2000 CDs and install a fresh copy of those operating systems.

With today's systems, you can also have a computer try to boot from a floppy disk, then a hard disk, then a CD-ROM, and finally a network. You determine the order to suit your needs, although typically, the floppy drive is checked first and then the hard disk. If you like, you can disable other devices in the boot order. You may change the startup order of bootable devices and disable different bootable devices through the CMOS setup program.

Passwords

In general, there are two types of passwords that can be set in CMOS: the power-on password and the administrator password.

The power-on password is required in order to power the computer on. It is part of the power-on process and occurs before the operating system displays. Many people like to call it a "hardware password," because the operating system won't have a chance to load unless the correct password is typed in. The implementation of power-on passwords may be especially useful in environments where security is a significant issue.

The administrator password is a password that you set through the CMOS setup program, which states that if someone is going to enter CMOS, they must know the administrator password. This will prevent unauthorized users from entering CMOS and changing the values that reside there.

When people get comfortable with computers, they start to explore the computer's options. In cases where users are hooked up to a network, companies often end up spending time and money fixing problems that arise from the exploration of these options. It may be useful to set an administrator password — that is, a password someone has to supply if they want to enter CMOS. The administrator password enables you to secure the workstation at the administrative level, as well.

Cross-Reference For detailed information about jumpers, refer to Chapter 8.

What happens if you forget one of these passwords? First, check whether a jumper exists on the motherboard that can be removed to make CMOS forget the passwords. You could also remove the battery from the motherboard. Remember that CMOS RAM retains its information because there is a battery supply power for CMOS. If you remove the battery, CMOS, including the passwords, is erased (hey — it's better than throwing the system away!). The only problem is that erasing CMOS erases all the information. The good news is that most of the information should be detected again on startup, such as the amount of memory installed and the size of the hard drive. The third solution — the one I like — is to get a CMOS utility, such as CMOS S&R v0.92, that will back up the CMOS information and then restore it when an emergency arises. I would back up the CMOS without a password, so that the CMOS can be restored without a password. CMOS utilities are popular and can be found on the Internet; they back the CMOS information up to a text file.

Plug-and-Play BIOS

If you have a newer system, you probably have a *Plug-and-Play BIOS*. The term "plug-and-play" refers to the idea that a device should be able to be plugged into the system and assigned resources dynamically from the system. To have a plug-and-play system, three conditions are necessary:

✦ You need a plug-and-play device.

✦ You need a plug-and-play operating system.

✦ You need a Plug-and-Play BIOS.

If you're missing any one of these conditions, the operating system will not be able to assign resources to a device on startup.

You can enable and disable plug-and-play in the CMOS program. If you have a mix of plug-and-play devices and legacy devices, you may wish to disable plug-and-play to make it easier to deal with both types of devices on the system.

Advanced CMOS Settings

Many of the newer systems maintain the basic CMOS parameters mentioned in the previous section, but are also supplemented by different advanced setup settings. This section will examine the purpose and characteristics of some of these advanced settings.

Globally Unique Identifier

The Globally Unique Identifier (GUID) is a 128-bit number, randomly generated for the system and entered into CMOS. The GUID uniquely identifies the system from any other. It enables the identification of individual computers and ensures that this identification method is one hundred percent unique.

Many features in today's computers make use of the GUID. For example, one of Windows 2000's installation tools (Remote Installation Services, or RIS) allows the administrator to go into a client computer's CMOS, make a note of the GUID, and then create a computer account within Windows 2000's Active Directory database for the workstation and associate the GUID with the account. If the client computer is booting off the network when it starts, it will contact the RIS server and start installing a Windows 2000 operating system on itself. The client computer will use the computer name of the computer account that its GUID is associated with.

Tip   IBM systems have adopted the term UUID instead of GUID, which stands for Universally Unique Identifier. Remember, you may see a UUID in CMOS instead of a GUID on these systems, but they're the same thing.

BIOS date

The date of your BIOS should be displayed somewhere in CMOS, usually under Summary Information. If you don't have a BIOS date, you may have a revision number or level. These entries in CMOS are important because you may be required to update your BIOS someday by going to the manufacturer's Web site and downloading the update. The first thing you will notice when doing this is that the manufacturer has built many different versions of BIOS for their systems. You need to make sure you get the proper update (the one for the date of your BIOS).

Universal Serial Bus

Universal Serial Bus (USB) devices have gained much recognition over the last two or three years. USB devices are high-speed serial devices that use a single connector style and can be chained together with a *USB hub device*. A USB hub device is a device that connects all USB devices together at a central point. The USB hub device may be its own unique device, or it may be just another device in the USB chain that has the capability of connecting other USB devices to it. For example, a USB monitor may have a USB port to allow a mouse to connect to it. Some popular USB-type devices include digital cameras, scanners, mice, and keyboards. You will even see a USB network adapter.

If you have any problem getting a USB device connected to your computer, make sure the USB port has been enabled in CMOS.

Built-in network adapter

Many systems today come with built-in network cards, which I think is great because you will not have to go out and purchase a specific network card for the system. However, built-in network cards (or any built-in device) may become faulty and then your system always tries to use this built-in faulty device. Note that you can usually enable or disable the built-in network card in the CMOS setup program.

When your system includes a built-in network adapter, you usually have the option of enabling or disabling the capability to boot off the network. Unless this option is enabled, you will not be able to boot off the network — even if you have specified a network boot in the boot order.

Tip   There are three options in CMOS you will have to check to boot off the network: whether your network card is enabled or not, whether your system has been told it is allowed to boot off the network, and the startup order of devices. (To boot off the network, you will probably want the network as the first boot device.)

Virus protection

Some BIOS systems have built-in virus protection—which is, for the most part, a good thing. Some viruses attack the system by altering the Master Boot Record (MBR). The virus protection built into the BIOS watches out solely for changes to the MBR and puts a stop to it.

Unfortunately, when you install a new operating system, it will also modify the MBR with its boot program files, which means that the built-in virus detection in CMOS will see that "something" is modifying the MBR and assume it's a virus. In this case, you would need to go into CMOS, disable the virus protection, and then restart the installation of your operating system.

On board cache

Chapter 4 discussed the benefits of cache and the two types of cache memory, L1 and L2. In CMOS, there should be an entry indicating how much cache memory exists on the system and how it can be disabled.

If enabling cache memory presents any compatibility problems with your system, you may try disabling the cache memory to see whether the problem goes away. If it doesn't, you would enable the cache memory once again.

Reserve resources

Many of the newer systems enable you to reserve resources that have been assigned to *legacy devices* in CMOS. Legacy devices are non–plug-and-play devices. This will ensure that a plug-and-play system will not hand the resources that are hard-coded into older devices out to plug-and-play devices, which would create a conflict.

Upgrading the System BIOS

When your system was designed, its program code was designed to work with very specific devices. As you know, computer technology changes very quickly, almost overnight. So, what if you have an older system and you want to update its capabilities? What can you do?

The BIOS dictates a system's capabilities. For example, assume that the BIOS on my old 486 is only aware of a 2GB drive, but I would like to install a 6GB drive into the system. I must first upgrade the BIOS so it's more aware of the change in drive dimensions.

To upgrade the BIOS, you need to obtain the update program from the manufacturer, which is probably in one of two places — in your back pocket right now, or on the manufacturer's Web site. (Chances are, you're hitting the Internet!)

Once you download the BIOS to a floppy disk, you will boot off the BIOS and the update will start. Just follow the directions on the screen. The update program will rewrite the program code stored in the BIOS chip that is normally read-only. Because you are writing to this ROM chip with a special program, they call the ROM a *Flash ROM*, where flashing is the process of rewriting the program code.

Key Point Summary

This chapter has introduced you to the common settings found in CMOS setup programs today. You have learned about the basic and advanced parameters in CMOS. The following points were covered:

✦ You will enter a system's CMOS setup program by using a keystroke such as F1 or F10.

✦ You can change the boot order of the different bootable devices.

✦ There are three parallel port modes — SPP, EPP, and ECP.

✦ You specify the hard drive size in CMOS usually by specifying a hard drive type.

✦ You may update your BIOS by downloading the BIOS update for your system from the BIOS manufacturer's Web site.

✦　　✦　　✦

STUDY GUIDE

This Study Guide presents 18 multiple-choice questions to test your knowledge of this exam topic area. It provides 3 scenarios to help you apply critical thinking skills to the solution of real-life problems and 1 lab to help you practice what you learned.

Assessment Questions

1. You have a USB camera in which you are trying to copy some of the pictures to the computer's hard disk. The computer does not seem to recognize the device. What should you do?

   A. Check to see that the boot order is correct.

   B. Make sure that the USB ports are enabled.

   C. Make sure that the serial port is enabled.

   D. Make sure that the operating system has not assigned the USB device resources to some other device.

2. The computer constantly prompts for the date and time. What does this indicate?

   A. The date and time are wrong.

   B. The time has fallen back by one hour.

   C. The battery on the motherboard is losing its charge.

   D. The time has increased by one hour.

3. On a plug-and-play system in which you have some non–plug-and-play devices, what should you do so that there are no conflicts with the legacy hardware resources and the resources assigned by the operating system?

   A. Replace the BIOS with a non–plug-and-play BIOS.

   B. Enable the Legacy Compatible option in CMOS.

   C. Replace the legacy devices with current plug-and-play devices.

   D. Go into the reserve resources area of the CMOS setup program and reserve the resources used by legacy devices. If you reserve the resources, then the system will not give those resources out.

4. Your manager is worried that someone will be able to start up any of the Windows 98 computers and view confidential information. What could you do to ensure that anyone starting the computer is supposed to be using that system?

   A. Set up a Windows logon.

   B. Set file permissions on the files that are confidential.

   C. Set a power-on password in CMOS.

   D. Use Microsoft Encrypting File System to protect the files from unauthorized access.

5. You are installing Windows 2000 on your computer and you know that the Windows 2000 CD is a bootable CD. You have tried a number of times to boot off the CD. What CMOS option would you look for?

   A. You must delete the existing partitions so that you can boot off the CD-ROM.

   B. Ensure that the CD-ROM device has been set up as the first device in the startup (boot up) order.

   C. Disable the hard disk in CMOS.

   D. Boot off a Windows 98 startup disk and access the CD-ROM from there.

6. You are worried that some of your advanced computer users on the network will start changing the settings within CMOS. What is the best thing you can do to protect these settings?

   A. Set a power-on password.

   B. Set an administrator password.

   C. Set a Windows logon password.

   D. Ask the advanced users not to change any of the CMOS settings.

7. When looking inside the My Computer icon, you notice that no floppy drive is listed. What should you check in CMOS?

   A. Make sure that the floppy drive is listed as a bootable device.

   B. Make sure that the hard disk is listed as a bootable device.

   C. Make sure the floppy drive is configured correctly in CMOS.

   D. Make sure the hard disk is configured correctly in CMOS.

8. Your built-in network adapter does not seem to be connecting you to the network. What is one of the first things you want to check for in CMOS?

   A. That the built-in network adapter is enabled in CMOS

   B. That the network adapter driver is loaded

   C. That the resources are not conflicting

   D. That the proper protocol is installed

9. You are trying to use Windows 2000 Server's Remote Installation Services, but the computer doesn't seem to boot off the network adapter. You have verified that the network adapter has been enabled in CMOS. What else should you check for within CMOS?

    A. That the network card has been disabled

    B. That the network adapter has been disabled

    C. That the CD-ROM has been configured as a bootable device

    D. That the network adapter is set up as a bootable device

10. You are experiencing a lot of problems running your customized software on some of the newer computers. What might you try disabling in CMOS to clear up the compatibility issue between the software and the system?

    A. RAM

    B. Cache memory

    C. Hard disk

    D. Floppy disk

11. You are having trouble installing a new operating system on your computer. Which of the following CMOS settings would you disable to help the system make it through the installation?

    A. Network adapter

    B. Bootable CD-ROM

    C. Antivirus

    D. Bootable network adapter

12. Which of the following is a typical method for updating your system BIOS?

    A. Replacing the old BIOS chip with a new BIOS chip

    B. Running a BIOS update program from a diskette that flashes the BIOS with a new version of the BIOS

    C. Replacing the old motherboard with a new one

    D. You cannot update the BIOS

13. Which of the following best describes the difference between BIOS and CMOS?

    A. BIOS contains the configuration information for the system, while CMOS is the low-level code that allows the devices to communicate.

    B. BIOS is stored in RAM, while CMOS is stored in ROM.

    C. BIOS is stored in RAM, while CMOS is stored in cache memory.

    D. CMOS contains the configuration information for the system, while BIOS is the low-level code that allows the devices to communicate.

14. Which of the following are typical keystrokes used to enter the CMOS setup program? (Choose two)

   A. F1

   B. Ctrl+Alt+Delete

   C. Alt+F10

   D. Del

15. You are deploying Windows 2000 Professional computers by taking advantage of Remote Installation Services. What CMOS setting will need to be looked up on the computer you are deploying the new operating system to?

   A. GUID

   B. Network adapter address

   C. Serial number

   D. ISBN number

16. You want to boot off your Windows 98 emergency repair disk and repartition the computer, but you cannot seem to boot off the floppy diskette. Which of the following CMOS actions would enable you to boot off the floppy? (Choose two)

   A. Make sure that a floppy drive is enabled in CMOS.

   B. Make sure the hard disk is disabled in CMOS.

   C. Make sure the floppy drive is the first bootable device in CMOS.

   D. Make sure the hard disk is the first bootable device in CMOS.

17. What hard disk type is typically used for custom settings?

   A. Type 2

   B. Type 10

   C. Type 74

   D. Type 47

18. Where is the CMOS configuration information stored?

   A. RAM

   B. ROM

   C. Cache memory

   D. Floppy disk

Scenarios

The following three scenarios will test your knowledge of some of the CMOS settings in their application to everyday problems.

1. Your manager is trying to hook a scanner up to the parallel port on her system, along with her printer, but cannot seem to get it to work. What steps would you take to get the scanner to work, and why?

2. You are trying to boot off the network and have specified that the network will be your first bootable device, then your floppy drive, and then your hard disk. You can't seem to boot off the network, although you have specified it as the first bootable device. What is the problem?

3. You have an old legacy network card installed in your system that is causing IRQ conflicts with COM1. You do not have either the setup diskette for the network card or access to the Internet. What could you do to solve the resource conflict?

Lab Exercises

Lab 5.1 Recording and Changing CMOS Settings

1. Power the computer on and enter the CMOS setup program for your system.

2. Record the information shown in the following table by finding it in your CMOS setup program.

Setting	Value
Amount of memory:	
BIOS date:	
Parallel port mode:	
Hard drive type:	
First startup device:	
Second startup device:	
COM1 IRQ:	
COM2 IRQ:	
LPT1 IRQ:	

3. Find out how to change the values of particular settings in your CMOS setup program. This is often done by using left and right arrow keys.

What method is used for changing values in CMOS?

_____

4. Find the power-on password setting (typically, in the advanced options or the security options). Change the power-on password to "password," and then save the changes and exit CMOS.

5. When the system restarts, you should be prompted for a password before the operating system displays. Type the password of "password" in, and then press Enter.

6. Remove the power-on password.

Answers to Chapter Questions

Chapter Pre-Test

1. CMOS stands for Complementary Metal-**Oxide** Semiconductor.

2. Some common methods of entering CMOS are **by pressing F1, F10, or Del** while booting.

3. You will use the **enhanced parallel printer mode** when hooking up a scanner.

4. Hard drive **type 47** is the user-defined hard drive type.

5. **IRQ 7** is the default IRQ for LPT1.

6. **IRQ 3** is the default IRQ for COM2.

7. **IRQ 4** is the default IRQ for COM1.

8. Enhanced Parallel Port Mode is a **bi-directional port that supports daisy chaining and has a transfer rate of 2Mbps**.

9. The default IO address of COM1 is **3F8-3FF**.

10. The default IO address for LPT1 is **378-37F**.

Assessment Questions

1. B. In today's systems, many of the built-in devices can be enabled or disabled in the CMOS setup program. When experiencing problems with a built-in device, the first thing I would check is whether the device is enabled. For more information, see the section labeled "Advanced CMOS Settings."

2. C. The CMOS configuration information is stored in CMOS RAM. This special RAM chip maintains its information by a small battery on the system board. If the battery loses its charge, then the CMOS RAM is flushed out, meaning that it will prompt you for the information as the system boots up. For more information, see the section labeled "Text."

3. D. The newer CMOS setup programs allow you to reserve resources so that the OS will not give those resources away. This way, when the legacy device initializes, the resource it tries to use is free. For more information, see the section labeled "Advanced CMOS Settings."

4. C. Although Choice B and Choice C are good answers, those options are only available on Windows NT or Windows 2000. Choice C is not dependent on any particular operating system because you are setting a hardware-level password. In order to power up to the operating system, you will have to type in the proper power-on password that has been set up in CMOS. For more information, see the section labeled "Basic CMOS Settings."

5. B. Many computers are set up to boot off the floppy drive, then the hard disk, and finally the CD-ROM, which means that if the system can boot off the floppy or hard disk, the opportunity will never arise to boot off the CD-ROM. Changing the startup order so that the CD-ROM is the first bootable device means that you can put the Windows 2000 CD-ROM in and setup will be invoked from it. Choice A would work, assuming that the CD-ROM device is listed anywhere in the bootable device order. Unfortunately, you have lost the contents of the drive because partitions have been wiped out, so Choice A is not the best answer. For more information, see the section labeled "Basic CMOS Settings."

6. B. An administrator password is a password someone will have to provide in order to enter the CMOS setup program and change the settings. Choice A is not the right answer, because you may not want to set up a password for when the computer turns on, but only if a user tries to enter the CMOS setup program. For more information, see the section labeled "Basic CMOS Settings."

7. C. The floppy drive is a device listed in CMOS. Not only do you want to make sure that the floppy drive is physically connected correctly, you want to make sure that CMOS sees the device. Check to make sure that the floppy drive is not disabled in CMOS. For more information, see the section labeled "Basic CMOS Settings."

8. A. One of the first things you want to do with a built-in device is ensure that the device has not been disabled in CMOS. If it has not been disabled, you should look at the other choices for the solution. For more information, see the section labeled "Advanced CMOS Settings."

9. D. When taking advantage of Remote Installation Services, you need to ensure that the computer not only has the network adapter enabled, but that the network adapter is signified as a bootable device, and maybe even the first bootable device. In this question, you have already verified that the network adapter has been enabled, so Choice D is the only possible answer. For more information, see the section labeled "Advanced CMOS Settings."

10. **B.** Many systems today have built-in cache memory. Although it's not that common, you may sometimes have problems with particular software not "liking the idea" of using information from cache instead of RAM. To test this, you may temporarily disable the cache memory. For more information, see the section labeled "Advanced CMOS Settings."

11. **C.** Viruses commonly attack the MBR of the hard disk, so virus software is constantly watching out for applications that try to make a change to this area of the disk. Some systems today have built-in virus detection, and because the installation of a new operating system will cause a change to the MBR, there may be incompatibilities between the operating system install and the virus protection built into the system. Disabling this virus protection in the CMOS will allow the installation to finish. For more information, see the section labeled "Advanced CMOS Settings."

12. **B.** To update your BIOS today, you will either get the update from the manufacturer on a floppy disk or download the update from the Internet onto a floppy. You will then boot off this diskette, and the update process will start. In the past, you would have to replace the entire ROM chip. For more information, see the section labeled "Upgrading the System BIOS."

13. **D.** CMOS is the "inventory list" of devices and their configuration, whereas the BIOS is the set of low-level instructions that tells these devices how to communicate. Choice B and Choice C are wrong because BIOS code is stored in ROM, not RAM. For more information, see the section labeled "Complementary Metal-Oxide Semiconductor."

14. **A, D.** Typical keystrokes used to enter CMOS while booting are the F1 keystroke and the Del keystroke. For more information, see the section labeled "Complementary Metal-Oxide Semiconductor."

15. **A.** When taking advantage of Remote Installation Services for Windows 2000, you will build a computer account in Active Directory and associate a GUID with the computer account. The GUID is located in CMOS and is a unique number associated with that system. For more information, see the section labeled "Advanced CMOS Settings."

16. **A, C.** You would first make sure that the floppy drive is a listed device in CMOS and then make sure it is configured properly. After checking that the device is listed in CMOS, make sure it is the first bootable device so that the system will boot off the floppy and not the hard disk. For more information, see the section labeled "Basic CMOS Settings."

17. **D.** Hard disk type 47 is typically associated with the hard disk custom setup. This will enable you to tell CMOS how many cylinders, sectors, and heads the drive has. For more information, see the section labeled "Basic CMOS Settings."

18. **A.** CMOS configuration information is stored in RAM, which maintains its information while the power is turned off by a small battery located on the motherboard. For more information, see the section labeled "Basic CMOS Settings."

Scenarios

1. Check to ensure that the parallel printer port mode is set to enhanced parallel port (EPP) mode — a parallel port mode that allows bi-directional communication up to 2Mbps, as well as daisy chaining.

2. Assuming that the network device is the first bootable device, there is another CMOS setting that you must enable: network booting. The system may not be booting off the network, because some of the systems today allow you to set the network adapter as the first bootable device, while the option to boot off the network is disabled.

3. Normally, you would change the resources of the network card to resolve the conflict. In this case, however, you don't have the setup disk for the network card and cannot download it from the Internet. The best solution in this scenario is to change the IRQ being used by COM1 in the CMOS setup program.

Ports, Cables, and Connectors

EXAM OBJECTIVES

Exam 220-201 ✦ A+ Core Hardware

- ✦ **1.4** Identify common peripheral ports, associated cabling, and their connectors. Content may include the following:
  - Cable types
  - Cable orientation
  - Serial versus parallel
  - Pin connections
- ✦ Examples of types of connectors:
  - DB-9
  - DB-25
  - RJ-11
  - RJ-45
  - BNC
  - PS2/MINI-DIN
  - USB
  - IEEE-1394

CHAPTER PRE-TEST

1. What are the two types of coaxial cable used for Ethernet networking?

2. When transferring files between computers, do serial or parallel connections offer the best performance?

3. How is Pin 1 identified on ribbon cables?

4. What is the typical use of RJ-11 connectors?

5. BNC is an acronym for _____?

6. What interface supports more devices: USB or IEEE-1394?

7. USB is an acronym for _____?

8. What type of network cable is used for fast Ethernet networks?

9. DB9 ports are usually associated with what type of connection?

✦ Answers to these questions can be found at the end of the chapter. ✦

In this chapter, you will examine the ports on the back of the computer, as well as the cables and connectors that are used to attach devices. Devices — such as printers, modems, internal drives, monitors, USB devices, and FireWire devices — are discussed in other chapters, but here we will look at getting them all connected.

Common Computer Ports

When connecting devices to your computer, you should first look at the different types of ports that can be found on it. You may already be familiar with some of the common ones, such as serial, parallel, and USB. This section will discuss IEEE-1394 ports as well, which are often called FireWire.

Serial versus parallel

Identify common peripheral ports, associated cabling, and their connectors
Content may include the following: Serial versus parallel

Two of the most common ports on the back of your computer are the serial ports and the parallel ports. Most computers have one parallel port and two serial ports. They are used to connect different types of devices to your computer.

Parallel ports send data over multiple wires simultaneously, while serial ports only send data over one wire at a time. Since parallel communication allows for multiple streams of data, it provides higher data transfer rates than serial communication.

Parallel ports were implemented on the personal computer when it was introduced by IBM in 1981. They used nine wires in cable to connect two devices together. This enabled them, at any given time, to deliver eight bits of data. However, because there was no way to accurately control the flow of the signal down each of the wires in the cable, it was recommended that the length of the cable be less than six feet. This became more of a factor when bi-directional communication was implemented over the parallel port. The standard for bi-directional communication was delivered in the IEEE-1284 specification, which allowed for high-speed communication over the parallel port. This also opened two new specifications for the port: the Enhanced Parallel Port (EPP) and the Extended Capabilities Port (ECP).

The EPP-type parallel port was used primarily for non-printer peripherals, while the ECP-type parallel port was designed to accommodate new high-speed printers and scanners. In order to better handle high-speed data communication, the ECP-type parallel port also implemented the use of a DMA channel.

Serial ports, on the other hand, deliver data sequentially down a single wire. Eight bits of digital data are converted into analog data using a system called *baud*. *Baud rate* refers to the number of state changes (tones) that are made on the wire in any given second. This is very different from bits per second (bps), which measures the amount of data that is transferred. At one point in time, 300 bps modems communicated at 300 baud, but compression standards adopted by the communications industry allowed more data to be delivered at the same baud rate. Today, 56Kbps (57,344 bps) modems communicate at 9,600 baud.

Depending on the baud rate used to transfer data, the length of the cable can range up to 5,000 feet. For data transfer rates at 9,600 baud, the maximum cabling length is 250 feet. The RS-232C standard, which is used as a basis of serial communication, recommends a maximum cable length of 50 feet.

Universal Serial Bus

Universal Serial bus, or USB, is a new release of the serial standard. The goal of USB was to revolutionize the way serial communication was conducted. In an effort to fulfill this goal, USB uses a new cabling system that allows up to 127 devices to be connected together. It also delivers power to the devices that are connected on this bus. To go along with this new cabling, the specification for USB dictates that all devices should support Plug-and-Play. With these two pieces of the puzzle put together, USB enables you to plug devices in and have them work. Some USB devices that require a large amount of power may use a supplemental power supply, but the USB bus will power most devices.

Cross-Reference For more information about USB, see Chapter 10.

FireWire (IEEE-1394)

FireWire is an Apple trademark for the IEEE-1394 standard. The 1394 standard implements a version of serial communication across a wiring network that is similar to USB. IEEE-1394 enables the connection of 64 devices on a bus that supports 50 to 400 Mbps. One of the goals of the IEEE-1394 standard was to replace SCSI.

Exam Tip On the exam, do not confuse IEEE-1394 (FireWire) with IEEE-1284, which deals with bi-directional communication over the parallel port.

While there have been disk drives implemented through the IEEE-1394 standard, it has seen the most growth in the area of data, voice, and video. While many PCs have been shipping for the last few years with USB ports, IEEE-1394 has not seen the same level of adoption by the PC manufacturing industry. Many device manufacturers are supporting IEEE-1394 in their devices, and interface cards are readily available to be added to your PC.

Keyboard

Since it's certain you will want to enter data into your computer, the keyboard connector on the back of your computer plays an important role. There are two main types of keyboard connectors: PS2 or mini-DIN 6 and DIN 5. The mini-DIN connector has now been fully adopted by AT PC standard. An illustration of the mini-DIN 6 connector can be found later in this chapter. (See Figure 6-12.)

Monitor

Since you will also want to see what you are doing, the monitor connector on the back of your PC plays an important role. With the demise of the CGA/EGA standards, and the release of VGA and SVGA, the monitor connector on the back of your computer moved from a DB9 female connector to a HD (high density) DB15 female connector. An illustration of the DB15 connector can be found later in this chapter. (See Figure 6-6.)

Cable Types

 Identify common peripheral ports, associated cabling, and their connectors. Content may include the following: Cable types

This section will examine several different types of cables and discuss the uses of each type.

Ribbon

Ribbon cables are often used to connect components inside a computer, such as floppy drives and hard drives. They are composed of several wires that are laid out parallel to each other. These wires are attached in such a way that they resemble a ribbon, as shown in Figure 6-1. These cables usually have keyed connectors on them, which prevents them from being incorrectly connected to devices. You should note the small tab halfway down the edge of the black connector. This tab will match a groove on the device that it is attached to.

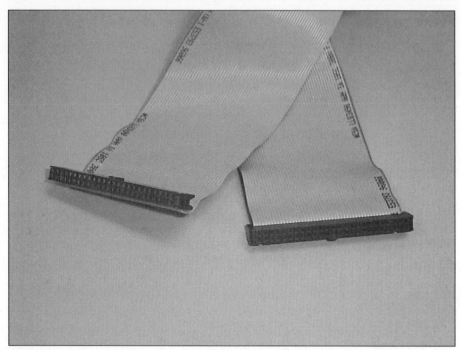

Figure 6-1: Ribbon cables are usually only found on the inside of your computer attaching devices to the motherboard.

Twisted pair

The following section provides a brief listing of the different types of twisted pair cables that are available. These cables consist of three or four pairs of wires. The grading level is based on how the wires are handled, rather than the number of wires. In Figure 6-2, you can see how each pair of wires is twisted together at a specific rate, and then how all of the pairs are twisted together. This procedure reduces the effect of cross talk between the pairs of wires and other external sources of interference. The differences between the different grades of cable include the quality of production material, and the overall number of twists per pair of wires per foot of cable.

Exam Tip   Pay close attention to the uses of CAT3, CAT4, and CAT5 cable types, since these map directly to network specifications. You will be tested on the minimum required for 10 Mbps Ethernet and 100 Mbps Ethernet.

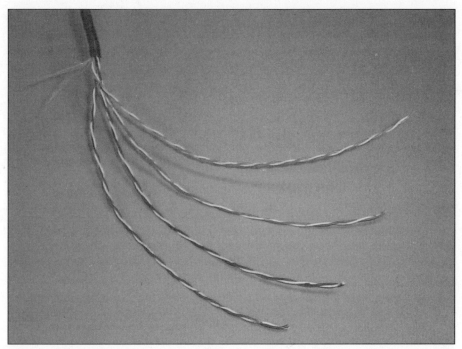

Figure 6-2: The twisting of the pairs of wire is one of the differences between the categories of cable.

CAT1

Category 1 wiring is unshielded twisted pair designed for transmission of audio signals. This wiring is intended to be used for transferring signals to speakers and other devices.

CAT2

Category 2 wiring is unshielded twisted pair used for low-speed transmissions. The pairs of wires have two twists per foot. The types of uses that were planned for this wiring dealt with analog telephone applications. CAT2 cables are also capable of carrying lower speed networking data, in the case of 4 Mbps Token Ring networking.

CAT3

Category 3 wiring is unshielded twisted pair cable that is designed with data networking in mind. The pairs of wires have three twists per foot. This category is similar in design to all of the newer categories, but some electrical characteristics are unique to each. CAT3 cables were used to carry 10 Mbps Ethernet data up to 100 meters (328 feet).

CAT4

Category 4 wiring is unshielded twisted pair cable that was designed to carry 16 Mbps Token Ring data up to 100 meters (328 feet). The pairs of wires have four twists per foot.

CAT5

Category 5 wiring is unshielded twisted pair cable that was designed to carry 100 Mbps Ethernet data 100 meters (328 feet).

CAT6

Category 6 wiring is a proposed standard for unshielded twisted pair cable that can carry 250 Mbps Ethernet data.

CAT7

Category 7 wiring is a proposed standard for unshielded twisted pair cable that can carry 600 Mbps Ethernet data.

Thick coax

Thick coax is rigid 0.5 inch coaxial cable that is capable of carrying 10 Mbps Ethernet data a distance of 500 meters. Thick coax is also referred to as Thicknet or 10Base5.

Thin coax

Thin coax is more flexible 0.25 coaxial cable that is capable of carrying 10 Mbps Ethernet data a distance of 185 meters. Thin coax is also referred to Thinnet or 10Base2.

Cable Orientation

 Identify common peripheral ports, associated cabling, and their connectors.
Content may include the following: Cable orientation

Cable orientation refers to how the cables connect together. Every cable and connection has the pins within it numbered. Each wire joins one particular connector on one end to a particular connector on the other end. Sometimes these differences are great, and other times they are very subtle (in the case of modem and null modem cables).

Pin connections for external cables

 Identify common peripheral ports, associated cabling, and their connectors.
Content may include the following: Pin connections

The first major difference between connectors is that most connectors have a male and a female component. The male connector is the connector with the pins on it, and the female connector has the holes. The only exception to this is the IBM Type 1 connector (shown in Figure 6-3), which is a hermaphrodite. Every connector can potentially be plugged into every other connector.

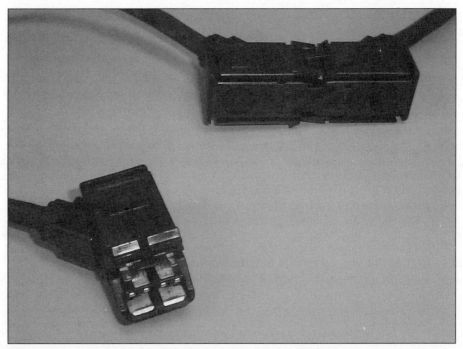

Figure 6-3: The IBM Type 1 data connector is a hermaphrodite.

Separate from the sex of the connector is the pin numbering. Every connector numbers the pins that are used in the connector. I use the term "pins" loosely here, since the receptacles in the female connector are also numbered. Numbering the pins on the connectors make it easier for us to describe what the cable is supposed to look like at the connector level. For example, a cable with a DB9 Female connector and a DB25 Female connector with pins 2-3, 3-2, 4-20, 5-7, 6-6, 7-4, and 8-5 connected would give you a null modem cable. Without a standard on numbering, this would not be possible. The most used connector on external cables is the D-shell connector (named for its shape), which is usually called DB.

The numbering of pins on male connectors starts with the top-left connector if you are looking at the connector and the D is pointing towards the ground. This is Pin 1, and the order goes across the connector and left to right for all subsequent rows. If you are dealing with a female connector, then Pin 1 is in the top right of the connector if the D is pointing down, and the other pins are numbered right to left. This allows Pin 1 on a male connector to match Hole 1 on a female connector.

Pin connections for internal cables

Identify common peripheral ports, associated cabling, and their connectors. Content may include the following: Pin connections

Internal cables also have a male and female connector. Most internal devices are connected using ribbon cables, in the case of drives, parallel ports, and serial ports. Some devices use unique cables, such as connecting your sound card to your CD-ROM drive. In many cases, these unique cables have molex connectors on the end that are keyed to prevent mistakes on connecting. Molex connectors are molded plastic connectors that are usually keyed. You will also see molex connectors on the power leads that are on your power supply.

There is one rule that can prevent most connection errors. If you are using a ribbon cable, Pin 1 will have the colored (usually red) stripe on it. This makes it easy to spot. On the device that you are connecting it to, Pin 1 is almost always the pin closest to the power connector, as shown in Figure 6-4. This same logic holds true when connecting cables to connectors on your motherboard. Pin 1 is closest to the power connectors on the motherboard. Most of the male slots that connect to the cable will be keyed to prevent errors, as long as the cable you are using is also keyed. Keyed connectors on your cards have a small notch cut out from the side of the connector, while the cables have a small lump or tab on them. The only way for the cable to be plugged into the connector is if the tab matches the notch, and there is only one way for that to happen.

Figure 6-4: Pin 1 for most slots will be found closest to the power connectors, while many connectors are keyed to prevent mistakes.

Connector Types

There are many, many types of cables that exist on the market these days: video cables, modem cables, printer cables, and extension cables, to name a few. One thing that is common to most cables is that there are relatively few connectors that have to be dealt with.

DB-9

 1.4 Identify common peripheral ports, associated cabling, and their connectors. Examples of types of connectors: DB-9

The DB-9 connector is the first D-Shell connector that you will examine. The term "D-Shell" is based on its shape. It also has nine connection points arranged in two rows. This connector used to be found on the back of your computer in its female form, to be used with a CGA or EGA monitor. It is still found on the back of your computer in its male form, as one of the two types of serial connections for your COM ports. Figure 6-5 shows a couple of DB-9 connectors.

Figure 6-5: The DB-9 connector

DB-15

1.4 Identify common peripheral ports, associated cabling, and their connectors. Examples of types of connectors include: DB-15

DB-15 or HD DB-15 has the familiar shape of the D-Shell connector, but contains three rows of five connection points rather than the traditional two rows. It is usually used for VGA and SVGA monitor connections, and should be found on your computer in its female form. Figure 6-6 shows the DB-15 connector.

Figure 6-6: The high-density HD DB-15

DB-25

1.4 Identify common peripheral ports, associated cabling, and their connectors. Examples of types of connectors include: DB-25

Once again, you will see the familiar shape of the D-Shell connector, but this time you will see 25 connections arranged into two rows. This connector is found on your computer in its male form in the role of a serial port, and in its female form as a parallel port. Figure 6-7 shows a parallel cable and a serial 9-25 pin converter. You will also find the 25-pin male connector on the back of most modems.

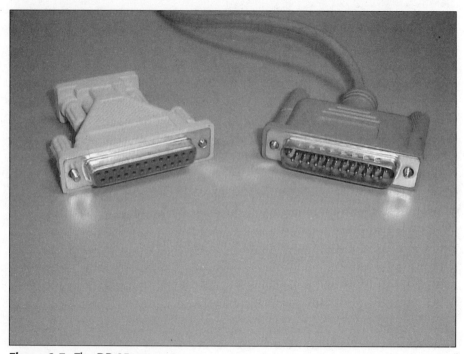

Figure 6-7: The DB-25 connector

Centronics 36 and 50

You have just read that one end of a parallel cable has a DB-25 connector. The other end of that cable is going to have a 36-pin male Centronics connector. You will find the female version of this connector on your printer. Also, you will often see Centronics connectors used with SCSI. Figure 6-8 shows 36-pin and 50-pin Centronics connectors.

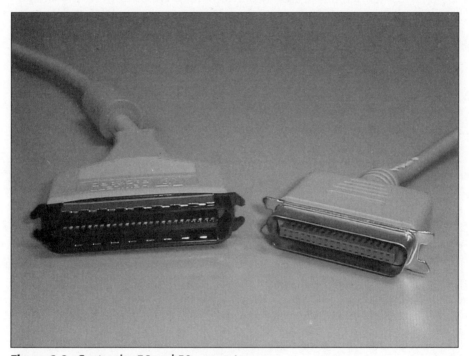

Figure 6-8: Centronics 36 and 50 connectors

RJ-11

 1.4 Identify common peripheral ports, associated cabling, and their connectors. Examples of types of connectors include: RJ-11

RJ is short for "registered jack," and the connectors are small modular connectors that clip into matching holes. The RJ-11 connector is a standard modular connector that is used for telephones. It accepts four wires, usually in the form of a flat wire. Analog telephone service is usually only on the two middle wires. You should see a female portion of this connector on the back of your modem. Figure 6-9 contains an RJ-11 connector.

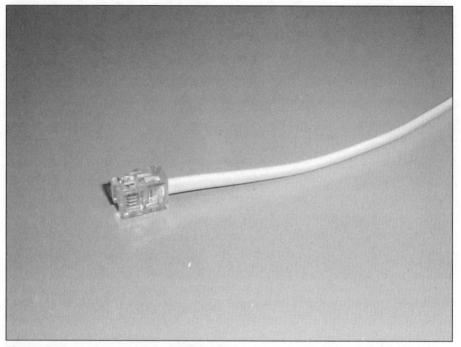

Figure 6-9: RJ-11 connectors should not be confused with RJ-45 connectors.

RJ-45

1.4 Identify common peripheral ports, associated cabling, and their connectors. Examples of types of connectors include: RJ-45

The RJ-45 connector is the larger cousin of the RJ-11 connector. They usually accept eight wires — or four pairs. This connector is used for 10BaseT, 10BaseTX, and Token Ring networking. (Basically, the RJ-45 is used anywhere UTP cables are used.) Figure 6-10 shows an RJ-45 connector. Officially, the RJ-45 connector was designed for voice grade circuits, and what is now referred to as an RJ-45 is officially known as an 8-pin connector.

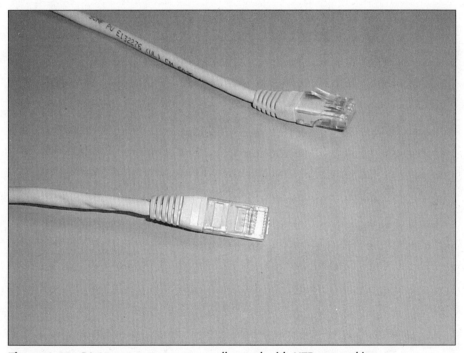

Figure 6-10: RJ-45 connectors are usually used with UTP networking.

British Naval Connector

1.4 Identify common peripheral ports, associated cabling, and their connectors. Examples of types of connectors include: BNC

The British Naval Connector (BNC) is also sometimes referred to as Bayonet Neil-Concelman connector, but this is a moot point for the exam. This connector is used for Thinnet networking. The male connector fits in a similar fashion to your home television connector. It also has a protruding point that fits into the female connector, at which time a ring is turned on the outside edge to lock the connectors together. The action of the ring is similar to a bayonet attaching to a rifle. Figure 6-11 contains a BNC T-connector and network card with a BNC connector.

Figure 6-11: Thinnet Ethernet makes use of the BNC connectors.

BNC T-connectors are used to attach two Thinnet cables to a network card on the back of your computer. The T-connector has a male connector to attach to your network card and then two female connectors to accept the two Thinnet cables. A Thinnet network segment makes one long chain out of all of the computers that are on the segment by using T-connectors.

PS/2 or MINI-DIN 6

 1.4 Identify common peripheral ports, associated cabling, and their connectors. Examples of types of connectors include: PS/2 or MINI-DIN

As mentioned earlier in this chapter, the PS/2 or Mini-DIN 6 connector is usually used for keyboards and mice for AT and ATX computers. This connector is now favored over the larger DIN 5 connector. Figure 6-12 provides an example of the Mini-DIN connector.

Figure 6-12: PS/2 connectors are used for keyboards and mice.

Universal Serial Bus

 1.4 Identify common peripheral ports, associated cabling, and their connectors. Examples of types of connectors include: USB

Universal Serial Bus, or USB, has recently had a performance boost up to 480 Mbps with the introduction of Version 2 of the USB standard. Your exam will still use 12 Mbps as the transfer rate of USB version 1.0 when discussing the speed of USB.

In either case, USB uses proprietary connectors (shown in Figure 6-13), to connect up to 127 devices together. All of these devices are required to be hot swappable, thanks to the specification for the standard.

USB Ports   USB Connector

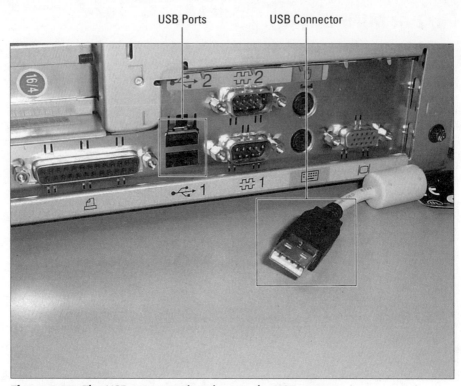

Figure 6-13: The USB connector is unique to the USB system.

IEEE-1394 (FireWire)

 1.4 Identify common peripheral ports, associated cabling, and their connectors. Examples of types of connectors include: IEEE-1394 (FireWire)

IEEE-1394 supports transfer rates of 400 Mbps, but a proposed new standard will take that speed up to 1.2 Gbps when it is released. Currently, there is no release date for this standard, but it is well into the development phase.

FireWire is an Apple Computers trademark for devices that match the IEEE-1394 specification. This specification allows 63 devices (without hubs) to be connected together in a single bus. It also uses a proprietary connector that is similar to the USB connector.

Adapters

There are many types of adapters that can be used to join different types of cables and devices together. This section will give a brief description of some of the major types.

Barrel connectors

The term "barrel connector" comes from Thinnet networking, where cables could be extended by means of a connector that accepted a male connector on either end — resembling a small barrel. This term is now often applied to any connector that extends the length of a cable by joining two cables together, but does not change the pin configuration. A barrel connector is displayed in Figure 6-14.

Figure 6-14: Barrel connectors enable you to extend the length of cables by joining two cables together.

Gender changers

Gender changers are a bit of a strange beast. They are straight through connectors, and do not change the order or connection of the pins; they only change the sex of the connector that they are attached to. They would look like a connector that either has two male or two female ends (as shown Figure 6-15), and when attached to a cable of one sex, the connector becomes the other. Gender changers are only used in rare cases.

Null modem

Null modem cables act as a replacement for two modems communicating with each other. If you have two computers that you want to connect directly together, then you can attach two modems, have one dial the other and transfer the files; or you can use a null modem cable. The null modem removes the modems from the equation, and connects the send pins on one serial port to the receive pins on the other, and vice versa. If you do not have a null modem cable, you can use a regular modem cable and a null modem adapter. The null modem adapter would look like a gender changer, except that it would not change the sex of the connection. The normal serial cable would have a female connector, and would still have it after attaching the null modem adapter.

The null modem adapter would actually look very much like a 9- to 25-pin or 25- to 9-pin adapter, but usually does not change the number of pins through the connection.

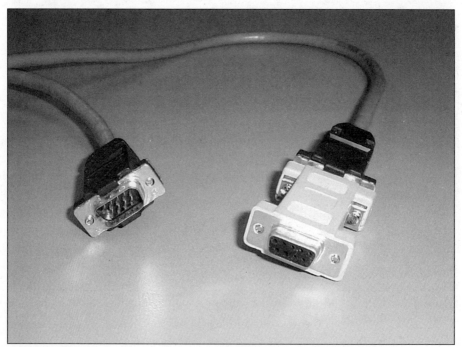

Figure 6-15: Gender changers are used to change the sex of a connector.

Key Point Summary

This chapter examined the primary functionality of different types of connectors. In the process, we examined the differences between serial and parallel communication, as well as the differences between USB and IEEE-1394 (FireWire). You learned about the different types of cables and connectors that are used in different areas of a computer system. You should now have a general understanding where the different cables and connectors are used in your system.

✦   ✦   ✦

STUDY GUIDE

This study guide presents 15 assessment questions to test your knowledge of the exam topic area. This chapter will not provide any scenarios or labs.

Assessment Questions

1. Which of the following ports offers the fastest throughput?

   A. Serial

   B. Parallel

   C. USB

   D. IEEE-1284

2. What type of connector is found on the back of your computer to accept a parallel cable?

   A. DIN-8 female

   B. DB-25 female

   C. DB-9 female

   D. DB-25 male

3. Which of the following is true about serial and parallel interfaces?

   A. Parallel cables are usually used for modems.

   B. Parallel cables often have DB-9 male connectors on the ends.

   C. Serial cables pass multiple bytes of data simultaneously.

   D. Serial cables are able to carry data longer distances.

4. Which of the following is not a feature of USB?

   A. Supports 128 devices

   B. Cabling to connect devices, also provides power

   C. All devices support Plug-and-Play

   D. Devices do not require IRQ resources

5. What type of port uses a three-row DB-15 connector?

    A. Serial

    B. SVGA

    C. Parallel

    D. Game

6. RS-232 is a term associated with which type of port?

    A. Serial

    B. Parallel

    C. SCSI

    D. Game

7. Ethernet network cards typically use what type of connector?

    A. RJ-32

    B. DB-9

    C. DB-25

    D. RJ-45

8. BNC connectors are usually used on your computer to provide which of the following?

    A. Serial connections

    B. Parallel connections

    C. Networking

    D. They are not used at all

9. Serial data is moved:

    A. Across multiple cables at the same time

    B. As a sequential stream of data

    C. Using a bidirectional information algorithm

    D. Using multi clock sequencing

10. Data transfer speed for the IEEE-1394 standard is:

    A. 10 Mbps

    B. 100 Mbps

    C. 400 Mbps

    D. 12 Mbps

11. Most keyboards connect to computers using which of the following types of connectors?

    A. DB-9

    B. Din 6

    C. Mini-Din 6

    D. RJ-45

12. Monitors usually connect to your computer through what type of connector?

    A. DB-15

    B. DB-25

    C. USB

    D. RS-232

13. CAT5 cables are defined by which of the following?

    A. Number of pairs of wires

    B. Length of the cable segment

    C. Type of shielding that is used

    D. Number of twists per foot in each pair of wires

14. Thin coaxial cable usually implements which type of connectors?

    A. BNC

    B. RJ-45

    C. RS-232

    D. IEEE-488

15. Pin 1 on a ribbon cable is usually identified by what?

    A. The number 1 inscribed on the connector

    B. A colored line on the wire leading to it

    C. A keyed connector

    D. Pin 1 is always on the left side of the connectors

Answers to Chapter Questions

Chapter Pre-Test

1. **Thick coaxial** (.5 mm) is used for 10Base5 networks, and **thin coaxial** (.25 mm) is used for 10Base2 networks.

2. **Parallel** offers higher transfer rates than does serial.

3. Pin 1 is usually identified **with a colored (red or blue) stripe on one side of the cable**.

4. RJ-11 connectors are usually used **with telephone systems**, while RJ-45 connectors are associated with Ethernet and Token Ring networks.

5. BNC is short for **British Naval Connector**.

6. **USB** supports 127 devices, but must implement the use of hubs, while IEEE-1394 supports 63 devices in a bus.

7. USB stands for **Universal Serial Bus**.

8. Fast Ethernet networks are designed to use **Category 5 cables**.

9. DB9 ports are associated with **serial connections**.

Assessment Questions

1. **C.** USB offers the highest transfer rates. USB 1.1 has transfer rates of 12 Mbps, while USB 2.0 offers transfer rates of 480 Mbps. This question may have been disputable if IEEE-1394 (FireWire) was in the question, since it has transfer rates of 400 Mbps. For more information, see the section labeled "Universal Serial Bus."

2. **B.** On the back of your computer, your parallel port has a DB-25 female connector. For more information, see the section labeled "DB-25."

3. **D.** Serial cables have a recommended maximum length of 30 feet based on the RS-232C specification, but are functional at 9,600 baud up to 250 feet. For more information, see the section labeled "Serial versus parallel."

4. **A.** USB only supports 127 devices. For more information, see the section labeled, "Universal Serial Bus."

5. **B.** VGA and SVGA use HD DB15 connectors that have three rows of five pins. For more information, see the section labeled "DB-15."

6. **A.** RS-232 is one of the standards associated with the serial port. For more information, see the section labeled "Serial versus parallel."

7. **D.** RJ-45 is typically used for networking. For more information, see the section labeled "RJ-45."

8. **C.** BNC connectors are used for Thinnet or 10Base2 Networking. For more information, see the section labeled "British Naval Connector."

9. **B.** Serial cables move data sequentially, one bit at a time, while parallel cables allow for all eight bits in a byte to be sent at one time. For more information, see the section labeled "Serial versus parallel."

10. **C.** FireWire or IEEE-1394 allows for transfer rates up to 400 Mbps. For more information, see the section labeled "FireWire."

11. **C.** Older PCs use Din 5 connectors, while newer ones use the Mini-Din 6 or PS/2 connector. For more information, see the section labeled "PS/2 or MINI-DIN 6."

12. **A.** VGA and SVGA monitors usually connect to your computer using a high density DB-15 connector. For more information, see the section labeled "DB-15."

13. **D.** CAT5 cables are defined by the type of copper wire that is used, and the number of twists per foot by each pair of wires. For more information, see the section labeled "Twisted Pair."

14. **A.** BNC connectors are used with Thinnet Ethernet networking. For more information, see the section labeled "British Naval Connector."

15. **B.** Pin 1 is identified by a colored line on the side of the cable that contains Pin 1. Keyed connectors prevent you from putting the cable in the wrong way, but do not specifically identify Pin 1. For more information, see the section labeled "Ribbon."

Printer Operations and Components

CHAPTER 7

EXAM OBJECTIVES

Exam 220-201 ✦ A+ OS Hardware

✦ **5.1** Identify basic concepts, printer operations, and printer components. Content may include the following:

- Paper feeder mechanisms
- **Types of printers:** Laser, Inkjet, Dot Matrix
- **Types of printer connections and configurations:** Parallel, Network, USB, Infrared, Serial

CHAPTER PRE-TEST

1. What printer type uses a cleaner blade?

2. What does a laser printer's fuser assembly do?

3. Complete the statement: Printer speed is measured by _____ _____ _____.

4. Why does toner contain iron oxide particles?

5. Which printer type heats the ink to transfer it to the paper?

6. Complete the statement: Printers typically attach to a computer through the _____ port.

7. In a TCP/IP environment, what must a network printer have to be accessible to users on the LAN?

8. What component of the printing process is susceptible to humidity?

9. Complete the statement: USB devices, including printers, can be in a daisy chain consisting of up to _____ USB devices.

10. What software component allows an operating system to communicate with a printer?

✦ Answers to these questions can be found at the end of the chapter. ✦

Troubleshooting, managing, and maintaining printers can be a chore that some technicians shy away from. Printers have long been a nemesis for the less-than-prepared technician—but the Certified A+ technician must understand the internal print process of a printer (as well as the communication process between printers and computers) and develop skills to repair and maintain a variety of print devices.

This chapter demystifies how a variety of printers work—and what to do when they don't. This chapter will examine the components of a printer and what each component is responsible for in the print process. The labs in this chapter provide adequate hands-on experience with a laser printer in preparation for the A+ exam.

Paper Feeder Mechanisms

5.1 Identify basic printer concepts, operations and components. Content may include the following: Paper feeder mechanisms

Paper. The goal of printing is to get what's on the computer's screen onto the paper. Sounds easy, right? Once the process is broken down, it's really not as mysterious as it all sounds.

Let's start with how the paper gets into the printer: through a feeder (technically, a paper feeder mechanism). A paper feeder mechanism is a simple way to describe the device that pulls or pushes the paper into the printer.

The type of printer a technician is servicing determines the paper feeder mechanism being used. All paper feeder mechanisms fall into one of two categories:

✦ Continuous form feed

✦ Friction feed

Continuous form feeders

Continuous form feed printers use paper that is connected into one long, long stretch of paper. This continuous form paper is typically perforated every 8.5 inches for letter size, or 14 inches for legal size forms. On both sides of the paper there is a .5-inch strip of perforated area, as well.

Within the .5-inch area of the perforated strip there are evenly spaced holes. These holes are used to pull and guide the paper into the printer assembly. When loading the continuous form paper, the holes of the first sheet of paper are placed over sprockets on the feeder assembly. The paper is then secured, typically, with a plastic hinge over the sprockets on either side.

The sprocket teeth are spaced so they move into the next series of holes on the continuous form as the wheel turns, feeding and guiding the paper into the assembly. Ingenious? Well, almost. The most common trouble with continuous form feed paper is that the box holding the paper must be aligned exactly with the sprockets. If the feed of paper is skewed or off-center, it can bring the whole process to a halt.

In the Real World

What printers use this type of form feed? Imagine a printer that prints hundreds of payroll checks weekly. The checks are attached in continuous form and fed from a box on the floor or a special paper tray. The software sends the information to the printer. The feeder advances the check into the print assembly. The check is printed and is ejected as the paper feeder advances the next check into the print assembly.

Friction feeders

Friction-feed printers are the most common type today, using friction to advance the paper into the assembly. These devices include laser printers, photocopiers, and fax machines.

A friction-feed printer works by loading individual sheets of paper from a tray into the printer. The paper feeder is a dual set of rollers that touch the first sheet in the paper tray and the rollers beneath, which ensure that only one piece of paper is allowed into the printer at a time.

As the printer gets the command from the operating system to print some image, the paper feeder slowly turns the rollers onto the paper. The rollers apply a gentle pressure as they turn in the direction the paper should move. Physics kicks in; the paper moves into the print assembly in a controlled, sequenced manner.

The friction feeders continue to move the entire sheet of paper into the assembly. As the paper moves through the print device, other rollers apply force and friction to advance the paper. If necessary, the process continues with subsequent pages of the document.

Tip

One gotcha with friction feed paper feeders is that rollers, which guide the paper into the print assembly, get worn down. Paper feeders are considered field-replaceable units, however, so here's a quick fix for worn or slick ones: With an emery board, gently scuff the D-shaped rollers that make contact with the top surface of the paper. That's it. The scuffed rollers eventually wear down again – and yes, they should be replaced – but this tech trick can save a day or two of downtime.

Types of Printers

 5.1 Identify basic printer concepts, operations and components. Content may include the following: Types of printers—Laser, Inkjet, Dot Matrix

Although many different manufacturers make printers, you're likely to encounter only three real categories of printers (so far). The three types of printers discussed in this chapter are:

✦ Laser Printers

✦ Inkjet Printers

✦ Dot-matrix Printers

The exam touches base on each of these, but the wise technician should focus on laser printers, not only for the exam's sake, but because these printers are the most common type in today's computing environment.

Laser printers

A laser printer was, at one time, also called a *page printer* because the computer's operating system instructs it to print an entire page at a time, rather than a dot at a time. It's the laser, the printer's process, and the code sent to the printer that makes this process not only possible, but fast.

Typically more expensive than its counterparts, the laser printer is also considered more reliable and its output of better quality. As a high-end, non-impact printer, the laser printer uses a combination of processes to print images: electricity, chemistry, magnetism, optics, heat, and friction. Each component of a laser printer has its own effect on the trip that a sheet of paper takes through the printer.

The paper feeder mechanism

As discussed earlier, laser printers use a friction feeder to feed paper into the print device. Most laser printers use a paper tray to hold the paper before it is printed on. Some printers, however, use gravity as a way to hold and begin the print process. These printers hold the paper vertical in a chute above the print components. Regardless of the feed device, each printer requires some mechanism to feed the paper into the printer.

The paper transport path

Paper moves through the printer by making contact with several sets of rollers that work much like the paper feeder. *Registration rollers* are synchronized with the print process so the paper doesn't lag or enter the printer too soon. *Fuser rollers* help fix the image to the paper in the final steps of the print process. *Exit rollers* (the final set) eject the finished, printed page.

The toner cartridge

The toner cartridge contains three indispensable elements of the printing process:

✦ **Toner.** This mixture of carbon, polyester, and iron particles does the job of ink. Carbon (the black, chalky substance) provides the outline of the image. Polyester helps the toner flow from the cartridge, through the print process, and onto the paper. Iron particles make the toner responsive to electrical charges and help it melt into the paper at the end of the print process.

✦ **Print drum.** A main component in the laser print process, this photosensitive cylinder holds an electromagnetic charge when not exposed to light — but loses its charge when exposed.

You do not want to fool around "rigging" your printer to be open while the printer attempts to print. Not only can this cause serious damage to the printer — it can cause serious damage to you as well. The print drum should never be exposed to direct light, as light causes the drum to lose its charge.

✦ **Cleaning blade.** This blade removes excess toner from the print drum as the drum rotates.

Always keep an extra toner cartridge on hand for each printer in your network. Not only does this save some grief when the printer is out of toner, it can also serve as a quick troubleshooting tool. For various troubles, a quick swap of the toner cartridge can tell the technician whether the problem is low toner, a bad cartridge, or something more serious.

The actual laser in the laser printer is contained in a special assembly that allows the laser to operate only when the printer is closed (direct laser light can damage your eyes). The laser shines on a mirror above the photosensitive drum; the reflected laser light shines on the turning drum. Because the drum cannot hold a charge when exposed to light, the laser and the drum work together to attract the charged toner to the drum — but only enough to make images on the paper. Toner will only be attracted to the areas on the print drum where the laser has shone.

Power supply

A laser printer requires high-voltage electricity to charge the corona wire and the transfer corona wire. The power supply charges these two components by converting standard AC current to a higher-voltage DC current, as required by each printer type. In addition, the printer requires DC power for the printer's cooling system, logic board, and the motors that turn the wheels to guide the paper through the device.

Transfer corona wire

The *transfer corona wire* gives the paper a positive electrical charge to attract the toner onto the paper (discussed in more detail in a moment). The transfer corona also contains a static-eliminator to remove the charge after the toner has passed onto the paper.

Fuser

This ominous-sounding device is responsible for fusing (melting) the toner into the paper. The fuser contains a halogen lamp to heat a Teflon-coated roller. Opposite the Teflon-coated roller is a thick rubber roller. As a sheet of paper passes between these rollers, the iron particles and toner are melted into the paper. This is why a laser-printed image is always warm when the paper is ejected from the printer.

The laser printing process

The components of a laser printer are the starting point; how they work together is the printing process. Knowing the process is the basis for effective printer support. Laser printers are far more complex than inkjets or dot matrix printers, so a more in-depth discussion is warranted.

Exam Tip   The CompTIA exam will focus more on laser printers than on ink jets and dot matrix printers. Know laser printers, their attributes, and how they work and you'll do fine on the printers portion of the exam.

Charging the drum

When the printer receives a command from the computer's operating system to begin the print process, the photosensitive drum is negatively charged (–600Vdc). This charging is why the printer requires a high-voltage power supply.

Exposing the drum

After the drum is charged, the laser flashes like a strobe light, the beam reflecting from the mirror to the negatively charged drum. In the areas where the light touches the drum, the charge changes from –600Vdc to approximately –100Vdc. As the drum spins, the laser creates the outline of the image on the drum by building a pattern of strongly charged and less-than-strongly-charged areas of negative voltage.

Developing the image

After the image is electromagnetically "written" to the drum, the toner must be applied to the print drum so the image can be transferred to paper. Adjacent to the print drum and the reservoir of toner is a smaller drum called the *developer*. Charged with –600Vdc by the high-voltage power supply, the developer attracts toner powder to itself as it rotates between the toner and the print drum. The print drum and the developer drum are both charged with –600Vdc, except for the areas of the print drum previously exposed to laser light. Those areas have a weaker negative charge, which attracts the toner. When the print drum has toner on only the areas of slight negative charge, then the image is ready for transfer to paper.

Transferring the image

Now the registration rollers feed the paper into the printer and over the transfer corona wire, which gives the paper a strong positive charge (+600Vdc). As the paper moves beneath the print drum, the weakly charged negative toner particles are strongly attracted to the positively charged paper. As always, opposites attract; the image, outlined in toner, moves onto the paper. The paper continues to move through the assembly, passing over a static eliminator strip that removes all electromagnetic charge from the paper. (This step is crucial; a positively charged piece of paper would be attracted to the still-negative print drum, stick there, and cause a major paper jam.)

Fusing the image

As the paper leaves the print drum, all that holds the toner on the paper is a slight positive charge and a bit of gravity. The *fuser* assembly finishes the printing by melting the toner into the paper as the sheet moves between a heated, Teflon-coated roller and a rubber roller. The paper is then ejected from the print device.

Cleaning up the mess

As with any good party, you have to clean up a mess when you're done. In this case, the actual mess is tiny — leftover toner in the cartridge. The cleaning blade in the cartridge scrapes the toner off the print drum in preparation for the next print job. Any unused toner is caught and held in a tray beneath the cleaning blade. (Don't worry — the tray won't fill up. You'll run out of toner first. Just be careful not to breathe the old toner when you change cartridges.)

Inkjet printers

An inkjet printer is a fine, acceptable printer for environments such as home, home office, or road trips (where large print runs probably don't take place). Though not as complex as a laser printer — nor as expensive — inkjets have evolved into high-quality short-run printers.

The early inkjet printers were clunky, unreliable, and messy. Their cartridges had an ink reservoir, a pump that forced the ink into a nozzle, and a reputation for leaking ink, ruining work, and staining hands.

Today's inkjets are much more civilized. The ink cartridge contains all the working elements needed to get an image from the computer onto a sheet of paper: compartments of ink sealed with a metal plate, thin tubes from the ink source to each well, and the *jet* at the bottom of each compartment (a tiny pinhole that sends ink onto the page).

When the print device receives the command from the computer's operating system to print an image, the printer starts the following process:

An electrical current warms the heating element, which is submerged in the ink source. As the element heats, the ink vaporizes, creating pressure in the compartments. The pressure forces the expanding ink out of the microscopic pinhole, one tiny bubble at a time. The cartridge doesn't spray ink like a squirt gun; the pressure in the cartridge is controlled by the degree of heat from the heating element. Only one drop at a time can escape from the ink cartridge—but it happens fast enough to create entire images in less than a minute.

Eventually the ink cartridge runs out of ink and should be replaced. Although kits are available for refilling your own ink cartridges, they can enlarge the pinhole, may contain a different formula of ink, and are generally messy and inefficient. Inkjet cartridges can also dry out if they are not used often. Most inkjet printers park the cartridge inside the printer when not in use. Other models have a separate storage unit that allows the cartridge to be removed from the print device.

Inkjet printers (especially color models) have grown in popularity with the advent of affordable digital cameras. Color inkjet printers often require two cartridges: one for black ink and one for the colors (whether red, green, and blue or cyan, yellow, and magenta). Cartridges that bundle the black ink with the other colors are called CYMK (for cyan, magenta, yellow, and black). Note that a "K," instead of a "B," designates "black." The printing industry has done this for years so as not to confuse "black" with "blue."

 Tip When replacing an ink cartridge (whether multicolor or single-color), always have an extra cartridge on hand. If you don't have an extra, put the old cartridge in a small plastic bag and take it with you when you purchase a new cartridge. This eliminates the guesswork when you're staring at 487 different types of printer cartridges.

Dot-matrix printers

Dot-matrix printers are *impact* printers; they strike an inked ribbon to put characters on paper. A dot-matrix printer triggers rows of pins that strike the ribbon in patterns, leaving closely grouped dots that make up numbers, characters, or even images.

The pins are actually *solenoids*—metal stubs wrapped with a short coil of wire, held in place with a spring and a small magnet. When a particular solenoid is needed to strike, an electrical current is sent to the coil of wires around the solenoid. This creates a miniature electromagnet, which causes the pin to repel against the magnet holding it in place – striking the ribbon and transferring a dot onto the paper in the process.

The *print head*, which houses the solenoids, moves across the paper, printing one line of dots—not characters or numbers—at a time. The rapidly striking pins make a whining screech. If you've never experienced the ear-splitting effect of a dot-matrix printer, you're lucky. Some models had plastic shields to suppress the noise—somewhat.

Early dot-matrix printers used only 9 pins to print; these *draft-quality* printers gave way to printers boasting 17 (or even 24) pins. They produced sketchy, crude-looking pages (compared to the output of today's printers), but they were faster than most typists.

Are businesses still using dot-matrix printers today? Sure. Overall, these reliable printers are excellent for filling in tractor-fed continuous forms—especially those that use special paper to create multiple copies of the form (for example, repair orders or sales receipts) at once.

Types of Printer Connections and Configurations

5.1 Identify basic concepts, printer operations, and printer components. Content may include the following: Types of printer connections and configurations—Parallel, Network, USB, Infrared, and Serial

Understanding how a printer does its job is half the picture (so to speak); the other half is how the printer receives its print-job instructions from the computer. Hundreds, if not thousands, of printer types are available today, but all have two things in common: They print images and they must communicate with an operating system.

Printers connect to the computer in one of five ways:

✦ Parallel cables

✦ Network connections

✦ Universal Serial Bus

✦ Serial

✦ Infrared

Parallel cable connections

Most printers can connect directly to a computer through a ribbonlike *parallel cable*, which attaches to your computer's parallel port through a male DB-25 connector and to the printer through a male 36-pin Centronics connector.

Most parallel cables are no longer than ten feet. Although some parallel cables can measure up to 50 feet, longer cables run the risk of crosstalk. *Crosstalk* is electrical interference from other equipment, fluorescent lights, and other cables.

A parallel connection transfers multiple bits (in groups of up to eight) from the computer to the printer, along the eight parallel wires that make up the ribbon. A parallel port can handle roughly 150 kilobytes per second.

Parallel printers and their cables should conform to the IEEE 1284 Standard for parallel cables. This standard addresses communication to and from the device attached to the cable, and defines the mode of operation as either duplex or half-duplex. Because *half-duplex* means communication can only occur in one direction at a time, you're likelier to see *full-duplex* (communication in two directions at once) used in up-to-date equipment.

The IEEE 1284 Standard accommodates five types of operation:

✦ **Compatibility mode.** Allows backward compatibility with older parallel printers. While this standard mode does allow backward compatibility, there are drawbacks. The processor must listen for activity on the cable, communication is using only half-duplex mode, and the maximum speed is limited to the standard 150 kilobytes per second.

✦ **Nibble mode.** Allows the printer to send information back to the computer. Nibble mode earned its name because the communication from the printer is sent back to the processor in two four-bit chunks called *nibbles*. This mode is also processor-intensive, as the processor must listen to the incoming traffic on the cable.

✦ **Byte mode.** Allows the printer to communicate with the computer at the same rate the computer speaks with the printer. Byte mode may also be called an enhanced bidirectional port. It allows older devices to go beyond the four-bit limit of nibble mode and use the full speed (150 kilobytes per second) to talk back to the computer.

✦ **Enhanced Capability Port (ECP) mode.** An advanced, bidirectional mode for fast communications between the computer and any device attached to the parallel port. Created by Microsoft and Hewlett-Packard to address the needs of high-speed printers and scanners, this mode reduces the dedicated CPU time required to move large chunks of data between devices.

✦ **Enhanced Parallel Port mode.** Designed by Intel, Xircom, and Zenith Data Systems to provide a common interface for devices besides printers (for example, scanners, external hard drives, or CD-ROM drives) that require speed.

Serial cable connections

Serial cables, which have a cylindrical (instead of ribbonlike) cross-section, connect to the computer's serial port, using either a 9-pin or a 25-pin connector to transfer data over the wire. A serial port connection allows only one bit at a time to be sent over the cable, which is why serial printers are typically older, slower models.

Serial cables do have one small advantage over parallel cables: They allow cable lengths of up to 25 feet; serial cables are not as susceptible to crosstalk as are parallel cables, since the data moves one bit at a time in a row over the cable.

Network cable connections

Network printers have integrated *network interface cards* (NICs) that connect the printers to a network cable so users can share them. Normally you find these printers managed in one of two ways: through software provided by the manufacturer, or through Telnet to ROM-based information in the printer.

In today's networked environment, chances are good the printer uses TCP/IP (Transmission Control Protocol/Internet Protocol). This network protocol requires that every network interface have its own unique IP address. The type of printer being used determines how the IP address can be assigned to the printer. Many printers are assigned IP addresses through a software interface. Other printers use DHCP (Dynamic Host Configuration Protocol) to obtain an IP address. A technician should always check with the manufacturer's documentation to ensure that the correct protocol and installation method are in use.

A network-based printer is an ideal solution for an environment where everyone needs to complete heavy-duty printing. Financial practicality argues against buying a laser printer for every user. A network-based printer allows all users to print to it (or to a set of printers) from any workstation on the network.

Access to the printer can still be set through permissions within your network operating system. For example, in Windows 2000, access to the printer can be granted to members of some groups and denied access to users in other groups.

A network-based printer has several advantages over an individual serial or parallel printer:

✦ **The network printer is available all the time.** This is true if the printer is connected directly to the network rather than through an intermediary print server.With a parallel printer or serial printer, should the server or workstation be offline, the printer is not available.

✦ **A dedicated print server is not required.** A network printer can be accessed from anywhere in the network.

Universal Serial Bus

Unless you've been living in a cave, you probably already know that Universal Serial bus, or USB is a very fast, reliable connection method for devices and operating systems. You can add a new device with a simple click; Plug-and-Play technology kicks in, recognizes the device, and it's ready to be used. No rebooting.

USB is emerging as a connectivity cure-all for devices that range from digital cameras to scanners and printers. No longer do you have to worry about how to connect a device to your computer or rip open the case, add a card, and *then* connect the device. USB is much closer to a *real* plug-and-play connection method.

How fast is fast? Well, it depends on the device using USB. A full-stream USB device can transmit data at a maximum of 12 megabits (MB) per second. Compare that with a parallel port's 115 kilobytes per second and you've got a rocket. But a printer can only print so fast; it's a physical, mechanical job. A printer using USB doesn't necessarily print the document any faster than an identical printer that uses a parallel connection.

Okay, then, why even bother with USB? Why not just leave well enough alone? Well, for starters, consider the unique features of USB:

✦ Plug-and-Play without the hassle of rebooting

✦ Daisychaining up to 127 devices (Daisychaining means to connect devices to devices in one long chain — like a chain of daisies.)

✦ No need to configure ports, IRQs, and DMA channels for each device

Infrared

Infrared technology allows the printer to be connected to the computer through infrared beams. It's the same technology of changing your television's channels with a remote control. The signal is carried through a beam of light. A computer sends pulses of infrared light to the printer to instruct the printer what to print.

To print to an infrared printer, you'll need an infrared transmitter/receiver connected to your printer and an infrared printer. The transmitter may be built into your computer — especially on laptops. For workstations, you'll most likely have to purchase a transmitter that will connect to your computer through a USB or serial port. The printer will have a transmitter/receiver built into the unit.

Infrared printers fall into one of three devices:

✦ **Reflective infrared**. Transmitters are aimed at a central unit, which then redirects the commands to the printer. This allows many users to print to a common printer.

✦ **Line-of-sight infrared**. As its name implies, the printer's receiver must be in a direct line of site with the computer's transmitter.

✦ **Scatter infrared**. This technology allows the signal to bounce off walls, ceilings, or people, all the way to the printer's receiver.

Key Point Summary

In this chapter, we've discussed three types of printers, how they work, and how they connect to the computer. Here's a quick summary of each:

Printer Types:

✦ Laser printers use light, electromagnetism, and heat to print a page.

✦ Inkjet printers use a heating element to vaporize ink and spray it through a microscopic pinhole to make characters on a page.

✦ Dot-matrix printers use solenoids to strike an inked ribbon, creating characters out of patterns of printed dots.

Printer Connections:

✦ Parallel connection (a standard, acceptable connection method for printers) sends the print-job information in batches of up to 8 bits over a cable made of 8 parallel wires.

✦ Serial connection (a slower connection method for printers) enables data to be sent to the printer one bit at a time over the serial connection.

✦ Network connection (a convenient method of connecting a shared printer to its users) allows access without requiring dedicated hardware resources, such as a print server.

✦ USB connection (an excellent connection method for connecting printers and other Plug-and-Play devices to computers) provides the nearest thing to true plug-and-play operation without having to reboot the computer.

✦ Infrared connection (a method of connecting to a printer through pulses of invisible light) is acceptable for smaller offices and home usage.

✦   ✦   ✦

STUDY GUIDE

This Study Guide presents 25 assessment questions, 2 scenarios, and 2 lab exercises to test your knowledge of the exam topic area.

Assessment Questions

1. What are the two types of paper feeder mechanisms?

   A. Continuous tractor feed

   B. Continuous form feed

   C. Friction feed

   D. Injected

2. What type of printer is most likely to use a continuous form feeder?

   A. Laser printer

   B. Inkjet

   C. Dot-matrix

   D. USB

3. Which of the following devices are most likely to use a friction-feed mechanism to load the paper into the print assembly? (Choose two)

   A. Laser printers

   B. Fax machines

   C. Dot-matrix printers

   D. A printer that prints hundreds of payroll checks

4. What is another name for a laser printer?

   A. Photoelectric printer

   B. Page printer

   C. CYMK printer

   D. Platen driver

5. Which of the following devices gives the paper a positive charge?

   A. The laser

   B. The print drum

   C. The registration rollers

   D. The transfer corona wire

6. Why is the print drum given a negative charge?

   A. To attract the toner to every area of the drum

   B. To attract the toner to the areas of the drum that have a stronger negative charge

   C. To attract the toner to the areas of the drum that have a weaker negative charge

   D. To attract the positively charged paper to the print drum

7. Why are both the developer drum and the print drum charged with –600Vdc?

   A. So the paper is attracted to neither

   B. So the toner is attracted to neither

   C. So the toner creates a fusion cloud between the two rollers and the paper

   D. So the toner is attracted only to weakly charged areas of the print drum

8. At what voltage is the paper charged?

   A. +600Vdc

   B. –600Vdc

   C. –100Vdc

   D. +100Vdc

9. What prevents the paper from rolling into the print assembly with the print drum?

   A. The registration rollers

   B. The static eliminator strip

   C. The fuser

   D. The electrical charge on the paper and the print drum

10. What is the fuser roller coated with?

    A. Teflon

    B. Aluminum

    C. Ink

    D. Rubber

11. What device removes unused toner from the print drum?

    A. Transfer corona wire

    B. Static eliminator strip

    C. Laser

    D. Cleaning blade

12. What best describes how an inkjet printer prints an image?

    A. One dot at a time to form a character

    B. Spray-painting a character

    C. Striking an inked ribbon

    D. Dropping ink onto the paper

13. What causes the ink to vaporize in an inkjet printer?

    A. Electrical pulses

    B. A heating element within the ink cartridge

    C. A solenoid in each chamber of the ink cartridge

    D. Drying of the ink when the cartridge has not been used for some time

14. What is another name for a dot-matrix printer?

    A. Impact printer

    B. Page printer

    C. Spray printer

    D. USB

15. What is a solenoid?

    A. An element in each chamber of an inkjet cartridge

    B. A component that heats the ink in an inkjet printer

    C. A pin assembly that strikes the inked ribbon in a dot-matrix printer

    D. A wire assembly that connects the print head to the print controller in any printer

16. How many pins were in the early dot-matrix print heads?

    A. 9

    B. 12

    C. 18

    D. 44

17. What type of paper-feed mechanisms do dot-matrix printers use?

    A. Continuous form feed

    B. Friction feed

    C. Friction continuous form feed

    D. Inverted gravity feed

18. What is the recommended maximum length for a parallel cable?

    A. 10 feet

    B. 20 feet

    C. 25 feet

    D. 50 feet

19. What printer cable uses a male DB-25 connector to attach to the PC?

    A. Serial

    B. Parallel

    C. USB

    D. Network

20. What is crosstalk?

    A. A parallel cable printing to a serial printer

    B. A serial cable printing to a parallel cable

    C. A type of interference in cables, caused by other equipment

    D. A type of interference in computers, caused by printers

21. What is ECP mode?

    A. A type of operation that allows a parallel port to speak with older printers

    B. A type of operation that allows the parallel port to communicate with devices

    C. A type of operation that provides fast bidirectional support for printers and computers

    D. A type of operation that allows the printer to speak to the computer at the same rate the computer uses to speak to the printer

22. Why is a serial port called serial?

    A. The pins in a serial port are all in one line.

    B. The printer is addressed as a serial number.

    C. Data for the printer is sent serially, one bit at a time.

    D. The serial ports are assigned serial numbers by the IEEE.

23. What is the maximum length for a serial cable?

    A. 10 feet

    B. 25 feet

    C. 30 feet

    D. 50 feet

24. What connection type allows a printer to connect to an RJ-45 connector?

    A. Parallel

    B. SCSI

    C. USB

    D. Network

25. How fast is a USB port?

    A. 10Mbps

    B. 12Mbps

    C. 75Mbps

    D. 100Mbps

Scenarios

This chapter has presented you with printing terms and concepts—and a lot of information about how printers should work. Identify a solution for each of the critical-thinking exercises that follow.

    1. You are an information-technology consultant. Your client has asked you to recommend a printer type that would allow all users in the office to print to a central printer. The workgroup has seventeen users; all computers are running Microsoft Windows 2000 Professional. You know that your client does not have a print server and is not interested in purchasing one. What printer type would best serve this network of users?

2. You are a technician for a manufacturing firm. The president of the company asks that you recommend a printer type for his home, where he uses a laptop running Windows 2000 Professional. He would like a printer type that is easy to configure, simple to connect, and would allow him to print color photos from his digital camera. What type of printer, and printer connection, would you recommend?

Lab Exercises

Lab 7.1 Identifying Laser Printer Components

This lab requires access to a laser printer. Because available models of laser printers may differ, consult your owner's guide. In addition, because active laser printers have hot parts that can be dangerous, you may want to power down, unplug, and allow the printer to cool for an hour before you begin this lab. You may also want to use a flashlight to see all the internal parts of the printer.

1. Power down the printer and disconnect the power cord.

2. Remove the paper tray and locate the rollers that make the initial contact with the paper. If you can, follow the path the paper takes to enter the print area.

3. Slowly open the printer cover. You should see a flap move slowly down over a gray-green cylinder. That cylinder is the print drum—don't touch it!

4. Locate a thin, mirrorlike strip opposite the print drum. This is the mirror that reflects the laser light onto the print drum. If you slowly close the printer, you may see the mirror align with the print drum.

5. If necessary, open the cover again. Notice the area with the warning messages about the heat? That is the fuser area—don't touch it! It can severely burn.

6. Your printer may use a transfer corona wire that charges the paper as it enters the printing chamber. The wire is thin metal thread. It's okay to look at the wire, but don't touch it; if it breaks, it's cumbersome to repair (which should happen rarely, if ever).

7. Close the print cover, replace the paper tray, and reconnect the power cord to the wall outlet. Power on the printer.

Lab 7.2 Connecting and Using a USB Printer

This lab requires access to a USB printer. If you do not have a USB printer, the exercise gives you some idea of how USB connectivity works.

1. Locate the USB port on your PC. On some computers this may be on the front of the PC. Locate the USB port on your printer. Attach the USB cable to the USB port on the printer.

2. Power on the printer.

3. Connect the USB device to the computer's USB port.

4. Windows 98 and Windows 2000 can detect the new USB device and (if necessary) prompt you for the CD so you can install the software drivers needed to communicate with the printer. If the device is already installed on the computer, you don't have to reinstall it.

Answers to Chapter Questions

Chapter Pre-Test

1. A **laser printer** uses a cleaner blade to clean the unused toner from the print drum.

2. A laser printer uses the fuser assembly to **melt the toner into the paper.**

3. Printer speed is measured in **pages per minute.**

4. Toner contains iron oxide particles **so it can be easily affected by electrical charges and melt easily into the paper during fusing.**

5. **Inkjet printers** use a heating element to heat and vaporize the ink before spraying it onto the paper, one drop at a time.

6. Most printers attach through the **parallel** port — still the most common method, although some printers use the serial or USB port.

7. Normally, a network printer already has a network interface card installed in the printer. This printer needs **an IP Address** so the users in the TCP/IP environment can connect to the device.

8. **Paper** is very susceptible to humidity. Always store your paper in a cool, dry place.

9. USB devices can be connected in a daisychain of up to **127**, provided all the connected devices are USB.

10. **A printer driver** is a piece of software that tells the operating system what the attached printer is capable of doing.

Assessment Questions

1. **B, C.** Paper-feeder mechanisms are devices that guide sheets of paper into the print device. A continuous form feed device is used most often with dot-matrix printers. A friction feed device is used primarily with inkjet printers and laser printers. For more information, see the section labeled "Paper feeder mechanisms."

2. **C. A.** Dot-matrix printers use a continuous form feeder. A continuous form is one long sheet of paper, perforated at intervals that correspond to the long sides of the eventual documents — 8.5 inches for letter size or 14 inches for

legal size. For more information, see the section labeled "Paper feeder mechanisms."

3. **A, B.** Friction feeders use rollers that apply a light pressure and friction to the top sheet in the paper tray to move it into the print device. Various pieces of equipment use such feeders, including laser printers and fax machines. For more information, see the section labeled "Paper feeder mechanisms."

4. **B. A.** A laser printer is also called a page printer; it can receive instructions from the operating system to print one page at a time. For more information, see the section labeled "Types of Printers."

5. **D.** The transfer corona wire charges the paper with a +600Vdc. The paper is charged so the negatively charged toner on the print drum is strongly attracted to the positive charge on the paper. For more information, see the section labeled "Types of Printers."

6. **C.** The print drum is charged with a strong negative charge, -600Vdc initially. As the laser shines the image onto the print drum, the lighted areas weaken their negative charge to nearly –100Vdc. This causes the toner (which is also charged at –600Vdc) to be attracted to the weaker charged areas. For more information, see the section labeled "Types of Printers."

7. **D.** The developer and the print drum are both equally charged. Objects that are equally charged are repelled from each other. The lesser-charged areas of the print drum attract the stronger charged toner to that area. For more information, see the section labeled "Types of Printers."

8. **A.** The corona transfer will charge the paper to a strong +600Vdc so the toner on the print drum, resting at –100Vdc, is strongly attracted to the much stronger, opposite charge on the paper. For more information, see the section labeled "Types of Printers."

9. **B.** The static eliminator strip, a feltlike pad, eliminates the charge from the paper. If it did not, the paper would continue to be attracted to the print drum, would curl around the drum, and cause a paper jam. For more information, see the section labeled "Types of Printers."

10. **A.** The fuser roller, which is typically made of aluminum, is coated with Teflon. The Teflon coating helps keep the melting toner from sticking to anything but the paper. For more information, see the section labeled "Types of Printers."

11. **D. A.** The cleaning blade scrapes against the print drum as it turns inside the toner cartridge. The small amount of unused toner is scraped off and collected in a small tray in a compartment inside of the toner cartridge. For more information, see the section labeled "Types of Printers."

12. **B.** An inkjet printer jets, or sprays, the ink onto the paper. A dot-matrix printer would print the characters, or images, in a series of dots. For more information, see the section labeled "Types of Printers."

13. **B.** Within the ink cartridge there is a heating element to cook the ink to the point of vaporization. This causes a pressure to build and the ink to "escape" through a tiny hole in the bottom of the print cartridge. For more information, see the section titled "Types of Printers."

14. **A.** A dot-matrix printer can also be called an impact printer as a solenoid strikes the inked ribbon to transfer a series of dots onto the paper to form a character. For more information see the section titled "Types of Printers."

15. **C.** A solenoid is a pin within an impact printer that strikes the inked ribbon to transfer a dot onto the paper. For more information see the section titled "Types of Printers."

16. **A.** Early dot-matrix printers used only 9 pins to create the dots on the paper. These printers with 9 pins in the print head were also called draft-quality printers. For more information see the section titled "Types of Printers."

17. **A.** Dot-matrix printers use a continuous form feeder. Recall that these printers print to paper that is in one long sheet, perforated every 8.5 inches or 14 inches for legal size documents. For more information see the section titled "Types of Printers."

18. **A.** Although there are parallel cables well beyond this 10 foot length, it is recommended that parallel cables remain at 10 feet or below to avoid crosstalk. For more information see the section titled "Types of Printer Connections and Configurations."

19. **B.** Parallel cables use a male DB-25 connector to attach to a PC and a 36 male Centronics connector to attach to the printer. For more information see the section titled "Types of Printer Connections and Configurations."

20. **C.** Crosstalk is interference a cable experiences from equipment, lights, and other cables in the vicinity of the cable. As the signal on the cable grows weaker (attenuation), cable is more prone to crosstalk. For more information see the section titled "Types of Printer Connections and Configurations."

21. **C.** ECP, Enhanced capabilities port, mode reduces the amount of dedicated CPU time required to move large chunks of data between devices. For more information see the section titled "Types of Printer Connections and Configurations."

22. **C.** Data sent across the serial cable is sent one bit at a time in a serial stream. For more information see the section titled "Types of Printer Connections and Configurations."

23. **B.** Serial ports have one advantage over parallel ports: their accepted length. Serial ports can range up to 25 feet from the source. For more information see the section titled "Types of Printer Connections and Configurations."

24. **D.** A network printer would connect to a cable with an RJ-45 connector. An RJ-45 connector is a standard connector for Category 5 UTP cables for Ethernet networks. For more information see the section titled "Types of Printer Connections and Configurations."

25. **B.** A USB port can have a maximum transfer of 12 Mbps. For more information see the section titled "Types of Printer Connections and Configurations."

Scenarios

1. A network printer would best serve your client, for several reasons. First, all the users need access to the printer. A network printer allows each user to install the printer on his or her Windows 2000 Professional workstation directly. Connecting the printer to a Windows 2000 Professional computer and sharing the printer through the operating system would not be a solution; Windows 2000 Professional allows only 10 concurrent connections, and the workgroup has 17 users who need access to the printer. Finally, since the office is already networked, a centrally-based network print device would be physically accessible to all users without imposing the prohibitive cost of giving each user a printer.

2. A USB color inkjet would best serve the president of this company. An inkjet printer is easy to configure, ideal for color photos, and easy to connect to the PC. In addition, many color inkjets are designed specifically for digital cameras. Finally, if the president already uses a digital camera, the camera probably connects to the computer via USB; he may already be familiar with the technology.

System Resources Used By Devices

EXAM OBJECTIVES

Exam 220-201 ✦ **A+ Core Hardware**

✦ **1.3** Identify available IRQs, DMAs, and I/O addresses and procedures for device installation and configuration. Content may include the following:

- Standard IRQ settings
- Modems
- Floppy drive controllers
- Hard drive controllers
- USB ports
- Infrared ports
- Hexadecimal/Addresses

CHAPTER PRE-TEST

1. Installing a device and assigning it IRQ 7 will conflict with which other device?

2. What is the purpose of an IRQ address?

3. What is the default IRQ assigned to LPT2?

4. What is the purpose of an I/O address?

5. What tool will display the IRQs being used in Windows 9x?

6. What does the abbreviation DMA stand for?

7. What is the I/O address of COM2?

8. What is the purpose of a DMA channel?

9. Where can I view I/O addresses on Windows NT 4.0?

10. What does the abbreviation IRQ stand for?

✦ Answers to these questions can be found at the end of the chapter. ✦

Suppose that one of your best friends calls you up one day to borrow your perfectly functional sound card and you tell him to come over and pick it up. Your friend (we'll call him Dan) comes over and picks up the sound card, and you show him that the thing works perfectly in your computer. You then remove it carefully and give it to him. Dan takes the sound card home, inserts it into his system, and boots up his computer. Windows loads up and installs the driver for the card, but after the driver has been loaded, Dan notices that there is no sound! Viewing the status of the sound card in the Windows 95 Device Manager reveals that the device is not functioning properly. So Dan is thinking to himself "Gee, the sound card worked before. What gives?"

Or worse still, say you purchase a sound card from the local computer store, insert it into your computer, properly install the drivers, and it doesn't work.

Problems like these are among the most common that technicians have with support systems today — a device that works in one computer doesn't initially work in another computer, even when the operating systems on both computers are identical.

This chapter will help you understand why these devices do not initially work in your system and identify what you can do to make them work. You will also learn the different types of resources that you will be required to troubleshoot and how to identify the default resources for any system.

Understanding System Resources

1.3 Identify available IRQs, DMAs and I/O addresses and procedures for configuring them for device installation and configuration. Content may include the following: Standard IRQ settings; Modems; Floppy drive controllers; Hard drive controllers; USB ports; Infrared ports; Hexadecimal/Addresses

In this chapter, when you see the term *system resource*, I would like you to think of a setting assigned to a device that allows the device to work with the computer. A device is anything that you can install on the computer — for example, a network card, a modem, or a sound card.

The three major system resources that can be assigned to different devices are I/O addresses, IRQ addresses, and DMA addresses. A fourth system resource, called a *memory address*, can sometimes be assigned to devices as well. In the following sections, we will discuss each of these system resources.

I/O addresses

It is extremely important to remember that the CPU is the traffic cop of the entire system. If something is going to happen on the system, then generally the CPU (processor) will enable the action. All devices in the computer need to communicate with the processor from time to time, and the processor needs a method of separating and prioritizing all these communications.

Because the processor needs to send information to a number of different devices and because those devices need to know which messages coming from the CPU are for them, each device is assigned an *I/O address*, or input/output address. The I/O address is a special port address that represents a pathway between the CPU and the device. So, for example, if the processor needs to send information to LPT1, it can send the information to pathway 378-37F, which is the pathway address that is leading to LPT1. I like to think of these pathways as tunnels; each device has its own tunnel that extends from the device to the processor.

Figure 8-1 shows a number of devices that are configured with IO addresses (note that the addresses are different in each system). If the processor needs to send information to the sound card, it knows that if it sends the information down I/O port address 220, then the sound card will receive the information. Conversely, when the processor receives information from I/O port address 220, it knows that the information comes from the sound card, because that address is assigned to only one device.

There are 65, 536 I/O port addresses available on the system. (There are actually fewer addresses than that, because when you assign an IO address to a device, you are really assigning a range of addresses.) The trick is to make sure that you have not assigned the same I/O port address to two different devices. If you do, you will get a resource conflict. A *resource conflict* is when two devices are using the same resource, such as an I/O address, IRQ, or DMA channel.

Note   The I/O address assigned to a device is really a range of values, such as 378-37F. Most people refer to the address block by the first value in the range.

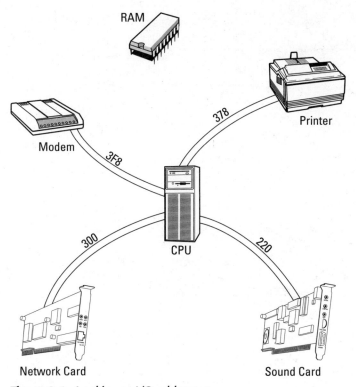

Figure 8-1: Looking at I/O addresses

To prevent resource conflicts, each device should have a unique I/O address, but the problem is, how do you know which I/O addresses existing devices already use? One way is to use the Windows 95/98 Device Manager to view I/O addresses being used on the system. The following Step By Step shows you how to view I/O addresses in use by your system.

STEP BY STEP: Viewing I/O Addresses in Use

1. Select Start ➪ Settings ➪ Control Panel.

2. Double-click the system icon.

3. Choose the Device Manager page tab.

4. Click Computer at the top of the device list and then click the Properties button to display the Computer Properties dialog box.

5. Select the Input/output (I/O) radio button on the View Resources tab (shown in Figure 8-2) of the Computer Properties dialog box. From there, you can scroll down to see all the address ranges that are in use by your computer and what device is using it.

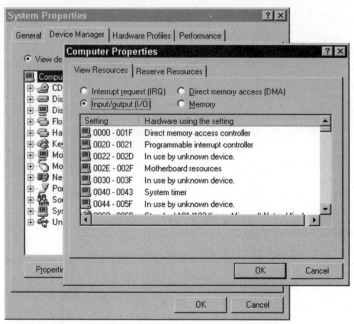

Figure 8-2: Viewing I/O addresses in use through Windows Device Manager

For the A+ exam, it is important to memorize the I/O addresses of standard ports, such as COM1, COM2, and LPT1. Table 8-1 lists these addresses.

Table 8-1
Standard I/O Address Assignments

Device	I/O Address Range
COM1	03F8 to 03FF
COM2	02F8 to 02FF
COM3	03E8 to 03EE
COM4	02E8 to 02EE
LPT1	0378 to 037F
LPT2	0278 to 027F
Math coprocessor	00F8 to 00FF
Primary hard disk controller	01F0 to 01F7

Device	I/O Address Range
Secondary hard disk controller	0170 to 0177
Sound cards	0220 to 022F
Floppy Disk	03F0 to 03F7

Note Although most systems come with COM1 and COM2, you may have additional serial ports, such as COM3 and COM4, because you have added an additional serial device to your system. An example of an additional serial device that could be added is an internal modem.

Interrupt request

Each device has its own tunnel for sending and receiving information to the processor, which is the function of the I/O port address that we detailed in the previous section. But how does each device get permission to send information to the processor, which as you know, is busy doing something important nearly all the time? Too much overhead would be created if the processor had to continuously poll each device to see if it had something that it needed the processor to do; instead, each device is responsible for notifying the processor if it has information for it. Devices need a way to interrupt the processor from its current processing to ask it if it will service their requests. The method that is used to interrupt the processor is called an *Interrupt request*, or IRQ line.

If you were standing beside someone who was involved in a conversation and you really wanted to talk to that person, what would you do? You might, for example, tap the person on the shoulder. Tapping the person on the shoulder is similar to what the IRQ line is used for; the IRQ line sends a signal from the device to the processor that grabs the processor's attention.

Tip Many people compare an IRQ to a bell sitting at the front desk of a restaurant or storefront. If you want service and no one is paying attention to you, you ring the bell for service — IRQs work the same way.

When a device taps the processor on the shoulder, the processor needs to know what device needs attention. That is why each device is assigned a unique IRQ line number. When a device sends a signal down the IRQ line to interrupt the processor, the processor checks which line the signal originated from and then attends to that device. For example, in Figure 8-3, if the network card wants to send information to the processor, the network card must first get the processor's attention by sending a signal down IRQ 10. This is like tapping the processor on the shoulder and saying "Hey, I have some information for you."

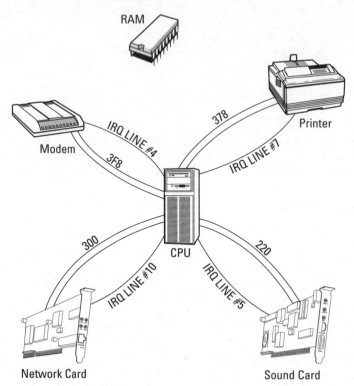

RAM

378

Printer

Modem

IRQ LINE #4

3F8

IRQ LINE #7

CPU

300

IRQ LINE #10

220

IRQ LINE #5

Network Card

Sound Card

Figure 8-3: Looking at IRQ lines

It is important to note that when information is sent to the processor, it is sent through the I/O address (the tunnel). So the IRQ is just to grab the processor's attention while the I/O address is used for the actual delivery of information.

Originally, there were only 8 IRQs available on XT (before 286) systems, but there are 16 IRQs available on AT (after 286) systems. In order to get 16 IRQs, another IRQ controller was added to the system, but having two sets of IRQs managed by two different controllers presented some technical problems. To help the two IRQ controllers act as one unit, the IRQs have cascaded (or linked) together, and the second controller goes through the first controller to send requests. Figure 8-4 shows the two controllers linked together.

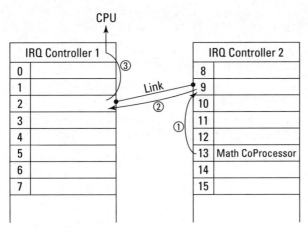

Figure 8-4: Looking at the two IRQ controllers cascaded together

In Figure 8-4, the path that the math coprocessor (which uses IRQ 10) would take to send an interrupt request to the processor is shown in three steps. These steps are as follows:

1. The math coprocessor sends a signal to the CPU, but because the second interrupt controller handles the math coprocessor, the signal is passed to IRQ 9, which forwards signals for the second interrupt controller.

2. IRQ 9 passes the signal to its linked partner, which is IRQ 2, which is managed by the first interrupt controller.

3. IRQ 2 then passes the signal through the first interrupt controller, which then sends the signal to the CPU.

 Tip For backward compatibility, only the first interrupt controller is allowed to send information to the CPU. This means that when interrupts 8 to 15 send information, they must pass it to the first controller, which in turn passes it to the processor on their behalf.

Like the I/O addresses, if you assign two devices the same IRQ value, you will get a resource conflict that results in at least one of the devices not working, or maybe both devices not working. To prevent assigning two devices the same resource, it is a good idea to understand what IRQ values you already have in use by your system.

The following Step By Step shows you how to view the IRQs that are being used (in Windows 95/98).

STEP BY STEP: Viewing IRQs in Use

1. Select Start ➪ Settings ➪ Control Panel.

2. Double-click the system icon.

3. Choose the Device Manager page tab.

4. Click Computer at the top of the device list and then click the Properties button to display the Computer Properties dialog box.

5. Select the Interrupt request (IRQ) radio button on the View Resources tab (shown in Figure 8-5) of the Computer Properties dialog box. From there, you can scroll down to see all the IRQ settings that are in use by your computer and what device is using each.

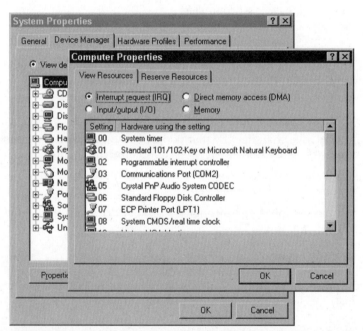

Figure 8-5: Viewing IRQs in use through Windows Device Manager

Exam Tip   For the exam, it is important to memorize the standard IRQs that are in use and which IRQs are generally considered available. Table 8-2 shows a listing of the IRQs on AT systems.

Table 8-2
Standard IRQ Assignments

IRQ Value	Device
0	System Timer
1	Keyboard
2	Link to second IRQ controller
3	COM2, COM4
4	COM1, COM3
5	LPT2
6	Floppy disk drive
7	LPT1
8	Real time clock
9	Available, but should not be used if IRQ 2 is being used
10	Available
11	Available
12	Available if not used by PS/2 mouse
13	Math Coprocessor
14	Hard disk controller
15	Available

Exam Tip   For the exam, it is important to know that the lower the IRQ value, the higher the priority the device will have with the processor.

Here are a few important points about IRQ assignments:

✦ **IRQs 10, 11, 12, and 15 are generally available.** If you are installing a new device into a computer and need to assign an IRQ, you would first try an available IRQ value.

✦ **IRQ 3 and IRQ 5 are used by COM2 and LPT2, respectively.** If you are not actually using COM2 or LPT2, you can consider IRQ 3 and IRQ 5 as available.

The following summarizes how I/O addresses and IRQs work together:

✦ When a device has information for the CPU, it first sends a signal down the IRQ line to grab the CPU's attention.

✦ After the device has the CPU's attention, it sends the information to the processor via its I/O address.

Exam Tip For the exam, it is important to memorize the default IRQs and I/O addresses of standard I/O ports.

Table 8-3 contains a listing of ports and associated addresses to memorize for the exam.

Table 8-3 Default IRQs and I/O Addresses		
Device	*IRQ*	*I/O Address*
COM1	4	3F8-3FF
COM2	3	2F8-2FF
COM3	4	3E8-3EE
COM4	3	2E8-2EE
LPT1	7	378-37F
LPT2	5	278-27F

Exam Tip You may be asked on the exam the IRQ of a modem plugged into a COM port. Know that an IRQ is not really assigned to a modem, but to the COM port the modem is using.

For the exam, you will also want to have an idea of where infrared and USB devices will sit as far as IRQs are concerned. Infrared ports attach themselves to virtual COM or LPT ports, which means that your infrared device will probably end up using IRQ 3 or 4. USB ports use the IRQ associated with the PCI bus, which can be anywhere from IRQ 9 and up.

Exam Tip On the exam, you may be asked the IRQ of an infrared device or a USB device. Infrared devices use either IRQ 3 or 4 and USB devices could use any IRQ from 9 on up.

Direct memory access

There are a number of different devices today that require constant access to system memory. Normally, devices must go through the CPU to write information to system memory, but using such a scheme can cause a lot of unnecessary overhead, so why not allow a device to access memory directly?

Cross-Reference For more information on memory, refer to Chapter 4.

To increase performance and to offload some of the work from the CPU, you can assign some devices a DMA (Direct Memory Access) channel. The DMA channel is a special pathway that allows the device to read and write information directly to system memory without passing the data to the processor.

For example, in Figure 8-6 you can see that the modem has been assigned DMA channel 6 and the printer has been assigned DMA channel 5 (like IO addresses, these addresses will be different on each system). This means that the modem and the printer can write information to memory directly, whereas the network card and the sound card must pass through the CPU.

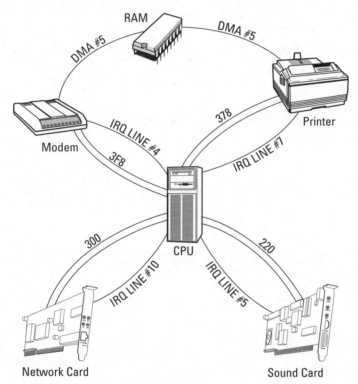

Figure 8-6: Looking at DMA channels

There are only 8 DMA channels available on your system, which should not be a huge problem because not all devices use DMA channels. Some examples of the different devices that you may run into that use DMA channels are sound cards, network cards, and, occasionally, CD-ROM drives. Table 8-4 shows a listing of common DMA channels.

Table 8-4
Common DMA Channel Assignments

DMA Channel	Device
0	Available
1	Sound or Available
2	Floppy Drive
3	Available
4	Cascade
5	Sound or Available
6	Available
7	Available

Like IRQs, there are two DMA controllers that are linked by a cascading DMA channel, DMA channel 4. DMA channels 0-3 are for 8-bit boards and cards; DMA channels 5-7 are used for 16/32-bit cards.

To view the DMA channels that are in use on your system, you can use the Windows Device Manager utility. The following Step By Step will walk you through viewing your DMA channels in use.

STEP BY STEP: Viewing DMA Channels in Use

1. Select Start ⇨ Settings ⇨ Control Panel.

2. Double-click the system icon.

3. Choose the Device Manager page tab.

4. Click Computer at the top of the device list and then click the Properties button to display the Computer Properties dialog box.

5. Select the Direct memory access (DMA) radio button on the View Resources tab (shown in Figure 8-7) of the Computer Properties dialog box.

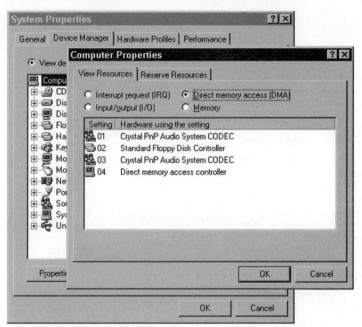

Figure 8-7: Viewing DMA Channels in use through Windows Device Manager

Memory addresses

A less common resource that may be assigned to devices is a memory address. A memory address is an area of upper memory where the device is allowed to store information.

If multiple devices have been assigned access to the same memory address, a device conflict will occur and one or both devices may not function. To view the memory addresses that are in use by the system, follow these steps:

STEP BY STEP: Viewing Memory Addresses in Use

1. Select Start ⇨ Settings ⇨ Control Panel.

2. Double-click the system icon.

3. Choose the Device Manager page tab.

4. Click Computer at the top of the device list and then click the Properties button to display the Computer Properties dialog box.

5. Select the Memory radio button on the View Resources tab (shown in Figure 8-8) of the Computer Properties dialog box.

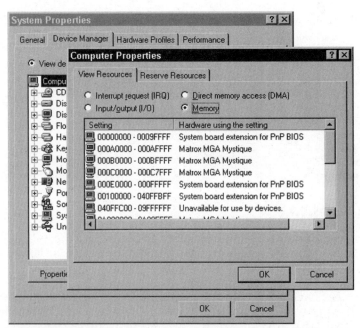

Figure 8-8: Viewing memory addresses in use through Windows Device Manager

Working with System Resources

In this section, you will be introduced to methods for viewing and editing system resource settings. One of the biggest issues in troubleshooting device-installation problems is being able to identify and solve resource conflicts.

Viewing resources in use

There are a number of different tools that you can use to view system resources, such as IRQs, I/O addresses, and DMA channels. Some of the tools are shipped with your operating system, and other tools are third-party products that you need to purchase.

Device Manager

Device Manager is a Windows 95/Windows 98 or Windows 2000 utility that you can use to view system resources and identify problems with devices. One of the benefits of the Windows Device Manager is that it not only shows you a device that has a conflict, but also the other device that it is in conflict with. Figure 8-9 shows a device with an IRQ conflict through the Windows 98 Device Manager.

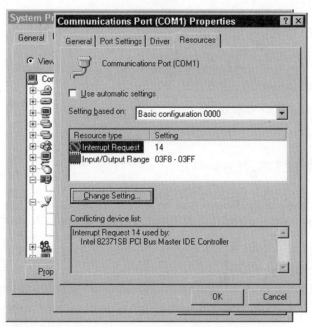

Figure 8-9: Identifying a conflicting device through Device Manager

Windows NT Diagnostics

In Windows NT 4.0, the operating system ships with a tool called Windows NT Diagnostics, instead of Device Manager. Windows NT Diagnostics (shown in Figure 8-10) serves the function of showing resources in use by devices and also gives you some reporting features to print the values of those resources. To print any page displayed in Windows NT Diagnostics, you will choose the File menu and then Print Report.

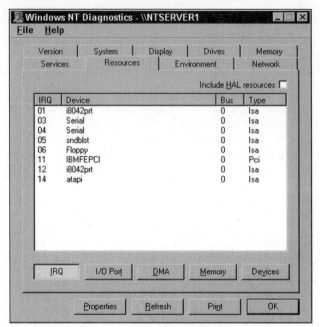

Figure 8-10: Looking at Windows NT Diagnostics

Changing system resources

Although viewing system resources and identifying devices that are causing a resource conflict are important, you also need to be able to make changes that will solve device conflicts. This section discusses different ways of changing system resources.

Troubleshooting techniques

Before changing a system resource, you need to have strategies for deciding the new value to assign to the resource. In general, the strategy is to look at all available resources and then reassign them such that each device is using an unused resource.

The manufacturer of the device generally limits the system resources that can be used to configure the device. In Figure 8-11, the sound card and network card only work with three IRQs each. The network card gives you the choice of using IRQ 4, 5, or 10; the sound card can function with IRQ 3, 4, or 5.

Suppose that you assign IRQ 4 to the network card and IRQ 3 to the sound card. (Remember that COM1 and COM2 normally use IRQ 3 and IRQ 4, so in reality, you would assign these resources only when all other resources were full. We are showing these system resources being assigned first for illustrative purposes only.)

Network Card	Sound Card
IRQ 4*	IRQ 3*
IRQ 10	IRQ 4
IRQ 5	IRQ 5

* = Assigned IRQ For That Device

Figure 8-11: Looking at an example of troubleshooting IRQs — Part 1

A few months later, you decide that you want to install an external modem on the computer. The modem must connect to COM1, which uses IRQ 4. Connecting the modem to COM1 generates a resource conflict that causes either the network card not to work, or both the network card and the modem not to work.

To fix such a resource conflict, you need to look at the IRQs that can be used for each device and start juggling them until you have all three devices working together on the same system. Figure 8-12 shows a modem being added to our scenario.

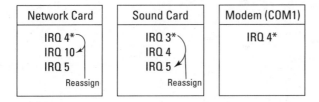

* = Assigned IRQ For That Device

Figure 8-12: Looking at an example of trouble-shooting IRQs — Part 2

You can see in Figure 8-12 that when the modem is installed, it will use IRQ 4 and conflict with the network card that is also using IRQ 4. At the same time, you notice that your sound card is using IRQ 3 (used by COM2), so to prevent future conflicts, you may be better off reassigning the IRQ for the sound card, as well. You decide to assign the network card to IRQ 10 so that the sound card can be assigned IRQ 5. The outcome of these reassignments is shown in Figure 8-13.

The final outcome of your decision on IRQ assignments allows all three devices to function without conflicts, and you are prepared for the day you decide to use COM2 by having that IRQ (IRQ 3) free.

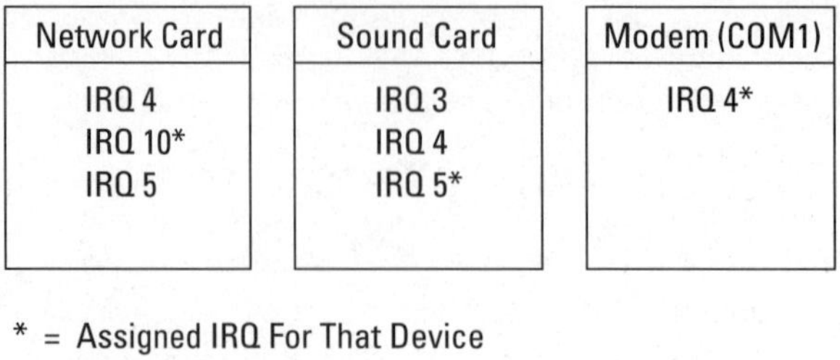

Network Card	Sound Card	Modem (COM1)
IRQ 4	IRQ 3	IRQ 4*
IRQ 10*	IRQ 4	
IRQ 5	IRQ 5*	

* = Assigned IRQ For That Device

Figure 8-13: Looking at an example of trouble-shooting IRQs — Part 3

Changing non–plug-and-play resources

In non–plug-and-play environments, such as Windows 3.1 or Windows NT, changing system resources on a device may take a little more research than making similar changes in a plug-and-play environment. To actually change IRQ values and I/O address values on older devices, you have to change *jumper* settings. A jumper (shown in Figure 8-14) is a set of pins on a card or board that applies a certain setting when a circuit is closed on a certain subset of the pins. Each jumper set on a card has a label associated with it that looks something like "J10".

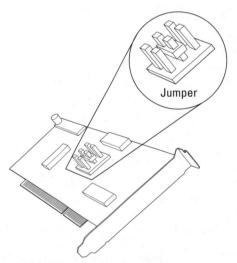

Jumper

Figure 8-14: Looking at jumpers

The documentation (finding the documentation is the challenge!) for the card tells you what the jumper set of J10 is actually used for. Suppose that the jumper set of J10 sets the IRQ value, and that the jumper set has 6 pins. The documentation for the card may tell you, for example, that you need to set the jumper across pins 1 and 2 to assign IRQ 4, across pins 3 and 4 to assign IRQ 5, and across pins 5 and 6 to assign IRQ 10.

Tip   You should keep all documentation for your system and any devices you purchase so that any information about jumpers is available. If you misplace the documentation, you can usually find the information on the manufacturer's Web site.

Another way to change the values of system resources is through software setup, which allows you to change the IRQ, I/O address, or other settings by running a setup program. The setup program usually comes on a floppy disk or CD-ROM and keeps you from worrying about messing with jumper settings (now you just have to worry about not losing the setup disk!).

Tip   It is a good idea to make a backup copy of the setup disk that comes with each device in case something happens to the original disk. If you misplace the setup disk or it becomes damaged, you can usually get them off the manufacturer's Web site.

When you run the setup program for the device, you usually have options to view and change the system resources. You change the system resources by saving the setup information to the EEPROM chip on the card (usually by pressing the F10 key). Figure 8-15 shows an example of a setup (diagnostic) disk.

Figure 8-15: Looking at changing resources through the setup disk of a device

Changing plug-and-play resources

In a plug-and-play environment, changing settings is a bit easier than in a non–plug-and-play environment. *Plug-and-play* systems automatically assign resources to devices dynamically as the operating system starts up. In order to have a full plug-and-play environment, you must have a plug-and-play operating system, such as Windows 95/98/2000, a plug-and-play device, and a plug-and-play BIOS.

If the operating system has assigned a resource to a plug-and-play device that you are not happy with, you can change it through Device Manager. In the Device Manager utility, you can change the IRQ or I/O address of a device by unchecking the Use Automatic Setting check box on the device, and then choosing a different resource (as shown in Figure 8-16).

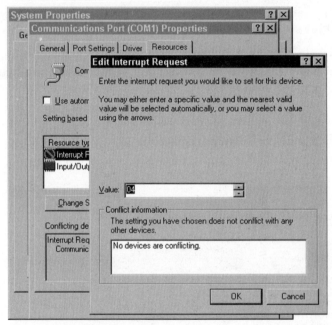

Figure 8-16: Looking at changing resource settings through Device Manager

A lot of systems today have a mixture of plug-and-play devices and non-plug-and-play devices (known as legacy devices), which can present problems. You want to ensure that the operating system does not use one of the resources that you have manually assigned to a device. To prevent this, what you can do is *reserve* that resource to prevent the operating system from assigning it to another device.

Reserving the resource can be done at two different levels, as the following list details:

✦ **Reserving a resource at the hardware:** Reserving a resource at the hardware level means that you would go into the CMOS setup program and tell the system what resources it is not allowed to give out.

✦ **Reserving a resource at the software level:** You can also reserve resources at the operating system level, which means that if you were running multiple operating systems, the resource would only be reserved for the operating system you put the reservation in for.

The following Step By Step displays the steps to reserve resources in Windows 98.

STEP BY STEP: Reserving Resources in Windows 98

1. Select Start ➪ Settings ➪ Control Panel.

2. Double-click the System icon to display the System Properties dialog box.

3. Click the Device Manager tab.

4. Click Computer at the top of the device list and then click the Properties button.

5. Click the Reserve Resources tab (as shown in Figure 8-17).

6. Select the type of resource that you want to reserve (IRQ, I/O, DMA, or Memory) and then click the Add button.

7. In the Edit Resource Setting dialog box, type the address of the resource and then click OK.

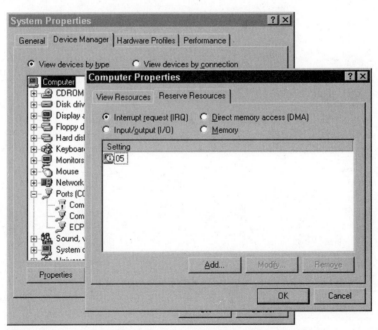

Figure 8-17: Looking at resources that have been reserved

In this section, you have learned different ways of configuring resources, such as IRQs, I/O addresses, and DMA channels. You have learned the three typical ways to configure a device for a resource; either through jumper settings, setup disk, or plug-and-play.

Key Point Summary

This chapter has introduced you to one of the most important topics with servicing computers today: managing resources. The following is a list of key points to remember when troubleshooting system resources.

✦ An I/O address is the pathway used by a device to send and receive information to the processor.

✦ An IRQ is a bell that a device can ring to interrupt the processor from its current task.

✦ A DMA channel is a device's direct pathway to memory so that it can read and write information to memory without bothering the processor.

✦ Changing resources on legacy devices usually involves changing jumper settings or running the diagnostic program for the device.

✦ Changing resources on plug-and-play devices involves going to Device Manager in plug-and-play operating systems and changing the resource for the device.

✦   ✦   ✦

STUDY GUIDE

This study guide presents 20 assessment questions, 1 scenario, and 3 lab exercises to test your knowledge of the exam topic area.

Assessment Questions

1. Device A has been configured for IRQ 3. Which of the following devices will Device A potentially conflict with?

    A. COM1

    B. LPT1

    C. COM2

    D. LPT2

2. What is the default IO address assigned to COM1?

    A. 02F8

    B. 0378

    C. 03F8

    D. 0278

3. Which of the following best describes DMA?

    A. DMA stands for Dynamic Memory Address, which means that the memory address is dynamically assigned to the device each time the system reboots.

    B. DMA stands for Direct Memory Access, which means that a device can use the operating system's area of protected memory without seeking permission.

    C. DMA stands for Dynamic Memory Address, which means that the device is assigned resources dynamically as the system boots.

    D. DMA stands for Direct Memory Address, which means that the resource is given a special pathway to memory so that it does not have to go through the processor.

4. You have assigned your network card to I/O address 0378. Which device will the network card create a conflict with?

    A. COM1

    B. COM2

    C. LPT1

    D. LPT2

5. What IRQ is assigned to COM1?

    A. 3

    B. 5

    C. 7

    D. 4

6. What is the default IO address assigned to COM2?

    A. 02F8

    B. 0378

    C. 03F8

    D. 0278

7. In order for a device to interrupt the CPU and request service, the device must be assigned what?

    A. IRQ

    B. IO address

    C. DMA channel

    D. Memory address

8. What is the default IO address assigned to LPT1?

    A. 02F8

    B. 0378

    C. 03F8

    D. 0278

9. What IRQ is assigned to COM2?

    A. 3

    B. 4

    C. 7

    D. 5

10. Which two ports use IRQ 4?

    A. COM1, COM4

    B. COM3, COM1

    C. COM2, COM4

    D. LPT1, LPT2

11. What is the default IO address assigned to LPT2?

    A. 02F8

    B. 0378

    C. 03F8

    D. 0278

12. What IRQ is assigned to LPT1?

    A. 2

    B. 4

    C. 5

    D. 7

13. What two ports use IRQ 3?

    A. COM1, COM3

    B. COM2, COM3

    C. COM2, COM4

    D. COM3, COM4

14. What IRQ is assigned to LPT2?

    A. 2

    B. 4

    C. 5

    D. 7

15. How many I/O port addresses are there in total?

    A. 8

    B. 16

    C. 16, 384

    D. 65,536

16. What is the IRQ value that is used to cascade the first 8 IRQs to the second 8 IRQs?

    A. 0

    B. 1

    C. 2

    D. 7

17. How many DMA channels are there in total?

    A. 8

    B. 16

    C. 16,384

    D. 65,536

18. How many IRQs are there on an AT system?

    A. 2

    B. 5

    C. 8

    D. 16

19. Which Windows utility can you use to view system resources in use?

    A. Windows Explorer

    B. Device Manager

    C. Internet Explorer

    D. Regedit

20. How many IRQs are there on an XT system?

    A. 5

    B. 8

    C. 16

    D. 32

Scenario

This chapter has introduced you to a number of ideas for working with and troubleshooting device resources. The following scenario will test your troubleshooting skills with IRQ settings.

1. You have the following three devices installed in your system: a sound card, a modem connected to COM1, and a serial mouse connected to COM 2.

   When you install the sound card, you could have used IRQ 3, 5, 10, or 12 and you went with IRQ 5. The modem is using the default IRQ for COM1, and the serial mouse is using the default IRQ for COM2.

   You are installing a network card into the system that can use IRQ 3, IRQ 4, or IRQ 5. What IRQ settings will need to be assigned to the four devices to allow them all to function at the same time?

Lab Exercises

Lab 8.1 Identifying IRQs in Use

1. Choose Start ➪ Settings ➪ Control Panel.

2. Double-click on the System icon and then click the Device Manager tab.

3. On the Device Manager tab, select the IRQ option button at the top of the screen.

4. In the following table, find the IRQs used by the devices listed:

Identifying IRQs	
Device	*IRQ*
LPT1	
Hard disk controller	
System timer	
COM1	
COM2	
Keyboard	
Floppy disk controller	
Math coprocessor	

Lab 8.2 Identifying I/O Addresses In Use

1. Choose Start ➪ Settings ➪ Control Panel.

2. Double-click on the System icon and then choose the Device Manager page tab.

3. On the Device Manager page tab, select the input/output option button at the top of the screen.

4. In the following table, find the I/O addresses used by the devices listed.

Identifying I/O Addresses	
Device	I/O Address
LPT1	
Hard disk controller	
COM1	
COM2	
Floppy disk controller	
Math coprocessor	

Lab 8.3 Changing an IRQ through Windows 98

1. Select Start ➪ Settings ➪ Control Panel.

2. Double-click on the System icon and then click the Device Manager tab.

3. On the Device Manager tab, double-click Ports (COM and LPT).

4. Select Communication Port (COM1); then click the Properties button.

5. Select the Resources tab. What IRQ is this port using _____?

6. Turn off the Use Automatic Settings check box. Doing so allows you to change the IRQ.

7. Ensure that Interrupt Request is selected and then click the Change Settings button.

8. A dialog box appears with a spinner that allows you to change the IRQ associated with this device. While watching the conflict information on the screen, click the Up arrow on the spinner until you get to a value of 15.

9. Click OK.

10. Click OK. A dialog box appears, warning you that if you manually change these settings, Windows will no longer manage the resource settings for this device to prevent conflicts if another device is added.

11. Click Yes and then click close.

Answers to Chapter Questions

Chapter Pre-Test

1. Installing a device and assigning it IRQ 7 will cause it to conflict with **LPT1** if LPT1 is in use.

2. An IRQ address is **an address that is assigned to a device that it uses to interrupt the processor if it has information that needs to be processed.**

3. The default IRQ assigned to LPT2 is **5.**

4. The purpose of an I/O address is **to give a device a path for sending information to and from the processor.**

5. Windows 95 and Windows 98 have a tool called **Device Manager** that will allow you to view IRQs that are in use by the system.

6. DMA stands for **Direct Memory Access.**

7. The default I/O address of COM2 is **2F8-2FF.**

8. A DMA channel **gives a device a path to memory so that it can read and write to it quickly.** If a device does not have a DMA channel, it then must go through the processor to access memory.

9. In Windows NT 4.0 there is **a tool called Windows NT Diagnostics** that will show you the I/O address in use.

10. The abbreviation IRQ stands for **Interrupt Request.**

Assessment Questions

1. **C.** If Device A is assigned IRQ 3, it will conflict with anything connected to COM2 because COM2 uses IRQ 3 by default. COM 1 uses IRQ 4 by default, LPT1 uses IRQ 7, and LPT2 uses IRQ 5 by default. For more information, see the section labeled "Understanding System Resources."

2. **C.** The default I/O address of COM1 is 3F8. The default I/O address of COM2 is 2F8, the default I/O address of LPT1 is 378, and the default I/O address of LPT2 is 278. For more information, see the section labeled "Understanding System Resources."

3. **D.** DMA (Direct Memory Address) is a device's unique path to memory so that it can read and write to memory quickly. The benefit of a device receiving a DMA channel is that it will not have to pass through the CPU each time it needs to access a block of memory. For more information, see the section labeled "Understanding System Resources."

4. **C.** LPT1 uses the default I/O address of 378, so installing a network card and configuring it for the same address will create an I/O address conflict. The default I/O address of COM1 is 3F8. The default I/O address of COM2 is 2F8, and the default I/O address of LPT2 is 278. For more information, see the section labeled "Understanding System Resources."

5. **D.** COM1 defaults to IRQ 4. IRQ 3 is used by COM2, IRQ 5 is used by LPT2 and IRQ 7 is used by LPT1. For more information, see the section labeled "Understanding System Resources."

6. **D.** COM2 uses the default I/O address of 278. LPT1 uses the default I/O address of 378, COM1 uses the I/O address of 3F8, and COM2 uses 2F8. For more information, see the section labeled "Understanding System Resources."

7. **A.** *IRQs* are used to interrupt the CPU and request service from the CPU. This is where the acronym IRQ (Interrupt Request) comes from. An *I/O address* is a device's communication channel to the CPU so that it can send and receive information to the CPU. A *DMA channel* is a device's direct path to memory so that it can quickly read and write to memory. A *memory address* is a device's address special block of upper memory for storing information. For more information, see the section labeled "Understanding System Resources."

8. **B.** The default I/O address assigned to LPT1 is 378. The default I/O address assigned to LPT2 is 278, the default I/O address of COM1 is 3F8, and the default I/O address of COM2 is 2F8. For more information, see the section labeled "Understanding System Resources."

9. **A.** IRQ 3 is the default IRQ of COM2. IRQ 4 is the default IRQ of COM1, while IRQ 7 is the default IRQ of LPT1. IRQ 5 is the default IRQ of LPT2. For more information, see the section labeled "Understanding System Resources."

10. **B.** The two ports that use IRQ 4 are COM1 and COM3. COM2 and COM4 use IRQ 3. For more information, see the section labeled "Understanding System Resources."

11. **D.** The default I/O address of LPT2 is 278. LPT1 uses 378 while COM1 uses 3F8 and COM2 uses 2F8 as the default I/O address. For more information, see the section labeled "Understanding System Resources."

12. **D.** LPT1 has the default IRQ of 7. IRQ 2 is the cascade IRQ that creates a link to the second IRQ controller. IRQ 4 is used by COM1 while IRQ 5 is used by LPT2. For more information, see the section labeled "Understanding System Resources."

13. **C.** The two ports that use IRQ 3 are COM2 and COM4. The ports of COM1 and COM3 use IRQ 4. For more information, see the section labeled "Understanding System Resources."

14. **C.** The default IRQ of LPT2 is IRQ 5. IRQ 2 is used to create a link to IRQ 9, which is cascaded to the second IRQ controller. IRQ 4 is used by COM1 and IRQ 7 is used by LPT1. For more information, see the section labeled "Understanding System Resources."

15. **D.** There are 65,536 I/O address ports available on the system. There are 8 DMA channels available and 16 IRQs available. For more information, see the section labeled "Understanding System Resources."

16. **C.** The IRQ that creates a cascade link to the second set of IRQs managed by the second IRQ controller is IRQ 2. The system timer uses IRQ 0, while IRQ 1 is used by the keyboard. IRQ 7 is used by LPT1. For more information, see the section labeled "Understanding System Resources."

17. **A.** There are 8 DMA channels on systems today. There are 16 IRQs and 65,536 I/O addresses available. For more information, see the section labeled "Understanding System Resources."

18. **D.** An AT system uses 16 IRQ channels that are numbered starting with zero and going up to 15. There were originally only 8 IRQ channels on XT systems, but a second set of 8 were created for AT systems. For more information, see the section labeled "Understanding System Resources."

19. **B.** Windows Device Manager is the tool that will allow you to view system resources, such as IRQs and I/O addresses. You can also use Device Manager to help solve resource conflicts. For more information, see the section labeled "Understanding System Resources."

20. **B.** There are only 8 IRQs available on XT systems, but an additional set of 8 have been created for AT (after 286 processors) systems, creating a total of 16 IRQs for AT systems. For more information, see the section labeled "Understanding System Resources."

Scenario

1. When you install the network card, you will have to assign it to IRQ 5 because COM1 and COM2 are using IRQ 4 and 3. The problem, however, is that the sound card is already using IRQ 5, so you will have to change it to use either IRQ 10 or 12. This will prevent the newly installed network card from conflicting with the sound card.

The following figure shows the solution of assigned IRQs and what was available for choice with each device.

Sound	Modem (COM1)	Mouse (COM2)	Network Card
IRQ 3 IRQ 5 IRQ 10* IRQ 12	IRQ 4*	IRQ 3*	IRQ 3 IRQ 4 IRQ 5*

* = Assigned Resource

Scenario Solution

Installing and Configuring Hardware

Part II deals with the installation of different pieces of hardware. It covers the installation of most of the major components of the computer, including internal drivers, IDE or ATA drives, and SCSI drives. Part II discusses basic installation of these components, as well as chaining multiple devices on either type of drive bus.

You will also cover the installation of most other components in the computer. You will deal with video configuration and types, modems, and other storage devices, such as floppy drives, USB, and IEEE 1394 devices. Part II also provides information about devices (for example, docking stations, keyboards, mice, and network cards) that would be dealt with differently when using a portable computer.

There is a large section devoted exclusively to portable devices, with topics that include installation of hard drives, memory, PCMCIA cards, processors, and video. It also covers devices that give the portable its power, such as AC adapters and batteries.

Internal Devices

EXAM OBJECTIVES

Exam 220-201 ✦ **A+ Core Hardware**

✦ **1.5** Identify proper procedures for installing and configuring IDE/EIDE devices. Content may include the following:

- Master/Slave

- Devices per channel

- Primary/Secondary

✦ **1.6** Identify proper procedures for installing and configuring SCSI devices. Content may include the following:

- Address/Termination conflicts

- Cabling

- Types (example: regular, wide, ultra-wide)

- Internal versus external

- Expansion slots (EISA, ISA, PCI)

- Jumper block settings (binary equivalents)

CHAPTER PRE-TEST

1. What is the Pin 1 rule?

2. What is the difference between SCSI and wide SCSI-2?

3. Why do IDE devices have to be set up in a master/slave configuration?

4. In what situation does the SCSI BIOS have to be enabled?

5. How is data written to a disk?

6. Where is the disk configuration information stored after a new disk is added to the computer?

7. How can the size of a disk be calculated?

8. How many pins will you find on an IDE hard disk controller?

9. How many pins will you find on an internal SCSI device?

10. A cluster is made up of _____.

✦ Answers to these questions can be found at the end of the chapter. ✦

One of the primary responsibilities of a PC technician is to manage hard disks. This responsibility involves more than just the partitioning and formatting of disks; it also entails installing disks into the computer system and configuring the system to recognize the newly added disks.

In this chapter, you will learn the skills that are required for installing, configuring, and troubleshooting hard disks. You will be introduced to a new world of terminology related to hard disk installation and configuration.

This chapter will also discuss the difference between IDE and SCSI devices, the steps required to install and configure IDE master/slave devices in a chain, and the steps required to install a SCSI bus.

Hard Drive Terminology

If you were to take some form of martial arts, the instructor would show you how to do some basic punches and kicks before teaching you to spar or compete. The instructor would be well aware that jumping into combat without the basics could do you more damage than good. PC repair works the same way: before discussing the installation and configuration of IDE and SCSI devices, it is important to cover some basics.

Disk geometry

This section will introduce you to disk geometry. You will learn some of the terminology that is required in order to understand the internal construction of a disk.

Platters

A *platter* is a physical object (actually, a plate) that resides inside the hard disk and is responsible for storing the data. A platter is similar to a record on an old record player — the main difference being that a hard disk has many platters, while a record player only holds one record at a time. Figure 9-1 shows the platters inside a hard disk.

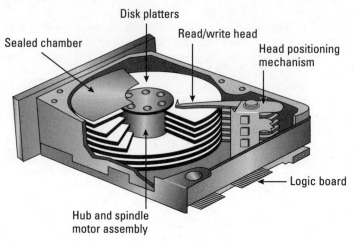

Figure 9-1: The internals of a hard disk

The platters are very much like records on a record player in the sense that they spin around in a circle on a spindle that runs through the center of all the platters. Each platter has two sides for storing information, and each side of the platter has a unique ID. The ID for the first side of the first platter is 0, and each side increases by 1. For example, if there were two platters in the disk, the first platter would have Side 0 and Side 1, while the second platter would have Side 2 and Side 3. Figure 9-2 illustrates this concept.

Figure 9-2: Sides of platters

Since there will be a writing mechanism — a head — for each side of the platter, many people use the terms "head" and "side" interchangeably. The head is more accurately called the *read/write head*, because it will move over the disk surface and read or write to the disk. Like a needle on a record player, the read/write head moves over the surface of the disk with the help of an arm, called the *actuator arm* (also known as the *head positioning mechanism*). Looking back at Figure 9-1, the figure shows the read/write head on an actuator arm (head positioning mechanism).

Tip There is a read/write head for each platter surface on the disk. When information is written to the disk, the read/write head will move to the same track on all platters in a single movement and then write to the same track on all platters. The actuator arm has multiple read/write heads on it.

Tracks

Just as there are grooves, or tracks, on a record or music CD, there are also *tracks* on each platter. These tracks are evenly spaced across the platter's surface.

Sectors

The platter is divided into pie slices, thus dividing the tracks into 512-byte sectors. Sectors are the actual storage areas for data, and each has an address that is made up of the platter side number, the track number, and the sector number on that track. Figure 9-3 illustrates the tracks and sectors on a disk platter.

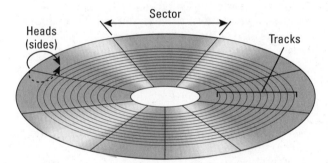

Figure 9-3: Tracks and sectors on a disk platter

Exam Tip For the Core Hardware exam, know that a low-level format is performed by the manufacturer and is responsible for preparing the disk for data storage by creating the tracks and sectors.

Clusters

A group of any number of sectors can make up a *cluster*. When a partition is formatted, the file system will determine the cluster size based off the partition size. For example, a partition that is 2GB in size formatted as FAT will use a 32K-cluster size. That same 2GB partition formatted as FAT32 will use only a 4K-cluster size.

Cross-Reference For more information on benefits of the different types of file systems, see Chapter 18.

Having a partition use a 4K-cluster size means there will be 8 sectors that make up a cluster. Keep in mind that once a file has been saved to the cluster, no other file can occupy that cluster. For example, if you had a 32K-cluster size and you saved a 3K file to the hard disk, the file would be saved to an empty cluster — but only 3K of it would be used, and the remaining 29K would be left unused. The remaining 29K is now considered unusable space; no other file can be saved to that unused 29 K.

Cylinders

Each platter in the disk contains the same number of tracks; these tracks are numbered from the outside in, starting with zero. For example, if there were ten tracks on a platter, the track closest to the edge of the platter would be Track 0, while the track closest to the center would be Track 9.

A cylinder consists of the same track on both sides of all the platters. In other words, when you reference Track 0, you reference a particular track on a particular platter, but when you reference Cylinder 0, you reference Track 0 on all platters.

If you know the number of cylinders, heads, and sectors per track, you can calculate the size of a disk. For example, if you have a drive that has 4,092 cylinders, 16 heads, and 63 sectors per track, the size of the disk would be 2,111,864,832 bytes (2.1GB). The formula to calculate the size of the disk is Cylinders × Heads × Sectors × 512 bytes per sector.

Read/write process

Platters are divided into 512 byte sectors. These sectors are the area on the platter that data is written to. The platters have a magnetic coating applied to them that is extremely sensitive to magnetism.

While the platters are rotating in a circle, the read/write heads are moved over the disk surface to the location where they need to write (or save) information. The read/write heads do not actually touch the surface of the disk platters; instead, they "hover" about ten micro-inches (or millionths of an inch) above — that's not even enough space to place a hair between the read/write head and the platter's surface. This design helps improve disk performance, because a read/write head that made contact with the platter would cause friction, slowing down the rotation speed of the disk.

While the platters spin around in circles, the read/write head moves from track to track until it reaches the desired one. Then it waits for the appropriate sector to move underneath it, at which time the read/write head is energized to apply a magnetic charge to the particles in the disk coating. This changes the particle binary state from zero to one, thus creating data.

Performance

Disk performance can be measured in terms of several important characteristics: seek time, latency, access time, and the spin speed of the disk. Table 9-1 describes these characteristics.

Table 9-1	
Measuring Hard Disk Performance	
Characteristic	*Description*
Seek time	*Seek time* is the time it takes to move the read/write heads to the desired track. Seek time is a calculated average, since the time it takes to move to the desired track will differ from one instance to another. For example, if the read/write heads are on Track 1, they will take a longer amount of time moving to Track 12 than to Track 3 (because the distance is greater between Track 1 and Track 12). Seek time is measured in milliseconds, or millionths of a second.
Latency	*Latency* is the time it takes for the appropriate sector to move under the read/write head. Latency is measured in milliseconds.
Access time	*Access time* is a term used to describe the overall speed of the disk. It is a combination of seek time and latency. The lower the access time, the better.
Spin speed	*Spin speed* is the speed at which the platters spin in a circle, measured in revolutions (rotations) per minute, or rpm. The larger the rpm value the faster the disk, which means less latency.

Figure 9-4 shows how seek time is measured.

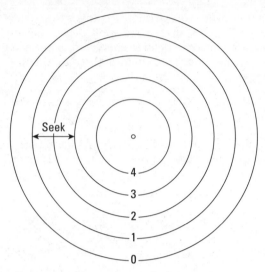

Figure 9-4: Measuring seek time

Master boot record

While I'm discussing disk geometry, I should make a brief comment about the Master Boot Record. The *Master Boot Record (MBR)* is the first sector on the first track of the first side of the first platter; it holds the operating system boot code that controls the loading of the operating system.

The MBR also holds drive characteristics — such as the partition table. During the boot process the system has to find a primary partition that is active and it will do this by looking in the boot record.

In general, if anything goes wrong with the MBR, you will be unable to boot the system. Since this boot record is always found in the same location on every disk, it becomes very easy for developers to write viruses that will modify or corrupt it. This is one reason you should always run virus detection software.

IDE Devices

 1.5 Identify proper procedures for installing and configuring IDE/EIDE devices. Content may include the following: Master/Slave, Devices per channel, Primary/Secondary

In this section, you will learn to install and troubleshoot IDE devices. First, you'll be given an overview of IDE devices and some of their features, and then you'll be shown a number of different configurations for installing IDE devices into a computer system.

IDE overview

The *hard drive controller* is responsible for converting signals made by the system CPU to signals that the hard disk can understand. These signals include instructions on where to find data and how to get there. The hard disk would perform its task and any data that needed to be returned would be sent to the controller from the hard disk. The controller would then convert the signals from the hard disk to signals that the system could understand.

In the past, the controller was found on an expansion card in the computer system, which then had ribbon cables going from the card to the drives. The goal of IDE was to make the installation of hard disks easier by including the controller on the hard disk, which is where the name comes from: *Integrated Drive Electronics* (*IDE*).

Today, controllers are integrated into the drive itself, meaning the drive is its own boss. There are also controllers on the motherboard—two perhaps (the primary IDE controller and the secondary controller).

Originally, IDE was only available in the flavor of hard drives, and the hard drives had a maximum capacity of about 528MB. Another important limitation with IDE is that there could only be two devices in a chain. SCSI is stronger in that respect: it supports at least eight devices in a chain.

IDE devices have a transfer rate of about 10Mbps and may have cache on the drive itself. The cache memory is a small amount of memory for storing data that is used frequently to increase drive performance.

 Cross-Reference   For more information on cache memory, see Chapter 4.

Due to its limitations, IDE has been replaced by EIDE (Extended Integrated Drive Electronics). EIDE devices have a transfer rate of about 16Mbps. Four devices are now allowed in an EIDE chain, with a greater variety available. For example, you may now add CD-ROMs and even zip drives to the EIDE chain. Note that the capacity of the drives has been dramatically increased to about 40GB! Table 9-2 summarizes the features of IDE and EIDE.

Table 9-2 IDE Versus EIDE		
Characteristic	**IDE**	**EIDE**
Size	528MB	40GB and higher
Devices in Chain	2	4
Transfer Rate	10Mbps	16Mbps
Types of Devices	Hard drives	Hard drives, CD-ROMs

Exam Tip On the Core Hardware exam, you may be asked the number of devices that IDE supports. IDE supports two devices, while EIDE supports four devices.

Installing IDE devices

This section will show you the steps to take when installing an IDE device. Because all hard drives are different, only the most popular solutions for installing hard drives will be presented.

First, you want to open up the casing of the computer and locate an empty bay to place or mount the new hard disk into. If you are removing the old hard drive, you will be able to use the same bay. However, if you are adding an additional hard drive, you will have to find an empty bay and mount the drive in place. Figure 9-5 shows an IDE drive being placed into the mounting bay.

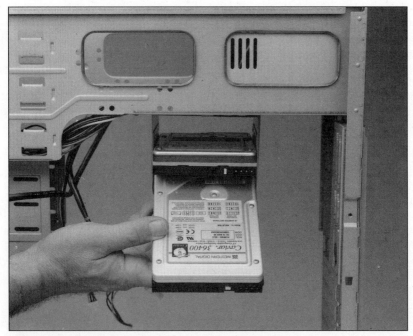

Figure 9-5: Mounting a drive into the mounting bay

Cabling

Once you have mounted the drive in place, you will have to take a 40-wire IDE ribbon cable and connect it to the controller on the motherboard and the controller on the hard disk. Figure 9-6 shows an IDE ribbon cable.

1st Wire

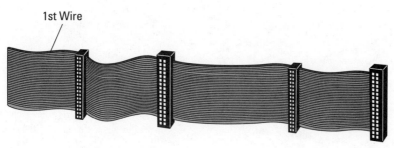

Figure 9-6: IDE ribbon cable

Exam Tip   For the exam, know that an IDE hard drive uses a 40-wire ribbon cable, while a floppy drive uses a 34-wire ribbon cable.

One of the wires (Wire 1) on the IDE ribbon cable is a different color than the others; usually, it's red, but it may be blue. Wire 1 must be placed over Pin 1 when connecting the ribbon cable to the hard drive and motherboard—a procedure known as the *Pin 1 rule*.

The big question is: how do you know which pin is Pin 1 when looking at the hard disk controller or the motherboard controller? Hopefully, the manufacturer has indicated Pin 1 by placing a small "1" in the place where Pin 1 should be. If you look at the controller on the hard disk or on the motherboard, and then at either end of the controllers, you may see a small "1" on one of the controller ends. That's where you need to place Wire 1 when connecting the ribbon cable.

Tip   Sometimes the manufacturer may not have enough space to indicate Pin 1, so they choose to do the opposite, which is to indicate Pin 40. This method gives you the same information, though: if you know what side Pin 40 is on, you know that Pin 1 is on the opposite side.

Once you have connected the IDE ribbon cable, you want to give the hard disk power from the power supply so that you can run the motor in the drive. Oftentimes, people forget this step. Figure 9-7 shows how to connect the ribbon cable and the power supply cable to the hard disk.

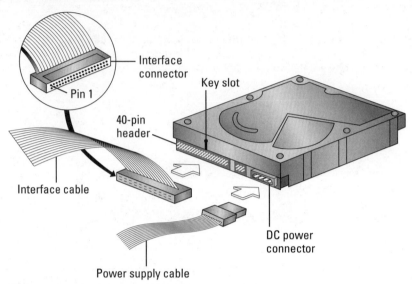

Figure 9-7: Connecting an IDE drive

Master/slave

If you are installing multiple IDE devices, you are creating an IDE chain. The chain will be made up of one 40-wire IDE ribbon cable and two drives connected to that IDE ribbon cable. The ribbon cable will be connected to the controller on the motherboard.

Once you have the two drives connected together, you will need to configure the drives into a master/slave configuration. Why this type of configuration? Because each drive has a built-in controller, which makes it act like its own boss.

When setting up a multi-drive system, you have two drives, each with a controller that can potentially send and receive signals to the processor. To save confusion, one of the drives is designated the master. The *master* drive will receive all signals from the processor and send back any data on behalf of both drives. The other drive is designated the slave. The *slave* drive will pass any information it wants to send to the processor up to the master, which will then forward that information to the processor. Figure 9-8 illustrates a multi-drive system.

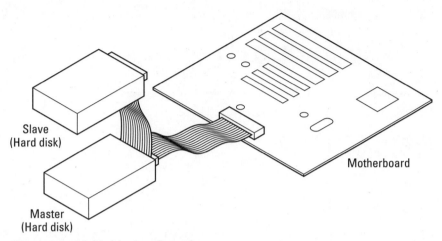

Figure 9-8: Multi-drive configuration

Once you have the drives connected to the ribbon cable, you will have to configure the jumper settings on the drives to tell the system who the master is and who the slave is. The idea of the procedure is similar for all drives, but the actual jumper setting may be different for each type of drive.

Many of today's drives have three jumpers that can be set to configure a master and a slave. One jumper setting designates the drive as a master (sometimes abbreviated "DS" for "drive select"), one jumper setting sets it as a slave (sometimes abbreviated "SP" for "slave present"), and a third jumper setting enables "cable select," or "CS" for short. Cable select would set the master and slave automatically, based off the order of the devices on the cable. This section discusses typical configuration examples of master and slave devices.

Typically, you would set the DS jumper on the drive you would like as the master, and then set SP on the drive you would like as the slave. Figure 9-9 shows the jumper configuration for setting up a master and slave between two drives.

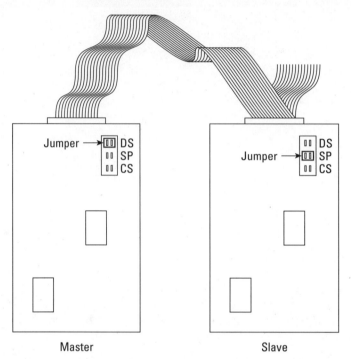

Figure 9-9: Looking at jumper configuration for a master/slave setup

 Tip   Sometimes the jumpers may be labeled simply "Master" and sometimes they may be labeled "Slave." These drives are usually pretty straightforward to configure. You place the jumper on the master setting for the drive you would like as the master, and you place the jumper on the slave setting for the drive you would like to configure as the slave drive.

Unfortunately, all drives are different. You may find that you do not have jumpers labeled DS, SP, and CS. You will have to check the documentation for the drive to see how the manufacturer would like the master and slave configured.

Many times, configuring your drives in a master/slave setup may not be as easy as discussed in these pages. What do you do when you cannot see a specific master or slave jumper setting? Many drives will place documentation on the back of the drive telling you how to configure the drive for master and slave setups. Unfortunately, this was not the case on a drive I had to configure in the office one day. So I went to the manufacturer's Web site and found out that this drive had a jumper labeled J20; the Web site documentation stated that if the drive was the only drive or was the master in a dual drive configuration, the jumper (J20) should be set. If the drive was the slave in the dual drive configuration, the jumper (J20) should be removed. Figure 9-10 shows the configuration for this example.

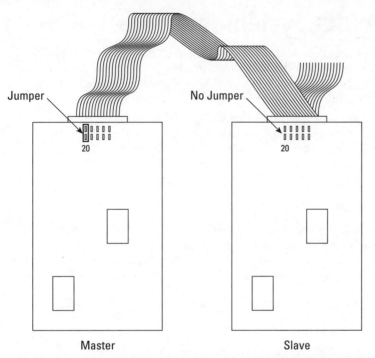

Figure 9-10: Additional jumper configurations for dual-drive setup

Today you are probably working with EIDE drives, which — as mentioned earlier — support up to four devices instead of two. In these systems, there are two controllers on the motherboard: the primary controller and the secondary controller. Each controller can have two devices, for a total of four devices. Typically, the devices can be either hard drives or CD-ROM devices. The steps are the same to master and slave a hard disk and a CD-ROM, but the CD-ROM will probably always be the slave (or may be the master device on the secondary controller).

 Tip   In today's systems you may encounter different types of devices that are IDE devices, such as hard drives, CD-ROMs, and zip drives.

After configuring the jumpers on the drive, you will power on the system. The computer should recognize that there is an additional drive and take you into the CMOS setup program. Your system should have the drive written into CMOS. You will just have to save the change and exit out of the CMOS setup program.

Small Computer System Interface

 1.6 Identify proper procedures for installing and configuring SCSI devices. Content may include the following: Address/Termination conflicts, Cabling, Types (example: regular, wide, ultra-wide), Internal versus External, Expansion slots (EISA, ISA, PCI), Jumper block settings (binary equivalents)

This section discusses a type of hard disk that is more popular in high-end machines (servers) than in personal desktop computers. First, I will discuss SCSI and some of its benefits. Then I will take a look at the steps involved in configuring SCSI devices.

SCSI overview

SCSI is an acronym for *Small Computer System Interface*. The important part of this term is "small computer." SCSI environments use a SCSI controller that is responsible for managing all SCSI devices and controlling the conversation on the SCSI chain.

SCSI technology has many advantages over IDE technology, such as:

✦ Types of devices supported

✦ Number of devices supported in a single SCSI chain

✦ Performance of SCSI over IDE devices

SCSI supports a multitude of devices, including hard drives and CD-ROMs. Remember that IDE devices typically only support hard drives and CD-ROMs. SCSI devices come in the following flavors:

✦ Hard drives

✦ CD-ROMs

✦ Scanners

✦ Printers

✦ Tape drives

You could have a SCSI chain that contains any of those devices, whereas IDE could probably support only two types of devices.

The other major benefit of SCSI is the number of devices that are supported in the SCSI chain, or what is known as the *SCSI bus*. Original SCSI supports up to eight devices in the chain, but one of those devices is the SCSI card that's added to the computer to give you the capability to use SCSI. Remember that IDE only allowed two devices in the chain, and EIDE supports four devices, so with SCSI you are not only allowed to have more types of devices, but you are also allowed to have more of those devices!

Original SCSI supports up to eight devices in the chain, but if the exam asks how many devices can be attached to a SCSI bus, the answer is seven (the test makers assume that the SCSI card is already there). Remember to watch the wording of the questions closely.

The last benefit of SCSI is performance. Original SCSI devices do not compare in the performance category with EIDE devices, but some of the latter SCSI technologies — such as SCSI-2 and SCSI-3 — can outperform IDE and EIDE. Later in this chapter, you will be given details on transfer rates of the different types of SCSI devices.

Host adapter

For the bulk of this chapter, assume that we are dealing with original SCSI, also known as SCSI-1. Towards the end of the chapter, I will discuss the newer types of SCSI.

When you install SCSI devices, you first need to install the SCSI host adapter. The SCSI host adapter is an expansion card that you add to the computer so you can chain SCSI devices off the adapter. In essence, the SCSI host adapter is the brains of the SCSI bus; it acts as the controller for the SCSI bus. Figure 9-11 shows the SCSI adapter being inserted into an expansion slot in the system.

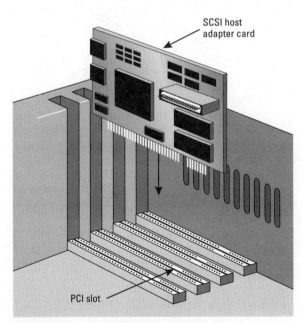

Figure 9-11: The SCSI host adapter

The SCSI controller (adapter) is responsible for sending and receiving all information to and from the SCSI bus, just like the IDE controller. When the system has information for one of the devices in the SCSI bus, the system will hand the information over to the SCSI controller, which will then hand the information to the appropriate device in the chain. Figure 9-12 shows a SCSI bus — made up of the SCSI host adapter (inside the computer) — and two SCSI devices.

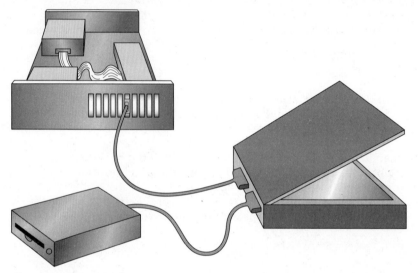

Figure 9-12: A SCSI bus

The beauty of the entire setup is that you have installed a SCSI adapter in the computer, which is a card that will be assigned resources like an IRQ and an IO address. Each device in the SCSI chain is not assigned these resources, because the processor will pass information to the SCSI controller and the controller passes the information to the device. This means that the system never talks to the devices directly, which means each device does not require an IRQ and an IO address.

When you go out to purchase the SCSI adapter, you will first have to look inside your system to figure out what type of expansion slots are free. Today, you will typically have some PCI slots, but you may have an ISA or an EISA slot, as well. The difference between these expansion slots is performance — PCI runs at 33 MHz, while ISA and EISA run at only 8 MHz. Also, PCI and EISA are 32-bit technologies, while ISA is only 16-bit. The bottom line is that if you have some PCI slots free, you will probably end up purchasing a PCI SCSI adapter.

Cross-Reference   For more information on expansion bus architectures, see Chapter 3.

When the controller receives information for a particular device, how does it send the information to that device?

Addressing

Each device is assigned an internal address in the SCSI bus, and the SCSI controller knows the address of each device. When the SCSI controller receives information for a particular device, the controller references that device by its ID in the SCSI bus. This way, there's no confusion as to who the data is destined for.

You assign the SCSI IDs when you connect each device to the SCSI chain. You will assign an ID either by jumpers or DIP switches if the device is an internal device, or by a "ticker" (yes, I made that term up) if the device is external. A ticker is an indicator on the back of the external SCSI device whose value you can change by pressing the button to increase or decrease the SCSI ID. Figure 9-13 shows the back of an external SCSI tape drive and how to change the SCSI ID.

Figure 9-13: Assigning a SCSI ID to an external device

Tip

In Figure 9-13, you can also see the type of connector used for external SCSI devices. This is a Centronics 50-pin connector.

If you are installing an internal SCSI device, you will most likely need to assign the SCSI ID by using jumpers. The internal SCSI devices will have a jumper set with three pairs of jumper pins. The decimal values of these jumpers, although probably not shown on the drive, are 4, 2, and 1 (from left to right). Table 9-3 shows this jumper setup.

Table 9-3
Jumper Block Settings

	J2	J1	J0
Decimal Value	*4*	*2*	*1*
SCSI ID 0	0	0	0
SCSI ID 3	0	1	1
SCSI ID 6	1	1	0

If you would like to assign the device a SCSI ID of zero, then you would not jumper any of the jumper pins. This is shown in Table 9-3 by having the off state (represented by zero) at each jumper location. Another example of setting a jumper ID would be if you wanted to assign the device a SCSI ID of 3, you would jumper the J0 pins and the J1 pins, but not the J2 pins. This would enable decimal values of 1+2. Table 9-3 also shows what would happen if you wanted to set the SCSI ID to six. You would enable jumper J1 and J2, which enables the decimal values of 2+4, while the first jumper has an off state.

The IDs you assign to each device are completely up to you, but note that the higher the number, the more important the device is to the SCSI bus. For example, if two devices need to send information through the bus at the same time, which device will the SCSI controller service first? The device with the higher SCSI ID is always given priority. This is why the SCSI host adapter is usually assigned the highest number in the chain (usually seven if the bus supports eight devices — the ID numbers start with zero).

So the host adapter is assigned an ID of seven, and a SCSI bootable hard drive is assigned a SCSI ID of zero. Outside of that, you decide what the ID numbers are for each device. As a rule of thumb, we give slower devices higher ID numbers so that they may get serviced when they need to.

Cabling

Different types of cabling are used to chain SCSI devices to the SCSI adapter. If the device is an internal device, a 50-wire ribbon cable will be used, which is very similar to the 40-wire ribbon cable used for an IDE device.

If the device is an external device, you will use a thick Centronics cable to connect to the Centronics 50 (typically used by SCSI-1) or the Centronics 68 (typically used by SCSI-2) connector on the back of the device.

Termination

Both ends of the SCSI bus must be terminated so that when a signal is sent down the SCSI bus, it is absorbed at the end of the bus by the terminator, which is acting as a resistor. The first device in the chain must be terminated along with the last device in the chain, the first device being the host adapter. If the device is an internal device, terminating usually involves playing around with jumpers. If the device is external, a terminator will be added to the back of the device. Figure 9-14 shows a terminator for external devices.

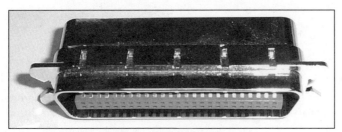

Figure 9-14: Looking at a SCSI terminator

Types of SCSI

Over the last number of years, SCSI has increased the performance of the devices over other types of devices, such as IDE and EIDE. This is one of the reasons why you will find network servers using SCSI hard drives instead of EIDE devices.

Original SCSI (SCSI-1), introduced in 1986, was an 8-bit technology and had a transfer rate of 5 Mbps — a slow speed compared to today's IDE devices, which run at about 10Mbps. A few flavors of SCSI-2 were introduced when SCSI-2 was developed as a standard in 1994. The first flavor was called *fast SCSI-2*, which increased the transfer rate from 5Mbps to 10Mbps, but kept it as an 8-bit technology. The other version of SCSI-2 was called *wide SCSI-2*, where the 8 bits were increased to 16 bits and the transfer rate is also increased to 10Mbps.

When developing the standards for SCSI-2 not only was there a Fast SCSI-2 and a wide SCSI-2 but a third version of SCSI was implemented that combined the features of fast SCSI-2 and wide SCSI-2. *Fast/wide SCSI-2* is a 16-bit technology that has a transfer rate of 20Mbps. There is also an *Ultra SCSI*, which has an 8-bit bus width and a transfer rate of up to 20Mbps. Ultra SCSI has a wide version, which increases the bus width to 16-bit; as a result, *Ultra-Wide SCSI* can transfer information at 40 Mbps.

Table 9-4 shows a chart summarizing the different types of SCSI and their characteristics.

Table 9-4 Types of SCSI			
Description	**Bus Width**	**Transfer Rate (Mbps)**	**Number of Devices**
SCSI-1	8	5	8
Fast SCSI-2	8	10	8
Wide SCSI-2	16	10	16
Fast/Wide SCSI-2	16	20	16
Ultra SCSI-2	8	20	8
Fast/Wide SCSI-3	16	40	16

Exam Tip   On the Core Hardware exam, you may encounter questions about the different types of SCSI. Therefore, I suggest memorizing the table of characteristics for different types of SCSI.

Installing SCSI devices

Once you understand the issues with SCSI, installing a SCSI bus is fairly simple. First, you want to assign a unique ID number to each device. I usually perform this step at the beginning so that when everything is connected, you won't have to play around figuring out how to change the ID of the devices.

When assigning the ID numbers, remember that you want to assign the bootable drive the ID of zero. You also want to enable the SCSI BIOS on the SCSI controller if you are booting off a SCSI hard disk. When you enable the SCSI BIOS, you will not be required to install a driver for the card, because the PC will recognize the device on startup. If you are booting off an IDE drive and using the SCSI disk as an additional drive, you should have the SCSI BIOS disabled and install a driver in the operating system.

Now that you have the ID numbers assigned to each device, insert the SCSI host adapter into the expansion slots of the PC. After inserting the SCSI card, chain all of the devices together.

Exam Tip   When preparing for the Core Hardware exam, it is important to know the different terms used for a particular technology. Another term for a SCSI chain is a daisy chain. When you chain the devices together, you are daisychaining.

Once you have the devices chained together, you want to make sure that each end on the SCSI bus is terminated. If the last device is an external device, you will need to put the terminator on the end of the device. If you are installing internal devices, you need to check the documentation on the internal devices to find out what jumpers to set.

At this point, the IDs are configured for each device, the SCSI card is inserted into the PC, and the devices are connected to the card to create a SCSI bus. We also terminated the SCSI bus at either end. Before installing the driver for the SCSI card in the operating system, I'll review the steps to install a SCSI device one last time.

To install a SCSI bus:

1. Assign unique IDs to each device.

2. Install the SCSI host adapter into the expansion slots.

3. Chain devices to the SCSI host adapter.

4. Terminate the SCSI bus at both ends of the chain.

5. Install the driver for the SCSI card if you are not booting off the first hard disk.

Since SCSI is a technology that is usually implemented in servers, the following sections outline the steps to install the driver in Windows NT 4.0 and Windows 2000.

Windows NT 4.0

Windows NT 4.0 is a non–plug and play type environment, so installing the device is a little different than in Windows 95 or Windows 98. With Windows 95 and 98, you could detect new hardware and take a chance on whether or not the operating system will see the SCSI card. With Windows NT 4.0, there is no hardware wizard that will install the device; you have to do it manually.

To install a SCSI host adapter in Windows NT 4.0, follow the steps outlined below.

STEP BY STEP: Installing a SCSI host adapter in Windows NT 4.0

1. Select Start ⇨ Settings ⇨ Control Panel.

2. Double-click the SCSI adapters.

3. In the SCSI Adapters dialog box, choose the Drivers tab.

4. Choose the Add button to add a driver.

5. In the Install Driver dialog box, choose the manufacturer of the host adapter and then choose the adapter on the right side. If the adapter is not in the list, choose the Have Disk button and provide the manufacturer's disk.

6. Click the OK button.

7. Restart the computer.

Windows 2000

Installing the SCSI host adapter in the Windows 2000 environment is a little bit different than installing the driver in Windows NT 4.0. A wizard will start up, asking whether you want to detect the device or install the driver. The following Step By Step shows you how to install a SCSI adapter in Windows 2000.

STEP BY STEP: Installing a SCSI host adapter in Windows 2000

1. Select Start ⇨ Settings ⇨ Control Panel.

2. Double-click the Add Hardware icon. The Add Hardware Wizard appears displaying the welcome screen to the wizard.

3. Choose Next.

4. Select Add or Troubleshoot A Device and then click the Next button.

5. In the Choose Hardware Device dialog box, select Add A New Device and then click the Next button.

6. If you know the host adapter you are installing, select "No, I want to select the hardware from a list." If you are unsure of the host adapter you are installing, then choose "Yes, search for new hardware." For these steps, you will choose the adapter to install, so select "No, I want to select the hardware from a list" and click Next.

7. The next screen will ask you what type of device you are installing. Choose SCSI and RAID controllers, then click Next.

8. In the list of devices on the left side select the manufacturer, and on the right side select the adapter to install. Click Next.

9. Click Finish.

10. Restart the computer.

Key Point Summary

In this chapter, you learned the terminology associated with troubleshooting hard drives and how hard drives are organized. This chapter also demonstrated the steps to install an IDE device, how to chain two IDE devices together, and how to install a SCSI chain and add devices to the SCSI chain.

✦   ✦   ✦

STUDY GUIDE

In this Study Guide, you will find 20 assessment questions to test your knowledge of the exam test areas. Two scenarios and two labs follow the assessment questions.

Assessment Questions

1. What is the size of a sector on a hard disk?

   A. 512K

   B. 1K

   C. 512 bytes

   D. 4K

2. How many devices can exist in an IDE chain?

   A. 1

   B. 2

   C. 3

   D. 4

3. What physical component of the disk is responsible for reading and writing data on the disk?

   A. Platter

   B. Sector

   C. Cluster

   D. Read/write head

4. How many wires can be found in an IDE ribbon cable for a hard disk?

   A. 40

   B. 34

   C. 50

   D. 66

5. Which of the following best describes seek time?

    A. The time it takes to move the appropriate sector under the read/write head

    B. The time it takes to move the read/write heads to the appropriate track

    C. The time it takes to find a file that is being deleted

    D. The time it takes to find an empty cluster to write to

6. In a SCSI chain, what devices are required to be terminated?

    A. The first device in the chain

    B. The last device in the chain

    C. Devices at either end of the SCSI chain

    D. Any hard disk in the SCSI chain

7. In a SCSI chain, what device should take a SCSI ID of zero?

    A. CD-ROM

    B. The bootable (first) hard disk

    C. The SCSI host adapter

    D. Printer

8. In an IDE chain, CD-ROM devices are usually the _____.

    A. Master

    B. Terminated devices

    C. Devices assigned ID zero

    D. Slave

9. Which of the following describes the cabling for internal SCSI?

    A. 40-wire ribbon cable

    B. 34-wire ribbon cable

    C. 50-wire ribbon cable

    D. None of the above

10. Which of the following best describes where the Master Boot Record is located?

    A. Last track on the disk

    B. First track on the disk

    C. First sector on the first track of the first side of the first platter

    D. First sector on the last side of the last platter

11. Which of the following take the highest priority in a SCSI bus?

    A. 0

    B. 7

    C. 5

    D. 1

12. When should the SCSI host adapter have the BIOS enabled?

    A. When the hard disk is the bootable device

    B. When the hard disk is the first device in the chain, but the computer is booting off an IDE drive

    C. When you have more than two devices in the chain

    D. When the host adapter is assigned SCSI ID seven

13. In Windows NT 4.0, where do you install the driver for the SCSI host adapter?

    A. Add/Remove Programs

    B. Add/Remove Hardware

    C. Add Printer

    D. Control Panel ⇨ SCSI Adapters

14. What is disk latency?

    A. The time it takes to move the read/write heads to the appropriate track

    B. The speed at which the disk spins

    C. The time it takes for the sector that needs to be read to move under the read/write head

    D. The time it takes to get the disk to spin at the maximum speed

15. In a multi-drive system with two IDE devices, which hard disk controller will communicate with the CPU?

    A. Both devices

    B. The master device

    C. The slave device

    D. The second device in the chain

16. What is the term used to describe the same track on all platters within a disk?

    A. Track

    B. Sector

    C. Head

    D. Cylinder

17. How many surfaces does a platter have?

    A. 1

    B. 2

    C. 3

    D. 4

18. Each physical plate within the disk is termed a _____.

    A. Platter

    B. Track

    C. Sector

    D. Cylinder

19. Which of the following is not a type of SCSI device?

    A. Hard disk

    B. CD-ROM

    C. Network card

    D. Scanner

20. How many devices exist in an EIDE chain?

    A. 1

    B. 2

    C. 3

    D. 4

Scenarios

This chapter has shown you how to install both IDE and SCSI devices. The following scenarios will give you real-life problems dealing with troubleshooting IDE and SCSI devices. The first scenario will give you an opportunity to research and verify the proper configuration of your IDE disk. The second scenario will give you an opportunity to analyze a problem and provide potential solutions to the problem.

1. As a technical support manager, you are required to provide documentation on the particulars of all hardware to the rest of your technical support team. You are required to find out what type of drive you have in your system, then go to the manufacturer's Web site to determine the access time, seek time, and maybe the transfer rate of the drive. You also need to find out how your particular drive should be set up in a dual drive solution. Document each of these items.

2. Your co-worker has set up a SCSI bus and has installed the proper driver in Windows NT 4.0, but the devices are still not accessible. What are some of the things you could check to troubleshoot the SCSI bus?

Lab Exercises

Lab 9.1 Identifying Master and Slave Configuration on your Hard Disk

The objective of this hands-on lab exercise is to gain experience searching for documentation on your hard drive. After retrieving the documentation and determining how to set up the system for multiple drives, you will install a second IDE drive and confirm the changes in your system CMOS.

In this hands-on lab exercise you will need a computer that you can work on, and two IDE hard drives that can be configured in a multi-drive configuration.

1. Power your computer off.

2. Take off the casing to the computer.

3. Take out the hard disk.

4. Somewhere on the hard disk, you should be able to see the manufacturer of the hard disk. You should also be able to see the make and model number. Record all this information in the spaces below.

Manufacturer:

_____

Make:

_____

Model:

_____

5. If you have not gone through Scenario 1, go to the manufacturer's Web site and find the documentation on your particular hard drive (this will probably be on some sort of support page). If you have already gone through Scenario 1, you have this information.

6. From the documentation, determine how you would set up a dual drive (master/slave) system using two of the same drives. Record your results on a piece of paper.

7. If you have a second hard disk and an IDE cable with three connectors, try to master and slave the two drives. Upon restarting the system after setting up the additional drive, you should have to save the information into CMOS.

Lab 9.2 Installing a SCSI Bus in Windows NT 4.0

The objective of this hands-on lab is to gain experience installing a SCSI device. To complete this lab, you will need a computer with Windows NT 4.0 installed. You will also need to know the administrator user account name and password, and you will have to have both a SCSI controller and a SCSI device (CD-ROM, Hard disk, Scanner).

1. Power off the computer.

2. Take the cover off.

3. Assign unique IDs to each of your SCSI devices. This may require researching the jumper settings on the devices if they are internal devices. If they are external devices, there should be a switch on the back of the SCSI device to change the ID number.

4. Place the SCSI card into an expansion slot.

5. Chain the devices off the SCSI card.

6. Place the cover back on the computer.

7. Power the computer on.

8. When you have the logon screen in Windows NT 4.0, log on as the administrator account.

9. Once logged on, select Start ⇨ Settings ⇨ Control Panel.

10. Double-click the SCSI Adapters icon.

11. In the SCSI Adapters dialog box, choose the Drivers tab.

12. Choose the Add button to add a driver.

13. In the Install Driver dialog box, choose the manufacturer of the host adapter and then choose the adapter on the right side.

14. Click the OK button.

15. Restart the computer.

Answers to Chapter Questions

Chapter Pre-Test

1. The Pin 1 rule is used when you are connecting a ribbon cable to a drive. **The colored wire on the ribbon cable has to match Pin 1 on the controller.**

2. **The data path of wide SCSI-2 (16-bit) is double that of SCSI's (8-bit).**

3. IDE devices have to be set up in a master slave configuration, because **both devices have controllers that act as the boss**, sending out instructions to the PC.

4. The SCSI BIOS has to be enabled **when you are booting off the first SCSI disk**.

5. Data is written to a disk **by the read/write heads moving over the disk surface and magnetizing the particles in the coating that resides on the disk.**

6. The disk configuration information is stored **in CMOS.**

7. The size of a disk can be calculated **by taking the number of cylinders multiplied by the number of heads multiplied by the number of sectors per track multiplied by 512 bytes.**

8. There are **40** pins on a hard disk controller.

9. There are **50** pins on an internal SCSI device.

10. A cluster is made up of **sectors.**

Assessment Questions

1. **C.** A single sector on the disk is 512 bytes in size. A group of these sectors makes up a cluster, which typically could be 4K, 16K, or 32K in size. For more information, see the section labeled "Hard Drive Terminology."

2. **B.** IDE supports only two devices in an IDE chain. EIDE improves on this limit by allowing four devices. For more information, see the section labeled "IDE Devices."

3. **D.** The read/write heads are responsible for moving over the disk surface and for writing data to the disk. A platter is one of the disk plates, a sector is where the data is written, and a cluster is a group of sectors. For more information, see the section labeled "Hard Drive Terminology."

4. **A.** The hard disk is connected to the motherboard with a 40-wire ribbon cable. A 34-wire ribbon cable is used to connect floppy drives, and a 50-wire ribbon cable is used for internal SCSI devices. For more information, see the section labeled "IDE Devices."

5. **B.** Seek time is the time it takes to move the read/write heads over the disk surface to the required track. Latency is the time it takes to move the appropriate sector under the read/write head after first being on the right track. For more information, see the section labeled "Hard Drive Terminology."

6. **C.** Devices at each end of the SCSI bus must be terminated. This is usually the SCSI host adapter, plus the last device in the chain. For more information, see the section labeled "Small Computer System Interface."

7. **B.** A bootable hard disk should take SCSI ID zero, while the host adapter usually takes an ID of seven. The other device can be assigned a number in the chain as long as it is a unique number. For more information, see the section labeled "Small Computer System Interface."

8. **D.** IDE CD-ROMs are slaves in an IDE chain. IDE devices do not get assigned IDs and do not have to be terminated. For more information, see the section labeled "IDE Devices."

9. **C.** An internal SCSI connector uses a 50-wire ribbon cable, an IDE device uses a 40-wire ribbon cable, while a floppy drive uses a 34-wire ribbon cable. For more information, see the section labeled "Small Computer System Interface."

10. **C.** The master boot record is the first sector on the first track of the first side of the first platter. For more information, see the section labeled "Hard Disk Terminology."

11. **B.** In a SCSI bus, the higher the number, the higher the priority the device has in the chain. It is recommended that the slower devices be assigned some of the higher values so that they can communicate in the bus when needed. For more information, see the section labeled "Small Computer System Interface."

12. **A.** The SCSI BIOS should be enabled when there is a SCSI hard disk in the chain and you will be booting off that device. For more information, see the section labeled "Small Computer System Interface."

13. **D.** You would install a SCSI adapter from the SCSI Adapters icon in Control Panel. For more information, see the section labeled "Small Computer System Interface."

14. **C.** Disk latency is the time it takes to move the sector that has the data under the read/write heads. For more information, see the section labeled "Hard Drive Terminology."

15. **B.** When setting up multiple IDE devices, you will have to choose which device will act as the master device. The master device is the device that is responsible for having its controller talk to the CPU. The slave device will use the controller of the master device. For more information, see the section labeled "IDE Devices."

16. **D.** The same track on all platters is referred to as a cylinder. People use the terms "tracks" and "cylinders" interchangeably because track 0 is cylinder 0. For more information, see the section labeled "Hard Drive Terminology."

17. **B.** Platters have two sides, just like a record. For more information, see the section labeled "Hard Drive Terminology."

18. A. Each plate within the disk is called a platter. A disk is typically divided up into three or four platters. For more information, see the section labeled "Hard Drive Terminology."

19. C. One of the benefits of SCSI is that the devices come out in all different flavors. There are hard disks, CD-ROMs, tape devices, printers, scanners, but no SCSI network adapter. For more information, see the section labeled "Small Computer System Interface."

20. D. There are four devices in an EIDE chain. IDE only supports two devices and the original SCSI supports eight devices in the chain. For more information, see the section labeled "IDE Devices."

Scenarios

1. There is no correct answer to this scenario. Everyone's answer will vary, because each system is unique and the drive characteristics will be unique to the drive. This scenario has given you time to learn to research information on the Internet that deals with your hardware — a talent in its own right.

2. The following list describes what you should check for when troubleshooting a SCSI bus:

   - ID numbers of devices have been assigned and every device has a unique ID.

   - Both ends of the SCSI bus have been terminated.

   - Everything is connected properly. (Double-check all cabling and make sure that the card is inserted correctly.)

CHAPTER 10

Installing and Configuring Peripheral Devices

EXAM OBJECTIVES

Exam 220-201 ✦ A+ Core Hardware

✦ **1.7** Identify proper procedures for installing and configuring peripheral devices. Content may include the following:

- Monitor/video card
- Modem
- USB peripherals and hubs
- IEEE 1284
- IEEE 1394
- External storage

✦ **Portables**

- Docking stations
- Keyboard
- Mouse
- NIC

CHAPTER PRE-TEST

1. What is resolution in regard to a monitor?

2. What does the refresh rate refer to on a video card?

3. What does a modem modulate?

4. In what unit is modem speed measured?

5. How many IDE drives can be installed in a computer at once?

6. What three fixed-disks file systems can Windows 2000 read?

7. How fast is USB?

8. What is one advantage of IEEE-1394 over USB?

9. What is a hardware profile?

10. What *must* a laptop have to connect to a network?

✦ Answers to these questions can be found at the end of the chapter. ✦

As a technician, you're likely to encounter many different scenarios where you'll have to install and configure hardware. An average day's work can range from setting the resolution on a video card to installing a NIC on a portable computer. As you become more experienced with different types of hardware, you'll learn that hardware devices are generally installed the same, maintained the same, and have common configuration methods. In addition, you'll see that devices, no matter what manufacturer, have similar nuances to their own class of hardware.

In this chapter, you dive into some common hardware installation and configuration, including laptops and their components. At the end of the chapter, there are two scenarios and two labs to offer you some hands-on experience.

Monitor/Video Cards

1.7 Identify proper procedures for installing and configuring peripheral devices. Content may include the following: Monitor/video cards

A *video card* is a device inside your computer that displays images on your monitor. Your monitor simply displays text, movement, and images that you input to the computer through your mouse, keyboard, or other input device. Put another way, a video card allows you to see into a PC — that's pretty incredible when you think about it.

Resolution

Whenever a discussion of monitors and video cards occurs, one question that is inevitably asked is: "What is resolution?" *Resolution* deals with the number of pixels required to draw an image on a monitor. Your monitor's screen is basically a grid of dots. How many dots? Well, that depends on (you guessed it) the monitor's resolution. For example, a resolution of 800×600 means 800 pixels across the monitor and 600 pixels down the monitor (do some math and you'll discover it takes 480,000 pixels to create that resolution).

Monitors

Monitors have evolved from simple monochrome displays to today's high-resolution Super VGA, which we'll discuss later in this chapter. Monitors vary in price because they also vary in quality. A monitor, no matter what its size, is only capable of producing so many colors and resolutions.

How a monitor works

How do all those colors get to the monitor?

The back of the monitor's screen, which is called a cathode ray tube (CRT), is coated with phosphors. Aimed at the CRT is an electron gun. As the video card sends a signal to the electron gun, the gun shoots electrons at the CRT, causing the phosphors on the CRT to glow.

The gun fires constantly at the CRT from left to right and from top to bottom. The glow of three phosphors, red, green and blue, creates 1 pixel. The combinations of lit pixels create a pattern recognizable to the human eye, and the speed at which the images on the screen change presents the illusion of movement and a flow of colors onscreen.

At some point, you may have run across a monitor's refresh rate, whether you read the monitor's manual or saw it on the monitor's specifications label. A monitor's *refresh rate* refers to how often the electron gun is capable of redrawing the screen.

Another term often included with the refresh rate is dot pitch. A monitor's *dot pitch* is simply the distance (in millimeters) between two dots of the same color on a monitor. For example, an average monitor would have a dot pitch of .28 millimeters. An above average monitor may offer dot pitch as tight as .24 mm.

Monochrome video

The first monitor type for PCs was a monochrome. As its name implies, with monochrome you got one color (well two if you count the black screen behind the colored text). Early monochrome monitors could display only text — no graphics — at a simple resolution of 720×350, which was fine for characters.

The Hercules Graphics card followed suit (1982) with the same resolution, but offered the ability to display graphics. Graphics could be displayed as the card used a library of characters for text mode and a more intense mode for drawing graphics. To the user, the switch between these two modes was invisible.

Color video

Most models of monitors available today are at least VGA. VGA (which stands for video graphics adapter) allows the monitor to send an analog signal to X that controls the flow and depth of colors more superbly than pre-VGA models allowed.

Super VGA-capable monitors allow monitors to display higher resolutions and richer colors. The amount of RAM on the video card determines the number of colors the monitor can display. Some monitors and video cards promise True Color, which allows for up to 16 million colors.

IBM introduced its first color monitors (1981) with the Color Graphics Adapter (CGA), which had the ability to use four colors at a pathetic resolution of only 320 × 200. The card could be switched to two colors, which would result in a slightly higher resolution.

In 1985, IBM introduced the Enhanced Graphics Adapter (EGA) that could display 16 colors at a resolution of 320 × 200 or 640 × 350.

IBM later introduced (1987) an adapter capable of even higher resolution with its Video Graphics Adapter (VGA). The original VGA card had 256K of memory and the ability to display 16 colors at 640 × 480 or 256 colors at 320 @ts 200. As you can see, the higher the amount of colors used results in a lower resolution. This card is the bare minimum for today's monitors and video cards. VGA uses analog and allows users to select from over 260,000 shades of colors.

Video Electronics Standard Association

As you can tell from reading the preceding sections, IBM was, for the most part, in control of the standards for color video adapters and monitors. The Video Electronics Standard Association (VESA) is a collection of manufacturers that later set out to improve on IBM's video technologies. The result was the Super VGA video card. While it's not the most creatively named card, it is, well, super (at least in comparison to its predecessor VGA).

SVGA can support:

✦ 256 colors at a resolution of 800 × 600

✦ 16 colors at 1,024 × 768

✦ 65,536 colors at 640 × 480

Installing a video card

Installing a video card is not hard to do. Of course, you'll need some tools to begin your work:

✦ A clean working area

✦ A standard computer toolkit

✦ A video card and installation instructions

STEP BY STEP: Installing a Video Card

1. Power off the computer and unplug it. Disconnect all cables from the computer and open the case according to the manufacturer's guidelines.

2. Based on your computer model, the current video card may be on board, or integrated. If not, remove the old video card and set it aside.

3. Confirm that the video card you are about to install has an available bus that matches the card type. If necessary, remove the metal plate to allow access to the back of the card once it is installed.

4. Insert the card into the appropriate bus (depending on the card type, it could be AGP, ISA, PCI, or even SCSI) until it snaps into place and fits snugly into the slot; then screw the video card's plate into place to secure the card.

5. Replace the computer cover and all of the cords, and then power on the computer and configure the video card, as described in the next section.

In the Real World As every manufacturer has its own method of opening the computer case, be certain you understand how your computer opens before you attempt to do so. As always, power off the computer and unplug the power cord and attachments before opening the case.

Configuring the video card

The kind of operating system your computer runs determines how you need to configure the video card. Windows 2000 and Windows 9x use a similar technology to find and detect the card: Plug-and-Play. Plug-and-Play is a technology to automatically detect new devices and, using information on the card, to install the drivers needed by the device to operate with the operating system.

Windows 9x and Windows 2000 use a similar method to configure the video card. The following Step By Step and the accompanying figures are for the Windows 2000 Professional workstation, but will work on 9x.

STEP BY STEP: Configuring a Video Card on Windows

1. Choose Start ➪ Settings ➪ Control Panel and then open the Display applet.

2. Click the Settings tab (see Figure 10-1).

3. From the Colors drop-down menu, choose a color palette that is applicable for your monitor.

4. In the Screen area field, move the slider to set the resolution of your monitor to the desired setting (make sure the setting you choose is one that your monitor can handle).

5. Click Apply to apply the changes and keep the Display properties applet open in case you'd like to change your mind. Click Cancel or OK, based on the settings you've selected.

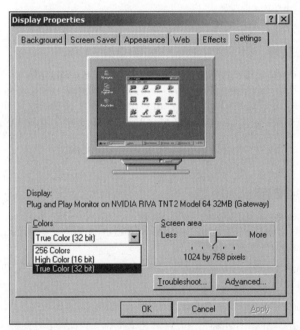

Figure 10-1: The Settings tab in the Display applet allows you to configure a monitor.

Modems

 1.7 Identify proper procedures for installing and configuring peripheral devices. Content may include the following: Modems

A modem is a device that modulates a digital signal into an analog signal. The signal then is demodulated back into a digital signal at the receiving modem. (If you haven't guessed, the term modulate was the basis for the word *modem*.) A modem allows a user to do a variety of tasks, including:

✦ Connect to the Internet

✦ Connect to a remote network

✦ Connect to another PC directly

✦ Send and receive faxes

✦ Accept incoming phone calls

Modem attributes

There are several attributes of a modem that will effect its installation and configuration: whether the modem is internal or external, the available resources on the computer, and the speed of the modem. The most prominent of these is the speed of the modem. Speed is measured in bits per second (bps) — and in today's world, the more bps the merrier. Realistically, as far as analog modems are concerned, dial-up connection speed begins promptly at 56K, or 56,000bps.

Installing a modem

Installing a modem is not difficult work. As most computers today ship with a modem installed already, you're likely to find yourself replacing modems more often than installing them from scratch.

STEP BY STEP: Installing a Modem

1. Power off the computer and disconnect all cords from the PC. Open the case of the computer according to the manufacturer's guidelines.

2. If you are replacing a modem, remove the old modem from its bus. If you're adding a new modem, confirm that the modem you're about to add has an available bus on the motherboard.

3. If necessary, remove the plate that allows access to the modem on the back of the PC. Insert the new modem into the appropriate slot. The card should fit snugly and firmly with a satisfying snap.

4. Screw the modem into place and replace the case's cover and all of the cords.

5. Most modems have two "jacks" or receptacles. The first jack connects to the telephone line. The second jack connects to a telephone, caller-ID station, or fax machine. The modem can route the call to the appropriate device if the call is not meant for it. Connect the modem directly to the incoming phone line and then connect the phone to the modem's second phone port. Modems accept RJ-11 connectors, the transceiver on the end of a standard phone line.

Configuring a modem

Windows 9x and Windows 2000 both use Plug-and-Play to detect and install modems. In some instances, the modem may not be detected properly through Plug-and-Play. You can use either the Device Manager in the System or Modems applets in the Windows Control Panel to confirm that your modem has been detected and installed properly. If you find that your modem has not been installed, you'll have to add your modem manually using the Add New Hardware Wizard in the Add/Remove Hardware applet of the Control Panel.

As with most hardware, the drivers for the modem are typically included with the modem on a floppy or CD. Additionally, the manufacturer's Web site should supply updated drivers for the device.

Storage Devices

1.7 Identify proper procedures for installing and configuring peripheral devices. Content may include the following: External storage

The term *storage devices* includes hard drives, but the term also includes media, such as Zip drives, tape drives, floppy disks, CD-Rs, and writeable DVDs. Storage devices must be formatted with a file system so that the operating system can write to the media.

Hard drives

Hard drives, or fixed (or not easily removable) disk drives, are internal devices used to store the operating systems, applications, and data. There are external hard drive devices that are used to back up data from the internal hard drive. These devices typically hold only data – not the operating system. Storage capacity for hard drives is measured according to gigabytes (GB), while capacity for smaller drives is measured in megabytes (MB). Drive speed is measured in milliseconds.

IDE drives

IDE drives (IDE stands for Integrated Drive Electronics) come with a controller right on the disk, and can connect to the motherboard or another controller card. These early drives were limited to a maximum capacity of 528 MB and you could only have two in a system.

EIDE drives

Enhanced IDE drives followed the IDE standard. EIDE drives are faster than their predecessors and allow for considerably larger drives (80gigabytes and beyond) and allow you to have up to four drives in one machine.

SCSI drives

SCSI (Small Computer Systems Interface) hard drives utilize a bus architecture, which allows each device on the bus to be identified through its own unique SCSI number. Internal SCSI drives use a 50-pin ribbon to connect each device in the chain. SCSI drives are very fast and reliable and are most common in servers.

Installing a hard drive

To install a fixed drive you may need all, or most, of the following items, depending on the drive and the computer current configuration:

✦ A standard computer toolkit

✦ A controller card

✦ Rails for the drive to rest on (Hard drives are often 3.5 inches wide. Bays for most computers are 5.25 inches. The rails "fill-in" the gap and secure the drive in place.)

✦ The hard drive

✦ The ribbon to connect the drive to the motherboard

STEP BY STEP: Installing an Internal (Fixed) Hard Drive

1. Power off the computer, disconnect all cords from the PC, and then open the case of the computer.

2. If this is a secondary drive, consult the drive's instructions on how to set the drive to be either a slave or master by moving the drive's jumpers to the appropriate positions.

3. If you are replacing a drive, remove the old drive and set it aside. If you're adding an additional drive, prepare the bay by removing the cover plate on the face of the computer, if necessary. As always, follow your manufacturer's guidelines for opening your computer.

4. If necessary, install the rails that your drive will rest on and then insert the drive into the rails (if there are any) and position the drive so it can be secured with screws. Once the drive is aligned on the rails, fasten the drive with the screws.

5. Connect the ribbon to the drive and to the motherboard or "controller card." The red stripe on the ribbon represents the first pin on the controller. Newer drives will only allow the ribbon to be connected to the drive if it is in the correct position.

6. Inside the computer, locate an available power connector. Connect the power source to the drive's power receptacle.

7. Replace the cover and cords and power on the computer; then refer to the next section, where we show you how to configure the drive.

Configuring the hard drive

After a hard drive is installed properly, you need to create a partition (or partitions) and format each partition with a file system so that the operating system can read and write to the drive. The operating system you are using determines how you will configure the drive.

Windows 9x configurations

In Windows 9x, hard drives are configured by using FDISK, an MS-DOS-based program that allows you to configure all aspects of a hard drive. When you run FDISK, the program asks if you'd like to enable large disk support. Large disk support allows you to create partitions larger than 512MB. If you enable large disk support, you'll be using the FAT32 file system (which we discuss in a moment).

After you choose whether or not to enable support for large disks, FDISK displays a menu that gives you the following options:

1. Create a DOS Partition or Logical DOS Drive

2. Set the Active partition

3. Delete Partition or Logical DOS Drive

4. Display Partition Information

If this is a new drive, you may have to boot from a Windows 98 startup disk to access the features within FDISK. For a new drive, you'll most likely use the following Step By Step to create a partition on the drive.

STEP BY STEP: Partitioning a New Hard Drive

1. Within fdisk choose the first option to create a DOS partition or Logical DOS Drive. The first partition you create is the primary partition and is typically your C: drive.

2. Designate the size of the primary partition. Some technicians find it best to create one large partition, as FAT32 partitions can be as large as 2TB (terabytes).

3. After creating the partition(s), you must reboot the system and enter FDISK again. However, if you are creating multiple partitions, you can create all your partitions in this one session of FDISK before rebooting.

4. Start FDISK again and choose the second option to set the active partition. An *active partition* is the partition from which the system's operating system boots from by default. When you're done, reboot again.

After the partition(s) are created, you need to format the drive with a file system so that Windows 98 can read and write to the disk. You can use the Format command at the MS-DOS-prompt. (If Windows 98 is already installed, you can right-click the new partition and choose Format within Windows Explorer.)

Windows 2000 configurations

Windows 2000 allows you to configure drives via two main methods: during the installation process and by using Disk Management. During a typical Windows 2000 installation, you are given the choice to format (or erase) the hard drive and partition it as you see fit. You can also choose a file system for the partition. After installing Windows 2000, you use the Disk Management tool to view, create, and format partitions. Figure 10-2 shows a hard drive viewed through the Disk Management utility.

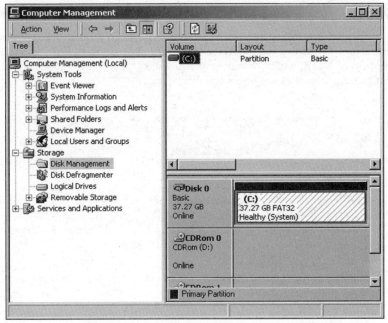

Figure 10-2: Disk Management controls the creation of partitions and volumes for Windows 2000 disks.

STEP BY STEP: Installing a Windows 2000 Disk Using Disk Management

1. Choose Start ➪ Programs ➪ Administrative Tools ➪ Computer Management.

2. Expand the storage container by clicking the plus symbol next to Storage. Click on Disk Management. Within Disk Management, a console shows all of the current drives and their storage features.

3. If a new drive has been added, the Write Signature and Upgrade Disk Wizard appear when you open Disk Management. A signature allows the disk to be read by Windows 2000. This utility walks you through the process of writing a signature to the drive (so Windows can access the drive) and upgrading the disk to a basic disk or a dynamic disk.

4. Right-click the drive and choose Create Partition to summon the Create Partition Wizard. This tool guides you through creating the partition, its type, and the file system to be used on the disk. (See the next section for more information on file systems.)

File systems

A file system allows an operating system to read and write to a hard drive (or any disk, for that matter). Windows 9x and Windows 2000 use common FAT file systems, with the exception of NTFS, which Windows 2000 works best with. Table 10-1 offers a more in-depth comparison of each file system.

Table 10-1
File Systems

File System	Description	Specifications
FAT	FAT means *File Allocation Table*. Uses a table to reference which cluster a file is in.	Simple file system. Can be read by Windows 95, 98, and Windows 2000 if dual-booting. Partitions are limited to 4GB.
FAT32	The preferred file system for Windows 98. Has the same general attributes as its predecessor, FAT, but allows for larger partitions with smaller cluster size for space conservation.	Simple file system. Can be used and read by Windows 98 and Windows 2000 if dual-booting. Partitions are limited to 2TB.
NTFS	NTFS stands for *New Technology File System*. This robust file system provides security, encryption, disk quotas, compression, and more.	Robust, powerful file system. Cannot be viewed by other operating systems in a dual-boot environment. Most secure of the Windows file systems.

Tape drives

Now that your drive is installed, you'll want to protect all that data, right? One of the best methods of securing data is through a tape backup. There is plenty of backup software available — including versions within Windows 9x and Windows 2000. Whatever backup software you decide to use, remember these things:

✦ Backing up data is a commitment to follow a set backup schedule and sticking to it.

✦ Tapes should be stored in a fireproof vault or off-site.

✦ A schedule should be created to archive tapes for disaster planning.

✦ Operating systems and applications do not need to be backed up as long as they can be reinstalled.

Backup types

Almost all backup software, including the backup software included with Windows 9x and Windows 2000, uses the same terminology to describe the type of backup to occur. Table 10-2 details each backup type and its advantages and disadvantages.

Table 10-2 Backup Types and their Features			
Backup Type	**Description**	**Advantages**	**Disadvantages**
Normal	Backs up all selected files and resets the archive bit.	Safely backs up all data regardless of last backup session.	Can result in a lengthy backup process.
Incremental	Backs up all files that have changed since the last backup session. Resets the archive bit.	Faster backup than a normal backup because only changed files are written to tape.	Can result in a slow restoration process, because many different tapes may be needed to restore all of the files that have been backed up at different times.
Differential	Backs up all files that have changed since the last full backup. Does not clear the archive bit.	Allows for a faster restoration of files, because less tape switching is required.	Can result in a lengthy backup process.
Daily	Backs up all files that were changed that day and does not clear the archive bit.	Safe, easy backup.	Can be a lengthy restore process as tapes from each day are required to restore the files to their most recent status.
Copy	Simple copy of all files. Does not clear the archive bit.	Good assurance of system status. Excellent way of archiving data on a given date.	Can be a lengthy process, depending on the amount of data to copy.

Tape drives

Installing a tape drive is very similar to installing an internal hard drive (which we discussed earlier in this chapter). The tape drive is installed in an open bay in the computer case and connects either through a controller or an internal SCSI bus. Some tape drives may be external and connect through a SCSI adapter.

Once the drive is installed you need to insert a tape into the drive and prepare the tape for backup. This usually involves formatting the tape through your backup software and creating a catalog of what is to be backed up. Finally, a schedule needs to be created of what backup types will occur and when the backup will take place. The backup software can guide you through these decisions and create an automated schedule in most instances.

Removable media

Removable media are storage devices that don't have to be constantly present to be accessible by the operating system. Floppies, CDs, ZIP drives, SuperDisks, and new technology allow data to be stored off of the PC or taken on the go.

Exam Tip   The CompTIA exam will quiz you on removable media: types, handling, and attributes.

Floppy disks

A floppy disk is a removable disk that allows you to store data off the PC for later retrieval, as a method for transferring data, or creating a boot disk. Some facts about floppies:

- ✦ Today's floppy disks are 3.5-inch diskettes.
- ✦ Floppies are actually polyester material coated in iron oxide.
- ✦ A sliding tab on the diskette can write-protect the disk.
- ✦ Floppies are typically capable of storing 1.44MB of data.
- ✦ Extra High Density floppies have a 2.88MB capacity.

Compact discs

Compact discs are excellent media for distributing applications, data, read-only information, artwork, and more. Some facts about compact discs:

- ✦ CDs can hold 650MB of data
- ✦ CDs can hold 74 minutes of sound
- ✦ Most CDs are written once, read many – or WORM
- ✦ CD-RWs allow a user to write to the CD multiple times through a CD-RW drive

Iomega drives

No discussion of removable media would be complete without mention of Iomega drives. Iomega was not the first company to offer high-capacity removable drives. SyQuest drives once led the removable storage industry, followed by Bernoulli drives. Iomega, however, was the first to move into the mainstream.

Iomega drives are internal or external. Facts about Iomega drives:

✦ These drives can connect through a parallel port, SCSI, or even USB

✦ Zip drives come with support for either 100MB or 250MB disks

✦ Jaz drives come with support for either 1 or 2GB disks

USB Peripherals and Hub

1.7 Identify proper procedures for installing and configuring peripheral devices. Content may include the following: USB peripherals and hubs

The advent of the Universal Serial Bus has brought many great things to the PC community. A USB is a fast connection between the computer and peripherals. USB-enabled devices allow for true Plug-and-Play experience. A user can take a USB device, such as a scanner, and connect it to a USB slot on their PC. The operating system then automatically detects the new device, installs the necessary software to run it, and lets the user begin utilizing the device.

Some basic facts about USB:

✦ USB is as simple as plugging in a cord; no configuring IRQs, DMAs, I/O ports or other resources

✦ Power to the devices may be delivered through the PC or the hub

✦ Allows for hot swapping (components can be swapped in and out of the USB connection without restarting the PC)

✦ USBs can operate at 12Mbps or 1.5Mbps

Installing a USB peripheral

Installing a USB device is very simple: connect the device to the USB port with a USB cable. Once a device has been installed and recognized by an operating system, the device won't have to be reinstalled every time the device is disconnected. For example, a digital camera most likely won't always need to be connected to the PC, only during the transfer of digital photos from the camera to the PC.

When the user returns to download images from the camera, she can simply connect the camera to the USB port and begin using the device as if it's been connected all along. When finished, she can remove the device from the USB port and the operating system doesn't mind at all. In fact, this feature allows other devices to be used intermittently as well.

How many USB ports do most PCs have? Most only have two. For those users that require more than two devices, there are a couple of options. First, a user can *daisy chain* USB devices together. For example, a USB keyboard may connect directly to the USB port. The USB mouse could then connect to one side of the USB keyboard. On the other side of the keyboard there may be an additional connection for another USB device, such as a digital camera or scanner. Theoretically, you can connect 127 USB devices at once.

Using a USB hub

If you have multiple USB devices, the purchase of a USB hub may be more practical than one long daisy chain of devices. A *USB hub* is a central station for connecting multiple USB devices to one PC. The hub connects to one of your computer's USB ports, and then devices connect directly to the hub. The computer won't know the difference; the USB port on the PC detects the devices that you've connected to the hub as if those devices were connected directly to the PC itself.

IEEE-1284

The IEEE-1284 is a set of rules that define communications to and from parallel ports. The IEEE-1284 Standard accommodates five types of operation:

✦ **Compatibility mode.** Allows for backward compatibility with older parallel printers. While this standard mode does allow for backward compatibility, there are drawbacks. The processor must listen for activity on the cable, communication is using only half-duplex mode, and the maximum speed is limited to the standard 150 kilobytes per second.

✦ **Nibble mode.** Allows the printer to send information back to the computer. Nibble mode earned its name because the communication from the printer is sent back to the processor in two four-bit chunks – called a *nibble*. This mode is also processor -intensive, as the processor must listen to the incoming traffic on the cable.

✦ **Byte mode.** Allows the printer to communicate with the computer at the same rate the computer speaks with the printer. Byte mode may also be called an enhanced bidirectional port. It allows older devices to go beyond the four-bit limits of nibble mode and use the full speed (150 kilobytes per second) to talk back to the computer.

✦ **Enhanced Capability Port (ECP) mode.** An advanced, bidirectional mode for fast communications between the computer and any devices attached to the parallel port. This technology was created by Microsoft and Hewlett-Packard to address the needs of high-speed printers and scanners. This mode reduces the amount of dedicated CPU time required to move large chunks of data between devices.

✦ **Enhanced Parallel Port mode.** Designed by Intel, Xircom, and Zenith Data Systems to provide a common interface for devices, in addition to printers (for example, scanners, external hard drives, or CD-ROM drives) that require speed. Devices could be scanners, external hard drives, or CD-ROMs.

These settings are enabled within your computer's BIOS. Not all parallel devices support IEEE-1284. When you go to connect the peripheral, you may need to access the setup program of your computer (the BIOS) to switch the communication mode of the parallel port to match the communication mode of the device. This is not an automatic feature like plug-and-play.

FireWire (IEEE-1394)

 1.7 Identify proper procedures for installing and configuring peripheral devices. Content may include the following: IEEE-1394.

IEEE-1394 is a definition for the management of communications between peripherals and computers. The devices connect to the computers through a special cable that allows data from the peripherals, such as digital video cameras, to be transferred much faster than USB or parallel cables. The thin connecting cable, commonly known as FireWire, allows for extremely fast transfer of data between the PC and connected devices. Devices in need of speed deal primarily with audiovisual equipment, such as video cameras, external storage devices, MIDI type equipment, and appliances.

While FireWire is very similar to USB capabilities, the primary difference is speed. FireWire makes USB look like the turtle racing the hare: FireWire speed ranges from 100Mbps, 200Mbps, and 400Mbps, while the fastest USB transmission is 1.5Mbps. A high-end digital video camera transferring a 30-minute recording through USB would be very painful, but through FireWire it's a breeze.

Microsoft promises more development with FireWire, but Windows 2000 and Windows 98 do offer limited support for FireWire components. Two restraints have kept Firewire implementation out of the mainstream-computing environment: price and demand. In Windows ME, users can network their PCs through FireWire cables rather than traditional network cables.

Portables

 1.7 Identify proper procedures for installing and configuring peripheral devices. Content may include the following: Portables — Docking stations

Portable computing has become an essential asset to any computing environment. Professionals all over the world, from archeologists, scientists, and traveling salesmen to students, are using portable computers in greater and greater numbers every day. It follows then, that as a technician you will no doubt encounter these devices and need to apply your hardware savvy to troubleshoot, upgrade, and configure these computers. The good news is that these devices use many of the same techniques you find in desktops. The bad news is that the components are much smaller (being mobile), and thus are generally more difficult to deal with.

Docking stations

A docking station makes a desktop system out of a portable computer. A user inserts, or *docks*, their laptop PC into a central *docking station*. Connected to the station is a regular keyboard, mouse, monitor, and any other peripherals. A docking station thus allows the user to have the functionality of a desktop PC without the sometimes-uncomfortable screen, keyboard, and mouse of a laptop.

When the user is ready to go on the move, the laptop portion of the PC is removed and the user is on their way — data intact! When the user returns, they simply dock the laptop again and have all the comforts of a desktop PC.

Windows 9x and Windows 2000 can detect when the PC is docked or mobile by using hardware profiles. A *hardware profile* is a collection of devices that should be initialized when the operating system is booted in a given environment. For example, when a docking station is on the road, the network card is most likely not needed but the modem probably is. A hardware profile then recognizes that the docking station is not present and loads the profile for the laptop configuration. A lab at the end of this chapter will have you manually create a hardware profile.

Keyboards

Mobile computers have small keyboards. Unless you have tiny fingers, they aren't the most comfortable keyboards to type on. Most portables have a connection for external keyboard connections. A user can simply take a regular keyboard and connect it to their PS/2 or USB adapter.

Some mobile computers have an expanding, butterfly-type keyboard that spreads out when the case is opened. These fancy units look neat the first few times you use them, but a fast typist can damage the keys by pressing too hard on them. They're difficult to repair and usually require replacement.

Keyboard attributes such as repeat delay and cursor blink can be managed through Windows 9x and Windows 2000's Keyboard Control Panel applet, as seen in Figure 10-3.

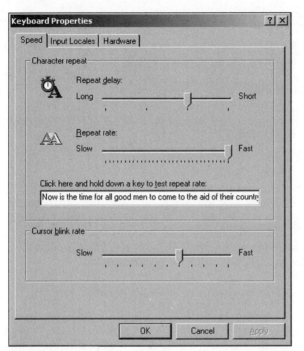

Figure 10-3: The Keyboard applet in the Control Panel allows you to configure your keyboard for both desktop and mobile PCs.

Mouse

A mouse on a mobile computer is not an average mouse. Input devices for mobile computers vary from manufacturer to manufacturer and may require special tools to service. The types of mice, or input devices, you can expect to encounter when dealing with mobile computers will vary, but here's a quick list of the most popular types:

✦ **Trackball:** Some mobile computers use a trackball mouse that attaches to the side of the monitor or is centered at the bottom of the keyboard area.

✦ **Touch pad:** Uses your finger to act as the mouse. These pads are typically centered below the keyboard.

✦ **Track point:** IBM laptops use little stick-like devices that are centered in the middle of the keyboard. You use your forefingers or thumbs to navigate with the track point.

✦ **Desktop mouse:** Most laptops allow a user to use a regular PS/2 mouse or USB mouse.

Network Interface Card

A Network Interface Card (NIC) on a mobile computer is usually a PCMCIA card (often called a PC Card)that attaches to the PC in an empty socket on the side of the computer. Many newer laptops include a built-in network connection. PC cards allow a mobile PC to access the network and Internet when appropriate.

Exam Tip   The CompTIA exam will use the terms *PCMCIA* and *PC cards* interchangeably to describe a NIC for a mobile computer.

Installing a NIC

Installing a NIC is pretty straightforward. The NIC for a mobile computer is a PC Card that is inserted into an empty socket in the laptop. Some laptops require the laptop to be rebooted whenever a new PC Card is inserted, but most allow hot-swappable cards. The NIC card then ejects (manually or automatically) a receiver for the network cable. Most of today's NICs are designed to accept an RJ-45 transceiver for connecting to an Ethernet 10/100BaseT network.

Protocols

Within the operating system, whether Windows 9x or Windows 2000, you have the same choice of protocols as on a desktop workstation. A protocol is the language computers speak on a network. For computers to speak to each other, a common protocol, or language, is required. The most common protocols and their attributes are:

✦ **TCP/IP:** The protocol created by the U.S. Department of Defense is the genesis of the Internet. This is the most widely used protocol today. A robust, routable protocol used for connecting dissimilar networks and accessing to the Internet.

✦ **NetBEUI:** A simple, non-routable protocol used widely in small networks. No configuration is required.

✦ **IPX/SPX (NWLINK):** A protocol used in conjunction with Novell's NetWare servers. This protocol is routable and robust.

Key Point Summary

In this chapter we've discussed installing and configuring peripheral devices, including devices for mobile computing. The key points discussed in this chapter were:

✦ Monitors and video cards

✦ Modems

✦ Storage devices

✦ USB devices and hubs

✦ IEEE-1394

✦ Portable computers and their attributes

✦   ✦   ✦

STUDY GUIDE

This Study Guide presents 25 assessment questions, 2 scenarios, and 2 lab exercises to test your knowledge of the exam topic area.

Assessment Questions

1. What is resolution on a monitor?

    A. The number of dots within one square inch

    B. The distance between two dots of the same color on a monitor

    C. The number of pixels required to draw an image on a monitor

    D. The number of pixels within one square inch

2. How many pixels are used in a resolution of 1024×768?

    A. Depends on the image being drawn

    B. 786,432

    C. Millions

    D. Depends on the size of the monitor

3. What substance is on the back of a computer's monitor screen?

    A. Phosphors

    B. Plasma

    C. Liquid crystal

    D. Electrons

4. What does an electron gun do?

    A. Shoots electrons at a monitor to cause the screen to redraw

    B. Regulates the amount of electricity into the monitor

    C. Sets the amount of voltage based on the resolution

    D. Shoots electrons out of the back of the monitor

5. What is a refresh rate?

    A. The number of times a screen "flickers" within one minute

    B. The number of times the electron gun redraws the screen

    C. The frequency at which the images on the monitor change

    D. The number of windows open on a computer monitor generates a higher refresh rate

6. What is dot pitch?

    A. The number of pixels on a screen

    B. The number of pixels within one square inch

    C. The number of pixels for a given resolution on a 15-inch monitor

    D. The distance between two dots of the same color on a monitor

7. What is the first step a technician should take when installing a video card?

    A. Change the resolution of the monitor to match that of the card about to be installed

    B. Power off the PC and remove all power cords

    C. Uninstall the old video card drivers

    D. Open the PC case's cover

8. Which of the following is a modem capable of? (Select two)

    A. Connecting a PC to a local network

    B. Sending faxes

    C. Acting as a fixed pager

    D. Connecting to Internet service providers

9. What is primarily required to achieve 56K modem speed?

    A. A modem capable of sending at 56K

    B. A software package capable of sending at 56K

    C. A cable modem

    D. A modem on both ends of the connection that can send and receive at 56K

10. What type of transceivers do modems use?

    A. RJ-11

    B. RJ-12

    C. UTP

    D. RJ-45

11. What Windows 9x applet would allow a technician to add a modem manually?

    A. System applet

    B. Regedit

    C. Modems applet

    D. Telnet

12. How large could a partition of an IDE drive be?

    A. 400MB

    B. 512MB

    C. 1,024MB

    D. 4GB

13. What is integrated into an IDE drive?

    A. The power source

    B. The controller

    C. The SCSI channel

    D. The ribbon to the motherboard

14. How many EIDE drives can be in one computer?

    A. 2

    B. 4

    C. 8

    D. 16

15. What size pin does an internal SCSI hard drive use?

    A. 36 pin

    B. 15 pin

    C. 32 pin

    D. 50 pin

16. With what utility are partitions created within Windows 9x?

    A. Windows Explorer

    B. Device Manager

    C. Disk Management

    D. FDISK

17. What two file systems are allowed for internal (fixed) hard drives in Windows 98?

    A. FAT

    B. FAT32

    C. NTFS

    D. HPFS

18. What is an active partition?

    A. A partition currently in use

    B. A partition being created

    C. A partition that an operating system can boot from

    D. A partition that an operating system can write to

19. How many active partitions can Windows 98 support?

    A. 1

    B. 2

    C. 4

    D. 7 – on a SCSI bus

20. How large can a FAT32 partition be?

    A. 4 GB

    B. 100 GB

    C. 2 TB

    D. 16 Exabytes

21. Which file system allows security to the file level?

    A. FAT16

    B. FAT32

    C. NTFS

    D. NTSF

22. Which backup type backs up only files that have changed since the last backup?

    A. Normal

    B. Incremental

    C. Differential

    D. Daily

23. How many minutes of music can an audio CD hold?

    A. 60

    B. 67

    C. 74

    D. 120

24. Which technology is best suited for digital video cameras?

    A. USB

    B. IEEE-1394

    C. SCSI

    D. Parallel

25. A docking station combines the portability of a laptop with the convenience of a _____.

    A. Modem

    B. Desktop

    C. Full-sized keyboard

    D. NIC

Scenarios

You learned much about peripherals and mobile computers in this chapter. The following scenarios give you the opportunity to apply what you've learned. Find a solution for the following two scenarios:

    1. You are a consultant for a small company. Your contact at the company informs you that she will be in and out of the office over the next few months. She asks you to help her find a configuration, device, or utility that will allow her to quickly and easily take her data with her from the office network and onto the road and back again. What are some options for this user?

2. You are a hardware technician for a marketing company. A user reports that he is having trouble configuring his new 21-inch monitor for desktop publishing and needs your help configuring the video card and monitor. What activities will you need to do to configure the card and monitor?

Lab Exercises

Lab 10.1 Configuring a Monitor on Windows 2000

1. Select Start ➪ Settings ➪ Control Panel.

2. Open the Display applet in the Control Panel and then select the Settings tab.

3. In the lower left-hand corner, you can change the color palette based on the type of video card you have installed. Choose a different color setting and then choose Apply to sample the new settings.

4. Windows asks if you'd like to keep these settings. Choose Cancel.

5. In the lower left-hand corner you can adjust the resolution. Move the slider to 640 × 480 and then click Apply to sample the settings.

6. Move the slide to the highest resolution your monitor supports and then click Apply.

7. Set the resolution for what is comfortable on your eyes. Apply and approve the settings.

Lab 10.2 Creating a Hardware Profile

1. Select Start ➪ Settings ➪ Control Panel.

2. Open the Systems applet and choose Hardware Profiles.

3. Click the Original Configuration and then choose Copy to create a new profile to work with.

4. Name this profile (something like On the Road is good).

5. Close the Control Panel and restart the computer. During the boot phase, choose the On the Road profile.

6. Choose Start ➪ Settings ➪ Control Panel and open the System applet.

7. Select the Device Manager tab and click the plus symbol (+) next to the Network Adapter container to collapse the list of devices, then select your network adapter card.

8. Open the properties for the card.

9. In the Device Usage section, disable the card in this hardware profile. Choose OK and exit the System applet. The card is now disabled whenever the On the Road profile is loaded. When the original configuration is loaded, the network card will be working.

Answers to Chapter Questions

Chapter Pre-Test

1. Resolution refers to **the amount of pixels required to draw an image on a monitor.** The more pixels used, the higher the resolution.

2. The refresh rate refers to **the amount of times the electron gun scans from left to right and from top to bottom to redraw the images on the monitor.**

3. A modem modulates **digital signal into analog signal.** On the receiving end, the analog signal is then demodulated back to digital.

4. Modems are measured in **kilobits per second.** For example, a 56K modem would transfer 56,000 bits per second.

5. A computer that houses IDE drives is limited to **two drives.**

6. Windows 2000 can read **FAT, FAT32, and NTFS file systems.**

7. USB can have speeds up to **12Mbps.**

8. IEEE-1394 **offers extremely fast data transfer** — upwards of 400MBps!

9. A hardware profile is **a computer configuration used to load certain devices in a given environment.**

10. A laptop must have **a network card installed and a properly configured protocol.**

Assessment Questions

1. **C.** Resolution refers to the number of pixels required to draw an image on a monitor. For more information, see the section labeled "Monitor/Video Card."

2. **B.** There are 786,432 pixels used for a screen resolution of 1024×768. To get this answer, multiply 1024 by 768. For more information, see the section labeled "Monitor/Video Card."

3. **A.** Phosphors on the back of a computer's screen glow when an electron strikes them. For more information, see the section labeled "Monitor/Video Card."

4. **A.** An electron gun fires a beam of electrons at the back of a computer monitor to redraw the screen. The gun shoots from left to right and from top to bottom. For more information, see the section labeled "Monitor/Video Card."

5. **B.** The refresh rate refers to the number of times the electron gun is able to redraw the screen. For more information, see the section labeled "Monitor/Video Card."

6. **D.** Dot pitch is the distance between two dots of the same color on a monitor. The closer the dots, the better the quality of the monitor. For more information, see the section labeled "Monitor/Video Card."

7. **B.** Safety first! Before performing any upgrade that requires the case's cover to be removed, you should always power down the computer and unplug all cables. For more information, see the section labeled " Monitor/Video Card."

8. **B, D.** A modem is capable of sending faxes, connecting to an Internet service provider, and performing many other jobs. A modem does not however, connect the PC to the local network—a network card does this. Nor does a modem act as a pager. For more information, see the section labeled "Modems."

9. **D.** For a true 56K connection, the caller and the receiver must both have a modem capable of speeds of 56K. For more information, see the section labeled "Modems."

10. **A.** Modems use RJ-11 transceivers. This is standard phone cord. Networks use RJ-45 cable, which looks similar to RJ-11 cable, but is larger in size. For more information, see the section labeled "Modems."

11. **C.** Should Windows 9x fail to detect a modem through Plug-and-Play, the modem can be added manually through the Modem applet in Control Panel. For more information, see the section labeled "Modems."

12. **B.** An IDE partition can only be up to 512MB in size. For more information, see the section labeled "Storage devices."

13. **B.** An IDE drive has the controller integrated into the drive housing. The ribbon from the drive connects to a connector on the motherboard or to a pass-through board, which, unfortunately, is sometimes referred to as a controller card. For more information, see the section labeled " Storage devices."

14. **B.** One advantage EIDE drives have over IDE drives is that up to four drives can be used in one computer (as opposed to two drives with IDE). For more information, see the section labeled "Storage devices."

15. **D.** An internal SCSI drive connects to a ribbon with a 50-pin connector. For more information, see the section labeled "Storage devices."

16. **D.** Windows 9x does not use a disk management tool to create partitions like Windows 2000 does. FDISK is the utility to create partitions in Windows 9x. For more information, see the section labeled "Storage devices."

17. **A, B.** Windows 98 allows you to format drives with FAT or FAT32. Partitions over 512MB should use the FAT32 file system for better performance. For more information, see the section labeled "Storage devices."

18. **C.** The active partition is the partition that the operating system uses to boot from. For more information, see the section labeled "Storage devices."

19. A. You can change the active partition if you need to boot under a different operating system, but you can still use only one active partition at a time. For more information, see the section labeled "Storage devices."

20. C. FAT32 partitions can be up to two terabytes in size. FAT16 partitions are limited to 512MB in size. For more information, see the section labeled "Storage devices."

21. C. NTFS allows security to the file level. This allows for files within the same directory to have varying permissions. For more information, see the section labeled "Storage devices."

22. C. Differential backups back up all files that have changed since the last backup. A backup operator can easily restore the data by restoring the last normal backup and then the last differential backup. For more information, see the section labeled "Storage devices."

23. C. A CD can contain 650MB of data and can contain up to 74 minutes of sounds. For more information, see the section labeled "Storage devices."

24. B. IEEE-1394, or FireWire, is best suited for digital video cameras as the technology offers high-speed connections between the device and the PC. For more information, see the section labeled "IEEE-1394."

25. B. A docking station allows a user to go on the road and back again with the same computer. There's no need for synchronization between two machines, as the user can use the docking station in the office and the laptop on the road. For more information, see the section labeled "Portables."

Scenarios

1. There are several options for this user, all varying in price and configuration. For starters, an external USB drive, such as a ZIP drive, allows the user to move data from her desktop to her PC on the road. Another option would be to install a modem on her workstation and laptop and then allow her to dial into her computer directly from the road. The final option, and probably the best, is to purchase a docking station for the user. She can then use the mobile computer as a laptop on the road and as a workstation while in the office.

2. To configure a monitor and video card, you need to examine the properties of the video card and confirm that the correct driver has been installed. You can do this through the Display applet in Control Panel. Once the correct driver has been installed for the monitor and video card, the monitor settings need to be configured. You need to configure the amount of colors to be used on the monitor; for desktop publishing, the highest color available is recommended. In addition, the resolution for the monitor will need to be set. Again, for desktop publishing purposes, a high resolution is most likely needed. Have the user test the colors and settings with you to confirm that they like the configuration before you're done setting up the PC.

Portable Devices

◆ ◆ ◆ ◆

EXAM OBJECTIVES

Exam 220-201 ✦ A+ Core Hardware

✦ **1.1** Identify basic terms, concepts, and functions of system modules, including how each module should work during normal operation and during the boot process. Examples of concepts and modules are: LCD (portable systems)

✦ **1.2** Identify basic procedures for adding and removing field replaceable modules for both desktop and portable systems. Examples of modules: Memory; Processor board; Hard drive; Keyboard; Video board. Portable system components: AC adapter; DC controller; LCD panel; PC Card

✦ **1.7** Identify proper procedures for installing and configuring peripheral devices. Content may include the following: Portables: PC cards

✦ **1.8** Identify hardware methods of upgrading system performance, procedures for replacing basic subsystem components, unique components and when to use them. Content may include the following: Portable systems: Battery; Hard Drive; Type I, II, and III cards; Memory

CHAPTER PRE-TEST

1. The four types of CMOS batteries are _____, _____, _____, and _____.

2. What are the functions of an AC adapter?

3. What hard disk characteristics influence its performance?

4. What is the function of a DC controller?

5. Type _____ PCMCIA card is used to add a hard drive to a portable computer.

6. Which PCMCIA cards provide network connectivity?

7. What are the different types of memory available on a video board?

8. Which LCD display category supports each pixel with its own transistor?

9. What is the most popular category of keyboards?

10. What type of memory does a portable computer normally use?

✦ Answers to these questions can be found at the end of the chapter. ✦

Do they have a computer I can use for my presentation? How do I carry and present all this information to the client? Familiar questions? If your job requires you to be on the move, these are questions that you frequently ask. What do you do? Carrying your computer may be the only solution that eliminates your apprehensions. But can you carry your computer?

A standard desktop computer can be carried, but it's inconvenient. It's large, heavy, awkward, and impractical because of the size and weight of the system and power-consumption by the CPU and monitor. Even if you can carry the computer, an appropriate wall outlet may be unavailable in cars, airplanes, and public places. Therefore, portable computers should be

✦ Easily carried, like a handbag or briefcase

✦ Equipped with their own power supplies

Note The first portable computers were *luggable.* They were lighter and smaller than standard desktop computers, but you still needed to be strong as a mule, and they needed an external power supply.

State-of-the-art design allows for truly portable computers that fulfill these requirements, so you can work on the go. These take the form of *laptop, palmtop,* and *suitcase* computers. Today, laptop computers are the most popular portables.

This chapter identifies, installs, configures, and upgrades special portable computer components, such as *batteries, hard drives, memory,* and *power systems.* Procedures in this chapter guide you through installation and removal of these modules.

Portable Computer Components

There are many vendors — such as Dell, Acer, IBM, and Compaq — that offer various makes of portable systems. Regardless of the make, all the portable systems have some components that are common. In other words, every make of portable computer includes a battery, AC adapter, DC controller, PC Cards, video board, processor board, LCD panel, keyboard, hard drive, and memory. Figure 11-1 displays these components.

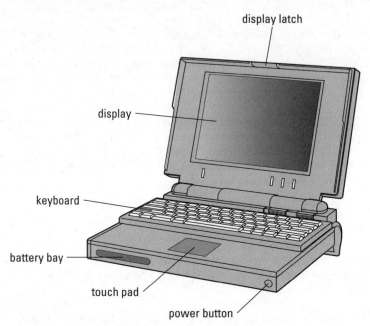

Figure 11-1: Major components of a portable system

The major components of a portable system are discussed in detail in the following list:

- ✦ **Batteries.** Free your system from wall sockets and extension cords.

- ✦ **AC adapters.** Convert analog signals to digital, so that your system can operate successfully. AC adapters also recharge the battery of your portable system.

- ✦ **DC controllers.** Protect voltage-sensitive devices (cards, chips, adapters, and circuitry) on the motherboard from sudden power surges.

- ✦ **Type I, II, and III cards.** Attach such components as external drives, modems, LAN adapters.

- ✦ **Video boards.** Remove color-display calculations from the microprocessor for sharp, faster display of images.

- ✦ **Processor boards.** Like the motherboard in a desktop computer.

- ✦ **LCD panels.** Display devices that replace standard CRT monitors.

- ✦ **Keyboard.**

- ✦ **Hard drives.** Storage devices that are physically smaller than desktop computer hard drives with the same capacity.

- ✦ **Memory.** Stores information. *SIMM* and *DIMM* cards are the common memory modules of a portable computer.

Batteries

1.8 Identify hardware methods of upgrading system performance, procedures for replacing basic subsystem components, unique components and when to use them. Portable Systems: Battery

A battery allows a portable computer to operate without an AC power source, thereby making it portable in the true sense. (Otherwise, you would need very long extension cords.)

Portable computers include *power management functions* (either built-in or through special device drivers). These functions make the portable PC "go to sleep" when there has been no input from the keyboard for a preset time period. The computer runs, but power drawing features like the screen are suspended until you "wake" your PC by pressing a key. When the PC is sleeping, the battery isn't being used, thus preserving the life of the battery.

A portable computer has two battery types:

✦ **Main battery.** Powers the computer while it runs. Also powers the RTC chip when the computer is switched off. There are four main battery types:

- **Alkaline.** Normally used in palmtop computers. These are the batteries that you use in calculators and TV remote controls.

- **NiCad (Nickel-Cadmium).** Common batteries in portable computers. These are the heaviest, least expensive batteries. They need to be recharged after 3 or 4 hours of use.

- **Li-Ion (Lithium-Ion).** Light, long-lasting alternative to NiCad batteries. They're very expensive.

 Exam Tip   On the exam, you might need to know which is the best battery for a portable PC. The answer is a Li-Ion battery. It may be more expensive than other types of CMOS batteries, but it provides the best durability, cost, and performance.

- **NiMH (Nickel-Metal Hydride).** Environmentally-friendly batteries that don't contain toxic metals. The same weight as NiCad batteries, but more expensive and can't be reused as many times.

✦ **CMOS battery.** Saves the computer's BIOS setup configuration, allowing the computer to successfully reboot every time. When the computer is switched off, this battery maintains the computer's date and time.

 Tip   A *smart battery* has its own power circuitry, which monitors the battery performance, output voltage, and temperature, and communicates the status to the processor. It's 15 percent more efficient than other batteries, and it's the most expensive type.

Handling batteries

Batteries contain toxic chemicals. If not properly handled, they can explode, harming you and your computer. Follow these guidelines:

✦ Keep batteries away from fire and water.

✦ Never open or dismantle batteries.

✦ Don't drop or throw batteries.

✦ Follow the manufacturer's guidelines.

Maximizing battery performance

To maximize portable computer battery performance, follow these guidelines:

✦ Fully charge and discharge a new battery, or a battery that has not been in use for a long time. A battery is generally discharged to increase its longevity. To discharge a battery, plug in your portable computer and leave it on overnight or longer, if necessary. Once the battery is discharged, the computer will shut down. You can then recharge the battery using the AC adapter.

Tip   You should charge and discharge a new battery, or a battery that hasn't been used for a long time, approximately two to four times to maximize its performance.

✦ Regularly charge and discharge batteries completely every two to three weeks, to keep them healthy. (You need not do this for a Li-Ion battery.)

✦ Keep batteries clean. This helps maintain a good connection between the battery and the portable device.

✦ Don't leave batteries dormant for long periods of time.

✦ Store batteries in a cool, dry, clean place away from heat and other metallic objects if you aren't planning to use it for a long time.

✦ Don't connect the PC to the AC adapter all the time. This wears the batteries faster than usual.

✦ Don't operate the PC while its battery is recharging.

✦ Switch off the PC when you aren't planning to use it for a while, even if it has sleep mode.

Changing batteries

Your computer generates the message "Invalid Configuration. Run Setup or press F1 to continue." But when you press F1, you get another message, "Invalid Drive Specification," and your computer stops functioning. It's time to change the computer's battery. To change the battery:

1. Record the current CMOS settings.

   To do this, turn on (or restart) the computer and display the CMOS settings.

   You can either jot down the settings or press the Print Screen key to print the displayed settings. You may need this information if you lose your computer's current settings.

2. Turn off the computer.

3. If the computer is connected to the AC adapter, unplug it.

4. Disconnect such peripheral components as printers, modems, and networks.

5. Remove the existing battery.

   The existing battery may be

   - In the holder at the bottom of the computer. (If so, the hatch slides out easily.)

   - Attached to the computer (in which case you may need to unscrew it, release a lock, or lift the keyboard).

6. Replace the old battery with the new one that you've purchased.

   Make sure that the battery is replaced in exactly the same configuration and polarity (+ and − settings). If in doubt, check the documentation.

Caution   After you have opened your computer, replace the battery immediately. If you delay, the battery or the computer may be damaged.

7. Close the computer and plug in the AC adapter.

8. Start the computer. Reset the computer date and time, if necessary.

AC Adapters

Objective   **1.2** Identify basic procedures for adding and removing field replaceable modules for both desktop and portable systems. Portable System Components: AC adapter

The *AC (Alternating Current) adapter* may not be new to you. It's used in a range of electronic devices, from electric shavers to PDAs (Personal Digital Assistants), and so on. Also known as an *AC/DC adapter*, it's an interface between your computer and the AC outlet. It converts the AC power from the wall socket into DC power. While it provides power to run your portable PC immediately, it also recharges the battery so you can use the computer later without plugging into a wall socket.

In desktop computers, adapters are typically printed circuit boards. For many portable computers, adapters are built into the computer. However, if adapters aren't built into the computer, they're integrated with a cable that plugs into the portable computer.

These adapters use the *Switchmode Power Supply* technology. Therefore, they're quite small and light. Since they use high frequency inverters, the outputs are regulated. They accept *universal power*—90 to 250 volts, AC or DC.

 Caution Always use an AC adapter that was shipped with your portable computer or is recommended by the manufacturer. Other adapters may fit your computer, but the voltage and amperage requirements may not match. In this case, you may damage or destroy your portable PC.

AC adapter problems

The most common problems related to the AC adapters are:

✦ Cable problems, such as broken wires either at the device end or at the wall outlet, due to excessive flexing of the cable.

✦ Internal electronic faults, such as blown fuse, bad startup resistor, and shorted or open semiconductors.

AC adapter troubleshooting and repair

If your computer is connected to an AC power supply, you may face a cable problem or an internal fault related to the AC adapter. If you don't look into these problems immediately, your computer may stop functioning. To repair broken wires, follow these steps:

1. Flex the cable to locate where it bends most easily. The cable will flex more easily where the conductor is broken.

2. Cut the cable where it's broken, then strip the cable until the copper wire is exposed.

3. Solder the wire ends together.

 Tip Different wires in an electrical system have different color codes. Make sure that you match the wire codes before soldering. This will help you avoid soldering wrong wires together. If in doubt, refer to the product manual.

4. Insulate the wire with several layers of electrical tape.

 Caution Ensure that you haven't interchanged the wires for DC output adapters. Also, verify polarity after the repair with a Voltmeter.

In case of blown fuses, bad startup resistors, and shorted or open semiconductors, the cost-effective solution is to buy a new AC adapter.

Tip Follow the same procedure if the break is at the device plug end. You may decide to buy a replacement plug rather than attempt to salvage the older one.

DC Controllers

 1.2 Identify basic procedures for adding and removing field replaceable modules for both desktop and portable systems. Portable system components: DC controller

The motherboard and other cards are sensitive devices that react badly to even minimal power surges. Even a slight variation in voltage can damage the board beyond repair. A *DC (Direct Current) controller* is an *IC (Integrated Chip)* that provides high performance adjustable power supply to the motherboard and other cards that require a very fast transient response and a high degree of accuracy (such as drives, memory, audio, and video). Generally, a DC controller uses the TTL-compatible five-bit digital code that adjusts the output voltage between 1.30V and 2.05V in 50 mV increments.

A typical DC controller in a portable system has these features:

✦ **Voltage monitor.** The DC controller monitors the supply voltage to both +5V and +12V pins.

✦ **UVLO (Under-Voltage-Lock-Out).** Initiates the *soft-start process* if the supply voltage passes the UVLO threshold. Soft-start controls the output peak voltage (both lower and higher).

✦ **OCP (Over-Current Protection).** Starts the *hiccup mode*, which reinitiates the soft-start process when the current exceeds its maximum limits. The process keeps the current within the maximum limit.

✦ **OVP (Over-Voltage Protection).** Prevents the output voltage from exceeding the maximum and minimum limits.

✦ **Internal Timer.** Controls the off-time of the circuit so that the switching-frequency is always 250KHz under steady-state operation.

PC Cards

 1.2 Identify basic procedures for adding and removing field replaceable modules for both desktop and portable systems. Portable system components: PC Card

 1.7 Identify proper procedures for installing and configuring peripheral devices. Portables: PC Cards

 1.8 Identify hardware methods of upgrading system performance, procedures for replacing basic subsystem components, unique components and when to use them. Portable Systems: Type I, II, III cards

Unlike desktop PCs, portable systems don't have standard expansion slots for the peripheral device connections. The expansion slots in a desktop computer allow additional devices to be attached to the computer. However, due to size and weight constraints, these slots are not available in the portable computers. Instead, they have expansion slots called *PC Card* slots or *Personal Computer Memory Card International Association* (PCMCIA) slots. PC Cards that can be inserted in these slots resemble a credit card in appearance and size, though they're slightly thicker. Originally, these slots were intended for memory expansion. But now, such devices as hard disks, CD-ROM, LAN cards, and modems can also be connected using these slots. A PC Card slot and a PC Card are shown in Figure 11-2.

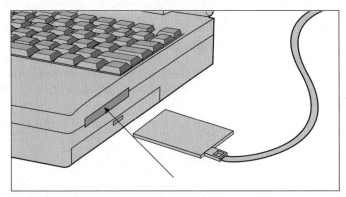

Figure 11-2: PCMCIA slot and card

A PC Card may have a data cable to the external power supply. For example, the card for a CD-ROM drive must be connected to a wall outlet for power supply. If the card doesn't contain the data cable, the care is *self-contained*, like a modem card that draws power from the battery instead of an AC outlet.

Depending on the size and number of connectors on the card, there are three standards for the PC Card slots:

✦ **Type I.** Up to 3.3 mm thick, with a single row of sockets. These usually add Static RAM (SRAM) to the portable system.

✦ **Type II.** Up to 5.5mm thick, with two rows of sockets and a pop-out RJ-45 or RJ-11 connector. These add modems and NICs to the portable system.

✦ **Type III.** Up to 10.5 mm thick, with three rows of sockets. These connect hard disk drives and adapters for CD-ROM, DVD, and tape drives.

Exam Tip   A common point of confusion in the A+ certification exam is which type of PC Card applies to a given situation. The rule of thumb for PC Cards is "the thicker the card, the higher its type." For example, a thick card needs a Type III slot. A thin card fits in a Type I slot.

Often, each type of slot is included in a portable PC. For better performance, look for a PCMCIA specification called *CardBus* slot. It's the latest slot type, and it increases I/O speed and supports 32-bit buses and low voltage.

To support PC Cards, the operating system in the portable computer must provide two services:

✦ **Socket service.** A BIOS-level service detects when a PC Card is inserted into or removed from the system and manages the sockets.

✦ **Card service.** This service provides the interface between the card and the device driver when the socket is closed. It manages the assignment and allocation of the system resources, such as I/O addresses and IRQs, to the PC Card.

Adding a PC card

One of the most popular features of a PC Card is *hot swapping*. This allows you to install a device while a computer is still running. The computer recognizes the device without rebooting. With this feature, you can remove a card and insert another without switching off the machine.

The steps for adding or installing a PC Card are:

1. Insert the card in the slot.

Make sure that the *notched* edge of the card goes in first.

Don't use extra pressure or force while inserting the card. You may damage the card and the slot.

2. Press the card into the connector so that it's firmly in place.

If the card is installed correctly, the Eject button (either inside the PCMCIA opening or on the side of computer next to the slot) pops out.

3. If a device driver comes with the card, install the driver.

Removing a PC Card

To remove a PC Card, press the Eject button. The card pops out. If it doesn't, either refer to the user manual or contact the support personnel.

Do not use the end of a paper and stick it in the slot. Portable computers are not as sturdy as desktop computers.

Caution   Make sure that any slots that aren't used are *closed* or *sealed.* The slot connectors are very small. Small amounts of dust can cause big trouble.

Video Boards

1.2 Identify basic procedures for adding and removing field replaceable modules for both desktop and portable systems. Examples of modules: Video board

The *video board* is the interface between the monitor and the computer. It converts the input from an application and instructs the monitor to depict the text or image. It's connected to the CPU by using the system bus. The bus speed can be a constraint on the speed of the image display. To solve this speed constraint and to depict the images in full color, the board has its own processor and memory. Newer video boards use the PCI bus and the AGP slot, which support 32-bit transfers at the speed of 533Mbps.

Tip   A video board is also known as a graphic adapter, graphic card, display card, or simply video adapter.

Here's how the video board functions:

1. Data travels from the processor/application via the system bus to the video chip set on the video board.

2. The video chip set writes the data to the video memory on the card.

3. The data is passed to the digital analog converter (RAM DAC). Here, it's converted from digital signals to analog.

4. The data is passed to the monitor, which displays the image.

Common video boards are:

✦ **Monochrome Display Adapter (MDA).** Displays text on a monochrome monitor. It's still used for servers and monitoring systems that don't need color display.

✦ **Color Graphics Adapter (CGA).** Displays four colors in a resolution of 320×200 and two colors with a resolution of 640×200. This was the first color adapter.

✦ **Enhanced Graphics Adapter (EGA).** Supports 16 colors at a resolution of 640×350. This is a digital adapter.

✦ **Video Graphics Adapter (VGA).** Supports 16 colors at a resolution of 640×480. At lower resolutions, it supports up to 256 colors.

✦ **Super VGA (SVGA).** Supports resolutions as high as 1280×1024, and up to 16 million colors. SVGA adds a few features to standard VGA.

Tip
Most new portable computers have SVGA or higher video boards, such as eXtended SVGA (XGA).

Video board features

A video board displays the output of an application as text or image on the computer screen. Although all the video boards provide varied video resolution capability and color depth and range, newer video boards have a video *coprocessor* that processes most of the display calculations. This leaves the processor with fewer video commands to process. These cards are also known as *accelerated video cards* or *graphics accelerators*. Watch for these important features when you choose a video board: resolution, colors, and interlacing.

Resolution and Colors

Resolution is determined by:

✦ The number of pixels that make an image

✦ How closely the pixels are packed

If you want a video board to support high resolutions, buy one that is powerful enough.

The number of colors that a video card supports also increases the memory requirement of the card. For example, CGAs can support up to 4 colors, EGAs can support up to 16 colors, VGAs can support up to 256 colors (at a resolution of 320×200), and SVGAs can support up to 16 million colors. Higher resolution and more colors require an expensive video card.

Interlacing

Interlacing is the frequency with which the image is refreshed per second. Frequent interlacing hampers the quality of the image, resulting in a flickering screen (also known as *ghosting* effect), eyestrain, and a headache. To escape these problems, you should ensure that the card is non-interlaced. The ideal vertical refresh rate is 72Hz.

Video memory

Since the amount of data required for a color display can be large, memory on a video card is justified. The memory on a video card is known as the *video memory*. Video memory is available in sizes of 256K, 512K, 1MB, and more. Original video memory was DRAM. It needed constant refreshing, when it became inaccessible. This hampered the card's performance. This led to the development of new memory types:

✦ **Video RAM (VRAM).** Needs lesser refreshing than DRAM. It can be read and written simultaneously. It's a dual-port memory, which means that the video chip set and the RAM DAC can access the video memory simultaneously. This considerably improves the performance of the card.

✦ **Multibank DRAM (MDRAM).** Designed so that the full width of the video bus can be utilized with lesser number of memory chips.

✦ **Windows RAM (WRAM).** Accessible in blocks/chunks, which makes the data transfer faster than more-expensive VRAM. It's also a dual-port memory that supports full-motion video.

✦ **Synchronous Graphics RAM (SGRAM).** A single-port memory, four times faster than other types of DRAM memory. It synchronizes with the CPU clock, which makes it faster.

✦ **3D RAM.** Designed for video processing involving 3-D graphics. 3-D processing logic is embedded in the card itself.

A video card has a separate device driver for each resolution or color depth. This is why you may need to reboot the computer (if you are running Windows 95 or earlier versions of Windows) when you change the display settings. Rebooting the computer loads the new device driver that you choose. However, you would not need to reboot the computer if it has a Windows 98 or later version.

Video board installation

To install the video card, open the system cover and follow these steps:

1. Insert the card into the corresponding slot.

   Make sure that the card is inserted properly, or the card may be damaged.

2. Turn on the computer to verify that the computer is booting properly.

3. Turn off the computer.

4. Secure the card in the slot with a screw.

Caution While securing the video board in the slot, don't exert extra force. It may harm the motherboard.

5. Turn on the computer and configure the drivers for the card, if necessary.

6. Close the system.

Processor Boards

1.2 Identify basic procedures for adding and removing field replaceable modules for both desktop and portable systems. Examples of modules: Processor boards

Portable computers have a strict restriction on space and size. As a result, portable PCs have a *closed architecture*. They don't have standard expansion slots. Instead, all the functions are built into the system board (or the motherboard) itself.

In a portable system, the processor board is where you find most of the logic circuitry of your computer. It also has interfaces to any external (peripheral) devices your computer may have. Also, the processor board is the host of the most important chip of your computer, the CPU (Central Processing Unit).

Processor board components

The typical components of a processor board include the Central Processing Unit (CPU), system clock, Complementary Metal-Oxide Semiconductor (CMOS), Read-Only Memory Basic Input/Output System (ROM-BIOS), Random Access Memory (RAM), system buses, and ports.

✦ **CPU.** The most common processors that you find in portable PCs are Intel's Pentium and 486. You may see an occasional 386 and 286, too. CPU models can be categorized as follows:

- **ZIF (Zero-Insertion-Force).** A lever next to the chip socket allows you to replace the CPU. It's soldered to the motherboard, which makes it slightly difficult to upgrade.

- **PGA (Pin-Grade-Array).** Looks like a conventional chip with pins at the bottom. It's one of the thickest CPU chips. It occupies more space, is heavier than the others, and generates more heat. It's found in the earliest portable PCs.

- **VRT (Voltage-Reduction Technology).** Accepts normal voltage (3.3V) from the system board, but uses less voltage (2.9V). This technology of converting a higher voltage to a lower voltage is known as *split-voltage technology*. This CPU generates less heat and consumes less power, thus increasing battery life.

- **TCP (Tape-Carrier Packaging).** It's pinless and smaller, thereby saving space. It also generates less heat and is capable of split-voltage. It's the best CPU for portable computers.

✦ **System clock.** Supplies common time to all the cards and chips connected to the motherboard by providing a continuous pulse even when the computer is switched off. This keeps all the devices *synchronized*, which is very important for them to communicate successfully with each other.

✦ **CMOS (Complementary Metal-Oxide Semiconductor).** Stores all the information needed by your computer to boot. This may include information about floppy drives, hard drives, RTC, keyboard, and all the other peripheral devices. CMOS is powered by the CMOS battery.

✦ **ROM BIOS (Basic Input/Output System).** The firmware that is built into your portable PC. It controls all the input/output functions of your computer, such as communication with hard drives, floppy drives, memory, monitor, and other peripheral devices.

✦ **RAM (Random Access Memory) and RAM Cache.** The primary storage device of a computer, which is represented by SIMM and DIMM modules.

✦ **System bus.** Connects the CPU with the RAM chips on the motherboard. (Also known as *memory bus* or *host bus*.)

✦ **Ports.** The physical connector at the back of the computer that allows the motherboard (and thus processor) to be connected to the various peripheral devices.

Power cords

Power cords provide power to all the components of the computer. They run from the power unit (SMPS) to all the boards and chips.

CPU, ROM BIOS chip, CMOS battery, RAM and RAM cache are known as *field replaceable units* because they can be replaced or upgraded without changing the processor board.

Selecting a processor board for a portable system

Buy a portable PC only after carefully considering the processor board that it uses. The processor board determines the following:

✦ Speed of your portable computer

✦ Type and size of memory (such as SDRAM, SIMMs, DIMMs, and EDO)

✦ Type and number of expansion slots (such as ISA, EISA, VESA, PCI, and AGP)

✦ ROM BIOS

✦ Various adapters and controllers

✦ Various ports (such as keyboard, mouse, COM, and LPT)

✦ Buses

Caution   If you are a novice, don't try to install or remove the processor board of your portable system. Removing or installing the processor board and the CPU without damaging them requires an expert's skill. Let an experienced technician handle it.

LCD Panels

 1.1 Identify basic terms, concepts and functions of system modules, including how each module should work during normal operation and during the boot process. Examples of concepts and modules are: LCD (portable systems)

 1.2 Identify basic procedures for adding and removing field replaceable modules for both desktop and portable systems. Portable system components: LCD panel

A Liquid Crystal Display (LCD) panel projects computer images from a desktop/ laptop onto a big screen by using an overhead projector. Apart from images, you can project from text, data, graphics, and animation with ease. Generally, this device is in classrooms and training centers for showing computer or video images to a larger audience.

The monitor of a portable system is essentially an LCD display. The biggest disadvantage of an LCD panel is that it's very expensive.

The major categories of LCD panels in portable computers are listed below:

✦ **Mono.** The original monochromatic LCDs belong to this category. They consume the least power and cost less.

✦ **Active matrix.** This category has a transistor for each pixel to create very crisp images with high resolution. These images are easy to view, even from an angle. Active matrix displays refresh themselves quickly so that the ghosting effect isn't visible. They're transistor-based, so they require a lot of power. Mostly you see them in your watches, but they're also very popular in portable computers.

✦ **TFT (Thin Film Transistor).** This is another category that is classed with active matrix displays. The difference is that the screen width of a TFT panel is less than the active-matrix display screen width. They're more expensive than the active matrix displays.

✦ **Passive matrix.** This category has a corresponding transistor for each vertical column of the pixels and one for each horizontal row of pixels. It doesn't use much power, but it's slower and produces lower-quality images. It has a narrower viewing area than active matrix displays, but some people prefer these for added privacy while traveling. Dual-Scan is classed with passive matrix.

In addition, you may come across Super-Twist (monochromatic and usually obsolete) and Plasma (bright orange and yellow LED, power consuming, and quite expensive) LCD categories, though both of them aren't much in use anymore.

There are different types of LCD panels, such as TN (Twisted Nematic), HTN (Higher Twisted Nematic), STN (Super Twisted Nematic), FSTN (Film Compensated STN), EL (Electro-Luminescent), LED (Light Emitting Diode) and CCFL (Cold

Cathode Fluorescent Light). LED is most popular because of low voltage consumption, long life (50,000 hours at an average), noiselessness, multi-colored display, and easy brightness adjustability.

Connecting an LCD panel to a computer

The monitor (or display) is fixed to your portable computer by hinges. To replace the old display with a new one, follow these steps:

1. In most modern portable systems, you press the spring of the hinges gently to detach the old LCD panel. Consult the owner's manual if you can't detach the panel.

2. Slide the new LCD panel firmly in place.

3. Close the system and reopen it to verify if you fixed the LCD panel correctly. If it easily closes and opens, you replaced the LCD panel successfully.

Caution

LCD panels aren't repairable. If you damage them while installing (even with your fingernails), you have to get them replaced. Be very careful!

Handling LCD panels

Take the following precautions while working with LCD panels:

✦ Make sure that the temperature and humidity is maintained within the correct range — humidity below 60 percent and temperature not more than 40 degrees C. Excessive temperature and humidity can cause polarization degradation or bubble generation, rendering your LCD panel unusable.

✦ Don't scrub the display surface vigorously or touch it with anything that has sharp edges. To clean the display surface, wipe it gently with a soft cloth soaked in petroleum benzene.

✦ Prevent contact with water or any other liquid for a long time. This could result in polarizer deformation, color fading, or corrosion of electrodes.

✦ DC voltage damages the LCD and shortens the display life. Therefore, don't use DC voltage for LCD panels. Also, store LCDs in dark places.

Caution

The LCD display is the weakest part of your portable PC. Don't lift the computer by its screen, and don't open it, close it or pull it with force.

Keyboards

1.2 Identify basic procedures for adding and removing field replaceable modules for both desktop and portable systems. Examples of modules: Keyboard

The *keyboard* is the most common PC input device, which helps you communicate with the computer by translating the keystrokes into corresponding letters, numbers, or commands in the following manner:

1. Pressing a key completes an electrical circuit to generate a *make code*.

2. Releasing the key breaks the circuit. This generates the *break code* signal.

3. The *keyboard microprocessor* generates the *scan code* (or *key id*) using the make code, break code, and location of the key on the keyboard.

4. The *keyboard driver* (part of system BIOS) converts the scan code into the corresponding character according to the language configured on the keyboard.

There are three common categories of keyboard interfaces that you generally come across in a portable PC, though XT and AT keyboards are nearly obsolete. The categories of keyboards are:

✦ **Enhanced keyboard.** It has 101 keys including 12 function keys, numeric keypad, cursor control keys, and screen control keys. The biggest benefit of this keyboard is that it's compatible with every other available keyboard interface. Also known as a *PS/2* keyboard, it's the most common type.

✦ **XT keyboard.** It has 83 regular keys and 10 function keys. In addition, it has a numeric keypad and cursor control keys integrated into a 5" × 3" area on the right side of the keyboard. The keyboard processor is located in the keyboard itself.

✦ **AT keyboard.** It has 84 regular keys, 10 function keys, and an additional SysReq (SysRq) key. The Return (Enter) key is bigger than the XT keyboard key. It was originally designed for OS/2 computers. The keyboard processor is located on the motherboard.

Note A fourth type of keyboard is an enhanced keyboard with built-in wrist-rest. It has an arched shape. This type of keyboard is known as the *ergonomic* keyboard.

Exam Tip On the exam, you might be asked what keyboard is generally found in the portable systems. The answer is the enhanced keyboard.

Depending on the key mechanism they use, two basic types of keyboards are used in portable computers.

✦ **Switch-based.** These keyboards use micro-switches for each key. The keys deteriorate with time and tend to get dirty. They aren't expensive.

✦ **Capacitive.** Also known as *membrane keyboards*. They're expensive, but more reliable. There is a large capacitive surface at the bottom of the keyboard. Each key pushes a spring, which pushes a paddle. This creates an impression on the capacitive surface, which sends a signal that is interpreted by the keyboard processor. This is the most common type of keyboard in portable computers.

Exam Tip   On the exam, you might be asked about the IRQ and the I/O address assigned to a keyboard. Like desktop keyboards, a keyboard in a portable system is assigned IRQ 1 and 060 as the I/O address.

The keyboard software of your system is of two types:

✦ **Firmware.** Stored on ROM, keyboard, or the motherboard. It has hardware and BIOS information, port assignments, and boot sequence support data.

✦ **Device driver.** Communicates directly with the device and the operating system, and acts as the software interface during normal operations.

Maintaining keyboards

You need to clean keyboards periodically. A lot of dust and other particles can accumulate between the keys. Because the portable PCs are small, the damage caused is more than on desktop PCs. Always ensure that the computer is switched off while you are performing the following maintenance activities:

✦ Turn the keyboard upside down and gently shake out loose dirt.

✦ Clean the key tops with a soft cloth dipped in an all-purpose cleaner.

✦ Clean between the keys with a lint-free swab.

Handling keyboard problems

Replacing a keyboard is far more efficient than repairing it. Use the following steps to troubleshoot any keyboard-related problems:

1. Check that the keyboard is seated correctly. You may have opened your computer and neglected to replace the keyboard correctly.

2. Switch off the computer and switch it on again. Rebooting the computer reloads the device drivers, which control the corresponding device.

3. Check the voltages of the connector pins (on the system unit) using a digital multimeter.

Tip If any voltages are less than 2V, or more than 5.5V, the problem is in the keyboard circuit in the system unit.

4. If nothing works, the keyboard needs to be replaced.

Hard Drives

Objective **1.2** Identify basic procedures for adding and removing field replaceable modules for both desktop and portable systems. Examples of modules: Hard drive

A hard drive is the *secondary storage* where you save most of your data (memory is the primary storage). This makes the hard drive one of the most valuable parts of your system. In contrast to memory, the data stored on the hard drive is permanent. This means that after switching off the computer, when you turn it on the next time, you can retrieve the data that you stored. Portable computers made before 1996 have 18mm full-height hard drives. Almost all new portable PCs use 2.5" slimline hard drives that are 11mm high.

Tip Drive A: and B: always refers to the floppy drive, whereas C: and onwards refer to the hard drives and CD-ROM drives.

Hard drive overview

Just like the hard drive of a desktop computer, the hard drive of a portable computer consists of at least two rigid circular metal disks, which are known as *platters*. These platters are stacked in an airtight compartment. Each side of the platter, also known as the *surface*, has a corresponding read/write head.

✦ Each surface is divided into concentric *tracks*. These tracks can range from 79 to 305, depending on whether the hard drive is an older or newer model. Figure 11-4 depicts the tracks on a hard drive.

✦ Each track is divided into a maximum of 63 *sectors* of 512 bytes each.

When similar numbered sectors on each surface of every head of the hard drive are aligned one over the other, they form a *cylinder*. An overview of the hard drive is shown in Figure 11-3.

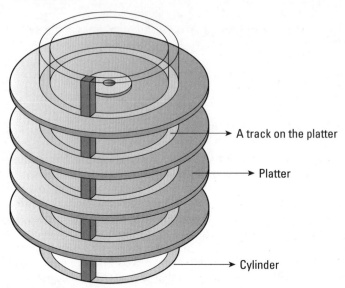

Figure 11-3: An overview of the hard drive

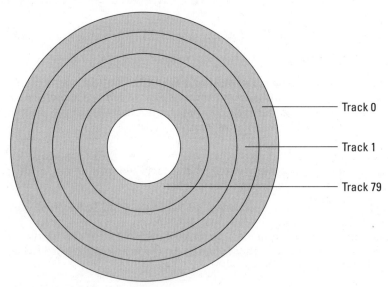

Figure 11-4: Tracks on a hard drive

Hard drive characteristics

There are a number of characteristics of a hard drive that influence the overall performance of your system—seek time, latency period, access time, and data transfer rate.

✦ **Seek time.** The time taken (5–16 milliseconds) by a head to position itself over a track. Lower seek times are critical for good drive performance. Seek times are a built-in characteristic of a drive. To improve a drive's seek time, replace it with a drive of better quality.

✦ **Latency period.** The time for a sector to move under the drive head. Like seek time, the latency period of a drive should also be as low as possible for better drive performance.

✦ **Access time.** The sum of the average seek time and the latency period. Both seek time and latency period should be as low as possible to improve the drive performance, so access time should be low, too.

✦ **Data transfer rate.** The speed with which the desired data is transferred to the RAM after it's located. The data transfer rate depends on such factors as *cache size available on the drive, access time of the drive,* and *the speed with which the drive interface can process the data.*

Tip

IDE drives are designed to provide maximum data transfer rate.

Interleave factor is the order in which the sectors are arranged when you low-level format the drive for the first time. Interleaving was introduced to eliminate the delays that occur when a drive cannot read or write the next sector after reading the previous sector. The latest PCs have an interleave factor of 1:1.

Hard drive performance

The following factors affect the performance of a hard drive:

✦ The drive should have considerable cache memory (64MB and more) to support high data transfer rates. At the same time, ensure that there isn't an excessive amount of cache memory; it may cause write-delays, which can reboot your computer without warning while you are working.

✦ Use drives with fast disk interfaces (such as IDEs and Enhanced IDEs) and fast buses. PCI- or VESA-based interface cards support the fastest buses.

✦ Install compression programs that help you effectively increase the amount of space that you can use. However, you should remember that the compression programs also slow down the data access rate. You'll have to carefully consider your priority.

✦ A PCMCIA hard drive helps improve the performance of your portable PC considerably.

✦ You can attach a removable media drive, such as a Zip drive, to the parallel port of your computer. This provides more disk space.

✦ Remove the current hard drive completely and replace it with a better or newer model.

Hard drive installation

There are many steps for installing a hard drive, but the steps may vary slightly for different drive types (such as SCSI, IDE, and EIDE). The steps for installing a hard drive are:

1. Assemble compatible hardware (drive, drive interface, and cables), depending on the type of hard drive you are installing. Your new hard drive should have capacity that fulfills your space requirement. The drive interface should support fast buses.

2. Open your computer. Some computers may need to be completely opened. For others, you just lift the keyboard by unsnapping it.

3. Locate the hard drive.

4. Remove the hard drive. For information, read the owner's manual or the documentation provided by the vendor.

   If you have more than one hard drive, you will need a second hard drive holder. Configure the drive jumper to ensure the drive's compatibility with other hard drives. You don't need to set jumpers if your system has a single hard drive. For multiple hard drives, place the jumper on the left-hand position (as shown in Figure 11-5) in the jumper block to make the drive the master. Set the jumper in the middle if the drive is a slave. These settings are depicted in Figure 11-6.

Tip   You should make the newer and faster drive the master.

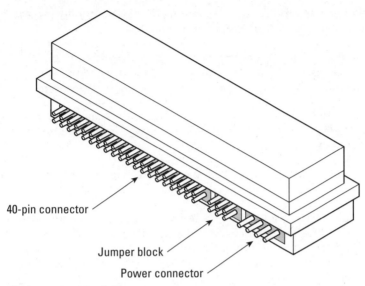

Figure 11-5: Hard drive

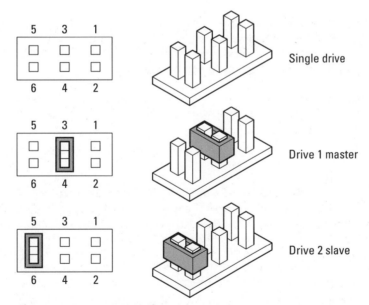

Figure 11-6: Jumper settings

5. Install the new hard disk in its mounting bracket. Carefully replace the bracket in the same position from where you detached it.

Caution   Make sure that the disk interface pins are properly aligned to the cable and connector to which they're attached. Otherwise, you may end up damaging the drive permanently.

6. Put the system back together completely. Carefully align and replace all the components (such as covers, snaps, and keyboard) in the order that you removed them.

Tip   Don't close the system as yet. You may need to open it if the installation wasn't successful.

7. Replace the battery and turn on the computer. If the memory test is complete, then the installation of the hard disk was successful. Otherwise, you have to repeat the process carefully. If the memory test runs successfully, the message "HDD Configuration Error" indicates that the hard disk is installed but not yet configured completely. This means that you are on the right track.

8. Configure the system's CMOS to store the information about the hard disk that you are installing.

Tip   CMOS is the built-in low-level software that controls your system's hard disk and stores all the operating system parameters. The new disk may not match your CMOS. In this case, you can get compatible BIOS, use utilities like BIOS Extender, or send it to an upgrade company to update your firmware BIOS.

9. If necessary, *low-level format* the disk. Usually, this is done during manufacturing. If your hard disk is already low-level formatted, skip to the next step.

10. Depending on your requirements, you may want the disk to act as a *single entity* or several smaller *logical drives*. In the latter case, you need to partition the hard disk.

Exam Tip   On the exam, you might be asked a question related to disk partitions. A partition is a portion of the physical hard disk that is treated by the operating system as a separate drive. You can use the FDISK, Disk Manager, or other utilities supported by the operating system you are using to create partitions.

11. High-level format the disk to get it ready for the operating system. The command is FORMAT <Disk_Name>. This command creates:

* DOS boot record (to start the operating system)

* FAT (File Allocation Table — the DOS file system)

* The root directory

12. When the computer is running, close it, put the keyboard back, and reinstall any screws that you removed in the process. Reconnect the printer, LAN card, and other peripherals that you disconnected in the beginning.

Memory

 1.2 Identify basic procedures for adding and removing field replaceable modules for both desktop and portable systems. Examples of modules: Memory

 1.8 Identify hardware methods of upgrading system performance, procedures for replacing basic subsystem components, unique components and when to use them. Content may include the following: Memory

Random Access Memory (RAM) is one of the most important components of your system. Your computer uses this memory to store program instructions, data, and intermediate results of processing. Even applications are first copied from the hard disk to the memory. Further execution and data processing takes place in the memory. Before anything is stored on the hard disk, it's temporarily stored in the memory. This is the reason why memory is known as the *primary storage device*. The amount of memory installed in your computer is a crucial factor affecting its performance.

 For more information regarding RAM and its different types, see Chapter 4.

Memory is a set of ICs (Integrated Chips) that store data (and instructions) as a series of 1s (on) and 0s (off). Memory requires constant power to store these patterns. In power failure, these patterns are lost and all the signals revert to off. This is why memory isn't a permanent storage device. Everything in the memory is lost after you switch off the PC or in case of power failure.

Most portable systems use *SIMMs (Single Inline Memory Module)* or *DIMMs (Dual Inline Memory Module)*, which are installed just as you install them in desktop computers.

Removing memory

To remove a memory module or card, follow these steps:

1. Switch off the PC, disconnect it from the AC adapter, and disconnect all the cables and peripheral devices.

2. Open up the system and locate the memory.

 Replace the existing memory, starting with the highest-numbered slot. Look for an indication of the memory slot with the highest number. You can get help on this by consulting the owner's manual. Otherwise, the company's tech support people can guide you.

3. Unhook the latches by pressing them away from the module. A gentle push does the job. Too much force may break the latches.

4. Tilt the module and slide it out gently to remove the memory module or slot.

Caution   Don't touch the connectors.

Upgrading memory

Upgrading memory is the most frequent improvement for better performance. In desktop computers, you can upgrade the RAM as much as you like, keeping the processor capability in mind. But in the case of portable systems, most of them have clear specifications on the type and speed of the RAM and the specific increments that you can add. Make sure that you get RAM faster than the existing RAM in your computer.

Tip   If your portable system has a proprietary module in place of generic SIMMs and DIMMs, you need to buy a single proprietary memory module of the exact size. Only one module can fit in such systems.

To upgrade the memory of your portable system, follow these steps:

1. You should always back up your hard disk before you do anything with your computer so that you can reload data if something goes wrong.

2. Make sure that the computer is turned off and disconnected from the AC adapter.

3. Remove the battery and disconnect all cables and peripheral devices.

   You should be well grounded and should touch something metallic before touching anything inside the system. This helps you discharge any static charge, which may be very harmful for your computer.

4. Open the computer to access the memory modules.

   Consult the system manual for information on how to locate them.

5. Insert the memory modules.

   If your system has prepackaged proprietary memory modules, you can simply slide the new memory module into the corresponding socket until it's in place.

   If your system has slots to accept SIMM or DIMM cards, you have to insert the card into an empty slot.

Caution   Make sure that you don't use much force or push the module until you feel the module snap-in. You may damage the memory module.

6. After the memory is correctly in place and installed, replace everything that you removed, such as drives, keyboard, cables, and battery.

7. Turn on the machine.

During the memory check, watch for the correct amount of memory. If the memory check finishes without a problem, you have installed the memory successfully. If not, repeat the installation process again.

Key Point Summary

In this chapter, you learned about various system modules of a portable PC and their functions, including:

✦ Battery

✦ AC adapter

✦ DC controller

✦ Type I, II, and III cards

✦ Video board

✦ Processor board

✦ LCD panel

✦ Keyboard

✦ Hard drive

✦ Memory

You learned in detail how each module works and the basic procedures for adding and removing these modules of a portable PC system.

✦　　✦　　✦

STUDY GUIDE

This Study Guide presents 22 assessment questions and 5 scenarios to test your knowledge of the exam topic area.

Assessment Questions

1. What is the most popular category of portable PCs?

    A. Notebook

    B. Laptop

    C. Palmtop

    D. Suitcase computer

2. Which battery type is the best for a portable computer?

    A. Alkaline

    B. NiCad

    C. Li-Ion

    D. NiMH

3. Which of the following system modules makes a PC really portable?

    A. Battery

    B. AC adapter

    C. DC controller

    D. PC Card

4. OCP, OVP, and UVLO are the characteristics of:

    A. AC adapter

    B. DC controller

    C. Video Board

    D. LCD Panel

5. Which of the following system modules supports hot-swapping?

   A. Keyboard

   B. Memory

   C. PC Cards

   D. None of the above

6. Which PCMCIA card type is used to connect a CD-ROM drive?

   A. Type I

   B. Type II

   C. Type III

   D. Type I and Type III collectively

7. Which of the following statements are true for card services? (Select all that apply)

   A. It provides an interface between the card and the slot when the card is inserted.

   B. It provides an interface between the card and the device driver when the card is inserted.

   C. It assigns I/O address and IRQ to the card.

   D. Both A and C.

8. Which of the following video adapters would you use for a Netware Server?

   A. MDA

   B. CGA

   C. EGA

   D. SVGA

9. What is a graphics accelerator?

   A. A type of video memory

   B. A function of video cards

   C. A video card with a video coprocessor

   D. A characteristic of video boards

10. Interlacing is the characteristic of which system module?

    A. Hard drive

    B. Keyboard

    C. Processor board

    D. Video board

11. Why do you need to reboot your computer after changing its display settings?

    A. To activate the video card

    B. To initialize the video memory

    C. To load the new device driver

    D. All of the above

12. LCD stands for:

    A. Liquid Crystalline Display

    B. Liquid Crystal Display

    C. Logical Crystal Display

    D. Liquid Crystal Device

13. Which statements are true for a passive matrix LCD display? (Select all that apply)

    A. It is slow.

    B. It displays crisp images.

    C. Each pixel is supported by its own transistor.

    D. Images are easy to read from angles.

    E. It displays low-quality pictures.

14. Which keyboard normally is used with portable PCs?

    A. Ergonomic

    B. AT

    C. XT

    D. Enhanced

15. Which of the following is NOT a disk performance characteristic?

    A. Interleaving

    B. Interlacing

    C. Data Transfer Rate

    D. Access Time

16. Which of the following are true for a hard drive? (Select all that apply)

    A. It is a primary storage device.

    B. It stores the data permanently.

    C. It is made of many platters.

    D. It is usually designated as A: and B:

17. Access time is:

    A. Seek time plus latency period

    B. Seek time minus latency period

    C. Latency period minus seek time

    D. Seek time times latency period

18. Hard drives of a portable PC have an interleave factor of:

    A. 1:3

    B. 3:1

    C. 1:1

    D. None of the above

19. Which of the following statements are NOT true regarding the memory of portable computers? (Select all that apply)

    A. It is the primary storage device.

    B. It is a permanent storage device.

    C. Intermediate results, data, and commands are stored in the memory until they're stored to hard disk.

    D. Portable PCs use SIMM but not DIMM.

20. What does the term *closed architecture* mean?

    A. The CPU is covered and protected.

    B. The processor board has all the functions hard-coded to compensate for the lack of expansion slots.

    C. The system board has expansion slots to provide connectivity to peripheral device.

    D. The hard disk platters are sealed in an air-tight box.

21. Which of the following processor board components is NOT field replaceable?

    A. CPU

    B. System Bus

    C. ROM BIOS

    D. CMOS Battery

22. CMOS stands for:

    A. Completely Metal-Oxide Semiconductor

    B. Complementary Metal-Oxide Socket

    C. Complementary Metal-Oxide Semiconductor

    D. None of the above

Scenarios

1. Anna is trying to install the PCMCIA modem card in her laptop, but even after inserting the card properly into the corresponding slot, the system doesn't recognize the card. What could be the problem?

2. Alan wants to buy a new AC adapter for his notebook. His vendor has convinced him to buy this new AC adapter that has been introduced in the market. When he plugs the AC adapter in his notebook, although it fits perfectly, his computer doesn't boot. What may be the problem?

3. Gregory is planning to upgrade the memory of his laptop from 8MB to 24MB. His laptop has two memory slots. Because he needs to add 16MB to the existing 8MB, he buys a 16MB memory card. After installing the card, the memory test fails when he reboots the machine. What may be the reason?

4. Amanda has replaced the old battery of her portable PC. However, her PC won't boot. What could be the problem?

5. The batteries of Tim's laptop seem to wear faster than his colleague's batteries, even though they use the same batteries and laptop. What could be the reason behind the short life of Tim's laptop batteries?

Answers to Chapter Questions

Chapter Pre-Test

1. The four types of CMOS batteries are **Alkaline, NiCad, Li-Ion, and NiMH.**

2. The AC adapter has two functions in a portable PC: **converting the AC signal from the wall socket into the DC signal that the computer understands, and recharging the battery of a portable PC.**

3. The characteristics of a hard drive that typically influence its performance are **seek time, latency period, access time, data transfer rate, and interleave factor.**

4. A DC controller **prevents motherboard and other voltage-sensitive cards from sudden power surges.**

5. **Type III** PCMCIA card slots add hard drives to portable computers.

6. **Type II** cards provide modem and NIC connectivity, thus providing network connectivity.

7. **VRAM, MDRAM, WRAM, SGRAM, and 3D-RAM** are the various types of memory available on a video card.

8. In an **Active matrix LCD display,** a separate transistor circuit supports each pixel.

9. **Enhanced** keyboards are the most commonly used keyboards.

10. **SIMM and DIMM** are the most common memory modules used in portable PCs.

Assessment Questions

1. **B.** Laptops are the most popular category of portable PCs. For more information, see the chapter introduction.

2. **B.** Li-Ion batteries are best suited for portable systems because they're lightweight and long-lasting. For more information, see the section labeled "Batteries."

3. **A.** Batteries provide users the freedom from AC outlets and extremely long extension cords, thus making PCs portable in the real sense. For more information, see the section labeled "Batteries."

4. **B.** These are the characteristics of a DC controller. For more information, see the section labeled "DC Controllers."

5. **C.** Hot-swapping is a characteristic of PC (PCMCIA) Cards. For more information, see the section labeled "PC Cards."

6. **C.** Type III cards connect CD-ROM drives to a portable PC. For more information, see the section labeled "PC Cards."

7. **B, C.** Card services of a PC Card provide an interface between the card and the device driver when the card is inserted. They're also responsible for assigning I/O addresses and IRQ to the card. For more information, see the section labeled "PC Cards."

8. **A.** A Netware server has a Character User Interface (CUI); that is, it isn't graphic-intensive. Therefore, Monochrome Display Adapter (MDA) would be preferable. For more information, see the section labeled "Video Boards."

9. **C.** A graphics accelerator (or accelerated video card) is a video card with its own coprocessor that allows the video card itself to process images instead of depending on the microprocessor. For more information, see the section labeled "Video Boards."

10. **D.** Interlacing is the frequency with which images are refreshed by the video card (or board). For more information, see the section labeled "Video Boards."

11. **C.** In order to load the new device driver (of the video card) that you've chosen, you should reboot your computer after changing its display settings. For more information, see the section labeled "Video Boards."

12. **B.** Liquid Crystal Display. For more information, see the section labeled "LCD Panels."

13. **A, E.** Passive matrix LCD displays are slow and produce low-quality images that aren't easy to read at angles. For more information, see the section labeled "LCD Panels."

14. **D.** Enhanced keyboards are the most popular category. For more information, see the section labeled "Keyboards."

15. **B.** Interleaving, DTR, and Access time are characteristics of a hard drive. Interlacing is the property of video boards. For more information, see the section labeled "Hard Drives."

16. **B, C.** A hard drive is the secondary storage device, which is usually designated as C: and higher. A: and B: are reserved for floppy drives. For more information, see the section labeled "Hard Drives."

17. **A.** Access time is the sum of average Seek time and Latency period. For more information, see the section labeled "Hard Drives."

18. **C.** The new PCs work at very high speeds, therefore the interleave factor is 1:1 (which means that the drive isn't interleaved at all). This prevents disk damage. For more information, see the section labeled "Hard Drives."

19. **B, D.** Memory is a temporary storage device that loses any data in case of power failure or when the PC is switched off. Portable PCs frequently use both SIMM and DIMM memory modules. For more information, see the section labeled "Memory."

20. **B.** To compensate for the size restriction of the computer, all the functions are built into the system board. For more information, see the section labeled "Processor Boards."

21. **B.** System bus is not a field replaceable component. The other components are field replaceable, because you can change or upgrade them without having to replace or upgrade the processor board. For more information, see the section labeled "Processor Boards."

22. **C.** Complementary Metal-Oxide Semiconductor. For more information, see the section labeled "Processor Boards."

Scenarios

1. One of the PCMCIA services, socket or card service, has failed. Either the card hasn't been properly detected by the socket service or the card service failed to allocate it system resources. Take out the card and insert it again carefully. If this doesn't work, the card may be damaged.

2. Alan probably bought an AC adapter that isn't compatible with his notebook and isn't on the list of AC adapters recommended by the manufacturer. The voltage and amperage requirements may not match, resulting in damage to the PC.

3. Gregory probably didn't consult his owner's manual before buying the new card. The old card (8MB) and the new card (16MB) don't match in their speeds. He should buy the new card according to the specifications in the owner's manual.

4. Amanda should make sure that the battery is seated correctly and has the same configuration and polarity.

5. Tim probably keeps his laptop connected to the AC adapter all the time. This can wear the battery faster. He should also remember to switch off the PC when he doesn't use it for long periods of time. He may also run his PC while the battery is recharging. These factors may reduce the life of his laptop battery.

Maintenance and Troubleshooting

Part III covers basic safety and troubleshooting procedures. This part examines some routine and preventive maintenance procedures that should be used with the computer. It discusses types of cleaners and ways to clean different components inside the computer. It covers power issues, such as UPSs, safety around high voltage devices, and Electrostatic Discharge. This part also covers the disposal of different components, such as batteries and toner cartridges.

Part III covers the replacement of components in the computer system, as well as the safe handling and storage of components. It covers the maintenance of printers, which includes routing maintenance of the printer and dealing with common problems when they arise.

This part finishes by covering most other troubleshooting procedures to diagnose normal problems — those that affect the major components in the computer system, such as processors, parallel ports, hard drives, and motherboards.

Preventive Maintenance and Safety Procedures

Exam 220-201 ✦ A+ Core Hardware

✦ **3.1** Identify the purpose of various types of preventive maintenance products and procedures and when to use them.

- **Content may include the following:** Liquid cleaning compounds, Types of materials to clean contacts and connections, Non-static vacuums (chassis, power supplies, fans)

✦ **3.2** Identify issues, procedures, and devices for protection within the computing environment, including people, hardware, and the surrounding workspace.

- **Content may include the following:** UPS (Uninterruptible Power Supply) and suppressors, Determining the signs of power issues, Proper methods of storage of components for future use

- **Potential hazards and proper safety procedures related to lasers:** High-voltage equipment, Power supply, CRT

- **Special disposal procedures that comply with environmental guidelines:** Batteries, CRTs, Toner kits/cartridges, Chemical solvents and cans, MSDS (Material Safety Data Sheet)

- **ESD (ElectroStatic Discharge) precautions and procedures:** What ESD can do, how it may be apparent or hidden, Common ESD protection devices, Situations that could present a danger or hazard

CHAPTER PRE-TEST

1. What is the purpose of practicing preventive maintenance with your computer?

2. Which utilities do you use to maintain the hard disk?

3. _____ is used to clean the keyboard and rollers in the mouse.

4. How does a brownout affect your computer?

5. What is a UPS?

6. How is a suppressor different from a UPS?

7. _____ is used to clean the lens of a CD-ROM drive.

8. _____, _____, and _____ are the protection devices that can be used to prevent damages due to ESD.

9. Fluctuation in voltage generates _____ and _____.

10. The _____ contains information on hazardous chemicals present in various computer components.

Does it scare you to think that just before the most important meeting of your career, you might fall sick and not be able to attend the meeting? What do you do to prevent this type of situation from happening? You undergo a regular medical checkup and take adequate precautions for your health. Furthermore, what would happen if you were expecting the most important client of your life one morning and your computer simply refused to function? All gone — your data, your effort, your aspirations, everything!

It's time to ask yourself a couple of questions. Do you conduct regular tests for your computer? Do you take adequate preventive measures to ensure that your computer is in working order at all times? If you can't answer these questions in the affirmative, you may be headed towards disaster.

Performing preventive maintenance activities for your computer is not optional. Your computer is a sensitive and delicate device, and if you do not devote adequate time and attention to it, it just might not work properly.

In this chapter we will look at the common and effective products and procedures that can be used to maintain the "health" of your computer. We will also look at the various safety measures that you should apply when you work with system components. (Computer components can be dangerous if not handled carefully.) Finally, we will examine proper disposal procedures for replaceable components, as well as some environmental issues that might affect you.

Preventive Maintenance

3.1 Identify the purpose of various types of preventative maintenance products and procedures and when to use them.

To ensure the smooth functioning of your computer and to prevent frequent problems, you need to maintain your computer. You reduce the chance of system failure and downtime — and minimize repair costs — by performing preventive maintenance activities. Keep the following points in mind to ensure that your computer runs smoothly:

✦ Switch off the power supply and remove all cables before you start work on your computer.

✦ Check all wires and connections for wear and tear.

✦ Disconnect all peripherals from the computer before you start cleaning them.

✦ Clean the peripherals regularly.

✦ Vacuum-clean the CPU at regular intervals.

✦ Check the voltage of all power supply equipment to see if it falls within the prescribed limits.

✦ If you use liquid cleaners to clean a component, ensure that the component is dry before you connect it to the computer.

Caution   If you are a smoker, make sure you don't smoke near your system. Cigarette smoke is not only hazardous to your health, it also reduces the life of the computer. The gunk from smoke accumulates on the mouse ball and rollers. It also affects the performance of the drive head adversely.

Now that you know some general rules of preventive maintenance, you may want to know what components require the most attention. In general, cleaning and maintenance is required for almost every component of the system, because dust accumulates almost everywhere and affects the efficient working of the components. System components that require regular maintenance include the following:

✦ Mouse

✦ Keyboard

✦ Floppy drive

✦ CD-ROM drive

✦ Hard disk drive

✦ Monitor

✦ Power supply

✦ Printer

When it comes to preventive maintenance, components may require different tools and methods; however, some tools are commonly used, such as liquid cleaning compounds, a vacuum cleaner, Uninterruptible Power Supply (UPS), and suppressors. You can use software utilities, such as Disk Defragmenter and ScanDisk, for maintaining floppy disks and hard disks.

Most vendors provide a PC maintenance schedule guide that describes the frequency of maintenance and maintenance actions for the components. If your vendor does not provide a maintenance schedule, you should create one and follow it. Table 12-1 shows a sample maintenance schedule that you can refer to when creating your own.

	Table 12-1	
	Sample Maintenance Schedule	
Component	*Frequency*	*Maintenance Action*
Mouse	Monthly	Clean the mouse ball and rollers
Keyboard	Monthly	Vacuum clean the keyboard
Monitor	Monthly	Clean the monitor screen with a lint-free soft cloth
System unit	Yearly	Vacuum clean the system unit
Floppy disk drive	As required	Clean using the floppy-drive cleaning kit

Ensure that your PC maintenance schedule includes all components.

Preventive Maintenance Tools

 3.1 Identify the purpose of various types of preventive maintenance products and procedures and when to use them. Content may include the following: Liquid cleaning compounds, Types of materials to clean contacts and connections, and Non-static vacuums (chassis, power supplies, fans)

You can broadly classify the tools used to maintain computer components in two categories: materials and equipment, and software utilities.

Materials and equipment

A common cause of computer problems can be attributed to dust, dirt, and erratic power supply. To keep components dirt-free, you can use various liquid cleaning compounds. You can take care of dust using a vacuum cleaner. To control erratic power supply, you can either use a UPS or a suppressor.

Liquid cleaning compounds

The most commonly used liquid cleaning compounds include various forms of alcohol — isopropyl and denatured alcohol — and soapy water. Before you use any liquid cleaning compound, it is important that you read the manufacturer's instructions and documentation to ensure that the compound does not have a detrimental effect on the component. You can also buy specialized cleaning compounds direct from the manufacturer.

Use a sponge dampened with mild detergent or soapy water to clean the monitor, outer case of the system unit, keyboard, and other peripherals.

Caution   If you decide to use a piece of cloth instead of a sponge, make sure that it is lint-free.

Vacuum cleaners

Dirt and dust particles get inside your system unit through its air ducts and lodge themselves almost anywhere. If the air ducts become clogged, air circulation is affected, causing the system to heat up. Other common problems caused by these particles include wear and tear of components and conduction of charge that leads to a risk of damage to the components. Thus, it is important to vacuum clean the interior of the system unit regularly. You can use small, portable vacuum cleaners, since they are economical and easy to manage.

Tip   Ensure that the speed of the vacuum cleaner is never set to "high," since high speed might damage the delicate components of the computer.

UPS and suppressors

Erratic power supply or voltage fluctuation might damage the components of the computer. Overvoltage or undervoltage in power supply can cause voltage fluctuations. Overvoltage generates spikes and surges.

✦ **Spike:** A short burst of electricity exceeding 100 percent of the normal voltage for an extremely short duration (microseconds), usually at 400–5,600 volts. A spike is also known as an impulse.

✦ **Surge:** Occurs when power exceeds 110 percent of the normal voltage for more than a few seconds. Surges are the most common cause of computer damage.

Undervoltage is also unfavorable to the computer. The most common undervoltage problems are brownouts and blackouts:

✦ **Brownout (or Sag):** A partial loss of voltage or power. Brownouts occur when the voltage drops below 110 volts for a few seconds. This might happen when the usage of the voltage in your area increases suddenly. Brownouts can cause frozen keyboards and unexpected system crashes, resulting in corrupt disks and lost data. Brownouts also reduce the life and efficiency of your computer.

✦ **Blackout:** A complete loss of power. Possible causes of blackouts are blown fuses, transformers, and downed power lines. Though a blackout might not lead to hardware damage, it can result in data and memory loss.

To protect the computer against damages that might be caused from overvoltage and undervoltage, you use power protection devices, such as Uninterruptible Power Supply (UPS) and suppressors.

A UPS monitors the power received from the AC source before sending it to the computer. It also acts as a backup power supply in the event of a power failure. A UPS has three components: an inverter, a battery, and a charger. The inverter, shown in Figure 12-1, converts AC supply to DC. Figure 12-2 shows the battery, which provides backup in case of power failure. The charger, as shown in Figure 12-3, charges the battery. There are two types of UPS: Standby UPS (SPS) and Online UPS.

✦ **Standby UPS:** Only provides backup power during a blackout. It does not take part in supplying normal power to the computer and therefore is not a good protection against the other types of power problems.

✦ **Online UPS:** Passes the power to the computer after conditioning it, thereby providing protection against surges, spikes, and brownouts.

A suppressor just takes care of the surges and spikes and provides voltage within the prescribed range. It does not act as a backup power supply.

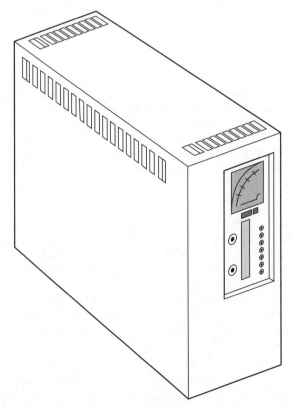

Figure 12-1: The inverter

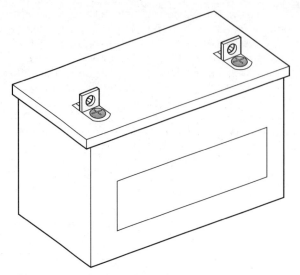

Figure 12-2: The battery

Software utilities

A considerable decrease in the performance of your computer could result from scattered data or fragmentation on the disk. Fragmentation occurs when you frequently create, modify, or delete the files on the hard disk. Large files are usually scattered among various clusters. When you try to access a file that is scattered across various clusters, the access time increases. This is because a search needs to be carried on all clusters to put a file together. Also, some clusters of the disks might have gone bad. These clusters need to be identified and marked to prevent applications from using them.

You can use software utilities, such as Disk Defragmenter and ScanDisk, for assessing and fixing disk problems. The Disk Defragmenter utility unites the separated blocks by moving the data to contiguous blocks. Since the data is no longer scattered, the performance of the system increases. It is advisable that you run the Disk Defragmenter utility regularly. The Scandisk utility is available with Windows 95, 98, and NT. However, the Disk Defragmenter utility is available only with Windows 95 and 98. To run the Disk Defragmenter, select Programs ➪ Accessories ➪ System Tools ➪ Disk Defragmenter from the Start menu. The Disk Defragmenter dialog box appears to guide you through the process, as shown in Figure 12-4.

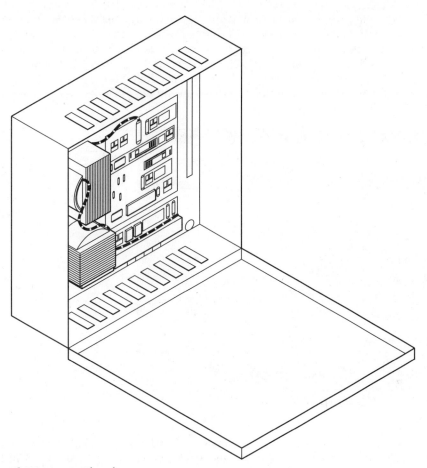

Figure 12-3: The charger

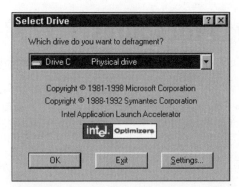

Figure 12-4: The Disk Defragmenter dialog box

The ScanDisk utility scans disks to mark out physical and logical errors on them. You can try to recover any valuable data that is present in the bad sectors. It is advisable to run the ScanDisk utility regularly to check for lost or bad clusters on the disks. To run the ScanDisk utility, select Programs ➪ Accessories ➪ System Tools ➪ ScanDisk from the Start menu. The ScanDisk dialog box appears, to guide you through the process of scanning the drive, as shown in Figure12-5.

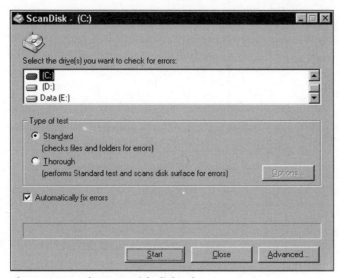

Figure 12-5: The ScanDisk dialog box

There are various third-party utilities, such as SpeedDisk and Disk Doctor, which can be used to assess and fix disk problems. However, you need to keep in mind the operating system your computer is using before deciding which utility to use.

Preventive Maintenance Procedures

 3.2 Identify issues, procedures, and devices for protection within the computing environment, including people, hardware, and the surrounding workspace.

As discussed earlier, almost all computer components require preventive maintenance. The methods and procedures to clean and maintain these components vary. The following sections discuss the preventive maintenance procedures of computer components in detail.

Mouse

Cursor movement becomes erratic when the mouse ball and/or rollers gather dirt. It's a good idea to keep the mouse covered when you are not using it. However, by no means can you eliminate accumulation of dirt. So, make sure that you clean the mouse ball and rollers monthly. To clean the mouse:

1. Disconnect the mouse from the computer.

2. Open the mouse ball cover from the bottom of the mouse and remove the ball. You can usually remove the mouse ball cover with a "press and turn" action.

3. Remove the dirt from the ball by washing it in soapy water.

4. Remove the dirt on the rollers using a cotton swab dipped in isopropyl alcohol.

5. Dry the rollers and ball well with a lint-free cloth before returning the ball and putting the mouse ball cover back in place. Connect the mouse to the computer.

Keyboard

Because the keyboard is the computer's primary input device—and one of the most used components—it gathers dust and dirt faster than any other component. When dust and dirt accumulate on the keyboard, they may cause the keys to stick when you press them. Also, dust may cause a short in the keyboard, resulting in incorrect characters being displayed on the screen. Liquids (for example, tea, coffee, or Coke) that are spilled on the keyboard may also cause a short.

In the Real World

Most of us have a habit of having snacks and drinks at our workstations. However, if you accidentally spill drinks on the keyboard, it can lead to a short circuit in the keyboard.

It is advisable to keep the keyboard covered when not in use. You should also clean the keyboard monthly to prevent accumulation of dirt. To clean the keyboard:

1. Disconnect the keyboard from the computer.

2. Remove the key tops from the keyboard and blow the dust using a vacuum cleaner.

3. Clean the key tops using a cotton swab dipped in denatured alcohol or spray cleaner.

4. Dry the key tops before putting them back on the keyboard and then connect the keyboard to the computer.

Printers

While printing, dust particles and bits of paper accumulate inside the printer. These particles can produce electrical charge that might damage the components of the printer. The dirt is also likely to cause mechanical wear and tear to the components of the printer. Ensure that papers with clean edges are inserted and that they are stacked evenly in the printer tray. It is recommended that you vacuum-clean the printer whenever you open it for repair. Use tweezers to remove bits of paper stuck in the printer.

Drives

Although drives are fixed inside the system unit, they gather dust over time. When dirt accumulates in a floppy drive, you might face problems in accessing floppies. At times, a floppy might become corrupt when you try to access it if the drive head is not clean. Figure 12-6 shows a floppy drive. You need to buy a floppy-drive cleaning kit to clean the floppy drive. The kit contains a cleaning disk and a bottle of isopropyl alcohol. To clean the floppy drive head:

1. Put a few drops of isopropyl alcohol in the access hole of the cleaning disk.

2. Insert the cleaning disk in the floppy drive. The disk spins over the head and cleans it.

 Tip   Ensure that the floppy drive cover is in place to reduce the accumulation of dirt.

You can clean a CD-ROM drive by using a CD lens cleaner that is available from your vendor. The CD lens cleaner resembles a CD but has a tiny brush on Track zero. To clean the CD lens:

1. Insert the CD lens cleaner in the CD-ROM drive.

2. Access the drive. The CD lens cleaner rotates, and the brush cleans the CD lens.

High-voltage equipment

You should be extremely careful when working with or handling high-voltage equipment (100 volts or more.) Carelessness while working with high-voltage equipment can lead to shock, severe burns, or electrocution. This equipment usually carries a warning or a caution label, which tells you about the potential damage that can be caused if the equipment is mishandled. The labels also carry a set of instructions that need to be followed while working with the equipment. You should also refer to the documentation provided by the manufacturer before you start working with high-voltage equipment. Also, ensure that you are properly grounded before you start working with high-voltage equipment. Grounding is a technique to get rid of static charge. In this technique, a ground wire facilitates the movement of charge from the equipment or your body to the ground. This prevents the equipment from any damages due to static charge. The following section describes high-voltage equipment that needs to be maintained regularly.

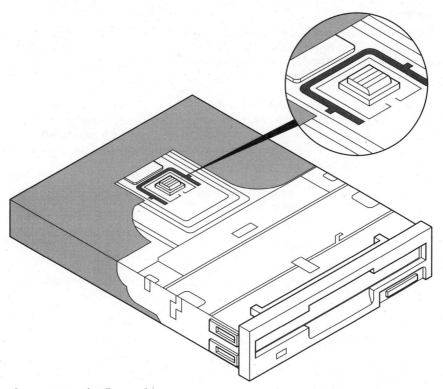

Figure 12-6: The floppy drive

Power supply unit

The power outlet provides alternating current (AC). The Power Supply Unit (PSU) converts this AC into direct current (DC) to be used by your computer. When the PSU converts the AC into DC, a significant amount of heat is generated, which can cause burns if you come in direct contact with it. Ensure that you switch off the main power when you are not using your computer. Also, allow the PSU to cool before you start working on it, or you might suffer from burns. The PSU contains capacitors that store electrical charge. If you try to open the PSU, there is a risk of shock or electrocution.

Caution   Even when the PSU has been switched off for a long time, the risk of getting a shock persists, as the capacitors inside the PSU continue to hold static charge even after the power is disconnected. So, never try to open the power supply unit until you are properly grounded.

CRT monitor

When you work with a cathode ray tube monitor (CRT), always remember that it is a piece of high-voltage equipment. It contains capacitors that store static charge for a long time even when the CRT is disconnected from the mains. Be very careful when handling the CRT, as this static charge can be fatal.

It is recommended that you do not try to repair the CRT unless you are experienced. Call a certified monitor technician, who will discharge the monitor before examining it. However, it is good to know how to discharge a monitor. All you need to discharge a monitor is a flat screwdriver with a well-insulated handle and a piece of metal wire. To discharge a CRT:

1. Tie one end of the wire to the metal part of the screwdriver and the other end to the frame of the monitor.

2. Touch the metal end of the screwdriver under the anode boot of the monitor. You'll see a flash and hear a loud popping sound, indicating that the monitor has been discharged.

3. Repeat this procedure after a few minutes to get rid of any residual charge that builds up.

Keep your monitor switched off when not in use, even if your computer has energy saving settings enabled.

Caution   Handle the monitor very carefully, as it is vacuum-sealed. If the glass breaks, it might implode violently.

In most high-voltage equipment, a static charge builds up that could lead to severe injuries and damage. Let's look in detail at the concept of static charge and the precautionary measures that you should take to handle it.

ElectroStatic discharge

ElectroStatic Discharge (ESD) is a phenomenon that occurs when two objects carrying dissimilar charge come in contact with each other. This results in the flow of static energy from one body to another to equalize the charge carried by the bodies. Sometimes you may experience a mild shock when you touch a metallic doorknob or walk on a carpet. This is due to ESD. Figure 12-7 shows how ESD is generated when you touch a metal doorknob. Human beings cannot feel the shock that occurs from a static charge less than 3,000 volts. However, computer components (such as chips) can be damaged by an ESD, which might be as low as 10 volts. Dirt and dryness contribute to ESD. Dirt holds the charge, and dryness in the atmosphere increases the ability of dirt to hold this charge.

How many times do we actually ensure that our shoes are dust-free before entering a computer room? People moving around a computer are one of the major causes of ESD, as they might carry dust and dirt along with their shoes.

Since ESD occurs naturally, it cannot be eliminated. You can, however, take precautionary measures to prevent damage to yourself and your computer's components due to ESD:

✦ Remove any jewelry you may be wearing, as metals are conductors of electricity.

✦ Do not wear clothes made of synthetic material, as this material is a good conductor of charge.

✦ Wear shoes with rubber soles to get rid of static charge.

✦ Ensure that the carpets are dust-free.

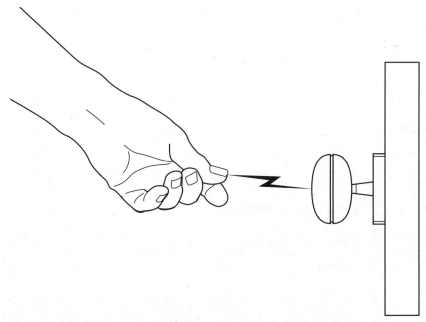

Figure 12-7: ESD is generated when you touch a metal doorknob.

The intensity of damage caused by ESD to a computer's components depends on the volts of charge transferred. ESD can damage a component either instantaneously or over a period of time.

You can use various protection devices, such as wrist straps, mats, and anti-static bags, to prevent damage from ESD.

✦ An ESD wrist strap is made of an insulated material, such as plastic, and has a wire attached to it. You need to ground this wire using an alligator clip to get rid of electric charge. The strap consists of a resistor that provides protection if the wire touches a charged object. It is advisable to stay close to the ground while working with the components to ensure that the wire is in contact with the ground.

✦ An ESD mat is also made of an insulated material and has two wires with alligator clips, one at the end of each wire. To use the mat, spread it on a flat surface that is near the ground. Attach one clip to the ground and the other to the computer. This ensures that the charge is transferred from the computer to the ground.

✦ An anti-static bag is used to store computer components when they are being shipped or stored. This bag ensures that dust and stray charges are kept away from the components.

✦ Anti-static sprays can be used on carpets to reduce ESD and thus prevent the damage.

When working with high-voltage equipment, ensure that:

✦ You don't have both hands on the equipment. This might be an inconvenience, but it will prevent the formation of a live circuit. In such a situation, the current enters from the equipment to one hand, travels through your body, and exits from the other hand. This will cause burns and severe pain.

✦ Humidity levels are between 50 and 70 percent.

Disposal of Components

 3.2 Identify issues, procedures, and devices for protection within the computing environment, including people, hardware, and the surrounding workspace. Special disposal procedures that comply with environmental guidelines.

Every computer component has a life span after which it needs to be replaced. Once you replace a component, you need to know how to dispose of it. Obviously, you cannot dump all of these components in landfills, since some components, such as CRTs, batteries, wiring, and toner cartridges, contain harmful chemicals.

Monitors contain heavy metals, such as lead and mercury. These chemicals will seep into the water table and contaminate our drinking water, resulting in adverse effects on the central nervous system of human beings and animals and plant tissues. These chemicals also have adverse effects on the environment.

Laws have been made that prevent people from dumping computers and monitors in landfills. You can expect to be fined if you break these laws. In every state, there are local laws that determine the disposal mechanism of the components. Contact your state's environment regulatory office to find the right way to dispose of the computer components. You can also contact the Environmental Protection Agency (EPA) for guidelines on how component disposal. These guidelines can be obtained from EPA's Hazardous Waste Resource Conservation and Recovery Act page at www.epa.gov/epaoswer/osw/hazwaste.htm.

To provide information on hazardous chemicals present in various materials, a Material Safety Data Sheet (MSDS) is available. The MSDS provides information about topics such as composition of ingredients, handling and storage methods, lethal dose information, and toxicology and ecology. The aim of MSDS is to inform people about the adverse effects of various chemicals and how to properly handle these chemicals. You can get more information on MSDS by visiting the Web site www.osha.gov.

Tip   Recycling computer components is gaining popularity these days. Most manufacturers take back the components and even pay you for them. Also, many charitable organizations accept used computer components for refurbishment and dispersal to the needy.

The following sections will discuss the disposal mechanisms for some hazardous components: batteries, CRTs, and toner kits/cartridges.

Batteries

Batteries contain metals, such as nickel and cadmium, which are environmentally harmful. Laws have been made to prevent people from dumping their batteries in trashcans. The Battery Act was passed in 1996 to ensure proper recycling or disposal of the nickel-cadmium batteries. Detailed information on the Battery Act can be obtained by visiting www.epa.gov/epaoswer/hazwaste/state/policy/pl104.txt.

Each state has different rules and regulations that govern the disposal of batteries. Make sure that you follow these rules when disposing of your used batteries. Contact your state's environmental regulatory office for more information.

CRTs

CRTs contain harmful chemicals and thus cannot be dumped in landfills. Old monitors that are still in working condition can be donated to churches and public schools. For such a donation, you also get a write-off on taxes. However, if the monitor is damaged and is not in working order, you can contact companies that buy monitors for spare parts or melt them for scrap metal.

Toner kits/cartridges

When you buy new toner kits or cartridges, vendors often take the old toner kits and cartridges and give you a small discount. These vendors then pass the toner kits/cartridges back to the manufacturers, who recycle them. However, if your vendor does not take the used toners and cartridges, you can contact the manufacturer or the environmental regulatory office for instructions on how to dispose of the toner kits and cartridges.

Ergonomics

 3.2 Identify issues, procedures, and devices for protection within the computing environment, including people, hardware, and the surrounding workspace.

Computers are beneficial in more ways that can be counted, but they can cause health problems. Ergonomics defines a set of standards to reduce or prevent Repetitive Strain Injuries (RSI). RSI basically affects the muscles and the tendons in the neck, shoulders, arms, wrists, and fingers due to repetitive movements or incorrect body posture. Other complications that can arise due to RSI are Carpel Tunnel Syndrome, tenosynovitis, and tendonitis. Do not ignore the signals that your body sends out to warn you. Figure 12-8 shows the advised sitting posture while working at the computer. Follow these guidelines to prevent yourself from strain injuries while operating a computer:

✦ Take frequent breaks. Most people work at a stretch without taking adequate breaks. This hurts the eyes and often leads to pain or swelling in body parts.

✦ Maintain a relaxed posture. An ideal posture is one where your feet are flat on the floor, the thighs and back are at ninety degrees, and forearms are parallel to the feet.

✦ Keep the keyboard and mouse at a comfortable distance. This ensures that you don't have to stretch your arms unnecessarily to reach these devices and that a proper posture is maintained.

✦ Adjust the monitor at eye level so that you don't have to bend or stretch your neck. The rays emitted by the monitor adversely affect your eyesight. Hence, the monitor should be kept at a distance of approximately two feet.

✦ Blink your eyes frequently and try to focus them on a distant object for a few seconds every 15-20 minutes. This gives a much-needed rest to your eyes.

✦ Use a wrist rest for the keyboard and mouse to ensure that you do not put unnecessary strain on your wrist muscles.

✦ If possible, use an ergonomic keyboard. This keyboard has a left and a right half set at a definite angle to reduce the strain on arm, wrist, and finger muscles. Use both your hands while typing. Also, do not pound the keys while typing.

✦ Use an adjustable chair with a firm back to provide lumbar support.

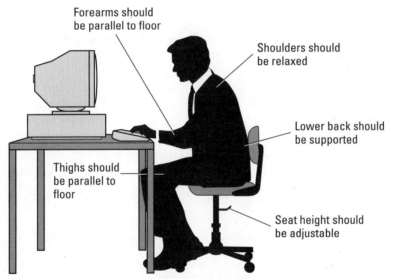

Figure 12-8: The advised sitting posture while working at the computer

Lasers can also be detrimental to human health. Lasers are high-intensity light rays that cause severe damage to human eyes, including blindness. Thus, never look directly into a laser beam in the laser printer. If the radiation of the laser beam comes in direct contact with skin, it can cause severe burns or even death, depending on the intensity. Avoid direct contact with laser beams.

The laser beams used in printers and CD-ROM drives are of significantly low intensity and thus do not cause harm to human skin. But as laser printers generate excessive heat, you should be careful when handling the inside of the printer.

Certain environmental conditions need to be maintained so that the performance of your computer is optimized. Keep the following guidelines in mind:

✦ The temperature of the room in which the computer is kept should be maintained at 60 to 75 degrees Fahrenheit (15.5 to 24 degrees Celsius). The computer should not be subjected to high temperatures, as this might damage the components.

✦ The room should ideally be dust-free. Because this is virtually impossible, ensure that the room is properly vacuumed.

✦ The circuits inside the CPU generate a lot of heat. There are in-built fans to take care of this heat. However, to aid proper air circulation, keep the computer at least six inches away from the wall.

✦ The relative humidity of the room should be maintained between 50 and 70 percent. Humidity less than 50 percent can lead to the formation of ESD that can cause damage to the components.

Key Point Summary

In this chapter, you learned about preventive maintenance. You also learned that preventive maintenance can be performed using tools, such as:

✦ Materials and equipments

✦ Software

You learned about preventive maintenance of computer components, such as mouse, keyboard, drives, and high-voltage equipment. You learned about ESD, its causes and effects on the computer components. You also learned how to dispose of various computer components, such as:

✦ Batteries

✦ CRT

✦ Toner kits and cartridges

Finally, you learned a few guidelines related to ergonomics and the workspace environment.

✦   ✦   ✦

STUDY GUIDE

This Study Guide presents 18 assessment questions and 3 scenarios to test your knowledge of the exam topic area.

Assessment Questions

1. Why should you perform maintenance activities? (Select all that apply)

 A. To prevent system failure

 B. To reduce computer downtime

 C. To reduce repair cost

 D. None of the above

2. Why do devices, such as the mouse and keyboard, need regular maintenance?

 A. They wear quickly

 B. They are breakable

 C. They gather dust easily

 D. None of the above

3. Tools that you use to perform maintenance activities are: (Select all that apply)

 A. Liquid cleaning compounds

 B. Suppressor

 C. PSU

 D. CRT

4. What is *not* true about the Disk Defragmenter? (Select all that apply)

 A. It is a system tool

 B. It should be run daily

 C. It marks bad sectors

 D. It unites separated chunks of data into contiguous blocks

5. You can clean the mouse by: (Select all that apply)

    A. Soaking it in soapy water

    B. Removing dirt from the mouse ball

    C. Removing dirt from the mouse roller

    D. Using a vacuum cleaner

6. Which of the following is high-voltage equipment? (Select all that apply)

    A. Printers

    B. CRTs

    C. PSUs

    D. Hard drives

7. Computer components can stand a static charge of:

    A. Up to 3,000V

    B. Less than 10V

    C. More than 10V but less than 3,000V

    D. 10V

8. ESD stands for:

    A. ElectroStationary Discharge

    B. ElectroStatic Discharge

    C. Electrostatic Disruption

    D. None of the above

9. While working with a PSU, you can hurt yourself because it: (Select all that apply)

    A. Generates a lot of heat

    B. Stores a lot of electrical charge

    C. Accumulates a dangerous amount of static charge over time

    D. Emits laser radiation

10. EPA stands for:

    A. Environmental Protection Association

    B. Environmental Preservation Agency

    C. Environmental Protection Agency

    D. Environmental Preservation Association

11. RSI stands for:

    A. Restive Strain Injuries

    B. Repetitive Strain Injuries

    C. Repetitive Self Injuries

    D. Restrictive System Injuries

12. What is *not* true about the environment at a workplace where many computers are used? (Select all that apply)

    A. There should be proper air circulation

    B. Temperature should be between 20 to 30 degrees Fahrenheit

    C. Humidity should be less than 50 percent

    D. Computers should be two inches away from the wall

13. The duration of a spike is measured in:

    A. Nanoseconds

    B. Minutes

    C. Seconds

    D. Microseconds

14. A brownout is:

    A. A partial loss of voltage or power

    B. A complete loss of power

    C. A short burst of electricity exceeding 100 percent of the normal voltage

    D. None of the above

15. When you get a shock from holding a metal knob, how many volts are generated?

    A. 3,000

    B. 10

    C. 5

    D. 200

16. You can prevent damage from ESD with the use of:

    A. Rubber gloves with matching cap

    B. De-ionizing fans

    C. A wrist strap

    D. A static meter

17. An ESD wrist strap contains:

   A. Surge protector

   B. Capacitor

   C. Voltmeter

   D. Resistor

18. The risk for electrostatic discharge is the greatest at:

   A. Daytime

   B. High humidity

   C. Low humidity

   D. Nighttime

Scenarios

1. ABC Inc. has decided to automate their system by migrating to computers from a manual system. They have bought 200 computers for this purpose. What should they keep in mind when planning the new office?

2. John, who has been continuously working for prolonged hours on his computer, has been experiencing severe pain in his shoulders and wrists. What measures do you think he should take to prevent this?

3. Diana has noticed in the past few days that the performance of her computer has deteriorated considerably. It takes a long time to access files from the hard disk. What should she do to increase the performance of her computer?

Answers to Chapter Questions

Chapter Pre-Test

1. Preventive maintenance **prevents system failures and reduces downtime and repair costs**.

2. The utilities used to maintain disks are **Disk Defragmenter** and **ScanDisk**.

3. **Isopropyl alcohol** is used to clean the keyboard and rollers in the mouse.

4. **The keyboard or mouse or applications that are currently running might stop responding** because of a brownout.

5. UPS provides a **consistent power supply**. It also acts as a **backup power supply** in the event of power failure.

6. A suppressor **does not act as a power supply backup in the event of a power failure**.

7. A **CD lens cleaner** is used to clean the lens of CD-ROM drive.

8. **ESD mats**, **wrist straps**, and **anti-static bags** are protection devices that can be used to prevent damages due to ESD.

9. Fluctuation in voltage generates **spikes** and **surges**.

10. The **Material Safety Data Sheet** contains information on hazardous chemicals present in various computer components.

Assessment Questions

1. **A, B, C.** You need to perform maintenance activities to prevent system failure and reduce computer downtime and repair costs. For more information, see the section titled "Preventive Maintenance."

2. **C.** Devices, such as the keyboard and mouse, gather dust easily and thus need regular maintenance. For more information, see the section titled "Preventive Maintenance."

3. **A, B.** Liquid cleaning compounds and suppressors are a few of the tools that you use to perform maintenance activities. For more information, see the section titled "Preventive Maintenance Tools."

4. **B, C.** The Disk Defragmenter should be run once a month. It unites separate chunks of data into contiguous blocks, but doesn't mark bad sectors. For more information, see the section titled "Preventive Maintenance Tools."

5. **B, C.** You should not clean the mouse by soaking it in soapy water or by using a vacuum cleaner. For more information, see the section titled "Preventive Maintenance Procedures."

6. **B, C.** CRTs and PSUs are high-voltage equipment. For more information, see the section titled "Preventive Maintenance Procedures."

7. **B.** Any shock greater than 10V can damage the computer components. For more information, see the section titled "Preventive Maintenance Procedures."

8. **B.** ElectroStatic Discharge occurs when two objects carrying dissimilar charge come in contact with each other. For more information, see the section titled "Preventive Maintenance Procedures."

9. **A, B, C.** A PSU generates a lot of heat, stores electrical charge, and accumulates static charge over time; thus, you need to be careful when working with it. For more information, see the section titled "Preventive Maintenance Procedures."

10. C. The Environmental Protection Agency provides guidelines on how the components should be disposed. For more information, see the section titled "Disposal of Components."

11. B. When you continuously work with your computer for prolonged periods of time, there is a chance of developing Repetitive Strain Injuries. For more information, see the section titled "Ergonomics."

12. B, C, D. The temperature of your workspace should be kept at 60 to 75 degrees Fahrenheit. Humidity should be maintained between 50 and 70 percent, and the computer should be placed at least six inches away from the wall. For more information, see the section titled "Ergonomics."

13. D. The duration of a spike is measured in microseconds. For more information, see the section titled "Preventive Maintenance Tools."

14. A. A brownout is partial loss of voltage or power. For more information, see the section titled "Preventive Maintenance Tools."

15. A. When you get a shock from holding a metal knob, 3,000 volts are generated. For more information, see the section titled "Preventive Maintenance Procedures."

16. C. You can prevent damage from ESD with the use of a wrist strap. For more information, see the section titled "Preventive Maintenance Procedures."

17. D. An ESD wrist strap contains a resistor. For more information, see the section titled "Preventive Maintenance Procedures."

18. C. The risk for electrostatic discharge is greatest at low humidity. For more information, see the section titled "Preventive Maintenance Procedures."

Scenarios

1. The following guidelines should be kept in mind while planning the office environment of ABC Inc.

   - The temperature of the room in which the computer is kept should be maintained between 60 to 75 degrees Fahrenheit (15.5 to 24 degrees Celsius).

   - The computer should not be kept in a room with a high temperature, as this damages its components.

   - The room should ideally be dust-free. Since this is virtually impossible, ensure that it is properly vacuumed.

   - The circuits inside the CPU generate a lot of heat. There are built-in fans to take care of this heat. However, to aid proper air circulation, keep the computer at least six inches away from the wall.

   - The relative humidity of the room should be maintained between 50 and 70 percent. Humidity greater than 70 percent can cause condensation inside the computer. Humidity less than 50 percent can aid in the formation of ESD that can cause damage to the components.

2. John should take the following measures to prevent RSI:

- Take frequent breaks.

- Maintain a relaxed posture. An ideal posture would be one where feet are flat on the floor, thighs and back are at ninety degrees, and forearms are parallel to the floor.

- Keep the keyboard and mouse at a comfortable distance.

- Adjust the monitor at eye level. The monitor should be kept at a distance of approximately two feet.

- Use the wrist rest for the keyboard to prevent unnecessary strain on the wrist muscles.

- If possible, use the ergonomic keyboard. This keyboard has a left and a right half set at a definite angle to reduce the strain on arm, wrist, and finger muscles.

- Use both hands while typing.

- Use an adjustable chair with a firm back to provide lumbar support.

3. One possible reason for the slow performance of Diana's computer is that it has scattered data or fragmentation on the hard disk. She should defragment the hard disk by using the Disk Defragmenter utility.

Managing Replaceable Components

Exam 220-201 ✦ A+ Core Hardware

- ✦ **1.2** Identify basic procedures for adding and removing field replaceable modules for both desktop and portable systems. Examples of modules:

  - System board

  - Storage device

  - Power supply

  - Processor/CPU

  - Memory

  - Input devices

  - Hard drive

  - Keyboard

  - Mouse

- ✦ **1.8** Identify hardware methods of upgrading system performance, procedures for replacing basic subsystem components, unique components and when to use them. Content may include the following:

  - Memory

  - Hard Drives

  - CPU

  - Upgrading BIOS

  - When to upgrade BIOS

CHAPTER PRE-TEST

1. Which cache memory can you upgrade?

2. Which system board size do you use for slimline desktops?

3. Which type of memory serves as secondary cache?

4. If your IDE controllers are full and you want to install a CD drive, what do you do?

5. What amount of secondary cache do most system boards accept?

6. The two types of keyboard connectors are _____ and _____.

7. While working with system components, what is the first thing you should do to avoid electrostatic shock?

8. The three types of mouse interfaces are _____, _____, and _____.

✦ Answers to these questions can be found at the end of the chapter. ✦

"Times they are a-changin'!" How true—especially if you look at the computer scene. Ever wonder why you keep hearing about faster processors, faster and more powerful memory, larger hard disks, and the like? Because the nature of computer technology is to change quickly and constantly. What's "in" today could be well and truly "out" tomorrow.

The components of your computer can become obsolete faster than you'd ever think. To stay at par with technology, upgrade your computer from time to time. The reasons for upgrades can vary from new, large, and complex applications to simply better, faster, and more powerful hardware. As the software scene keeps expanding, the hardware market also keeps growing to meet the expanding needs of newer software.

If you want to keep abreast of the latest technology, you should be familiar with replacing and upgrading common components of your computer. Even if you prefer not to upgrade your system components, it is essential that you know how to replace them; they may fail despite preventive measures and troubleshooting. You may also decide to upgrade certain components if you're looking for better performance (faster speed and less time).

In this chapter, you identify the possible need to upgrade different replaceable components—such as CPU, memory, power supply, system board, storage devices, and input devices. You also get a look at the standard procedures for upgrading these replaceable components.

CPU/Processor

 1.2 Identify basic procedures for adding and removing field replaceable modules for both desktop and portable systems. Examples of modules: Processor/CPU

 1.8 Identify hardware methods of upgrading system performance, procedures for replacing basic subsystem components, unique components and when to use them. Content may include the following: CPU

The Central Processing Unit (also called the CPU or microprocessor) determines the computer's speed and performance. Processor technology is advancing to meet the growing requirements of larger and more complex applications. As a result, even a system with the latest CPU is likely to become obsolete in a few years. To maintain a competitive edge, you may have to upgrade almost constantly to enhance performance.

Different types of CPUs are available from different manufacturers such as Intel, Advanced Micro Devices (AMD), and Cyrix. The type of CPU determines the software that can run on your computer; the same is true of the operating system. For example, an old 8088 CPU can't run Windows NT or OS/2 (or, for that matter, the software designed for them). When you buy a CPU, choose one that suits your performance requirements. Also, when you buy a new software package, check its system requirements to ensure that it runs properly on your computer.

Checking CPU compatibility

CPUs are manufactured by a number of different vendors, but no vendor has provided a CPU that is compatible with all available hardware platforms. Make sure your new CPU is compatible with your system BIOS before you install it. Certain CPUs come with a disk that helps you diagnose whether your system BIOS is compatible. If you have installed a CPU that won't work with a non-flashable system BIOS, then you have to install a new BIOS to work with the new CPU. The good news is that if your system has flashable BIOS, you can upgrade it without having to install a new BIOS.

You can upgrade a flashable BIOS by using a special software that your computer vendor can provide. Before you do so, however, first determine the model of your computer and its system board, as well as the make and version of your current BIOS. (This information is displayed during bootup.) The bootup information tends to zip by on-screen; you can press the Pause or the Scroll Lock key to freeze the content so that it is readable.

Upgrading the CPU

Replacing your computer's processor with a newer, faster model makes sense if the older one can't run the current version of your software (or another program that you want to use) at a reasonable speed. Before you upgrade the CPU, take a couple of precautions:

✦ Back up your hard disk so you don't risk losing valuable data.

✦ Store the current BIOS settings so you can configure the new CPU properly.

To replace a CPU, follow these steps:

1. Shut down the computer, disconnect the power cable, and remove the outer casing.

2. Leave the system idle for about half an hour so the CPU cools down.

3. Avoid electrostatic shock (which can damage delicate components) by grounding yourself to a static mat (which usually has a cord that attaches to your wrist).

4. Remove the new CPU from its packaging and place it pins-up.

5. Locate the old CPU. To do so, you may need to remove other components that block access to the CPU.

6. Locate the latch that holds the CPU and pull it up gently so the CPU is released from the socket.

7. Remove the CPU by holding it with your thumb and forefinger and pulling it (gently) straight upward.

Tip You can use a tool called "Chip-Puller" to remove the CPU. A Chip-Puller is U-shaped, and has small fingers on the ends that slip between the socket and the chip itself. These fingers ensure that the force used to pull the chip from the socket is spread equally between the two sides to reduce the possibility of damage to the chip.

Caution Ensure that you don't tilt the CPU while removing it or you may break some pins.

8. Store the old CPU safely in an anti-static bag.

9. Hold the new CPU and orient it so its Pin 1 aligns with Pin 1 in the CPU socket.

10. Place the CPU into the socket.

Tip Align the edges of the CPU and the socket so that the pins seat smoothly into the socket holes. Otherwise, the pins might break and cause permanent damage to the CPU.

11. Gently push the CPU into its socket to make sure that all pins are in contact with the socket; then lower the latch to keep the CPU in place.

12. Plug in your computer and start it.

Caution Do not disturb the other components inside the system unit while replacing the CPU. Otherwise, the computer might not start — or if it starts, it might give errors.

13. If the machine boots normally, then the new CPU is installed successfully. Replace the outer case.

Tip The systems that use Pentium, Pentium MMX, K5, K6, 6x86, and M II processors include Zero Insertion Force (ZIF) sockets. The ZIF sockets have an easily accessible lever to socket and desocket the CPU. The ZIF sockets make it simple to insert and remove the CPU. Newer systems (such as Pentium II and later) use Slot 1 connectors that make removing and inserting a CPU even simpler.

Memory

 1.2 Identify basic procedures for adding and removing field replaceable modules for both desktop and portable systems. Examples of modules: Memory

 1.8 Identify hardware methods of upgrading system performance, procedures for replacing basic subsystem components, unique components and when to use them. Content may include the following: Memory

Memory has two parts: system RAM and cache memory. To meet the growing memory requirements of applications, constant memory upgrades are a fact of life. Without adequate memory, your CPU takes longer to retrieve data from the hard disk. Even if your CPU is fast, inadequate memory leads to an overall slowing of system performance.

 For more information about different types of RAM, see Chapter 4.

Managing memory

To improve system performance so you can use the latest applications effectively, you have to add memory from time to time. You can identify your computer's current memory requirements by using the memory utilities of your operating system.

Windows 95/98, Windows NT, and Windows 2000 provide many utilities that you can use to determine the information about the system memory. Some of the utilities are described below:

✦ **POST memory diagnostic:** During the boot process, in the POST routine, the BIOS checks the system memory and displays the information. You can use the Pause key to freeze the screen and note down the information. You can also use the Print Screen key on your keyboard to print the information displayed on the screen.

✦ **System Properties dialog box:** The amount of system RAM is displayed in the General and Performance tabs of the System Properties dialog box. To display this dialog box, right-click the My Computer icon and from the short cut menu, choose Properties.

✦ **System Monitor dialog box:** The System Monitor displays details about the available memory and also displays information about the processor usage, network data packets, and file access. To display the System Monitor dialog box, select Start, Programs, Accessories, System Tools, System Monitor.

✦ **System Information dialog box:** The System Information displays details about the range of memory addresses used by different devices along with the memory status. To display the System Information dialog box, select Start, Programs, Accessories, System Tools, System Information.

Identifying when to upgrade memory

You can identify when to upgrade the memory by observing the system performance. Upgrade the memory when:

✦ There is a constant disk activity even when you are running only a few applications.

✦ It takes a long time to open large files and to switch between applications.

Choosing compatible memory

If you decide to upgrade the system RAM, get one that is compatible with your computer. You can find the amount of memory available on your computer by using any of the memory utilities. To identify the type of RAM compatible with your computer, refer to your computer's documentation or the cryptic numbering on the memory modules.

Before deciding what type of RAM to buy, run down the following checklist:

✦ Refer to the system documentation to identify the system memory technology.

✦ Check to see whether the BIOS supports parity and ECC operations.

✦ Identify the RAM speed. The RAM speed is inscribed on the memory modules.

✦ Refer to the system documentation to identify the voltage at which the RAM operates.

✦ Identify the type of connectors that your RAM should have.

After you've identified the type of memory for your computer, decide the amount of memory you want. Three factors can help you decide:

✦ The applications you want to use

✦ The amount of memory those applications need

✦ The number of free slots available on your motherboard

Tip

You must install SIMMs in pairs; you can install DIMMs singly. The SIMM pairs should have the same capacity, speed, and should be preferably from the same manufacturer. Otherwise, the computer might not work because of the differences in the memory modules.

Adding system memory

After you've decided the amount of memory you need, you can replace the existing memory modules or add more memory modules. To add a memory module, follow these steps:

1. Ground yourself to a static mat.

2. Shut down the computer, unplug it, and remove the outer case.

3. Remove the existing memory module if necessary. Push the tabs on the edges away from the module so the module is released from the slot and falls forward.

4. Hold the new module, line up the notched bottom edges of the module with the notch in the memory socket, and insert the module into the socket at an angle of 45-degrees. See Figure 13-1.

Figure 13-1: Adding a RAM module

5. Rotate the module to an upright position slowly so the tabs fall in place and the module is locked.

6. Plug in the computer and boot the system. Check to see whether the RAM is automatically recognized by the system. If the new RAM is not recognized, enter the CMOS setup, make necessary changes, save the settings, and exit.

7. Shut down the system and replace the outer case.

Managing cache

Modern systems use additional SRAM as cache to enhance performance, as SRAM is six to eight times faster than the normal system memory of DRAM. Your system can have primary cache or secondary cache. But if the available cache is not enough for you, you can upgrade it. Primary or L1 cache is built into the processor. So, to upgrade L1 cache, replace the CPU with one that has more built-in SRAM. But secondary or L2 cache is placed on the motherboard. Upgrading the L2 cache is possible in some systems in which the SRAM modules are placed in sockets on the motherboard. However, upgrading the L2 cache in systems with Pentium Pro and Pentium II processors is simply impossible, as the SRAM is built into the motherboard. In such cases, replace the motherboard if your L2 cache requirements are not adequate.

Identifying the cache compatibility

Before upgrading the secondary cache, know the following to ensure that no compatibility problems crop up later:

✦ **The amount of cache that can be installed on your system board:** Refer to your system documentation to find this. Most system boards accept up to 512KB of secondary cache, while some can accept as high as 1024KB.

✦ **The type of cache that your system board supports:** You can refer to your system documentation for details.

✦ **The SRAM speed:** The cache speed should not be slower than the rate required by the system board. Refer to your system documentation to find out the speed that you should look for in the SRAM.

Upgrading the cache

You can upgrade the cache once you have taken compatibility issues into account. To upgrade the cache, follow these steps:

1. Ground yourself to a static mat.

2. Shut down the computer, unplug it, and remove the outer case.

3. Locate the L2 cache module. It is an independent module close to the CPU.

4. Remove the cache by holding the cache module at the top and pulling it straight up and out of the socket. Put it in a safe place.

5. Hold the new cache module and lower it into the socket. Ensure that the notched corner of the module is aligned with the notched corner of the socket.

6. Secure the module into the socket by using the gold edge connectors.

7. Plug-in the computer and boot the system.

Normally, the new cache is automatically detected. However, if your system does not detect the cache, enter the BIOS setup, make necessary changes, and save the settings.

Power Supply Unit

 1.2 Identify basic procedures for adding and removing field replaceable modules for both desktop and portable systems. Examples of modules: Power supply

All components in the computer draw power from the Power Supply Unit (PSU). The PSU should therefore be able to handle the load. As you upgrade the system hardware, you may need to upgrade the PSU to supply adequate power. Also, when the PSU fails, even after preventive maintenance and troubleshooting, you'll need to replace it.

Identifying a failing PSU

You probably have a failing power supply unit when at least one of the following occurs:

✦ The power lights constantly flicker or are dimming.

✦ The keyboard and/or the system locks up frequently.

✦ Your computer reboots itself randomly.

✦ The fan noise is completely absent or the noise is louder and rougher than usual.

✦ The power supply chassis is extraordinarily hot to touch.

Caution   Although the power supply unit can be repaired, the high voltage that stays inside it makes it dangerous to repair. Power supply units are relatively inexpensive; replacing the old, failing power supply unit with a new one is cheap insurance.

Choosing the right PSU

If you decide to replace the power supply unit, you must keep the following in mind before you buy a new one:

✦ **The power requirement:** You can estimate the power requirement for different components according to the type of the computer. It is advisable to buy a PSU that has more capacity than you need.

✦ **Size:** The PSU must fit into the existing space inside your computer. To get a PSU of the right size, take a note of the dimensions of the existing PSU and buy a new one that has the same dimensions.

Replacing a PSU

The procedure that you should follow to install a PSU in your computer is as follows:

1. Ensure that you are properly grounded.

2. Shut down the computer, unplug the power supply, and open the outer case.

3. Remove the power cable connectors that are attached to the system board and disk drives.

Tip
Label each connector cable by using a masking tape and marker so you remember which disk drive or socket each connector matches with.

4. Remove the power supply unit from the front panel switch. To do so, disconnect the front panel switch first. If the switch is soldered, unfasten it from the computer chassis.

5. Remove the screws that hold the power supply chassis.

6. Remove the power supply unit.

7. Replace the new power supply unit in place of the old one.

8. Secure the power supply unit to the chassis. To do so, use the screws provided.

9. Attach the 20-pin connector to the matching connector on the system board.

10. Attach the disk drive connectors.

Caution
Align the pins of the connectors carefully. Otherwise, the pins might get damaged.

11. Connect the switch wires.

System Boards

Objective
1.2 Identify basic procedures for adding and removing field replaceable modules for both desktop and portable systems. Examples of modules: System board

The *system board*, also called the *motherboard*, is the most important component of your computer. All other components (such as the graphics card, disk drives, CPUs, and RAM) are plugged into the system board and communicate with each other by using the board connections. The system board determines how quickly and efficiently the different components can communicate and work together.

The system performance can be improved by upgrading components, such as the CPU, memory, or the graphics card. However, the overall system performance is still limited by the speed of the system board. Replacing the system board is extremely expensive; consider the option of purchasing a new computer instead. Following are some questions that you could ask about your present system before deciding whether to upgrade the system board or buy a new computer:

✦ Does the system support Plug-and-Play?

✦ Is the system BIOS-flashable?

✦ Does the system use 30-pin RAM sockets?

✦ Does the system have PCI expansion slots, or do the PCI slots support bus-mastering facilities?

If you answered no to the preceding questions, then buying a new computer is probably more cost-effective than investing in a system-board upgrade. If the components in the following list are up to date, however, then upgrading a system board is a good idea:

✦ Internal disk drives: hard disk, floppy disk, and CD-ROM drive

✦ External devices: keyboard, mouse, monitor, and modem

✦ System RAM

✦ Power supply unit

✦ Add-in cards, such as graphics, sound, and network cards

If you can keep these components, then you can save on the cost of getting a new computer.

Choosing the right system board

If you want to buy a new system board, you must consider compatibility, upgradability, performance, and cost factors, as you do for any other component. Also, the system board must fit within the space in the system. Three common sizes of system board are as follows:

✦ **AT and Baby AT:** For older 486 and Pentium desktops and minitowers.

✦ **ATX and Baby ATX:** For Pentium and faster computers.

✦ **NLX:** For slimline desktops.

Upgrading the system board

Make certain preparations before you start the system board upgrade. First, back up your data. Then, note down the current system configuration. If you are using Windows 95, you can use the Device Manager to print a detailed record of your system configuration. If you're running Windows 98, you can use the System Information utility to do the same job.

Removing the old system board

Follow these steps to remove the system board:

1. Ground yourself to a static mat.

2. Shut down your computer, unplug the power cord from the power supply, and remove the outer case.

3. Remove all cables that are attached to external devices, such as the monitor, modem, keyboard, and mouse.

4. Remove the add-in cards. To do so, unscrew the cards and pull them out one by one by applying firm but gentle upward force.

5. Pull out the RAM modules if you plan to use the existing RAM in the new system board.

Ensure that you keep the old memory module in a place free of static electricity, such as anti-static bags. Otherwise, the memory modules might get damaged and become unusable.

6. Locate and unplug the floppy and IDE connectors from the system board, but keep them connected to the disk drives.

7. Locate the serial and parallel connectors if the system board type is AT. Unplug their cables from the system board sockets. Unscrew the connectors from the backpane of the chassis.

For ATX system boards, you can ignore this step; these connectors are directly attached to the system board.

8. Remove the wires that connect the power supply unit and the white connector near the edge of the board.

9. Remove your existing CPU if you want to use it with the new system board.

10. Disconnect all wires that are attached to the power and disk-activity lights, as well as those connected to on/off and reset switches.

Make sure that you identify each wire with a label before you remove it from the system board socket. You can do so by using masking tape and a marker.

11. Remove all screws that attach the system board to the bottom of the case. Loosen the fasteners to free the system board. Keep the fasteners; you can use them with the new system board. Put aside the system board you removed.

Adding the new system board

Adding the new system board is fairly straightforward. Follow these steps (refer to the system documentation whenever you are in doubt):

1. Tape the cables and wires to the edge of the case to keep them out of the way.

2. Place the system board in the chassis to align the keyboard port with the matching hole in the case. Secure the board to the case with the screws.

3. Attach the CPU to the system board. For non-Pentium II system boards, lift the lever, align the edge of the CPU with Pin 1 of the socket, and lower the CPU gently into the holes. When the CPU is seated, lower the lever to secure it. (Pentium II system boards provide a Slot 1 connector; slide the CPU vertically into Slot 1.)

4. Attach the fan to the CPU as mentioned in the fan's documentation. Then connect the power wire of the fan to one of the free wires from the power supply unit.

5. If you are reusing old memory modules, unplug them from your old system board and plug them into the open sockets of the new system board. If you have purchased new memory modules, install those as well.

6. Reconnect the main power cable. For AT style system boards, make sure that the twin power cables are plugged into their respective connectors.

7. Attach the serial and parallel port assemblies to the case. Refer to the system documentation to identify the COM1 and COM2 ports. For the ATX systems, you do not need to screw these assemblies, as they are built in.

8. Plug in the connectors that came with the new board. Be careful to identify Pin 1 on the cables with Pin 1 on the ports.

9. Connect the lights and buttons at the front of the case to the sockets along the front edge of system board. Refer to the system board documentation to properly connect these.

10. If your system uses an IDE CD-ROM drive, plug the hard disk's cable into the primary IDE interface. Plug the CD-ROM drive into the secondary IDE interface. Plug the floppy drive's cable into the dedicated connector for the floppy disk drive. Attach power leads to these devices.

11. Attach the add-in cards to the system board and secure them with a screwdriver.

12. Reattach the monitor, modem, keyboard, and mouse.

13. Plug the power cord into the power supply.

14. Start the system and observe the initial displays; check to make sure everything is working.

When the computer does not function smoothly after replacing the system board, there might be a problem with the hard disk. To identify the source of the problem, you need to perform one of the following:

✦ Check if the drive cables are firmly set.

✦ Verify that the drive is getting power by observing the drive activity during the boot process.

✦ Verify that the jumper settings are correct.

✦ Check if the automatic hard disk detection option is selected in the BIOS settings.

Another source of computer failure after system board upgrade could be the peripherals. This might be due to the conflict with the operating system or the new system board resources. You can locate the malfunctioning peripheral by following these steps:

1. Shut down the computer and remove the power cable.

2. Unplug any unnecessary external devices, such as modems and printers. Also, remove any unnecessary internal cards and devices, such as sound boards, LAN cards, and I/O cards.

3. Start the computer; the operating system should recognize the missing devices.

4. Reboot the computer. If the computer functions properly, the peripherals were the source of the problem. So, start installing devices one at a time. This way, you can identify the device causing the problem.

Storage Devices

 1.2 Identify basic procedures for adding and removing field replaceable modules for both desktop and portable systems. Examples of modules: Storage device

 1.8 Identify hardware methods of upgrading system performance, procedures for replacing basic subsystem components, unique components and when to use them. Content may include the following: Hard drives

The different categories of storage devices include hard disks, floppy disk drives, CD-ROMs, DVD-ROMs, and tapes. With operating systems and applications getting larger and more complex day by day, storage requirements likewise keep increasing. For that reason, storage devices are the most common components in need of upgrading.

Hard disks

Hard disks are the primary storage devices and store all your applications and data. You'll need to upgrade your hard disks to make room for applications and/or data, to improve your system performance, or if your disk has crashed. Consider a hard-disk upgrade if the following conditions apply:

✦ You can't install a new application due to insufficient disk space.

✦ You notice an unusual slowdown in your applications.

✦ You suddenly have to search your hard disk for files to delete before you can save a document in a running application — and the system didn't give you an insufficient-disk-space warning.

✦ You encounter disk errors continuously, even after performing troubleshooting operations.

Deciding between replacing or adding a new hard disk

Instead of upgrading the existing hard disk, you may decide to add a new disk drive to your computer. If the old hard disk is performing well — without disk errors — but has run out of space, adding another disk can save time and cost (provided you have free controllers and a drive bay available).

Tip　　If you add a larger disk drive, designate the larger disk as the boot drive.

On the other hand, if you encounter frequent hard disk errors, then probably your hard disk is bad and deteriorated. In such a situation, replace the current disk drive with a new, larger, and more efficient hard disk.

Choosing the right hard disk

If you have decided to upgrade your hard disk, choose the one that meets your system's requirements. Keeping the following points in mind can help:

✦ **Capacity:** Hard disks of different capacities, such as 2GB, 8GB, or 16GB are available. Determine the capacity of the hard disk that you need. You can determine the capacity by identifying the applications that you want to run. Also, since the application and data files only get larger with time, you should plan for a big hard disk.

✦ **Controller type:** Decide the type of hard disk controllers, IDE, EIDE or SCSI. The SCSI controller supports faster data transfer and provides flexibility in adding devices, but are more expensive.

You should also look at the disk's stated performance specs, manufacturer's warranty and service policies, and the overall dimensions of the new disk drive; if you've chosen an internal hard disk, it should fit into the available drive bay.

Installing a hard disk

After you have purchased the hard disk that meets your system's needs, you can install it by performing the following procedures in order, consulting the descriptions of each procedure that appear in this section:

1. Back up your data.

2. Use jumpers to set up the new hard disk as a master or slave.

3. Replace the old hard disk.

4. Set the CMOS.

5. Partition the new hard disk.

6. Perform a high-level format on the new hard disk.

Backing up your data

Take a full backup of your data in case you are replacing the current disk drive so you can later copy all the data back onto your new hard disk. However, backing up data is a good idea even if you are simply adding a new hard disk.

Setting up the disk drive

An IDE device can be either a master or a slave. If you are adding a second hard disk, specify the boot drive (which should also be the larger one) as the master and the other as the slave before you start the drive installation. To do so, set the jumper switches. Generally, manufacturers of IDE hard disks configure them as master drives for one-drive setups. If your new hard disk is a replacement, you need not modify the jumpers. If the new hard disk is an addition (and you set it up as a slave), you may have to set a jumper on the original hard disk to indicate that a slave is now present.

Replacing the hard disk

To replace the old hard disk with a new one, follow these steps:

1. Ground yourself to a static mat.

2. Shut down the system, disconnect the power cable, and open the case.

3. Remove the data cable and power cable from the old disk drive. (Data cables often include a white strap at each connector.)

Caution

Be careful when you remove or replace ribbon cables; their connectors are often cheaply made and pull apart easily, which ruins the cable.

4. Unscrew the mounting screws that hold the old disk drive. If your disk drive is in a slot-type disk-drive bay, remove the brackets on either side of the disk drive.

5. After you remove all the mounting screws, slide out the old disk drive.

6. Insert the new hard-disk unit and slide it into the drive bay.

Tip   If the new disk drive is smaller than the original disk drive, you must first attach the mounting brackets so the smaller box fits properly into larger bracket frame.

7. Screw in the mounting screws; do not overtighten them.

8. Reconnect the data and power-supply cables to the computer.

9. Close the computer cover and connect the power cable.

Setting the CMOS

After you have physically installed the new hard disk, change the CMOS settings so your system recognizes the new disk drive. If it's an IDE drive, your computer may support auto-detection — if so, enter the CMOS setup utility and set the IDE drive setting to Auto. If your computer does not support auto-detection, enter the drive information (such as cylinder, head, and sector/track) manually.

If your new hard disk is a SCSI drive, the SCSI host adapter has its own BIOS that handles all SCSI devices attached to it. Note, however, that sometimes the boot drive should have a specific SCSI ID.

Low-level formatting a new hard disk

Low-level formatting outlines the positions of clusters and sectors, defines the interleave factor (the way the sectors are organized), records bad sectors, and hence prepares the disk for a particular type of disk controller. Even after low-level formatting, the disk cannot store programs and data. High-level formatting writes the file system structure on the disk, which makes the disk usable by the operating system.

Sometimes your hard disk needs a low-level format, though generally you won't have to do that; it's usually done during manufacturing. You can identify whether or not a disk is low-level formatted from the disk cover or the manual that comes with the disk. To low-level format a disk, you can use the low-level formatting utility of the BIOS, or the utilities provided by the vendors. If your hard disk is already low-level formatted, you can skip this step and move to the next.

Partitioning

Depending on your requirements, you may want the new hard disk to act as a single entity or as several smaller logical drives. In the latter case, you can use the FDISK utility to create partitions on the hard disk.

High-level formatting a new hard disk

To get the disk ready for the operating system, perform a high-level format on it. The command to do so is FORMAT <Disk_Name>. This command creates the DOS *boot record* (used to start the operating system), FAT (File Allocation Table, the DOS file system), and root directory. If you have designated the new drive as the boot drive, you must install the system files on it (to do so, use the /S switch with the FORMAT command). Then you can copy all the applications and data from your backup disk drive to the new hard disk.

Floppy disk drives

Floppy disk drives were among the first removable storage media for the computer. Floppies are ideal when transferring or backing up a small amount of data. Floppy disks come in two sizes, 5¼ and 3½ inches. Drives that handle the old-fashioned 5¼-inch floppy disk (which can hold no more than 1.2MB), are gone from nearly all new machines. Most floppy drives currently available are designed for the 3½-inch disks (which have a capacity of about 1.44MB). As with hard disks, floppy disk drives undergo wear and tear with time. Consider replacing a floppy disk drive if you consistently encounter read errors with different disks, even after troubleshooting.

Replacing a floppy disk drive

Floppy disk drives reside in their own controller ports. Before you replace a floppy disk drive, follow these steps:

1. Ground yourself to a static mat.

2. Shut down the system, disconnect the power cable, and remove the computer case.

3. Remove the data and power cable from the floppy disk drive.

4. Unscrew the mounting brackets that hold the disk drive in place.

5. Remove the disk drive out of the drive bay by sliding it out.

6. Screw in the mounting brackets if the new disk drive is smaller than the original disk drive.

7. Connect the data and power cables to the back of the new floppy drive unit.

8. Slide the new disk drive in the drive bay.

9. Secure the disk drive in place with the help of screws.

10. Close the computer cover and connect the power cable.

11. Start the system.

The new floppy disk drive should be automatically recognized by your system; most recent systems support Plug-and-Play. If your system does not detect the new floppy drive, change the corresponding CMOS settings.

Floppy disk drive successors

Floppy disks have low capacities, and thus cannot hold large files. As a step forward, new removable storage technologies, such as Zip and Superdisk drives, have been developed. These new technology drives are called *floppy disk drive successors*, as they offer much larger storage capacities. Some of the newer PC models include these new drives. However, you can add these drives to your PC when needed.

The Zip disk drive, introduced by Iomega Corporation, uses proprietary 3½ inch disks. These disks are twice as thick as the standard 3½ inch floppy disks, and have 100MB of storage capacity. For newer Zip drives, disks with a capacity of up to 250MB are also available.However, Zip drives cannot read traditional floppy disks.

Superdisk drives, introduced by Imation, use high-density disks and provide faster data transfer rates. You can use 1.44MB and 720KB 3½ inch floppy disks with Superdisk drives. The higher disk rotation in Superdisk drives allows a faster data transfer rate than the traditional floppy drives.

CD-ROM drives

Compact discs are currently the most popular medium for mass storage. Storing up to 650MB of data, they can transfer large applications, multimedia software, and large data files (such as sound files or graphics) from one computer to another. Early CD-ROM drives (called 1X drives) had data-transfer rates of 150 kilobytes per second (Kbps). Later CD-ROM drives brought higher speeds — 2X, 4X, 32X, 40X, to 52X.

As with hard disks, CD-ROM drives come in both IDE and SCSI controller types. Both types are similar in terms of performance. Therefore, you can select either type for your system. However, the IDE type is less expensive and easy to install. On the other hand, if you already have a SCSI controller and your IDE controllers are full, you can consider a SCSI CD-ROM.

Generally, the CD-ROM drives are reliable, but as the technology changes, you have to replace your CD-ROM drive according to your requirements. You can consider a CD-ROM replacement if:

　　✦ Your CD-ROM generates constant read errors, even after troubleshooting.

　　✦ Your CD-ROM constantly makes a loud noise, even after troubleshooting.

　　✦ Your current disk drive has difficulty reading CD-R (recordable) discs.

Before you add a new CD-ROM drive, make sure that you modify the jumpers on the IDE controller if you are using the IDE CD-ROM. However, if you are using a SCSI CD-ROM, set a proper SCSI ID and termination setting. To do so, set the jumpers on your CD-ROM drive to a unique SCSI ID. Then, if the disk drive is at the end of a SCSI chain of devices, set the termination jumpers. To add a new CD-ROM drive:

1. Ground yourself to a static mat.

2. Shut down the system, remove the power cable, and open the outer case.

3. Remove the front placeholder panel.

4. Make sure that you set all the jumpers and terminators.

5. Attach the slide rails if your drive bay requires them.

6. Connect the controller cable and the power cable.

7. Connect the audio cable from the CD-ROM drive to the sound card. The audio port is adjacent to the power cable port on the CD-ROM drive. To find where the connector goes on the sound card, refer to the sound card's documentation.

8. Slide the CD-ROM drive into the drive bay.

9. Close the computer case and reconnect the power cable.

Replacing Input Devices

 1.2 Identify basic procedures for adding and removing field replaceable modules for both desktop and portable systems. Examples of modules: Input devices, Keyboard, Mouse

You interact with your computer by using a number of different input devices, such as keyboard, mouse, touch screens, light pens, and scanners. Among all the input devices, keyboard and mouse are the most commonly used — but the keyboard is especially important. (For example, a Macintosh won't start if the keyboard is not connected.) Most computers come equipped with keyboard and mouse; this section explains how to replace them when necessary.

Keyboard

Keyboards are connected to COM ports of your computer through keyboard connectors. Of the two major types of keyboard connectors — DIN-5 and Mini DIN-6 — the smaller Mini DIN-6 has a size advantage.

Of all input devices, you use the keyboard most; it's prone to wear and tear. Your keyboard can live a long life if you use preventive measures and clean it from time to time, but eventually it wears out and you have to replace it. Your old keyboard may stop working properly (right in the middle of a crucial document) or you may simply want to get the latest keyboard that has some attractive new features. Before you buy a new keyboard, you should make sure that it matches the port on your system. Otherwise, you should have bought the right adapter to match the plug to the port (for example, some adapters enable you to plug larger keyboard connectors into Mini DIN-6 ports, and vice versa). To install a keyboard, just connect the keyboard to an available serial port and then install the keyboard-driver software.

For more information about the preventive measures for a keyboard, see Chapter 12.

Mouse

The mouse is the most commonly used pointing device used to interact with graphical user interface (GUI). A mouse has a ball that rotates rollers as it moves. The rollers produce a corresponding movement of the cursor on the screen. You may have to replace a mouse if the rollers get damaged.

For more information about the preventive maintenance of a mouse, see Chapter 12.

A mouse can be connected to your computer in different ways. The way a mouse is connected to the computer is called the mouse interface. The three major mouse interfaces are Serial, Bus, and PS/2. Each type is installed and configured differently. However, with portable systems, the mouse is built-in as a part of the keyboard. These keyboards are pressure-sensitive and the movement of fingers moves the pointer in the desired direction.

Serial mouse interface

The mouse is connected to a serial port on your system by using its DB-9 connector. If the serial port uses the 25-pin variety, you can plug the mouse's DB-9 connector into the adapter that comes with the mouse.

A mouse that uses the serial interface is easy to install. To install the mouse, you just have to connect the mouse to an available serial port and then install the driver software.

Bus mouse interface

Using a cylindrical DIN-6 mouse connector, a *bus mouse* connects to a special, 8-bit interface card installed on the computer's bus. As input devices go, a bus mouse is faster because its signals travel directly into the computer's bus. Also, unlike a serial mouse, the bus mouse does not need a COM port — so you can use one on systems that are short of COM ports. One disadvantage to a bus mouse, however, is that the bus card uses an interrupt — it can only use IRQ 2, 3, 4, or 5 — and the card does take up an expansion slot in the computer.

Installing a bus mouse requires three steps:

1. Install the bus card in one of the possible IRQ choices.
2. Connect the mouse to the bus mouse port.
3. Install the driver software for the operating system you're using.

PS/2 mouse interface

A mouse connected to a PS/2 mouse port uses the same connector that a bus mouse uses. The only significant difference between a PS/2 mouse and a bus mouse is that the PS/2 mouse does not use the bus card; the PS/2 mouse port is integrated into the system board.

To install a PS/2 mouse, connect the mouse to the PS/2 mouse port and install the mouse-driver software.

Key Point Summary

This chapter briefed you on managing the replaceable components of your computer by identifying the need for their replacement or upgrade. You also learned the standard procedures to disassemble/assemble these components.

✦ CPU/ Processor: Before upgrading your system CPU, you should back up your hard disk and store the current BIOS settings. If your replacement CPU is not compatible with your system BIOS, upgrade the BIOS. However, you can upgrade only the flashable BIOS by downloading the BIOS code from the vendor's Web site.

✦ Memory: Before upgrading the system memory, you should find the memory information that your computer is currently using. To check the amount of your system's available RAM, use one of the memory utilities. However, the memory information, such as memory type, parity, or volts, can be found from the system documentation.

✦ Power Supply Unit: Before buying a new PSU for your system, identify the power requirements and the size of your system's power supply.

✦ System Board: When the upgrades of the components, such as CPU, memory, or graphics card cannot improve the system performance because of the system board performance, consider upgrading the system board or buying a new system.

✦ Storage devices

  • Hard disks: If you encounter frequent or continuous disk errors after repetitive troubleshooting, the hard disk must be replaced.

  • Floppy disk drives: The floppy disk drives reside on their own controller ports. Therefore, no jumper settings are needed when installing a floppy disk drive.

  • CD-ROM drives: CD-ROM drives are available in different speeds, ranging from 1-X to 52-X. Replacing a CD-ROM drive is a fairly straightforward procedure.

✦ Input devices

  • Keyboard: The two types of keyboard connectors are DIN-5 and Mini DIN-6 (which is smaller).

  • Mouse: The three types of mouse interfaces are serial, bus, and PS/2.

✦   ✦   ✦

STUDY GUIDE

This Study Guide presents 20 assessment questions, 4 scenarios, and 2 lab exercises to test your knowledge of the exam topic area.

Assessment Questions

1. Which type of memory cannot be upgraded without replacing a CPU?

   A. RAM

   B. L1 cache

   C. L2 cache

   D. None of the above

2. Which type of the system BIOS can be upgraded?

   A. Flashable

   B. Non-flashable

   C. Both types

   D. None

3. Which of the following utilities cannot be used to identify the amount of system memory?

   A. POST memory diagnostic

   B. System Properties

   C. Format

   D. System Monitor

4. The Windows System Monitor utility is used to identify the _____. (Select all that apply)

   A. Amount of system RAM

   B. Memory type

   C. Processor usage

   D. Voltage at which the memory operates

5. What do you do to enable your computer to run multiple applications simultaneously?

    A. Upgrade the CPU

    B. Add a hard disk with larger capacity

    C. Add more RAM

    D. All of the above

6. A SCSI interface requires which specific setting?

    A. Unique SCSI ID

    B. Jumper setting

    C. Controller ID

    D. None of the above

7. Which component do you check if a parity error occurs?

    A. Hard disk

    B. RAM

    C. Software

    D. Controller

8. Which of the following processes displays the complete system configuration?

    A. Power-on startup process

    B. Power-up boot process

    C. Power-on self-test

    D. Startup utility test

9. What type of memory is the secondary cache made of?

    A. SRAM

    B. DRAM

    C. SDRAM

    D. VRAM

10. Which type(s) of memory do you find mounted on the system board? (Select all that apply)

    A. RAM

    B. L1 cache

    C. L2 cache

    D. L1 cache and L2 cache

11. What is the most common capacity of CD-ROM drives?

    A. 1,000MB

    B. 250MB

    C. 650MB

    D. 300MB

12. Which disk drives do not require changes to the jumper settings before installation?

    A. Floppy disk drives

    B. CD-ROM drives

    C. Hard disk drives

    D. Floppy disk drives and hard disk drives

13. Of the following, which utility displays detailed information about your system configuration?

    A. FDISK

    B. Device Manager

    C. ScanDisk

    D. Disk Defragmenter

14. Which type of interface provides fastest data transfer?

    A. Parallel

    B. SCSI

    C. Serial

    D. IDE

15. Your PC has only one IDE adapter and you want to add a second hard disk, keeping the first hard disk as the boot drive. How should you configure the second hard disk?

    A. Master

    B. Secondary

    C. Slave

    D. Primary

16. What is the correct sequence for installing a hard disk that serves as a boot drive?

    I. Auto-detection (or configure manually) in CMOS

    II. Partition

    III. Jumper setting

    IV. High-level formatting with /S switch

    A. I, III, IV, II

    B. III, I, II, IV

    C. III, II, I, IV

    D. III, IV, II, I

17. Where do you connect the CD-ROM audio cable?

    A. Speaker

    B. Power supply

    C. Sound card

    D. BIOS

18. In which of the following ports do you insert a keyboard connector?

    A. LPT

    B. COM

    C. DIN-5

    D. Mini DIN-6

19. Which of the following memory modules are installed singly?

    A. SIMM

    B. DIMM

    C. Both SIMM and DIMM

    D. None of the above

20. Which of the following is the correct IRQ that a bus mouse can use?

    A. IRQ 1

    B. IRQ 2

    C. IRQ 8

    D. IRQ 10

Scenarios

1. Alan wants to upgrade the CPU of his PC. After he replaces the old CPU with the new one and boots up the system, the system does not boot properly. What could be the reason?

2. Gregory's PC is having problems, such as random system reboots, keyboard and system lockups, louder and rough fan noise. What problem area should he look into?

3. Anna bought a PC ten years ago. She is very fond of using the latest software, so she has upgraded different system components from time to time. Now she wants to upgrade her system board so she can use the latest technology. Her PC does not support Plug-and-Play; the system uses 30-pin RAM cards. Should Anna upgrade the system board or buy a new PC?

4. Tina's PC uses only one hard disk, which she decides to replace because of continuous disk errors. To do so, she has bought a disk drive that matches all the compatibility issues of her PC. Should she change the jumper settings before replacing the disk drive?

Lab Exercises

Lab 13.1 Replacing the CPU

1. Refer to your system documentation to identify the type of CPU that your computer supports.

2. Remove the computer case and the old CPU.

3. Insert the new CPU into the socket.

4. Restart the computer.

Lab 13.2 Replacing a Hard Disk

1. Select the hard disk of the appropriate size and capacity. Also refer to the system documentation to find out the controller type.

2. Back up your data.

3. Set the disk drive, if necessary.

4. Replace the old disk drive with the new one.

5. Restart the computer and make any necessary changes in the CMOS settings.

6. Perform low-level formatting, if necessary.

7. Partition the disk, if necessary.

8. High-level format the hard disk.

Answers to Chapter Questions

Chapter Pre-Test

1. You can upgrade only **the secondary cache** (also called the L2 cache).

2. You use the **NLX system board size** for slimline desktops.

3. **SRAM** serves as secondary cache.

4. If your IDE controllers are full, **you can use the SCSI controller to install a CD drive.**

5. Most system boards accept **512KB** of secondary cache.

6. The two types of keyboard connectors are **DIN-5 and Mini DIN-6.**

7. While working with system components, the first thing you should do to avoid electrostatic shock is to **ground yourself to a static mat.**

8. The three types of mouse interfaces are **serial, bus, and PS/2.**

Assessment Questions

1. **B.** L1. cache can be upgraded only by replacing the CPU; you can upgrade other memory separately. For more information, see the section labeled "Managing cache."

2. **A.** Only flashable BIOS can be upgraded. Upgrading flashable BIOS requires special software that you can obtain from the vendor. For more information, see the section labeled "Checking CPU compatibility."

3. **C.** The Format command does not find the amount of memory; instead, it performs a low-level disk format. For more information, see the section labeled "Installing a hard disk."

4. **A, C.** The Windows System Monitor utility can identify the amount of RAM, the processor usage, network data packets, and file access. Use the PC's documentation to identify the memory type and voltage at which the system memory operates. For more information, see the section labeled "Managing memory."

5. **C.** Adding RAM enables your computer to run more applications simultaneously. For more information, see the section labeled "Memory."

6. **A.** A SCSI interface requires that you specify a unique SCSI ID. For more information, see the section labeled "Storage Devices."

7. **B.** If a parity error occurs, check RAM. For more information, see the section labeled "Choosing compatible memory."

8. **C.** The complete system configuration is checked and displayed during the Power-on self-test process. For more information, see the section labeled "CPU/Processor."

9. **A.** The secondary cache (also called L2 cache) is made up of SRAM chips. For more information, see the section labeled "Managing cache."

10. **A, C.** RAM and L2 cache memory are mounted directly on the system board. For more information, see the section labeled "Memory."

11. **C.** CD-ROM drives commonly store 650MB of data. For more information, see the section labeled "CD-ROM drives."

12. **A.** Floppy disk drives do not need a jumper setting while you are installing them. For more information, see the section labeled "Floppy disk drives."

13. **B.** Device Manager is the utility that displays detailed information about system configuration. For more information, see the section labeled "CPU/Processor."

14. **B.** The fastest data transfer is provided by a SCSI interface. For more information, see the section labeled "Storage Devices."

15. **C.** When your PC has only one IDE adapter and you want to add a second hard disk, keeping the first disk drive as the boot drive, you should configure the second disk drive as slave. For more information, see the section labeled "Storage Devices."

16. **B.** The correct sequence for installing a hard disk as a boot drive is as follows: Jumper setting, auto-detection (or configure manually) in CMOS, partitioning, and high-level formatting. For more information, see the section labeled "Installing a hard disk."

17. **C.** The CD-ROM audio cable is connected to the sound card (or to the system board if your sound card is integrated into it.) For more information, see the section labeled "CD-ROM drives."

18. **B.** A keyboard connector is connected to a COM port (serial port). For more information, see the section labeled "Keyboard."

19. **B.** Only DIMM modules are installed singly. For more information, see the section labeled "Adding system memory."

20. **B.** The IRQs that a bus mouse can use are IRQ 2, IRQ 3, IRQ 4, or IRQ 5. For more information, see the section labeled "System Boards."

Scenarios

1. The CPU is probably not compatible with the system BIOS. In such a situation, Alan has to upgrade the system BIOS (provided it's flashable). If the BIOS is not flashable, he must install a new BIOS.

2. The symptoms — random system reboots, keyboard and system lock-ups, and louder, rough fan noise — indicate a failing power supply unit. Therefore, Gregory should check the power supply unit and get it replaced.

3. Anna is using quite an old computer that lacks many features (such as Plug-and-Play) and it has old RAM SIMMs. Investing in a new system board by itself does not give the required results. Anna needs a new system.

4. Tina does not need to change any jumper settings. A system with only one hard disk recognizes that disk automatically as the master disk.

Maintaining Printers

CHAPTER

14

EXAM OBJECTIVES

Exam 220-201 ✦ A+ Core Hardware

✦ **5.2** Identify care and service techniques and common problems with primary printer types. Content may include the following:

- Feed and output
- Errors (printed or displayed)
- Paper jam
- Print quality
- Safety precautions
- Preventive maintenance

CHAPTER PRE-TEST

1. What print device uses a tractor feeder mechanism?

2. What device melts the toner into the paper before ejecting the paper?

3. What software component allows an operating system to speak with a printer?

4. What is a spool file?

5. What would cause a vertical line on each page of a document?

6. What printer type requires head alignment?

7. The quality of a printer is measured in its _____ per _____.

8. What can be done to fix a clogged ink cartridge?

9. What is the best method to clean up spilled toner?

10. Why is it important to not overload a paper tray?

✦ Answers to these questions can be found at the end of the chapter. ✦

In a large multi-user networked environment, maintaining printers can be a full-time job. Printers can create mysterious jams, smudged ink, blemishes, and other undesirables at practically any moment. Laser printers may work fine with one brand of paper, but jam with another. Dot matrix printers can fade text, tear the continuous form paper, and cause headaches in general. And software? Software drives can disappear, become corrupt, or forget the printer is attached.

This chapter will examine printer trouble and how to avoid it. It will detail problems with each type of printer — laser, inkjet, and dot matrix — and how these problems can be resolved, or better yet, avoided. The labs in this chapter will provide hands-on experience with common printing problems and maintenance.

Feed and Output

5.2 Identify care and service techniques and common problems with primary printer types. Content may include the following: Feed and output

Most users think a printer is working properly when the printer spits out their paper and everything looks acceptable. And this is how it should be. After all, a printer's main purpose is to print. It's not some mystical device that we need to spend all our energy worrying about. A printer should hum contentedly in the corner, wait for a print command, and then nonchalantly print the page.

Unfortunately, printers seem to have a magical way of forgetting what their real job is. Many, if not most, problems with a printer will happen at one of two places in the print process: feed and output.

The goal of printing is to transfer information from a PC into hard copy. Essentially, there are two major steps to accomplishing this process: getting the paper into the printer and then getting the paper to come out of the printer. This section will examine this process in detail for laser, inkjets, and dot matrix print devices.

Friction feeders

Laser printers typically use friction feeder mechanisms. Friction feeders use a set of rollers to apply some amount of pressure to the top sheet of paper to guide the sheet into the printer assembly.

There are various types of friction feeders. Some use a set of ribbed wheels that "catch" the top sheet of paper between the grooves on each wheel. As the wheels turn, the paper moves with the ribbed wheel as the next rib applies the friction to keep the sheet moving onto the registration rollers.

Another popular method of friction feed involves a D-shaped wheel that applies a small amount of friction to the top sheet of paper in the paper tray. As the wheel moves slightly, the paper trips onto a second set of wheels, both on top and bottom, which continue to feed the paper into the printer assembly.

Troubleshooting friction feeders

Most friction feeder problems begin when the paper is loaded into the printer. In general, laser printers can use a broad range of paper types. Keep in mind, however, that if the paper can be sent through a photocopier, it can probably also go through a laser printer. If you are uncertain if the paper can print in your laser printer, check the manufacturer's Web site and the product manual.

Exam Tip   Paper weight is determined by the weight of the paper, before it is cut to finished size, in stacks of 500 sheets. Typical printer paper is 20-pound bond, or 20 pounds per 500 sheets in its original uncut size, which is 17 × 22 inches. On the exam, know that the weight of the paper correlates to the ability of the printer to print on the paper.

Inkjet printers, which also use friction feeders, can also use the same type of paper laser printers use. However, paper mills have perfected paper specifically for inkjet printers. The primary difference between laser printer paper and inkjet paper is that photocopier paper is porous, or to be more technical, has cellulose fibers. So? A porous paper will soak up the ink from an inkjet rather than hold the ink on the surface of the paper. With paper made for inkjet printers, you'll notice less "cockling" or buckling of the paper.

The second problem with paper has to do with humidity. Paper can, and does, accept and release humidity. Paper should be stored in a cool, dry place. Of course, paper isn't wine — it doesn't need its own storage cellar — but if you store paper flat and dry, your printer will be happier.

Finally, sometimes the paper is just too slick for the friction feeder to guide into the printer. This problem can usually be remedied by using the manual feed tray. On inkjet printers, where the paper tray is exposed, you may be able to use your finger to push the paper with the friction feeder to get the paper moving.

The mechanics of a friction feeder are not difficult to understand. The wheels that first touch the paper flip the paper into printer assembly. Eventually, most printers will experience problems with these wheels, because they will wear down and have to be replaced. The original price of the printer will determine whether or not you'll want to replace the feeder rollers or the entire printer.

If you decide to replace the feeder assembly on your printer, always disconnect the power supply, remove the toner, and read the manufacturer's installation manual for detailed instructions on how to replace the feeder. Because there are so many different models of printers, it would be impossible to discuss feeder assembly replacement for each type in the context of this chapter.

In some extreme cases, friction feeder problems can stem, not just from the printer rollers, but from something more serious. It is possible for the engine that turns gears along the perimeters of the paper path to fail. The printer may still have power, but the rollers cannot move to pull and guide the paper through the printer. In general, the cost for a new engine will be proportionate to the cost of the printer: the more expensive the printer, the more expensive the engine. In most cases, replace the entire printer, not just the print engine.

Troubleshooting continuous form feeders

Dot matrix printers use continuous form feeders. These beasts are great for forms, checks, and documents that don't require the fancy output a laser or inkjet printer can provide. A continuous form feeder, sometimes called a tractor feeder, uses two wheels to pull the paper into and through the printer.

The printer is typically set above a box of continuous forms—one long sheet of paper perforated every 8.5 inches or so. The continuous forms have a .5-inch strip of holes on each side of the page. These holes are designed to correspond to the sprockets on the wheels of the printer. Two or three holes of the paper, depending on the printer model, are aligned onto the sprockets to begin pulling the paper through the feeder. On most dot matrix printers, a hinge-like clamp secures the paper onto the wheels.

As the printer begins to print, the wheels turn in tandem with the print head to advance the paper one line at a time through the printer. As the paper advances, successive holes along the edge of the paper fit magically onto the next sprocket to continue the advancement of the paper.

Although continuous form feeders are generally very reliable, they may start to malfunction if the box holding the paper becomes askew. In such a case, the printer may begin pulling the paper more to one side than the other, which may cause the paper to jam or rip. Newer dot matrix printers are equipped with their own tray or storage area for the continuous forms, which keeps the paper neat and straight.

Troubleshooting paper output

When I bought my first printer, I asked the sales guy how it worked. He said, "Simple. The paper goes in here and comes out here." Well, that sounded easy enough for me.

Paper output problems can arise with any printer. However, the type of printer allows you to troubleshoot specific problems.

Laser printers

On a laser printer, the paper passes through a fuser. The fuser, which is responsible for fusing, or melting, the toner into the paper, is an aluminum roller coated with Teflon. Opposite this Teflon roller is another roller to help the paper eject. A halogen bulb heats the aluminum roller. As the paper passes through the fuser assembly, the toner is melted into the paper and ejected from the printer.

You can see your printer's fuser assembly by opening the cover of the printer. Look for the rectangular box near the printer exit that contains a warning about the temperature. Do not touch this rectangular box — it is the fuser! If you do, you'll learn why the manufacturer printed "Achtung!" on the device.

Paper output from a laser printer is generally reliable. The exit path should remain clear — a stack of papers blocking the path could create a nasty jam inside the printer. In addition, the fuser may eventually wear down or die. It is possible to replace the fuser assembly yourself, although the manufacturer may strongly recommend that it be replaced by one of their certified technicians.

Inkjet printers

With inkjet printers, the paper is nearly output when the printing is complete. Most inkjets use a C-pattern for their print process. The paper is pulled from a tray below the print mechanism and curls under the print head. It is the bottom of the top sheet of paper that is printed on. As the engine advances the paper, the print head drops the ink onto the paper a line at a time. By the time the printed image is finished, the paper is nearly out from under the print head.

The engine may turn another .375-inch increment to pass the paper all the way out of the device. Some models suspend the printed page on a trapdoor–like mechanism. When the image has finished printed, the doors move to enable the paper to drop into a simple paper tray.

Output problems in an inkjet printer will most likely stem from the engine that advances the paper into and out of the printer assembly. When this engine fails, the printer is usually beyond repair and should be replaced. This failure is rare, however — chances are, you'll want to replace your inkjet for some new technology before the engine fails to grip and advance the paper.

As with the laser printer, a stack of pages in the inkjet printer's exit paper tray may cause interference with newly printed sheets.

Dot matrix printers

Dot matrix printers use a very simple in-and-out method of printing. The continuous form feeds into the printer and a line of dots is printed. As the print head moves to either end of the printer assembly, the paper advances one line — enabling the print head to move back across the paper with the next line of dots.

Interestingly enough, the dot matrix printer's feeder mechanism is also responsible for ejecting the paper from the device. The sprockets that pull the next sheet of paper into the print device are simultaneously ejecting the sheet above it — one line at a time.

The trouble with dot matrix printers and their "ejection system" is that the paper can trip against objects around the exit. A twist in the output of the paper can cause the printer to pile up the paper and eventually jam. For optimum performance, the printer's exit path should be clear of any objects that could disrupt the exit path. Superior dot matrix devices have a bin that catches the paper as it exits and folds the paper back into form.

In the Real World Dot matrix printers were fine printers — when that was all the world had. Today, however, technicians won't (or hopefully won't) encounter dot matrix printers on a regular basis. With today's inexpensive laser printers and high-quality ink jet printers, there is not a huge demand for dot matrix devices.

Errors

Objective **5.2** Identify care and service techniques and common problems with primary printer types. Content may include the following: Errors (printed or displayed).

Errors can evolve from software, hardware, or an inexperienced user.

Software-based errors stem from software drives, applications, and operating systems. Hardware-based errors are generally caused by hardware that is old, worn down, or defective. In this section, we will examine both types of errors and how they can be resolved.

Software-based errors

When you first begin troubleshooting a printer and you suspect the trouble is software-related, try to experience the problem firsthand. If possible, attempt to print the same document the user is attempting to print so that you can see the print command, sense a potential slowdown on the system, and listen for any print device attempting to start the print process. Ask yourself these questions:

✦ Can the error be reproduced?

✦ Does the printing error occur from only one application or from all applications within the operating system?

✦ What type of application is being used: a 16-bit application or a 32-bit application?

✦ If the printer is shared, do other users experience the same problem?

✦ Is the correct printer selected within the operating system?

For general troubleshooting, start by printing a test page for the printer. A test page enables you to test several things:

✦ Communication between the PC and the printer

✦ Communication between the operating system and the printer

✦ The validity of the driver

✦ The possibility of hardware failure versus software failure

STEP BY STEP: Printing a Test Page

1. Select Start ➪ Settings ➪ Control Panel.

2. Double-click the Printers folder.

3. Right-click your printer and choose Properties.

4. Click the Print Test Page button.

5. Click the OK button if the page printed properly or the Troubleshoot button if the page did not print correctly.

Most software errors are the result of drivers that have become corrupt or been installed incorrectly. But first, what's a driver? A driver is a piece of software that enables the operating system to communicate with the associated hardware device — in this case, a printer.

A printer driver comprises three different components:

✦ **Printer graphics driver** — For composing the information for the printer.

✦ **Printer interface driver** — Enables a user to control the attributes of the printer.

✦ **Characterization data file** — Enables the operating system to understand just what this printer can do.

A driver that becomes corrupt is not an uncommon thing. It often happens that your users will be printing along just fine — and then, nothing. You'll know something's wrong with the printer driver when you open the properties on a printer and Windows 2000 ignores your request. To repair the problem, delete the printer you've installed and reinstall the printer.

Windows 95, 98, and Windows 2000 all use a spooling mechanism to control the print process. The spooler service is responsible for moving the job from the application through the printer drivers and onto the print subsystem.

In Windows 2000, a print job may become corrupt and refuse to print. What will also happen, however, is that the print job hangs out in the printer queue — even when you chose to cancel the printing.

In these instances, you need to stop and restart the spooler service to flush the stubborn print job from the queue. When you stop the spooler service, the print jobs are completely deleted. The service will need to be restarted with no items in the queue. See Figure 14-1 for the Spooler Service Properties, which is accessed through the Services applet.

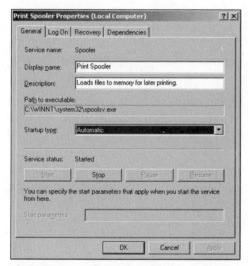

Figure 14-1: Editing the spooler services properties for a Windows 2000 computer

If print jobs consistently become stuck in the queue or you receive out-of-storage errors when attempting to print, the partition that houses your spool folder is too full. There are a couple of options to remedy this problem.

The spooled jobs are stored by default in your `%systemroot%\system32\spool\printer` directory. The `%systemroot%` is a method to identify the partition where Windows 2000 is installed. You can first remedy this by cleaning up the partition. There may be unneeded files, old applications, and temp files hogging space. Free up some room and the spooler service may be just fine.

The second method is a little more involved. It consists of moving the spool directory to a new folder.

The following Step By Step will walk you through the process of changing the spool folder for a Windows 2000 computer:

STEP BY STEP: Changing the Spool Folder

1. Select Start ➪ Settings ➪ Control Panel.

2. Double-click the Printers folder.

3. Click the File menu and choose Server Properties.

4. Click the Advanced tab as seen in Figure 14-2.

5. Enter the path of the new Spool folder. If storage or drive speed is your motivation, this should be on a different partition or drive.

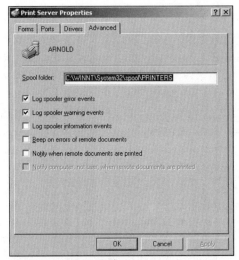

Figure 14-2: Changing the Spool folder on a Windows 2000 computer

Hardware-based errors

Software is not always the culprit when it comes to a printing error. Hardware failure can contribute to errors — though usually with less frequency than with software. Clues for hardware-based errors include strange noises from the printer, flashing lights on the console, or smeared toner on the printed pages. Use the following checklist when you begin to troubleshoot hardware-based errors.

✦ Do you have power? Check first for activity lights on the console of the print device, a hum from the printer, and the existence of power. Check to confirm the power cord is plugged into the printer and a working receptacle.

✦ Are the connections secured? Make sure that there's a secure connection at both ends between the printer and the computer. If your printer is network-based, make certain the printer is connected to a working network cable that is attached to the network.

✦ Are there messages on the LCD display? Often, problems are reported on the LCD display. Based on your printer type, the messages may contain codes listed in the printer's reference manual, or simple text such as "Out of Toner" or "Paper Jam."

✦ Is there paper in the paper tray? Take the tray out of the printer and examine the paper in the tray. Make certain the paper is loaded into the tray properly and not overloaded. Look into the paper feed area. Are any sheets of paper blocking access to the printer?

As with any hardware device you are troubleshooting, the problem may not be with the hardware but with the user attempting to use the device. With printers, users can inadvertently unplug printers, overload paper trays, select the wrong print device in their operating system, or a variety of other low-level errors. The above checklist will certainly uncover "misconfigurations" induced by your average user. Of course, as a great technician, you should treat the user with respect while educating the user on what has caused the error.

Cables to the printer should be securely fastened to the printer and to the PC. These cables should also not be crimped or pinched by the positioning of the PC or the printer. If you are using a parallel printer cable, confirm that the printer cable is less than ten feet. Cables over ten feet are susceptible to crosstalk and attenuation. If a cable over ten feet is required, try to position the cable away from other cables, equipment, and fluorescent lights. These devices contribute greatly to EMI (Electromagnetic Interference) on all cables. EMI can cause the print job to never reach the printer or distort the information en route to the print device.

An empty toner cartridge can lead to mysterious printing problems. Remove the toner cartridge and determine if it's empty. If the cartridge is nearly empty, give it a shake. This action can revive any remaining toner and enable the printer to get a last few pages out of the cartridge. Replace the toner cartridge when necessary.

A "textbook" problem with toner cartridges is that the eager technician forgets to remove the protective tape that seals the toner in its chamber. On each toner cartridge, there is a tag, usually green, that is pulled out of the cartridge and discarded. If this tag is not removed, the toner cannot print, and only blank pages emit. No error is reported, but obviously something is not right. The solution? Open the printer, remove the toner cartridge, and pull out the tape!

Inkjet printer problems typically result from their ink cartridge. The nozzle on the bottom of the ink cartridge can become clogged with ink. Remove the ink cartridge that refuses to print and clean the bottom of the cartridge with a cotton swab and isopropyl alcohol. Allow the alcohol to evaporate and then reinstall the ink cartridge.

Anytime you remove an inkjet's printer cartridge, you need to align the ink cartridge again. This is done through the print driver of the software. Some manufacturers, such as Hewlett-Packard, have separate software packages to communicate and manage the alignment of the ink cartridge.

Tip   Do not refill an empty ink cartridge. This process is messy and can damage the ink cartridge. Also, it is generally not as cost-effective as replacing the entire ink cartridge.

Paper Jams

Objective   **5.2** Identify care and service techniques and common problems with primary printer type. Content may include the following: Paper jam

You know the story. You're in a rush — you want to print this piece of information and go! And then what happens? Argh! Paper jam! In this section, we'll discuss the cause of those pesky bugs and what to do when they show up. In general, the type of printer you are servicing will determine how the paper jam is created and how it is resolved.

Laser printers

There are many different places a piece of paper can decide to get stuck in a laser printer. Let's walk through each stage of the print process and examine the jam and solution.

Paper feed

For any jam that occurs at the start of the print process, confirm that the paper is the correct media being used, that the paper tray is not overloaded, and that there are enough sheets of paper in the tray.

If the paper is crinkling and wadding up as it attempts to enter the print area, the printer rollers are probably dirty and need to be cleaned. We'll discuss cleaning your printer in the preventive maintenance section within this chapter.

If the page is simply slipping out of the tray but does not enter the print area, then most likely the feeder wheels are worn down and need to be replaced.

Occasionally, your feeders may attempt to allow two sheets of paper into the printer, resulting in a jam. When this occurs, there could be one (or more) possible reasons:

✦ Paper is the incorrect media for the printer.

✦ The feeder wheels are dirty and need to be cleaned.

✦ The feeder wheels are worn down and need to be replaced.

✦ The paper tray is overloaded.

Transfer corona assembly

Jams that occur after the page has entered the printer could be related to the transfer corona assembly. Recall that this device is responsible for charging the paper with a +600Vdc and then stripping the charge away from the paper upon exit. The positive charge on the paper attracts the toner to the paper — as opposite charges attract. If the transfer corona wire were damaged, it could not charge the paper properly and no toner would be attracted to the paper.

Should the static eliminator strip get damaged or removed, the paper could be continually attracted to the –600Vdc charged print drum and cause a print jam. Examine the transfer corona wire (or component) for damage. The wire is located close to the point of entry for the paper. The static eliminator strip is often a felt strip located near the exit path for the paper. Damage to either of these components calls for replacement.

The paper rollers

There are registration rollers throughout the printer to guide and move the paper through. Damage to any of these rollers could disrupt the flow of the paper and cause a jam. Most likely, a roller may receive a buildup of toner and cause the paper to shift and eventually cause jams.

Inkjet printers

Inkjet printers jam for a variety of reasons, but the most common reason is improper media type (for example, the paper may be too thick, slick, or porous). Like laser printers, inkjet printers can experience many jams at the point of entry for the following reasons:

✦ Incorrect paper for the type of printer

✦ Dirty feeder wheels that need to be cleaned

✦ Worn feeder wheels that need to be replaced

✦ Overloaded paper tray

Besides improper media type, paper jams that occur during the print process may result from the way the paper is loaded into the printer. Many inkjets have a compartment where paper is added rather than a separate, removable paper tray, which creates new challenges. Should the paper shift or creep away from the front edge of the "paper compartment," the feeder wheels cannot properly grip the paper and may pull a sheet in at an angle, resulting in a jam.

The solution? First load the paper correctly:

1. Fan through the paper (to air out any dust or shreds leftover from being cut at the mill).

2. Square the paper and insert it into the paper holding area for the printer.

3. If your printer has a plastic tab to hold the paper flush against the grips of the feeder wheels, make certain to use it! If your printer does not have such a device, square the paper occasionally with your hands to ensure a good grip by the feeder wheels.

Dot matrix printers

Dot matrix printer paper jams are usually related to the positioning of the continuous feed paper. The paper should be positioned in a somewhat straight path below the feed of the printer. Most continuous forms are in a covered cardboard box. The paper slips through a slat on top of the box and runs to the printer.

Should the path of paper become skewed, the printer may pull one side of the paper more than the other, causing a print jam. The nasty thing about dot matrix printers and print jams is that the print head may continue to attempt to print and chew the paper up into its mechanism.

To resolve this jam, power off the printer. Rip the sheet off of the continuous form below the print head and then twist the knob for manual advance for the paper. You may have to reverse the paper out of the printer. For the paper that has jammed into the print head, carefully tug the paper away from the print head to remove it. Some models may allow the print head to back away from the platen to allow you to remove such jams.

Paper jams may also result from the exit of the paper. As mentioned earlier, the exit path of the paper should remain clear so the paper can exit freely. Should the paper exit path become blocked, the paper may not be able to exit as quickly as the printer expects it to. This, of course, causes the printer to print over lines that have already been printed and eventually jam.

Finally, mechanical failure of the dot matrix printer can cause print jams. The print head shifts from side to side when printing on a dot matrix printer. If you look closely, you can see a rubber belt attached to the print head that controls the speed, motion, and placement of the print head. This belt can break or become stretched and eventually need to be replaced. Consult with the manufacturer as to the replacement belt and instructions for replacing the part.

Print Quality

 5.2 Identify care and service techniques and common problems with primary printer types. Content may include the following Print quality

Print quality is dependent on the type of printer you're working with. Obviously, a dot matrix printer is not going to print as crisply as a laser printer. Within each printer type, there are some nuances that affect print quality. A discussion of these printers follows.

Laser printers

A laser printer's quality is measured in terms of dpi (dots per inch). Dpi refers to the amount of dots that a device can print within one square inch. Most of today's laser printers start at 600 dpi and go up from there.

Blank pages

A blank page, while frustrating, at least tells you that the printer's engines and rollers are operational. The printer may be spewing blank pages for the following reasons:

- ✦ Corona transfer wire broken. The corona transfer wire will charge the paper to attract the toner from the print drum.

- ✦ HVPS Failure. HVPS supplies the voltage to charge corona assembly to charge the paper and print drum. Without it, the toner is not attracted to anything.

- ✦ No toner in the printer. And without toner....

Ghosted images

A printer producing ghosted images will print a sheet of paper as normal — only the current print job will have a lighter image of the last document through the printer. This scary problem is usually due to the erasure lamp that wipes the image from the print drum. Should the lamp fail, the previous print job will print again — only ghosted out from the original. You'll most likely have to replace the lamp and the fuser when this problem happens.

Vertical line

This problem is most often due to a scratch on the print drum. Typically, replacing the toner will resolve the problem. If the problem persists after replacing the toner, the vertical line could result from a problem with the laser shining on that area of the drum or a smudge of toner loose in the printer. This could be a major malfunction of the laser within the printer, which would generally require the laser component to be replaced (or more likely, the entire printer). If the vertical line is smeared, rather than printed, on the page, the rollers are dirty and need to be cleaned.

Smeared pages

If you pick up a sheet of printed paper and the toner smears off, then the fusing process has failed. Most likely, the halogen lamp has failed and needs to be replaced. Use caution when working with the fusing assembly, as there are extremely hot temperatures involved. Before changing, or checking, the halogen lamp, allow the printer to cool completely.

Speckled pages

This problem may result from a variety of reasons:

✦ A scratch in the print drum where toner collects and then is attracted to the paper when the image is transferred. Cleaning the printer to remove loose toner should resolve this problem. As a worst case scenario, replacing the toner should also resolve this problem.

✦ Flecks of toner collecting on the rollers. Loose toner in a printer can cause problems for months after the initial spillage. Use a shop vacuum to thoroughly clean the loose toner and follow this task with a thorough cleaning of the print device.

✦ Failure of the fusing assembly. The fusing assembly is a dangerous and essential piece of the printing process. Should the fuser not properly melt the toner into the paper, replace the fuser or (if it makes more economical sense) the printer.

✦ The toner cartridge could be leaking toner. Replace the toner and clean the innards of the printer to resolve this issue.

Inkjet printers

Inkjet printers that produce poor quality are not uncommon. Most often the issue is related to the ink cartridge. The ink cartridge can be cleaned if ink is still inside, as described in the following Step By Step.

STEP BY STEP: Cleaning an Ink Cartridge

1. Prepare a clean, dry work area, since the ink may leak. Wear appropriate clothes and, if desired, latex gloves.

2. Remove the ink cartridge from the inkjet.

3. Power down the printer and unplug it.

4. With a small amount of isopropyl alcohol on a cotton swab, clean the outer case, including the ink nozzle on the bottom of the printer.

5. With a clean cotton swab, clean the inside of the print head where the cartridge rests.

6. Allow the alcohol to evaporate. Confirm that no remnants of the cotton swab are on the ink cartridge.

7. Replace the cartridge and use the manufacturer's directions to align the ink cartridge if necessary.

You can increase the print quality of your inkjet printer by using an inkjet-compatible paper. Color inkjets in particular work well with paper designed for printing photographs.

Dot matrix

Dot matrix printers have never been fantastic in their ability to print stunning images. Still, print quality can be controlled. The number one problem with dot matrix printers and poor quality has to do with the ribbon that the printers have to strike. When the images begin to fade, the inked ribbon has to be replaced.

In some instances, the print head has to be replaced. The print head is on the carriage that moves back and forth across the page. While this is not as common as replacing a ribbon, print head replacement every few years is a necessary evil for a dot matrix printer. What happens is that the solenoid that is electromagnetically firing onto the ribbon begins to stick or break from usage. The page will then have dots missing, causing the page to look splotchy.

Safety Precautions

5.2 Identify care and service techniques and common problems with primary printer types. Content may include the following: Safety precautions.

Printers, like all electrical appliances, can cause you severe bodily harm. For starters, when doing major work on a printer, such as cleaning the printer or replacing a component, turn off the power and unplug the printer from the electrical source. Some printers use a stand-by mode even when the power switch is in the off position. Unplugging the power cord is a safe way to distance yourself from danger.

Don't be fooled into a false sense of security though. Like a PC, a printer can still hold a charge even when the power is off. Use caution around the power supply and the corona transfer assembly.

Most printers have latches that ensure the printer is closed before operating. Don't attempt to rig the latches to watch the miracle of printing. Not only can you tear up the printer, you can hurt yourself or others.

The fuser can remain hot for some time after the printer has been turned off. Don't assume it's cool just because the power is off. You can severely burn your fingers by touching the fuser assembly. It's hot enough to melt iron.

One of the worst messes around a printer is toner that has leaked. Not only does this stuff stick to everything, it can burn your eyes, irritate your skin, and get in your nose. Nasty stuff. When dealing with toner cleanup, do not be tempted to use a regular vacuum as a quick solution. The toner is so fine it may seep through the bag and blow out the exhaust of the vacuum.

Some vendors offer toner-capable vacuums the size of a briefcase. These vacuums have very tight filters to trap the toner. In addition, the vacuum is typically grounded to avoid any electrical shortages within the printer. Finally, these service vacuums have special gadgets for cleaning around areas like the corona transfer wire and the fuser.

If you get toner on your hands, try to gently brush it off with a soft, dry towel. Water, especially warm or hot, tends to melt and spread the toner. If you will be servicing many printers in your career, you may want to invest in waterless cleaning towels that absorb toner and the like from your skin, some fabric, and work areas.

Preventive Maintenance

 5.2 Identify care and service techniques and common problems with primary printer types. Content may include the following: Preventive maintenance

Printers get dirty, dusty, and ignored throughout their lifetime. Be good to your printers and occasionally — at least once a year — spend some time with them. Consider it an anniversary.

All printers need to be cleaned. First, power off the printer and remove the power cord. Move the printer to a clean, uncluttered work area. Clean the outside of the printer with a lint-free cotton cloth and a small amount of isopropyl alcohol.

Remove the paper tray and remove the paper. Clean the inside of the tray, removing dust and scraps of paper.

If possible, clean inside the area where the paper tray meets the feeder rollers. These rollers may have a thin line of crud around them. It is acceptable to use a sponge or small brush to clean these rollers.

Open the printer and remove the toner cartridge — no need to clean it in detail, other than knocking any dust or excess toner off of it. Inside the printer, clean each roller from edge to edge, all the way around each cylinder. If you have a service vacuum, you can use it to remove any dust or excess toner inside the printer.

Check your printer's manual to see if your printer uses an ozone filter. An ozone filter is typically used with printers that use a corona transfer wire. They aid in reducing dust and residual toner — and in proper ventilation for your printer. A yearly change on these is a fine idea.

When you've cleaned the printer completely, clean the area where the printer is stationed. This will prevent an immediate buildup of dust in the printer and allow any excess alcohol on the printer to evaporate. Put the toner back in place, reposition the printer, reconnect the cables, and do a test print. Always do a test print after a cleaning to ensure that no parts have been damaged or are missing from your cleaning duties.

When you position your printer, make certain there is plenty of unobstructed area around the printer. A good six inches is adequate for cooling and ventilation. The printer cables should not be pinched or jammed against the wall.

Key Point Summary

In this chapter, we discussed the type of work and challenges a technician will encounter when maintaining and servicing printers. The major points of printer maintenance include:

✦ Feed and output of paper

✦ Errors from hardware and software

✦ Resolving paper jams

✦ Print quality expectations

✦ Using safety when maintaining printers

✦ Implementing preventive maintenance strategies

✦   ✦   ✦

STUDY GUIDE

This Study Guide presents 20 assessment questions, 2 scenarios, and 2 lab exercises to test your knowledge of this exam topic area.

Assessment Questions

1. What are the two most common places in a printer where paper jams occur?

    A. The fuser

    B. The feeder assembly

    C. The output assembly

    D. The print drum

2. Why should an inkjet use paper created for an inkjet printer?

    A. Regular laser printer paper cannot print through an inkjet printer.

    B. Inkjet paper is slightly smaller than laser printer paper.

    C. Inkjet paper is coated with ozone, which repels any charge — laser printer paper is not.

    D. Inkjet paper is less porous than laser printer paper.

3. What can be done if the paper is too slick for the friction feed to enter the printer?

    A. The edge of the paper can be slightly wrinkled.

    B. The edge of the paper can be dog-eared so the gripper area is thicker.

    C. The paper should be fed through the manual feeder.

    D. The printer rollers should be tightened to apply more pressure to the first sheet of paper in the tray.

4. What would cause all of the internal gears to quit moving even though the printer is powered on?

    A. The toner is empty.

    B. The toner is low.

    C. The print engine has failed.

    D. The fuser's halogen bulb is broken.

5. Why do continuous forms have holes down either side of the actual printing area?

    A. The holes guide the paper into the printer.

    B. The holes trigger the print head to print the next line.

    C. The holes trigger the solenoids to print each block.

    D. The holes are used to pull the paper out of the printer by a tractor sprocket.

6. What is so dangerous about the fuser assembly in a laser printer?

    A. The fuser houses the laser.

    B. The fuser charges the corona transfer wire.

    C. The fuser melts the iron particles and toner into the paper.

    D. The fuser houses the HVPS for the laser printer.

7. What component in an inkjet printer would be responsible for advancing the paper out of the printer?

    A. The ink cartridge

    B. The print head

    C. The print motor

    D. The tractor feeder

8. What component in a dot matrix printer is responsible for ejecting the paper from the printer?

    A. The solenoid

    B. The sprockets that pull the paper into the printer

    C. The print head

    D. The sheet ejector

9. A test page to a printer establishes what two things?

    A. Communication from the printer only

    B. Communication between the OS and the print device

    C. The validity of the driver

    D. The status the print driver

10. What portion of a driver reports information on the printer's capabilities?

   A. Printer graphics driver

   B. Printer interface driver

   C. Characterization data file

   D. EMF

11. What service controls the Windows 2000 print process?

   A. Net logon

   B. Browser

   C. Spooler

   D. Print subsystem

12. What must be done if a print job refuses to leave the print queue in Windows 2000?

   A. Delete the printer and reinstall it

   B. Restart the computer

   C. Turn the printer off and then on

   D. Stop and restart the spooler service

13. Why would a technician want to move the spool folder from one partition to another?

   A. To set permissions on the printer

   B. To clear jobs out of the print queue

   C. To customize the print process

   D. To speed up the printing process

14. What can remedy a print that jams and crushes the paper into the feeder assembly on a laser printer?

   A. Restart the printer

   B. Clean the feeder rollers

   C. Add more paper to the paper tray

   D. Replace the print engine, as it is moving the paper too fast into the printer

15. What would happen if the corona transfer wire were broken?

   A. The printed page would be blank

   B. The paper would not feed into the printer

   C. The printed page would be solid black with toner

   D. The printed page would be very faded

16. What is the most common reason an inkjet printer jams?

   A. Dirty or clogged ink cartridge

   B. Failure of the print engine

   C. Failure of the printer driver

   D. Incorrect media type

17. A vertical line on every page of a printed document means there is a
   _____ on the print drum.

   A. Fleck of toner

   B. Scratch around the cylinder

   C. Light leakage

   D. Fingerprint

18. What would cause a speck to show on each page of every printed document?

   A. A fleck of toner on the print drum

   B. Scratches on the print drum

   C. Weakness in the fuser

   D. Improperly charged paper

19. Why should a regular vacuum not be used to clean toner that spilled?

   A. The vacuum may not fit into the printer assembly

   B. The vacuum will cause the HPVS to fail

   C. The vacuum will emit the toner through its exhaust system

   D. The vacuum will not pick up toner, as the toner is too fine

20. What should a technician do after a thorough cleaning of a printer?

   A. Complete a test page from the operating system

   B. Restart the computer it is attached to

   C. Restart the spooler service

   D. Reinstall the printer on the operating system

Scenarios

You've learned a great deal about maintaining and troubleshooting laser, inkjet, and dot matrix printers in this chapter. The following two critical thinking exercises will test your ability to apply what you learned.

1. You are a consultant for a small company that has 25 users on a network. Their primary printer, a laser printer, has recently stopped printing. You confirm that the printer has power, and you can hear the printer attempt to print when you send a test page. What steps would you take to determine the problem and resolve the issue?

2. You are a technician responsible for nearly eighteen printers. One printer, a color inkjet, has started printing splotchy patterns, and the color red seems to be shifted out of the image. What steps can you take to resolve this problem?

Lab Exercises

Lab 14.1 Installing a Windows 2000 Printer

1. Select Start ⇨ Settings ⇨ Printers.

2. Double-click the Add Printer icon.

3. Choose Next and then click the radio button for the local printer. For this exercise, confirm there is no check next to "Automatically detect and install my Plug and Play printer." Click Next.

4. Choose an available port, such as LPT2, and then click Next.

5. For this exercise, choose any manufacturer and then choose a model. For example, select HP and then select HPLaserJet4V. Click Next.

6. Supply a friendly name for this printer. If you have other printers connected to this machine, do not make this new printer your default printer. Click Next.

7. If you are on a network, you can choose to share this printer. Click Next.

8. In most instances where a printer is actually attached to the port, you can choose to print a test page. In this exercise, there is no need to do so.

Lab 14.2 Cleaning an Ink Cartridge

1. Remove the ink cartridge from your laser printer. Some laser printers require the printer to be powered off; others require you to press a button to move the print head to a parked position. If you are uncertain, check your printer manual.

2. Place the ink cartridge on a clean cloth where it won't matter if it gets dirty. With a small amount of isopropyl alcohol on a cotton swab, gently clean the exterior of the ink cartridge. Clean the connectors on the back or sides of the cartridge. Clean the area around the nozzle on the bottom of the ink cartridge.

3. Set the ink cartridge aside. Power off the inkjet if necessary and remove the power cord.

4. Gently clean the interior of the print head where the ink cartridge rests. Allow any moisture on the ink cartridge and the clean print head to evaporate.

5. Replace the ink cartridge. Power on the printer.

6. Use the manufacturer's software, if applicable, to complete an alignment and test print.

Answers to Chapter Questions

Chapter Pre-Test

1. A **dot matrix printer** uses a tractor feed mechanism to move the continuous form paper through the printer.

2. In a laser printer, the **fuser** melts the toner into the paper as it exits the printer.

3. A **driver** allows a computer to communicate with the printer. Drivers are software that allow operating systems to speak with hardware.

4. A spool file is **the print job that has been submitted to the print queue**.

5. A vertical line running the length of a document is most likely caused by **a scratch on the print drum**.

6. **Inkjet printers** often require the head to be aligned when changing the ink cartridge.

7. Printer quality is measured in the number of **dots** per **inch**, abbreviated as dpi.

8. The best method for repairing a clogged ink cartridge is to **clean the cartridge**.

9. Spilled toner should be cleaned **with a service vacuum or a treated shop towel designed to attract and absorb spilled toner**.

10. Too much paper in a paper tray **can cause the printer to jam with duplicate sheets, or prevent the feeder rollers from working properly, if at all**.

Assessment Questions

1. **B, C.** Most jams occur during the paper feed process or the exit process. For more information, see the section titled "Printer Feed and Output."

2. **D.** Inkjet printers spray their ink onto the paper. Regular laser printer paper, which will pass through an inkjet, absorbs the ink into the paper rather than holding the ink on top of the paper. For more information, see the section titled "Troubleshooting Friction Feeders."

3. **C.** Paper that is too slick for the feeder wheels to grip should be fed into the printer through the manual feed tray. For more information, see the section titled "Troubleshooting Friction Feeders."

4. **C.** The printer engine is responsible for turning the wheels and gears to move the paper through the printer. Should this engine fail, the printer may continue to receive power, but will not begin the print process. For more information, see the section titled "Troubleshooting Friction Feeders."

5. **A.** The holes on either side of the printer are responsible for moving the paper through the printer. The holes fit over sprockets in the dot matrix print assembly. As the sprockets turn, the paper advances through the print assembly. For more information, see the section titled "Troubleshooting Continuous Form Feeders."

6. **C.** The fuser is extremely hot and can severely burn. Do not touch the fuser assembly without first powering down the printer and allowing it to cool completely. For more information, see the section titled "Troubleshooting Paper Output."

7. **C.** An inkjet printer uses a friction feed mechanism to load the paper into the print assembly. The print engine turns the cylinder that moves the paper under the ink cartridge and ultimately out of the printer. Should the print engine fail, the paper will not advance. For more information, see the section titled "Troubleshooting Friction Feeders."

8. **B.** Dot matrix printers use sprockets to advance and eject the paper from the printer. For more information, see the section titled "Troubleshooting Continuous Form Feeders."

9. **B, C.** The ability to print a test page from the operating system confirms that the computer and the print device can communicate. A test print will also confirm that the printer's driver is still valid and working in the OS. For more information, see the section titled "Software-Based Errors."

10. **C.** The characterization data file tells the operating system what the printer is capable of doing. For example, information on paper sizes, language, and resolution is included in the file. For more information, see the section titled "Software-Based Errors."

11. C. The spooler service is responsible for the print process. When an application prints, the print job is handed to the spooler service to convert the data into the code expected by the printer. For more information, see the section titled "Troubleshooting Continuous Form Feeders."

12. D. Should a print job become stuck in the print queue, a technician can stop and restart the spooler service to clear the queue. Restarting the computer would also work, as the service would stop and restart, but there is no real reason for a reboot. For more information, see the section titled "Software-Based Errors."

13. D. The Spools folder is where the print jobs stay while they are being submitted to the print device. A technician could move the Spools folder to a partition on a faster drive to speed up transmission. For more information, see the section titled "Software-Based Errors."

14. B. If a printer is jamming and crushing the paper as soon as the print process begins, the feeder rollers are most likely dirty and need to be cleaned. Use a small amount of isopropyl alcohol to remove the crud from the wheels and try printing again. For more information, see the section titled "Laser Printers."

15. A. The corona transfer wire is responsible for charging the paper so the toner will be attracted to the positive charge on the paper. Without the charge, the paper will not attract the toner. For more information, see the section titled "Laser Printers."

16. D. Inkjet printers can become jammed when paper that is not created for an inkjet is used. While most laser-approved papers will print through an inkjet printer, heavier stock paper will not. For more information, see the section titled "Troubleshooting Friction Feeders."

17. B. A scratch around the cylinder of the print drum allows toner to collect into the scratch and then deposit onto each printed page during the toner transfer. For more information, see the section titled "Laser Printers."

18. B. This problem is similar to a vertical line on each printed page of a document. Specks on every sheet of paper could be a result of scratches on the print drum. As toner is transferred to the drum, it collects in the scratches. When the positive paper moves beneath the print drum, the toner in the scratches will move to the paper. For more information, see the section titled "Laser Printers."

19. C. A regular vacuum can pick up the toner—but cannot usually hold. The toner may seep through the vacuum's dust bag and blow out the exhaust, creating an even bigger mess. For more information, see the section titled "Laser Printers."

20. A. After a thorough cleaning, a technician should submit a test page to the printer to confirm that all of the parts are in working order. For more information, see the section titled "Laser Printers."

Scenarios

1. A printer may stop printing for a variety of reasons. First, confirm that the printer is properly connected to the network and does indeed have power. Next, the printer should be checked for paper jams. Third, check the feeder wheels to see if they are slick or dirty. If the wheels are worn down, they should be replaced; if they're dirty, clean them. Check the toner to confirm that the toner is loaded properly and has the protective strip of tape removed from the toner chamber. Finally, consult the printer manual to find directions on testing the print engine and its ability to move the internal working parts of the printer. If the engine has failed, determine if it makes financial sense to replace the engine or to replace the entire printer.

2. An inkjet that prints splotchy colors and that has its colors misaligned needs to have its ink cartridge cleaned and then its heads realigned through the printer software. Remove the ink cartridge and clean it with a cotton cloth and a small amount of isopropyl alcohol. Power off the printer and clean the interior of the compartment where the ink cartridge rests. Restore the cartridge and power on the printer. Launch the printer's software to align the print head on the inkjet. Finally, confirm that the paper is loaded properly and is the correct media type for the inkjet printer. Print a sample page to the printer.

Troubleshooting Procedures and Guidelines

EXAM OBJECTIVES

Exam 220-201 ✦ A+ Core Hardware

- ✦ **2.1** Identify common symptoms and problems associated with each module and how to troubleshoot and isolate the problems.

  - **Content may include the following:** Processor/Memory symptoms; Mouse; Floppy drive; Parallel ports; Hard Drives; Sound Card/Audio; Monitor/Video; Motherboards; Modems; BIOS; USB; CMOS; Power supply; Slot covers; POST audible/visual error codes; Troubleshooting tools, e.g., multi-meter; Large LBA, LBA

- ✦ **2.2** Identify basic troubleshooting procedures and how to elicit problem symptoms from customers.

  - **Content may include the following:** Troubleshooting/ isolation/problem determination procedures; Determine whether hardware or software problem; Gather information from user regarding, e.g., Customer Environment, Symptoms/Error Codes, Situation when the problem occurred

CHAPTER PRE-TEST

1. The three types of hard drive errors are _____, _____, and _____.

2. POST tests the calculated checksum and verifies it against a value stored in _____.

3. During POST, the _____ error code indicates a keyboard problem.

4. The first thing you should do in case your modem does not respond is check that the cord from the phone line is plugged into the _____ port.

5. While trying to read a floppy disk, you get the error "Write protect error writing drive A:" What will you check for?

6. What tool do you use to check the resistance of wires?

7. Why does a monitor flicker? Give three reasons.

8. Name some troubleshooting tools.

✦ Answers to these questions can be found at the end of the chapter. ✦

What do you do if a problem crops up with your computer? Do you rush to call the technical support team? Or do you panic and think that it's the end of the world? In this chapter, we will examine some procedures to help you troubleshoot common computer problems. Troubleshooting is all about knowledge — knowing where to look for the problem; about skill — performing the correct action once you locate the problem area; and about attitude — how to approach a problem. In this chapter, we will look at each one of these troubleshooting aspects.

A note about the way this chapter is organized: technical problems are discussed in the order in which they are most likely to occur when you work with your computer. For example, the problems we examine first are those that may occur at startup. This is followed by an in-depth examination of problems and possible solutions related to various system components. In the final sections, the chapter focuses on how a good troubleshooter should approach a problem (systematically and precisely), some do's and don'ts for a troubleshooter, and how to bring out all relevant information that will help identify the problem area.

Troubleshooting

An important part of setting up and maintaining your computer is learning how to troubleshoot common problems. Troubleshooting is the process of identifying the source of a problem in order to eliminate the problem. In this chapter we will learn how to troubleshoot problems that commonly occur during booting and with various hardware devices.

POST

 2.1 Identify common symptoms and problems associated with each module and how to troubleshoot and isolate the problems. Content may include the following: POST audible/visual error codes

The POST, or Power On Self Test, resides in the ROM BIOS of the computer. It checks if the system hardware is in proper working condition. If POST identifies an error, it communicates the type and cause of the error using a variety of error codes, such as beeps and displays. Each BIOS manufacturer has its own set of beep codes. To find out the specific beep codes for your motherboard, visit your computer manufacturer's Web site. Table 15-1 lists some common beep codes and the probable causes for them.

Table 15-1
Common Beep Codes

Beeps	*Probable Causes*
One short beep	Normal startup
One long beep	Keyboard error
One short, one long beep	Monitor problem
Two short beeps	The POST numeric code appears on the monitor
Repeating short beeps or a continuous beep	Power problem
One long, one short beep	System board problem
One long, two or three short beeps	Monitor/Display error
One beep, followed by three, four, or five beeps	System board problems, possibly with DMA, CMOS setup chip, timer, or system bus
Two beeps, followed by three, four, or five beeps	First 64K of RAM has errors
Three beeps, followed by three, four, or five beeps	Keyboard controller or video controller failed
Four beeps, followed by two, three, or four beeps	Serial or parallel port, system timer, or time of day problem

The flags and register of the processor are tested using a checksum value generated by the CMOS. If this value does not match the checksum value stored in the ROM, the system halts. If the checksum value matches, the DMA controller is checked. If the DMA controller fails, then again the system halts.

Next, the interrupt controller is checked. If this fails the POST, the system sounds a long beep followed by a short beep and halts.

Then, the timer is checked to see if it is running at the proper speed. If this fails, you again hear a long beep followed by a short beep, and the system halts.

The next check is done on the serial and parallel ports, followed by the display card. If the display card is not functioning properly, you might hear two short beeps.

If the display card passes the POST, the RAM is checked. Next in line is the keyboard. If the keyboard does not function properly, Error Code 301 is displayed on the screen, and a long beep is heard. For POST, the Error Code range for a keyboard is between 300–399.

The disk drives and their controller cards are checked for functionality against the information stored in the CMOS. If these are not operational, you hear a short beep, and the DRIVE MISMATCH ERROR message is displayed. Error Code 601 is displayed if the drive motors fail the POST. The POST Error Code range for a floppy drive is between 600–699.

Finally, the various adapters are checked. If the adapters are fine, a short beep is sounded, and the POST loads the boot record.

Beep codes are not always the most reliable information regarding the errors that crop up during the POST. Often, power supply problems or a malfunctioning system board are causes of misleading beeps. Other causes of misleading error codes include incorrect setting of PC/XT memory configuration switches and certain expansion boards on IBM systems.

CMOS

2.1 Identify common symptoms and problems associated with each module and how to troubleshoot and isolate the problems. Content may include the following: CMOS

CMOS, or Complementary Metal-Oxide Semiconductor, is used to create a special RAM that stores the hardware configuration. A rechargeable battery on the motherboard supplies power to this RAM even when the computer is switched off, so that the configuration information is retained. This RAM is commonly referred to as the CMOS. If a CMOS error occurs, the related hardware will not function. CMOS errors usually occur due to a mismatch in the configuration stored in the CMOS and the actual hardware being used. To resolve most CMOS errors, you need to enter the CMOS setup and change the data. Some common CMOS errors and the ways to resolve them are presented in the following list:

- ✦ **CMOS display type mismatch** — Enter the CMOS setup to change the CMOS video settings.

- ✦ **CMOS system options not set** — Re-enter all the CMOS settings. Check if the CMOS backup battery is working properly.

- ✦ **CMOS memory size mismatch** — Specify the correct amount of RAM installed on your computer in the CMOS setup.

- ✦ **CMOS battery state low** — Replace the old battery pack with a new one.

- ✦ **CMOS checksum failure** — Check the CMOS battery. If it is fine, then you probably need to replace the motherboard.

- ✦ **CMOS time and date not set** — Set the date and time in the CMOS setup.

You might also encounter CMOS errors related to incorrect hard disk parameters, wrong floppy disk types, incorrect memory, or I/O wait states. For these errors, enter the CMOS setup and specify the correct information.

BIOS

 2.1 Identify common symptoms and problems associated with each module and how to troubleshoot and isolate the problems. Content may include the following: BIOS

BIOS, or Basic Input/Output System includes a set of software routines that test the hardware at startup. It also provides low-level software routines and boots the operating system. If errors are found during the test at startup, BIOS reports it using beeps.

One beep — DRAM refresh failure

To resolve this kind of error, try reseating the memory. If that doesn't help, you might have to replace the memory.

Two beeps — Parity circuit failure

Probably the only solution to this problem is replacing the motherboard.

Three beeps — Base 64K of RAM failure

Again, check if reseating or replacing the memory helps. If not, you might have to replace the motherboard.

Four beeps — System timer failure

Replace the motherboard. That's probably the only solution.

Five beeps — CPU failure

If you hear five beeps, ensure that the CPU is fixed properly and that a heat sink is attached to it. Ensure correct jumper settings on the motherboard. Check the system documentation for the correct settings. If all else fails, try replacing the CPU chip.

Six beeps — Keyboard controller/Gate A20 failure

To resolve this error, try resetting the keyboard controller chip. If that doesn't work, try replacing the keyboard with one that you know is working. If you still get the error, you might have to replace the motherboard.

Seven beeps — Virtual mode exception error

There's not much you can do to solve this problem. Replace the motherboard.

Eight beeps — Display memory read/write failure

Reseat the display card. If the problem persists, replace the display card memory. If that doesn't help, replace the display card itself.

Nine beeps—ROM BIOS checksum failure

This indicates a faulty BIOS. Try reseating the ROM chips in the sockets. You might have to replace the ROM chips.

Ten beeps—CMOS shutdown register read/write error

Replace the motherboard.

One long, and two or three short beeps—Display card failure

Reseat the display board. If that doesn't help, replace it.

Motherboard

 2.1 Identify common symptoms and problems associated with each module and how to troubleshoot and isolate the problems. Content may include the following: Motherboards

The motherboard is an integral part of the computer. When troubleshooting the motherboard, you should take as many clues as possible that POST might offer. The beep codes often provide a sufficient amount of information if you can interpret them. For help in interpreting the beep codes, refer to the ROM BIOS manufacturer's Web site.

When troubleshooting motherboard problems, first strip your computer to bare-bones—motherboard, processor, memory, display card, and a drive to boot the system. Once the barebones working system is in place, check the connections of each component.

Apply correct jumper settings for the processor type, speed, voltage, and bus speed. Then return all BIOS settings to the default values. Check for physical damage on the motherboard. Specifically, check for broken or bent pins on the connectors and cracks on the board.

Check the power supply. Ensure that necessary power is available. Also check the voltage coming from the power supply. Inappropriate voltage might cause good components to malfunction.

Run diagnostic programs, such as PC Technician or IBM Diagnostics, to detect hardware errors. If the diagnostic programs detect hardware errors, you might have to change the CPU, the BIOS, the RAM, or the motherboard itself. Try reseating these components before deciding that you need to replace them.

If you are unable to resolve the problems, you should try disassembling the computer and then reseating the cables, adapters, DIMMs, SIMMs, and socketed chips. Sometimes, corrosion or simply a bad connection between the components causes a motherboard to fail.

Don't forget to check the CMOS settings, DIP switches, and jumpers. A weak battery might also cause the CMOS configuration to be lost.

Another possible problem might occur if the computer is unable to recognize all the SIMMs and DIMMs. First, check the CMOS settings. Then, see if the SIMM and DIMM modules are seated properly. Try a different memory slot for each. Check if the part numbers on the SIMMs are correct. The speed (in nanoseconds) and size (in megabytes) of all the SIMMs must be the same. Finally, look for physical damage. If you decide to replace the memory modules, replace one module at a time. This ensures that you don't change the good modules.

If you notice a broken trace (a fine printed circuit) or a bad socket, you might have to replace the motherboard. Before you do so, ensure that the voltage from the power supply is correct. Fluctuating or high voltage might damage a good motherboard.

Processor/memory

2.1 Identify common symptoms and problems associated with each module and how to troubleshoot and isolate the problems. Content may include the following: Processor/Memory symptoms

The memory is one of the most important parts of your computer. Any problems with the memory could severely hamper the computer's functionality, or even cause it to stop working. To remove any problems related to the memory, you must identify the cause of the problem and act accordingly. Potential problems with memory management, symptoms, and solutions to these problems are discussed in the following sections.

A TSR does not load

TSR is a Terminate-and-Stay-Resident program that is loaded into the memory by AUTOEXEC.BAT, but not immediately executed. This program is executed later, when some special key (or "hot" key) on the keyboard is pressed, or a special hardware action occurs. An example of a TSR is the screen capture program that is activated by the Print Screen key. When you are using any application software, you can press the Print Screen key to activate this TSR, and save a copy of the screen to any graphic application. Suppose that in the CONFIG.SYS file, you have included the commands DEVICE=HIMEM.SYS, DEVICE=EMM386.EXE, and DOS=UMB. You then tried to load a TSR high, by using either the DEVICEHIGH= command in CONFIG.SYS or the LOADHIGH command in AUTOEXEC.BAT. But the MEM/C report shows that the load high instruction did not work and that the TSR is still in conventional memory.

Tip

Loading a TSR into some blocks in the upper memory addresses is called "loading a TSR high." A TSR, or any program, is loaded into the upper memory by using either the DEVICEHIGH= command in CONFIG.SYS or the LOADHIGH command in AUTOEXEC.BAT, after making the upper memory blocks available by using three commands in the CONFIG.SYS file: DEVICE=HIMEM.SYS, DEVICE=EMM386.EXE, and DOS=UMB.

The problem could either be that there was not enough space in the UMB assigned to the TSR, or that there were no free UMBs available for it.

This problem could also occur because some TSRs do not work from upper memory. Test the TSRs before you proceed with other methods to isolate and remove the problem. Then check the command lines in the CONFIG.SYS and AUTOEXEC.BAT files to see if they are correct. You should also check the order of the DEVICEHIGH= commands in CONFIG.SYS to see if the larger TSRs are placed first and allocated the larger UMBs. Even if all TSRs don't fit into the upper memory, allocating the largest UMBs to the largest TSRs will free the maximum possible amount of conventional memory. If in doubt, you can try to use MEMMAKER to choose the best order of loading the TSRs.

A device does not work, or the system hangs

Suppose you have a scanner that works properly with the scanner card installed on your computer. However, when you install a network card, the scanner stops functioning. Even the network does not work properly.

It's possible that both the network card and the scanner card are using the same upper memory address. If your system does not respond or a device does not function, the probable cause could be a memory conflict. A memory conflict occurs when two or more programs or data are assigned the same memory address. Memory conflicts that can cause devices or the computer to stop working occur if:

✦ Two expansion boards use the same upper memory

✦ DOS uses the memory used by an expansion board to create and use a UMB

If a device stops functioning after you install a new device, the chances are that both of the devices are using the same upper memory. One of the devices has to be assigned a different upper memory address for both devices to work properly. You can do this by using the DIP switches that come with some expansion boards to replace one set of memory addresses with another. You might also add a parameter to the command line that loads the device driver for the expansion board to change the memory address.

The problem might remain if neither of the devices accepts an alternate set of memory addresses. This means that the two devices cannot be installed on the same computer. To check which memory address is assigned to a device and whether the device can accept a different set of addresses, you need to consult the documentation of the device or its device driver.

The other possible cause of the system not responding or a device not functioning could be that DOS uses the same memory to create and use a UMB that is also used by a device. Sometimes DOS does not know what memory addresses the devices are using, until the system boots and the devices are activated. Due to this delay, DOS might consider an address to be free and not being used by any device, and use it to create a UMB and load a TSR into it. As a result of this conflict, the system might stop responding and the TSR and/or the device might not work properly.

To resolve this conflict, you first need to identify the memory used by the devices, which can be done by consulting the documentation that was provided with the device. Some device drivers display the memory address they are using during the boot process. Look for this information on the screen during startup. You can also use MSD (Microsoft Diagnostics) to see how memory is being used.

Then, you can change the EMM386.EXE command line in CONFIG.SYS to exclude the range of addresses that the device is using. You can do this by using the Exclude (X) option. For example, if you find out that the device uses the address range BC000-BFFFF, exclude this range from the address used by the UMBs with the following command:

```
DEVICE=C:\DOS\EMM386.EXE NOEMS X = BC00 - BFFF
```

Finally, you have to reboot your computer to make the changes effective and to resolve the memory conflict.

If your system hangs intermittently when you run certain applications, a CPU error is probably indicated. To identify the source of the problem, you can try running some diagnostic programs, such as AMIDAIG from AMI or The Troubleshooter from ALLMicro. If the diagnostic tools point to the CPU as the cause of the errors, you might have to replace the CPU. However, if the computer hangs irrespective of the application being run, then a thermal failure is indicated. Check to see if the cooling fan is operational. You can try installing a heat sink in the CPU.

Floppy drive

 2.1 Identify common symptoms and problems associated with each module and how to troubleshoot and isolate the problems. Content may include the following: Floppy drive

The mechanical nature of a floppy drive makes it prone to a number of problems. We will address common floppy drive problems, their causes, and possible remedies in this section.

You might see a 601 Error, or a Floppy Drive Controller Failure Error, when the system boots up—an indication that the floppy drive did not pass the POST. This error could be caused by an erroneous power supply, a bad drive, a bad cable, or an incorrectly configured controller board. To verify if the motherboard DIP switches (for an XT system) or SETUP (for an AT system) are configured properly, you can run the CMOS setup.

Even if the floppy drive passes the POST, you may still not be able to access the disks. To troubleshoot drive problems, you should first perform some basic checks. For example, take out the disk and check if the shuttle window moves freely. Ensure that there is no dust or dirt on the disk's Mylar surface. Dust—and objects, such as blades of grass or hair—often prevent the disk from functioning properly. Also check if the disk spins freely inside the plastic cover. Some new disks need a little loosening up. After checking these things, try using the disk. Your problem may have been solved.

You should also check if the light on the correct drive goes on when you try to access the disk. You might just be accessing drive A when the disk is in drive B.

Before attributing a problem to the drive, you should try to access other disks using the same drive. If you can do so, the problem is probably with the disk and not with the drive. However, this is not always true. It's possible that a drive is out of alignment, in which case it will not be able to read disks other than those it has formatted with its own alignment. Try using several disks and note if the drive only reads the disks that it has formatted recently. If so, then the drive is probably out of alignment and you will need to change the drive.

If the light on the drive does not come on at all, there could be a problem with either the software or the hardware. Try to access the disk by using other programs, such as the DIR A: command in DOS, or the CHKDSK A: command. Try to access the disk from Windows Explorer or File Manager. If the light still does not come up, the problem is more likely with the power supply to the drive or the cable connection. If you have another floppy drive installed, check if that light comes on. If the light does not come on for either drive, the problem could be caused by the power supply or the floppy drive controller card.

If the cable is not aligned properly to Pin 1, the drive light could come on and stay on at the boot process, which might mean that the disks in the drive are not being accessed. You need to check the edge of the cable to see if it is properly aligned with Pin 1.

Sometimes, errors are caused if the system setup loses CMOS data. For example, you are using a 1.44MB drive, but the system treats it as a 720K drive. You should check the drive specifications in the system CMOS setup and supply the correct configuration.

Sometimes, the drive might not work properly if the read/write heads are not clean. You should use a head cleaning kit that includes a paper disk and a cleaning solution to clean the read/write heads of the drive. If you do not know how to use the kit, refer to the directions available with the kit.

Finally, you can try rebooting the computer. Though not conventional, this is often a solution to many computer problems. Try a hard boot if a soft boot does not do the trick.

If, after taking all these simple steps, the drive still does not respond, you might decide to open the casing and take a look at the hardware inside. There are a number of hardware components that might cause a drive to fail: the power supply, the power cable, the floppy drive controller, the cable from the controller card to the drive, the system board, and, of course, the drive itself. It will help if you have components in hand that you know are working fine. You can then replace each of the above-mentioned components, one at a time, until the problem is resolved.

Tip   When you know for certain that a particular device works properly, it is called a *known-good device*.

When resolving a hardware problem, you should first check all the connections from the system board to the drive. Then you should check the power supply and the power cable connection. If the problem persists, try using a different power cable. Then try changing the data cable. Make sure that you align the data cable properly with Pin 1. Try changing the controller card, and finally the drive itself. Make sure that you try to access the drive after changing each component.

If the drive still does not work after checking all the components, then the problem probably lies in the system board or the ROM BIOS on the system board.

Some common error messages generated by floppy drive problems and how to interpret and resolve them:

✦ `Non-system disk or disk error. Replace and press any key when ready.`

This message appears when you try to boot from a non-bootable disk. To solve the problem, all you need to do is remove the disk and press any key. The system then bypasses the floppy drive and loads the operating system from the hard drive. If you want to boot from the floppy, COMMAND.COM and the two hidden DOS system files that are necessary to load DOS must be present in it. Recall that the two system files for Microsoft DOS are IO.SYS and MSDOS.SYS, whereas the system files for IBM DOS are IBMBIO.COM and IBMDOS.COM. You can also boot from a Windows 9x rescue disk or a startup disk, if you have created one.

If the drive is empty but the same message appears, some critical operating system files are corrupted or missing from the hard disk. You should then boot from a bootable floppy disk or rescue disk to check if any of the necessary system files have been accidentally deleted from the hard disk.

✦ `Invalid or missing COMMAND.COM`

This message appears if you try to load DOS from a disk that has the two hidden system files, but COMMAND.COM is either missing or is corrupted. In such a case, you should first boot from a bootable floppy and then copy the COMMAND.COM file to the disk from which you were trying to boot.

✦ `Invalid Drive Specification`

You might see this message if you try to access a drive that the operating system does not recognize. The OS might not recognize a drive if the drive fails the POST. For example, during startup you see a message indicating that the BIOS cannot access the hard drive. You boot from a floppy and then from the A prompt, you type C: to access the hard drive. Then you might see this message because the hard drive has failed the POST. Check the CMOS setup for correct specifications of the drive.

✦ Not ready reading drive A:, Abort, Retry, Fail?

This message will appear if the system cannot read the disk in drive A —
perhaps because the disk is not inserted properly or is missing. If you insert
the disk properly and the problem persists, you may have bad sectors in the
disk, a bad boot record, or errors in the FAT. Try using some utilities, such as
Norton or Nuts & Bolts, to check errors in the disk.

✦ General failure reading drive A:, Abort, Retry, Fail?

This message may appear if you try to read a disk that is not formatted or is
corrupted. The message could also mean that the floppy drive itself is bad. To
determine the problem area, try accessing other disks. If the disk is the problem but the disk is formatted, then the disk is probably unusable — perhaps
due to a bad master boot record.

✦ Track 0 bad, disk not usable

This message is most likely to occur if you try to format a disk using the
wrong disk type. Check the FORMAT command. Don't try to format a disk
using the wrong density.

✦ Write-protect error writing drive A:

This message indicates that you are trying to write to a disk that is write-
protected. Check the write-protect tab on the disk. If you are using a 3½ inch
floppy, the write-protect hole must be closed, with the switch (also called a
tab) towards the center of the disk. For a 5½ inch floppy, ensure that the write-
protect notch is uncovered.

Sometimes, you may encounter a strange problem: You insert a floppy in the drive
and read its contents (using the DIR command, for example). Then you remove it
and insert a different disk. But when you try to read it, you find that the contents of
the previous floppy are displayed again. No matter which disk you insert, the contents displayed remain the same. The most probable cause of this kind of a problem
is a scratched or bad floppy cable. Replace the cable before you use other disks in
the drive. If you do not replace the cable, you might end up losing information from
good floppies. Another possible cause for this type of problem is that your system
does not have change-line support. Change-line is a signal from the drive to the controller indicating that the floppy drive door has been opened since a disk was last
read. If this is not enabled, the system might not recognize a change of disk and
therefore display the contents it read last. To check if your system has change-line
support and to find out how to activate it, consult the system documentation.

Hard drives

2.1 Identify common symptoms and problems associated with each module and
how to troubleshoot and isolate the problems. Content may include the following: Hard drives

A hard drive failure can be attributed to one of three types of failures: disk access
failure, file access failure, or boot failure. The following section discusses each type
of error in detail.

Disk access failure

In Windows 9x, NT, or 2000, you may sometimes not be able to see the drive icon, or in DOS you may get the error message

```
Invalid Drive Specification
```

when you try to read from the hard drive. These errors indicate that the operating system is unable to access the drive. In such a situation, you will not be able to access any data from the hard disk. These kinds of problems are probably caused by disk controller failures, drive failures, or errors in the partition table.

The first step in troubleshooting a drive access failure is to boot from a floppy and then run the FDISK utility to check the partition information. If the partitions are not created, you need to build them. If the partition information is correct, try formatting the partitions. After formatting, you should be able to access the disk, but you will lose all the data stored. If you have backups, you can recover the data.

If FDISK is unable to recognize the hard disk, the problem might be a faulty disk or a defective disk controller. Check the disk controller card to remove any possible IRQ or address conflicts. Then, check if the cables and the power supply are connected properly.

If you have an IDE disk, check the CMOS settings to ensure that the master/slave information is correct and that the disk controller is enabled. If you have a SCSI disk, check for the drive ID and the SCSI chain termination.

If you are still unable to access the disk, the problem could either be the disk itself or the controller card. To check where the problem lies, remove the hard disk and install it in a machine that you know to be working fine. If you are able to access the disk in the other machine, you probably need to replace the controller card. Otherwise, you need to replace the disk.

File access failure

Sometimes, you might be able to access the hard disk, but not access all or some files in it. In DOS, you may see the following messages:

```
Sector not found
Error reading drive C:
General failure error reading drive C:
```

Inability to access files might be attributed to a corrupt directory structure, corrupt files, or media failure. SCANDISK is a very useful utility that takes care of multiple file access related problems, including corrupted directory structures. Third-party utilities, such as Norton Disk Doctor, are also extremely helpful in troubleshooting file access errors.

If these utilities are not able to solve the problem, you might need to format the hard disk. But remember to make a backup of all the accessible files. If the file access errors recur, the problem is more likely due to media failure. Formatting the disk usually rectifies media failure problems. If formatting does not help, you probably need to replace the disk.

Boot failure

If a boot failure occurs, your computer becomes unusable. Either a disk access error or a file access error might cause a boot failure. When the computer boots, BIOS first tries to load the boot files from Drive A:. If the floppy drive does not contain a disk, then BIOS searches the hard disk for the relevant files. If the system files are missing from the hard disk or if they are corrupted, you might encounter a boot failure. An error message appears and the boot process halts. To solve this problem, you need to boot from a floppy. Run the SYS.COM utility and from A:, issue the SYS C: command. This copies the system boot files to the hard disk. You should then be able to boot from the hard disk. Sometimes you might have to format the hard disk. In such a situation, use the FORMAT C: /S command to format the hard disk and copy the system files to it.

Cross-Reference For more information about creating emergency repair disks, see Chapter 22.

If there is a drive access error, the boot process will always fail. You need to troubleshoot this problem first and then copy the boot files to the hard disk.

LBA, large mode

Objective

2.1 Identify common symptoms and problems associated with each module and how to troubleshoot and isolate the problems. Content may include the following: Large LBA, LBA

If you use a hard drive that has a capacity greater than 504MB, the BIOS uses either the ECHS or large mode, or the LBA mode to support the hard drive. To find out which mode your system BIOS supports, look at the CMOS settings.

To use either the large mode or LBA to support large capacity hard drives, the system BIOS and the hard drive controller BIOS (present within the hard drive casing) must support translation. Translation is the method by which the BIOS communicates information regarding the hard disk to the operating system. Translation occurs in the large mode or the LBA mode. Consult the system documentation to find out which mode you should use to support the hard drive.

If your system BIOS does not support a large capacity drive, you need to upgrade the BIOS. But ensure that the new BIOS relates correctly to the system board chip set. Select a new BIOS based on the recommendations of the system board manufacturer.

Some old BIOSs will work with a large capacity hard disk if they treat the large capacity hard disk as a smaller hard disk that they can support. In this case, the BIOS simply assigns a drive capacity smaller than the actual. This leads to wastage of disk space.

There are some drives that come with disk manager software installed on them. The software enables the BIOS to recognize the complete hard disk as separate partitions or logical drives.

Most large capacity drives come with a disk that is designed to perform the translation between the older BIOS and the large capacity disk. To use the software provided, boot from the disk and follow the on-screen instructions.

You might also decide to upgrade the entire system board.

Mouse

 2.1 Identify common symptoms and problems associated with each module and how to troubleshoot and isolate the problems. Content may include the following: Mouse

The most common mouse problem occurs when the on-screen cursor doesn't move according to the movement of the mouse. Why? Because the rollers inside the mouse casing that are responsible for moving the cursor collect dust and dirt from the surface that the mouse moves on. To rectify this problem, you need to clean the rollers occasionally. To do so, open the mouse ball cover from the bottom of the mouse and remove the ball. You can usually remove the mouse ball cover with a press-and-turn action. Use a cotton swab dipped in a very small amount of some liquid cleaning compound, such as isopropyl alcohol, to clean the rollers.

In case cleaning doesn't help, check the mouse drivers to see if the right drivers are present and if they are set up correctly. You should also check the port to which the mouse is connected.

Another common problem that you might face while working with the mouse is a missing or inoperative mouse cursor. This problem can be attributed to either the software or the hardware. To resolve this problem, ensure that the mouse is plugged in properly and that the mouse cable is not physically damaged. You might also encounter this problem if the correct drivers are not installed, if the drivers are disabled, if the port is defective or disabled, or if there is a device conflict. Check if the correct drivers are installed and are enabled. Also check the device settings, remove the conflict, and reboot the computer to resolve the problem.

If the mouse buttons are failing, you probably need to replace the mouse. However, before replacing it, run the manufacturer's diagnostics (if they are available) to see the button operations.

Sound card/Audio

2.1 Identify common symptoms and problems associated with each module and how to troubleshoot and isolate the problems. Content may include the following: Sound Card/Audio

The common symptoms of an audio problem are distorted sound and complete absence of sound. Sometimes, you may not be able to play the sound files. If you encounter such a problem, first check if the speakers are properly plugged in and the volume is turned up. If you are using speakers that have their own power unit, check if the power supply is operational and the speakers are receiving power. Also ensure that the connection cable is plugged into the correct sound card jack. Try using a set of known-good speakers to discern whether the problem lies with the speakers that you are using. In case the good speakers are also not operational on your computer, you might have to replace the audio drivers.

Distorted sound might also result from an IRQ/DMA conflict or an I/O address conflict. Check to see if a free IRQ is assigned to the sound card.

Monitor/Video

2.1 Identify common symptoms and problems associated with each module and how to troubleshoot and isolate the problems. Content may include the following: Monitor/Video

Common symptoms of a monitor problem include distorted images, incorrect colors, or no display on the screen. As always, you should do some basic troubleshooting first. Very often, problems are due to faulty connection or improper power supply. However, display problems might also be caused by display adapter problems, insufficient VRAM, and IRQ conflicts. The following section will examine some common display problems and ways to resolve them.

Blank screen/Power light (LED) does not glow

First, ensure that the wall outlet, to which the monitor is connected, is functional. Try plugging in a lamp or some other device to see if the power supply works.

If the power cord of the monitor is directly connected to an external power strip, check if the power strip and the monitor are switched on. If the monitor power cord is connected to the back of the computer, ensure that the connection is tight and secure. Check if the computer is switched on and is receiving power.

Check if the power socket voltage is rated between 104–130 volts. If you use a monitor with a switch at the back that lets you choose from the range of 110–220 volts, ensure that the switch is in the right position. If your monitor has a fuse at the back, remove it and check for broken wires that indicate a bad fuse.

Tip

A fuse at the back of a monitor looks like a black knob that you can remove without opening the monitor cover. All monitors do not have these fuses.

Power light glows, but no display on screen

The first thing you should do in this situation is check the brightness and contrast adjustment. If brightness and contrast are set to the minimum value, you will not be able to see anything on-screen, even if the monitor is working properly.

If you don't observe any change, check if the display signal cable connection with the computer is secure. If the monitor-to-computer cable can be detached, try using one that you know is working fine. If this works, reconnect the old cable and recheck the connection.

Next, check the system configuration. If your computer has an older system board that uses a jumper or a DIP switch, you can use it to select the monitor type. Check the CMOS settings to verify the specifications. In case you are using Windows 9x, you also need to verify the software configuration. If possible, boot in the safe mode. When the computer boots in safe mode, it selects a generic driver and a low resolution. If the problem is resolved, the problem was most likely due to incorrect drivers or a bad resolution. Try changing the driver and/or the resolution and see if your problem is solved.

If the procedures specified above are unable to solve the problem, you might need to investigate inside the system unit. Check the video card. Remove it and then reseat it. Try putting the card in a different expansion slot. Clean the edge connectors using a contact cleaner or eraser, but ensure that eraser crumbs don't fall in the expansion slot.

Try swapping the video card with one that you know is good. If possible, use the video card on a known-good computer, and also use a known-good card on your computer. This will help you identify the problem area. If the video card of your computer has socketed chips, a loose chip might also cause a display problem. Press down the corners of each chip firmly using a screwdriver. If you determine that the problem is a bad video card, the best solution is to replace it.

If all of these procedures fail, you probably need to replace the monitor or take it to a service center. Try using a known-good monitor with your computer and see if that works.

Monitor displays wrong characters

If wrong characters are displayed, your monitor is probably fine. The problem is most likely with the video card. Try using a good one. Sometimes, wrong characters can also be displayed as a result of a bad chip, ROM or RAM on the motherboard. Use a good motherboard to see if the problem is resolved.

Monitor flickers/has wavy lines

The most common cause of this problem is a cable connection error. Check the connections. This problem can also be caused due to electrical/magnetic signal interference. If your computer is placed near a source of high-volume electrical noise, you will likely face this problem. Examples of sources producing a high

Modem

 2.1 Identify common symptoms and problems associated with each module and how to troubleshoot and isolate the problems. Content may include the following: Modems

In order to connect to remote computers, your modem needs to be working properly. The following section discusses some problems you might face with your modem and procedures that will help you resolve them.

The modem does not respond

If your modem is not responding, first check if the phone cord from the wall outlet is plugged into the line-in jack in the modem. Modems have two RJ-11 ports. Make sure that the phone cord is plugged into the correct (line-in) port.

If you are using an external modem, make sure that it is securely connected to the computer.

Check if the phone line is operational. Plug in a phone directly to the wall socket and check if you hear the dial tone. Ensure that the modem dials any extra characters necessary to access an outside line, such as 9 or 8.

Check the COM port and the IRQ settings for the modem. Ensure that they match the settings for the software. Also check that no other device is assigned the same COM port and IRQ. Check if you specified the correct modem type to the software. Otherwise, the software might be sending incorrect initialization commands to the software.

Try using a known-good serial cable to connect the external modem to the computer. If the modem uses a serial port card, you could move the serial port card to a different expansion slot and reinstall the modem. If you have an internal modem, you might have to reseat it in the expansion slot. You might try a different expansion slot, as well.

The modem can't identify the dial tone

You can hear the dial tone when you plug a phone directly to the wall outlet, but the modem does not identify it. Once again, check if the phone cord from the wall outlet is plugged into the correct port. If other devices, such as a fax machine or a credit card machine, are connected to the same phone line, remove them and try again. Ensure that the phone cables are straight and not crossed up with other electrical cables.

If the modem is still unable to detect the dial tone, try issuing the ATX0 command. On specifying the ATX0 command, the modem does not need to hear the dial tone first, and it will also not hear a busy signal. This state is known as Blind dialing. You can issue this command in the Advanced Connection Settings dialog box. To open this dialog box, select Settings ➪ Control Panel from the Start menu. In the Control

volume of electrical noise include bad fluorescent lights, large speakers, or other electrical devices that are connected to the same power outlet as the monitor.

Another cause of this problem is a low refresh rate at which the images on the screen are drawn (vertical scan frequency). Typically, a refresh rate below 60 Hz is likely to display flickering images. If your monitor supports a higher refresh rate, change it. If it does not, you need to buy a new monitor that solves your problem.

If there is not enough VRAM, or if the socketed VRAM has a different speed than the soldered memory, or if the video card that you are using does not support the resolution that you have selected, you might encounter flickering screens on your monitor.

Monitor cannot display graphics

If you find that your monitor is unable to display graphics or becomes blank when trying to open certain applications, there is a problem with either the VRAM or the graphics card. Check if your computer has a graphics, or video accelerator, card. Without one of these, graphics cannot be displayed. If the graphics card is present, check to make sure it's not defective. Try replacing the card you suspect to be bad with a good one. If the card is fine, the software that you are using might not be configured to support graphics, or it might not recognize the installed card.

There are other possible causes that lead to this problem. You might have selected a resolution and color depth that the video card in your computer does not support. The VRAM might not be adequate, or the socketed chips in the VRAM (if any) might have a different speed than the soldered memory. These problems might also lead to a poor-quality color display, if you can see the images at all.

Picture out of focus

Use the buttons on the outside of the monitor to readjust the screen dimensions, screen positions, color, brightness, and contrast. If that does not solve your problem, you might have to take you monitor to a service center, where some adjustments will be made inside the monitor.

Screen goes blank after a certain period of inactivity

You might observe that your computer screen becomes blank if the computer is left unused for a while. This is generally not a problem. Some computers follow the energy-saving standards. The monitors in these computers are sent into a standby mode or a sleep mode after a specified period of inactivity. You can usually identify if your monitor is in the power-saving mode if the LED light changes to orange from the usual green. Pressing a key or moving the mouse will bring the display back. You might be able to change the power-saving settings through the CMOS settings, or if you are using Windows 9x, by going to the Display Properties dialog box and selecting the Screen Saver tab.

Finally, it is also important that you use the correct display drivers and adapters for a high-quality display.

Power light glows, but no display on screen

The first thing you should do in this situation is check the brightness and contrast adjustment. If brightness and contrast are set to the minimum value, you will not be able to see anything on-screen, even if the monitor is working properly.

If you don't observe any change, check if the display signal cable connection with the computer is secure. If the monitor-to-computer cable can be detached, try using one that you know is working fine. If this works, reconnect the old cable and recheck the connection.

Next, check the system configuration. If your computer has an older system board that uses a jumper or a DIP switch, you can use it to select the monitor type. Check the CMOS settings to verify the specifications. In case you are using Windows 9x, you also need to verify the software configuration. If possible, boot in the safe mode. When the computer boots in safe mode, it selects a generic driver and a low resolution. If the problem is resolved, the problem was most likely due to incorrect drivers or a bad resolution. Try changing the driver and/or the resolution and see if your problem is solved.

If the procedures specified above are unable to solve the problem, you might need to investigate inside the system unit. Check the video card. Remove it and then reseat it. Try putting the card in a different expansion slot. Clean the edge connectors using a contact cleaner or eraser, but ensure that eraser crumbs don't fall in the expansion slot.

Try swapping the video card with one that you know is good. If possible, use the video card on a known-good computer, and also use a known-good card on your computer. This will help you identify the problem area. If the video card of your computer has socketed chips, a loose chip might also cause a display problem. Press down the corners of each chip firmly using a screwdriver. If you determine that the problem is a bad video card, the best solution is to replace it.

If all of these procedures fail, you probably need to replace the monitor or take it to a service center. Try using a known-good monitor with your computer and see if that works.

Monitor displays wrong characters

If wrong characters are displayed, your monitor is probably fine. The problem is most likely with the video card. Try using a good one. Sometimes, wrong characters can also be displayed as a result of a bad chip, ROM or RAM on the motherboard. Use a good motherboard to see if the problem is resolved.

Monitor flickers/has wavy lines

The most common cause of this problem is a cable connection error. Check the connections. This problem can also be caused due to electrical/magnetic signal interference. If your computer is placed near a source of high-volume electrical noise, you will likely face this problem. Examples of sources producing a high

Sound card/Audio

2.1 Identify common symptoms and problems associated with each module and how to troubleshoot and isolate the problems. Content may include the following: Sound Card/Audio

The common symptoms of an audio problem are distorted sound and complete absence of sound. Sometimes, you may not be able to play the sound files. If you encounter such a problem, first check if the speakers are properly plugged in and the volume is turned up. If you are using speakers that have their own power unit, check if the power supply is operational and the speakers are receiving power. Also ensure that the connection cable is plugged into the correct sound card jack. Try using a set of known-good speakers to discern whether the problem lies with the speakers that you are using. In case the good speakers are also not operational on your computer, you might have to replace the audio drivers.

Distorted sound might also result from an IRQ/DMA conflict or an I/O address conflict. Check to see if a free IRQ is assigned to the sound card.

Monitor/Video

2.1 Identify common symptoms and problems associated with each module and how to troubleshoot and isolate the problems. Content may include the following: Monitor/Video

Common symptoms of a monitor problem include distorted images, incorrect colors, or no display on the screen. As always, you should do some basic troubleshooting first. Very often, problems are due to faulty connection or improper power supply. However, display problems might also be caused by display adapter problems, insufficient VRAM, and IRQ conflicts. The following section will examine some common display problems and ways to resolve them.

Blank screen/Power light (LED) does not glow

First, ensure that the wall outlet, to which the monitor is connected, is functional. Try plugging in a lamp or some other device to see if the power supply works.

If the power cord of the monitor is directly connected to an external power strip, check if the power strip and the monitor are switched on. If the monitor power cord is connected to the back of the computer, ensure that the connection is tight and secure. Check if the computer is switched on and is receiving power.

Check if the power socket voltage is rated between 104–130 volts. If you use a monitor with a switch at the back that lets you choose from the range of 110–220 volts, ensure that the switch is in the right position. If your monitor has a fuse at the back, remove it and check for broken wires that indicate a bad fuse.

Tip   A fuse at the back of a monitor looks like a black knob that you can remove without opening the monitor cover. All monitors do not have these fuses.

Panel, double-click Modems. Select the modem from the list and click the Properties button. Next, select the Connection tab and click the Advanced button. The Advanced Connection Settings dialog box is displayed in Figure 15-1. If the ATX0 command does not help, be sure to remove it.

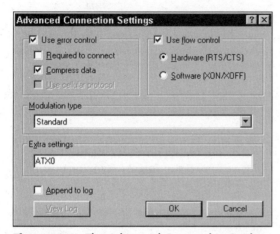

Figure 15-1: The Advanced Connection Settings dialog box that can be used to specify an extra AT command to the modem

The modem indicates that the other end is busy

This problem occurs if the modem does not recognize the incoming signal as a ring. Try using the ATX0 command to resolve this problem. Straighten the cables and remove any additional equipment that might be connected to the phone line.

The sending and receiving modems take a long time to establish the connection

The possible cause of this problem could be a noisy phone line. Try calling again. If you have a different number, try using it. Remove any additional equipment from the phone lines. Turn off error checking and data compression. Also, use a lower modem speed before you try again. You should try all of this, even if it sounds like the handshaking starts again during the connection. A handshake is a series of signals that acknowledge that the transfer of data can take place between the modem and other devices.

Tip
Sometimes, if you are connecting over a noisy phone line, it might sound as if the handshaking starts again during the connection. This is called *retraining* and it occurs when data becomes corrupt due to noisy phone lines. Retraining might solve the problem at times, as the modems reestablish the connection to compensate for the noisy phone lines.

File transfers are slow

File transfers will be slow if data compression is not enabled. Try to configure your modem to use data compression. In Windows 9x, you can use the Control Panel to access and change the modem properties.

The connection is very slow or is lost at times

This error is probably caused by the speed at which the communication software is set. The software needs the port speed, not the modem speed. Check if an error has been made in assigning the proper speed to the communication software.

Tip   The port speed that the communication software needs should be about four times the speed of the modem for an efficient connection.

Again, a noisy phone line is a possible cause. Try to straighten the cables and remove any extra equipment. Ensure that the phone line from the wall outlet to the modem is not more than four feet long. Otherwise, it might create electromagnetic interference that leads to slow or lost connections.

If all else fails, reinstall the modem. When using Windows 9x, let the operating system detect the modem and install the drivers.

The connection is lost and the modem gives the NO CARRIER message

If you see the NO CARRIER message, it is very likely that the remote modem has dropped the connection first. This problem is likely to occur when someone tries to use a phone extension on the line that you are using, or if call waiting is enabled. Disable call waiting, straighten the phone cables, and remove any additional equipment from the phone line. Disable error control, and try using a different modulation in the Advanced Connection Settings dialog box. Try using a lower port speed — 9600 or lower.

Tip   Some communications software provides a setting to disable call waiting. If that setting is not available, however, try using *70 before the number you are trying to dial. Use the ATX0 command along with this.

The modem is unable to transfer large files

You might keep losing the connection while trying to transfer a large amount of data. Even if the data is transferred, you might find that some of the data is lost or that you receive only garbage across the connection. Try using a lower port speed and a lower modem speed. If the port speed is too high for the Universal Asynchronous Receiver-Transmitter (UART) chip, it might cause loss in data, or junk display. Ensure that hardware flow control is enabled and that software flow control is disabled for the COM port, the software, and the modem. Use the correct connection preferences — Data bits: 8, Parity: None, and Stop bits: 1. Also ensure that the correct terminal emulation is set for the software (in most cases, VT-100).

There is dual display for each character

When using a modem, you may have a double display for each character that you type. This problem can usually be resolved by switching the local echo off. Local echo causes the modem to display each character as it is typed in from the keyboard. If remote echo is enabled in the other computer, each letter that the modem receives is transmitted back. So each character is displayed twice.

Parallel ports

2.1 Identify common symptoms and problems associated with each module and how to troubleshoot and isolate the problems. Content may include the following: Parallel ports

If a parallel port stops functioning, the parallel interface devices—such as printers that are connected to it—will also stop working. A parallel port might not function properly if it is disabled at the BIOS level. Check the CMOS settings to ensure that the port is enabled. You should also check that a free IRQ is assigned to the port. If you use a single parallel port (LPT 1), IRQ 7 is usually assigned to it. In case of multiple parallel ports (LPT 1, LPT 2, or LPT 3), ensure that a different IRQ is assigned to each. You might want to run a diagnostic program, such as Norton Utilities or IBM Diagnostics, to identify the root cause of the parallel port problem. If the cause is a configuration error, you can rectify it by changing the CMOS settings. However, if the problem turns out to be hardware-related, you might need to change the controller card or the motherboard, depending on where the port controller is located.

USB

2.1 Identify common symptoms and problems associated with each module and how to troubleshoot and isolate the problems. Content may include the following: USB

USB, or Universal Serial Bus, is easier to install, configure, and manage than ordinary serial or parallel ports. But many older system boards do not support USB. If you use an older system board and want to use a USB port, you can upgrade your computer by adding a PCI-to-USB controller card in a PCI slot to provide a USB port.

USB must be supported by the operating system to work. Windows 95, with the USB update, supports USB. Windows 98 and NT have built-in USB support. Windows 98 provides a much improved USB support.

If you are using USB ports or controllers, ensure that these are enabled in the CMOS setup. USB is a comparatively new I/O bus. For more details regarding USBs, visit www.usb.org.

Power supply

2.1 Identify common symptoms and problems associated with each module and how to troubleshoot and isolate the problems. Content may include the following: Power supply

A problem with your computer's power supply may manifest itself in a number of different situations:

✦ Your computer boots successfully at times and at other times it halts during booting.

✦ Your computer hangs for apparently no reason at all and sometimes even reboots itself.

✦ You keep getting error codes or beep codes during startup, but inconsistently.

✦ You encounter memory problems sporadically.

✦ Data is not correctly written on the hard disk.

✦ The keyboard suddenly stops working and then starts again.

✦ The motherboard fails.

✦ The power supply is too hot to touch.

Each of these cases indicates a power supply problem. The PSU, or power supply unit, is an important component because it supplies power to all other components in the system. So if you face any problems regarding the power supply, you should try to resolve them by performing some fundamental checks.

First, check the power from the wall socket. If the external power supply is fine, you need to get inside the system unit.

Clean the PSU and the system. Dust acts as an insulator and could retain the heat generated by the PSU inside the computer itself.

Use a voltmeter to check the output voltage in the PSU. Apply the voltmeter leads to an unused PSU power connector. Ensure that the PSU output voltages are –5VDC, +5VDC, –12VDC, and +12VDC. At least one of the power connectors from the PSU should be connected to a device. In the absence of any load, the output voltage will not be depicted correctly.

Check the power outlet. Set a VOM meter or a multimeter to read AC voltage. The acceptable power outlet range is 104–130 volts of AC.

If the voltages are not within the acceptable limits, the PSU needs to be replaced.

You might find that the fan on the power supply makes a lot of grinding noise. This might be caused by a bad fan or by a short that occurred elsewhere in the system. Replace the entire PSU (it is a more cost-effective solution than trying to repair the fan). If the problem persists, you can eliminate the fan as the problem area. Then you should remove all connections from the PSU and turn the power on. If the fan works, the problem lies with one of the components. Try connecting one component at a time to find out the root cause of the problem — most likely the drives, motherboard, power cords or interface cards. Replace the faulty component with one that works.

Caution

Be extremely careful while working with the power supply unit. Do not subject yourself to high voltages (over 110V). Wear protective gear and follow safety procedures. For more information about handling high-voltage equipments and safety procedures, see Chapter 12.

System covers

2.1 Identify common symptoms and problems associated with each module and how to troubleshoot and isolate the problems. Content may include the following: Slot covers

The numerous circuits and devices inside the computer are quite likely to create problems. But sometimes even the system cover causes the computer to malfunction. Though easily rectifiable, you should know the common problems related to the system cover.

The system cover could be damaged if the computer overheats, which might occur if the forced cooling system provided by the fan does not work properly. The cooling system is effective only when the system unit cover is in place and properly secured. Ensure that you keep the system cover properly secured at all times using all the screws provided.

At times, you might find that the computer runs but the power indicator LED light does not glow. Ensure that the connection between the power indicator and the motherboard is secure. You might also check whether reversing the leads on the LED connection solves the problem.

If you find that pressing the Reset switch does not restart the computer, the cause of the problem is probably a loose connection between the Reset switch and the motherboard. Secure the connection to solve the problem.

Troubleshooting tools

2.1 Identify common symptoms and problems associated with each module and how to troubleshoot and isolate the problems. Content may include the following: Troubleshooting tools, e.g., multimeter

Troubleshooting tools include diagnostic, measurement, and rescue tools. Most important of these are the rescue tools, which include a bootable disk for DOS and a rescue disk for Windows 9x.

Bootable disk for DOS

You can use a DOS bootable disk to boot from the floppy and attempt some kind of recovery in case the hard drive fails. You should make the bootable disk using the same DOS version as the one in the hard drive. To create a DOS bootable disk, issue the following command:

```
C:\>FORMAT A: /S
```

This command formats the disk, and the /S option copies the system files needed to load DOS to the floppy. This includes the two hidden DOS files and COMAND.COM. To make this disk act as a rescue disk, you can copy some DOS utilities to it. Some files that you might find useful are:

✦ ATTRIB.EXE

✦ CHKDSK.EXE

✦ EDIT.COM (also QBASIC.EXE if necessary)

✦ EMM386.EXE

✦ FDISK.EXE

✦ FORMAT.COM

✦ MSCDEX.EXE

✦ SCANDISK.EXE

✦ SYS.COM

✦ DEFRAG.EXE

✦ HIMEM.SYS

✦ UNDELETE.EXE

Rescue disk for Windows 9x

Use the options provided by the operating system software to create rescue disks. In Windows 95, you should also copy the files that you need to access the CD without hard drive support. In Windows 98, these real-mode drivers are automatically placed on the disk.

Diagnostic tools

Diagnostic tools include diagnostic cards and utilities, which are very helpful in diagnosing PC problems. Common utilities include PC Technician from Windsor Technologies, Nuts & Bolts from Network Associates, Norton Utilities from Symantec, and First Aid 2000 from McAfee.

Common measurement tools include VOM meters, voltmeters, ohmmeters, ammeters, and multimeters.

VOM meters

VOM meters are multipurpose meters used to read volts and ohms. They can be either analog or digital.

Voltmeters

A voltmeter is used to read the voltage coming from power outlets. A voltmeter has a calibrated wire in series with the meter movement. The resistor drops the line voltage, and the rest of the voltage is used to deflect the meter. To read AC voltage, some voltmeters have a rectifier added to the circuit that converts AC to DC. With the rectifier, the meter circuit acts like any other DC voltmeter.

Ohmmeters

An ohmmeter measures resistance. When you are using an ohmmeter, ensure that the component you are checking is isolated and not switched on. If the circuit is switched on, the large amount of current flowing through the circuit might damage the ohmmeter. It is also not safe to check resistance with the circuit switched on.

Caution   If you are checking an IC (Integrated Circuit), be very careful. An ohmmeter supplies current to the component being checked. This is potentially harmful for the IC chips.

Ammeters

An ammeter is used to check the flow of current. It is a basic meter that is connected in parallel to a calibrated resistor. When the testing leads are brought in contact with the circuit, the current is divided between the meter movement and the calibrated resistor. Most of the current flows through the calibrated resistor.

Multimeters

Multimeters are similar to VOM meters in operation. Multimeters can be analog as well as digital. Digital multimeters are, however, more stable and accurate. An analog multimeter uses a needle that deflects on a scale to show the values. A digital multimeter uses LCD, or Liquid Crystal Display. A digital multimeter is usually handheld and has two testing leads, also called probes. AC and DC voltages, resistance and current can be measured with a multimeter. While measuring DC voltages, it is important to maintain the correct polarity. Maintaining the polarity is not necessary for AC voltages.

Tip   To maintain a good working condition for your multimeter, change the battery at scheduled time intervals. Also remember to get your multimeter professionally calibrated at least once every year.

Troubleshooting Procedures and Good Practices

2.2 Identify basic troubleshooting procedures and how to elicit problem symptoms from customers.

The knowledge of troubleshooting techniques is essential, but in order to troubleshoot computer problems effectively, you need to follow certain basic approaches and procedures. In this section, the basic guidelines and procedures to be followed for troubleshooting are discussed.

Troubleshooting and problem isolation procedures

2.2 Identify basic troubleshooting procedures and how to elicit problem symptoms from customers. Content may include the following: Troubleshooting/isolation/problem determination procedures

Troubleshooting, like everything else, has a few fundamental rules that make your work easier and more efficient.

Start at the beginning

From the beginning, work your way through the system in a very thorough and systematic way. This is the one rule you should never forget. Conduct a very logical walkthrough to determine the problem. If you don't find the problem the first time, repeat the walkthrough more carefully, double-checking to find which step you overlooked the first time.

Don't overlook the obvious

We expect computer problems to be so difficult that we forget to look for the obvious. When you start, check the basics first. Is the computer switched on? Are the monitor and computer properly plugged in? Is the monitor switched on?

Divide and rule

To overcome a problem, you need to isolate it. Remove one hardware or software component after another from the system, until the problem is isolated to one component. Remember to remove only one component at a time and test the system after removing each component. Trade a suspected-bad component for a known-good component and try again.

Try simple things first

Check the things that are easiest to replace first. For example, if you have a display problem, try replacing the monitor before you decide to replace the video card.

Don't assume things

If you try to solve problems with a user's computer, don't make deductions based on what the user is saying. The user might have overlooked things. Don't trust the system documentation completely. Software or hardware documentation might not always be accurate. See for yourself what happened. Investigate the problem yourself.

Don't assume the worst. Nothing is lost until you cannot recover it.

Establish your priorities

What do you want to do? Recover lost data, or get the system up and running as soon as possible? Get your priorities straight and concentrate on them.

Keep your cool

Think and act. Take all practical precautions to protect data and OS files. Don't assume data is lost before you try to recover it. Don't hurry. Plan your actions.

Start afresh

A fresh start might bring to light some steps that you had missed or some problem that you had overlooked. It is also good to know what your starting point should be. Listen carefully to the problem, analyze, and start.

Research

If you face a problem that you cannot solve easily, be tenacious. Read, and read more. Make phone calls. Read the system documentation. Browse the net. Use every available resource to learn. Keep learning until you solve the problem.

Take notes

Writing down things is a good habit. Keep writing down what you learned about the problem. It is always easier to analyze things if they are written down. Make diagrams to reach the root cause of the problem. Writing down what you learn will help you solve the problem more efficiently and also provide invaluable notes for the future.

Determine whether it is a hardware or software problem

 2.2 Identify basic troubleshooting procedures and how to elicit problem symptoms from customers. Content may include the following: Determine whether hardware or software problem

Sometimes it is difficult to isolate the problem as a hardware problem or a software problem. This is especially true if the computer does not boot successfully. In such a situation, you should apply the rule of "eliminating the unnecessary." First, try booting from a disk that has only the hidden system files and COMMAND.COM. The disk should have a minimal OS configuration, which means no CONFIG.SYS or AUTOEXEC.BAT. This eliminates all the applications software loaded at startup on the computer, all the TSRs loaded at startup, and a major part of the OS, especially if it is Windows 9x. If you are able to boot from such a disk, the problem is either with the software or with the hard drive.

In Windows 9x, you can boot from the safe mode and eliminate most of the OS customized configuration and try to boot again. If the boot is successful, then the problem can be attributed to the operating system files. Install the OS again.

If you suspect a bad device or faulty hardware, eliminate the hardware one at a time to isolate the problem. Trade a known-good device for a suspected-bad one and try again.

Gather information from users

2.2 Identify basic troubleshooting procedures and how to elicit problem symptoms from customers. Content may include the following: Determine whether hardware or software problem; Gather information from user regarding, e.g., Customer Environment, Symptoms/Error Codes, Situation when the problem occurred

To efficiently isolate and solve a problem, you might need some information from the user. The best way to know is to ask. You should ask the user questions to find out about the environment, the situation when the problem occurred, and the symptoms and error codes that the user might have seen. When you ask questions regarding the environment, make sure you cover both the physical environment as well as the software environment.

It is also important to know the context in which the problem occurred. Try to re-create the circumstances that existed when the computer stopped working. What procedure was taking place at the time? What recent changes had been made? What program was the user working on? Did the user see any error messages? What exactly happened when the computer stopped working?

Probe the user to find out the error messages that might have been displayed. Also ask the user to tell you about any symptoms the user may have noticed.

The following questions may be useful when you're trying to get important information:

✦ When did you first encounter the problem?

✦ What exactly happened?

✦ Did you see any error messages on the screen? Was there any unusual display?

✦ Which program or software were you using?

✦ Did you move the system recently?

✦ Was there a thunderstorm or electrical problem recently?

✦ Did you make any hardware changes?

✦ Did you install any new software?

✦ Did you make any changes to the configuration setups of the software?

✦ Has anyone else used your computer lately?

✦ When did the computer last work properly?

✦ Did anything considerable happen in the meantime?

Even when you ask these questions, don't forget to use diplomacy. For example, instead of asking, "Did you make any hardware changes?" be a little more indirect and say, "Have any hardware changes been made?"

Keep the following points in mind when interacting with users:

✦ Don't patronize the user

✦ Don't start work without permission

✦ Don't use the phone without permission

✦ Provide the user with alternatives whenever possible

✦ Protect the confidentiality of the data

Key Point Summary

In this chapter, you learned how to troubleshoot some common problems related to various devices. You learned to troubleshoot problems that are encountered during startup, such as CMOS errors and BIOS errors. Then you learned to troubleshoot various hardware components, such as the mouse, floppy and hard drives, motherboard, and modem. You also learned some fundamental troubleshooting procedures and best practices.

✦   ✦   ✦

STUDY GUIDE

This Study Guide presents 20 assessment questions and 5 scenarios to test your knowledge of the exam topic area.

Assessment Questions

1. The correct voltages in the PSU are:

   A. +5 VDC, –5 VDC, +10 VDC, –10 VDC

   B. +5 VDC, –5 VDC, +11 VDC, –11 VDC

   C. +5 VDC, –5 VDC, +12 VDC, –12 VDC

   D. +5 VDC, –5 VDC, +13 VDC, –13 VDC

2. You encounter a 601 Error during the POST. This indicates an error with the:

   A. Keyboard

   B. Mouse

   C. Hard drive

   D. Floppy drive

3. During POST, one long beep indicates _____.

   A. Memory failure

   B. Keyboard error

   C. Normal startup

   D. Monitor error

4. During a connection using your modem, you notice that there is a dual display for each character that you type. What should you do to resolve this problem?

   A. Switch on local echo

   B. Switch off local echo

   C. Switch on remote echo

   D. Switch off remote echo

5. If you find that the monitor displays wrong characters, what is the most likely cause of the problem?

    A. Bad monitor

    B. Bad video card

    C. Insufficient VRAM

    D. Bad keyboard

6. You hear seven beeps at startup, indicating a BIOS virtual mode exception error. How can you resolve this problem?

    A. Change the CMOS battery

    B. Upgrade the RAM

    C. Replace the motherboard

    D. Replace the hard drive

7. How does BIOS report a parity circuit failure?

    A. One beep

    B. Two beeps

    C. Error message on-screen

    D. This error is not reported

8. If the computer has a single parallel port, which IRQ is usually assigned to it?

    A. 3

    B. 4

    C. 6

    D. 7

9. What three files are necessary to load Microsoft DOS?

    A. CONFIG.SYS, COMMAND.COM, IO.SYS

    B. COMMAND.COM, MSDOS.SYS, IO.SYS

    C. CONFIG.SYS, AUTOEXEC.BAT, MSDOS.SYS

    D. COMMAND.COM, AUTOEXEC.BAT, CONFIG.SYS

10. You are using Windows 98 and a new system board that has USB ports. However, when you connect a USB device, you find that it doesn't work. What could be the possible reason?

    A. Windows 98 does not support USB.

    B. USB port is disabled in the CMOS setup.

    C. A USB port has to be connected to a PCI port.

    D. A USB device must be connected to a serial port.

11. What should be the maximum length of a phone line from the wall outlet to the modem so that electromagnetic interference does not occur?

    A. 3 feet

    B. 4 feet

    C. 8 feet

    D. 10 feet

12. If you encounter a hard disk access failure, what command will you use to check the partition table information?

    A. CHKDSK

    B. FDISK

    C. SCANDISK

    D. FORMAT C:

13. During bootup, you do not hear a beep. What is the possible problem?

    A. The calculated checksum value does not match the value stored in the ROM.

    B. The interrupt controller fails the POST.

    C. There is no problem. It's a normal startup.

    D. The display card is not working.

14. You insert a disk in the floppy drive and read its contents. Then you insert a second disk and try to read its contents. But you find that the contents of the first floppy are displayed. What is the problem?

    A. The floppy disk controller is corrupt.

    B. The second disk is unreadable.

    C. The computer has a virus.

    D. The floppy cable is scratched.

15. Your computer does not boot. What is the first thing you should do to identify whether it is a hardware problem or a software problem?

   A. Upgrade the operating system.

   B. Replace the motherboard.

   C. Format the hard drive and reload the software.

   D. Boot using a bootable floppy disk.

16. The power indicator on the monitor glows, but the screen is blank. What is the first thing you should check for?

   A. The brightness and contrast adjustments are not set to the minimum.

   B. The display drivers are correct.

   C. The video card is not corrupt.

   D. The CMOS settings are correct.

17. During a connection, it seems that the handshaking starts all over again. What is the most likely cause?

   A. The modem is not connected properly to the computer.

   B. The phone line is noisy.

   C. The COM port assigned to the modem is also assigned to another device.

   D. There is an IRQ conflict.

18. You encounter a CMOS memory size mismatch. What is the possible problem?

   A. The CMOS battery is not working.

   B. The motherboard is not working.

   C. The actual amount of RAM installed on your computer is not specified in the CMOS setup.

   D. The memory modules are bad.

19. What is the acceptable range of power outlet?

   A. 104–130 volts AC

   B. 104–130 volts DC

   C. 110-220 volts AC

   D. 110–220 volts DC

20. What command do you use to find out in what order TSRs are loaded?

    A. DIR /TSR

    B. DIR C: /TSR

    C. MEM /T

    D. MEM /C

Scenarios

Five scenarios are provided that will test your ability to apply what you have learned in this chapter.

1. Jack goes to a customer to resolve some problems with the customer's computer. On inspection, Jack finds that the machine is not booting. The user says it worked well the last time he used it. What steps should Jack take to isolate and solve the problem?

2. You are trying to install some devices in the upper memory of the computer. You want to load a TSR high. In the CONFIG.SYS file, you have included the commands DEVICE=HIMEM.SYS, DEVICE=EMM386.EXE, and DOS=UMB. You then tried to load a TSR high by using either the DEVICEHIGH= command in CONFIG.SYS or the LOADHIGH command in AUTOEXEC.BAT. But the MEM/C report shows that the load high instruction did not work and that the TSR is still in conventional memory. What will you do now to resolve the problem?

3. Jack was called to check and troubleshoot Bill's computer. However, when Jack arrived at the site of the machine, Bill was not around. So, Jack placed his tools on top of Bill's papers and started working. He observed that the computer wouldn't boot. He booted from a floppy, and because the boot was successful, he decided to format the hard disk. (He decided that trying to recover the files would be too much of an overhead.) He wanted to install Windows 98 from his company file server. He started calling the technical support group to install the operating system. Analyze this scenario and state how Jack performed as a troubleshooter. Did he do anything he shouldn't have? How would you suggest he present himself to clients in the future?

4. You get a call from one of your customers, who simply states that "the computer does not start." What questions would you want to ask the customer to obtain the information you need to successfully troubleshoot the problem?

5. A user complains that his internal modem is not responding. He says that he has attached the phone cord from the wall socket to the modem. He also says that the phone line is fine. What steps would you undertake to enable the user to connect again?

Answers to Chapter Questions

Chapter Pre-Test

1. The three types of hard drive errors are **disk access failure**, **file access failure**, and **boot failure**.

2. POST tests the calculated checksum and verifies it against a value stored in **ROM**.

3. During POST, the **301** Error code indicates a keyboard problem.

4. The first thing you should do in case your modem does not respond is check that the cord from the phone line is plugged into the **line-in** port.

5. This message indicates that you are trying to write to a write-protected floppy disk. **Check the write-protect tab on the disk.**

6. You use an **ohmmeter** to check the resistance of wires.

7. A monitor might flicker for several reasons: **cable connection error**, **electromagnetic interference**, **low refresh rate**, and **insufficient VRAM**.

8. Some troubleshooting tools include **DOS bootable disk**, **Windows 9x rescue disk**, **diagnostic tools such as PC Technician and Norton Utilities**, **VOM meters**, **voltmeters**, **ohmmeters**, **ammeters**, and **multimeters**.

Assessment Questions

1. **C.** Apply the voltmeter leads to an unused PSU power connector. Ensure that at least one of the power connectors from the PSU is connected to a device. For more information, see the section labeled "Power supply."

2. **D.** Error 601 is displayed if the floppy drive fails the POST. For more information, see the section labeled "POST."

3. **B.** If you hear one long beep during POST, a keyboard error is indicated. For more information, see the section labeled "POST."

4. **B.** Dual display of characters can be avoided by switching off local echo. Local echo causes the modem to display each character as it is typed in from the keyboard. For more information, see the section labeled "Modem."

5. **B.** The most likely cause is a bad video card. Try replacing it and check if it solves the problem. The other possible causes are corrupt RAM or ROM. For more information, see the section labeled "Monitor/Video."

6. **C.** The only solution to this problem is to replace the motherboard. For more information, see the section labeled "BIOS."

7. **B.** BIOS reports a parity circuit error by sounding two beeps. The solution to this problem is to replace the motherboard. For more information, see the section labeled "BIOS."

8. **D.** IRQ 7 is usually assigned to a single parallel port. For more information, see the section labeled "Parallel ports."

9. **B.** COMMAND.COM, along with the two hidden system files (MSDOS.SYS and IO.SYS), are necessary to load DOS. For more information, see the section labeled "Floppy drive."

10. **B.** To use a USB port or controller, -USB must be enabled in the CMOS setup. For more information, see the section labeled "USB."

11. **B.** Beyond the length of four feet, phone lines are more susceptible to electromagnetic interference. For more information, see the section labeled "Modem."

12. **B.** FDISK is used to check the partition table and also create partitions if they do not exist. For more information, see the section labeled "Hard drives."

13. **A.** If the calculated checksum value does not match the value stored in the ROM, the system hangs up. For more information, see the section labeled "POST."

14. **D.** If the floppy cable is scratched or broken, you might not see the contents of the new floppy that you insert. The contents of the first floppy are displayed over and over. For more information, see the section labeled "Floppy drive."

15. **D.** Try booting from a floppy disk. If you are successful, the problem is very likely with the software. For more information, see the section labeled "Determine whether it is a hardware or software problem."

16. **A.** Don't overlook the obvious. It's possible that the brightness and contrast are set to the minimum. For more information, see the section labeled "Monitor/Video."

17. **B.** Sometimes, if you are connecting over a noisy phone line, it might sound as if the handshaking starts again during the connection. For more information, see the section labeled "Modem."

18. **C.** If the amount of RAM specified in the CMOS setup does not match the actual amount of RAM installed, you might encounter a CMOS memory size mismatch error. For more information, see the section labeled "CMOS."

19. **A.** Use a VOM meter or multimeter to check the AC voltage. The acceptable range is 104–130 volts of AC. For more information, see the section labeled "Power supply."

20. **D.** The MEM /C report shows where the TSRs are loaded. For more information, see the section labeled "Processor/memory."

Scenarios

1. If the computer does not boot successfully, Jack should apply the rule of "eliminate the unnecessary." First, Jack should try booting from a disk that has only the hidden system files and COMMAND.COM. The disk should have a minimal OS configuration, which means no CONFIG.SYS or AUTOEXEC.BAT. This eliminates all the applications software loaded at startup on the computer, all the TSRs loaded at startup, and a major part of the OS, especially if it is Windows 9x. If he is able to boot from such a disk, he can attribute the problem to either the software or the hard drive.

   If the user is using Windows 9x, Jack should boot from the safe mode and eliminate most of the OS customized configuration and try to boot again. If that works, he can attribute the problem to the operating system files. He will have to install the OS again.

   If Jack suspects a bad device or faulty hardware, he should eliminate the hardware one at a time to isolate the problem. He could trade a known-good device (if he has one) for a suspected-bad one and try again.

2. You might face this problem either because enough space is not available in the UMB assigned to the TSR, or because no free UMBs were available for it. This problem could also occur if the TSR does not work from upper memory.

   First, check the TSRs before you proceed with other methods to isolate and remove the problem. Then, check the command lines in the CONFIG.SYS and AUTOEXEC.BAT files to see if they are correct. You should also check the order of the DEVICEHIGH= commands in CONFIG.SYS to see if the larger TSRs are placed first and allocated the larger UMBs. Even if all TSRs don't fit into the upper memory, allocating the largest UMBs to the largest TSRs will free the maximum possible amount of conventional memory. If in doubt, you can try to use MEMMAKER to choose the best order of loading the TSRs. Once you have isolated the problem, you can change the CONFIG.SYS and AUTOEXEC.BAT files to rectify the problem.

3. As a troubleshooter, Jack has missed some basic diplomacy and etiquette issues. First, Jack should not have placed his tools on top of the user's papers. Next, before formatting the hard disk, Jack should have taken permission from the user. The user might have stored important data in the hard disk, and formatting the hard disk before recovering the files could cost the user days of hard work. Again, before using the customer's phone, Jack should have asked him for permission.

   In the future, Jack should remember not to start working in the user's absence. If he must start his work, he should ensure that he does not damage any of the user's property, including physical papers and data stored in the computer. He should also ask the user for permission if he needs to use the telephone.

4. You will want to ask your customer the following questions:

- Is the power indicator glowing?

  If yes, you need to probe further. Otherwise, the problem may be with the connection.

- Did you move the system recently?

  This will give you an idea as to whether or not some connection is loose or whether some component has moved within the system unit.

- Was there a thunderstorm or electrical problem recently?

  If so, you could possibly attribute the problem to the power supply. There may be burnt or damaged system components.

- Did you see any error messages on the screen? Was there any unusual display?

  If an error message was displayed, it will help you identify the possible cause of the error.

5. First, you will have to check if the phone cord from the wall outlet is plugged into the line-in jack in the modem. Modems have two RJ-11 ports. Make sure that the phone cord is plugged into the correct (line-in) port.

Next, check the COM port and the IRQ that the modem is set to. Ensure that they match the settings for the software. Also, check that no other device is assigned the same COM port and IRQ. Check if you specified the correct modem type to the software. Otherwise, the software might be sending incorrect initialization commands to the software.

Finally, reseat the modem in the expansion slot. You might try using a different expansion slot, as well.

Operating System Basics

Part IV introduces you to topics covered in the OS Fundamentals exam, including the basic operating system functions and the major differences between the Windows 9*x* and Windows 2000 operating systems discussed in Chapter 16.

This part discusses the command prompt. Even though the exams will not be covering MS-DOS or Windows 3.11, they will probably ask you several questions about command prompt applications, such as `fdisk.exe`, `attrib.exe`, `defrag.exe`, and `format.com`. You will also be tested on your knowledge of many of the system files that are found on your computer and the role that each of these files plays within the OS.

This part includes a section that deals with basic memory management and several sections that deal with ways to set or check your current system configuration with either Windows 95 or Windows 2000.

This part also discusses working with files and directories. It covers file attributes, file naming conventions and restrictions, new features of the Windows 2000 file system, and disk management from the OS level. The disk management section will discuss different types of drives, backing up and restoring data, fragmentation, and the differences between the types of file systems that you would likely encounter with Windows-based operating systems.

Operating System Functions

✦ ✦ ✦ ✦

Exam 220-202 ✦ A+ OS Technologies

- ✦ **1.1** Identify the operating system's functions, structure, and major system files to navigate the operating system and how to get to needed technical information. Content may include the following:

  - **Major Operating System functions:** Create folders, Checking OS Version

  - **Major Operating System components:** Explorer, My Computer, Control Panel

  - **Contrasts between Windows 9X and Windows 2000**

CHAPTER PRE-TEST

1. Can you solve Windows 9x performance problems with the Performance Monitor tool?

2. Virtual memory is composed of what two components?

3. Windows 2000 protects the OS memory by doing what with applications that start?

4. New folders can be created at a command prompt with what command?

5. Windows 9x uses what to execute MS-DOS based applications?

6. Windows 2000 can implement security restrictions on which of the following: files, system time, logon to computer, or Registry values?

7. How can you prevent people from installing untested drivers on a Windows 2000 computer?

✦ Answers to these questions can be found at the end of the chapter. ✦

Just as the engine is the driving force behind an automobile, the operating system (OS) is the driving force behind your computer. Your choice of engine in your automobile affects the performance of its system, and also affects what you can do with your vehicle. You will find that the performance and functionality of your computer is different if you use MS-DOS, Windows 3.1, Windows 95, Windows 98, Windows NT Workstation 4.0, Windows 2000, or some other operating system. Because the A+ exam focuses on Windows 9x and Windows 2000, this chapter focuses on these two operating systems.

The operating system is responsible for several major functions on your computer, so you should take a look at some of these functions. In order to achieve its purpose of managing your computer, the operating system relies on its major components. This chapter examines these components and how they interrelate to effectively manage the computer. By the end of this chapter, you will know some of the differences between choosing Windows 9x or Windows 2000 as your operating system.

Major Operating System Functions

 1.1 Identify the operating system's functions, structure, and major system files to navigate the operating system and how to get to needed technical information. Content may include the following: Major Operating System functions

The operating system is responsible for two major functions: managing the hardware devices that are on the system and managing the software and data on the system. Each operating system is responsible for both of these areas. Some do a better job than others, but all must attempt to do their management to the best of their abilities.

Managing hardware devices

Managing the hardware is a big job. The operating system must deal with each device on the system. To do this job, the OS has to register the fact that the device is present, communicate with it, allow other components to communicate with it, and ensure at all times that it is functioning properly. Plug-and-play is part of most hardware on the market these days, and knowledge of the plug-and-play processes and how the devices operate will make dealing with them easier. Devices that follow the plug-and-play specification automatically announce themselves to the operating system. The only problem with this is that the OS must have drivers for it.

Each new version of Windows has managed to ship with more device drivers; in fact, each new version ships far more device drivers than the previous version of Windows. The *device driver* is the programming code that tells the OS how it is able to communicate with the appropriate device (see Figure 16-1). This code provides the OS with a detailed list of what the device is actually capable of and how the OS is able to control it. If the driver is missing a control to a function — even if the device is capable of that function — the OS will not be able to manage that function. This places a lot of importance in the hands of the device driver.

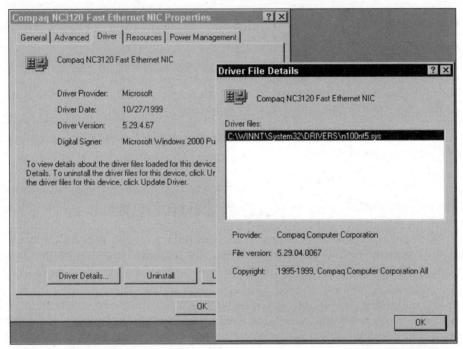

Figure 16-1: Device drivers for each device control interaction with that device.

Operating system vendors, such as Microsoft, lay out a set of standards that device manufacturers should follow when they are writing their drivers. If the hardware vendor follows these steps, then the device provides better interoperability with the OS. These standards are set in order to give each device manufacturer the best chance of making their driver behave well by not interfering with other device drivers on the computer. These standards also aid in device management, so that the OS can manage all similar devices the same way. You can see this by looking at a Device Manager, as shown in Figure 16-2.

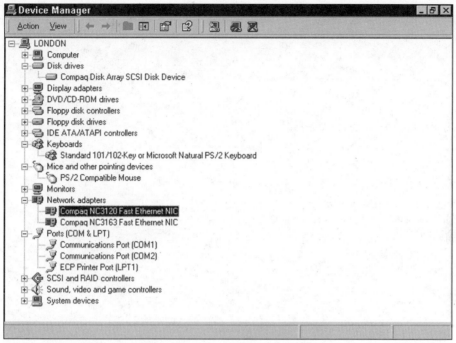

Figure 16-2: Device Manager represents the standardization in the hardware management interface.

Hardware management is only half of the OS's job; the other half is presenting a consistent interface for the user.

Benefiting from the user interface

The responsibility of the OS regarding user interface consists of displaying an interface that always reacts the same way, and makes it easy for the user to perform needed tasks. MS-DOS has a Command Line Interface (CLI), but Windows provides a Graphical User Interface (GUI). This GUI attempts to make it easy for the user to employ intuitive actions to carry out the tasks that they desire. In an attempt to provide a space for applications to run, and for the user to manage his or her environment, Microsoft has employed the "desktop" metaphor (see Figure 16-3). This metaphor declares the desktop as a work area on which you have a computer, a place to store items (My Documents), and a waste bin. In this environment, you start applications from the Start menu, and keep track of running tasks with the taskbar at the bottom of your screen.

Figure 16-3: The desktop illustrates the common user interface for applications.

The continuity of the GUI is extended to the applications that run within the environment. Again, the OS vendor puts forth a set of standards to establish interface consistency and interoperability of applications that are running on the system. This also allows for applications to share components that are created at the application or OS level. You can see an example of this in the sharing between applications of components like Save and Open dialog boxes (see Figure 16-4).

The hardware and software get tied together in the location where everything happens: memory.

Understanding memory management

Memory is the playing field where hardware and software mix. Memory management is the responsibility of the OS. The OS makes sure that the hardware and software components work within their own confines of memory. As memory resources are requested, the OS releases them either to the hardware device driver or to the application. The OS then takes steps to make sure that only the application accesses the memory areas that have been allocated to that particular application. If an application attempts to access memory that has not been allocated to it, then the OS has to decide what to do with the application.

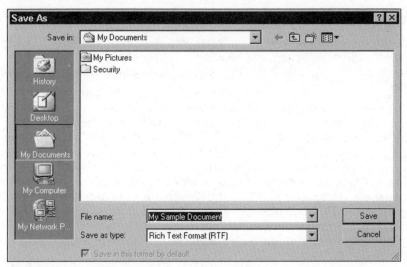

Figure 16-4: Most functions can share OS level resources, which is illustrated in the sharing of dialog boxes.

In all cases, the attempts to access the memory space of other applications are denied. Usually the denied application does not know what to do when this happens, so you get an application that "hangs" or terminates through a General Protection Fault (GPF). Most applications really never expect to be denied anything. Hangs and GPFs are annoying because the failed application is now flushed from memory and data may have been lost. On the positive side, the other application whose memory was almost accessed should still be working. The goal is to protect the other application by terminating the application that exceeded its boundaries.

As part of the management of memory on the system, the OS keeps track of physical memory on the computer, as well as hard drive space that is used to expand the memory available on the computer. Access time to physical memory is measured in nanoseconds, and access time to disk drives are measured in milliseconds. These scales are widely different, and so is the access time of information from these memory locations. Both types of memory are lumped together to make up Virtual memory. Sometimes the term *Virtual memory* is applied to the hard drive space that is used to simulate memory, but at the OS level, the term is used to refer to all of the memory available for storage on the system.

As applications launch and get loaded into memory, physical memory is used. When this space becomes limited, the OS moves some data out of RAM and onto the hard drive. The OS records the change in the actual location, so that when the application requests that information again, the information can be moved back into physical memory and accessed.

Working with folders

1.1 Identify the operating system's functions, structure, and major system files to navigate the operating system and how to get to needed technical information. Content may include the following: Major Operating System functions — Create folders

The OS is responsible for keeping things organized for you on your computer. When you first get your computer, it should be fairly well organized. The OS has segmented the application's use of memory so that it won't interfere with other applications on the system. You may have noticed that the disk of your computer is fairly well organized as well. At the hard drive level, things are organized in directories or folders. The term *directory* refers to a listing of items. When working with MS-DOS, you must ask to see a listing of the files that are on your hard drive with a directory command. The term *directory* does not blend in nicely with the desktop metaphor, so it has been renamed *folder*. There is no difference between the two, although when people refer to folders through the command prompt interface, they often call them *directories*.

You derive the same benefits from using folders on your computer as you do from using folders in your office. You use folders to organize vast quantities of data, so you can retrieve data quickly and efficiently. If you don't have folders on your hard drive, then you are faced with tens of thousands of files in one location. Some of these files are used for the OS, some for your applications, and some for your documents and working files. This is insanity! Enter folders, which help you separate out these different types of files. And if you get too many files in any one folder, all you have to do is to create a new one.

To create folders, you can either use the GUI or command line. Creating folders with the GUI is extremely easy. Find a location or folder in which you want to create a new folder, and then either right-click in an open space and choose New ⇨ Folder (see Figure 16-5), or choose File ⇨ New ⇨ Folder. You now have a new folder that is actually named *New Folder*. The name of your new folder is ready for editing — it has a box around it and the text is selected. You can type a new name and then press Enter to change the name. If anything happens and you don't get the name changed, you can change it at any time in the future by clicking twice on the name, or by right-clicking the folder and choosing Rename. After you've created your folder, you can start organizing your files by dragging them into the folders.

If you choose to create your folders at the command prompt, then you can use the make directory command — mkdir or md. A sample of the syntax is:

```
mkdir "c:\my documents\my_test_directory"
```

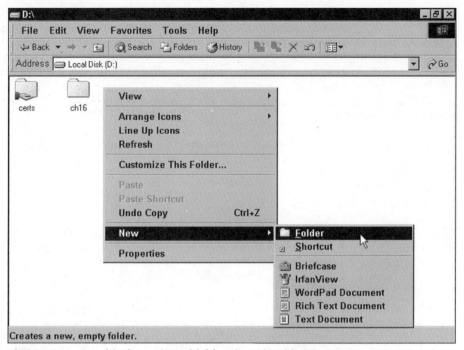

Figure 16-5: Graphical creation of folders is an intuitive process.

This code creates a new directory in the My Documents directory. To create a new directory in your current directory, use this code:

```
mkdir my_test_directory
```

For more information about managing folders from the command prompt, see Chapter 17, which examines other commands for folder or directory management, such as `rmdir`, `chdir`, and `deltree`.

You should be aware of two limitations when dealing with folders: One limitation is the total number of directory entries available on a drive, and the other limitation is the number of directory entries in the root directory of a drive. The *root directory* is the directory at the top of the drive, or the directory that you see when you double-click a drive in My Computer. The limit for directory entries on the root directory of a FAT or FAT32 partition is 512 entries, while floppy disks have a limit of 112 entries. This means that you can only have 512 files or directories in the root directory of your hard drive. You may find that the value is even less than that, because Windows supports long file names, and they occupy more than one directory entry. See Chapter 19 for more information.

If you want to find out how many directory entries that your drive supports, you can use the scandisk.exe command in Windows 9x, or the chkdsk.exe command in either Windows 9x or Windows 2000. scandisk.exe is a command line application, but if you run it from the Windows GUI, it automatically launches scandskw.exe, which is the Windows version. ScanDisk is used to repair errors with the files on your hard drive. The full use of ScanDisk is discussed in Chapter 17 and Chapter 27. To use ScanDisk to determine the number of directory entries on your hard drive, just follow these steps:

✦ Launch ScanDisk for Windows by choosing Start ➪ Programs ➪ Accessories ➪ System Tools ➪ ScanDisk

✦ Select the radio button for Standard

✦ Choose the Start button

After the test is completed, you are presented with a ScanDisk Results dialog box for the drive that you were just scanning (see Figure 16-6). This displays the size of each allocation unit (number of bytes), total number of allocation units on the drive, and the number of allocation units that are currently available.

If you are using Windows 2000, then scandisk.exe is not available to you, but chkdsk.exe is. *CheckDisk* is a command-line application that checks many of the same things that ScanDisk checks. The final output of the commands is very similar. Prior to the release of ScanDisk, CheckDisk was the command that was used to correct disk problems. Now you may be asking, If Windows 2000 is the newest OS, why does it only use CheckDisk, if ScanDisk is new and better? The answer to this question is the fact that Windows 2000 is based on Windows NT, and Windows 9x is based on Windows 3.11 and MS-DOS. ScanDisk started out as a MS-DOS command. The CheckDisk included with Windows 2000 is as powerful and functional as the ScanDisk included with Windows 9x. The command that you must enter to get information about your drive with CheckDisk is chkdsk c: (we use Drive C here, but you can use any drive letter). The output of the command looks something like the following:

```
The type of the file system is NTFS.

WARNING!  F parameter not specified.
Running CHKDSK in read-only mode.

   2803342 KB total disk space.
   1609942 KB in 18863 files.
      6968 KB in 1114 indexes.
         0 KB in bad sectors.
     73582 KB in use by the system.
     10752 KB occupied by the log file.
   1112850 KB available on disk.

      2048 bytes in each allocation unit.
   1401671 total allocation units on disk.
    556425 allocation units available on disk.
```

You should note that it provides the same type of information about the size and number of allocation units on the disk.

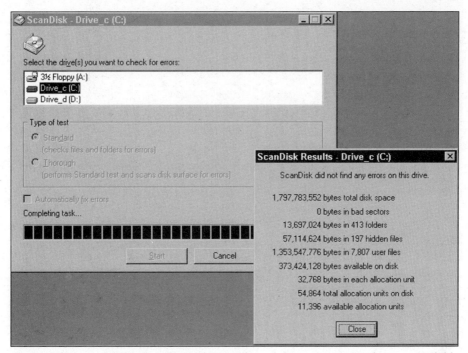

Figure 16-6: Scandisk can tell you the number of directory entries that are available.

Checking the OS version

1.1 Identify the operating system's functions, structure, and major system files to navigate the operating system and how to get to needed technical information. Content may include the following: Major Operating System functions — Checking OS Version

No matter which OS you are using, at some point you will need to know the exact version of the OS that you are using. This is often the case when you are considering installing new software, which requires a specific version of the OS. Many of the methods for retrieving this information are similar between Windows 9x and Windows 2000. In this section, you examine the methods that are available to each OS.

The System control panel in Windows 9x or Windows 2000 lets you know which version of the OS you are actually running (see Figure 16-7).

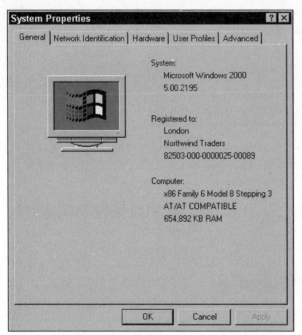

Figure 16-7: The System control panel is available
in all versions of Windows.

You can launch the System control panel in the following ways:

✦ Open My Computer ➪ Control Panel ➪ System.

✦ Right-click My Computer and select Properties.

You see the version number of the OS listed in this dialog box screen. Some of the
version numbers you may see are listed in Table 16-1.

Table 16-1
OS Version Numbers

Operating System	*Version Number*
Windows 95 Retail/Upgrade	Windows 95 [4.00.1995]
Windows 95 OSR2	Windows 95 [4.00.1111]
Windows 98	Windows 98 [4.10.1998]
Windows 98 Second Edition	Windows 98 [4.10.2222]
Windows Millennium Edition	Windows ME [4.90.3000]

If you are using Windows 98, then you also have the System Information tool available to you. To launch the System Information tool, select Start ➪ Program ➪ Accessories ➪ System Tools ➪ System Information. The System Information tool includes the version number on the main window, which is displayed when you launch the tool (see Figure 16-8).

If you are using Windows 2000, then you still have a couple of options for finding your version number. With Windows 2000, the version number is always `build 2195` or `Microsoft Windows 2000 Version 5.00.2195`. As patches and upgrades become available for Windows 2000, Microsoft releases a service pack. The installation of a service pack adds to the end of a build number, a service pack identifier. The new version number looks like `Microsoft Windows 2000 [Version 5.00.2195] Service Pack 1`.

To find out which version of Windows 2000 you have, you can either use the System control panel or the System Information tool. The System control panel is accessible the same way it is in Windows 9x. The System Information tool can either be launched through the Start menu, or you can use the Run command, and type `winmsd`. `winmsd` (Windows NT Microsoft Diagnostics) is the name of the Windows NT 4.0 tool that would have provided the same information, but running it launches the System Information tool. When using System Information, you find the version and build numbers on the main window, as shown in Figure 16-9.

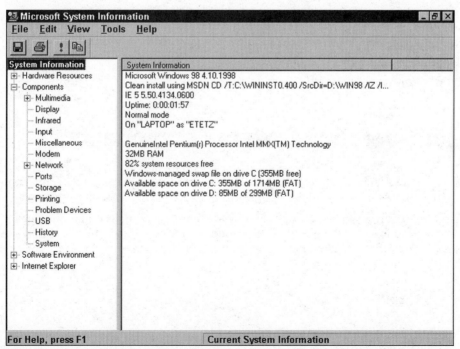

Figure 16-8: The System Information tool provides a large amount of information.

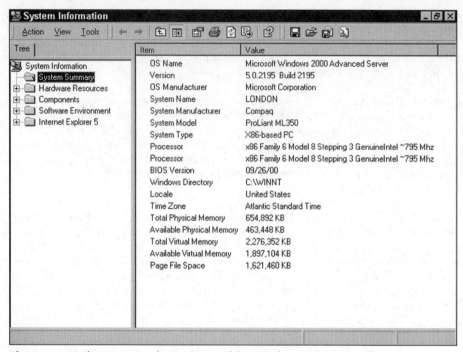

Figure 16-9: The System Information tool for Windows 2000 provides more detailed information.

After you know which version of the software you are running, you can take a look at what makes up your OS.

Major Operating System Components

1.1 Identify the operating system's functions, structure, and major system files to navigate the operating system and how to get to needed technical information. Content may include the following: Major Operating System components

In this section, you briefly examine how applications actually run on both Windows 9x and Windows 2000 computers. For a more complete description of how applications are supported, see Chapter 24.

Getting into the architecture

System architecture refers to how the components of the OS communicate with each other to allow the system to operate. Windows 9x and Windows 2000 differ distinctly in how they allow their components to operate. The first OS that you examine is Windows 9x.

Windows 9x has inherited many of its features from MS-DOS 6 and Microsoft Windows 3.11. The boot process still contains a 16-bit real mode component, which then starts the primarily 32-bit protected mode component of Windows OS. During the real mode boot, some of the hardware devices are initialized, system-wide environment variables are set, and some global resources are reserved. At the end of the real mode boot, the Windows kernel is loaded, and then the protected mode boot is started.

After the protected mode boot is completed, the Windows kernel operates from within a System Virtual Machine. All Windows-based applications run from this environment, keeping 16-bit applications separated from each 32-bit application. MS-DOS based applications run from their own MS-DOS Virtual Machine. This layout separates some processes on the computer, such as message queues, while other processes are still sharing resources and services. This is shown in Figure 16-10.

Windows 2000 was a complete rewrite of the OS, and as such, Microsoft was able to do things that they couldn't do with Windows 9x. When the OS boots, it immediately enters a 32-bit protected mode state. The entire OS operates from this 32-bit state, and the kernel is loaded into Ring 0, which Microsoft refers to as *Kernel Mode* (see Figure 16-11). All processes running in Kernel Mode are protected from any processes running in Ring 3 or User Mode.

Tip   The Intel processor design divides operation of the code into four separate execution levels called *rings*. Ring 0 is at the middle of this arrangement, and Ring 3 is at the outside. These are the only two rings that Microsoft has implemented during the development of Windows 9x and Windows 2000.

The kernel is responsible for keeping User Mode processes separated from each other. Each application is started up in its own discrete area. The application is not directly allowed to interact with other applications, and must pass such requests through Executive Services, which operate in Kernel Mode. This isolation of the applications from each other and the rest of the OS are some of the keys to the Windows 2000 operating system stability.

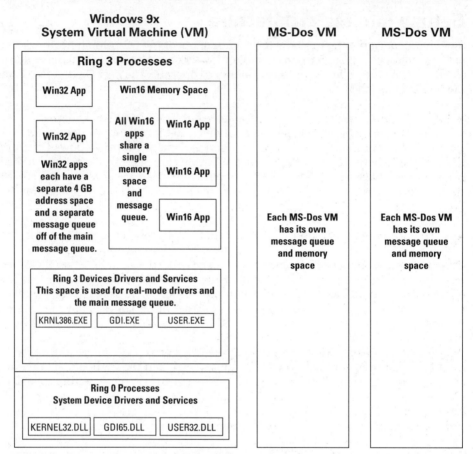

Figure 16-10: The Windows 9x architecture

Kernel mode processes are kept separate from User Mode processes, but are vulnerable to corruption by other User Mode processes. The processor's architecture is all that protects Kernel Mode processes from each other, and it often fails in its job. This means that STOP events (a.k.a., Blue Screen of Death), which reboot the system, are usually caused by a conflict by the processes that are running Kernel Mode.

Although both Windows 9x and Windows 2000 use Intel's Ring Architecture to improve system stability, Windows 9x implements substantial OS code in the Ring 3 area.

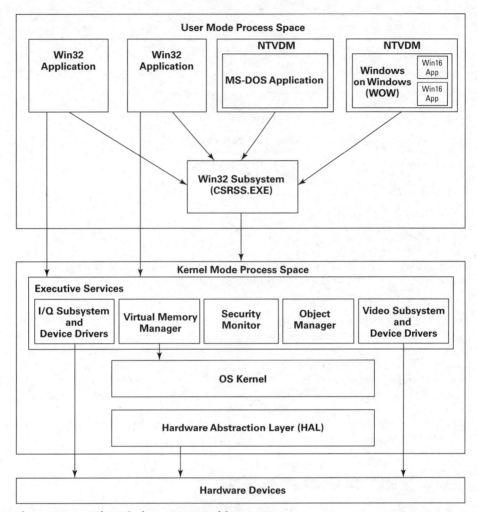

Figure 16-11: The Windows 2000 Architecture

Paging your memory

Both Windows 9x and Windows 2000 make use of hard drive space to extend the amount of memory that is available to applications. The total pool of memory that is available is referred to as the *Virtual Memory Page Pool* or *Virtual memory*, and is maintained by the Virtual Memory Manager (VMM). Figure 16-12 shows how these systems relate to each other. The Virtual Memory Manager is responsible for keeping track of where different kinds of information are located in memory. As applications request to have information placed in memory, the VMM places the information in an area of RAM. If RAM is getting full, then some information is moved from RAM to an area on the hard drive. The location that is used on the hard drive is either called a *swap file* in Windows 95 or a *page file* in Windows 2000. As applications request stored data, then the VMM moves information around so that the data is available in RAM.

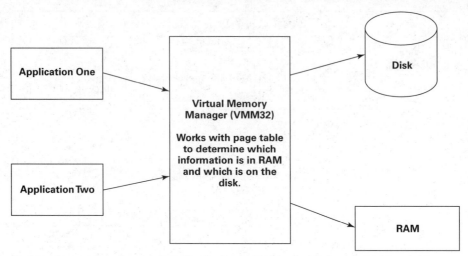

Figure 16-12: Virtual memory is composed of both physical RAM and hard drive space. This is a sample of Virtual memory within the Windows 2000 OS.

Windows 9x refers to the memory file on the hard drive as a *swap file*. The default settings for Windows 9x let the OS control the size and location of the swap file. This is the recommended setting. Under certain circumstances, you may want to modify these default settings. To change the swap file location or size, go to the System control panel by right-clicking the My Computer icon on your desktop and selecting Properties. In the System Properties window, choose the Performance tab and then the Virtual Memory button. This action places you in the Virtual Memory dialog box (see Figure 16-13), where you can choose to adjust the settings, or even disable Virtual memory altogether.

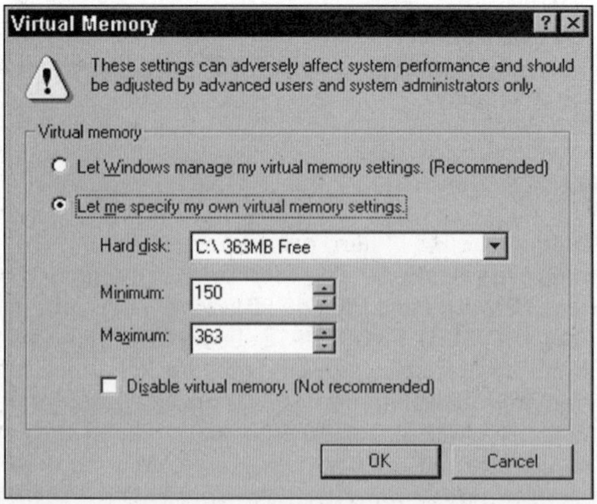

Figure 16-13: Page file settings for Windows 9x

Some of the reasons to adjust your Virtual memory settings when using Windows 9x include:

✦ Running low on hard drive space on the default drive (usually the C: drive). You can then move the swap file to another drive.

✦ You have installed a much faster drive on your computer, and moving the swap file to that location improves Virtual memory access times.

✦ You want to minimize disk contention with the rest of the OS when you are using a computer with multiple hard drives.

✦ You only want to disable Virtual memory when you are troubleshooting the source of a system problem. If you suspect that you may have a file corruption problem with your disk, then you may want to disable Virtual memory all together.

If you are using Windows 2000, then you must follow a different procedure to adjust your page file settings. The configuration of the page file is also done in the System control panel, which you can get to by right-clicking the My Computer icon on your desktop, and selecting Properties. In the System Properties dialog box, choose the Advanced tab, the Performance button, and then the Virtual memory button (see Figure 16-14). In this dialog box, you are able to set an initial and maximum size for the page file on each logical drive. Some of the reasons you may want to adjust the page file size include:

✦ You are running out of space on your boot partition (the one with the `winnt` directory).

✦ You want to improve paging performance by reducing disk contention with the OS. In this case, you can move the page file to a different physical disk if you have one.

✦ You want to improve paging performance by load balancing the page file between different physical drives. Unlike Windows 9x, Windows 2000 allows you to have multiple page files each on a different disk.

Tip

If you reduce the size of the page file on your boot partition below the size of the physical RAM on your system, you are warned that some of the recovery options will be disabled. The page file is used as a storage space for the `memory.dmp` file that is generated during a STOP error.

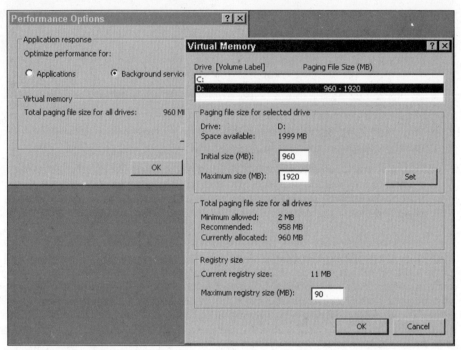

Figure 16-14: Page file settings for Windows 2000 can be used to improve performance.

Contrasts Between Windows 9x and Windows 2000

1.1 Identify the operating system's functions, structure, and major system files to navigate the operating system and how to get to needed technical information. Content may include the following: Contrasts between Windows 9X and Windows 2000

There are many similarities between Windows 9x and Windows 2000, but most of the similarities stop at the user interface. This section will examine the differences between the two operating systems in areas such as architecture, security, and hardware management.

Examining the architecture

Figures 16-10 and 16-11 illustrate the internal system architecture of Windows 9x and Windows 2000. Due to the architectural design, Windows 2000 has more stability as an OS, but in building for stability, Microsoft has to sacrifice backwards compatibility. There is a high level of compatibility within the arena of 32-bit applications, but there are limits placed on compatibility with 16-bit Windows and MS-DOS based applications. These limits are necessary, and without them there would be even less system stability. Windows 9x was designed for backward compatibility, but as the versions have been changing, some compatibility has been removed in each revision, to improve the overall system stability.

Windows 9x has been evolving since the original release of Windows 95 as Microsoft adds code to make it more stable. Even with the changes that have been made to Windows 9x, there are still major architectural differences between Windows 9x and Windows 2000.

Counting on the file systems

Another area of difference between Windows 9x and Windows 2000 is in the types of file systems that they support on disks. Windows 9x supports FAT16 and FAT32, and Windows 2000 supports FAT16 and FAT32, plus NTFS version 5.0.

Tip   When discussing file systems, FAT is generally used to describe the FAT16 file system, while FAT32 is usually referred to as FAT32.

FAT32 offers larger partition sizes than the 2GB FAT16 limit. Windows 9x is capable of creating FAT32 partitions from 512 megabytes up to 2 terabytes in size. Windows 2000 allows you to work with FAT32 partitions up to 2 TB in size, but only lets you create partitions up to 32GB in size. The reasoning behind this is that NTFS is a more stable file system, and if you are working with partitions in excess of 32GB, Microsoft recommends going with NTFS anyway.

Exam Tip   FAT32 was introduced as a file system with Windows 95 OSR2. Earlier versions of Windows 95 only had support for the FAT file system.

Another difference between the types of partitions is the size of their clusters. Cluster sizes for the different partition types are summarized in Table 16-2.

Table 16-2 Cluster Size Comparison			
File System	**2GB**	**4GB**	**8GB**
FAT16	32,768 bytes (32 K)/ 65,536 units	65,536 bytes (64 K)/ 65,536 units*	131,072 bytes (128 K)/ 65,536 units*
FAT32	4,096 bytes (4 K)/ 524,288 units	4,096 bytes (4 K)/ 1,048,576 units	8,192 bytes (8 K)/ 1,048,576 units
NTFS	2,048 bytes (2 K)/ 1,048,576 units	4,096 bytes (4 K)/ 1,048,576 units	4,096 bytes (4 K)/ 2,097,152 units

*FAT16 partitions between 2GB and 16GB are only supported in Windows NT. Windows 2000 uses FAT32 for partitions in excess of 2GB.

NTFS provides the best usage of space on a drive, due to the small size of its clusters (see Figure 16-15). The least amount of space that a file can use on a drive is one cluster; it doesn't actually matter if the file itself is only one byte. Almost every file on your drive will contain one cluster that is partially full, and therefore will waste a small amount of space. If this space is wasted on a large number of files — at an average rate of half a cluster per file — then it starts to make a difference on the storage space available to a drive.

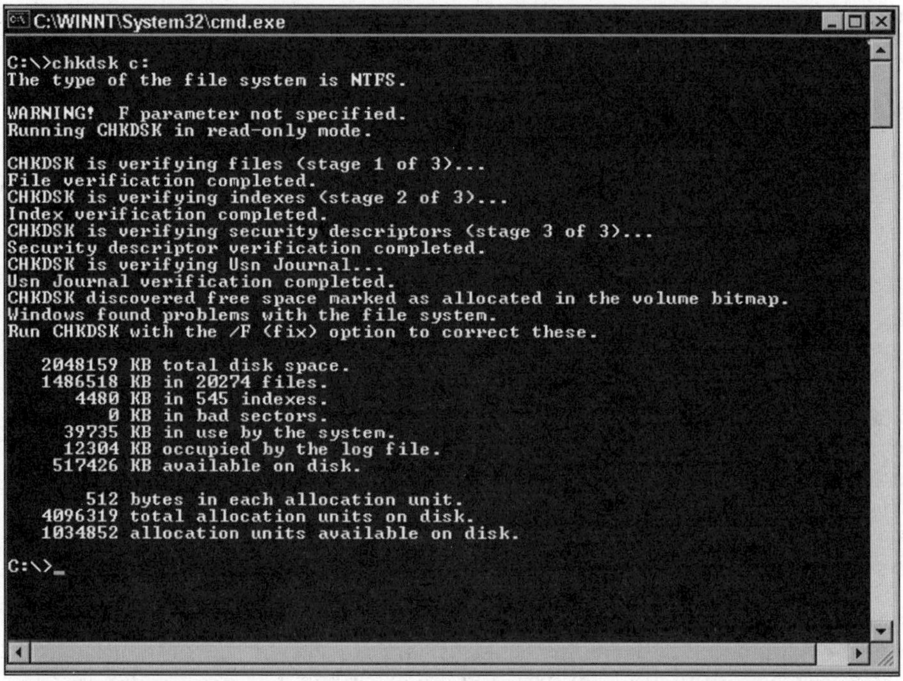

```
C:\WINNT\System32\cmd.exe                                        _ □ X

C:\>chkdsk c:
The type of the file system is NTFS.

WARNING!  F parameter not specified.
Running CHKDSK in read-only mode.

CHKDSK is verifying files (stage 1 of 3)...
File verification completed.
CHKDSK is verifying indexes (stage 2 of 3)...
Index verification completed.
CHKDSK is verifying security descriptors (stage 3 of 3)...
Security descriptor verification completed.
CHKDSK is verifying Usn Journal...
Usn Journal verification completed.
CHKDSK discovered free space marked as allocated in the volume bitmap.
Windows found problems with the file system.
Run CHKDSK with the /F (fix) option to correct these.

   2048159 KB total disk space.
   1486518 KB in 20274 files.
      4480 KB in 545 indexes.
         0 KB in bad sectors.
     39735 KB in use by the system.
     12304 KB occupied by the log file.
    517426 KB available on disk.

       512 bytes in each allocation unit.
   4096319 total allocation units on disk.
   1034852 allocation units available on disk.

C:\>_
```

Figure 16-15: chkdsk shows that NTFS uses small cluster sizes to optimize space usage on your drive.

The file allocation table allows a maximum number of entries for both FAT16 and FAT32. For FAT16 partitions, the maximum number of table entries is 65,536, and FAT32 supports 2,096,896 entries. This is the biggest reason why FAT32 supports smaller cluster sizes — it supports more clusters. You can always work out the cluster size by dividing the number of allocation units on the drive into the number of kilobytes:

```
5,242,880 KB / 1,048,576 = 5 KB
```

This value must then be rounded up to the next base 2 (2^x), which is 2^3K or 8K.

The NTFS file system offers more efficient use of space — it also offers security.

When creating NTFS partitions inside of the Windows 2000 OS, the size of the allocation units on a 2GB partition are 2,048 bytes, but if the partition is converted to NTFS during the installation of the OS, the cluster size is 512 bytes. In Table 16-2, the information on your computer may appear as 512 bytes per allocation unit with 4,194,304 units on a 2GB drive.

Implementing security

Windows 2000 has several security features built into the OS. These features are totally non-existent in Windows 9x. These include security on the file system, Registry, and other components on the computer.

NTFS permission can be used to apply security restrictions on either a file, a directory, or a drive on the system. To apply NTFS permissions to an object, select the object, right-click the object and then select Properties. In the Properties dialog box, select the Security tab and set the permissions on the object (see Figure 16-16). When setting permissions, you are able to add or remove users or groups from the Name pane, and set their level of security in the Permissions pane. By default, folders and files inherit their permissions from their parent object, but permissions can be set or modified at any level.

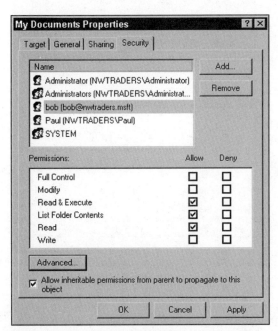

Figure 16-16: File system permissions restrict access to files.

Unlike the Registry in Windows 9x, the Windows 2000 Registry allows you to place security on it. The Registry is composed of three components, which are:

✦ **Keys:** The containers or folders that contain the values that have the actual data.

✦ **Values:** The names that have been assigned to the individual Registry entries.

✦ **Data:** The actual values that are stored in the Registry.

Security and permissions are much the same in appearance as NTFS permissions, after you get to the dialog box to apply the permissions (see Figure 16-17). Permissions can only be applied to Keys or folders in the Registry. To open the security dialog box in the Registry, launch `regedt32`, not `regedit`, and then select the key that you want to modify and select Permissions from the Security menu. At this point you can grant Read or Full access to the selected key.

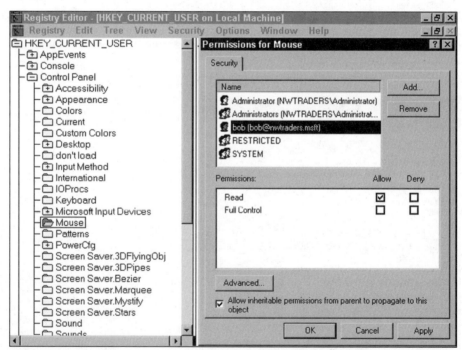

Figure 16-17: Security can be applied to specific Registry entries.

The last major place that you can modify user access to a system is by granting User Rights. These are implemented through *policies*. Policies with Windows 2000 can be applied through Active Directory or to a local computer. If Active Directory policies conflict with the local policies, then the Active Directory policy set by the network administrator prevails.

To set local User Rights, you have to launch the Local Security Settings administrative tool. This is accessible through the Administrative Tools control panel. Figure 16-18 shows where in the Local Security Settings the User Rights Assignment is located. They are under Security Settings ⇨ Local Policies ⇨ User Rights Assignment. If you are using Windows NT 4.0, then they are located in the User Manager application as User Rights in the Policies menu.

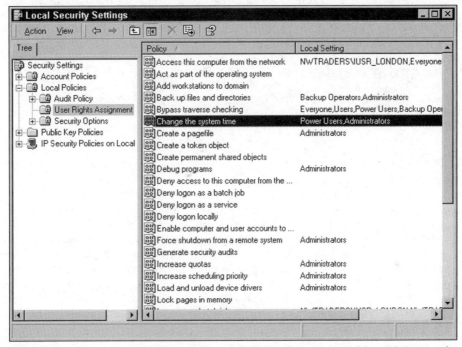

Figure 16-18: User Rights restrict what an individual user is capable of doing on the system.

User Rights range from changing the system time to acting as part of the operating system. Some common User Rights include:

✦ Access this computer from the network

✦ Add workstations to domain

✦ Back up files and directories

✦ Change the system time

✦ Log on locally

✦ Remove computer from docking station

✦ Restore files and directories

✦ Shut down the system

Most of the listed rights are self explanatory, but in the event you have more questions about individual rights, consult Windows 2000 Help and type `privileges` on the Index tab and then double-click `available (list)` in the list box. These rights can be assigned to any users on your system. This gives you a high degree of local control as to what users are capable of doing on the system. These features are just not available to the Windows 9x OS.

When you consider User Rights Assignments, together with the mandatory logon that is required with Windows 2000, you have a highly secure OS using Windows 2000.

Managing hardware

Hardware management is another area where major differences exist between Windows 9x and Windows 2000. These differences show up in the Driver Signing feature, and the system monitoring tools that are available to the operating systems.

Configuring Driver Signing

Driver Signing was incorporated into the Windows 2000 OS to prevent the installation of untested drivers on the system. Hardware vendors have an option to send their completed drivers to Microsoft for testing. After testing the driver, and confirming that it doesn't have any apparent problems within the OS, Microsoft returns the driver to the vendor with a signature file. This signature file contains information about the original driver file to ensure that the driver was not modified since it was sent to Microsoft. When loading drivers, Windows 2000 checks for the existence of the signature file. If the signature is not available, then you can configure what you want to have happen on the system. Your choices are:

✦ Ignore the missing signature and install the drivers.

✦ Warn the user of the missing signature, but still give them the option of installing.

✦ Block the installation of the driver.

These settings are configured in the System control panel, using the Driver Signing button on the Hardware tab (see Figure 16-19). If you are logged in as an administrator on the computer, you can save these settings to affect all users.

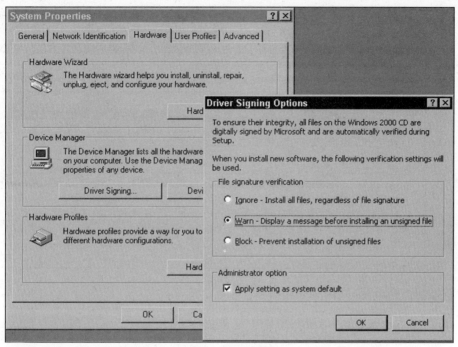

Figure 16-19: Driver Signing prevents the installation of unwanted drivers.

System monitoring

System monitoring is a required skill to allow you to maximize the performance on your system. Again, a huge world of difference exists between Windows 9x and Windows 2000 when it comes to system monitoring tools.

With Windows 9x, the best monitoring tool you have is the System Monitor tool, located in the Start menu in Programs ➪ Accessories ➪ System Tools. This tool has some rudimentary counters for monitoring the system. It supports three types of charts:

✦ Line (shown in Figure 16-20)

✦ Bar

✦ Numeric

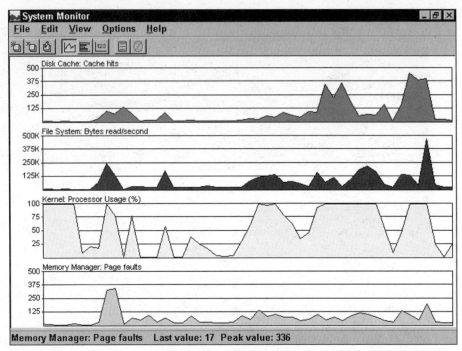

Figure 16-20: The System Monitor tool for Windows 9x provides basic information.

You can diagnose several problems with the System Monitor tool, but you have to do this with the level of detail that is available to the counters. The list of categories for your counters changes depending on what you have installed on your computer, but as a base, it includes:

✦ Dial-Up Adapter

✦ Disk Cache

✦ File System

✦ Kernel

✦ Memory Manager

✦ Microsoft Network Client

These counters allow you to gather information about a wide number of objects on your system, including processor utilization and available memory.

If you are using Windows 2000 instead of Windows 9x, then you have a more advanced tool available to you. This tool is the Performance MMC snap-in or Performance Monitor (see Figure 16-21). Performance Monitor allows you to gather very detailed information about a wide number of objects on your computer.

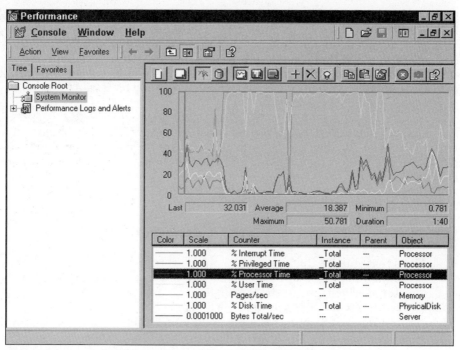

Figure 16-21: Performance Monitor can provide very detailed data.

Like System Monitor on Windows 9x, the list of counters and objects change, based on the specific components installed on your computer. For example, you see counters related to Microsoft SQL Server 2000 if you have it installed on your computer. Your data can be displayed as a line chart, a histogram (bar chart), or a numeric report. In addition to this functionality, Windows 2000 is able to store selected objects in a log file, which you can view at a later date; or you can have Windows 2000 monitor the counters and generate alerts when the values of the counter exceed threshold values.

Which one is right for me?

This is a very good question. Ideally, Windows 2000 Professional is the right OS for everyone. The only problem with this statement is that not everyone has the required hardware to run this OS. If you have limited hardware available to you, then Windows 98 or even Windows 95 may be the best OS for you. Even though the minimum requirements for Windows 2000 Professional are a Pentium 133 with 64MB of RAM, you should not consider using Windows 2000 Professional with less than a Pentium 200 with 96MB of RAM. The additional RAM reduces paging when multiple applications are running, and the more memory you have, the more applications you are able to open at any time.

If you have a computer with less hardware than is recommended for Windows 2000 Professional, then you have to run Windows 9x. If you have a computer that just meets the requirements for Windows 2000 Professional, then you find that the performance and speed that you get with Windows 9x exceeds the stability and security benefits derived from running Windows 2000 Professional. If you are not willing to trade stability and security, then you have to upgrade hardware to properly support Windows 2000 Professional.

As previously mentioned, this is a good question, because it is dependent on your requirements for security and performance. You are the only person who is able to determine which OS is right for you, and that depends on what you actually feel is important.

Navigating Around Your Computer

It is crucial that you are able to get to your files when you need them. If you were at the command prompt, you would be able to work with cd (change directory) and dir (directory), which are covered at length in Chapter 17. When you are using Windows (either 9x or 2000), you are able to make a choice between Windows Explorer (not Internet Explorer) and My Computer. Either one may be used, and the reason for choosing one or the other will be personal preference.

My Computer

1.1 Identify the operating system's functions, structure, and major system files to navigate the operating system and how to get to needed technical information. Content may include the following: Major Operating System components — My Computer

My Computer is the most common way people start accessing files on their computer, mostly because of its location at the top left-hand corner of your desktop. When you double-click My Computer, a large window is displayed (shown in Figure 16-22), listing the drives that are in your computer. You can then double-click your C: drive to see what files are located on the drive.

Some tasks are more easily accomplished with an additional open window, such as copying files from one folder to another. To open an additional window, you can either double-click My Computer on the desktop, or hold down your Ctrl key as you double-click a folder.

The toolbar at the top of the My Computer window features navigation buttons that allow you to go back to the previous folder or up to the parent folder. There are also a set of Cut, Copy, and Paste buttons that allow you to move files between folders.

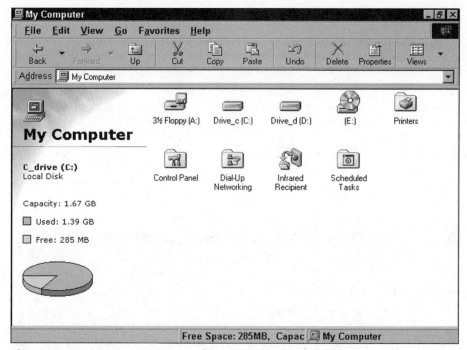

Figure 16-22: My Computer starts drive navigation at the drive.

If you do not like the way the files in the My Computer window are being displayed, then you can use the View button on the toolbar to change the view from Large Icons, to Small Icons, List, or Details. Details view offers the advantage of listing file sizes and modification dates, which is often useful when trying to locate specific files.

The address line near the top of the My Computer window allows you to type in the name of the folder that you want to go to, and directly switch to it. For example, you could type c:\My Documents to switch to that folder.

When you select an item in the My Computer window, you will see properties for that item in a panel on the left-hand side of the window. This is dependent on whether the window is large enough to display the information for you.

If you want to explore many of the options for displaying information in the My Computer window, then open the Folder Options dialog from the Tools menu if you are using Windows 2000, or the View menu if you are using Windows 9x.

Explorer

1.1 Identify the operating system's functions, structure, and major system files to navigate the operating system and how to get to needed technical information. Content may include the following: Major Operating System components — Explorer

To open Windows Explorer, select Start menu ➪ Programs ➪ Windows Explorer for Windows 9x computers, or Start menu ➪ Programs ➪ Accessories ➪ Windows Explorer for Windows 2000 computers. This will open a window like the one shown in Figure 16-23. This window has a right-hand pane that resembles My Computer using Details view, and a left-hand pane that hierarchically displays all folders or containers on your computer, starting with the Desktop. The left-hand pane is called the navigation pane or window.

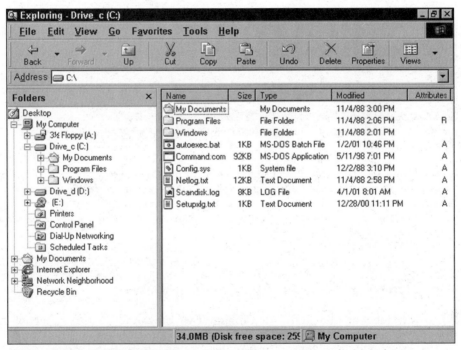

Figure 16-23: The hierarchical view of the folder structure makes Windows Explorer a very useful application.

The left-hand pane is what makes Windows Explorer different from My Computer. Now we will see that Windows Explorer does not really exist. In the top right corner of the navigation pane is a small x, which is the close box for the navigation pane. If you select My Computer in the navigation pane, close the navigation pane, and change the view to Large Icons, you will see that this window is the same as the My Computer window. To show the navigation pane, select the View menu ➪ Explorer

Bar ➪ Folders. The navigation pane allows you to quickly move from one folder to another, or copy files from one folder to another without opening multiple windows. Many Windows users prefer the Explorer view to the My Computer view of their files. Both views of your files use the same program, and it is not actually Windows Explorer that does not exist — it is My Computer, since both views make use of `explorer.exe`.

Tip   The original retail version of Windows 95 did not allow the navigation pane to be closed, but did use one program (`explorer.exe`) to display both My Computer and Windows Explorer.

If you want to quickly open Windows Explorer, right-click on My Computer and choose Explore from the shortcut menu.

Control Panels

Objective

1.1 Identify the operating system's functions, structure, and major system files to navigate the operating system and how to get to needed technical information. Content may include the following: Major Operating System components — Control Panel

Most of the settings for your computer are stored in the Registry, but the Registry is a place where errors can require that you re-install your operating system. To help make your life foolproof, Microsoft created the Control Panel folder. This folder contains Control Panel applets that allow you to change many system settings without requiring you to make direct changes to the Registry. Control panels are the recommended method for changing most of your system settings. Table 16-3 summarizes how each Control Panel applet is used and identifies if they belong to Windows 9x, Windows 2000, or both operating systems.

Table 16-3 Control Panel Applets	
Control Panel Applet	**Description**
Accessibility Options	Changes the settings for accessibility features of the computer for people who have physical limitations when using the computer.
Add New Hardware (9x)	Runs a hardware detection of your computer to detect new hardware devices or allows you to manually select devices to install.

Continued

Table 16-3 *(continued)*

Control Panel Applet	Description
Add/Remove Hardware (2000)	Performs Plug-and-play detection, full hardware scan, device configuration, or device removal.
Add/Remove Programs	Allows you to start the installation of programs, displays a list of installed programs that can be removed, allows you to add or remove operating system optional components (like games), and — for Windows 9x computers — allows you to make a Startup Disk.
Administrative Tools (2000)	Opens a folder that contains the Administrative Tools for Windows 2000. These tools allow you to configure, manage, and control your Windows 2000 computer.
Date/Time	Changes the system date, time, and time zone.
Desktop Themes	Desktop Themes are colorful and playful sets of wallpapers, system sounds, screen savers, and icons that can be used to personalize your desktop environment.
Display	Provides an interface to video configuration of your computer. This includes video card settings, screen resolution (dimensions like 800 x 600), color depth (number of colors), and color scheme.
Folder Options (2000)	This allows you to change to default folder options for your computer. These are the same options that are available through Windows Explorer's Tools menu ⇨ Folder Options.
Fonts	Displays a list of fonts that are installed on your computer, allows you to see what the fonts look like, and allows you to delete fonts or copy fonts into the folder.
Game Controllers	Allows you to add or remove game controllers and joysticks.
Internet Options	Allows you to configure Internet options and connection settings. It also allows you to clear your Temporary Internet Files and History.
Keyboard	Allows you to change the sensitivity settings for your keyboard and the layout for your keyboard.
Licensing (2000)	This is only available on Windows 2000 server and it allows you to configure the number of client access licenses that you have purchased.

Control Panel Applet	Description
Mouse	Configures the orientation, motion, and double-click settings for your mouse.
Multimedia (9x)	Configure settings for audio and video recording and playback.
Network and Dial-up Connections	Configure connections to your network or other networks.
Phone and Modem Options (2000)	Configures dialing rules and modem settings.
Modems (9x)	Configures modem settings.
Network (9x)	Configures network settings such as protocols and computer name.
Power Options (2000)	Configures power management settings for your computer.
Power Management (9x)	Configures power management settings for your computer.
Printers	Add, remove, or configure printer settings and queues.
Regional Options	Configure the operating system to support different currency, numeric, date, and time settings for specific countries.
Scanners and Cameras (2000)	Configure installed scanners and cameras.
Scheduled Tasks (2000)	Add, modify, or delete scheduled tasks. This shows up in My Computer for Windows 9x computers, but it is not in the Control Panel folder.
Sounds and Multimedia (2000)	Configures sounds for system events, like window open or new mail, and allows you to configure audio or multimedia hardware.
Sounds (9x)	Configures sounds for system events, like window open or new mail.
System	Configures advanced system settings for hardware and performance.
Telephony (9x)	Configures dialing properties.
Users (9x)	Configures user profiles and user settings.

Key Point Summary

This chapter takes a look at what functions make up the major roles of the operating system. These include hardware and software management. In the area of hardware management, you examine memory management. You also look at folder management on the disk, and examine some of the ways to create and remove folders from your hard drive. When dealing with folders, you also look at how many files can be created on a disk, and how the file system alters the values.

When dealing with software, you look at the different versions of the various OSs, and how to determine which version you are running. You also examine some of the major differences between Windows 9x and Windows 2000.

✦   ✦   ✦

STUDY GUIDE

Now that you have taken a look at the major functions of an OS, this Study Guide provides 15 assessment questions to check your knowledge of the exam topic area.

Assessment Questions

1. Phil is using a Windows 98 computer. He has opened two 32-bit applications, two 16-bit applications, and two MS-DOS applications. How many Virtual Machines does he have in use?

    A. 1

    B. 3

    C. 5

    D. 6

2. Virtual Memory is composed of which of the following? (Choose all that apply)

    A. Physical Memory

    B. Extended Memory

    C. Hard drive space

    D. Compressed Memory

3. Jill has tried to create a new folder (d:\items), but received an error message stating the she was out of space. She checked the D: drive and found that she has 500MB of free space. What is likely the problem?

    A. The folder was automatically created on her C: drive.

    B. The folder name was already in use.

    C. The folder she was creating was larger than the free space that is available.

    D. She has used up all of the free directory entries in the root of her drive.

4. Jamie needs to load File and Printer Sharing services. She has three Windows 95 CDs and needs to identify the correct version before placing it in her CD drive. What can she do?

   A. Open the System control panel, and check the version number.

   B. Open a command prompt and type `version`.

   C. Double-click the My Computer icon, and then read the version number.

   D. Get the Properties of Network Neighborhood and read the version number.

5. Bill is looking for the version number on his Windows 95 computer. He went to the Start menu ⇨ Programs ⇨ Accessories ⇨ System Tools, but does not see the System Information Tool. Which of the following may have caused this?

   A. The component was not installed.

   B. Bill is not in the Administrator's group, so he does not have access to the application.

   C. Bill is using the retail version of Windows 95.

   D. The System Information Tool is only available with Windows 2000.

6. The total number of available directory entries on your hard drive affects what?

   A. The number of directories you can create on your hard drive

   B. The number of files you can create on your hard drive

   C. Both of the above

   D. None of the above

7. You have a 500-character text file that you are about to save to your hard drive. You have three partitions that are all 2GB in size. Each of the partitions has been formatted with a different file system. On which drive will this file use the least amount of space?

   A. The drive formatted with FAT16

   B. The drive formatted with FAT32

   C. The drive formatted with NTFS

   D. The file uses the same amount of space on any drive

8. You require the version number of your installation of Windows 2000. Which of the following are methods of obtaining the number?

    A. The Version control panel applet

    B. Reboot the computer

    C. The System Version Tool

    D. The Properties of My Computer

9. You have launched an MS-DOS application on your Windows 2000 computer. When you open Task Manager to see how much processing time the application is taking, you don't see it listed. Why?

    A. The application is running inside of a NTVDM.

    B. MS-DOS applications are not listed on the Processes tab.

    C. The application is listed, but the Processes tab is using the name stored in the header of the application, rather than the executable name.

    D. You should check the list again because all running processes are listed, and you must have missed the name.

10. Your computer has just suffered from a STOP event (a.k.a., Blue Screen of Death). What is the most likely cause of the error?

    A. A multimedia application

    B. A background application

    C. Solar flares

    D. A system device driver

11. Tommy is trying to set the time on his Windows 2000 computer, but is denied access. What must he do to be able to set the time?

    A. Log on as Administrator

    B. Make sure his computer is in the correct time zone

    C. Be granted the User Right, Change the System Time

    D. Log on as an authorized user, rather than guest

12. Bill has just attempted to delete a file from the root of the C: drive on his Windows 2000 computer. He was denied access. What are some of the reasons for this?

    A. The file has the Read-only file attribute

    B. The file has only the Read NTFS permission

    C. The file is shared as Read-only

    D. The file has the Deny-delete file attribute

13. Jason has a user on his network that needs the ability to edit five Registry values on a Windows 2000 computer. They all exist under different keys in the Registry. Can Jason restrict the user to editing just the five values?

   A. Yes

   B. No

14. Mary has just attempted to install a new video driver for the video card on her Windows 2000 computer. She received a message stating that the driver she was installing was not signed. Should Mary continue with the installation?

   A. She can continue, but should be aware that the driver may not work.

   B. She should stop the installation, because the driver was not signed, and it won't work with Windows 2000.

   C. She can continue. If there are any problems with the driver, it won't install.

   D. She should stop the installation and run: `drvsgn <driver.dll>` to sign the driver files. Then it should install without any problems.

15. Jane is having a problem with her Windows 98 computer. It seems that everything is running very slowly. What tools can she use to try to identify why her computer is running slowly?

   A. Memory Monitor

   B. Performance Monitor

   C. System Information Monitor

   D. System Monitor

Answers to Chapter Questions

Chapter Pre-Test

1. The correct answer is **no**. Performance problems with Windows 9x computers can be solved with System Monitor. Performance Monitor is a similar tool for Windows 2000 computers.

2. Virtual memory is actually composed of both **hard drive space** and **physical RAM**. Many people intend to refer to the hard drive space when they talk about Virtual memory.

3. Windows 2000 protects the OS memory from applications **by starting applications up in the User Mode area of the OS**. This prevents stay requests from applications from affecting the OS.

4. `md` **or** `mkdir` are command-line tools for creating folders or directories.

5. Windows 9x uses an **MS-DOS Virtual Machine (VM)** to execute MS-DOS based applications.

6. Windows 2000 can implement security restrictions on **files, system time, computer logon, and Registry values**.

7. **Changing the driver signing options to block the installation of unsigned drivers** achieves that goal.

Assessment Questions

1. **B.** There are three Virtual Machines in use: one for the System VM, which executes all of the Windows-based applications, and one for each of the MS-DOS–based applications. For more information, see the section titled "Getting into the architecture."

2. **A, C.** Virtual memory is composed of both physical RAM and a swap or page file on the hard drive. For more information, see the section titled "Paging your memory."

3. **D.** If you have used up all of the available directory entries in the Root directory (usually 512 entries), then you are prevented from creating additional files in the directory. For more information, see the section titled "Working with folders."

4. **A.** If she was to use the command prompt, then she should type `ver`. With the My Computer icon, she should right-click and get the properties. For more information, see the section titled "Checking the OS version."

5. **C.** The System Information tool was only included with the OSR2 version of Windows 95 and with Windows 98. For more information, see the section titled "Checking the OS version."

6. **C.** The number of directory entries affects both the number of files and the number of folders. Each file or folder uses up one directory entry. For more information, see the section titled "Working with folders."

7. **C.** This file takes up one cluster or one allocation unit on any drive that it is placed on. At 2GB the cluster size of an NTFS partition is smaller than FAT16 and FAT32 at 2K. For more information, see the section titled "Contrasts Between Windows 9x and Windows 2000."

8. **C, D.** If you are using Windows NT 4.0, then you can also get the information during the boot process. Finally, there isn't a Version control panel. For more information, see the section titled "Checking the OS version."

9. **A.** The application is running inside of one of the NTVDM's that are listed. For more information, see the section titled "Getting into the architecture."

10. **D.** Most Blue Screen errors are the result of driver conflicts. This is not to say that the multimedia application may not have made some unsupported calls to a sound or video card to cause the problem, but this would have been the second choice. For more information, see the section titled "Getting into the architecture."

11. **A, C.** By default, only users in the Administrators and Power Users groups have the User Right of "Change the System Time." This right can be granted to any user. For more information, see the section titled "Contrasts Between Windows 9x and Windows 2000."

12. **B.** Share permissions won't apply to Bill because he can access the files locally. There isn't a Deny-delete file attribute. The Read-only file attribute seems likely, but with other OSs, this would have been the correct answer. For more information, see the section titled "Contrasts Between Windows 9x and Windows 2000."

13. **B.** No, unless each value is under a key that doesn't contain any other values. This is because you can only implement permissions at the key level. For more information, see the section titled "Contrasts Between Windows 9x and Windows 2000."

14. **A.** If unsigned drivers are not being blocked, then she is able to install the driver. She should be aware that there may be problems with the driver because it has not been tested at Microsoft. For more information, see the section titled "Contrasts Between Windows 9x and Windows 2000."

15. **D.** System Monitor returns information about her system. Memory Monitor does not exist, and Performance Monitor is designed for Windows 2000. For more information, see the section titled "Contrasts Between Windows 9x and Windows 2000."

Command Prompt Procedures

EXAM OBJECTIVES

Exam 220-202 ✦ A+ OS Technologies

- ✦ **1.1** Identify the operating system's functions, structure, and major system files to navigate the operating system and how to get to needed technical information. Content may include the following:

  - Command Prompt Procedures (Command syntax): DIR, ATTRIB, VER, MEM, SCANDISK, DEFRAG, EDIT, XCOPY, COPY, FORMAT, FDISK, MSCDEX, SETVER, SCANREG

CHAPTER PRE-TEST

1. What is the primary difference between the `copy.exe` command and the `xcopy.exe` command?

2. What command will tell you how much space `config.sys` drivers are taking in memory?

3. If you don't use the `sys.com` command, how can you create a system disk from the command prompt?

4. What is the name of the utility that will find and repair some errors with files and the directory structures?

5. What will the command `attrib.exe +h *.*`, cause to happen on your computer?

6. What types of file formats can you save with `edit.com`?

✦ Answers to these questions can be found at the end of the chapter. ✦

This chapter will take a look at several command prompt utilities and a few graphical utilities. Even in the age of Windows, statements that can be issued from command prompt are still required knowledge for support professionals. This knowledge will help you automate processes — such as batch files — and solve problems when the graphical operating system is not functioning. After reading this chapter, you should have a good understanding of many of the basic commands that are available from the command prompt. MS-DOS supports internal and external commands. Internal commands are commands that are built into the `command.com` file, while external commands are found on your disk. The usual location for external commands when using MS-DOS is in the `C:\dos` directory. When using Windows, you will usually find external commands in either `C:\windows` or `C:\windows\command`. Some of the commands that will be covered in this chapter are internal commands and some are external commands. The external commands will end with either `.exe` (executable) or `.com` (command), while internal commands will not have a file extension.

As an added benefit, you will also learn how to build a basic batch file, with some controls in it. This will be done at the end of the chapter, as you will not be tested directly on that knowledge.

Managing Directories

All files that are saved on a disk are stored in a hierarchical directory structure. All the files could be placed at the top of this structure, but it would be disorganized, and therefore poorly managed. Also, most top-level directories, or "root" directories, have a limited number of files they can hold. This directory structure is allowed to have as many nested sub-directories as you want. The commands discussed in this section enable you to get listings of files, as well as create and delete directories on your disk.

dir

1.1 Identify the operating system's functions, structure, and major system files to navigate the operating system and how to get to needed technical information. Content may include the following: Command Prompt Procedures — DIR

The first command that you will see is the directory command (`dir`). This command is used to get a listing of the files that are in a directory on your disk. Typing `dir` by itself will enable you to see the listing of your current directory. The current directory is usually listed in the command prompt, like this:

```
C:\WINDOWS\COMMAND>_
```

The `dir` command is extremely useful, and has several options that are discussed later in this section. First, though, you will have to get a firm grasp of wildcards, relative paths, and absolute paths.

There are two wildcards that can be used to help modify what results you are given back. They are * and ?. The * represents one or more characters. Here is an example of its usage to retrieve a list of files that match a certain pattern. The command:

```
dir WIN*XE
```

returns the following:

```
WINMINE.EXE
WINHELP.EXE
WINHLP32.EXE
WININIT.EXE
WINVER.EXE
WINFILE.EXE
WINPOPUP.EXE
WINIPCFG.EXE
WINREP.EXE
```

The results that were returned include all files that start with win and end with xe, with any number of characters in between — even zero. This information will also be useful when we discuss copy commands later in the chapter.

The ? works a little differently from the * since it represents one or zero characters. Here is an example of the ? in action, as it looks for all files that were created on the 5th of any month after Jan 01, 2000. The command:

```
dir ??052???.TXT
```

returns the following list of files:

```
1052000.TXT
5052000.TXT
10052000.TXT
11052000.TXT
12052000.TXT
4052002.TXT
12052003.TXT
6052008.TXT
```

The ? in the command will not return any files that have more than two characters before the 05 and will not return any more than three characters after the 2 in the dir statement. This is often helpful when files in a directory are named with six- or eight-character numeric dates with the pattern of mmddyyyy.txt, and you are looking for all of the files that are named for the 5th of any month.

When you type dir, you will be given a directory listing for your current directory. If you want to see the listing for a different directory, Table 17-1 provides several options available to you in choosing a different directory. All the command examples in the table use the c:\parent_dir\child_dir\grandchild_dir directory structure, with the current directory set to c:\parent_dir\child_dir.

Table 17-1
Ways to Specify Directory Paths

Command	*Directory Result*
Dir	Returns the listing for the current directory c:\parent_dir\child_dir.
dir c:	Returns the listing for the current directory on the C drive c:\parent_dir\child_dir.
dir c:\parent_dir	Returns the listing for c:\parent_dir.
dir \	Returns the listing for the root of the current drive c:\.
dir ..	Returns the listing for the parent directory of the current directory c:\parent_dir.
dir ..\..	Returns the listing of the parent directory of the current directory c:\.
dir ..\child_dir	Returns the listing of a directory named child_dir, which is a child of the parent directory c:\parent_dir\child_dir.
dir grandchild_dir	Returns the listing of a child directory named grandchild_dir, c:\parent_dir\child_dir\grandchild_dir.

Caution It is very easy to unintentionally delete files (or delete the wrong files) when working with relative paths. When possible, use full path names to avoid mistakes.

Whenever a full path is specified, starting with the drive letter, it is referred to as an absolute path. If you do not specify the full path, you are using a relative path. Care should always be taken when using relative paths with commands. Look, for example, at the following code sample:

```
dir sub_dir
del *.*
```

In this example, a directory listing is taken of a subdirectory, while the following delete command was working on the entire contents of the current directory. This is an easy mistake to make. When working with relative paths, the double period (..) notation refers to a parent directory, and the single period (.) refers to the current directory.

Most programs and commands can have their actions modified by providing options on the command line. These options are usually represented by one or more letters and are introduced to the command with either / or -. The - is usually used with commands that come from (converted from) the UNIX OS, while most MS-DOS programs have implemented the /. These options are referred to as "switches." Here is an example of the `dir` command using switches:

```
dir /on /s
```

Table 17-2 summarizes some of the most important options for the `dir` command.

<table>
<tr><td colspan="2" align="center">Table 17-2
Options for dir</td></tr>
<tr><td>*Switch*</td><td>*Description*</td></tr>
<tr><td>/ad</td><td>The /a switch is short for "attributes." This switch provides a listing of files that have matching attributes. In this particular case, the attribute is the "directory" attribute This switch must be used in conjunction with an additional letter to provide results. There are five letters that may be used: (d)irectory, (a)rchive, (h)idden, (s)ystem, and (r)ead-only. Using a minus sign (e.g., /a-d) will show you things that are not directories.</td></tr>
<tr><td>/b</td><td>The /b command displays a bare listing. The bare listing does not include a separate section in the output that tells you the directory that you are working with, but rather displays a single line listing, like this:

c:\windows\hosts.txt

c:\windows\lmhosts.txt</td></tr>
<tr><td>/od</td><td>The /o switch is short for "order by." This switch is similar to /a in that /o by itself will not work, and it required an additional letter to tell it how to order or sort. The options that are available for sorting are: (n)ame, (s)ize, (e)xtension, (a)ccessed date - earliest first, (d)ate modified - earliest first. If you use a minus sign (e.g., /o-d), the order is reversed. If you use the letter g after the o (e.g., /ogd), then directories will be grouped at the top of the list rather than mixed in.</td></tr>
<tr><td>/p</td><td>This switch will pause the screen after each full screen of text and wait for a key to be pressed. If you do not use this option, you can use the pipe-more command which would look like this: dir c:\windows*.exe | more. Since not all commands support a pause feature, the pipe-more command is a useful option.</td></tr>
</table>

Switch	Description
/s	This switch will include in the directory listing, listings for each subdirectory under it.
/w	This switch will display the text in a wide listing. It enables more text to be displayed on a screen by using multiple columns.
/x	This switch is used on Windows 2000 computers to display the short file names, as well as the long file names.

If you want to use the same set of switches each time you execute the dir command, you can use the dircmd environment variable. This variable can be set in the autoexec.bat file or at a command prompt, like this:

```
set dircmd=/on /w
```

Now, every time you type dir, you will get output that looks like this:

```
Volume in drive D is DRIVE_D
 Volume Serial Number is FFFF-FFFF

 Directory of D:\DOS

[.]            [..]           CHOICE.COM      DELTREE.EXE     DOSHELP.HLP
DOSKEY.COM     EXPAND.EXE     FC.EXE          FDISK.EXE       HELP.COM
HELP.HLP       HIMEM.SYS      INTERLNK.EXE    INTERSVR.EXE    LOADFIX.COM
SMARTDRV.EXE   TREE.COM
               15 File(s)         525,943 bytes
                2 Dir(s)      446,431,232 bytes free
```

You should note that the list is presented in wide format, and sorted by name.

mkdir

mkdir, or md, is used to create directories. There is no difference between the two commands, other than the fact that they are spelled differently. Many of the commands that are used with MS-DOS originated in other operating systems, and in some cases, new short forms were created. In an effort to provide backward compatibility, support for the older spelling of the command was kept. With this command, you will be able to script the creation of directories. The directory created will be in the current directory, unless you provide an alternative path to the command, like this:

```
mkdir "c:\temp\my new directory"
```

chdir

chdir, or cd, is used to change the current directory for a drive to another directory. The drive need not be your current drive, as this command can set a current directory on another drive. For example, if your current drive is C:, you could still type cd d:\my_dir_on_d to change the current directory for the D drive. You will not see a difference on your screen, but if you change to the D drive by typing d:, you will see that the current directory is set to d:\my_dir_on_d. The current directory is important when you want to use other file operation commands, such as copy. If you only specify the drive that you want to work with, then you will be working with the current directory on that drive. Take a look at this example:

```
c:
cd \
mkdir d:\old_configs
cd d:\old_configs
copy a*.bat d:
copy c:\c*.sys d:\old_configs
```

The first line changes your current drive to C. The second changes to the root directory of the current drive (c:\). The third creates a new directory on the D drive, and the fourth sets old_configs as the current directory on the D drive. You will see the copy command later in this chapter, but the fifth line copies all files in the current directory that start with a and end with .bat to the current directory on the D drive (currently old_configs). The last line copies all files from c:\ that start with c and end with .sys to d:\old_configs. Lines 5 and 6 copy files from the same directory (c:\), while the relative path is used in line 5, and the absolute path is used in line 6. The destination directory in line 6 is also absolute, while the relative path or current directory is used in line 5. In both statements (line 5 and 6), the same directories are used as the source and destination directories. Relative paths can save on typing, but can also cause errors if you are not careful.

rmdir

rmdir, or rd, is used to remove or delete directories or your drive. There are two rules that are imposed on you: the directory must be empty, and it cannot be the current directory. You can empty a directory by using the del command to delete the files. To remove a directory, just specify its location after the rmdir command:

```
rmdir c:\remove_me
```

If you are using Windows 2000, there is an optional switch, /s, that will automatically delete subdirectories and files.

Deltree.exe

If you have many files and folders to delete, `deltree.exe` is the command for you. `deltree.exe` enables you to delete directories, even if the directories contain files or subdirectories. If you specify a file, rather than a directory, when using the `deltree.exe` command, then the file will be deleted. Wildcards, such as `*` and `?`, may be used with this command.

 Tip   If you have a large number of files in a directory that you need to selectively delete (such as several files on the root of the C: drive), you can use `deltree.exe` as a solution.

When removing Windows NT or Windows 2000 from a FAT formatted partition, I regularly have to delete several files of a directory. The problem with this action is that many of the files have attributes of hidden, read-only, or system, which prevents them from being deleted with the `del` command. In order to quickly delete these files, I use `deltree.exe` . as a solution. When using this command, you will be prompted with the name of each file or directory and asked if you would like to delete it `[yn]`. Please use caution when doing this — if you answer incorrectly, then you will have deleted files or directories. The command:

```
deltree.exe .
```

would ask the following questions (the "y" or "n" at the end of the lines represent my choices):

```
Delete directory ".\SUB_DIR1" and all of its subdirectories? [yn] y
Delete directory ".\SUB_DIR2" and all of its subdirectories? [yn] n
Delete file ".\FILE_ONE.TXT"? [yn] n
Delete file ".\FILE_TWO.TXT"? [yn] y
Delete file ".\FILE_THREE.TXT"? [yn] n
Delete file ".\FILE_FOUR.TXT"? [yn] y
```

`deltree.exe` is a Windows 9x command, and does not work with Windows 2000. To delete full directories with Windows 2000, use `rmdir /s`.

Copying and Moving Files

Doesn't it seem like once you finally get things organized, it's time to start all over again? When organizing and backing up files, you will often be required to copy or move files to new locations, either in another directory or on another disk. The following sections provide an overview of the commands that will let you do this.

copy

1.1 Identify the operating system's functions, structure, and major system files to navigate the operating system and how to get to needed technical information. Content may include the following: Command Prompt Procedures (Command syntax) — COPY

The copy command expects you to give at least the name of the file you would like to copy. If you only provide one filename, then the selected file will be copied into the current directory. If you provide a source filename and a destination directory using a command such as

```
copy c:\source\myfile.txt c:\destination
```

then the file will be copied into the destination directory. You will also be able to rename files while you are copying them by using a command like:

```
copy c:\source\*.bat c:\destination\*.old
```

The previous command would copy all of the files with an extension of .bat from the source directory and rename with an .old extension in the destination directory.

If you are about to overwrite an existing file, you will be prompted to confirm the operation. This can be suppressed if you use /Y at the end of your copy command. /Y tells the copy command to answer "yes" to all confirm overwrite questions. If you want to consistently overwrite destination files, you can set the copycmd environment variable to /Y in the same manner that you set the dircmd variable earlier in this chapter.

xcopy.exe

1.1 Identify the operating system's functions, structure, and major system files to navigate the operating system and how to get to needed technical information. Content may include the following: Understand Command Prompt Procedures (Command syntax) — XCOPY

Many times, you will have to copy entire directory structures from one location to another. If you were to do this with the copy command, you would first have to create all of the destination directories using the md command. With the xcopy.exe command, you can perform this task in a minimal amount of time. To copy an existing directory named source to a new directory named destination, you would type the following command:

```
xcopy.exe c:\source\*.* c:\destination\*.*
```

If you wanted to copy all the subdirectories as well, you would use:

```
xcopy.exe c:\source\*.* c:\destination\*.* /s
```

To also include empty directories, add /e (empty) to the end of the command. To include just files with the archive attribute set, add the /a (archive) switch.

Like the copy command, /Y will overwrite files without asking for confirmation. The /Y tells the command to answer "yes" to all overwrite prompts.

Move.exe

The move.exe command will move files from one directory to another. It is also used to rename directories. To use the move.exe command, you have to specify the name of the files you want to move, and then specify the destination directory, like this:

```
move.exe c:\source\source_file.txt c:\destination
```

This example moves the file source_file.txt into the directory c:\destination. If you wanted to rename the directory c:\source, you would use:

```
move.exe c:\source destination
```

del

To delete or remove files or directories, you can use del or erase. Once again, these two commands are synonymous. If you want to delete multiple files, you will have to use the * and ? wildcards. Windows 9x will allow you to delete only files with this command, while Windows 2000 will also delete directories.

Performing Diagnostics and Tuning Performance

There are a few commands — such as defrag.exe, scandisk.exe, and mem.exe — that can be used to optimize and diagnose your computer. The MS-DOS or command prompt versions of the defrag.exe and scandisk.exe utilities have now been replaced by Windows 9x and Windows 2000 versions. scandisk.exe for Windows 9x comes in two flavors: a command shell version, and a Windows 9x GUI version, while Windows 2000 only has one version.

Defrag.exe

1.1 Identify the operating system's functions, structure, and major system files to navigate the operating system and how to get to needed technical information. Content may include the following: Understand Command Prompt Procedures (Command syntax) — DEFRAG

The purpose of the defrag.exe utility is to fix speed and performance problems. As files are written to and then deleted from a disk, they leave holes or blank areas scattered around your drive. When you write files to a disk, they will always write to the largest open spaces that are available to them. There will then be times that the largest area is not large enough and the file will have to be split into pieces. Fragmented files will be slower to access, since the disk head has to keep moving to a new location on the drive. If you want to defragment the files that are on your hard drive, you can use Computer Management in Windows 2000, or defrag.exe in Windows 9x, as shown in Figure 17-1.

Cross-Reference   For more information about the use of Computer Management in Windows 2000 and defrag.exe in Windows 9x, see Chapter 20.

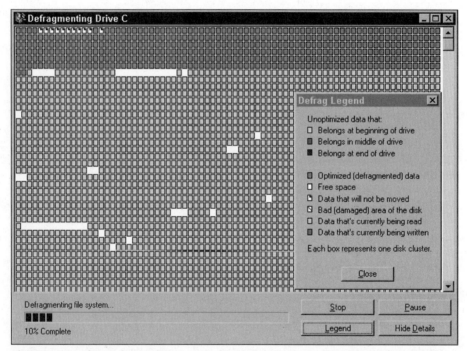

Figure 17-1: The Defragmentor in Windows 9x is an easy-to-use graphical utility.

scandisk

Objective   **1.1** Identify the operating system's functions, structure, and major system files to navigate the operating system and how to get to needed technical information. Content may include the following: Understand Command Prompt Procedures (Command syntax) — SCANDISK

`scandisk.exe` serves an important purpose within the Windows operating system. Its job is to inspect all the files on the disk, and to check for worn out areas of the disk. Its purpose is to reduce the chance of data loss by catching corruption early, and by fixing small problems before they become larger.

Cross-Reference For more information about `scandisk.exe`, refer to Chapter 20.

mem.exe

Objective **1.1** Identify the operating system's functions, structure, and major system files to navigate the operating system and how to get to needed technical information. Content may include the following: Understand Command Prompt Procedures (Command syntax) — MEM

The `mem.exe` command is used to display usage information about your memory. This is often useful when trying to optimize the boot process, or when trying to maximize the amount of memory available to MS-DOS–based applications. `mem.exe` will run from within MS-DOS.

Running the command by itself will display basic information about how much memory is available to the MS-DOS environment. There are two main switches that are available to the `mem.exe` command. `/c` (classify) is used to determine how much space applications are using in upper memory and conventional memory. `/d` (debug) is used to give you a detailed breakdown of what is stored in the first 1MB of RAM.

Working with the Rest

The rest of the utilities in this module, which defied classification, are presented in the following sections. Although they serve a wide range of functions, they are all important in your computer's usage.

attrib.exe

Objective **1.1** Identify the operating system's functions, structure, and major system files to navigate the operating system and how to get to needed technical information. Content may include the following: Understand Command Prompt Procedures (Command syntax) — ATTRIB

All files have four basic attributes: read-only (`r`), hidden (`h`), system (`s`), and archive (`a`). The `attrib.exe` command allows you to change these attributes. The attributes are added or removed from files by specifying the attribute with a + or - in front of the file name, as in the following statement:

```
attrib.exe -s -h +a +r c:\*.sys
```

The previous statement would remove the system and hidden attributes, while adding the archive and read-only attributes. If /s was added to the end of the line, then this would have been done to all of the files in the subdirectories, as well.

As their name suggests, read-only files cannot normally be deleted, nor can they be modified. Hidden files are not usually visible. System files have special file protection, so that you may not delete or modify them. Archive files are files that have been modified. The archive attribute is used by some backup utilities to identify changed files for incremental backups.

fdisk.exe

1.1 Identify the operating system's functions, structure, and major system files to navigate the operating system and how to get to needed technical information. Content may include the following: Understand Command Prompt Procedures (Command syntax) — FDISK

The fdisk.exe command is used to create initial boundaries on your computer's hard drive. These boundaries are referred to as partitions. Your drive must be partitioned and formatted prior to being used to store data.

For more information about the fdisk.exe command and partitions, consult Chapter 20 and Chapter 27.

Format.com

1.1 Identify the operating system's functions, structure, and major system files to navigate the operating system and how to get to needed technical information. Content may include the following: Understand Command Prompt Procedures (Command syntax) — FORMAT

The format.com command prepares a disk to be used by your computer. The purpose of this command is to check to see if all of the clusters on the partition are in working order, and to create the directory table. On FAT partitions, the directory table is referred to as the File Allocation Table. The directory table's job is to maintain a list of where each file starts on the disk.

The format.com command requires a drive letter and supports additional switches. The proper syntax to format you're A: drive would be:

```
format.com a:
```

You could modify the command with /q to perform a quick format of the drive. The quick format does not check the integrity of the sectors on the drive, but only deletes and re-creates the directory table.

If you are using Windows 9x, you will also be able to use the /s (system files) switch. This will copy over the system files that are required to boot.

For information about the boot process, see Chapter 22.

sys.com

The `sys.com`, or system command, enables you to get the files that are required for booting your computer to a disk that has already been formatted. This is sometimes the case after you have formatted a disk and copied files to the disk, or if the system files on the disk have been corrupted or deleted. By default, the system files will be copied from your current drive to the drive specified in the command. You can copy the files from an alternate location, but you cannot copy them to your current drive. Here are two examples:

```
sys.com a:
sys.com d:\sysfiles a:
```

Since the files have to be placed in a specific location on the disk, there is a chance that you will be told that there is no room on the disk, if that area is already occupied.

mscdex.exe

1.1 Identify the operating system's functions, structure, and major system files to navigate the operating system and how to get to needed technical information. Content may include the following: Understand Command Prompt Procedures (Command syntax) — MSCDEX

The Microsoft CD Extension (`mscdex.exe`) is used to access your CD-ROM when using MS-DOS. It is important to know how this utility works, especially when you need to make a bootable disk that is capable of reading your CD-ROM. This command is loaded in `autoexec.bat` or after the boot process completes. In order for this command to function, you will have to have loaded drivers for your CD-ROM in your `config.sys` file, using a statement such as:

```
device=c:\windows\vide-cdd.sys /d:cdrom
```

The `/d` (device name) is the switch that assigns a name to the device. The name will be used as a reference by `mscdex.exe`. The command to allow access to the CD-ROM looks like this:

```
mscdex.exe  /d:cdrom /l:f
```

The `/l` (letter) switch in the previous line is used to assign the first CD-ROM drive letter (F:). If there was more than one CD-ROM in your computer, then the other drives would be G:, H:, and so on.

ver

1.1 Identify the operating system's functions, structure, and major system files to navigate the operating system and how to get to needed technical information. Content may include the following: Understand Command Prompt Procedures (Command syntax) — VER

The `ver` command indicates what version of the command prompt you are running. This will vary between copies of Windows 9x and Windows 2000, as shown in Table 17-3.

Table 17-3 Windows ver Output	
Version	**Output of ver Command**
Windows 95 Retail	Windows 95. [Version 4.00.0095]
Windows 95 OSR2	Windows 95. [Version 4.00.1111]
Windows 98	Windows 98. [Version 4.10.1998]
Windows 98 SE	Windows 98. [Version 4.10.2154]

setver.exe

1.1 Identify the operating system's functions, structure, and major system files to navigate the operating system and how to get to needed technical information. Content may include the following: Understand Command Prompt Procedures (Command syntax) — SETVER

Many MS-DOS based applications are designed to work only with specific versions of MS-DOS. This is a problem when the version of MS-DOS that you are using is the version that is required by the application. The exact problem is summed up in the following error message:

```
Incorrect DOS version
```

The previous straightforward message lets you know that you are using a different version of MS-DOS. If you check the documentation for the application, you may be able to tell what version of MS-DOS is required. If you are able to locate the correct version number, then you will be able to implement a fix using `setver.exe`.

`setver.exe` is a TSR whose job is to report the version of MS-DOS that is in use back to applications that make a request. By using `setver.exe` you will be able to report back the required version, rather than the one that is currently in use. In order to use `setver.exe`, you will first have to load it by adding the following line to your `config.sys` file:

```
device=c:\windows\setver.exe
```

To see the list of programs that `setver.exe` has already been configured to work with, just type `setver.exe` at a command prompt. To add programs to the list, type `setver.exe <program> <MS-DOS version>`. An example of this with a program named `test.exe` that requires MS-DOS version 6.22 would look like this:

```
setver.exe test.exe 6.22
```

To remove programs from the list, type `setver.exe`, followed by the name of the program and the delete switch, like this:

```
setver.exe text.exe /delete
```

scanreg.exe

1.1 Identify the operating system's functions, structure, and major system files to navigate the operating system and how to get to needed technical information. Content may include the following: Understand Command Prompt Procedures (Command syntax) — SCANREG

`scanreg.exe` is the Windows Registry Checker. This utility is capable of backing up, restoring, and fixing the system Registry.

To back up the Registry, you would use this command:

```
scanreg.exe /backup
```

The file is backed up into the `c:\windows\sysbckup` directory and is incrementally numbered `rb000.cab`, `rb001.cab`, `rb002.cab`, `rb003.cab`, `rb004.cab`, and `rb005.cab`. There are only ever five backup files, so `scanreg.exe` will rotate through previously used filenames when necessary.

To restore your Registry from a backup, you will have to exit Windows using the Start menu ➪ Shutdown ➪ Restart in MS-DOS mode, and then use this command:

```
scanreg.exe /restore
```

After entering the previous command, you will be presented with a list of your Registry backups, and you will be able to choose which one you would like to restore. Usually, you will restore the last one that was backed up. When restoring the Registry, the bad or previous version of the Registry will be named `rbbad.cab`. This will allow you to examine the settings that were in use prior to restoring your Registry.

You may want to attempt to fix the Registry prior to restoring it, or if you do not have a backup of the Registry. To attempt to fix the Registry, you will have to exit Windows as with the restore procedure, and then use this command:

```
scanreg.exe /fix
```

This will scan the Registry for valid entries, and then rebuild the Registry with just the valid entries. If your Registry is badly damaged, the fix may not result in a working version of the Registry, and you will have to restore an older backup or reinstall Windows 9x.

 Cross-Reference To get more information on scanreg.exe, refer to Chapter 27, where it is covered in greater detail.

Working with the Edit Command

 Objective **1.1** Identify the operating system's functions, structure, and major system files to navigate the operating system and how to get to needed technical information. Content may include the following: Understand Command Prompt Procedures (Command syntax) — EDIT

Most of the configuration files on your computer can be edited with any text editor. If you have the Windows interface loaded, you will probably prefer to use a graphical program like notepad.exe or wordpad.exe. In the event that you do not have a computer that is currently running Windows, you can always use the edit.com command.

Opening files

To open files, you first have to launch the editor. This can be done by typing edit.com in any command window. If you know the name of the file that you want to edit, you can specify it after the edit.com command, like this:

```
edit.com a:\config.sys
```

If you have the editor open and you want to open a file, you have to type Alt to get access to the menu, then f to access the File menu, and o for open. This will bring you to the Open dialog box shown in Figure 17-2. By default, you will be in the File Name position, with the current name of *.* selected. If you type in the full path and file name of a file, you will be able to open the file. If you choose to browse for your file, it gets a little more complicated.

Figure 17-2: At first glance, navigating the MS-DOS-based dialogs can be confusing.

There are two ways to navigate the Open Dialog window. First, you can use the Alt key on the keyboard. You will notice that in several places in the dialog box, there is a white letter. By choosing Alt and a letter, you will be able to go to a section of the dialog. For example, pressing Alt+d will move the cursor to the Directories pane, and Alt+f will move it to the Files pane. You will be able to use the arrow keys on your keyboard to scroll through either of these lists, and the Enter key to select choices. The first entry is in the Directories pane, to navigate to the parent directory; and the last entries in that pane are all of your drive letters, to switch to different drives.

The second way to navigate from pane to pane in this dialog box is to use the Tab key. If you press the Tab key in succession, you will move through the panes, fields, and buttons from left to right, from top to bottom. The exact order for this dialog would be: File Name, Files, Directories, Open Read-only, Open Binary, OK, Cancel, Help. After completing the dialog, you would cycle back up to the File Name field. By holding the Shift key while tabbing, you will move in the reverse order. To select the check boxes, you should use your spacebar when the option is highlighted.

Once the correct file has been selected, you can press Enter or select the OK button to open the file.

Saving files

Saving files also requires that you first get access to the menu bar by pressing the Alt key. f will open the file menu, and either s to Save or a for Save As. If the file has already been saved, then saving will update the original, but if the file has never been saved, then either option will open the Save As dialog box. (See Figure 17-3.) This dialog is similar to the Open dialog with regard to navigation. Once you have selected a directory and provided a name, select the OK button.

Figure 17-3: When saving, choose a location and then a file name.

Searching and replacing

One of the more powerful features of edit.com is its ability to search and replace text in your file. To perform a replace, use the Alt key to access the menu, and then type s to access the Search menu. The Replace dialog box can be opened by typing r. (See Figure 17-4.) You can then type the string that you are looking for, as well as the string that you would like to replace it with.

To narrow down the search, you can also tell the editor to only search whole words, and to match the case. Searching for whole words means that when you search for cat, for example, you will not find it as part of the words cats or categories. Matching case means that cat would not be found if you were searching for Cat.

Closing the editor

To close the editor, gain access to the menu with the Alt key, then select f for File, and x for Exit. If you have unsaved changes, you will be prompted to save your changes, as shown in Figure 17-5.

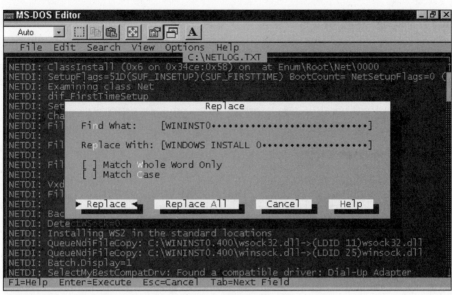

Figure 17-4: Search and replace is a powerful feature.

Figure 17-5: If there are unsaved changes when you close the `edit.com`, you will be prompted to save them.

Batch File Basics

You now know several basic commands that make the command prompt easier to use — as well as a powerful ally to you. In the following section, you will learn how to write a batch file, which will make the command prompt an even more powerful tool. A batch file is simply a string of commands that could have been typed at a command prompt and chained together to automate a process.

Starting your file

Open the editor of your choice and create a new file. If you are using a Windows-based editor, such as `notepad.exe`, and the operating system option of "Hide file extensions for known file types" is still enabled, you will have to enclose your file name in quotation marks when saving it. Save your file with a `.bat` extension. If you want to show or hide your file extensions, use the following steps:

1. Open My Computer.

2. Choose Folder Options from the Tools menu.

3. Select the View tab.

4. Clear or check the box next to "Hide file extensions for known file types."

5. Press the OK button.

You can now type any commands you want, but remember to put only one command per line in your file. You can use this file to create files, copy files, delete files, or anything else that you could do from the command prompt.

Getting your directions

Many people want to be able to direct text out of their command line, or more rarely, into their command line. There are a couple ways to do this using either ⟨, ⟩, or |. Table 17-4 summarizes the differences between the options. All of these options require that your program is generating output going to `stdout` (standard output), or accepting input from `stdin` (standard input). These are actually C routines for handling input and output.

Table 17-4
Redirection Symbols

Symbol	Function
<	Sends the contents of a file listed on the right into the command on the left. This is useful when you want to provide an answer to a question that a command will be prompting for (e.g., when the format command is prompting for confirmation). Creating a one-character text file with just Y and a return, you will be able to pass a yes into the format command.
>	By specifying a command on the left and a text file or nul on the right, you will be able to prevent output of a command from going to the screen. Instead, the output will be passed to the file that is listed on the right-hand side. If the file exists, it will be overwritten. This is extremely useful if you would like to log the results of certain statements.
>>	Similar to the > symbol, except that the output will be appended to the destination file if it already exists. If the file does not exist, then it will be created.
|	Referred to as a pipe. It pipes or directs the output of the file that is listed on the right side into (as input) the command that is listed on the left. This may allow you to bypass the creation of a text file.

Working with parameters or starting arguments

You can get a lot more mileage from your batch files if you pass and use arguments or parameters with them. There are ten that you can use. This really drops off to nine, since the first parameter is %0, and that represents the name of the running batch file. %1 through to %9 can be used as parameters for your batch file. If you have created a batch file that copies files from one directory to another, you can make your batch file more reusable by working with parameters. Here is an example of this concept:

Old batch file — StaticCopy.bat:

```
xcopy.exe c:\dos\*.* c:\dosback
```

This file could be made more generic with these modifications:

New batch file — DynamicCopy.bat:

```
xcopy.exe %1 %2
```

This new batch file would be run by typing:

```
dynamiccopy.bat c:\dos\*.* c:\dosback
```

It's true that you are typing more to achieve the same result. But you have to consider that this line could be in a much larger batch file, which could make use of the two parameters (%1 and %2) in many different ways. Since the parameters can be used rather than hard coding the paths or parameters, this could actually save you a lot of typing when creating and editing your batch file.

This system works fine until you find yourself in a position where you need more than nine parameters passed to your batch file. However, if you plan the order in which you are going to use your parameters, you can actually support many more than nine. This will be done with the shift command. Each time you use shift in your batch file, all of the parameters that are passed to your batch file will be shifted over one position. For example, %2 becomes %1, %3 becomes %2, and so on

Making decisions

So far, you have seen some ways to make your batch file more generic. Now I'll show you how to make it think for itself, or at least think for you. There are two ways to get your batch file to make some decisions, although after you've read this section, you may argue that there is only one way.

First, the if statement introduces simple program flow logic. For example, if you knew that you needed two parameters passed to your batch file for it to work properly, you could use something like this in your batch file:

```
if not !%2==! goto correct

:Instructions
echo.
echo Please provided two parameters. The first is the
echo source directory, and the second is the destination.
echo.
goto end

:correct
xcopy.exe %1 %2
goto end

:end
```

You may be questioning the use of the exclamation marks in the previous example. If they were not used and a second parameter was not provided, the logic would be "If ==". You would probably agree that that looks odd, and your computer would think so as well. With the exclamation marks (or any other letter or symbol), the statement now looks like "If !==!", which gives the computer something to test. If you are using a parameter like %1 on either side of the test equation, you should add a character to both sides of the equation to address the possibility that the parameter was not provided. You should also take note of the use of the word not to reverse the results of the test.

This example also showed you how to work with labels and the goto statement. The goto statement only uses the first eight characters of the label, so try to keep label names unique. The goto statement requires a destination in the batch file to be sent to, and that is where the labels come in. Although end is a label that is meaningful to you, to the batch file it is just another label. Remember, if you use a goto in your batch, you must have a matching label, or you will get errors and your batch file will not work.

The last method of controlling the flow of your batch file is using the choice.com statement. The choice.com statement allows you to pause your batch file to wait for input. Input to the choice.com statement is a single character. Here is an example of how to use the choice.com statement:

```
@echo off
choice.com /c:ynm You choose
if errorlevel == 3 goto m
if errorlevel == 2 goto n
if errorlevel == 1 goto y
goto end

:y
echo You chose Yes.
goto end

:n
echo You chose No.
goto end

:m
echo You chose Maybe.
goto end

:end
```

The choice.com statement uses the list of parameters after the /c: to listen to input. One of those choices must be provided. The choice.com statement will actually ignore any other input and wait for one of those choices.

Also, take note of how to handle the input afterwards. Each choice is assigned a number, based on its order: Y = 1, N = 2, M = 3. The if statement should actually be read as, "If the errorlevel is greater than or equal to x goto label". Due to the way the computer handles the if statements, always test the error levels from the highest to the lowest. If you test the values in the wrong order, then everything will satisfy the first test, since all values would be greater than or equal to one.

The `if` and `choice.com` statements add many options to the design of your batch files; they will enable you to make batch files that are flexible and comprehensive.

Looping

I hate having to repeat myself, and if you are the same, then loops are for you. Loops can be used inside or outside of batch files, with only a small modification. The loop is a `for` loop, and requires a list of values that are assigned to a variable and a statement that uses that variable. The variable is assigned with a % sign in front of it outside of a batch file, and two % signs when used with a batch file. Here is an example of a loop at the command prompt:

```
echo off
for %x in (hello world) do echo %x
```

The output of the previous loop would be:

```
hello
world
```

If this was done in a batch file, it would look like this:

```
echo off
for %%x in (hello world) do echo %%x
```

Loops may cut down your work when you have several repetitive lines in your batch file.

Locating commands

When you type a command at a command prompt in a batch file, or at the Run command, your computer follows a set of steps to locate the command. The steps include:

✦ The current directory

✦ All directories listed in the Path environment variable

If the command is not located (possibly because you misspelled it), then you will see the following message:

```
Bad command or file name
```

If you see the previous message, check the spelling of the command and try it again.

The Path variable can be set in the `autoexec.bat` file for all Microsoft operating systems. It is the only environment variable that can be set without using the `set` command. To set the path variable, you can use either:

```
set path = c:\windows;c:\windows\system
```

or:

```
path = c:\windows;c:\windows\system
```

The only advantage of the latter is that it uses four fewer keystrokes. If both `c:\windows` and `c:\windows\system` are in the path, then they will be checked when the command that is typed is not in the current directory.

Windows 2000 computers provide an additional location for setting the path environment variable. To change the path on a Windows 2000 computer, open System control panel, select the Advanced tab, and choose the Environment Variables button. You will be able to use the Environment Variables dialog box to modify the path for the computer.

Key Point Summary

The most important things to remember in this chapter are what the different commands are used for, and the major difference between similar commands. Here is a quick review:

- ✦ `attrib.exe` is used to change file attributes, such as read-only, hidden, system, and archive.
- ✦ `copy` is used to copy one or multiple files from one directory to another.
- ✦ `defrag.exe` is used to defragment your hard drive to increase performance.
- ✦ `dir` displays a list of files in a directory or directories.
- ✦ `edit.com` is used to modify text or ASCII files.
- ✦ `format.com` is used to prepare a disk for accepting data, or to erase a disk.
- ✦ `mem.exe` displays information about memory usage.
- ✦ `mscdex.exe` assigns a CD-ROM a drive letter, so that it can be accessed.
- ✦ `scandisk.exe` checks a disk for errors that could cause data loss.
- ✦ `scanreg.exe` is used to backup, restore, and fix the system registry.
- ✦ `setver.exe` sets the MS-DOS version that is reported to an application.
- ✦ `ver` displays the version of Windows that is in use.
- ✦ `xcopy.exe` is like `copy`, but can be used to copy entire directory structures.

✦   ✦   ✦

STUDY GUIDE

This Study Guide presents 15 assessment questions to test your knowledge of this exam topic area. A lab exercise follows the questions.

Assessment Questions

1. You are working on the help desk, and you receive a call from Mary. She is looking for a file that is saved on her hard drive. She has forgotten the name she gave it, but she knows that the title contains the budget, and that it is a Microsoft Excel spreadsheet. What command will best help her locate her document?

   A. `dir *budget.xls`

   B. `dir *budget*.xls /b`

   C. `dir *.budget*.xls /s`

   D. `dir *budget*.xls /b /s`

2. Sitting at your computer one day, you attempt to open a file with the `edit` command, but you see in the title bar that the file is opened as read-only. How can you get the file opened for editing?

   A. Open the file using `edit.com <filename> /modify`

   B. Before opening the file, type `attrib.exe -r <filename>`

   C. After the file is open, type `attrib.exe -r <filename>`

   D. When you attempt to save the file, check off the Overwrite Existing File option

3. You need to regularly back up files in a directory, but you want to only back up files that changed. What commands can you use to accomplish this in the easiest way possible?

   A. `fc.exe` and `xcopy.exe`

   B. `attrib.exe` and `copy`

   C. `fc.exe`, `changes.exe`, and `xcopy.exe`

   D. `xcopy.exe` and `attrib.exe`

4. You want to copy a directory structure (complete with subdirectories), so you type in: `copy c:\dir1\*.* c:\newdir /s /e`. What will you find in the `newdir` directory?

    A. All of the files that were in `dir1`

    B. All of the files and subdirectories that were in `dir1`

    C. Nothing—the command is improperly constructed and will generate an error

    D. None of the above

5. What is the purpose of the `ver` command?

    A. To switch output from other commands to verbose mode

    B. To imitate older versions of the command shell to improve backward compatibility

    C. To display the version of the operating system that you are using

    D. To enable advanced logging options

6. You receive a call from a user on your network, and they complain that their computer is slow. You ask a few more questions and find out that they feel that the speed of their hard drive is much slower than when they got their computer. What command would you suggest running?

    A. `diskfix.exe`

    B. `quikdisk.exe`

    C. `scanfix.exe`

    D. `defrag.exe`

7. You have placed a floppy disk in your drive and typed `format a:`, but then realized that it is the wrong disk. It has just counted up to 90%. Can you do anything to retrieve your files?

    A. After it completes, type `undofrmt.com a:`

    B. Press Ctrl+C to cancel the existing format, then run the `recover.com` command

    C. Press Ctrl+C to cancel the existing format

    D. There is nothing you can do

8. What command is used to assign a drive letter to a CD-ROM?

    A. `mscdex.exe`

    B. `cdletter.exe`

    C. `drvmnt.exe`

    D. `cdmount.exe`

9. You have just been told that an MS-DOS application that you are supposed to run requires 550K of conventional memory. How can you check to see if you have that much memory available?

    A. convchck.exe

    B. memchck.exe

    C. mem.exe

    D. freemem.exe

10. Which file on your computer sets the initial path environment variable?

    A. config.sys

    B. path.sys

    C. autoexec.bat

    D. config.bat

11. You need to copy an entire directory structure from floppy disk over to your hard drive. Which command should you use?

    A. xcopy.exe

    B. pathcopy.exe

    C. copy.exe

    D. dircopy.exe

12. You have a text file on your hard drive, and you need to add a listing of the files that are found in the c:\files directory to the end of this text file. What command will let you do this?

    A. dir c:\files|filelist.txt

    B. dir c:\files>filelist.txt

    C. dir c:\files>>filelist.txt

    D. dir c:\files<filelist.txt

13. You are using a Windows 9x computer and would like to remove the c:\files directory. This directory is not empty. What command would you use?

    A. deltree.exe

    B. rmdir

    C. deldir.exe

    D. nukedir.exe

14. You are using a Windows 2000 computer and would like to remove the c:\files directory. This directory is not empty. What command would you use?

　　A. deltree.exe

　　B. rmdir

　　C. deldir.exe

　　D. nukedir.exe

15. What character is used to identify a label in a batch file?

　　A. *

　　B. |

　　C. ?

　　D. :

Lab Exercises

Lab 17.1 Creating a Batch File to Automate a Task

This lab exercise requires a blank disk.

1. Create a batch file that will format a disk, configure it to be bootable, and copy over to it himem.sys, smartdrv.exe, and edit.com.

Answers to Chapter Questions

Chapter Pre-Test

1. xcopy.exe will copy entire directory structures, while copy will only copy files from one directory to an existing destination directory.

2. mem.exe /c or mem.exe /d will let you know how much memory drivers and devices have taken up in memory.

3. You could use format.com a: /s. This will format the disk and transfer the system files.

4. scandisk.exe will repair some errors with the file system and with some files.

5. This command will **hide all of the files in the current directory.**

6. edit.com can be **used to create text or ASCII files only.**

Assessment Questions

1. D. Although C looks like a good choice as well, using the subdirectory switch, it has an additional period in the search string, so will not return as many files and will only work if Mary's document has a period in front of the work budget. For more information, see the section labeled "dir."

2. B. The edit.com command will only let you change the attribute before the file is opened. For more information, see the section labeled "attrib.exe."

3. D. The attrib.exe command can be used to remove the archive attribute from all of the files in a directory structure. As files are modified, you can use xcopy.exe *.* c:\backuplocation /s /a to copy all of the files to a new location. If you want your next copy to copy the files that were modified since the last copy, you will have to use the attrib command to remove the archive attribute again. For more information, see the section labeled "xcopy.exe."

4. C. This command will cause a syntax error, and nothing will be copied. The copy command does not support either /s or /e. For more information, see the section labeled "xcopy.exe."

5. C. ver is used to display the version of the operating system. For more information, see the section labeled "ver."

6. D. defrag.exe is used to reorganize files, which will speed up access to the disk. For more information, see the section labeled "defrag.exe."

7. C. While the percentage is counting up, the disk is being checked for errors. The files are not actually erased, but appear to be when the FAT is rewritten at the end of the formatting process. For more information, see the section labeled "format."

8. A. mscdex.exe is used to assign a drive letter to a CD-ROM. For more information, see the section labeled "mscdex.exe."

9. C. mem.exe will tell you how much conventional memory is available to your applications. For more information, see the section labeled "mem.exe."

10. C. autoexec.bat is used to set the path environment variable. For more information, see the section labeled "Locating Commands."

11. A. xcopy.exe can be used to copy entire directory structures. For more information, see the section labeled "xcopy.exe."

12. C. >> will add the output of a command to a text file that already exists. For more information, see the section labeled "Getting Your Directions."

13. A. deltree.exe will remove directories on a Windows 9x computer, even if they contain files. For more information, see the section labeled "deltree.exe."

14. B. rmdir will remove directories on a Windows 2000 computer, even if they contain files. For more information, see the section labeled "rmdir."

15. D. The colon (:) is used to identify a label in a batch file. For more information, see the section labeled "Making Decisions."

Lab Exercises

Lab 17.1 Working Batch Files

A possible answer would be `systemdisk.bat`:

```
c:
format.com a: /v:startup /q /u<c:\resp.txt
sys.com a:
cd \windows
for %%f in (himem.sys smartdrv.exe command\edit.com) do_
copy %%f a:\*.*
```

where the file `c:\resp.txt` is a three-line test similar to the following:

```
Y
N

```

The last line of the file is blank.

Major System Files and their Purpose

EXAM OBJECTIVES

Exam 220-202 ✦ A+ OS Technologies

✦ **1.1** Identify the operating system's functions, structure, and major system files to navigate the operating system and how to get to needed technical information. Content may include the following: Major system files: what they are, where they are located, how they are used and what they contain. Identify the major system files and their purpose:

- **System, Configuration, and User Interface files:** IO.SYS, BOOT.INI, WIN.COM, MSDOS.SYS, AUTOEXEC.BAT, CONFIG.SYS, COMMAND LINE PROMPT

- **Memory management:** Conventional, Extended/upper memory, High memory, Expanded memory, Virtual memory, HIMEM.SYS, EMM386.EXE

- **Windows 9x:** IO.SYS, WIN.INI, USER.DAT, SYSEDIT, SYSTEM.INI, SETVER.EXE, SMARTDRV.EXE, MSCONFIG (98), COMMAND.COM, DOSSTART.BAT, REGEDIT.EXE, SYSTEM.DAT, RUN COMMAND, DriveSpace

- **Windows 2000:** Computer Management, BOOT.INI, REGEDT32, REGEDIT, RUN CMD, NTLDR, NTDETECT.COM, NTBOOTDD.SYS

CHAPTER PRE-TEST

1. What is the purpose of `io.sys`?

2. How large is conventional memory?

3. How large can virtual memory be?

4. Where is extended memory located?

5. How do you get TSRs in your `autoexec.bat` to use upper memory?

6. What is the name of the fully functional program that edits the Windows 2000 Registry?

7. What command must be called in order to load Computer Management for another computer on your network?

✦ Answers to these questions can be found at the end of the chapter. ✦

Your operating system is a useful tool once it is installed on your computer However, there may be times when you want to either get more functionality out of it or correct errors that have appeared in certain files. This chapter will examine several of the basic configuration files that exist under Windows 9x and Windows 2000. A solid understanding of these files will prepare you for the exam and for working with these systems in the field.

First, the chapter will discuss some of the common files that have been around since MS-DOS, and then move into a discussion about memory management. Even with the advent of Windows 9x, knowledge of these topics is crucial—you still need to get the OS initially loaded. Good memory management will only help you once you move into Windows 9x.

This chapter will close with a look at the files that are specific to Windows 2000. Many Windows 2000 files will bear little resemblance to the other files discussed in this chapter.

Examining Basic System and User Interface Files

1.1 Identify the operating system's functions, structure, and major system files to navigate the operating system and how to get to needed technical information. Content may include the following:

Major system files: what they are, where they are located, how they are used and what they contain—System, Configuration, and User Interface files.

This section gives an overview of the files that are required to get a system functioning.

For more information about the boot process in which the basic system files play a major role, see Chapter 26.

io.sys

io.sys is one of the first files accessed by both MS-DOS and Windows 9x. This file is the system boot loader. It resides in the boot sector of the active partition on the drive. The boot sector is checked by the computer hardware in an attempt to locate an OS on the drive. In the event that a boot loader program is found, control is given over to it. io.sys is such a boot loader.

io.sys is responsible for loading the rest of the OS. It must locate the components that comprise the OS, such as the kernel, then load the kernel into memory and pass control over to it. The 16-bit Real-mode kernel for MS-DOS and Windows 9x is command.com. There is no configuration that can be done to io.sys directly, but when attempting to diagnose boot problems, it is one of the files that should be checked.

Also note that io.sys is very version-dependent. It has been written to load only one version of the OS, which means that there is a version to load MS-DOS 6.22, one to load Windows 95 Upgrade/Retail, one to load Windows 95 OSR2, and one to load Windows 98. This should also be remembered as part of the process of diagnosing boot problems.

Exam Tip   Remember that io.sys is OS version-specific, and that each version of the OS has its own version of io.sys.

The Windows 2000 boot process does not use io.sys.

msdos.sys

io.sys attempts to load the 16-bit Real-mode kernel, but reads configuration information out of the msdos.sys file. This file contains settings and configuration information about the initial Real-mode environment.

For MS-DOS systems, the msdos.sys file is in a binary format, but for Windows 9x systems, it is in an ASCII or text format (which means it is easily editable). The msdos.sys file contains paths to the bootable Windows directory and other boot settings.

Cross-Reference   For a complete list of values that can be added to the msdos.sys file, consult Chapter 22.

The Windows 2000 boot process does not use this file.

config.sys

The config.sys file is used to load system-level devices and to make additional changes to the initial environment that will be used by command.com. The config.sys file would be used to load the drivers for your CD-ROM if you wanted to use it prior to launching Windows 9x. If the config.sys file does not exist, Windows 9x will proceed with default drivers and settings.

Windows 2000 does not generally use this file. If the file was edited and saved as an OS/2 text file, Windows 2000 will look at the file and extract any OS/2 configuration information. This information will be written to the registry and used for running OS/2 applications from within the Windows 2000 OS. This process does not happen with Windows 9x — only with Windows NT and Windows 2000.

autoexec.bat

As with the `config.sys` file, Windows 9x will function without `autoexec.bat`—though it will use it to set environment variables and load TSRs (Terminate Stay Resident programs). If the `autoexec.bat file` was missing under MS-DOS, you would be prompted to confirm the date at every bootup.

 Note TSRs (Terminate Stay Resident) are applications that load and run but do not normally occupy space in the user interface. A good example is `doskey.com`. When you run `doskey.com` from a command prompt, it doesn't appear to do anything, but it does: it runs, loads itself into memory, and then returns the command prompt back to you. This return of control is different from a command such as `xcopy.exe`, which will control the command prompt while it runs. It then completes its task and exits (terminates). When it terminates, it removes itself from memory, and is no longer running.

Windows 2000 will read the `autoexec.bat` file, but it will ignore lines that execute programs or load TSRs. The only items or lines that are used out of the `autoexec.bat` file are statements that set environment variables, such as the system path.

boot.ini

The `boot.ini` file is also a text file, and it is only used by Windows 2000 and Windows NT. It contains a boot menu that is presented to users of the OS to let them decide how they would like to boot the OS or what OS they want to boot.

 Cross-Reference For more information about the `boot.ini` file, consult Chapter 26.

win.com

In order for Windows to operate properly, it needs to load base operating system components. These base components are loaded by `win.com`. `win.com` loads the kernel, user, and GDI components, which constitutes the core of the Windows OS.

Command prompt

Before launching Windows 9x—and before the GUI (Graphical User Interface) loads—you are faced with a command prompt. If you are unfamiliar with the command prompt, you may ask yourself, "Now what?" The command prompt, which is composed of a `c:>` and a hypnotically blinking underscore, looks back at you unyieldingly. Unfortunately, it will never share its secrets (unless you ask nicely!)

In the Real World If you have a full version of MS-DOS installed on your computer, then you will be able to get help for commands by typing `help` or `help` with a command (e.g., `help xcopy`). If you have Windows 9x or Windows 2000 installed, you will find help on many MS-DOS commands in the Windows help file (Start menu ➪ Help). Last but not least, try typing the name of the command followed by the /? switch. One of these options should provide some information about the command you want to use.

Asking the command prompt for help implies that you know what to ask, or at least the name of the command that you need help on. In the case of the GUI, you are given hints and a fairly intuitive way of moving around and accessing information. However, basic functionality at the command prompt requires only that you know a small handful of commands. These commands, covered in Chapter 17, include navigation commands, such as `dir`, `cd`, and `md`; movement commands, such as `ren`, `copy` and `xcopy.exe`; disk level commands, such as `fdisk.exe` and `format.com`; and text manipulation commands, such as `type` and `edit`.

All of these commands happen at the command prompt. You will often have to revert to the command prompt within Windows 9x and Windows 2000 to execute command line programs. In the case of Windows 9x, you may also have to resort to the command prompt when you are not able to get the GUI loaded due to errors in the system configuration.

Utilizing Memory Management

Objective 1.1 Identify the operating system's functions, structure, and major system files to navigate the operating system and how to get to needed technical information. Content may include the following:

Major system files: what they are, where they are located, how they are used and what they contain — Memory management

If you are lucky enough never to have created a boot disk for your computer, then you have never had to get into the down-and-dirty world of memory management. If you have to support MS-DOS–based applications within the Windows environment, or if you need to create custom boot disks that will load your network drivers, you will want to pay attention to this section. Memory management skills are becoming a lost art in the world of Windows.

Exam Tip On the exam, expect some basic questions about what driver file is required to access which type of memory. You may also be asked about the load order of the drivers.

Conventional memory

When MS-DOS was first being developed, the world was just starting to imagine that computers would actually have 1MB of memory. The first IBM PC released in 1981 only shipped with 320K of memory. Within 18 months of its release, the IBM PC was followed up by a new version of MS-DOS and an unheard of 1MB of memory. It was seriously believed (shortsightedly) that computers would not progress beyond the 1MB mark in the near future. A decision was made early on to slice this 1MB pie into a couple of pieces. This slice cut out the first 640K of memory and called it conventional memory.

Conventional memory was "conventional" because it was the place where normal applications would run. All applications run in the conventional memory space. Many TSRs and drivers also load into this space, each taking a piece of the space away from other applications. Since there is a finite amount of memory available in this 640K area, care has to be taken to load the required drivers, while leaving space for applications to run. Lab 18.1 at the end of this chapter examines the use of memory, and how to free up space in conventional memory. Even with Windows 9x, conventional memory will still have an effect on you, until you launch the Windows GUI.

The rest of the memory below the 1MB mark was to be used for loading device drivers and supporting different levels of video displays.

Expanded memory

The limit of 640K of conventional memory became troublesome for many people, and by 1984, there were several methods available to expand the memory on your computer. By adding additional memory on expansion cards, more memory could be made available to applications. Lotus, Intel, and Microsoft created the LIM EMS (Lotus Intel Microsoft - Expanded Memory System) standard to standardize the implementation of memory expansion. Memory added through expansion cards was — very logically — called expanded memory. Although all of the system's "action" takes place in conventional memory, the expanded memory area gave applications an area where they could store information.

Expanded memory could only be beneficial if applications were written that made use of it, and eventually, many applications grew to rely on the extra storage space provided by expanded memory. Expanded memory resulted in increased application performance. After the introduction of the 80286 processor in 1984, preference was given to extended memory, and expanded memory cards became a thing of the past. Nowadays, applications that require expanded memory use an emulator, `emm386.exe`. `emm386.exe` will be discussed later in this chapter.

Extended memory

Eventually, computer manufacturers devised a way to enable hardware to address more than 1MB of memory, and the amount of available memory then jumped to 2MB or 4MB. Unfortunately, the MS-DOS real-mode operating system was hard coded to limit applications to 640K. In order to enable access to the additional memory, and at the same time allow Windows to use the additional memory, the idea of a memory manager was born. The memory manager would control access to the extension to the 1MB memory chips.

Allowing a memory manager, such as `himem.sys`, to swap information in and out of extended memory gave applications access to a larger block of memory. All memory that was being accessed had to be below the 640K mark, but it could be swapped into the extended memory area at other times. With the release of protected mode Windows 3.0 in 1990, Windows was able to access extended memory directly.

High memory

When the driver (`himem.sys`) was created to enable access to extended memory, something odd happened. With MS-DOS 5.0, it turned out that MS-DOS was able to access the first 64K of extended memory (from 1,024K to 1,088K). This area was referred to as the High Memory Area (HMA).

MS-DOS is able to load a portion of its code into the High Memory Area. This is done by adding the `dos=high` command to `config.sys`.

Upper memory

Upper memory refers to a portion of the memory that exists between the 640K and 1MB marks. A large portion of this area was originally allocated for use by system devices, such as your video display. With Windows 9x, you are able to use this area either to emulate expanded memory, to load drivers, or both. When you use this area for either of these purposes, you will need to load the `highmem.sys` and `emm386.exe` drivers, as high memory is used to gain access to the Upper Memory Area. Both of these drivers — and some of their options — are covered later in this chapter.

Virtual memory

As improvements were made in the field of RAM, and as computers with more and more memory continued to ship, software developers created applications that made use of the new memory. Because users often found themselves short of memory, they would cheat the systems by using hard drive space as temporary RAM. This hard drive space, or temporary RAM, was referred to as Virtual Memory.

Access speeds of hard disks are measured in milliseconds (10Exp-3), while memory access is measured in nanoseconds (10Exp-9). It should not be hard to guess that this means that virtual memory is extremely slow memory.

Use of Virtual memory should be limited to times that a small amount of additional memory is required. Most operating systems implement virtual memory to allow applications with high memory requirements to function, but greater performance will be achieved by adding more physical RAM to the system.

Windows uses virtual memory in the form of a *swap file* on the hard drive. Information is moved in and out of the swap file by the Virtual Memory Manager (VMM). All information must be located in physical memory to be accessed. When an application needs to store information to memory, it passes the request to the VMM. VMM stores the information into RAM, but may move the information at a later time to the swap file on the drive.

When the application makes a request for the information, the VMM checks to see if the information is in RAM (see Figure 18-1). If the information is in RAM, it is simply returned to the application. If not, VMM checks to see if there is enough space in RAM to retrieve the information from the swap file. If there is enough space to retrieve the information, then the information is retrieved from the drive and stored into RAM. If there is not, VMM will check for things that can be passed from RAM down to the drive. Once enough information is moved to the swap file, the requested information is moved into RAM, and then returned to the application.

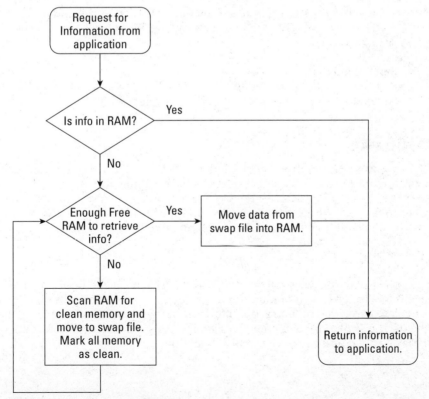

Figure 18-1: The swap process

During the scan of RAM for information to swap, any information in RAM that has not been accessed is considered to be clean. Dirty information has either been read or written. All information that is left in RAM is marked as clean during the scan. If a second scan is required, information that is dirty or was accessed since the first scan is left in memory. This algorithm is referred to as the Least Recently Used (LRU) algorithm.

Whenever possible, the active use of virtual memory should be avoided to maximize your computer's performance.

himem.sys

`himem.sys` is a high memory manager that allows computers to access memory above the 1MB mark. It is loaded in the `config.sys` file with the following line:

```
device=c:\windows\himmem.sys
```

An optional switch (`/testram:off`) can be used to bypass the memory test. This test is considered redundant by some people, since RAM is tested during the POST (Power On Self Test) process.

On Windows 9x systems, `himem.sys` is automatically loaded at the end of processing `config.sys` — that is, if it hasn't been already. The Windows GUI requires `himem.sys`.

The addition of the line `dos=high` anywhere in your `config.sys` file will cause a portion of `command.com` to be loaded into the HMA. Windows 9x systems automatically process `dos=high` if it is not present in the `config.sys` file.

emm386.exe

`emm386.exe` is not required for use by Windows, but is either used to optimize memory configurations, or to support MS-DOS–based applications.

If you want to use `emm386.exe` to support your applications that require expanded memory, you can load it with the following line in your `config.sys` file.

```
device=c:\windows\emm386.exe ram
```

Loading `emm386.exe` this way will create a 64K page frame in the upper memory. This page frame is composed of four 16K pages. `emm386.exe` uses extended memory to simulate expanded memory, but information that is being manipulated must reside below the 1MB mark of memory. To achieve this, information from extended memory is swapped into the page frame 16K at a time.

If you know that you will not be using applications that require EMS, you can make additional space available as Upper Memory Blocks (UMB) by using the following lines in config.sys:

```
dos=umb
device=c:\windows\emm386.exe noems
```

Not all driver files and TSRs can be loaded into UMBs, but for those that can, you can modify device lines in config.sys to devicehigh, as shown in this example:

```
devicehigh=c:\windows\command\ansi.sys
```

You can also modify TSR lines in autoexec.bat by placing an lh (load high) at the beginning of the line, like this:

```
lh c:\windows\smartdrv.exe
```

You can check on your success from the command prompt by using the mem /c command. This will give you a listing of what has loaded into conventional memory, and what has loaded into upper memory. Any drivers or TSRs that loaded into UMBs will have reduced conventional memory requirements. The following is a sample of the output from the mem command.

```
Modules using memory below 1 MB:

  Name        Total           Conventional      Upper Memory
  --------    ----------      ----------------   ---------------
  SYSTEM      34,592  (34K)   10,656   (10K)     23,936  (23K)
  HIMEM        1,168   (1K)    1,168    (1K)          0   (0K)
  EMM386       4,320   (4K)    4,320    (4K)          0   (0K)
  COMMAND      8,224   (8K)    1,056    (1K)      7,168   (7K)
  RAMDRIVE     1,456   (1K)        0    (0K)      1,456   (1K)
  ANSI         4,320   (4K)        0    (0K)      4,320   (4K)
  DOSKEY       4,688   (5K)        0    (0K)      4,688   (5K)
  SMARTDRV    32,192  (31K)        0    (0K)     32,192  (31K)
  Free       722,624 (706K)  638,080  (623K)     84,544  (83K)

Memory Summary:

  Type of Memory      Total         Used          Free
  ---------------    -----------   -----------   -----------
  Conventional          655,360        17,280       638,080
  Upper                 158,304        73,760        84,544
  Reserved              393,216       393,216             0
  Extended (XMS)     82,679,200     8,717,728    73,961,472
  ---------------    -----------   -----------   -----------
  Total memory       83,886,080     9,201,984    74,684,096

  Total under 1 MB      813,664        91,040       722,624

  Largest executable program size      638,064   (623K)
  Largest free upper memory block       84,256   (82K)
  MS-DOS is resident in the high memory area.
```

You should note that drivers such as ramdrive.sys and ansi.sys have loaded into upper memory, and TSRs such as doskey.exe have also loaded into upper memory.

By using the include switch, you can include areas of upper memory that are reserved for other components. For example i=B000-B7FF would include the area that is reserved for monochrome monitors, and i=E000-EFFF would include an area that is reserved for IBM PS/2s.

Touring Windows 9x System Files

 1.1 Identify the operating system's functions, structure, and major system files to navigate the operating system and how to get to needed technical information. Content may include the following:

Major system files: what they are, where they are located, how they are used and what they contain — Windows 9x.

Several files are core to the Windows 9x operating system. This section will provide an overview of each of them.

io.sys

io.sys is the system boot loader for MS-DOS and all Windows 9x versions. It is responsible for initiating the loading of the OS from the hard drive. It starts this process by creating a real-mode environment using settings found in both msdos.sys and config.sys. It also ensures that certain required system level device drivers get loaded (such as himem.sys).

command.com

command.com is the real-mode operating system kernel. It is responsible for the execution of all commands prior to the loading and initialization of the Windows kernel. It is loaded by io.sys, and executes the lines of autoexec.bat prior to starting to load the Windows kernel.

system.ini

Prior to Windows 95, all configuration settings for applications were stored in .ini files. All .ini files have a similar structure, which is represented in the following code section:

```
[section one]
setting one = "my mystery word"
setting two = 42
```

```
[section two]
setting one = "another mystery word"
setting two = 75
```

The `system.ini` file specifically contains settings that are used by Windows. The type information that is found in this file includes device settings and settings that are used when loading the Windows kernel. The `system.ini` file is not used as much these days, compared to Windows 3.x; but it still finds use when you need to load 16-bit MS-DOS real-mode drivers. If you check your `system.ini` file, you should see settings for your mouse and video. Here is a sample of what to expect:

```
[386Enh]
device=*vshare
device=*dynapage
device=*vcd
device=*vpd
device=*int13
mouse=*vmouse, msmouse.vxd
woafont=dosapp.fon
COM1Fifo=0
keyboard=*vkd
display=*vdd,*vflatd

[boot]
system.drv=system.drv
drivers=mmsystem.dll power.drv
user.exe=user.exe
gdi.exe=gdi.exe
sound.drv=mmsound.drv
dibeng.drv=dibeng.dll
comm.drv=comm.drv
shell=Explorer.exe
keyboard.drv=keyboard.drv
fonts.fon=vgasys.fon
fixedfon.fon=vgafix.fon
oemfonts.fon=vgaoem.fon
386Grabber=vgafull.3gr
display.drv=pnpdrvr.drv
mouse.drv=mouse.drv
*DisplayFallback=0
SCRNSAVE.EXE=
```

In the `[386enh]` section, file and printer sharing is initialized with `*vshare`, and real-mode support for the mouse and video display are loaded with `*vmouse`, `msmouse.vxd`, `*vdd`, and `*vflatd`. In the `[boot]` section, power management support is loaded with `power.drv`; the sound card is initialized with `mmsound.drv`; serial communication is initialized with `comm.drv`; and the system shell application is set with `shell=Explorer.exe`.

If the `system.ini` file was lost or corrupted, you would likely have problems with all the devices that rely on it. Since video configuration is included in this file, you tend to see problems quickly. If the `system.ini` file is missing, Windows 9x will create a new one and start loading the settings back in.

win.ini

Like `system.ini`, `win.ini` was heavily used by both the Windows 3.x operating system and its applications. Today, it is used primarily for backwards compatibility with older applications. There are still some settings that are stored and used out of this file. Here is a sample of some of the information that is found in a `win.ini` file:

```
[windows]
run=Qtstub.exe
NullPort=None
ScreenSaveActive=1
UninstallPath=C:\
device=EPSON Stylus COLOR 600,EPS600,LPT1:

[Desktop]
Wallpaper=C:\WINDOWS\APPLIC~1\MICROS~1\INTERN~1\INTERN~1.BMP
TileWallpaper=0
WallpaperStyle=0
Pattern=(None)

[Extensions]
txt=notepad.exe ^.txt
bmp=C:\Progra~1\Access~1\mspaint.exe ^.bmp
vdo=VDOLIV32.EXE ^.vdo
gra=C:\PROGRA~1\COMMON~1\MICROS~1\MSGRAPH5\GRAPH5.EXE ^.gra
Q98=C:\APPS\QUICKTAX\QTAX98.EXE ^.Q98
Q97=C:\QCKTAX97\QTAX97.EXE ^.Q97
Q99=C:\QUICKTAX\Qtax99.exe ^.Q99
```

This sample illustrates common items that you will find in your `win.ini` file. `run` lines automatically load applications when the shell loads. `device` lines in the `win.ini` file will make hardware devices available for older applications that need to use them. Wallpaper and desktop settings are here, as well. Finally, for more backward compatibility, there is a mapping of some of the registered file extensions.

Caution   Corruption or deletion of the `win.ini` file tends to be less noticeable than that of the `system.ini` file, but it will still cause problems with older applications that refer to the information that is found in the file. If you have a problem with an older application, then you should be able to fix the problem by re-installing the application.

regedit.exe

Caution

Extreme care must be taken when editing the Registry. Although it is not uncommon to have to edit the Registry to correct some system problems, incorrect changes could leave your system in an unusable state. Please follow the safety procedures listed in the "Using `regedit.exe`" section of Chapter 27.

regedit.exe is a program that can be used to edit the system registry. The Registry is Microsoft's newest location for storing application and system settings. These settings exist on your hard drive in the Windows directory within `user.dat` and `system.dat`. Since these two files are in a binary format, `regedit.exe` gives you a user interface through which to edit the files. Extreme care must always be used when editing the Registry, since without it, your computer will not be bootable, and Windows will have to be reinstalled.

`regedit.exe` has a two-pane window when you open it (see Figure 18-2). The left pane contains a listing of keys and subkeys, which are illustrated as folders. The right pane contains values and their data. These values control or store most of the settings on your computer.

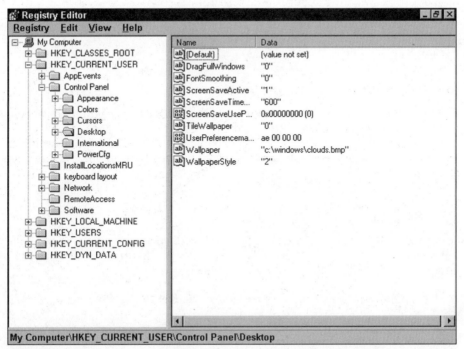

Figure 18-2: `regedit.exe` has two panes—one for navigation and one for editing.

Cross-Reference For complete details about how to use `regedit.exe`, see the regedit.exe section in Chapter 27.

system.dat

Within the Registry, settings are stored in two major sections: Hkey_Local_Machine and Hkey_Current_User. All of the information that is displayed in Hkey_Local_Machine is actually stored in the file `system.dat`. This file is backed up when the computer boots up. If the file is examined at boot and it appears to be correct, then Windows backs the file up as `system.da0`.

Caution `system.dat` should only be edited through the Registry Editor. This is the only editor that is approved by Microsoft, and corruption of your Registry may require you to re-install Windows.

user.dat

Hkey_Current_User represents user-related settings on your computer and is stored as `user.dat` in your Windows directory. This file is examined at boot; if it appears to be correct, it is backed up as `user.da0`. If you are using user profiles, then `user.dat` will be in your profile directory.

Cross-Reference For more information about user profiles, consult Chapter 16.

sysedit.exe

The System Configuration Editor (shown in Figure 18-3) gives you quick access to your main configuration files — `win.ini`, `system.ini`, `protocol.ini`, `config.sys`, and `autoexec.bat`. It is capable of editing and saving these files. This task could have been accomplished with any text editor, but it is far easier to just type `sysedit`.

setver.exe

Some applications are designed to only work with specific versions of MS-DOS. `setver.exe` is used to fool the application into believing that it is running on a different version of MS-DOS.

Cross-Reference For more details on `setver.exe`, consult Chapter 17.

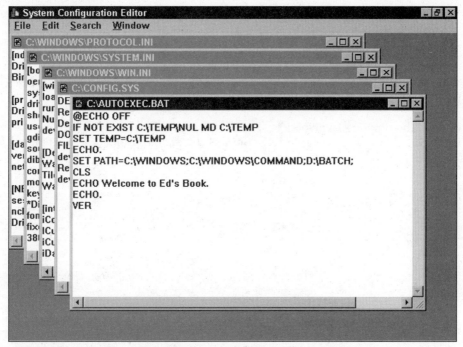

Figure 18-3: Sysedit makes getting at configuration files easier.

smartdrv.exe

Caching within computers has been implemented at different levels. Smart Drive (smartdrv.exe) represents one of those levels. smartdrv.exe is a disk caching program, which means that it reads additional data from the drive in anticipation of your program's request. Anticipating reads is the read caching feature of smartdrv.exe. smartdrv.exe also performs write caching, which is when it collects the write requests from several seconds, and then commits all of the data to the disk at once. Disk caching improves drive I/O performance by reading and writing to the drive in larger units, which requires less drive head movement than normal.

smartdrv.exe is usually only loaded when creating a boot disk or installing Windows 9x. Windows 9x has its own disk caching software built into the operating system. If you have some older applications that will not work with Windows 9x's disk caching, you can disable it, and load smartdrv.exe.

smartdrv.exe can be loaded through either config.sys or autoexec.bat. If you have an old disk controller that will not work with memory that is provided by emm386.exe, then you will have to load smartdrv.exe through config.sys with the double_buffer option. Most hard drives, definitely not new drives, do not require double buffering. To load `smartdrv.exe` in your `config.sys` file, use the following command:

```
device=c:\dos\smartdrv.exe /double_buffer
```

The `smartdrv.exe` line must be prior to the line that loads `emm386` if you are using the `/double_buffer` option.

Most of the time, you will load `smartdrv.exe` from the command prompt or through `autoexec.bat`. Table 18-1 contains the main options that you will use with `smartdrv.exe`.

Table 18-1
smartdrv.exe Switches

Switch	Description
drive_letter + or -	Allows you to enable or disable caching on specific drives using this command: `smartdrv.exe a- c+ d-` When you load `smartdrv.exe`, it automatically enables read and write caching on all hard drives, read caching on floppy drives and CD-ROM drives, and it ignores network drives and Flash memory-card drives.
InitialCacheSize	If you specify a size in kilobytes after the `smartdrv.exe` command, then it will be treated as the initial cache size. This tells `smartdrv.exe` how big to make the cache. Table 18-2 describes how the default cache sizes are set. This value can be set as high as 16,383K. In general, the larger the cache, the less often you will have to read from the drive. To set the cache size to 2MB, you would use the command: `smartdrv.exe 2048`
WindowsCacheSize	If you only specify one size in kilobytes after the `smartdrv.exe` command, then it sets the initial cache size, and the Windows cache size is still based on the values in Table 18-2. If you want to control the Windows cache size as well, then you will have to provide two values after the `smartdrv.exe` command. To set the initial and Windows caches to 4MB, you would use this command: `smartdrv.exe 4096 4096` The initial cache always has to be as large or larger than the Windows cache. If you set the Windows cache to a value that is higher than the initial cache, `smartdrv.exe` will use the Windows cache size for the initial cache size.

Switch	Description
/X	Disables write caching on all drives. It takes several seconds after your application tells smartdrv.exe to write to the drive and the information is actually written to the disk. If the power is interrupted during this time, the data will be lost. If you are concerned about the loss of data, then you will want to disable write caching.
/C	This switch is used from the command prompt to instruct smartdrv.exe to write all outstanding information to the drive.
/V	Verbose mode makes smartdrv.exe display status and error messages when it loads.
/Q	Quiet mode makes smartdrv.exe hide status messages when it loads. It will still display error messages.
/S	Displays the status of smartdrv.exe.

Caution   You should always make sure that your computer has finished writing information to the drive by typing: smartdrv.exe /c. smartdrv.exe will automatically commit data to your drive if you reboot using Ctrl+Alt+Delete.

The initial cache size and Windows cache sizes can be set when loading smartdrv.exe, but will default to the values listed in Table 18-2. The default values are based on the amount of extended memory that is on the computer.

Table 18-2
SmartDrive Default Cache Sizes

Amount of Extended Memory	Initial Cache Size	Windows Cache Size
0 MB–1MB	All extended memory	0
1.xMB–2MB	1MB	256K
2.xMB–4MB	1MB	512K
4.xMB–6MB	2MB	1MB
6.x MB and up	2MB	2MB

msconfig.exe for Windows 98

If you are using Windows 98, you have the opportunity to use the System Configuration Utility (msconfig.exe). You can see msconfig.exe running in Figure 18-4. It is truly a pumped-up version of sysedit.exe, capable of editing config.sys, autoexec.bat, system.ini, and win.ini.

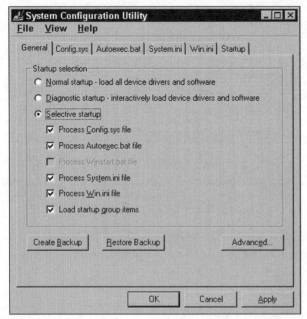

Figure 18-4: msconfig.exe is an easier to use form of Sysedit.

msconfig.exe also enables you to perform the following procedures:

✦ Back up and restore the four files that it edits

✦ Configure startup applications from the RUN key in the Registry

✦ Cancel loading of the Startup group in the Start menu

✦ Edit msdos.sys to enable different settings, like displaying the boot menu or disabling Scandisk from running

The View menu in the System Configuration Utility also allows you to launch various other utilities, such as:

✦ Device Manager

✦ Printers Folder

✦ Display Settings

✦ Multimedia Settings

✦ Fonts Folder

The editing of files with `msconfig.exe` is done in a very Windows-like fashion, as seen in Figure 18-5.

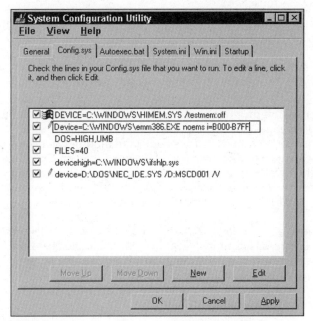

Figure 18-5: `msconfig.exe` makes file editing a breeze.

dosstart.bat

Windows 9x loads most drivers through the Registry or `system.ini`. If you choose to boot only as far as the command prompt (using F8 or the Ctrl key during boot), then you will not have these drivers loaded. The drivers will also not be loaded if you choose to "Restart in MS-DOS" from the Shutdown dialog box. If you want to use the MS-DOS Real Mode version of these drivers, you can load them though `c:\windows\dosstart.bat`. `dosstart.bat` is a text file, and can contain items such as sound card, mouse, and CD-ROM drivers.

If you choose the shutdown option of "Restart in MS-DOS mode," then `dosstart.bat` is automatically processed after the Windows GUI is unloaded. If you choose to boot to the command prompt, then you will have to run `dosstart.bat` to enable the drivers that it loads.

If you are running an MS-DOS application that required special configuration files (`config.sys` and `autoexec.bat`), you can return to your normal version of the files, and Windows by typing `win.com /w` or `win.com /wx` (which suppresses the "Press any key to continue. . . ." message).

For more information about running MS-DOS applications that require special configuration files, refer to Chapter 24.

DriveSpace

DriveSpace is a drive compression program that works with Windows 9x computers. MS-DOS 6.22 includes DriveSpace 1.0, while Windows 95 (Retail/Upgrade) included DriveSpace 2.0, and the Windows 95 Plus Pack, and all other versions of Windows 9x included DriveSpace 3.0. The primary difference between the different versions of DriveSpace is the level of compression that they offer. This section will summarize the differences between DriveSpace 2.0 and DriveSpace 3.0. There are no major differences between DriveSpace 1.0 and DriveSpace 2.0.

DriveSpace does not work with Windows 2000. To compress data on NTFS partitions, you will use the Compress file attribute. FAT and FAT32 partitions are not able to contain compressed data, and Windows 2000 will not be able to read data that is in a DriveSpace Compressed Volume File.

DriveSpace 2.0 supports the following features:

✦ Compressed Volume files up to 512MB

✦ Compression using 8K cluster sizes (This sets the working unit for compression to 8K.)

DriveSpace 3.0 supports the following features:

✦ Compressed Volume files up to 2GB in size

✦ Compression using 32K cluster sizes (Working with larger units than DriveSpace 2 provides better performance, since there is a lower number of disk I/O requests.)

✦ 20% performance increase over DriveSpace 2.0 at standard compression

✦ Supports HiPack and UltraPack compression formats

Even though the compression formats differ, standard compression for both DriveSpace 2.0 and DriveSpace 3.0 are achieved in the same manner.

Exam Tip DriveSpace may only be used to compress data on FAT partitions. You are not able to compress data on FAT32 partitions.

Before looking at the process, you should become familiar with the terms in Table 18-3.

Table 18-3 DriveSpace Terms	
Term	**Definition**
Token Replacement	Token replacement is one of the methods that is used to provide more space to save data on your disk. Within each file (binary or text) are strings of characters that are the same as other strings in the file. Token replacement records the position of the first occurrence of a common string, and then deletes subsequent occurrences, leaving only an offset marker. During decompression, the offset marker is used to locate the original data.
Compressed Volume File (CVF)	The Compressed Volume File is a file on your Host Drive that contains compressed files. These files are compressed using token replacement to obtain a space savings. There is an additional space savings achieved by how the file is saved to the disk. A 2GB FAT partition uses a 32K cluster size (the smallest storage unit), which means even a one-byte file will occupy 32K of space. The CVF is one large file that spans several clusters. A file that is written to the CVF is able to share a cluster with other files, since the CVF is occupying the entire cluster. The CVF changes the smallest space for a file to occupy down to 4K. For a one-byte file, 28K of space is saved by writing it to the CVF, rather than the drive directly. You access the CVF through a drive letter in My Computer.
Compressed Drive	The virtual drive that contains compressed data. This is a virtual drive, since you are using a drive letter to access data that is on a CVF.
Host Drive	The drive that contains the CVF.

Continued

Table 18-3 (continued)	
Term	**Definition**
Compression Ratio	The ratio that is used to report free space on the CVF to the user. If the compression ratio is set to 2:1 and there is physically 500MB of free space in the CVF, then the compressed drive will report 1GB of free space. The default compression ratio is 2:1, but can be set from 1:1 to 16:1, based on the estimated compression of files that you will be copying into the CVF. For example, BMP files often compress with a high level of compression, while JPEG files (already in a compressed format) tend to have a low level of compression. If you are saving mostly JPEG files, you would set the compression level closer to 1:1, so the free space will be reported more accurately.

To enable compression on your drive, you will use `drvspace.exe`, which is found in your Start menu under Programs ➪ Accessories ➪ System Tools ➪ DriveSpace. To work with compression, you can either create a new compressed drive or compress an existing drive.

To compress an existing drive, you will choose a drive and then select "Compress . . ." from the Drive menu. This will present a dialog box that describes the amount of space that will be left on your drive after compression. An Options button opens a dialog box that lets you choose a host drive letter, set the amount of free space on the host drive after compression, and decide if you want to hide the host drive.

To create a new compressed drive from free space on another drive, choose the drive you want to act as the host drive, and then select "Create Empty . . ." from the Advanced menu. You will then be able to choose a drive letter to be used for your new CVF, and determine how much of your host drive you would like to use for the CVF.

You can change the compression ratio of your CVF file or compressed drive by choosing the drive and selecting "Change Ratio . . ." from the Advanced menu. You should set the ratio based on the level of compression you expect to receive from the files that you save to the drive.

If you are using DriveSpace 3.0, you will be able to change the level of compression you are using by selecting "Options . . ." from the Advanced menu. Your options are "No compression," "No compression unless drive is x% full" (where the default for x is 90%), "Standard compression," and "HiPack compression."

Using "No compression" will still save you some room on the disk, since the actual cluster size is ignored, and 4K units are used to save files. FAT32 uses smaller cluster sizes than FAT partitions, and this is one of the reasons that compression is not supported on FAT32 partitions. The amount of space saved with compression would be limited to token replacement only. "No compression" provides some space savings, but allows for the fastest access to files, since no other manipulation of the file data is required, as in the case of token replacement.

Cross-Reference

For more information about file systems and their features, consult Chapter 20.

"Standard compression" provides all of the benefits of "No compression," but adds in token replacement — sometimes called encoding. Standard compression uses the same DriveSpace encoding algorithm that is used in all current Microsoft compression techniques, such as compression under Windows NT and Windows 2000. When performing token replacement, standard compression searches only the recently read portion of the file for patterns to remove.

In the Real World

Although Windows NT and Windows 2000 use the DriveSpace algorithm to compress files, they implement compression at the file level and do not require a CVF. In fact, they are not able to read Windows 9x or MS-DOS based CVFs.

"HiPack compression" operates in the same way as standard compression and uses an identical compression algorithm, but it searches the entire file for matching patterns that can be removed. As a result of this intensive searching, it removes more data through token replacement than standard compression does. Microsoft recommends that HiPack compression should only be run on Pentium class computers or better. HiPack compression uses more RAM and processor time than standard compression.

The last type of DriveSpace compression is UltraPack. UltraPack cannot be set through the DriveSpace application, but is implemented through the Compression Agent (cmpagent.exe). The Compression Agent can be run with either a drive letter (e.g., D:) or the /all switch to process all drives. You can also use the /noprompt or shorter /nop switch to suppress all messages, except error messages. The UltraPack compression algorithm is different from the normal DriveSpace algorithm and increases the level of compression at a cost of more processor time and RAM during the compression and decompression phases. UltraPack is only recommended for fast computers (Microsoft recommends Pentium or faster) and should only be used for files that are not accessed regularly (e.g., less than 30 days ago).

If you launch the compression agent with no switches, you will see the entire user interface, which enables you to configure settings for compression. The settings for the Compression Agent include which directories you would like to process, the activity level for files (for example, compress files not accessed for 30 days), and any files that you would like to exclude.

Once configured, you can start the Compression Agent manually or with the System Agent (now called the Task Scheduler). When using the Task Scheduler to start the Compression Agent, you can set it to run on a specific schedule or when your computer is idle.

RUN command.com and the command-line prompt

Although Windows 9x is a graphical operating system, there are many instances when you will need to revert to the command prompt. You can get to the command prompt in several different ways, including the following:

✦ Start menu ➪ Accessories ➪ MS-DOS prompt

✦ Start menu ➪ Run, then type `command.com`

The command prompt looks like the command prompt that you saw before you started Windows. This command prompt will be required in order to run many older MS-DOS-based applications and utilities. You could run many commands directly from the Start menu ➪ Run, since MS-DOS applications will usually cause `command.com` to be loaded; but these applications will also close the command window when the program finishes execution — not allowing you to see the output.

Windows 9x keeps several copies of `command.com` on the hard drive. They exist in the following locations:

✦ `c:\command.com`

✦ `c:\windows\command.com`

✦ `c:\windows\command\ebd\command.com`

The redundant copies of `command.com` give you some level of safety in case one becomes corrupted. To find out which one is being used by your system, open a command prompt and type `set`. The output will look similar to this:

```
TMP=C:\WINDOWS\TEMP
TEMP=C:\WINDOWS\TEMP
PROMPT=$p$g
winbootdir=C:\WINDOWS
COMSPEC=C:\WINDOWS\COMMAND.COM
PATH=C:\WINDOWS;C:\WINDOWS\COMMAND;
windir=C:\WINDOWS
BLASTER=A220 I5 D1 T4
```

The `comspec` value identifies the `command.com` file that is used when the operating system requires access to `command.com`. This value is regularly checked by the system when calling for a new command window to be opened.

Touring Windows 2000-Specific Files

 1.1 Identify the operating system's functions, structure, and major system files to navigate the operating system and how to get to needed technical information. Content may include the following:

Major system files: what they are, where they are located, how they are used and what they contain — Windows 2000.

Windows 2000 uses many of the files that are used by Windows 9x. However, there are many files that are specific to Windows 2000. This section provides an overview of Windows 2000-specific files.

Computer Management

Within Windows 9x, there is a program called Device Manager that is used to manage hardware on your computer. Windows 2000 includes a more robust version of Device Manager, but also includes a more complete tool called Computer Management. Computer Management is accessible through the System control panel applet; by right-clicking on My Computer and selecting Manage (see Figure 18-6); or from your Administrative Tools. Windows 2000 has taken the idea of a management tool several steps further with the Computer Management MMC snap-in.

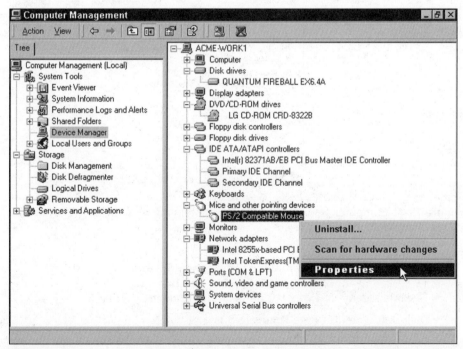

Figure 18-6: Computer Management includes Device Manager in its list of components.

Device Manager was capable of associating drivers and configuring system resources, while Computer Management does so much more. Computer Management contains system tools, such as:

✦ Event Viewer

✦ System Information (See Figure 18-7.)

✦ Performance Logs and Alerts

✦ Shared Folders

✦ Device Manager

✦ Local Users and Groups

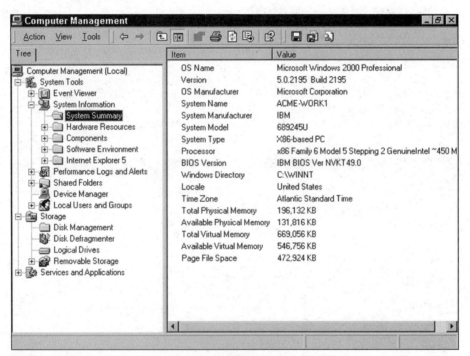

Figure 18-7: Computer Management displays system information, as well as other types of information.

Disk management tools in Computer Management include:

✦ Disk Management, for partitioning and formatting drives

✦ Disk Defragmenter (See Figure 18-8.)

✦ Logical Drives, to view Property Information

✦ Removable Storage, for offline storage of information and media management

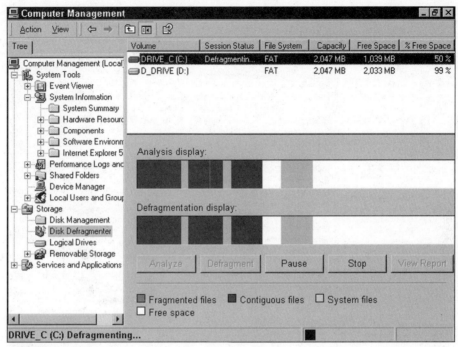

Figure 18-8: Computer Management ships with several disk tools, including a Disk Defragmenter.

Services and Applications in Computer Management allow for the configuration and management of several different services, such as:

✦ Telephony, for serial communication configuration

✦ WMI Control — Windows Management Instrumentation (WMI) service is really the Web-Based Enterprise Management (WBEM) configuration tool

✦ Services — allows for the configuration of all system services (See Figure 18-9.)

✦ Indexing Service

✦ DNS — Domain Name System management tool

✦ Internet Information Services (IIS)

Computer Management is really a full remote or local computer management tool. It is capable of configuring most of the system services and resources. By using the computer management icon in either of the following locations, you will be able to manage the local system:

✦ Start menu ➪ Programs ➪ Administrative Tools ➪ Computer Management

✦ Start menu ➪ Settings ➪ Control Panels ➪ Administrative Tools ➪ Computer Management

✦ My Computer ➪ Control Panels ➪ Administrative Tools ➪ Computer Management

Figure 18-9: Services and other tools complete the Computer Management application.

If you want to manage a remote computer, follow these steps:

1. Start menu ⇨ Run.

2. MMC, then choose the OK button. This will open an empty Console Root window, as shown in Figure 18-10.

3. Go to Console ⇨ Add/Remove Snap-in to open the snap-in management window.

4. Choose the Add button.

5. Select the Computer Management snap-in and then choose the Add button.

6. You will now have the option of typing in the name of the computer that you want to manage through this snap-in, as shown in Figure 18-11.

7. Select the Finish button, then the Close button, and then the OK button to return to the console. You should now have the computer listed in the console.

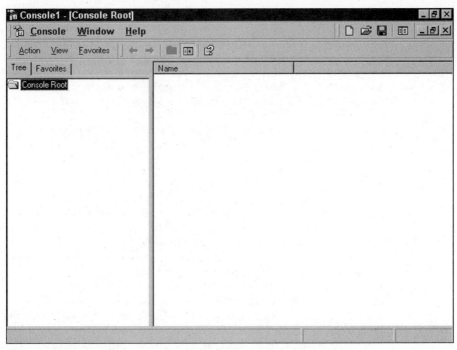

Figure 18-10: Loading a custom console gives you many options.

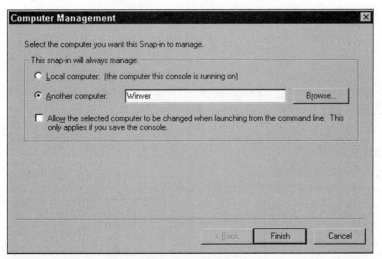

Figure 18-11: Remote administration is possible through Computer Management.

NTLDR

NTLDR is the system boot loader for Windows NT and Windows 2000. When either of these versions of Windows is installed on your computer, then NTLDR is installed in the boot sector of the active partition. When your computer boots, NTLDR runs and reads the boot.ini file to display the boot menu. It then either starts the boot process for MS-DOS/Windows 9x or Windows NT/Windows 2000.

Cross-Reference   For more information about NTLDR and the Windows 2000 boot process, consult Chapter 22.

boot.ini

The boot.ini file is called by ntldr during the boot process and is used to display the list of operating systems that can be started on this computer. It is used when you have more than one operating system installed on your computer. If you only have one copy of Windows 2000 installed, then you will not see the boot menu at all, but if you have another OS installed, such as Windows 95, Windows NT 4.0, or another copy of Windows 2000, then you will see the Boot menu displayed. The entries in the boot.ini file fall into two major sections: [boot loader] and [operating systems]. The boot loader section controls what operating system should be booted and how long the menu is visible, while the [operating systems] section lists the different operating systems that will be presented as choices. You should expect to see something similar to this structure:

```
[boot loader]
timeout=10
default=multi(0)disk(0)rdisk(0)partition(5)\WINNT
[operating systems]
C:\="Microsoft Windows 98"
multi(0)disk(0)rdisk(0)partition(4)\WINNT="Windows 2000 Advanced Server"
multi(0)disk(0)rdisk(0)partition(5)\WINNT="Windows 2000 Professional"
```

Cross-Reference   For more information about the boot.ini file, see the section "Examining boot.ini" in Chapter 22.

ntdetect.com

ntdetect.com performs a comprehensive hardware check of your computer to determine what devices are attached, what type and number of processors are in use, and resources (for example, IRQ, I/O, and DMA). It reports all of this information back to NTLDR and it is eventually used to build the Hardware key in the Registry.

For more information about `ntdetect.com` and the Windows 2000 boot process, consult Chapter 22.

ntbootdd.sys

When you boot your computer from an IDE/ATA drive or a SCSI drive from a SCSI controller that supports its own BIOS, you will not see this file on your computer. If you are loading Windows 2000 from a SCSI drive on a controller that does not have its own BIOS, then you will have `ntbootdd.sys` on the root of the drive that has `NTLDR` on it. `ntbootdd.sys` is the SCSI driver for your SCSI controller, but it has been renamed.

For more information about `ntbootdd.sys` and the Windows 2000 boot process, consult Chapter 22.

regedt32.exe

Extreme care must be taken when editing the Registry. Although it is not uncommon to have to edit the Registry to correct some system problems, incorrect changes could leave your system in an unusable state. Please follow the safety procedures listed in the section "Using `regedit.exe`" in Chapter 27.

`regedt32.exe` is actually a Windows NT 3.x application. It has been ported over to Windows NT 4.0, and now to Windows 2000. As far as the application goes, no major changes have been made to it since Windows NT 3.x. It is geared specifically to the Windows NT Registry. Compared to the Windows 9x Registry, the Windows NT Registry accepts some different data types (REG_MULTI_SZ and REG_EXPAND_SZ), as well as security restrictions that can be placed on each and every key (see Figure 18-12). To accommodate these features, you should use `regedt32.exe` over `regedit.exe`. If the work you are doing in the Registry does not utilize either of these components, you can use whichever editor you are more comfortable with.

Unlike the Windows 9x Registry, which is made up of only two files, the Windows 2000 Registry is made up a series of files that are called hives when they are loaded in to the editor. The hives for Hkey_Local_Machine are found in `%systemroot%\system32\config`, and include the files `software`, `system`, `sam`, and `security`. The hives for Hkey_Users and Hkey_Current_User include `%systemdrive%\documents and settings\%username%\ntuser.dat` and `%systemroot%\system32\config\default`.

Chapter 27 contains more information about how to work with `regedt32.exe` in the "Using `regedt32.exe`" section.

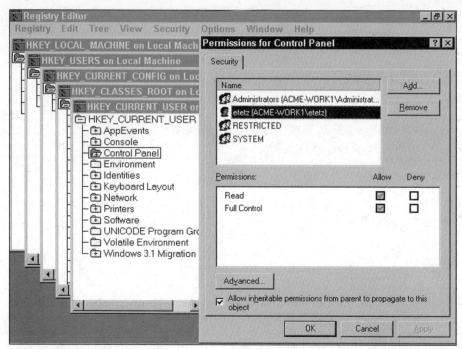

Figure 18-12: Modifying permissions on Registry keys is an option for the security-conscious.

regedit.exe

This version of regedit.exe has been updated since Windows NT 4.0. It now supports reading and editing some of the Windows NT/2000-specific data types, such as REG_MULTI_SZ and REG_EXPAND_SZ. Creation of these data types is still limited to regedt32.exe. Other features that are new to this version of the Registry editor include:

✦ Favorites — so you can build a list of the most edited keys. The Favorites list is unique to the Registry editor, and is not shared with the default OS Favorites list.

✦ Saving of position when exiting the editor, so you return to your last position

✦ Connecting to remote Registries

Cross-Reference   Chapter 27 contains more information about how to work with regedit.exe and regedt32.

Run cmd

Just as many utilities in Windows 9x are command line–based, many of the really useful utilities in Windows 2000 are command-based. Windows 2000 gives you two options for running command line utilities: command.com and cmd.exe.

command.com is a 16-bit version of a command prompt for use with utilities and applications that will not work from the default command prompt. When command.com is running, you will see an NTDVM listed on the Processes tab of Task Manager. NTDVM is short for Windows NT Virtual DOS Machine. This is the environment that all 16-bit MS-DOS applications and 16-bit Windows applications run in. For more information about supporting these applications, refer to Chapter 24.

cmd.exe is used when running all other applications. It is a 32-bit command prompt with a number of enhancements, including:

✦ The ability to run 16-bit and 32-bit command line utilities

✦ The ability to run Posix and OS applications

✦ Built-in doskey support for saving and executing commands

To launch command.com, choose Start menu ➪ Run, type command.com, and choose OK. This will open a window that tells you that you are running Microsoft Windows DOS, as shown in Figure 18-13. The display of the version is a sure way to let the user know they are running command.com rather than cmd.exe.

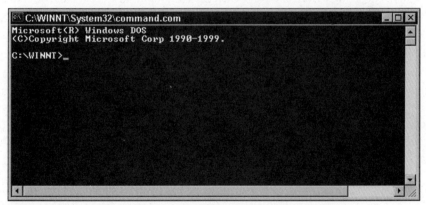

Figure 18-13: You should always know when you have opened command.com, since the window will claim that DOS is running.

To launch cmd.exe, you can do either of the following:

✦ Go to Start menu ➪ Run, type cmd.exe, and choose OK

✦ Go to Start menu ➪ Programs ➪ Accessories ➪ Command Prompt

When you choose either option, you will be graced with a window that tells you that you are running Microsoft Windows 2000 (see Figure 18-14). Even though it is a command prompt interface, it is Windows 2000.

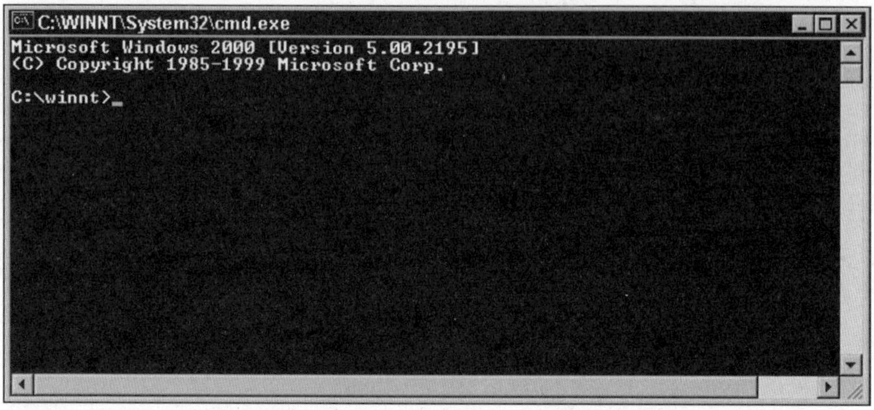

```
C:\WINNT\System32\cmd.exe
Microsoft Windows 2000 [Version 5.00.2195]
(C) Copyright 1985-1999 Microsoft Corp.

C:\winnt>_
```

Figure 18-14: cmd.exe is the Windows 2000 command prompt

Key Point Summary

This chapter examined the major system files that are used in the Windows operating systems. These files were broken down into some major categories, such as:

✦ System, configuration, and user interface files

✦ Memory management

✦ Windows 9x files

✦ Windows 2000 files

The system and configuration files included `io.sys`, `boot.ini`, `msdos.sys`, `autoexec.bat`, and `config.sys`. These files are important to the boot process and to set the initial configuration of the Windows 9x operating system.

In terms of memory management, this chapter provided an overview of the different types of memory that you might deal with from the OS level, as well as the files that help you manage your memory, specifically `himem.sys` and `emm386.exe`.

This chapter also discussed files that were specific to one or both of the operating systems discussed in this chapter, such as `io.sys`, `win.ini`, `sysedit.exe`, `msconfig.exe`, `regedit.exe` and `regedt32.exe`.

✦   ✦   ✦

STUDY GUIDE

This Study Guide presents 15 assessment questions to test your knowledge of this exam topic area. It also features a lab exercise in which you optimize command memory for a system boot disk.

Assessment Questions

1. What is the first file that is loaded as part of the Windows 9x boot process?

    A. `msdos.sys`

    B. `autoexec.bat`

    C. `ntldr`

    D. `io.sys`

2. You have several TSRs that you must start up after the boot process completes. If you are able to incorporate these files into the boot process, what file must you edit?

    A. `autoexec.bat`

    B. `config.sys`

    C. `msdos.sys`

    D. `boot.ini`

3. What is the purpose of `himem.sys`?

    A. It provides access to upper memory blocks.

    B. It is a memory manager.

    C. It verifies the validity of RAM and then starts the networking subsystem.

    D. It provides a virtual RAM disk.

4. Which of the following lines includes the monochrome monitor range into your default upper memory blocks?

    A. `device=c:\windows\himem.sys noems i=B000-B7FF`

    B. `device=c:\windows\emm386.exe noems i=E000-EFFF`

    C. `device=c:\windows\emm386.exe noems i=B000-B7FF`

    D. `device=c:\windows\himem.sys noems i=E000-EFFF`

5. What driver is used to access upper memory?

    A. himem.sys

    B. emm386.exe

    C. boot.ini

    D. ramdrive.sys

6. What driver is used to access virtual memory?

    A. ramdrive.sys

    B. himem.sys

    C. emm386.exe

    D. none of the above

7. What type of memory exists between 640K and 1024K of RAM?

    A. High memory

    B. Extended memory

    C. Expanded memory

    D. Exploded memory

8. What are valid options to be included with emm386.exe? (Select all that apply.)

    A. ram

    B. noems

    C. testram:off

    D. except=b000-bfff

9. What files make up the Windows 9x Registry?

    A. ntuser.dat

    B. system.ini

    C. user.dat

    D. system.dat

10. If you need to quickly edit win.ini, autoexec.bat, and config.sys, what command(s) could you use? (Select all that apply.)

    A. sysedit.exe

    B. cfgedit.exe

    C. msconfig.exe

    D. notepad.exe win.ini autoexec.bat config.sys

11. Which of the following cannot be managed through Computer Management?

    A. `boot.ini`

    B. Services

    C. DNS

    D. Disk Partitions

12. Which of the following is not an enhancement of the Windows 2000 command prompt?

    A. Automatic `doskey.com`

    B. Support for Posix applications

    C. Support for MacIntosh applications

    D. Ability to run 16-bit command line applications

13. What is the first file that is loaded as part of the Windows 2000 boot process?

    A. `io.sys`

    B. `ntbootdd.sys`

    C. `ntbooter`

    D. `NTLDR`

14. What is the name of the utility that manages drive compression on Windows 9x systems?

    A. `drvspace.exe`

    B. `compressor.exe`

    C. `compact.exe`

    D. `dblspace.exe`

15. What levels of disk compression are available with Windows 98 drive compression? (Select all that apply.)

    A. Basic

    B. HiPack

    C. UltraPack

    D. SuperPackLab Exercises

Lab Exercises

Lab 18.1 Optimizing Memory for a System Boot Disk

For this lab exercise, you need a blank floppy disk and a computer with Windows 95 or Windows 98 installed on it.

1. Open a command prompt window. Go to the Start menu ➪ Programs ➪ MS-DOS Prompt.

2. Insert your floppy disk in the drive.

3. Type `format.com a:` to initiate the formatting of the disk. This will erase everything on the disk. You will be asked to give the disk a name after formatting. Press `<enter>`. Then choose `n` to format additional disks.

4. Make the disk a system disk by typing `sys.com a:`. If you preferred, you could have added `/s` to the format command in Step 3.

5. You should now have a bootable disk. Before you reboot, you will copy some files from your `<windows>\command` directory to the root of your `a:` drive. These files include:

   - c:\windows\command\more.com
   - c:\windows\command\edit.com
   - c:\windows\command\mem.exe
   - c:\windows\command\ansi.sys
   - c:\windows\command\doskey.com
   - c:\windows\himem.sys
   - c:\windows\emm386.exe
   - c:\windows\ramdrive.sys
   - c:\windows\smartdrv.exe

6. Leave the disk in your floppy drive and reboot. When your computer starts up, it should boot from the floppy. After it completes, type `mem.exe`. This will give you some statistics on the amount of free memory on the computer. Record the following:

   - Upper (Used):
   - Upper (Free):
   - Extended (Used):
   - Total Memory (Free):
   - Total Memory under 1MB (Used):
   - Total Memory under 1MB (Free):

- Largest Executable Program Size:
- Largest Free Upper Memory Block:

Now type `set` to see what environment variables have been configured. You should have values for the following:

- path = :
- prompt = :
- comspec = :

7. Create a new `config.sys` file by typing `edit.com a:\config.sys`. This will open the editor. Type the following:

```
device=a:\hemem.sys /testram:off
dos=auto,high
```

This will load the high memory manager, and instruct `command.com` to load a portion of the real mode kernel into the High Memory Area. To save the file, press Alt+F, and then press S. To close the editor, press Alt+F, and then press X. Then reboot your computer with either the reset button, or by pressing Ctrl+Alt+Del.

8. After rebooting, type `mem.exe`, and record the following information:

- Upper (Used):
- Upper (Free):
- Extended (Used):
- Total Memory (Free):
- Total Memory Under 1MB (Used):
- Total Memory Under 1MB (Free):
- Largest Executable Program Size:
- Largest Free Upper Memory Block:
- Is MS-DOS Resident In The High Memory Area?

You should notice that the amount of extended memory has changed.

For more information about memory usage, you can use the classify switch with the `mem.exe` command: `mem.exe /c | more`. The `more` option will cause the command to stop and wait for a keystroke after filling the screen.

9. Now you will create a new `autoexec.bat` file by typing `edit a:\autoexec.bat`. This will open the editor. Type the following:

```
a:\doskey.com
a:\smartdrv.exe 4096 4096
```

`doskey.com` will load, which enables you to scroll through previously typed commands. SmartDrive will also load, which is a disk caching program to speed up disk access. To save the file, press Alt+F, and then press S. To close the editor, press Alt+F, and then press X. Then reboot your computer with either the reset button, or by pressing Ctrl+Alt+Del.

10. After rebooting, type `mem.exe`, and record the following information:

- Upper (Used):
- Upper (Free):
- Extended (Used):
- Total Memory (Free):
- Total Memory Under 1MB (Used):
- Total Memory Under 1MB (Free):
- Largest Executable Program Size:
- Largest Free Upper Memory Block:
- Is MS-DOS Resident in the High Memory Area?

You should notice that the amount of free memory has decreased with the loading of TSRs in `autoexec.bat`.

For more information about memory usage, use the classify switch with the `mem.exe` command: `mem.exe /c | more`. The `more` option will cause the command to stop and wait for a keystroke after filling the screen.

Examine the amount of memory that both `doskey.com` and `smartdrv` are using.

11. Now you will edit the `config.sys` file with the following command: `edit.com a:\config.sys`. This will open the `config.sys` file in the editor, then modify the file to look like this:

```
device=a:\hemem.sys /testram:off
device=a:\emm386.exe
device=a:\ramdrive.sys 4096 /E
device=a:\ansi.sys
dos=auto,high
```

The new `config.sys` file will load the expanded memory manager and a RAM drive in extended memory. To save the file, press Alt+F, and then press S. To close the editor, type Alt+F, and then press X. Then reboot your computer with either the reset button, or by pressing Ctrl+Alt+Del.

12. After rebooting, type `mem.exe` and record the following information:

- Upper (Used):
- Upper (Free):
- Extended (Used):
- Total Memory (Free):
- Total Memory Under 1MB (Used):
- Total Memory Under 1MB (Free):

- Largest Executable Program Size:
- Largest Free Upper Memory Block:
- Is MS-DOS Resident in the High Memory Area?

You should notice that the amount of extended memory that is free has decreased again, as the RAM drive is using extended memory for the drive.

Type `mem.exe /c | more`. You should notice that you are not using any upper memory. You have an application that requires 590K of conventional memory to run, but you must still load all the items you currently have. From this point on in the lab, you will be looking at ways to free up additional conventional memory.

13. Edit the `config.sys` file with the following command: `edit.com a:\config.sys`. Modify the `config.sys` file to look like this:

```
device=a:\hemem.sys /testram:off
device=a:\emm386.exe noems
device=a:\ramdrive.sys 4096 /E
device=a:\ansi.sys
dos=auto,high,umb
```

The `noems` switch tells the expanded memory manager to use all of the available space between 640K and 1MB to load drivers, rather than to emulate expanded memory. You have also told MS-DOS that it is able to use that memory as Upper Memory Blocks. To save the file, press Alt+F, and then press S. To close the editor, press Alt+F, and then press X. Then reboot your computer with either the reset button, or by pressing Ctrl+Alt+Del.

14. After rebooting, type `mem.exe` and record the following information:

- Upper (Used):
- Upper (Free):
- Extended (Used):
- Total Memory (Free):
- Total Memory Under 1MB (Used):
- Total Memory Under 1MB (Free):
- Largest Executable Program Size:
- Largest Free Upper Memory Block:
- Is MS-DOS Resident In The High Memory Area?

You should notice that the amount of Extended memory that is free has decreased again, as the RAM drive is using extended memory for the drive.

Type: `mem.exe /c | more`. You should notice that you are not using any Upper Memory. You have an application that requires 620 KB of conventional memory to run, but you must still load all of the items you currently have. The next steps in this lab will look at freeing Conventional Memory.

15. Now you will edit the `config.sys` file with the following command: `edit.com a:\config.sys`. This will open the `config.sys` file in the editor, then change the file so that it looks like this:

```
device=a:\hemem.sys /testram:off
device=a:\emm386.exe noems
devicehigh=a:\ramdrive.sys 4096 /E
devicehigh=a:\ansi.sys
dos=auto,high,umb
```

The devicehigh lines tell MS-DOS to load those items into the Upper Memory Blocks. To save the file, press Alt+F, and then press S. To close the editor, press Alt+F, and then press X. Then reboot your computer with either the reset button, or by pressing Ctrl+Alt+Del.

Now you will edit the `autoexec.bat` file by typing `edit a:\autoexec.bat`. This will open the editor, then type:

```
lh a:\doskey.com
lh a:\smartdrv.exe 4096 4096
```

The `lh` lines tell MS-DOS to load those items into the Upper Memory Blocks. To save the file, press Alt+F, and then press S. To close the editor, press Alt+F, and then press X. Then reboot your computer with either the reset button, or by pressing Ctrl+Alt+Del.

16. After rebooting, type in `mem.exe`, and record the following information:

- Upper (Used):
- Upper (Free):
- Extended (Used):
- Total Memory (Free):
- Total Memory Under 1MB (Used):
- Total Memory Under 1MB (Free):
- Largest Executable Program Size:
- Largest Free Upper Memory Block:
- Is MS-DOS Resident in the High Memory Area?

You should notice that the largest executable program file is now close to, or over, 620K. Also, you should still have a large amount of free memory in Upper Memory Blocks. This is a very optimized memory configuration for your application.

Type `mem.exe /c | more`. You should note that you are now using upper memory. You should have more than the required 620K of conventional memory to run the application. If you need a little more space, you can attempt to give yourself more upper memory by using the "include" option. The include option will free upper memory areas that are reserved for devices that you may not be using, such as monochrome monitors or PS/2 mice. You may then be able to move additional drivers into upper memory. Try changing the `emm386.exe` line in `config.sys` to the following:

```
device=a:\emm386.exe i=E000-EFFF i=B000-B7FF noems
```

After rebooting, you should see an increase in the amount of upper memory that is available to you. The two ranges that you just included are for Monochrome monitors and IBM PS/2s.

If you were to use a utility such as `memmaker.exe`, you may be able to get a small amount of additional free memory out of this configuration.

Hopefully, you have realized how much can be done to optimize your memory utilization with just a small amount of work. Not all drivers and applications can be loaded into the Upper Memory Blocks.

Answers to Chapter Questions

Chapter Pre-Test

1. `io.sys` is the boot loader for Windows 9x. It is **responsible for the initial loading of the OS**.

2. Conventional memory is **640K** in size.

3. Virtual memory can be **as large as the free space on your hard drive**.

4. Extended memory is **composed of all the memory above the 1MB of RAM**.

5. In order to get the TSRs that are willing to load into upper memory, **preface their lines in** `autoexec.bat` **with** `lh`.

6. The fully functional version of the Windows 2000 Registry editor is `regedt32.exe`. `regedit.exe` lacks some features, such as certain supported data types.

7. You must call or load the MMC prior to loading a custom Computer Management that points to another computer.

Assessment Questions

1. **D.** `is.sys` is the boot loader for Windows 9x systems. For more information, see the section labeled "io.sys."

2. **A.** `autoexec.bat` is used to launch TSRs. For more information, see the section labeled "autoexec.bat."

3. **B.** `himem.sys` is a high memory manager for Windows 9x and MS-DOS. For more information, see the section labeled "Extended memory."

4. **C.** The monochrome monitor memory range is B000-B7FF. For more information, see the section labeled "emm386.exe."

5. B. emm386.exe is used to access upper memory. For more information, see the section labeled "Upper memory."

6. D. Virtual memory reserves space on the hard drive to be used as RAM. It is managed by VMM32 and is loaded by Windows. For more information, see the section labeled "Virtual memory."

7. C. Expanded memory is found between 640K and 1024K. For more information, see the section labeled "Utilizing Memory Management."

8. A, B. ram and noems are valid options when loading emm386.exe. For more information, see the section labeled "emm386.exe."

9. C, D. user.dat and system.dat are the two files that make up the Windows 9x Registry. For more information, see the section labeled "Touring Windows 9x System Files."

10. A, C. sysedit.exe and msconfig.exe provide quick means of editing the listed configuration files. For more information, see the section labeled "Touring Windows 9x System Files."

11. A. boot.ini is a text file and can be edited directly or through the System control panel. For more information, see the section labeled "Touring Windows 2000 Specific Files."

12. C. Support for MacIntosh applications has nothing to do with the command prompt, but doskey.com, Posix support, and command line applications do. For more information, see the section labeled "Run cmd."

13. D. NTLDR is the first file that loads as part of the Windows 2000 boot process. For more information, see the section labeled "Touring Windows 2000 Specific Files."

14. A. DriveSpace (drvspace.exe) is the utility that manages drive compression for Windows 9x computers. For more information, see the section labeled "DriveSpace."

15. B, C. HiPack and UltraPack are disk compression formats for DriveSpace 3, which is used on some versions of Windows 95 and all versions of Windows 98. For more information, see the section labeled "DriveSpace."

Managing Files and Directories

EXAM OBJECTIVES

Exam 220-202 ✦ A+ OS Technologies

✦ **1.2** Identify basic concepts and procedures for creating, viewing and managing files, directories and disks. This includes procedures for changing file attributes and the ramifications of those changes (for example, security issues). Content may include the following:

- File attributes — Read Only, Hidden, System, and Archive attributes

- File naming conventions (Most common extensions)

- Windows 2000 COMPRESS, ENCRYPT

CHAPTER PRE-TEST

1. What are the four basic file attributes?

2. What three extended attributes does Windows 2000 NTFS provide?

3. What is the maximum file length in Windows 9x?

4. If a file is named `Letters home from bob.doc`, what is the likely MS-DOS–compatible short file name for the file?

5. When a file is hidden, it is always invisible to all users on the system. True or False?

6. Read-only files may not be deleted. True or False?

7. Encrypted files may only be modified and deleted by the person who encrypted them, and the recovery agent. True or False?

8. Indexing files provides what benefit?

9. Compressing files provides what benefit?

✦ Answers to these questions can be found at the end of the chapter. ✦

Most people would agree that money management is important: when you put your money somewhere, it's good to have an organized system so that you can remember where the money is and be able to retrieve it as needed. Similarly, file management is an important part of any operating system. You need a way to organize the data on your drive so that it is easily retrievable, as well as a way to identify files that are used for certain purposes.

This chapter will examine the topics of file identification and management. In addition, you will learn what long file names are and how Windows 9x and Windows 2000 supports them. The chapter will end by discussing some of the settings that exist under Windows 9x that can help optimize your file system performance.

Filenaming Conventions

1.2 Identify basic concepts and procedures for creating, viewing and managing files, directories and disks, This includes procedures for changing file attributes and the ramifications of those changes (for example, security issues). Content may include the following: Filenaming conventions (Most common extensions)

This section will discuss the changes that filenaming conventions have undergone over the years. It will also examine the difference between file names and directory entries.

When MS-DOS was the premier OS on the market, it set the standard for what is referred to as the eight-dot-three (8.3) character file name. This file system was created using thirty-two character fields (bytes) for the file names. If you work out all of the math, you probably wonder where the extra characters are. Eight plus three is eleven, and that leaves twenty-one outstanding characters. Table 19-1 summarizes how each byte is used.

Tip

Most limits that exist on computers are set using the binary number system. Often, some overhead is associated with these limits. If you look at any limit on your computer, you should be able to trace it back to one of these base 2 numbers (2^x). In the case of FAT directory entries, the number is 2^4, or 16 characters. Common base 2 numbers include 2, 4, 8, 16, 32, 64, 128, 256, 512, 1024, 2048, and 4096.

Table 19-1 Directory Entry Format	
Use	**Size**
File name	8 bytes
Extension	3 bytes
Attribute	1 byte
Reserved	10 bytes — FAT 32 makes use of two of these entries
Time	2 bytes
Date	2 bytes
First Cluster	2 bytes
Size	4 bytes

When dealing with file attributes, there is one byte, or eight bits, used to store these settings. There are not, however, eight attributes. Table 19-2 summarizes the values that are possible for file attributes. If several attributes were applied to a file, you would add the values together to get a final result that is 255 or less (255 is the maximum value of one byte). If the file were Read Only, System, and Archive, then the value of the attribute byte would be 1 + 4 + 32 — or 37. Thirty-seven could only represent a file with these attributes.

Table 19-2 File Attributes		
Bit Position	**Value (Decimal)**	**Attribute**
1	1	Read Only
2	2	Hidden
3	4	System
4	8	Volume Label
5	16	Subdirectory
6	32	Archive
7	64	Unused
8	128	Unused

For the exam, you will only be asked about the Read Only, Hidden, System, and Archive attributes. But you should be aware of the Volume Label and Sub-directory attributes for real-world applications. You do not need to know the bit positions or values for the exam.

The 8.3 naming convention quickly proved to be very limiting. Extensions were often used to allow for longer names, and were not directly associated with individual applications. When Windows came onto the market, people began making proper use of the file extensions. Within Windows, the extension was used to identify the application that was used to make a particular document. Other OSs placed different limits on the length of a file name. Macintosh limited the length of file names to 31 characters, and OS/2 limited them to 254 characters. While 8.3 was very limiting, 254 characters seems excessive.

Long file names

Windows 9x and Windows 2000 both allow for long file names on a FAT16 partition. These file names are limited to 255 characters, while some applications, such as Windows 2000 Explorer, will only display 199 characters (including the period separator for the file extension), and Windows 98 Explorer will only display 235 characters. If you want to use even longer names, you have to name your files someplace other than Windows Explorer.

On a FAT16 or FAT32 partition, you are still limited to the 8.3 naming convention. Windows 9x and Windows 2000 get around this problem by cheating the file system. When you save a file, it is saved using one directory entry, and it is saved with a short 8.3 character file name. The short file name is created by using the first six characters of the file name, followed by a tilde (~) and an incremental number. If you are using Windows 2000, then after creating four files with the same six starting characters, the formula for creating short names is changed. The first two characters are used, followed by a randomly generated four-digit hexadecimal number, a tilde, and the number one. Table 19-3 lists the names of six files that are created in the same directory and what their short file name entries are. To get a listing of the short file names, you can use `dir /x` or get the properties of each file. If you are using Windows 9x, then the file names continue to increment until you run out of directory entries or a disk, or hit the limit of 65,536 entries in any given directory. As the increments move to ~10 or ~100, the number of characters at the start of the name decreases to five and then four.

Microsoft has published information stating that Windows 9x will not allow more than 99 files to be created in a directory with the same starting of a short file name. So the last file that can be created in a directory is `myfil~99.txt`. This published fact, however wrong, has been brought up in many Microsoft exams, but is unlikely to be on CompTIA's OS Technologies exam.

Table 19-3
Short File Names in Windows 2000

Long File Name Entry	Short File Name Entry
ShortFileTest1.txt	SHORTF~1.TXT
ShortFileTest2.txt	SHORTF~1.TXT
ShortFileTest3.txt	SHORTF~1.TXT
ShortFileTest4.txt	SHORTF~1.TXT
ShortFileTest5.txt	SHD022~1.TXT
ShortFileTest6.txt	SHAF9C~1.TXT

You have now seen how the short file names are generated, but where are the long file names? The long file names are stored in additional empty directory entries. The characters for the long file names are stored using 11 characters per additional directory entry. So a file with a name of `My financial report for 2000.txt` would take one directory entry of the short file name (possibly `myfina~1.txt`), and then one additional entry for each 11 characters in the file name, or an additional three entries. That means that this one file would actually occupy four directory entries on your drive. These long file name directory entries have non-standard attributes of Read Only, Hidden, System, and Volume Label. If MS-DOS systems see these entries, they will ignore them rather than generate an error.

One of the problems with long file names occurs when the long file name entries disappear. This can happen if you use MS-DOS–based disk utilities on your disk. Some of these utilities will tell you that you have a problem with your directory entries and offer to fix them. Unfortunately, "fixing" means deleting all of the invalid entries, which means you lose all of your long file names. That's not a good thing.

In the Real World   Microsoft makes conflicting claims about the compatibility of MS-DOS 6.x versions of `scandisk.exe` and `defrag.exe`. Some of their documentation states that MS-DOS 6.x utilities will not harm the long file name entries, while other documentation states that you should not use any MS-DOS–based file utilities. Anytime I have used MS-DOS 6.x versions of `defrag.exe` on my disks, I have lost the long file name entries, which makes me think that these utilities are not compatible with the long file name entries.

For Windows 9x, Microsoft provides a utility called `lfnbk.exe`. This program runs with one of two switches, either `/b` or `/r`. The first switch will back up all of your long file name entries into a file on the root of your drive (`lfn.dat`). It also strips the current names from your file system so that older utilities can be run. After using your utilities, you can then use `lfnbk /r` to restore your long file names to their original state.

`lfnbk.exe` is available on the Windows 95 Retail CD in the `\admin\app-tools\lfbback` folder or from the Windows 9x Resource Kit.

There may come a time when you attempt to copy files to a destination that does not support long file names. This used to happen when files were copied to NetWare 3.x servers that had not enabled long file name support (OS/2 namespace). In such cases, a rename file dialog box would appear, like that shown in Figure 19-1, for each file with a long file name.

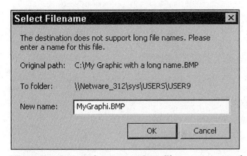

Figure 19-1: When copying files, you may be prompted to rename files if the destination does not support long file names.

File associations

Associates are people who work together. A file association is just a mapping of the three-letter file extension of a file to a program that can be used to open the file. When dealing with Windows, file associations are used to let the OS know what program should be used to open a specific type of file. This information is stored in the Registry but can be accessed from a number of locations. If you have any files that are not associated with an application, they will have a generic Windows logo on their icon (see Figure 19-2).

Tip The Macintosh OS does not use file extensions for associations; instead, each file that is saved with both a data and resource portion. The resource portion contains file type and associated application information. Windows-based files are only saved with a data portion.

Figure 19-2: Each file has an icon that represents its file association.

How to associate files

There are a number of different ways to associate files to applications, such as:

✦ Double-clicking on unassociated files

✦ Pressing Shift while right-clicking on associated files

✦ Using the Folder Options dialog box

✦ Editing the Registry

As always, since there are ways other than the Registry, editing the Registry is not recommended.

Caution   Microsoft does not recommend editing the Registry directly with the Registry editor, even though it is required from time to time. If you make a mistake with the Registry, you may have to reinstall the operating system. For more information about editing the Registry, consult Chapter 27.

For any files that are not currently associated with another file, you can create an association by simply double-clicking the file to open it. Windows will check its list of associations and when it can't locate one, it will prompt you for the name of the application that should be used, as shown in Figure 19-3. One of the options provided in the Open With dialog box is "Always use this program to open this file." This particular option will place an association with file extension in the Registry. This is by far the easiest way to create file associations.

Tip If you are not sure about the program you should be using, you can clear the check box, and the file will be opened by the application. This will not put an association in place, so if you have used the wrong application, you can just double-click on it again to choose another application.

Figure 19-3: File associations can be created through the Open With dialog box.

If you make a mistake or need to change the application that is used to open a file, you can use the shortcut menu. First, select the file (if you forget this step, the Open With option will be missing). Then press Shift while right-clicking the icon. In the shortcut menu, you should see an option for Open With. When you choose Open With, you will see the same dialog you saw with unassociated files (refer back to Figure 19-3). Once again, by choosing "Always use this program to open this file" you will be able to associate the document extension with another application.

If you are looking for a few more options, you can look at the Folder Options dialog box. To get to Folder Options, open any directory window, such as My Computer. If you are using Windows 9x, you will choose Folder Options from the View menu. If you are using Windows 2000, you will choose Folder Options from the Tools menu. You will be able to see all of the associations on the File Types tab.

Windows 2000 makes this dialog a little easier to work with, since a list of all the file extensions appears in the top pane, as shown in Figure 19-4. To change the program that is associated with an application, click the Change button. This will open the Open With dialog box that was shown in Figure 19-3. You will now have to choose a new application for that extension.

Figure 19-4: Folder Options is easier to use in Windows 2000 than in Windows 9x.

If you click the Advanced button, you will see the dialog box featured in Figure 19-5, and you will be able to set additional options for this type of file. These options include:

✦ Confirming file open after downloading the file using Internet Explorer

✦ Always showing the file extension for this file, even when Explorer is set up to hide them

✦ Browse in same window when loading these files into Internet Explorer

Figure 19-5: Advanced options allow you to always have the extension of certain files displayed.

If you select one of the listed actions, you will be able to modify how the action is performed by choosing the Edit button (see Figure 19-6). In doing so, you will be able to specify the full path to the program to open this file and any switches that should be used. For example, if the extension has both an open and a print action, open may look like this:

```
C:\WINNT\system32\NOTEPAD.EXE %1
```

while print may look like this:

```
C:\WINNT\system32\NOTEPAD.EXE /p %1
```

Tip Not all applications support printing for the Windows Explorer shell, but for those that do, you can either right-click on them and choose Print, or drag them to a printer.

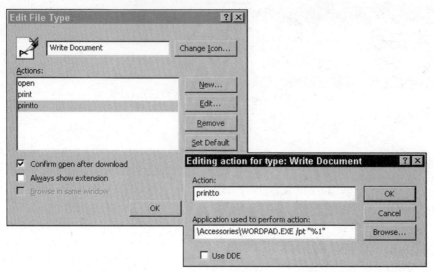

Figure 19-6: Write Documents can be opened, printed, or printed to (a device) through Windows Explorer.

If you are using Windows 9x, then the File Types tab resembles the one shown in Figure 19-7. This tab is a little difficult to use if you are trying to locate a file that is used with a specific extension. The listing at the top of the tab contains mostly official object types registered on the computer. For example, instead of listing pdf for Adobe Acrobat files, the "Registered File Type" list displays Adobe Acrobat Document. If you select the file type, the details at the bottom of the screen will list the actual extension, the mime type that is used by your Web browser to decide what to do with the file, and what program will open the file.

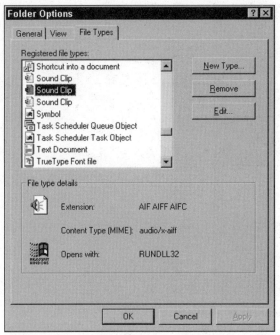

Figure 19-7: The Windows 9x File Types tab displays registered file types in the list box.

If you click the Edit button for the selected file type, you will be presented with the dialog shown in Figure 19-8. This dialog enables you to change the following:

✦ Description for the type of file.

✦ Mime content type.

✦ Actions that are available to the file. These actions are the same as the actions for Windows 2000.

✦ Whether Quick View can open the file.

✦ Continuous display of the file extension.

✦ Whether to confirm open after downloading the file with Internet Explorer.

✦ Whether the file is supposed to open in the current Internet Explorer window.

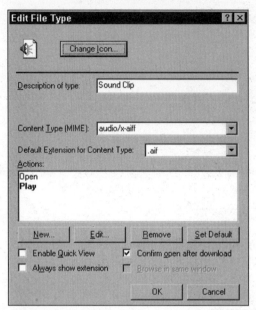

Figure 19-8: Editing a file association in Windows 9x is similar to Windows 2000, although the dialog has a different layout.

Editing the actions (such as Open, Print, and Print to) is the same as editing the actions for Windows 2000 discussed earlier in this chapter.

File extensions and what they are used for

1.2 Identify basic concepts and procedures for creating, viewing and managing files, directories and disks. This includes procedures for changing file attributes and the ramifications of those changes (for example, security issues). Content may include the following: File naming conventions (Most common extensions)

This section will take a look at some of the major types of file extensions you should expect to see within your operating system. By default, file extensions for registered file types are hidden. To display file extensions within Windows 9x:

1. Open any directory window, such as My Computer.

2. Select Folder Options from the View menu.

3. Select the View tab (shown in Figure 19-9).

4. Clear the check box in front of the text "Hide file extensions for known file types".

5. Choose the OK button.

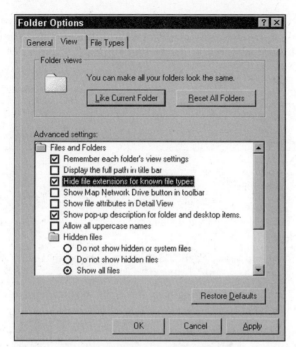

Figure 19-9: The Folder Options dialog box is used to display file extensions on your files.

Tip
The View tab for the original retail version of Windows 95 only allows you to set Hidden files, displaying the full path in title bar, and the hiding of file extensions. Windows 95 OEM versions, Windows 98, Windows NT 4.0, and Windows 2000 all display many more settings.

The process for displaying file extensions in Windows 2000 is a little different from that of Windows 9x, since you go to the Tools menu rather than the View menu to find Folder Options.

Now let's take a look at common file extensions and how they are used on your computer. The common file extensions can be categorized as:

✦ Executables

✦ Major applications by suite

✦ Compression utilities

✦ System files

✦ Other files

Executables

Executables are files that can be run and perform tasks on the system. They are usually programs with the `.exe` extension. Table 19-4 summarizes some of the executable file extensions.

Table 19-4
Executable File Extensions

Extension	Description
.bat	Batch files. Batch files are a series of commands that have been sequentially typed into a text file.
.cmd	OS/2 command files. Command files usually execute with only a command shell interface.
.com	MS-DOS command files. Like the OS/2 command files, these files usually execute with only a command shell interface.
.exe	Command line or graphical programs. This is the most common extension for executable files.
.vbs	Visual Basic Script files are not executable themselves, but rather require either `wscript.exe` or `cscrript.exe` to be executed. They are a cross between Visual Basic applications and batch file.

Major applications

There are several popular applications on the market today, and you should be familiar with a few of their extensions—especially if you're asked, "Which program do I use to open a file with an .xyz file extension?" Some of these extensions are listed in Table 19-5.

Table 19-5
Application File Extensions

Extension	Description
.doc	Document files are usually associated with Microsoft Word, but are sometimes used by installations of WordPerfect.
.dot	Document templates for Microsoft Word. `normal.dot` is the template used for default documents.
.ppt	Microsoft PowerPoint document.
.wks, .wk4	Lotus 1-2-3 worksheet files. The number at the end denotes that a specific version of Lotus 1-2-3 was used.

Extension	Description
.wpd	WordPerfect document. `.wpd` and doc are common extensions for documents.
.wpg	WordPerfect Graphic. Their proprietary graphic format.
.xls	Microsoft Excel document.

Compression utilities

Over the years — and across operating systems — there has been a need to reduce the size of files that are on a disk, which means there have been a variety of formats that have been used to compress data. Table 19-6 lists some of the common compression file extensions and where they are used. Although some utilities are based in one OS or another, today you can find compression and decompression tools for most formats in most operating systems.

Table 19-6
Compression File Extensions

Extension	Description
.ace	A new high compression format.
.arc	Traditional Linux and Unix utility.
.arj	Traditional archive utility for MS-DOS.
.bhx, .hqx	Bin-Hex is a Macintosh encoding format.
.cab	A Microsoft format for distributing software.
.rar	New high compression format that is used on most operating systems.
.sit	The most popular Macintosh compression format.
.tar	Traditional and very popular compression format for Linux and Unix. Short for Tape Archive. It is used for its ability to back up directory structures, rather than compress.
.tgz	A popular, traditional compression format for Linux and Unix. This is actually a GZIPped TAR file.
.uu, .uue	UUEncode is one of the most popular encoding algorithms for Linux and Unix.
.zip	The grandfather of PC compression formats and still the most popular format for the MS-DOS and Windows worlds.

System files

Your computer uses many types of files to drive the operating system. Some of the extensions you should expect to see are included in Table 19-7.

Table 19-7
System File Extensions

Extension	Description
.386	Windows-based driver file.
.ani	Animated cursor file.
.bak	Backup file. Used as a default extension by a number of applications.
.bin	Binary drive. Used for a few system drivers, such as `drvspace.bin`.
.cpl	Control Panel file.
.cur	Cursor file.
.da0	Backed up `dat` file. Used with the Registry `system.dat` and `user.dat`.
.dat	Data file. Used with the Registry files `system.dat` and `user.dat`.
.dll	Dynamic Link Library. These files contain common and reusable code that can be called by any application. This reduces the amount of code that has to be placed within specific applications, and makes the code easily reusable.
.drv	MS-DOS or real-mode driver file.
.ini	Initialization file. These text files contain settings for applications, but they are being phased out, with preference being given to the Registry.
.msc	Microsoft Console. This is a saved Microsoft Management Console settings file. You will see this extension a lot with Windows 2000, and a bit with Windows NT 4.0.
.msg	These files contain error messages that are supposed to be displayed in the event of an error. These were used with the MS-DOS network client, and were only required if you wanted to see a text description of error codes.
.msi	Microsoft Installer document. This is a new file format that is used to distribute software to computers that are running the Windows Installer service (`msiexec.exe`).
.scr	Windows screen saver file.
.sys	System driver file. Used with MS-DOS, and with Windows for backward-compatibility.
.ttf	True Type Font definition file.
.vxd	Virtual Device Driver.

Graphics files

Graphics have been an important part of computers from the beginning. A number of different graphic formats have become popular, and with the expansion of the Internet, the number of major graphic formats has greatly increased. For a listing of formats, see Table 19-8.

Table 19-8
Graphics File Extensions

Extension	Description
.bmp	Bitmap image, used by MS-Paint.
.eps	Adobe Encapsulated Post-script. Used by several major graphics applications.
.gif	Graphic Interchange Format. Originally owned by CompuServe, but now by AOL. It was designed to minimize download times.
.jpg, .jpeg	Joint Photographics Experts Group file format. A compression format that discards data thought to be invisible to the human eye. Discarding data to compress files is referred to as "lossy."
.pcd	Kodak Photo CD format.
.pcx	PC Paintbrush file.
.pdf	Adobe's Portable Document Format. It is readable with the Adobe Acrobat Reader.
.png	Portable Network Graphics. A newly developed (six-year-old) open (free-to-use) photo standard. It is planned as a replacement for .gif and .jpeg formats, as it supports all the benefits of both formats. It uses a zip type algorithm for compression.
.tif, .tiff	Aldus Tagged Image File Format. Used as a common interchange format between most graphics applications. Very popular with photographic manipulators. Supports LZW (Lempel-Ziv-Welch) compression format to reduce file sizes. LZW compression is "lossless," as it does not discard data.

Other file extensions

Table 19-9 lists some additional file extensions that are worth noting.

Table 19-9	
Miscellaneous File Extensions	
Extension	*Description*
.asp	Active Server Page files are server-side scripted HTML files.
.cda	CD Audio files are used to store audio data on audio CDs.
.css	Cascading Style Sheet files are used to store HTML-style data.
.htm, .html	HyperText Markup Language (HTML) files are used to store data that will be displayed on Web sites. Web servers use the Hyper Text Transfer Protocol (HTTP) to send the information to your Web browser. HTML is gaining popularity as a way to locally display information as well. Many vendors send help files in this format so that they can be used on their Web sites.
.tmp	Temporary file.
.txt	Text file. These files are ASCII text, which is readable on every operating system.
.wav	Windows Audio format.

Exam Tip There is no need to memorize all the data on the preceding tables for the exam, but you should be familiar with many of the extensions that are used by applications, especially those for system files.

File Attributes

Objective

1.2 Identify basic concepts and procedures for creating, viewing and managing files, directories and disks. This includes procedures for changing file attributes and the ramifications of those changes (for example, security issues): Content may include the following: File attributes — Read Only, Hidden, System, and Archive attributes

Starting with the first versions of MS-DOS and the FAT file system, files have exhibited some basic attributes. The full list of file attributes was provided at the beginning of this chapter. This section will deal only with the visible attributes: Read Only, Hidden, System, and Archive. The discussion will focus first on how to change and examine file attributes, then the basic attributes, and finally the extended attributes with Windows 2000.

Changing attributes

There are many different ways to change the attributes on the files. The first method — the command line — is the only way that is common to all of the Microsoft operating systems.

Command line

In order to change file attributes from the command line, you have to use the `attrib` command. The basic syntax for the command is:

```
attrib <attribute to set> <files to modify>
```

Setting of the attributes includes a plus (+) or minus (−) sign to specify if the attribute should be enabled or disabled, and the one-letter code for each attribute. The one-letter codes are:

✦ H—Hidden

✦ S—System

✦ R—Read only

✦ A—Archive

If the `attrib` command is used without any options, it displays a listing of the current attributes, like this:

```
A            C:\7flen.crt
A    SHR     C:\arcldr.exe
A    SHR     C:\arcsetup.exe
A            C:\AUTOEXEC.BAT
A    SH      C:\boot.ini
A            C:\CONFIG.SYS
A    SHR     C:\IO.SYS
A    SHR     C:\MSDOS.SYS
A    SHR     C:\NTBOOTDD.SYS
A    SHR     C:\NTDETECT.COM
A    SHR     C:\ntldr
A            C:\uninst.log
```

If you use an attribute without specifying a file name, you will set the attribute on all the files in the current directory. Here is an example of the command and the attribute that would be set:

```
attrib -a -s -h -r

            C:\7flen.crt
            C:\arcldr.exe
            C:\arcsetup.exe
            C:\AUTOEXEC.BAT
            C:\boot.ini
            C:\CONFIG.SYS
            C:\IO.SYS
            C:\MSDOS.SYS
            C:\NTBOOTDD.SYS
            C:\NTDETECT.COM
            C:\ntldr
            C:\uninst.log
```

You can specify a file after the `attrib` command to see the current attributes on that file, or with the attribute to set. The last option is /s, which instructs the `attrib` command to process the files in all subdirectories. This does not change the attribute on the subdirectories. If you are using Windows 2000, /d will change the attributes of the directories as well.

There are some restrictions on changing attributes with the `attrib` command. Hidden and system files will not have their attributes changed, and these attributes have to be added or removed in the same command.

Windows 9x

If you want to change the attributes on a file or folder (not the contents) then you only have to right-click on the folder and get the properties. The attributes are listed at the bottom of the properties window (see Figure 19-10). Select the appropriate attributes and select OK. Microsoft has decided not to let you change the system attribute to prevent the accidental deletion of system files.

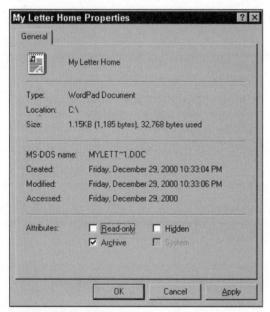

Figure 19-10: Properties of a file will let you set attributes in Windows 9x.

Windows 2000

Changing attributes in Windows 2000 is similar to the way it is done in Windows 9x, with a few exceptions. When you right-click on a file, you will only see the options for Read Only, Hidden, and Archive when working FAT partitions. If you are working with NTFS partitions, then the Archive check box is replaced with an Advanced button. See Figure 19-11.

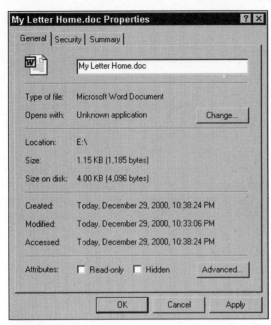

Figure 19-11: On NTFS partitions, you will only see the Hidden and Read Only attributes.

Clicking the Advanced button will let you set the Archive attribute, as well as the Windows 2000 advanced attributes of Compressed, Encrypted, and Indexed. See Figure 19-12.

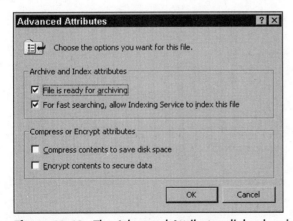

Figure 19-12: The Advanced Attributes dialog box is only available on NTFS partitions.

The basic attributes

There are four basic attributes that you will find on all files on your computer:

✦ Read Only

✦ Hidden

✦ System

✦ Archive

In addition to these four, there is an attribute that is usually set on your hard drive, called the Volume attribute. It is usually only applied to one directory entry per drive (excluding the ones that are used for long file name entries). It stores the volume label for the drive. The directory entry that contains the label can be modified through one of the following methods:

✦ Using the label command at a command prompt

✦ Editing the name Label field in the properties window of your drive (see Figure 19-13)

✦ Using the rename command in the My Computer window (Windows 2000 only)

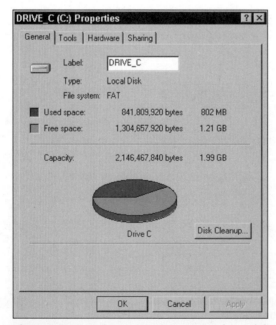

Figure 19-13: Drive properties are used to relabel drives in Windows 9x or Windows 2000.

Descriptions of the four common attributes are listed in Table 19-10.

	Table 19-10 **File Attributes**
Attribute	**Description**
Read Only	Files with this attribute can't be deleted from the command line and can't be written to or saved over.
Hidden	These files are not visible to us unless they have changed their viewing options to display hidden files. Hidden files cannot have their attribute changed by the `attrib` command.
System	System files are flagged as being required by the operating system. They can't have their attributes changed by the `attrib` command.
Archive	Files with the Archive attribute set are ready for archiving or backing up. This attribute is used by some backup programs so that they can perform incremental backups. Currently, the `xcopy` command supports an `/a` switch, which will only copy files that have the Archive attribute set. When the file is modified, the Archive attribute will automatically be reset on it.

Windows 2000 attributes

1.2 dentify basic concepts and procedures for creating, viewing and managing files, directories and disks. This includes procedures for changing file attributes and the ramifications of those changes (for example, security issues). Content may include the following: Windows 2000 COMPRESS, ENCRYPT

There are three attributes that are specific to Windows 2000 and NTFS partitions:

✦ Compress

✦ Encrypt

✦ Index

Compress

The Compress attribute allows the compression of files. To enable the Compress attribute, you will have to right-click on the file or folder and choose Properties, then choose the Advanced button. You will be able to compress the file or folder by selecting the "Compress contents to conserve disk space" check box. See Figure 19-14.

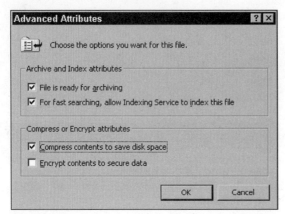

Figure 19-14: The Compress attribute is set on a file-by-file basis.

 Exam Tip   If you are asked about extended attributes on your exam, remember to look at the OS that is mentioned in the question. If the question deals with Windows NT 4.0 rather than Windows 2000, remember that Windows NT 4.0 also supports the Compress attribute, but not the Encrypt or Index attributes.

When you compress a file, the file attribute is changed to Compress, and then the file is actually compressed. There is a small chance that something may go wrong during the compression phase, so that some of the files on your hard drive may have the Compress attribute set, but may not actually be compressed. One situation that may cause this inconsistent Compress attribute to happen would be a power interruption during the compression process, so that the attribute change was made, but the compressed version of the file was not saved. To ensure that this has not happened, you could use the command line utility, compact.exe.

Compact.exe can be used to compress or decompress files from the command line. It supports switches that will allow it to process subdirectories as well.

If you move a compressed file within a partition, the file will retain its Compress attribute, but if you copy a compressed file to a folder, it will inherit the Compress attribute that is set on the folder.

Encrypt

If you choose to compress your files, you may not encrypt them. Windows 2000 does not allow you to both encrypt and compress the file, because compression requires the file to be rewritten, but encryption doesn't permit it. The file header contains the file encryption key for the file. This key is protected by the public key of the user who encrypted the file, as well as the public key of the encrypted file recovery agent. The encrypted file recovery agent is specified in the local public key policies of the computer or in Active Directory. When a file is encrypted, the only person who can read it is the user that enabled encryption (and the recovery agent).

The file is only protected against being read. This means that the file can be moved to another location on the same partition, as this only requires modifying the directory table and does not constitute a read to the file. The file may also be deleted if the appropriate NTFS permissions have not been applied to it.

If the encrypting user moves or copies a file between NTFS partitions (even between computers), the file will remain encrypted. This is very different from Compression or NTFS permissions. If the file is copied to a non-NTFS partition, then the file is unencrypted.

`cipher.exe` can be used to encrypt or decrypt files from the command line. It supports switches that will allow it to process subdirectories as well.

Index

Indexing the file system will greatly improve the length of time it takes to search your hard drive, but in return demands space on your drive. The default catalog is called System and is found in the `System Volume Information` directory of your Boot drive.

To enable basic indexing of your drive, right-click on your drive in My Computer and select Properties (see Figure 19-15). Then select the check box for "Allow Indexing Service to index the disk for fast file searching." This will enable indexing, provided that the Indexing Service is running.

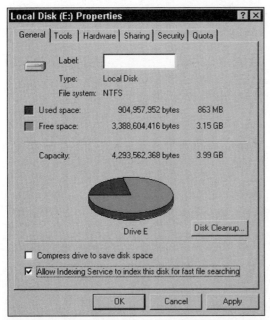

Figure 19-15: Indexing can be enabled for your whole drive, or just a folder.

To ensure that the Indexing Service is running, go to the Start menu and click Search ⇨ For Files or Folders. If the Index Service status not already visible, select Search Option, just below the Search Now button. This will display a small pane that includes a link to the Indexing Service, and it will tell you if the Indexing Service is running. If the Indexing Service is not running, click on the blue link. This will open a new dialog box that will allow you to enable indexing (see Figure 19-16).

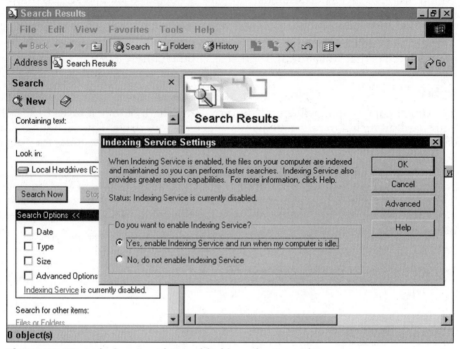

Figure 19-16: Indexing must be enabled in order to work.

Key Point Summary

This chapter discussed the management of files and directories on your hard disk. You learned how long file names are supported and the limits on the length of these names under Windows 9x and Windows 2000. You also looked at some of the more common file extensions and what they are used for.

File attributes were examined, and you saw how to apply attributes both from the command line and the GUI. You learned what the four major attributes (Read Only, System, Hidden, and Archive) do. Lastly, you looked at NTFS attributes that can be assigned to Windows 2000.

✦   ✦   ✦

STUDY GUIDE

This Study Guide presents 15 assessment questions and 2 lab exercises to test your knowledge of this exam topic area.

Assessment Questions

1. What is the maximum length of a file name under Windows 2000?

  A. 64 characters

  B. 128 characters

  C. 254 characters

  D. 255 characters

  E. 256 characters

2. You get a call from Billy. You find out that he has a problem with several of the files on his hard drive. He claims that Windows 95 has renamed many of his files and directories. After questioning him, you find out that he has just defragmented his hard drive with an MS-DOS 6.0 boot disk and the MS-DOS version of `defrag.exe`. What is the likely cause of the problem, and is there a solution to correct it?

  A. The MS-DOS version of `defrag.exe` was unaware of the long file name directory entries and overwrote the directory entries. There is no easy fix for this problem.

  B. The long file name entries have just become unassociated from the files. Run `assoc c: /repair` to re-establish the associations.

  C. The file name entries are fine. They were automatically backed up, and you just have to run `lfnbk` from the root of each drive.

  D. Everything is fine. Billy just needs to reboot.

3. Tom was copying files to a NetWare server on his network, and he was prompted to rename his file. What is the likely reason that this happened to him?

  A. The NetWare server already has a file with the same name.

  B. Tom does not have sufficient permissions on the server.

  C. The server does not support long file names.

  D. The server needs to be rebooted.

4. Which of the following can be used to associate file extensions with an application? Choose all that apply.

    A. `attrib.exe`

    B. `assoc.exe`

    C. Shift + Right-click ⇨ Open With

    D. Tools ⇨ Folder Options ⇨ Associate tab

5. Which of the following are extensions of executable files?

    A. `.ini`

    B. `.prg`

    C. `.exe`

    D. `.cmd`

6. Which of the following are associated with compression programs?

    A. `.com`

    B. `.zip`

    C. `.cmp`

    D. `.cab`

7. Which of the following are attributes that are associated with files on your hard disk?

    A. Restrict-Modify

    B. Archive

    C. Visible

    D. Hidden

8. When you copy an NTFS-compressed file to a FAT32 partition, what happens to the file?

    A. The copy action is denied.

    B. The file is copied but remains compressed, so it is unreadable.

    C. The file is copied but becomes uncompressed.

    D. The file can only be copied if the FAT32 partition has been compressed with DriveSpace compression.

9. You are moving several of Bob's files from one directory on a server to another directory. What message should you receive when you encounter an encrypted file?

    A. You should not receive a message. The file will just be moved.

    B. You should get an access denied message.

    C. You should get a message stating that you could not read the file, and that it may be corrupted.

    D. You should get a message stating the file cannot be moved because it is encrypted.

10. You are now attempting to move the same files to a FAT32 partition. What message should you receive when you encounter an encrypted file?

    A. You should not receive a message. The file will just be moved.

    B. You should get an access denied message.

    C. You should get a message stating that you could not read the file, and that it may be corrupted.

    D. You should get a message stating the file cannot be moved because it is encrypted.

11. What is the length of a file name when using MS-DOS?

    A. 10.3 characters

    B. 4.4 characters

    C. 8.3 characters

    D. 9.4 characters

12. You need to compress files on your Windows 2000 computer and you want to write a batch to perform the task for you. What is the name of the command that you will use in your batch file?

    A. compact.exe

    B. compress.exe

    C. shrink.exe

    D. makelittle.exe

13. In order for the Index attribute to have an effect on your search times, what must be running on your computer?

    A. File Replication service

    B. indexer.exe

    C. scanner.exe

    D. Index service

14. What is the name of the utility that will allow you to encrypt files from the command line?

    A. `cipher.exe`

    B. `encrypt.exe`

    C. `encode.exe`

    D. `scramble.exe`

15. What file extension is associated with Windows Scripting Host files?

    A. `.sht`

    B. `.scr`

    C. `.wsh`

    D. `.vbs`

Lab Exercises

Lab 19.1 Setting and Working with File Attributes at the Command Line

In this exercise, you will need a computer running Windows 9x or Windows 2000.

1. Open a command prompt by going to the Start menu ➪ Programs ➪ Accessories ➪ Command Prompt.

2. Create a new directory on the root of one of your drives and four files using the following commands:

```
mkdir c:\attribtest
c:
cd \attribtest
dir c:\*.* >c:\attribtest\read.txt
dir c:\*.* >c:\attribtest\hidden.txt
dir c:\*.* >c:\attribtest\system.txt
dir c:\*.* >c:\attribtest\archive.txt
```

3. Set the following attributes with the `attrib` command:

```
attrib +r read.txt
attrib +h hidden.txt
attrib +s system.txt
attrib +a archive.txt
```

4. Now remove the Archive attribute from all files in the directory using the following command. Record any errors below.

```
attrib -a
```

_____

_____

5. Check the existing attributes using:

```
attrib
```

Notice that only `archive.txt` and `read.txt` have had the Archive attribute removed.

6. Open `read.txt` with the `edit.com` command using:

```
edit read.txt
```

Then add or remove some text and record your error message below.

_____

Exit without saving your changes by pressing Alt+F, and then X.

7. Now open and edit `archive.txt` with the `edit` command. When you are done, close and save your changes by pressing Alt+F and S, then Alt+F and X.

8. Check the existing attributes on `archive.txt` using:

```
attrib archive.txt
```

`archive.txt` should now have the Archive attribute set on it again.

9. Delete all of the files in the attribtest directory using the command:

```
del c:\attribtest\*.*
```

Confirm the deletion.

10. You should not have been able to delete the file `read.txt`. Remove the Read Only attribute on the file and delete it again.

```
attrib -r read.txt
del c:\attribtest\*.*
```

11. Remove the test directory using:

```
cd c:\
rmdir c:\attribtest
```

12. Did the last command work? Why not?

_____

13. Remove the directory using the following commands:

```
attrib -h c:\attribtest\hidden.txt
attrib -s c:\attribtest\system.txt
del c:\attribtest\*.*
rmdir c:\attribtest
```

Lab 19.2 Working with File Associations

In this exercise, you will be working with file associations. You will require a computer with Windows 9x.

1. Create a new text file on your desktop by right-clicking the desktop, and then selecting New ➪ Text Document. Use the default name.

2. If you do not see the `.txt` extension at the end of the file name, open My Computer, and then choose Folder Options dialog from the View menu. Then choose the View tab and uncheck the box labeled "Hide file extensions for known file types." Press the OK button to close the dialog.

3. Right-click on the file to rename it. Change the name to `testfile.luk`. The file's icon should change to a document with a Windows logo in it. If it does not, then the `.luk` extension is already in use on your computer. Try changing it to something else.

4. If you double-click on the file to open it, you should see a dialog box asking you to choose a program to open it. Choose Wordpad and the check box at the bottom of the dialog. Wordpad should open, displaying the blank document. Type your name, and then close the program and save the file.

5. Open the File Types dialog using, My Computer ➪ View menu ➪ Folder Options ➪ File Types. Look through the list for LUK File and select it. You should see the program that is associated with LUK files.

6. Select LUK File and choose the Edit button. Then select the Open command in the Actions pane, and choose the Edit button.

7. You are now going to edit this file so that it opens with the Notepad program. In the "Application used to perform action" text box, type:

   `c:\windows\notepad.exe "%1"`

   Press the OK button. Then press OK, Close, and Close to return to the My Computer window. Close the My Computer window.

8. Double-click on the `test.luk` file on your desktop. Did it open with Notepad? If not, repeat steps 5–7 to see what went wrong.

9. Delete the file `test.luk` from your desktop.

Answers to Chapter Questions

Chapter Pre-Test

1. **Read Only, System, Hidden, and Archive** are the four basic attributes.

2. **Compress, Encrypt, and Index** are the three extended attributes that are provided with Windows 2000.

3. **255 characters** is the maximum file length in Windows 9x and Windows 2000.

4. `Letter~1.doc` is the likely short file name. If other files in the directory already begin with the same six letters, then the digit would be incremented. If there are more than nine files, the last letter would be dropped and the last two digits would be numbers.

5. **False.** Any user that has their viewing options set to `show all files` will be able to see the hidden files.

6. **False.** When using the Graphical User Interface, there is no problem deleting files from the system. However, you won't be able to modify them.

7. **False.** Encrypted files may only be opened by the person who encrypted them and the encrypted files recovery agent, but they can be deleted by anyone with the appropriate NTFS permissions.

8. Indexing files provides **faster searching capabilities.**

9. Compressing files **saves space**, but increases the access time to the files.

Assessment Questions

1. **D.** The maximum length of a file name is 255 characters. For more information, see the section labeled "File Naming Conventions."

2. **A.** You should only use Windows 9x or Windows 2000 utilities to maintain your disks. For more information, see the section labeled "File Naming Conventions."

3. **C.** When copying files to destinations that do not support long file names, then you are prompted to rename your files. For more information, see the section labeled "File Naming Conventions."

4. **A, C.** `assoc.exe` does not exist, and the correct path on a Windows 2000 computer would have been Tools ➪ Folder Options ➪ File Types. For more information, see the section labeled "File Associations."

5. **C, D.** `.ini` is an initialization file, and `.prg` was a made-up extension. `.cmd` files are text files similar to batch files, but are treated as executable. For more information, see the section labeled "File Associations."

6. **B, D.** Pkzip files use the `.zip` extension, and `.cab` files are a proprietary Microsoft compression format. For more information, see the section labeled "File Associations."

7. **B, D.** The four basic attributes are Read Only, Hidden, System, and Archive. The advanced NTFS attributes are Compress, Encrypt, and Index. For more information, see the section labeled "The basic attributes."

8. **C.** Compressed files copied from NTFS volumes to any other type of disk will become uncompressed. If they are copied to other NTFS volumes, they will inherit the compression attribute from the destination folder. For more information, see the section labeled "Windows 2000 attributes."

9. **A.** As long as the move is within one partition, the files will just be moved. If the directories are on different drives, you will receive an access denied message. For more information, see the section labeled "Windows 2000 attributes."

10. **B.** Since the files are being moved to a different drive, and you are not the person who encrypted the files, you will be denied access. If you owned the files, the files would have been decrypted as they were copied. For more information, see the section labeled "Windows 2000 attributes."

11. **C.** MS-DOS file names must not exceed the 8.3 character naming convention. For more information, see the section labeled "File Naming Conventions."

12. **A.** `compact.exe` is the name of the command that is used to compress files at the command line. For more information, see the section labeled "Compress."

13. **D.** The Index service is required to be running in order to build and use indexes. For more information, see the section labeled "Windows 2000 attributes."

14. **A.** `cipher.exe` is the name of the command line utility that is used to encrypt files. For more information, see the section labeled "Windows 2000 attributes."

15. **D.** `.vbs` (Visual Basic script) is the extension that is commonly associated with Windows Scripting Host. For more information, see the section labeled "File Associations."

Managing Disks

EXAM OBJECTIVES

Exam 220-202 ✦ A+ OS Technologies

✦ 1.2 Identify basic concepts and procedures for creating, viewing and managing files, directories and disks. This includes procedures for changing file attributes and the ramifications of those changes (for example, security issues). Content may include the following:

- IDE/SCSI

- Internal/External

- Backup/Restore

- Partitioning/Formatting/File System — FAT, FAT16, FAT32, NTFS4, NTFS5, HPFS

CHAPTER PRE-TEST

1. How do you perform a ScanDisk-type function in Windows NT?

2. Which file system allows you to create a partition of up to 2000GB?

3. What operating systems can access NTFS partitions?

4. What partition type is responsible for holding logical drives?

5. What utility in Windows 2000 allows you to manage partitions?

✦ Answers to these questions can be found at the end of the chapter. ✦

To support today's desktop operating systems, a PC technician must know how to manage disks. The fundamentals of disk management involve the following tasks:

✦ Understanding different file systems

✦ Organizing and formatting partitions

✦ Ensuring data recoverability

✦ Ensuring data integrity

✦ Ensuring optimal performance of the file system

In this chapter, you learn to perform these fundamental tasks by using the utilities that Windows 2000 provides for managing different file systems — Backup and Restore, Disk Defragmenter, and tools to check the integrity of the disk.

Understanding File Systems

 1.2 Identify basic concepts and procedures for creating, viewing and managing files, directories and disks. This includes procedures for changing file attributes and the ramifications of those changes (for example, security issues). Content may include the following: File System — FAT, FAT16, FAT32, NTFS4, NTFS5, HPFS

The file system dictates how information is organized on the disk. (For example, the file system determines how large the *allocation unit*, or storage unit, is for a particular disk.) If you create a 12KB file, how much space is that file really using — 12KB, 16KB, or 32KB? Such organizational issues are what the file system deals with.

This section introduces the different types of available file systems and the operating systems that support them.

The FAT file system

The *File Allocation Table (FAT)* file system has been the most popular file system up until the last few years. Although the FAT file system is the most common file system (it can be used by all operating systems), it is losing the popularity contest to its successor — Mr. FAT32. The FAT file system was the file system used by DOS, Windows 3.1, and Windows 95, and is continued in Windows NT, Windows 98, and Windows 2000.

FAT's biggest strength is that it's the file system most widely understood by different operating systems — but it has many shortcomings. One of the major shortcomings is that the FAT file system cannot create a partition larger than 2GB. (A discussion of partitions is coming up in a little while; for now, consider a partition simply as a discrete portion of disk space on the disk.) The two-gigabyte size limit was not a major limitation until hard drives grew to an average size of about 20GB. Using FAT on one of these recent drives would mean dividing the drive into ten different partitions — an impractical and inappropriate use of space. (Can you imagine being required to divide your home up into ten different rooms whether you wanted to or not? Instead of five spacious rooms, you'd get ten cramped rooms.)

Chapter 9 describes the characteristics of a disk, including *clusters* — groups of sectors (each sector taking up 512 bytes). The problem with clusters is that once their standard size is determined (according to the file system used and the partition size), that same size determines the allocation unit (storage area) provided for a file when it is saved. If, for example, you have a 32KB cluster size (which requires a 2GB FAT partition) and you save a 12KB file, then you waste 20KB of hard disk space. Over time, as more files are saved, this could add up to a lot of wasted space.

The FAT file system has an inefficient use of cluster sizes; Table 20-1 lists cluster sizes next to the partition sizes that determine them.

Table 20-1
FAT Partitions and Their Cluster Sizes

Partition Size	Cluster Size
0–127MB	2KB
128–255MB	4KB
256–511MB	8KB
512–1023MB	16KB625
1024–2048MB	32KB

One other limitation of the FAT file system is its lack of built-in security. In fact, if you ran Windows NT 4.0 or Windows 2000 (which are well respected for their file-system security) on the FAT file system, you would lose that built-in security because it's not available on FAT.

So — besides serving as the file system that all operating systems can run on, what is the FAT file system good for? Well, the versatility of FAT may be its only major benefit, but that's considerable. For example, if you're supporting an organization that has planned an upgrade to Windows NT from Windows 95, and much of the crucial data was generated in an old accounting application that doesn't run on Windows NT, then you may have to run both operating systems on the accounting department's computers. The accountants use Windows NT until they need to run their accounting application, at which time they have to reboot to the Windows 95 operating system. A computer that can boot multiple operating systems is called a *dual-boot system*; the only problem is that drive C: has to use a file system that both operating systems understand. . . you guessed it — FAT.

There are a number of reasons you may want to have a dual-boot system; (1) Software will not run smoothly on one operating system so you install an additional operating system and boot to that OS to run your software. (2) You are part of the help desk team in an organization that runs two different operating systems—you will need to boot to the appropriate OS to find solutions to problems. (3) You are studying for the A+ exams and need to run Windows 98, Windows NT, and Windows 2000, but don't have three different computers.

The FAT32 file system

After the retail release of Windows 95, an update to the operating system was created which was known as Windows 95 OSR2 (OEM Service Release 2). Windows 95 OSR2 introduced an updated FAT file system called FAT32. One of the apparent benefits of FAT32 was that the maximum partition size was increased from 2GB to 2000GB. Now when you go out and buy that 20GB drive, you don't have to divide it into ten different partitions.

The other major benefit to FAT32 is that it has dramatically decreased the cluster size to make better use of disk space. Table 20-2 compares the cluster size of FAT partitions with the cluster size of FAT32 partitions. Table 20-2 shows that FAT32 is not a supported file system for partitions less than 512MB, you may only use the FAT32 file system when you're creating partitions over 512MB.

<table>
<tr><td colspan="3" align="center">Table 20-2
Comparing Cluster Sizes</td></tr>
<tr><td>*Partition Size*</td><td>*FAT Cluster Size*</td><td>*FAT32 Cluster Size*</td></tr>
<tr><td>0MB–127MB</td><td>2KB</td><td>Not Supported</td></tr>
<tr><td>128MB–255MB</td><td>4KB</td><td>Not Supported</td></tr>
<tr><td>256MB–511MB</td><td>8KB</td><td>Not Supported</td></tr>
<tr><td>512MB–1023MB</td><td>16KB</td><td>4KB</td></tr>
<tr><td>1GB–2GB</td><td>32KB</td><td>4KB</td></tr>
<tr><td>2GB–8GB</td><td>Not Supported</td><td>4KB</td></tr>
<tr><td>8GB–16GB</td><td>Not Supported</td><td>8KB</td></tr>
<tr><td>16GB–32GB</td><td>Not Supported</td><td>16KB</td></tr>
<tr><td>Over 32GB</td><td>Not Supported</td><td>32KB</td></tr>
</table>

One of the shortfalls of FAT32 is that MS-DOS, Windows 3.1, the original release of Windows 95 and Windows NT 4.0 do not support it. This means that Windows 95 OSR2, Windows 98 and Windows 2000 can access data on a FAT32 partition, which is great considering these are the popular operating systems today. The problem: If you're dual-booting between Windows 98 and Windows NT 4.0, you have to give drive C: a maximum partition size of 2GB; any other partitions in Windows 98 that use FAT32 are not available to Windows NT.

Tip

Windows 98 has a drive converter application that converts from FAT to FAT32 without the need to reformat the drive. The drive converter program doesn't allow you to convert back to FAT; you need third-party software to do that.

NTFS

Windows NT 4.0 implemented its own native file system called NTFS (New Technology File System). NTFS makes better use of the space available on a particular disk by using 512 Bytes as the cluster size.

Windows NT also supports the FAT file system but not the FAT32 file system. NT relies heavily on NTFS; if you go with the FAT file system, you lose some NTFS functionality. For example, if you want to use the file-system security features (or compression features) in NT, you have to use the NTFS file system.

One of the biggest complaints with Windows NT 4.0 (on the server side) is that it has no way to limit how much disk space a user could use. As a result, users could waste hundreds of megabytes of hard disk space on the server. Stopping such waste was one benefit of NTFS version 5.0, implemented with Windows 2000.

NTFS 5.0

A notable improvement over the NTFS file system that shipped with NT is the new version of NTFS that shipped with Windows 2000: NTFS 5.0. This version has a few extra features, one of which has been long overdue: Disk Quotas. In Windows NT 4.0, the lack of quotas (limits on restricting the total amount of disk space a person can use) has peeved network administrators for years.

Another feature of NTFS 5.0 is the encrypting file system. The *Encrypting File System* uses the public key/private key technology to encrypt a file stored on the hard drive. Only the Recovery Agent and the person who has encrypted the file can open the file, even if another user has permission to view the resource. The encrypting file system is a big selling point for organizations with lots of mobile users who need to protect the privacy of the data that sits on their laptops.

Cross-Reference

For more information on the Encrypting File System, refer to Chapter 19.

HPFS

The *High Performance File System* (HPFS), which gained its popularity with OS/2, was a major improvement over the FAT file system years ago. When looking at the benefits of HPFS, you may be thinking "What is the big deal, I get that with FAT32?"; the big deal is that HPFS was released well before FAT32, or even before Windows 95 was designed. Some of the benefits of OS/2 is that it supports long file names, up to 254 characters (including the path). HPFS also supports partition sizes up to 2000GB and uses a cluster size of 512 bytes!

The disadvantage of HPFS is that it is not widely supported. Operating systems such as DOS and Windows cannot access HPFS volumes.

Installing a Hard Disk

1.2 Identify basic concepts and procedures for creating, viewing and managing files, directories and disks. This includes procedures for changing file attributes and the ramifications of those changes (for example, security issues). Content may include the following: IDE/SCSI, Internal/External

Setting up a computer often requires knowledge of how to place the hard disk inside the computer and prepare it to store information. This section briefly describes the steps for installing a hard disk at the operating-system level.

Basic safeguards

Before you start to service any computer using partitioning tools, save the computer's data and create an emergency repair disk to safeguard both the data and the computer. The emergency repair disk contains system files that the system can use to boot from if it suddenly can't boot from its hard disk. Booting from the floppy disk means you can still run formatting and partitioning tools; saving the data beforehand is still a prudent idea.

To save the data on the computer, either back up the data with the operating system's backup utility or copy the files to a location on the network (or onto a CD-ROM). For more information on performing backups, see the "Backup and restore" section later in this chapter.

When you have backed up the data, created your emergency repair disk, and installed the actual drive, you're ready for the next step — installing the hard disk at the operating-system level. This type of installation means partitioning and formatting the disk.

To install a hard disk at the operating-system level, follow these steps:

1. Create a primary partition.

2. Create an extended partition.

3. Create a logical drive in the extended partition.

4. Format the drives to create a file system.

5. Install the operating system.

Exam Tip   Understanding the order of the steps for partitioning and formatting a disk is important for the exam.

IDE versus SCSI

When installing hard drives in your system, chances are you are installing one of two types of drives: an IDE/EIDE or a SCSI drive.

IDE devices are popular with personal computers and originally had a limitation of about 504MB. An extension to IDE, called EIDE, allowed for larger drives (today that is reaching an average of 40GB!). IDE/EIDE became a popular standard because of the ease of installation for these types of devices.

Cross-Reference   For more information on IDE/EIDE devices and their installation, consult Chapter 9.

SCSI devices gained popularity because organizations that were implementing network servers needed a high performing disk and IDE just wasn't fast enough. SCSI also supports seven drives connected together (IDE only supported two). You probably will not encounter a SCSI hard disk in a system unless you are working on a server.

Cross-Reference   For more information on the benefits of SCSI and how to install SCSI devices, refer to Chapter 9.

Internal versus external

When installing a hard drive on a system, you can have internal or external flavored drives. Typically, IDE drives are implemented as internal drives, so to install an IDE drive, you will remove the computer casing and mount the drive inside the system. Internal IDE drives are connected to the motherboard with a 40-wire ribbon cable.

SCSI drives are implemented as either internal or external devices. If you have an internal SCSI hard drive to install in the system, you will have to remove the casing and mount the drive to the system. Internal SCSI devices typically use a 50-wire ribbon cable.

SCSI drives are also implemented as external devices. If the device is external, it is connected to the back of a SCSI card that has been installed in the system by a cable and is sitting on the outside of the computer.

Cross-Reference For more information on installing IDE and SCSI drives, refer to Chapter 9.

The next sections of this chapter provide you with details about managing partitions and formatting these partitions.

Managing Partitions

Objective

1.2 Identify basic concepts and procedures for creating, and managing files, directories and disks. This includes procedures for changing file attributes and the ramifications of those changes (for example, security issues). Content may include the following: Partitioning/Formatting

A *partition* is a defined segment of the hard disk, created by dividing the disk logically. Partitions come into existence for various reasons — whether as a simple means of organization or as a way of running multiple operating systems on the same machine.

Whatever their reason for being, the purpose and management of partitions is important for the exam. This section examines different types of partitions and provides steps for creating, deleting, and formatting them.

Frequently a partition is a means of providing better access to the information stored on a disk. For example, telling the kids that their games are on the D: drive is usually easier than describing a complex path to the folder that holds the games.

Two types of partitions are the most common, regardless of operating system:

✦ **Primary partition.** This is the partition that the computer boots from; the operating system's boot files are loaded from here. Because you may have multiple primary partitions (say, if you're running several operating systems on the same computer), you must designate one as the *active partition* — the partition from which your normal operating system loads.

✦ **Extended partition.** This partition is, in effect, the space that remains after the primary partition is defined. The extended partition does not have an actual drive letter assigned to it; it's simply a container that holds all the logical drives that you build. (A *logical drive* is a logical division of the hard disk that the computer treats as if it were a separate disk drive; it's the actual area of the extended partition to which documents are saved.)

Tip   Knowing the steps that you must take to boot from a partition could save you hours of troubleshooting when the system has boot problems. If (for example) you have formatted a drive as a system drive and you can't boot from it, you should check to make sure that the primary partition has been set as the active partition.

As an example, suppose you're partitioning a 6GB hard disk, using the original release of Windows 95 (which only supports the FAT file system). FAT cannot define partitions larger than 2GB; you have to divide this drive into at least three different partitions: The first partition you define, then, is primary partition — a 2GB partition that also becomes the active partition (drive C:). What's left is a 4GB extended partition that can store two logical drives (D: and E:), each of which can be no larger than 2GB. Figure 20-1 shows this partition configuration.

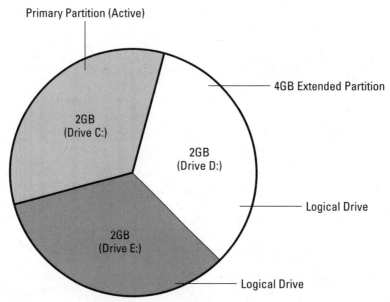

Figure 20-1: Partitioning a hard disk

Note that extended partition itself has no drive letter assigned to it. The extended partition is just a container to hold the logical drives — and they take the drive letters.

Under FAT, a hard disk can contain no more than four partitions, only one of which can be the extended partition. This means you could have three primary partitions and one extended to hold any logical drives. Having three primary partitions also shows why you have to set the active partition. A primary partition is a bootable partition. What if I have three primary partitions? Which one do I boot from? The answer is simple — the one defined as the active partition.

Creating partitions with Windows FDISK

To create or delete partitions in Windows 95 or Windows 98, you must use the fdisk.exe utility. This utility (an old friend from the MS-DOS days) is still the primary tool for managing partitions in Windows.

The Windows 95 OSR2 (OEM Service Release 2) and Windows 98 versions of fdisk.exe have somewhat different startup screens because they both support the FAT32 file system. When you start fdisk.exe under one of these operating systems, a message box asks whether you want to enable large disk support. Figure 20-2 shows the startup screen of fdisk.exe in Windows 98.

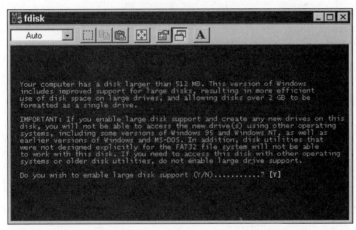

Figure 20-2: Enabling large disk support in Windows 98

Enabling large disk support means that if you create any partitions over 512MB for that fdisk session, they are created as FAT32 (instead of FAT) partitions. Any partitions you create in that session that take up less than 512MB are defined as FAT partitions.

The following Step By Step shows creating a 2GB primary partition—and marking it as the active partition—in Windows 98. The steps then create a 4GB extended partition with two logical drives of 2GB each.

STEP BY STEP: Creating Partitions with Windows FDISK

1. Select Start ➪ Run.

2. In the Run window, type fdisk and choose the OK button.

3. Fdisk starts up and shows you the initial screen, asking whether you want to enable large disk support. Choose Y for yes.

fdisk shows you the main menu of actions that can be performed with partitions (see Figure 20-3).

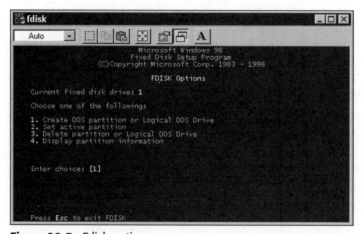

Figure 20-3: Fdisk options

Option number 1 creates partitions or logical drives.

Option number 2 sets an active partition.

Option number 3 deletes partitions.

Option number 4 shows you the partition table so you can see how the drive is currently partitioned.

4. Choose option number 1 to create a partition.

Fdisk shows you a submenu asking which type of partition you want to create. In this screen (shown in Figure 20-4), you may choose to create a primary partition, an extended partition, or a logical drive within the extended partition.

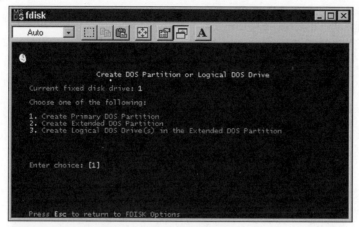

Figure 20-4: The Create Partition submenu

5. Choose option number 1 to create a primary partition.

6. The next screen asks whether you want to use the entire available space on the disk. Since you only want to use 2GB for the primary partition, press N for no.

7. Fdisk then asks you how large the primary partition will be. Type the amount in MB and press Enter.

8. When you have created the primary partition and you are back at the main menu in fdisk you will make sure that you set the active partition. Choose option 2 to set the active partition and press Enter.

9. A dialog box appears, asking which partition will be the active partition; choose partition 1 and press Enter.

   Back at the main menu, you want to create an extended partition, so choose option 1 to create a partition and press Enter.

10. In the create partition screen, choose option number 2 to create an extended partition and press Enter.

11. Type in the size of the extended partition and press Enter.

12. Press Escape once and Fdisk will ask you the size of the first logical drive in the extended partition; type in the desired size of the first logical drive and press Enter.

    You should see at the top of the screen that a drive D has been created.

13. Repeat Step 12 until all the space in the extended partition is used.

14. Press Escape a few times to exit fdisk.

15. Reboot the computer off a startup disk.

When you have created the partitions and exited the fdisk.exe program, it will be time to format the disk and prepare it for use.

Windows NT's Disk Administrator

Creating partitions in Windows NT's Disk Administrator program is a little easier because it is a Windows-based application. Depending on the type of Windows NT computer you are sitting at, either workstation or server, you will be able to create different types of partitions. Figure 20-5 shows the Windows NT Disk Administrator application.

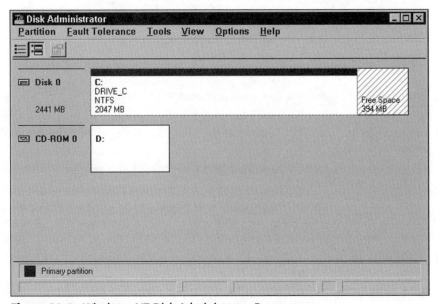

Figure 20-5: Windows NT Disk Administrator Program

Creating partitions with Disk Administrator

The Disk Administrator program allows you to create primary and extended partitions along with logical drives, but it also allows you to create volume set. A *volume set* is a partition made up of two or more areas of free disk space that are not contiguous. These areas of free disk space could be of different sizes and on separate disks. For example, on disk 1 you may have 75MB of free disk space and on disk 2 you have 210MB of free disk space. Instead of creating two separate smaller partitions, you can join the two areas of free space to create a larger volume (partition) of 285MB. A volume set may also be extended, or increased in size, at a later time if another disk is added to the system, as long as the volume is formatted as NTFS.

STEP BY STEP: Creating Partitions with Disk Administrator

1. Select Start ➪ Programs ➪ Administrative Tools ➪ Disk Administrator.

2. In the Disk Administrator program, select an area of free disk space and choose the Partition menu, then choose Create.

3. A warning displays, indicating that the partition scheme may not be compatible with MS-DOS. Choose OK.

4. The Create Primary Partition dialog box, shown in Figure 20-6, appears. Type in the desired size of the partition and choose OK.

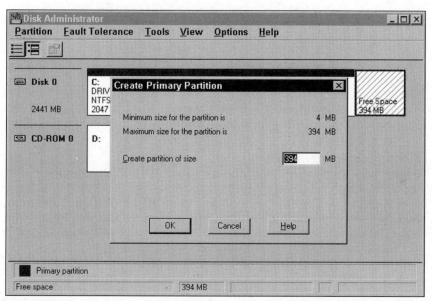

Figure 20-6: Creating a Primary Partition in Windows NT's Disk Administrator

5. To create an extended partition, select an area of free space and choose the Partition menu, then choose Create Extended.

6. The Created Extended Partition dialog box appears, asking the desired size of the partition. Type the size you want for the extended partition, and choose the OK button.

7. When you've marked the area as being the extended partition area you can now select that area of free space again, and from the Partition menu choose Create.

8. The Create Logical Partition dialog box appears, asking the size of the logical partition. Type in the desired size, and choose OK.

9. In the Partition menu, choose the "Commit changes now" option.

10. When you're prompted to save the changes, choose the Yes button.

11. When a dialog box confirms that the update has been saved, choose OK.

12. Close the Disk Administrator.

Fault tolerance and RAID

Windows NT Server has (built into the operating system) a software implementation of RAID (Redundant Array of Inexpensive Disks). RAID puts *redundancy* — duplicated information — on your RAID disks; if one disk fails, the other disk(s) can provide the missing information. Several different levels of RAID are possible; Windows NT Server supports only RAID level 1 and RAID level 5.

Note   Windows NT Server also supports RAID level 0, called *stripe sets*. There is no redundant information stored on stripe sets, which is why stripe sets are classified as RAID 0 (think of it as zero level of RAID).

Mirroring/duplexing (RAID 1)

Disk mirroring is the use of two disks on a single controller to create full redundancy; whatever is placed on one disk is copied to the second disk. When you create the mirror, you use two areas of free space in the Disk Administrator program; then you select the Fault-tolerant menu and choose Establish Mirror. The two areas of free disk space must be two different drives; if one drive fails, the other drive can still function.

When the mirror is established and the system is rebooted, then you will have a new drive letter that's accessible from the My Computer icon. This drive actually shows the data stored on *both* disks; if you save a file to this drive, it's written to both disks that make up the mirror.

Disk duplexing is the same idea as disk mirroring — but requires the installation of an additional hard disk controller. Disk mirroring is fault-tolerant if a drive fails (because the other drive is available) — but you are not in a fault-tolerant solution if the hard disk *controller* fails (because there is only one). If you add an additional hard disk controller and place one drive on one controller and the other drive on the other controller you are fully fault-tolerant. If one drive fails, you have the other; if a controller fails, you have the other drive running off the other controller. Figure 20-7 shows the difference between a mirror and a duplex.

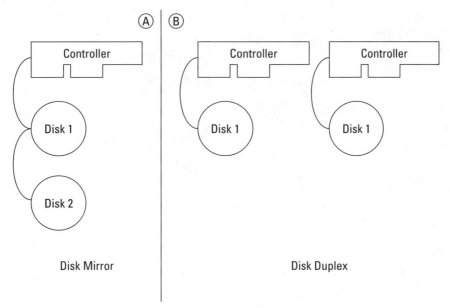

Figure 20-7: Comparing disk mirroring with disk duplexing

Stripe set with parity (RAID 5)

The problem with RAID 1 is that you lose 50% of the money you have spent on hard drives because under normal conditions you are only using one disk. There is a RAID solution that will get you a better use of disk space for the dollar. This RAID solution is called *Stripe set with parity*.

Stripe set with parity uses from 3 to 32 disks and writes information across all disks in the array and writes one piece of duplicated information per row. Figure 20-8 shows three drives in a Stripe set with parity.

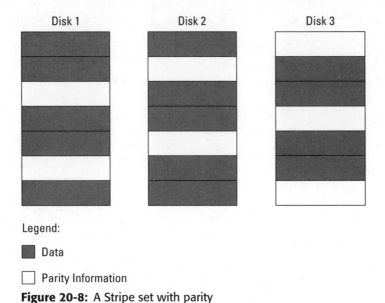

Legend:

■ Data

☐ Parity Information

Figure 20-8: A Stripe set with parity

Information written to a Stripe set with parity is written across the disk by row; one disk per row carries the *parity information* — the duplicated information provided by the fault-tolerant disk driver. If some data is missing on one of the disks for that row, Windows NT can regenerate the missing data by referring to the parity information.

Disk Management in Windows 2000

Windows 2000 has changed the look and feel of the disk-administration tool that ships with the operating system. This tool now resides in the Computer Management Console found in the Administrative Tools program group (accessed via the Start button). Figure 20-9 shows the Disk Management utility in Windows 2000.

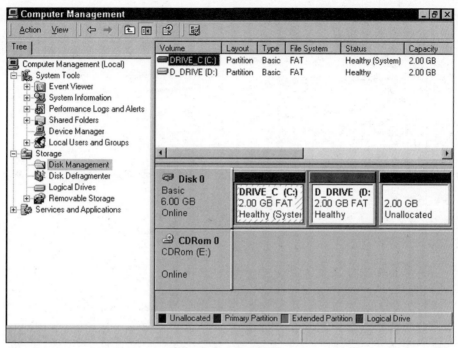

Figure 20-9: Disk Management in Windows 2000

Although the interface has changed a little bit, to create partitions in the Disk Management is pretty much the same idea as creating partitions in Windows NT's Disk Administrator program, only easier. The following Step By Step shows you how to create a partition in the Disk Management utility.

STEP BY STEP: Creating a Partition in Windows 2000

1. Select Start ⇨ Programs ⇨ Administrative Tools ⇨ Computer Management.

2. When the Computer Management application has started, select Disk Management in the left side of the screen. Figure 20-10 shows the Disk Management utility.

3. Over on the right side, in the bottom half of the screen, right-click the unallocated space and choose Create Partition. Figure 20-10 shows how to create a partition.

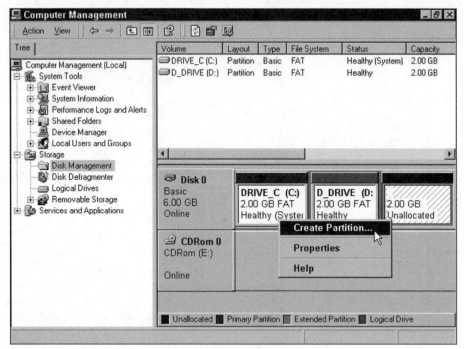

Figure 20-10: Creating a partition in Windows 2000

4. The Create Partition wizard starts and displays a welcome screen. Choose Next.

5. The wizard asks what type of partition you will be creating; select Primary Partition and choose Next. Figure 20-11 shows the Select Partition Type window.

6. Type the desired size of the primary partition and choose Next.

7. Choose the drive letter you want to associate with this partition, and then choose Next.

8. Choose the file system you want to format the partition as, and then choose Next. Figure 20-12 shows how to choose the file system.

9. Choose the Finish button.

10. You will notice that the drive starts to format in the background and it indicates the percent complete in the Disk Management utility.

11. Close the computer management utility.

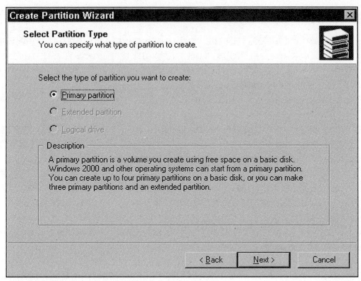

Figure 20-11: Choosing a partition type

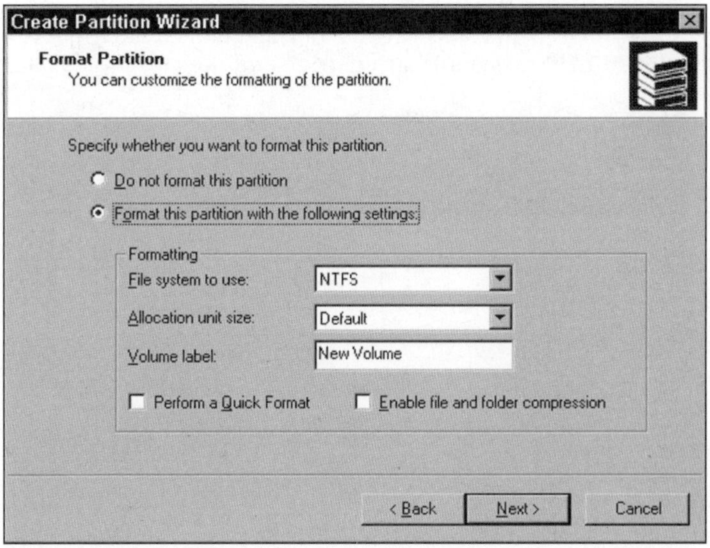

Figure 20-12: Choosing the file system to format the partition

Formatting the partitions

When you have created the partitions, your next step is to format these partitions. Before you can format the partitions, you will want to review the different types of file systems and the advantages and disadvantages of each. When you format the partitions, which now show as drive letters in the My Computer icon, you will be choosing which file system to format them as.

Formatting a drive prepares the drive for storing information. The `format` command will create a root directory on the disk and two file allocation tables used to store information about the files and to aid in the retrieval of these files.

The first table is the *Directory Entry Table*; it lists all the files stored on the drive, along with the date the file was last modified. It also stores the starting cluster for the file. When the system goes to open this file it will look in the directory entry table for the file, find out what cluster the file starts in and go to that cluster to begin the retrieval of the file.

The second table is the FAT Table. The *FAT Table* lists each cluster, showing us which cluster is used and which clusters are free. The FAT Table also indicates any clusters that have been marked as bad. When a file spans multiple clusters, the FAT Table will show that the first cluster is linked to the next cluster by indicating the next cluster value as part of the FAT entry. When all clusters have been linked, the operating system will know that it is the end of the file because there is an end of file marker. Figure 20-13 shows a formatted drive and the two tables on the drive.

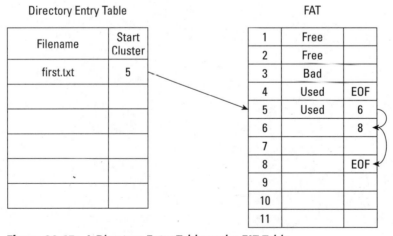

Figure 20-13: A Directory Entry Table and a FAT Table

In Figure 20-13 a file named first.txt is listed in the directory entry table with the beginning cluster location of 5. When the file is open, it looks for the file in the directory entry table and then is directed to the first part of the file, which is cluster 5. When the system looks at cluster 5 in the File allocation table it sees that cluster 5 is being used and that it continues on to cluster 6, and then continues on to cluster 8. Cluster 8 is the last cluster that makes up the file and this is indicated with the EOF marker.

When cluster 5 is pointing to cluster 6, two links are established; cluster 5 is linked to cluster 6, which is linked to cluster 8. The file system could get confused and point the links to the wrong location. (This situation is referred to as *cross-linked files.*)

The `format` command supports the switches listed in Table 20-3.

	Table 20-3
	Format Command Switches

Switch	Description
/S	Formats the drive as a system disk; copying the system files to the drive after formatting it.
/U	Formats the drive *unconditionally*; the drive cannot be unformatted because `format` does not save the information required to do an unformat.
/Q	Formats the drive quickly. The drive must have been formatted before to do a quick format and the quick format does not check the surface of the disk for errors.
/V:	Formats the drive and adds a volume label to the drive.

This section reviewed different types of partitions used to organize a hard disk, as well as the tools used to manage those partitions (and the steps needed to format the partitions) in each of the popular operating systems.

Understanding Management Tools

1.2 Identify basic concepts and procedures for creating, and managing files, directories and disks. This includes procedures for changing file attributes and the ramifications of those changes (for example, security issues). Content may include the following: Backup/Restore

After partitioning the disk and formatting the drive, some maintenance still needs to be done on a regular basis. Drive maintenance helps you address three areas of concern that have an impact on a user's data:

✦ **Data recoverability.** This is the extent to which a computer's data can be recovered, no matter what the disaster is. The usual way to address this concern is to back up your data on a regular basis.

✦ **File system optimization.** This means getting the best performance from your file system. If you can open the files stored on a computer but they open much slower than they did two months ago, your system needs optimizing.

✦ **Data integrity.** This means having files that are uncorrupted so the data is intact and accessible. Sometimes a file opens slowly (or not at all) because the file system has lost parts of the file — in which case you must restore and ensure the integrity of the file. It's a separate issue from file system optimization.

The following section describes some operating-system tools that can help you accomplish these three goals as you maintain your system.

Backup and restore

Ensuring data recoverability involves performing a backup (normally to another type of medium) in addition to storing the file on the hard disk. This medium could be (for example) a floppy disk, another hard disk, a tape drive, a Zip drive, or a CD-ROM.

Windows 95/98

The Backup utility in Windows 95/98 is similar to the typical Windows interface. It has the Explorer look and feel; a directory list appears on the left and a file list appears on the right. The following Step By Step takes you through the steps needed to do a backup in Windows 98. Figure 20-14 displays the Windows Backup application.

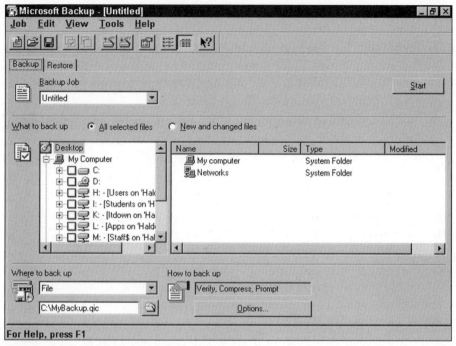

Figure 20-14: The Windows 98 Backup utility

STEP BY STEP: Using Backup in Windows 95/98

1. Select Start ➪ Programs ➪ Accessories ➪ System Tools ➪ Backup.

    A welcome screen appears, showing you information about the three steps of the backup process.

2. Choose the OK button.

    Another dialog box appears, stating that the backup software has created a full backup set, which will back up all files and the Registry.

3. Choose the OK button.

    You may get another dialog box informing you that you do not have a tape drive. If so, choose OK.

    The Windows Backup application appears.

4. Select the files or folders that you want to back up by enabling the check box beside each file or folder.

5. Choose the Next Step button that appears in the upper-right corner of the screen.

6. Select where to back the files up to (typically a floppy drive, tape drive, or another hard disk).

7. Choose the Start Backup button in the upper-right corner.

    You are prompted for the backup set name. A *backup set* is all the files you intend to back up during this operation. The backup set is the actual file that has the contents of the files you are backing up.

8. Type the name that you want to use for the backup set (the file to which the original files are backed up). This file has a .QIC extension.

    You may also password-protect the file so no one else can restore the contents of the backup set.

9. Choose OK.

    Backup starts backing up the selected files; a Confirmation dialog box appears when the operation has completed successfully.

10. Choose OK on the Confirmation dialog box.

11. Close the Backup program.

As you perform regular backups, you should also perform a Restore operation periodically to make sure your backups are working correctly. The Restore operation takes the files stored in the backup set and puts them back on your system.

The following steps show how to perform a Restore procedure.

STEP BY STEP: Performing a Restore in Windows 98

1. Select Start ⇨ Programs ⇨ Accessories ⇨ System Tools ⇨ Backup.

    A welcome screen shows you information about the three steps of the backup process.

2. Choose the OK button.

    Another dialog box appears, stating that the backup software has created a full backup set which will back up all your files and the Registry.

3. Choose the OK button

    You may get another dialog box informing you that you do not have a tape drive. If so, choose OK.

    The Windows Backup application appears.

4. Click the Restore Page tab in the upper-left hand corner.

5. Choose the backup-set file that you want to restore. Typically you can find it on the floppy drive or the tape drive (or on another hard disk).

6. Choose the Next Step button in the upper-right corner of the screen.

   Windows Backup shows the contents of the backup set file.

7. Select the file or folder you want to restore.

8. Choose the Start Restore button in the upper-right corner of the screen.

   The Restore process starts, showing you a Confirmation screen when completed.

9. Choose the OK button on the Confirmation screen.

10. Close Windows Backup.

Backups with Windows NT 4.0

The Windows NT backup software (called NTBackup) has the typical Windows look and feel. The NTBackup is rather limited, even though it comes with Windows NT Server as well. NTBackup has no scheduling capabilities built in; as a result, the NT administrator must use the operating system's scheduler to schedule a batch file to perform the backup.

In addition, NTBackup only backs up to and from a tape drive; you can't use other media with it. NTBackup can't back up open files (which you need the capability to do if you're backing up resources on a server).

Backups with Windows 2000

The Windows 2000 backup software is much improved over NTBackup. This software picks up where its predecessor left off, allowing you to schedule regular backups without having to be on site to perform them—to nearly any medium you like (including, but not limited to, tape drives).

Defragmentation utilities

After a drive is formatted and you start storing information on it, the information is written to one cluster at a time. This means that on a freshly formatted drive, the contents of a file are written to clusters on the disk that are side-by-side. This will ensure optimal performance when opening a file, because the read/write heads don't have to jump from one end of the disk to another to open a single file. Unfortunately the disk will not stay in this state, because as you are adding contents to files and deleting files, the contents of these files are being scattered throughout the disk. Figure 20-15 shows a fragmented disk.

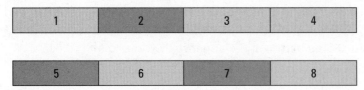

Figure 20-15: Data Stored in Block on Hard Disk

In the example shown in Figure 20-15, you can see that Block 2, 5, and 7 belong to the same file but are scattered throughout the disk. This will cause a performance decrease when accessing the file. Disks defrag applications clean this up by taking all the clusters of a single file and placing them in clusters that reside side-by-side. Figure 20-16 shows what this would look like after a Windows defrag.

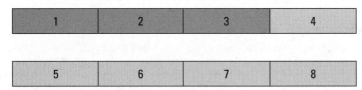

Figure 20-16: Optimized Disk after Defrag

The following section shows you how to run a defrag utility in the different Windows-based operating systems.

Defrag with Windows 95/98

The Windows 95/98 defrag utility organizes the files so all parts of a particular file are grouped together and placed at the beginning of the drive, while all free space is located at the end of the drive.

Windows 98 keeps track of your most popular applications by logging your use of them in a log file directory (`C:\windows\applog`). Within this directory, Windows 98 creates log files with names that follow the pattern *applicaton*`.lgd`. The *application* part of the file is the name of the application (like `winword  -`); the letter *d* in the syntax is the letter that identifies the drive on which the application resides. If you run Microsoft Word from drive C:, its corresponding file is called `winword.lgc`.

Windows 98 uses the log file when performing a defrag; it looks at all the applications (and the associated .DLL files) required to start a particular program and places them side by side. This dramatically increases performance and reduces application startup time.

Defrag with Windows 2000

Windows 2000 has a Disk Defragmenter utility in the Computer Management MMC snap-in. This great little tool has an analyzer that you can run first — it checks the selected disk and reports where the used space is and where the free space is. This tells you whether you have to perform a defrag. Figure 20-17 shows the Disk Defragmenter utility in Windows 2000 after analyzing drive C:.

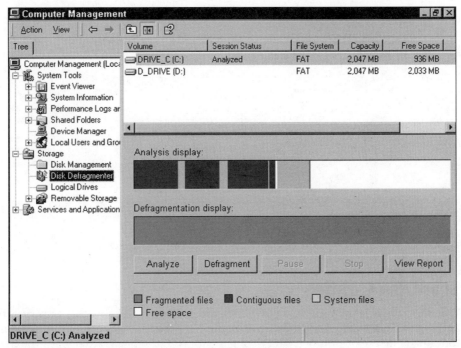

Figure 20-17: The Windows 2000 Disk Defragmenter

After the hard drive has been analyzed, you can also view a report that shows you detailed information about the analysis just performed. When you're happy with the analysis, you can perform the defrag by choosing the Defrag button. Figure 20-18 shows the report generated by the analysis of drive C:.

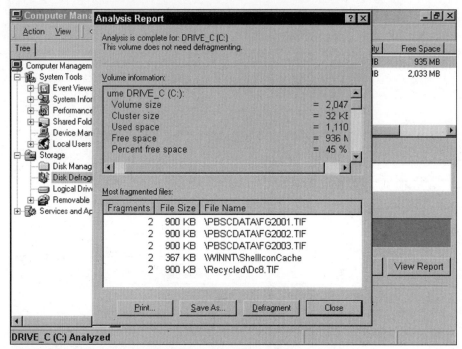

Figure 20-18: The Analysis Report in Windows 2000

ScanDisk Utilities

When a drive is formatted, two FAT tables are created — the Directory Entry Table and the FAT table. The FAT table links all the clusters that make up a file. What if that link is lost — or points to the wrong location? If the file system loses the link that joins two clusters together, the file becomes unreadable and has lost its data integrity. ScanDisk not only looks for lost links, but also scans the disk surface for bad blocks (clusters that cannot be written to), marking them as bad so they are not used.

ScanDisk with Windows 95/98

There are two different versions of ScanDisk in Windows 95/98. There is the command-prompt version, called ScanDisk.exe, and there is the Windows version, scandsk.exe. The command-prompt version is also the version found on your startup disk.

If Windows is shut down improperly, Windows will invoke a ScanDisk (the command-prompt version) automatically on startup. The reason for this is that shutting down Windows in the past has been a big cause for loosing the links between two clusters that make up the same file.

The ScanDisk for Windows will fix a number of problems, the most common being:

✦ File system problems (crossed linked files, lost clusters)

✦ Long file name problems

✦ Directory tree structure problems

✦ Disk surface Problems (bad sectors)

To perform a ScanDisk, go to your system tools option in Programs ⇨ Accessories. Figure 20-19 shows the ScanDisk screen.

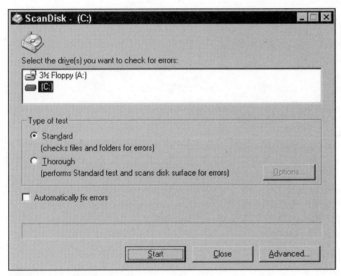

Figure 20-19: ScanDisk

If you perform a standard test it will check the file and folders at the file system level to ensure that they are readable, whereas if you perform a thorough test it will perform the standard test plus scan the surface of the disk for bad blocks. Notice in Figure 20-19 that you can also ask ScanDisk to automatically fix the errors.

ScanDisk with Windows NT/Windows 2000

Windows NT has a drive checker that is the equivalent of ScanDisk — it looks for problems with the file system and disk surface. The following Step By Step shows you how to run ScanDisk in Windows NT/2000.

STEP BY STEP: Verifying the Integrity of a Disk in Windows NT/2000

1. Open the My Computer icon and select the drive.

2. Right-click the drive and choose Properties.

3. On the Tools page tab, select the Check Now button. Figure 20-20 shows the dialog box that appears.

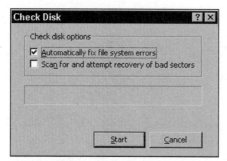

Figure 20-20: Check disk options in Windows 2000

You may choose to automatically fix any file system errors and specify whether you want Windows NT to scan the surface of the disk and attempt to fix any problems with sectors.

4. Select the two options.

5. Choose the OK button.

In this section you have learned the purpose of running utilities like ScanDisk and disk defrag tools on a regular basis. You have also seen some of the backup utilities available in the different operating systems to help protect data loss.

Key Point Summary

This chapter has introduced the importance of hard disk management and the utilities used to perform the management of the hard disk. The following list provides some key points to remember when managing hard disks:

✦ A cluster is the allocation unit for a file.

✦ The cluster size for a partition is based on the file system being used and the size of the partition.

✦ The FAT file system is limited to a maximum partition size of 2GB. FAT32 has increased the maximum allowable partition size to 2000GB.

✦ Windows NT implemented its own file system, called NTFS. NTFS has a number of benefits, some of which are security, auditing, and compression. Windows 2000 implemented NTFS 5.0, where the Encrypting File System and Quotas have been added to the benefit lists.

✦ To optimize your drive, you run a defrag tool often.

✦ To verify the integrity of the drive, you run a scandisk often.

✦ A primary partition is the bootable partition for the system and must be set active. An extended partition holds logical drives for the storing of information.

✦   ✦   ✦

STUDY GUIDE

This Study Guide presents 15 assessment questions to test your knowledge of this exam topic area. Two scenarios present real-life problems to test your skills in generating solutions to those problems. Finally, two labs demonstrate the material covered in this chapter.

Assessment Questions

1. What does ensuring data integrity involve?

A. Performing a backup

B. Running a ScanDisk

C. Running a defrag

D. Running convert.exe

2. Which file systems can be used by Windows NT 4.0?

A. FAT32

B. FAT

C. NTFS

D. NTFS 5.0

3. Which of the following tools will help optimize the file system?

A. Backup

B. Defrag

C. ScanDisk

D. Format

4. What is the maximum capacity for a partition using the FAT file system?

A. 2GB

B. 2MB

C. 2000GB

D. 16GB

5. What utility will manage partitions in Windows 98?

   A. Disk Administrator

   B. Disk Management

   C. Backup

   D. Fdisk

6. What type of partition is used to boot the computer?

   A. Extended

   B. Primary

   C. Mirror

   D. Stripe set with parity

7. Which of the following lists the benefits of NTFS?

   A. Security

   B. Maximum partition size is 2GB

   C. All operating systems can boot from NTFS

   D. Auditing

8. You notice that the computer seems to be taking a long time to open files. Which utility would you run to improve performance?

   A. Restore

   B. Defrag

   C. ScanDisk

   D. Fdisk

9. You have just partitioned your disk and you want to format drive C to boot with the Windows 98 operating system files. What command should you use?

   A. `format c: /s`

   B. `format c:`

   C. `format d:`

   D. `format c: /u`

10. What is the allocation unit for the storage of a file?

   A. Sector

   B. Track

   C. Partition

   D. Cluster

11. What utility will manage partitions in Windows NT?

    A. Disk Administrator

    B. Disk Management

    C. Backup

    D. Fdisk

12. Which file system includes encryption technology?

    A. NTFS

    B. FAT

    C. NTFS 5.0

    D. FAT32

13. What is the maximum capacity for a partition using the FAT32 file system?

    A. 2GB

    B. 16GB

    C. 4GB

    D. 2000GB

14. What utility will manage partitions in Windows 2000?

    A. Disk Administrator

    B. Disk Management

    C. Backup

    D. Fdisk

15. What type of partition must be flagged as being active?

    A. Extended

    B. Logical

    C. Primary

    D. All partitions

Scenarios

This chapter discussed the different file systems and the partitioning utilities in different operating systems. The following scenarios help you apply your knowledge of these topics to real-world situations.

1. You are required to determine a partition scheme for all the laptops running Windows 98 that belong to your sales team. You want to plan ahead and store all the source files for drivers and give a specific area for the salespeople to store data. The drives are 10GB. What partitions would be created and what file systems would be used?

2. Describe the order of steps used to build the partitions you used in the solution from scenario number 1.

Lab Exercises

Lab 20.1 Creating an Extended Partition in Windows 95/98

1. Select Start ⇨ Run, and then type `fdisk` in the open text box.

2. Choose OK.

3. If you're asked to enable large disk support, choose Y and press Enter.

4. When the `fdisk` main menu appears, choose option number 1 to create a partition.

   Choose option number 2 to create an extended partition.

5. A screen appears, asking how large you want to make the partition in MB; type 30, and press Enter.

6. A screen appears, displaying a summary; you should be able to see the extended partition as your second partition. Press Esc.

7. A screen appears, stating that you should create a logical drive in the partition and asking what size you want to make that logical drive; accept the default, and press Enter.

8. A summary of logical drives is shown. Press Esc to continue.

9. Press Esc to exit fdisk.

10. Restart the computer.

Lab 20.2 Formatting a Partition in Windows 95/98

1. Open the My Computer icon.

2. Select the drive that was created in Lab 20.1.

3. Right-click the drive, and choose Format.

4. The Format dialog box appears; choose Full, and then type D_Drive as your label.

5. Choose the Start button.

6. A warning appears, informing you that all data will be lost; Choose OK.

7. When the format is complete, summary information appears; choose Close.

8. If the Windows Help appears, close that window.

9. Choose Close in the Format dialog box.

10. Close My Computer.

Answers to Chapter Questions

Chapter Pre-Test

1. You would **go to the properties of the drive in My Computer. On the Tools page tab, choose Check Now.**

2. **Fat32** allows you to create a partition of 2000GB.

3. **Windows NT 4.0 and Windows 2000** are the only operating systems that can access a NTFS partition.

4. An **extended** partition must be created before logical drives can be created.

5. The **Disk Management utility** (found in the Computer Management MMC) manages partitions in Windows 2000.

Assessment questions

1. **B.** Ensuring data integrity means that you're interested in making sure that you can open the file. You're not really concerned with how long it takes to open the file, as long as it opens. For more information, see the section titled "Understanding Management Tools."

2. **B, C.** Windows NT 4.0 can only access drives formatted with FAT or NTFS. Windows NT 4.0 cannot access FAT32 drives created with Windows 95 OSR2, or Windows 98. For more information, see the section titled "Understanding File Systems."

3. B. A defrag will optimize the file system. It will reorganize the clusters on the disk so all the data that makes up a file is in the same area so the read/write heads will not have to jump around from one end of the disk to the other. For more information, see the section titled "Understanding Management Tools."

4. A. FAT file systems can only access 2GB partitions. FAT32, which can access 2000GB, is a big improvement however. For more information, see the section titled "Understanding File Systems."

5. D. The fdisk utility manages partitions in Windows 95 and Windows 98. Disk Administrator is used in Windows NT 4.0, and Disk Management is the name of the utility in Windows 2000. For more information, see the section titled "Managing Partitions."

6. B. A primary partition is the type of partition that is bootable. Extended partitions are used to hold logical drives. Stripe set with parity is used as a RAID solution on servers. For more information, see the section titled "Managing Partitions."

7. A, D. Security and auditing are the two relevant NTFS features. Security involves setting up permissions on files or directories; auditing involves monitoring who accesses those files and directories. For more information, see the section titled "Understanding File Systems."

8. B. The Defrag utility organizes files so they open faster. For more information, see the section titled "Understanding Management Tools."

9. A. When you format the drive after building the partition and want to include the operating system boot files, you must format the drive with the /s switch to copy the system files over after formatting the drive. For more information, see the section titled "Managing Partitions."

10. D. Files are written to clusters on the disk. Only one file can occupy a cluster, regardless of whether the file fills the entire cluster. For more information, see the section titled "Understanding File Systems."

11. A. Disk Administrator is the utility you will run under Windows NT to manage partitions. For more information, see the section titled "Managing Partitions."

12. C. The Windows 2000 version of NTFS, called NTFS 5.0, implemented the Encrypting File System. For more information, see the section titled "Understanding File Systems."

13. D. FAT32 partitions can be up to 2000GB in size. This is a major benefit of FAT32 over original FAT. For more information, see the section titled "Understanding File Systems."

14. B. The disk management utility in Windows 2000 allows you to manage partitions. For more information, see the section titled "Managing Partitions."

15. C. Primary partitions are the type of partitions that are flagged as being active. You may have two or three primary partitions on your drive. The primary partition that is flagged as being active will be the partition the system boots from. For more information, see the section titled "Managing Partitions."

Scenarios

1. Since you want a place to put the source files for drivers and data, I would probably put those files on a separate partition. The solution should have at least two partitions — one to store the operating system and applications, the other to store the data and drivers. Rebuilding the laptop is a lot easier, should anything go wrong with the operating system. The partition sizes would depend on how many applications are installed on the laptop. I would say 5GB for each partition; they will be using FAT32 as the file system.

2. The steps would be as follows:

   a. Boot from floppy disk

   b. Create primary partition of 5GB

   c. Create extended partition of 5GB

   d. Create logical drive in extended partition of 5GB

   e. Restart system

   f. Format drive C: with a /S to make to copy system files

   g. Format drive D:

   h. Install Windows 98 on drive C:

Installing and Configuring Operating Systems

Part V walks you through the process of bringing a system to a usable state by learning to install an operating system. It also covers the steps a system takes to boot up and which files are needed to boot for the different operating systems.

Once you understand how to install an operating system, you will learn to install devices in the Windows 9*x* and Windows 2000 operating systems.

An important part of troubleshooting systems today involves understanding how different applications run in the different operating systems. Thus, the last topic in this part will discuss how DOS applications, 16-bit applications, and 32-bit applications run in the Windows environment.

Installing and Upgrading Windows

EXAM OBJECTIVES

Exam 220-202 ✦ A+ OS Technologies

- ✦ **2.1** Identify the procedures for installing Windows 9x and Windows 2000 for bringing the software to a basic operational level. Content may include the following:

  - Start up

  - Partition

  - Format drive

  - Loading drivers

  - Run appropriate setup utility

- ✦ **2.2** Identify steps to perform an operating system upgrade. Content may include the following:

  - Upgrading Windows 95 to Windows 98

  - Upgrading from Windows NT Workstation 4.0 to Windows 2000

  - Replacing Windows 9x with Windows 2000

  - Dual boot Windows 9x/Windows NT 4.0/2000

CHAPTER PRE-TEST

1. What is the setup switch that is used to tell the Windows 9x setup program to run scandisk in the foreground?

2. How can a user who has saved the system configuration during a Windows 98 installation uninstall the newly added operating system?

3. How much RAM is required for a Windows 95 installation?

4. What type of Windows 95 setup would you do on a system that has limited hard disk space?

5. What command would you use to create the three Windows NT 4.0 setup boot disks?

6. What setup switch can you use with the Windows NT 4.0 installation program to pass it the name of an unattended answer file called acme.txt?

7. A Windows NT 4.0 Workstation can be upgraded to what type of Windows 2000 operating system?

8. How much RAM is required to install a Windows NT 4.0 workstation?

9. How can you create the four setup boot disks for a Windows 2000 installation?

10. What file is created on the hard drive if Windows freezes up during the hardware detection phase?

✦ Answers to these questions can be found at the end of the chapter. ✦

Although the installation of operating systems has gotten easier over the last few years, it is still important to understand some of the issues surrounding the installation and the upgrading of operating systems.

This chapter will give you some background on the issues that surround the installation of Windows 95, Windows 98, Windows NT 4.0, and Windows 2000 operating systems. It will walk you through these installations step-by-step.

Preparing for Installation

After talking to many people in the industry about installing servers and different operating systems, I have come to realize that one thing we can always spend more time on is planning. Many people tell me that they can't do any actual work until their head office sends them the server. However, the best time to do your planning and disaster planning may be while the server is being shipped. Planning your installation or deployment of the operating system on the desktops can save you time and money in the long run, by foreseeing any issues that may arise and having the solutions ready when the time comes.

This section will help you identify some points you need to consider when installing a new operating system, first with Windows 95 or Windows 98, and then with Windows NT 4.0 and its successor, Windows 2000.

Windows 95/98

Because Windows 95 and Windows 98 are similar in design, I will refer to them collectively in this section as "Windows." This section will examine six different aspects of a Windows installation:

✦ Hardware requirements

✦ Startup disk

✦ Partitioning the disk

✦ Formatting the disk

✦ Application support

✦ Upgrade or not

Hardware requirements

When preparing for the installation of any operating system, first find out its hardware requirements so you can decide whether or not you need to update the hardware on the systems that the operating system will be installed onto.

Table 21-1 displays the *minimum* hardware requirements for both Windows 95 and Windows 98. Remember, having just minimum hardware requirements may not be practical for a business environment.

Table 21-1 Windows 9x Minimum Hardware Requirements		
Hardware Component	*Windows 95*	*Windows 98*
Processor	386DX 20 MHz	486DX 66 MHz
Memory	4MB	16MB
Hard disk space	50–55MB	300MB

The minimum hardware requirements listed above will, at the very least, get your operating system installed and functioning. They answer textbook-type questions, such as "What do you need to run Windows 95?" Table 21-2 lists the recommended hardware requirements to run Windows

Exam Tip   For the exam, it is important to remember the minimum hardware requirements for the Windows 9x operating systems.

Table 21-2 Windows 9x Recommended Hardware Requirements		
Hardware Component	*Windows 95*	*Windows 98*
Processor	486 DX 33	Pentium
Memory	16MB	32MB HD
Hard disk space	60MB	300MB

After you have evaluated the hardware required to install the operating system, you will need to think about how the hard drive will be partitioned and what file system you will use.

Startup disk and partitioning the disk

When installing the Windows operating system, you will need to build some sort of startup disk to boot the computer, and then set the partitions up on the drive. You will want to think about how many partitions you should have and what the sizes of those partitions are going to be. For a more detailed discussion about partitions as they relate to the installation of the operating system, see the "Understanding Partition Issues" section later in this chapter.

File system

If you are installing the original release of Windows 95, you really don't have a choice about which file system to use. You can only go with the FAT file system. If you are installing Windows 95 OSR2 or Windows 98, you can choose between the FAT file system or the FAT32 file system. For more information about why you would choose one file system over the other, see the "Understanding Formatting Issues" section later in this chapter.

You will want to test the applications that will be running on the operating system for compatibility issues. For example, suppose that your company has built a customized accounting application for use in-house. You will want to make sure you test that in-house application on each of the different operating systems and verify that it functions correctly. If you test the application on Windows and it functions normally, and then install the application on Windows NT and it fails, you have a better idea of what operating system to choose. (You are obviously not going to install Windows NT on each user's computer.)

Upgrade or not

Another planning consideration with your operating system installation is whether you will be performing an upgrade or whether you are going to install the operating system from scratch. If you are installing the operating system from scratch, you will either partition the drives and then format them, or you will leave the partitions that are intact and just do a format. For more information on upgrading operating systems, see the section "Understanding How to Upgrade to Windows" later in this chapter.

I want to offer a final planning tip for your OS install: always perform backups of the current state of the system before making any major changes. This best practice applies to upgrades rather than to clean installations.

Cross-Reference For more information on performing backups, consult Chapter 20.

Windows NT/2000

In this section, the designation "Windows NT" also refers to Windows 2000, because both are based on Windows NT technology. Many of the installation issues for Windows NT 4.0 apply to Windows 2000 as well, and the setup procedure is similar for both operating systems.

Once again, prepare for the installation of an operating system by finding out its hardware requirements. Table 21-3 shows the minimum hardware requirements for Windows NT operating systems.

Table 21-3
Windows NT Minimum Hardware Requirements

Hardware Component	Windows NT Workstation	Windows NT Server	Windows 2000 Professional	Windows 2000 Server
Processor	486 66MHz	486MHz	Pentium 133MHz	Pentium 133MHz
Memory	12MB	16MB	64MB	128MB
Hard Disk Space	350MB	500MB	650MB	900MB

Many of the issues regarding Windows 95/98 installations apply to Windows NT, as well. However, a Windows NT installation exhibits some unique issues related to:

✦ Computer role

✦ Computer name

✦ Workgroup/domain

✦ File systems

✦ Application support

Computer role

When preparing to install Windows NT, you should plan the role of each Windows NT installation. The role implies the computer's responsibility on the network, the role being the installation of a Windows NT Workstation or Windows NT Server. You would use Windows NT Workstation instead of Windows 95/98, and Windows NT Server would be used as a machine that would provide resources out to the network. If you are installing a server, however, you will need to choose one of three different types of installations: a primary domain controller, backup domain controller, or member server.

A *primary domain controller* is a machine that manages a list of user accounts for the network, while a *backup domain controller* receives a copy of everything that the primary domain controller has in the database for fault tolerance. Both the primary domain controller and backup domain controller are responsible for answering user logon requests.

A *member server* is a machine that does not contain the list of user accounts for the entire network, so a member server is not responsible for answering logon requests when users log on to the network. Member servers are not responsible for answering logon requests, because member servers do not have a copy of the user account database for the network. In Windows NT 4.0, you choose the roles of these machines during the installation.

Note In Windows 2000, all servers get installed as member servers. Then you run DCPROMO to make the member server a domain controller when necessary.

Computer name/domain name

When you install Windows NT, you choose a computer name for the machine you are installing and then you choose the domain that you would like to join. A *domain* is a group of computers that have a central database for storing the username and password of each user on the network. This gives the user the capability to log on to the network only once and gain access to all of the resources on the network the user has permission to.

File systems

Windows NT supports two file systems: FAT16 and NTFS. The primary advantage of using the FAT file system is that it is the shared file system for all operating systems, whereas NTFS is only available to Windows NT operating systems. The FAT file system has its limitations, however — it can only handle 2GB partitions.

Cross-Reference Windows 2000 supports FAT16, FAT32, and NTFS file systems. For more information on the differences between these file systems, consult Chapter 20.

Application support

Make sure you test each application that will be running on the operating system completely to verify that it functions correctly. You may find that Windows NT loses the race to Windows 95 or Windows 98 with respect to application support. Windows NT will not allow applications to access resources directly, so if an application tries to access the resources directly, Windows NT shuts the system down.

Booting for Installation

Objective **2.1** Identify the procedures for installing Windows 9x and Windows 2000 for bringing the software to a basic operational level. Content may include the following: Start up, Loading drivers

When starting an operating system installation, your first step is to collect the tools that you will need to do the job: (1) a startup disk and (2) a CD-ROM driver added to the startup disk. Adding the CD-ROM driver to the startup disk enables you to boot off the diskette, repartition the disk, and then install the operating system from the CD. Without the CD-ROM driver, you will not be able to access the CD.

Windows 95/98 startup disk

Windows 95 and Windows 98 allow you to create a Windows startup disk that will act as your primary tool for troubleshooting installation and bootup problems. To create a Windows 95/98 boot disk, follow these steps:

STEP BY STEP: Creating a Windows 95/98 Startup Disk

1. Select Start ➪ Settings ➪ Control Panel.

2. Double-click the add/remove programs.

3. Choose the Startup Disk page tab.

4. Choose "Create Disk".

Once the startup disk is created, you can boot off the setup disk and repartition the drive. After repartitioning the drive, you can then format the drive and install the operating system.

You will want to make sure that you have loaded the appropriate CD-ROM drivers on the startup disk so that after formatting the drive, you can run the operating system setup program from CD. To install the CD-ROM driver, you will need to obtain the driver from the manufacturer of the CD-ROM, usually from their Web site.

Tip   The Windows 98 version of the startup disk will load a generic CD-ROM driver automatically for you so that you can access a CD after booting off the startup disk.

Windows NT/2000 setup disk

Windows NT/2000 is a little bit different from Windows 95 and Windows 98. In Windows NT, you can install the operating system by creating the "setup boot disks." The reason why these diskettes are called "setup boot disks" instead of "startup boot disks" is because you are not actually booting to the operating system with the "setup boot disk" — you are booting to an installation of Windows NT/2000. The "setup boot disks" invoke the installation of Windows NT/2000. There are three setup boot disks; you will boot off the first diskette to get a setup invoked. One of the purposes of these three diskettes is that they load generic CD-ROM drivers and then continue setup from the CD! This means you don't have to fuss around, trying to get familiar with the system you are troubleshooting and trying to find a driver for the CD-ROM device.

To create the setup boot disk in Windows NT 4.0, you run the winnt.exe setup program with the /OX switch. This switch will run the Windows NT setup program only for the purpose of creating the setup boot disk. To create the setup boot disk in Windows 2000, you will run the makeboot.exe program found on the Windows 2000 CD.

Another way to boot the operating system into a setup program is to boot off the Windows NT CD-ROM, which will invoke a setup automatically — assuming that you have a BIOS that supports bootable CD-ROM devices.

To summarize, Windows NT and Windows 2000 can be installed in two different ways: by creating the Windows NT setup boot disks, or by booting off the CD for Windows NT and Windows 2000 and having the setup start automatically.

Understanding Partition Issues

 2.1 Identify the procedures for installing Windows 9x, and Windows 2000 for bringing the software to a basic operational level. Content may include the following: Partition

Once you boot off your operating system boot disk, you can begin to define partitions on the drive. Partitions are logical divisions in the disk that you can use to help separate the different types of information stored on the system.

In this section, we will overview partition issues with Windows 9x and Windows NT operating systems. For more information about types of partitions, refer to Chapter 20.

Windows 95/98

When installing Windows 95 or Windows 98, keep your startup disk on hand to manage the partitions before the installation of the operating system. When you are ready to build partitions to install an operating system onto, you will boot off the startup disk.

If you are booting off a Windows 98 startup disk, you will be asked if you want CD-ROM support. If you do, loading CD-ROM support from the Windows 98 startup disk will load a generic CD-ROM driver for your system so that you can access the CD for the operating system and perform the install. Having a generic CD-ROM driver on your startup disk is a great feature of the Windows 98 startup disk. You will not need to go through the trouble of finding out what driver is needed for a specific CD-ROM — your Windows 98 startup disk has one that will load automatically.

 If you support a number of different types of machines, I would highly recommend carrying around with you a Windows 98 startup disk. When you need to reinstall an operating system, you can boot off the Windows 98 startup disk and then partition and format the drive. After formatting the drive, you can then access the CD-ROM and install your new operating system. It's as easy as that!

Once you have booted off the startup disk, you can run fdisk to manage or create your partitions. If you are using a Windows 95 OSR2 or a Windows 98 startup disk, you will be asked if you want to enable large disk support. If you choose yes, any partitions you build over 512MB will use the FAT32 file system when formatted. If you choose no to enabling large disk support, any partitions created will use the FAT16 file system.

When installing an operating system with no partitions defined, you will create partitions in the following order:

✦ Primary partition

✦ Extended partition

✦ Logical drives in extended partition

Exam Tip   For the exam, it is important to understand the steps to building partitions on a hard disk.

Windows NT/2000

When installing Windows NT 4.0 or Windows 2000, you could manage the partitions with a Windows 9x startup disk first, and then run the setup of Windows NT or Windows 2000 from the CD. Or you could manage the partitions within the setup program of Windows NT/2000.

Within the Windows NT/2000 setup program, you can build the partitions by choosing an area of free space and then choosing the letter "c" (for create). The setup program will ask you the size of the new partition. There is also a delete command, which enables you to delete any existing partitions. After creating the partitions and then choosing a partition to install the Windows NT/2000 operating system on, you will be asked what file system you wish to use.

In the Real World   When installing Windows NT you do not have any control over the types of partitions that are created during the setup. For this reason, it is best to only create one partition (used to install the operating system) during the installation of the operating system, and then after the operating system has been installed use Disk Administrator to create the remaining partitions. For more information on using Disk Administrator, see Chapter 20.

Understanding Formatting Issues

Objective   2.1   Identify the procedures for installing Windows 9x, and Windows 2000 for bringing the software to a basic operational level. Content may include the following: Format drive

Once the partitions have been defined, you will need to format them. Formatting the partitions will prepare the disk to store information by building the root directory and the file allocation table.

Windows 95/98

After you have booted off the Windows floppy disk and have built the partitions, you will need to reboot the system and boot off the floppy disk again (because there is no file system on your partitions yet). Once you have booted off the floppy disk again, you can format the partitions, which now appear as drives.

To format the primary partition (which should be Drive C), you will need to format the drive but apply the operating system boot files. To do this, you will run `format c: /s`, which will format the disk, and then apply the operating system boot files and write the boot sector.

Note   Remember that if you have enabled large disk support, any partitions you build over 512MB will be FAT32. Also remember that operating systems like Windows 95 or Windows NT 4.0 do not understand FAT32.

You now have a bootable partition that you can install an operating system on. If you already have your CD-ROM driver loaded, at this point you would execute the setup program for the Windows operating system.

Windows NT/2000

After you have partitioned the disk during your Windows NT installation, you will be asked what file system you want to use for the partition you are installing the operating system to. If you choose to install to a FAT partition, the installation program will format the newly created partition as FAT; if you choose to use the NTFS file system, it will format the partition as NTFS.

Note   If you choose to install to a FAT partition in Windows 2000 and that partition is larger than 2GB, Windows 2000 will format using FAT32 as the file system.

If you decide that you want to install Windows NT or Windows 2000 to a partition that already exists, you will still be asked what file system you want to use. If you decide you want to use NTFS, the installation program will install the operating system using FAT and then convert the file system to NTFS later in the installation.

Running the Setup Program

Objective

2.1   Identify the procedures for installing Windows 9x and Windows 2000 for bringing the software to a basic operational level. Content may include the following: Run appropriate setup utility

This section will start with an overview of the installation process for Windows 95 and Windows 98. Although we use Windows 95 in our example, keep in mind that the installation process is much the same for Windows 98. After discussing the Windows 95/98 setup, the Windows NT/2000 setup process will be covered. The setup process for both Windows NT and Windows 2000 is much the same, so the discussion will focus on Windows 2000.

Windows 95/98

To install the Windows 9x operating system, you will need to run the setup.exe program located on the CD-ROM or the floppy diskettes (if you have them). Remember that you can customize the way setup performs its task by passing it some switches. Table 21-4 lists some of the popular switches for the Windows 95 setup program.

Table 21-4
Windows 95 Setup Switches

Switch	Description
/IS	This switch will tell Windows setup not to perform a scandisk before the installation of the operating system. IS stands for "ignore scandisk."
/ID	This switch will tell Windows setup not to perform the disk space check. ID stands for "ignore disk space."
/L	This switch will enable your Logitech mouse during setup.
/IQ	This switch prevents setup from checking for cross-linked files.
/IH	This switch causes scandisk to run in the foreground.

After you have placed the Windows 95 CD into the CD-ROM tray, you can execute the setup.exe program by typing setup at the DOS prompt or by choosing the run command from within Windows. When you run the Windows 95 setup program, it will ask you to press Enter to continue with setup or ESC to exit.

If you press Enter, the setup program will first run a scandisk (shown in Figure 21-1) to check the integrity of the disk. It checks the file allocation table and the file system to make sure that no areas are corrupt.

Although it is recommended to allow setup to run the scandisk before the setup, you can skip the scandisk portion of setup by executing setup /is. This is useful when automating the setup procedure so that you have as little user intervention as possible (usually you need to press exit when scandisk is finished — if scandisk does not run, you will not have to choose exit).

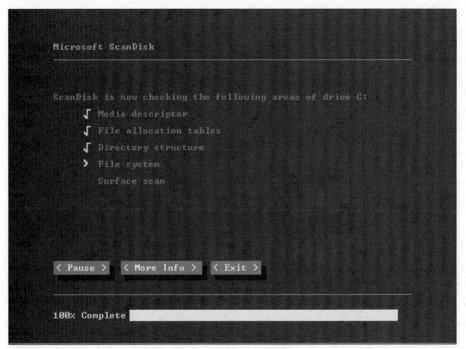

Figure 21-1: Windows 95 installation runs a scandisk

Once the scandisk has finished checking for errors, you can tab to the exit option in the installation screen. This will exit the scandisk and continue with the installation. When setup continues, it copies enough files to run a minimal Windows GUI interface so that the installation is as user-friendly as possible.

After some temporary files have been copied, you should get a welcome screen from the Windows setup program. Once again, you can choose to continue with setup or choose the exit setup option (shown in Figure 21-2).

After choosing to continue with setup, you will be presented with the end-user license agreement (shown in Figure 21-3). Read through the terms of this agreement carefully and continue with setup by choosing the Yes button.

In the Real World

If you run setup with the /IW switch, setup will not display the license agreement screen. This is useful for creating automated installations so that you have as little user intervention as possible. Getting rid of the license agreement screen means one less dialog box you will have to deal with during setup.

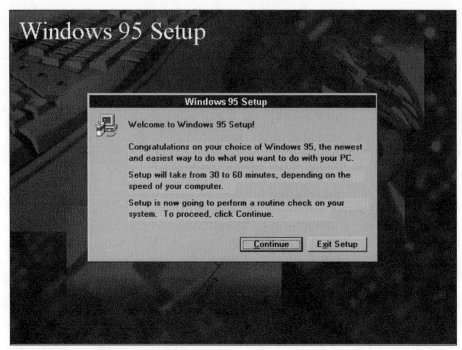

Figure 21-2: Windows 95 setup welcome screen

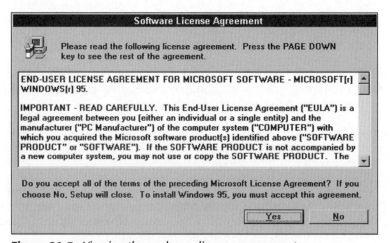

Figure 21-3: Viewing the end-user license agreement

Windows 95 setup goes through the following three phases:

✦ **Phase 1:** Collect information about the system (such as your name and organization, the type of installation you want to perform, and the components you want to install).

✦ **Phase 2:** Perform the major file copy operation of all the files needed to run Windows 95 on your system.

✦ **Phase 3:** Reboot and finalize setup by setting up your regional settings and printer.

Figure 21-4 shows the Setup Wizard screen explaining the three stages.

Figure 21-4: Windows 95 Setup Wizard

After choosing the Next button on the Windows 95 Setup Wizard screen, setup will ask you for the directory to install Windows into (shown in Figure 21-5). At this point, you need to make a decision as to whether or not you want to do an upgrade from a previous version of Windows. For example, if you are already running Windows 3.1 in the c:\windows directory and you want to upgrade your Windows 3.1 environment to Windows 95, you would install Windows 95 into the same folder. When you install Windows 95 into the Windows 3.1 folder, all your existing applications migrate into the newly added Windows 95 operating system. This will save you the time of having to reinstall all of your applications again once you have the new operating system. If you are not convinced that you would like to migrate to a

Windows 95 environment, you can install Windows 95 into a separate folder, which will preserve your Windows 3.1 environment and allow you to run both operating systems. You will, however, be required to install any applications you wish to use in Windows 95 all over again.

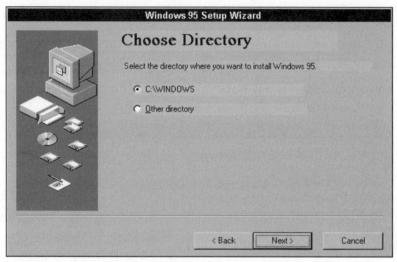

Figure 21-5: Choosing a directory to install Windows 95 into

Once you have selected the directory where you want to install Windows 95, you can continue with the installation by choosing the Next button. Setup will verify that you have enough hard disk space to install Windows 95, and then present you with the Setup Options dialog box (shown in Figure 21-6). Now you will decide on the type of installation that you want to perform.

It is important to understand the different types of setups available, because each installation you perform will require different features of the operating system. For example, if you install Windows 95 on a laptop, the user of the laptop may wish to have some of the mobile features installed, such as dial-up networking and direct cable connect. On the other hand, a desktop computer in an office environment may not require those features. Table 21-5 describes the four setup options available.

Table 21-5	
Windows Setup Options	
Setup Type	*Description*
Typical	Should be used for most setups. All of the common components are installed that will be needed with everyday use.
Portable	Should be used if installing Windows on a laptop computer. This option will install remote features such as direct cable connect and dial-up networking.
Compact	Should be used in low disk space scenarios. This option will install just enough of the Windows components to get the operating system running.
Custom	Should be used if you are familiar with the setup options you would like to install and would specifically choose the options that are desired for the installation.

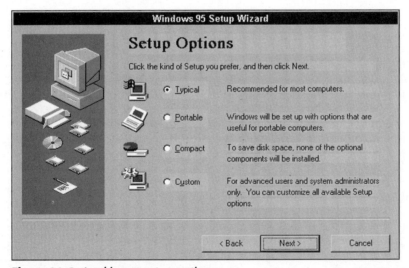

Figure 21-6: Looking at setup options

For this installation, we will choose a custom install. Once you choose the custom option, you then click the Next button. You will be prompted for the 10-digit CD Key (shown in Figure 21-7). You will find the CD Key on the CD case.

Figure 21-7: Entering product identification

After entering the CD Key and clicking Next, you will be prompted for your user information (specifically, your name and company). It is this user information that will eventually get written into the registry. Because this information displays each time you install new software, you may want to use something generic if you're installing on a system in a business. If, for example, job roles change and someone sits at a computer with an old employee's name registered on it and installs software, the old employee's name will appear as the computer that is being registered to. The new employee will eventually ask for a method to change the name that displays when new software is installed. You can prevent this scenario by using something generic like "IT Support" for the name and the company's name for the company (as shown in Figure 21-8)

Setup then asks you if you want the setup program to detect all of the different types of hardware that are installed on the system or if you want to specify the type of hardware that setup is to look for. In most cases, it is recommended that you get the setup program to detect all hardware, then choose Next.

During the hardware detection phase, all of the devices that are detected are recorded into a hidden file called detlog.txt, which is located on the root of the C drive. Another file that is important to the setup process, setuplog.txt, is a record of all of the steps during the setup process.

A third file, detcrash.log, is created if setup crashes (or freezes during the hardware detection phase). This file tells setup which device has caused it to crash during the hardware detection. If you encounter a system that freezes during hardware detection, power the system off for ten seconds and then power it back on, choose the safe recovery option and setup will continue skipping the step that caused it to crash, which it is reading from detcrash.log file.

Figure 21-8: Entering user information

Tip

If you encounter a system that freezes during the hardware detection phase, power the system off for ten seconds and then power it back on. Choose the safe recovery option to continue the setup, skipping the step that has caused setup to hang the first time around.

Setup then wants to know if you have a CD-ROM or network card installed; if you don't, it won't bother trying to detect for those devices (as shown in Figure 21-9). This will speed up the time that it takes to detect for the hardware. If you have a CD-ROM or network card, you can select them from the list, and then choose Next.

Setup starts detecting your hardware, which could take a few minutes. At any point during the hardware detection, if you notice that the setup program has frozen, you can power the computer off (this will not work if you press Ctrl+Alt+Delete), and then power the computer back on. The setup program is keeping track of all of the stages of the installation and will skip any step that causes it to crash when it hits that point in setup again.

Once the hardware has been detected, you will be presented with the Get Connected dialog box, where you can specify whether or not you want to install Windows Messaging; choose Next.

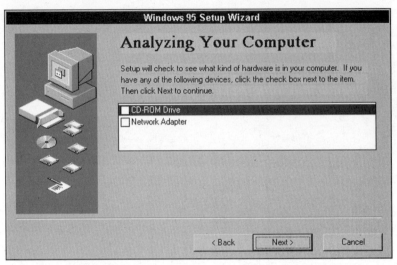

Figure 21-9: Selecting additional devices for hardware detection

Because you have decided to do a custom installation, setup wants you to choose the Windows components you wish to install (as shown in Figure 21-10). You can install components now or later on — after the operating system has been installed. In fact, you can select components through the Add/Remove Programs icon in Control Panel at any point in time.

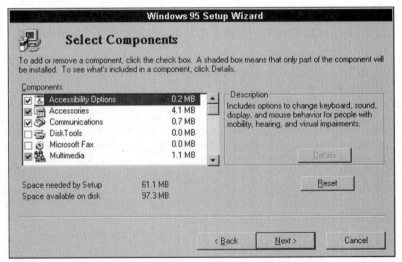

Figure 21-10: Selecting Windows components to install

After selecting the Windows components to install (if you're looking for the games, they're in Accessories!), click the Next button. Setup now wants to know what your networking configuration is. It does have some default protocols loaded, and it should have detected your network card (shown in Figure 21-11). For more information on the networking configuration of Windows, see Chapter 29. When you are satisfied with your networking settings, click the Next button.

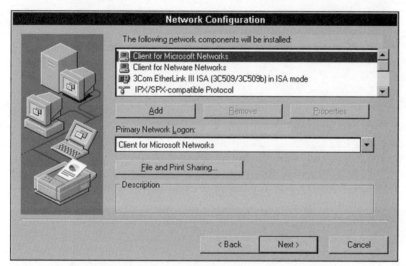

Figure 21-11: Looking at networking configuration settings

You are next asked about the computer's identification information (shown in Figure 21-12). This is the part of setup where you give your computer its unique 15-character name. You can also give it the name of the workgroup or network name that you are to become a part of and a friendly description about the computer. For more information on computer identification, see Chapter 29.

After filling in your computer name, choose the Next button. The setup program now displays the Computer Settings dialog box, where you have an opportunity to change some of the devices that the computer has detected during the setup process (as shown in Figure 21-13). Typically, this might be the time where you change the display adapter if you are not happy with what it has detected.

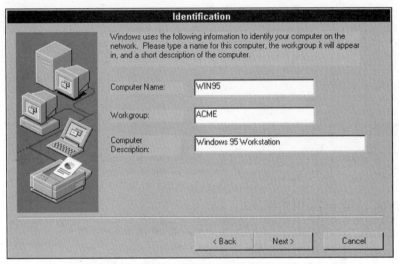

Figure 21-12: Identifying the computer to the network

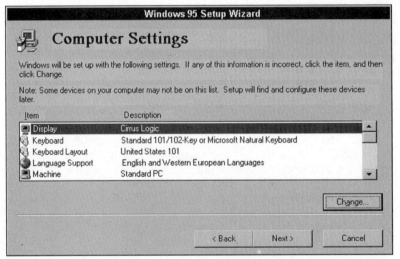

Figure 21-13: Viewing computer settings detected by the Windows 95 setup program

After verifying that setup has detected the appropriate computer settings, you can continue setup by choosing the Next button. An important part of a new operating system installation is ensuring that you have an emergency boot disk (startup disk) for that operating system. At this point, the Windows setup program is asking you if you would like to make a startup disk. If you currently don't have one for this operating system, it is a good idea to make one. You will be required to insert a floppy disk, and after setup has made the startup disk, setup will then continue. Figure 21-14 shows the startup disk prompt.

After choosing whether you want to build a Windows 95 startup disk, you can then click the Next button. The Windows 95 setup program then informs you that it is ready for the second stage of the Windows 95 installation program. Based on your answers to the previous questions, it is now ready to copy files to your computer (as shown in Figure 21-15).

Figure 21-14: Windows 95 setup prompting you to create a startup disk

You can choose Next to begin the file copy stage. This stage of the installation takes the longest amount of time, so you may want to start filling out those product registration cards! After the file copy stage, the setup program is ready to restart and finish setup, which is the third and final stage of the setup program. When prompted, you can choose the Finish button to reboot the computer.

Windows restarts and sets up any plug-and-play devices by dynamically assigning them resources. Windows then continues by setting up the Control Panel and Start menu items, configures Help, and then asks for your time zone (as shown in Figure 21-16) and whether you wish to install a printer.

Figure 21-15: Stage two in Windows 95 setup

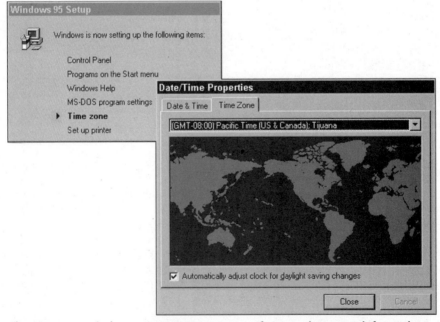

Figure 21-16: Windows 95 setup prompts you for your time zone information

After you have selected your time zone and chosen whether you wish to install a printer, Windows finishes setup and then displays a welcome screen, indicating that the operating system installation is complete.

Windows NT/2000

The installation program for Windows NT is winnt.exe if you are installing the operating system from anything other than a previous version of Windows NT. If you are installing Windows NT 4.0 on a previous version of Windows NT, you can use the winnt32.exe program to perform the setup.

The installation program for Windows 2000 is much the same, but you will run winnt32.exe to install Windows 2000 on a previous 32-bit operating system. If you are installing Windows 2000 on a DOS system, you will run winnt.exe. Table 21-6 shows some of the setup switches supported by the Windows NT/2000 setup program.

Table 21-6 Windows NT/2000 Setup Switches	
Switch	**Description**
/B	Floppyless installation. Windows NT 4.0 will create three setup boot disks during the installation unless the /b switch is used.
/OX	Running the setup program with only a /OX will only create the three setup boot disks. This switch does not work in Windows 2000. To create the setup boot disks in Windows 2000, use the makeboot.exe program on the Windows 2000 CD.
/U:<file>	This switch is used to tell the installation program the name of a file that has all of the answers to the questions that will be asked during the installation. This is used to automate the setup.
/UDF:number,<file>	This switch will point to a database file (really a text file) that has a list of unique settings per computer. This is another file used in automating setup.
/S:<path>	This switch specifies the source path to the Windows NT/2000 installation files.

Windows NT and Windows 2000 both have bootable CDs, so if you have a bootable CD-ROM, the installation will be fairly easy. All you need to do is place the CD in the CD-ROM tray and boot the system up. The setup program is invoked automatically (as shown in Figure 21-17).

When the setup program starts for Windows 2000, you are asked whether you want to install Windows 2000 or whether you are looking to repair an installation of Windows 2000. Repairing an installation of Windows 2000 usually involves a repair disk that will allow you to recover from missing or corrupt operating system files. In this example, you are looking to install a copy of Windows 2000, so press Enter.

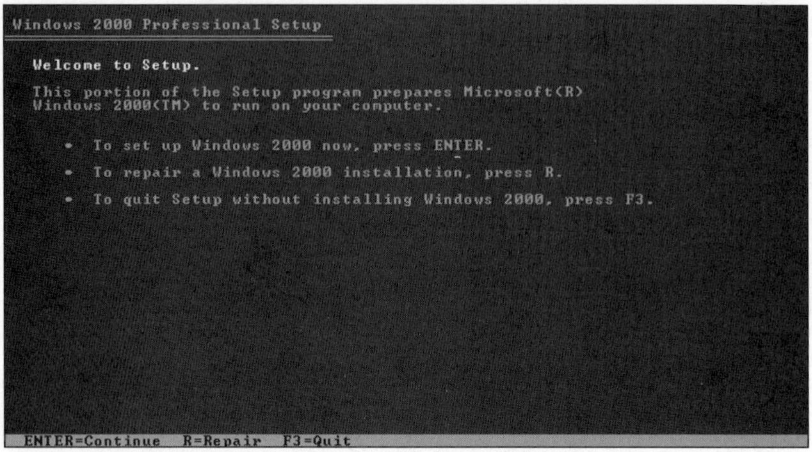

Figure 21-17: The start of a Windows 2000 installation

If you are installing Windows 2000 on a system that has not yet defined any partitions, Windows 2000 will display a screen that warns you that there is an empty disk or a disk running an operating system that Windows 2000 does not understand (as shown in Figure 21-18). To continue with setup, you can type "c."

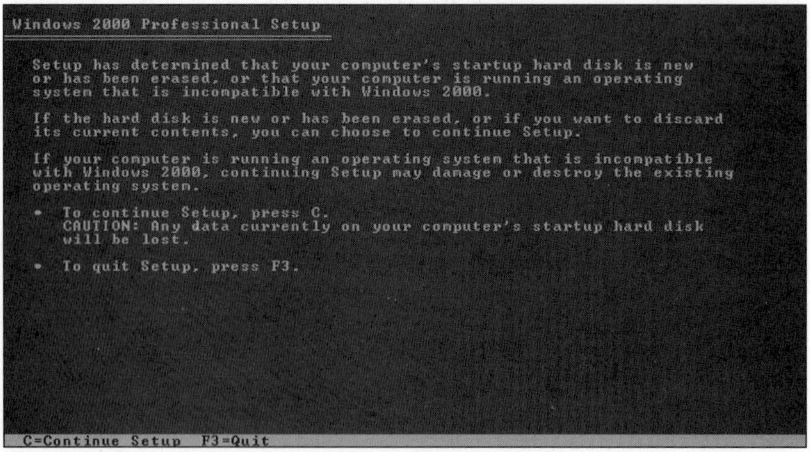

Figure 21-18: Partition warning in Windows 2000

When you continue with the setup program, you will be required to read over the license agreement and agree to its terms (as shown in Figure 21-19). To scroll through the agreement, press the Page Down button. When you are finished, press F8.

After you have agreed to the licensing terms, Windows 2000 shows you a screen where you choose the partition you wish to install the operating system to (as shown in Figure 21-20). If you want to change your partition information by creating and deleting partitions, you can do so by choosing "c" for create and "d" for delete.

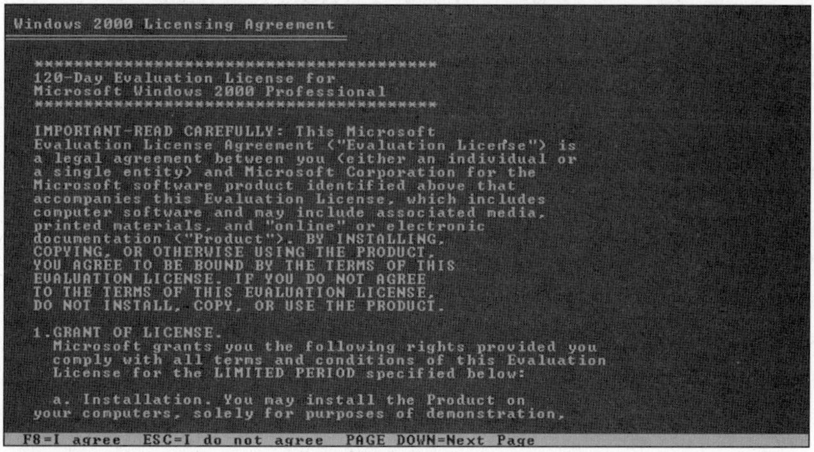

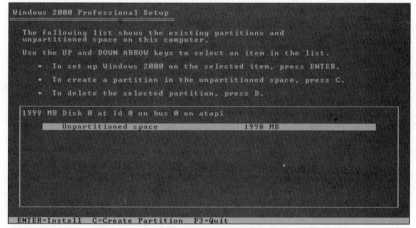

Figure 21-19: Agreeing to the terms of the license

Figure 21-20: Choosing a partition to install Windows 2000 to

Once you have chosen the partition that you want to install Windows 2000 onto, you will be asked what file system you want to use for that partition (as shown in Figure 21-21).

```
Windows 2000 Professional Setup

  The partition you selected is not formatted. Setup will now
  format the partition.

  Use the UP and DOWN ARROW keys to select the file system
  you want, and then press ENTER.

  If you want to select a different partition for Windows 2000,
  press ESC.

  Format the partition using the NTFS file system
  Format the partition using the FAT file system




  ENTER=Continue   ESC=Cancel
```

Figure 21-21: Choosing a file system during the Windows 2000 installation

Setup will then begin copying the files that are required for the installation to your hard disk. After the files are copied to your system, Windows 2000 will load the GUI phase of the installation where the rest of the setup will continue. During this time, the Windows 2000 setup program will be detecting the hardware that is installed on your system. This part of the installation may take anywhere from three to five minutes, depending on your system (as shown in Figure 21-22).

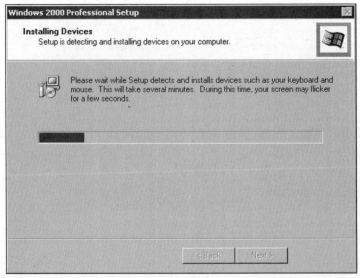

Figure 21-22: Windows 2000 setup detects your computer hardware

After Windows 2000 has detected the hardware in your system, it will then continue with the installation and ask for your local settings and your keyboard layout settings. If you would like to change these settings, you may click the Customize button (shown in Figure 21-23).

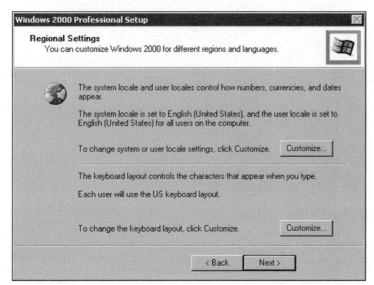

Figure 21-23: Selecting your locale and your keyboard layout

Once you have entered the keyboard layout and the locale that you will be using, setup will ask you to personalize your software. Specifically, it asks for your name and the organization name (as shown in Figure 21-24). It's probably a good idea to use a generic name, such as "IT Support," instead of your real name. Any new software that is installed will display this information.

Once you have entered your personal information, setup prompts you for the product key of the operating system. This product key can be found on the CD case of Windows 2000.

After you enter the product key, you will be required to enter a computer name and a password for the administrator account (as shown in Figure 21-25). The administrator account is an account that has full access to the system. You will want to make a password that is unique and difficult for someone to guess, which you can do by composing the password as a mixture of numbers and letters and also by including capitalized characters at different points in the password (passwords are case-sensitive). Note that you are not asked for the administrator's name. Each Windows NT and Windows 2000 installation has an administrative account that has full access to the system. When you install the operating system, that administrative account automatically has an account name of 'Administrator'. You are only responsible for assigning a password to that account during the installation of the operating system.

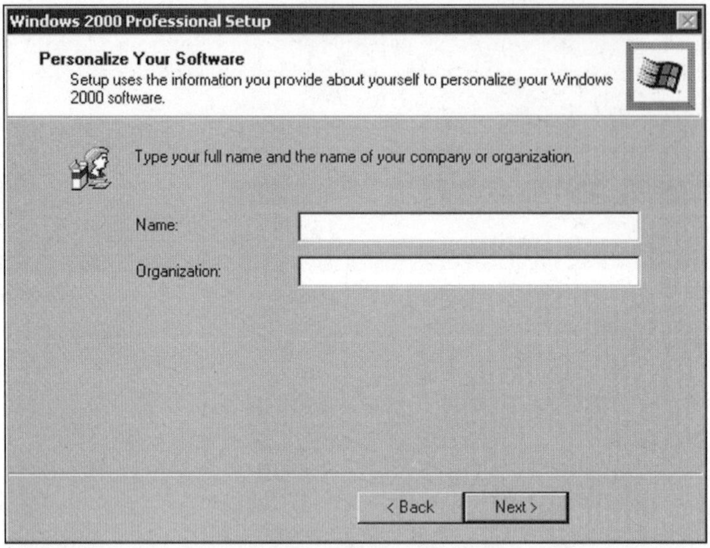

Figure 21-24: Entering personalized information during Windows installation

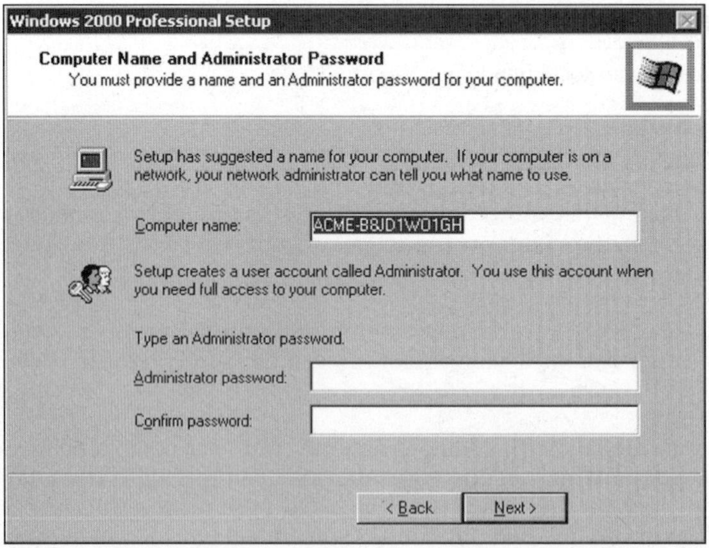

Figure 21-25: Assigning a computer name and administrator password

After the installation program asks for the name of the computer and the administrator password, it will ask you to verify the date and time. You may also choose whether you would like the operating system to adjust the time automatically to accommodate daylight savings (as shown in Figure 21-26). This is something that can be changed at any time through the Windows Control Panel.

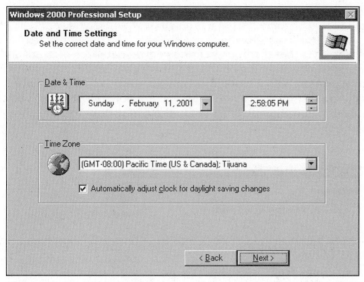

Figure 21-26: Selecting the date and time during the Windows 2000 installation

When you continue with the installation, the installation wizard informs you that it is configuring the networking components of the operating system. Setup then asks whether you would like to install typical network settings or if you would like to customize your network settings (as shown in Figure 21-27). If you choose "Typical Settings," setup will install Client for Microsoft Networks, File and Print Sharing for Microsoft Networks, and the TCP/IP protocol configured for DHCP.

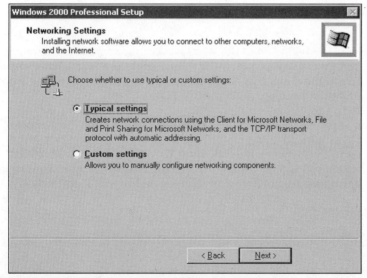

Figure 21-27: Choosing a network installation type

After you choose your network installation type, the installation wizard asks whether you would like to become part of a domain or whether you would like to be installed into a workgroup (as shown in Figure 21-28). The difference between a domain and a workgroup is that the domain has a central database of users and computers for people who wish to log on to the network and use certain network resources, such as a printer. With a workgroup environment, you do not have a server that has a central list of user accounts. If you are not sure whether you are in a domain environment, choose the first option in the dialog box. You can always join the domain later on.

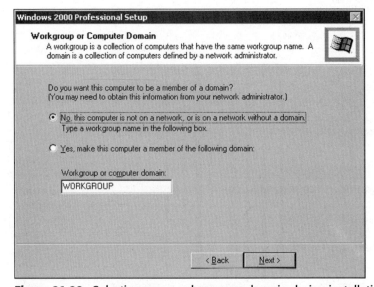

Figure 21-28: Selecting your workgroup or domain during installation

Windows continues by installing all of the Windows components that are required by the operating system for day-to-day use. It then sets up the Start menu, registers components on the machine, and finally cleans up any temporary files that were created by the installation program (as shown in Figure 21-29).

Once the finalizing stage has completed, you will have to click the Finish button on the wizard so that Windows 2000 will restart the computer. Upon restart, Windows 2000 will take you into the Network Identification Wizard, where you are to tell Windows 2000 whether you will be using the same username and password to log on each time so that Windows can automatically log on for you. If you would rather the system require you to log on manually each time, you may select that option as well (shown in Figure 21-30).

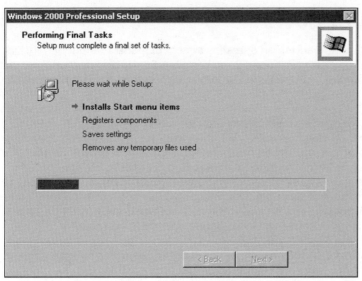

Figure 21-29: Finalizing the Windows 2000 installation

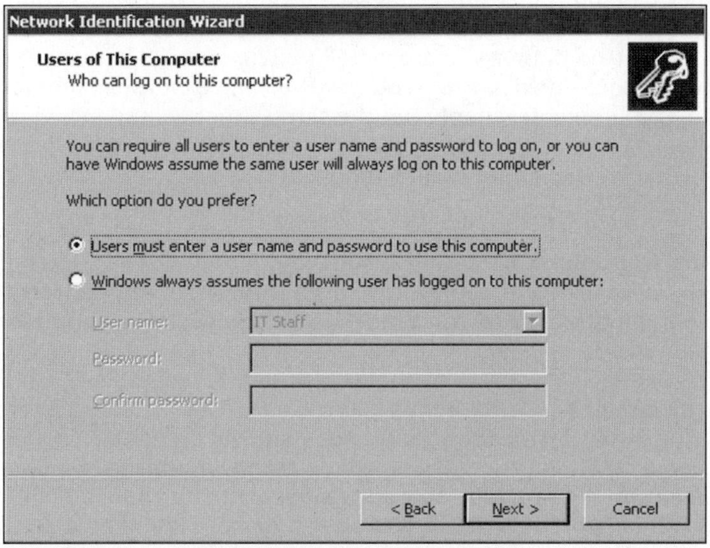

Figure 21-30: Configuring Windows 2000 logon

Once you have finished the Network Identification Wizard, the installation is complete and you may need to log on to the computer if you have chosen the option that states everyone must provide a username and password. Congratulations! You have completed the installation of Windows 2000.

Upgrading Windows

 2.2 Identify steps to perform an operating system upgrade. Content may include the following: Upgrading Windows 95 to Windows 98; Upgrading from Windows NT Workstation 4.0 to Windows 2000; Replacing Windows 9x with Windows 2000

Many of today's businesses run a Windows operating system, so it is important to understand how to upgrade from a previous operating system (such as 9x) to a current operating system (such as 2000). Whether you are installing the operating system from scratch or performing an upgrade, the installation process is pretty much the same. Although with an upgrade, you may find that there are fewer steps because many decisions have already been made from the installation of the previous operating system. For example, when you upgrade a Windows NT 4.0 computer to Windows 2000, you will not be asked the name of the computer to be installed — this information is inherited from the previous operating system.

This section will provide an overview of upgrades to the different major operating systems and the different types of upgrades that are possible.

Windows 95 to Windows 98

One very important question is: "How do I upgrade from my Windows 95 computer to a Windows 98 computer while maintaining all of the applications I currently use?" First, verify that the computer you are installing Windows 98 onto meets the Windows 98 hardware requirements. After you have verified that the computer meets the hardware requirements, simply run the setup program and install the new operating system. When you install Windows 98 into Windows 95's directory (usually c:\windows) all of the Windows and application settings are carried from Windows 95 to Windows 98.

When you install the Windows 9x operating system into a previous Windows directory, it will carry all of the user and application settings forward. This is true if you wish to upgrade from Windows 3.1 to Windows 95, or if you wish to upgrade from Windows 95 to Windows 98.

When you run the installation of Windows 98 and choose to install into the previous operating system's directory (typically c:\windows) you will be performing an upgrade. During the installation process, you will be asked whether you wish to save the system files from the previous operating system. If you choose yes to this question, two files will be stored on the root of your C drive: winundo.dat and winundo.ini. The winundo.dat file contains all of the system files that have been modified during the upgrade. The winundo.ini file is a listing of each of the files contained in the winundo.dat and a pointer to where they belong if you restore the system back to its previous operating system.

By saving the previous operating system files, you will then be able to uninstall the current operating system through the Add/Remove Programs icon in Control Panel. For example, if you have upgraded Windows 95 to Windows 98 and saved the system files, then in the Control Panel of the Windows 98 computer will be an option to uninstall Windows 98 on the Add/Remove Programs icon in Control Panel.

Tip You can also uninstall the operating system if you have saved the system files by booting off the Windows 9x startup disk and running uninstal.exe.

If you have not saved the system files, or have deleted the winundo.dat and winundo.ini files, you will not be able to uninstall the operating system through Add/Remove Programs. If you have not saved the system files from the previous operating system, the only way to remove the operating system would be to sys the drive that hosts the operating system, remove the Windows directory and reinstall the previous operating system. By performing this process, you are not technically performing an uninstall because you have lost all the previous operating system settings, which is the goal of being able to uninstall an operating system.

Windows NT to Windows 2000

Windows NT 4.0 cannot be upgraded from a previous operating system. If you are running Windows 3.1, Windows 95, or Windows 98 you will have to install Windows NT 4.0 into its own directory (usually c:\winnt) and then remove the previous operating system if you want.

Keep in mind that if you are installing Windows NT 4.0 on Windows 95 OSR2 or Windows 98, those operating systems may be using the FAT32 operating system. Windows NT 4.0 does not recognize the FAT32 file system — it only understands FAT and NTFS. So if your C drive is using FAT32, you will be unable to run Windows NT 4.0.

Tip There is no upgrade path from Windows 9x to Windows NT 4.0.

Windows 2000, on the other hand, enables you to upgrade from a previous operating system such as Windows 95 or Windows 98. You can also upgrade your Windows NT 4.0 machine to Windows 2000. Table 21-7 lists the upgrade paths for the different Windows operating systems.

Table 21-7
Client Upgrade Paths to Windows 2000

Current Operating System	Upgrade To. . . .	Then To. . . .
Windows 3.1	Windows 95/98	Windows 2000 Professional
Windows 95	Windows 2000 Professional	
Windows 98	Windows 2000 Professional	
Windows NT Workstation 4.0	Windows 2000 Professional	

Caution It is important to perform a backup of the system and important data before any major upgrade to the operating system.

You can see that if you are upgrading from Windows 9x or Windows NT 4.0 Workstation, you can upgrade directly to Windows 2000 Professional. But if you are looking to upgrade a Windows 3.1 computer, you can only upgrade to Windows 2000 Professional if you first upgrade to Windows 95 or Windows 98.

Tip To find out whether there's any incompatible software or hardware before upgrading to Windows 2000, you can run the setup in the check upgrade mode by typing `winnt/checkupgradeonly`.

When you are upgrading from Windows NT 4.0 to Windows 2000, you are not likely to run into any major upgrade issues because the structure of the operating systems is very similar. The similarities between Windows NT 4.0 and Windows 2000 include the following:

✦ Registry structure

✦ File systems

✦ Security

To perform an upgrade from Windows NT 4.0 to Windows 2000, you will run the winnt32.exe program. Winnt32.exe is the upgrade program designed to run from a 32-bit operating system for the purpose of upgrading to Windows 2000. When you run winnt32, many of the operating system's settings are carried into the installation program from Windows NT 4.0 — this means that you will have fewer questions to answer during the installation.

Be sure to review the hardware requirements of Windows 2000 before you perform the upgrade and make sure to set up a test environment where all applications and existing hardware have been thoroughly tested.

Dual Booting Windows Operating Systems

 2.2 Identify steps to perform an operating system upgrade. Content may include the following: Dual boot Windows 9x/Windows NT 4.0/Windows 2000

Dual booting is the concept of running multiple operating systems on the same computer. Dual booting is the exact opposite of performing an upgrade. With an upgrade, all of your applications and their settings carry forward into the new operating system. When you dual boot, you are installing each operating system into a different directory, which means that the applications will not carry forward into your new operating system.

One of the reasons you may want to dual boot multiple operating systems is to test or support applications in the different operating systems. You may also want to dual boot if your company is running an application that will not function on your primary operating system (for example, Windows 2000), but works great in an older operating system (for example, Windows 98). You could install both operating systems on the computer and then install your application that does not work in Windows 2000 on Windows 98; any time you wish to use that application, you will need to boot to Windows 98.

In order to dual boot multiple operating systems, the following criteria must be met:

✦ The bootable drive (usually drive C) must have a file system supported by all operating systems.

✦ You must install each operating system into its own folder.

If you would like to dual boot Windows 98, Windows NT, and Windows 2000 all on the same computer, the first thing you will need to do is make sure that your bootable partition (drive C) is using the file system common to all operating systems (in this example, FAT16). Once you have ensured that you are using a common file system, you may then install each operating system. Remember that you will install each operating system into a different directory. For this example, assume you have installed Windows 98 in c:\windows, and have installed Windows NT 4.0 into c:\winnt.

You now have a system that dual boots between Windows 98 and Windows NT 4.0. So how do you choose which operating system you wish to boot to? Windows NT has a boot menu that will display the different operating systems; when it appears, you select one of the operating systems.

Now that you have Windows 98 and Windows NT functioning on the same system, you can dual boot these operating systems with Windows 2000 by installing Windows 2000 into its own directory (say, c:\win2000). Now you have a system that can boot between three different operating systems (Windows 98, Windows NT 4.0, and Windows 2000). To accomplish this, all you needed to do was install each operating system into its own directory.

Note   In dual boot scenarios, it is important to note that any applications that are installed in one operating system must be reinstalled into any additional operating systems.

Key Point Summary

This chapter has introduced you to some of the setup guidelines for installing the different Windows operating system. Some of the key points to remember are:

✦ Install Windows 95 and Windows 98 by using setup.exe.

✦ Install Windows NT 4.0 and Windows 2000 by using winnt.exe or winnt32.exe.

✦ Remember that only Windows NT 4.0 and Windows 2000 understand the NTFS file system, and that Windows 95 OSR2, Windows 98, and Windows 2000 understand FAT32.

✦ A Windows 98 startup disk has a generic CD-ROM driver that will be loaded if you boot off the startup disk, whereas a Windows 95 startup disk requires you to add your own CD-ROM driver.

✦ You can boot off the Windows NT/Windows 2000 startup disks (or CD-ROM), which invoke an installation and continue it from the CD-ROM automatically.

✦ When you upgrade Windows 95 to Windows 98, if you save system files you will be able to uninstall the Windows 98 operating system through Add/ Remove Programs in Control Panel. This will return your operating system to its previous state (Windows 95).

✦ To dual boot multiple operating systems, you will need to ensure that the file system on drive C is understood by each operating system, and then install each operating system into a different directory.

✦   ✦   ✦

STUDY GUIDE

This Study Guide presents 20 assessment questions, 1 scenario, and 3 labs to test your knowledge of the exam topic area.

Assessment Questions

1. What command starts a Windows NT 4.0 installation?

   A. Server.exe

   B. Winnt.exe

   C. Workstation.exe

   D. Setup.exe

2. What command, found on the Windows 95 startup disk, will uninstall the operating system?

   A. Uninstall.exe

   B. Setup.exe /u

   C. Uninstal.exe

   D. Install.exe /u

3. What is the setup switch that tells Windows 9x to run scandisk in the foreground?

   A. /IS

   B. /ID

   C. /HI

   D. /IH

4. What is the setup switch that provides the Windows NT installation an answer file?

   A. /U: <file>

   B. /UDF:<file>

   C. /UDF:number,<file>

   D. /A:<file>

5. What are the minimum processor requirements for Windows 95?

    A. 486SX

    B. 386DX

    C. 486DX

    D. Pentium

6. What type of setup would you use to install Windows 95 on a laptop?

    A. Typical

    B. Custom

    C. Portable

    D. Minimum

7. What are the minimum RAM requirements for Windows 98?

    A. 8MB

    B. 4MB

    C. 12MB

    D. 16MB

8. You are going to a customer's site to install Windows NT Server. You would like to install the server without having to dig up CD-ROM drivers for your customer's machine. What can you do before you go to the customer's site?

    A. Run winnt.exe /b

    B. Run setup.exe /ox

    C. Run winnt.exe /ox

    D. Run setup.exe /b

9. Where can you create a Windows 98 startup disk?

    A. Add/Remove programs in Control Panel

    B. Run makeboot.exe off the Windows 98 CD

    C. Run makeboot.exe from the Windows folder

    D. Run makedisk.exe off the Windows 98 CD

10. What are the minimum RAM requirements for Windows NT Workstation?

    A. 32MB

    B. 8MB

    C. 12MB

    D. 16MB

11. Which of the following files does the setup program in Windows 9x create on the root of Drive C?

    A. logsetup.txt

    B. setuplog.txt

    C. setup.txt

    D. autoexec.bat

12. What would be the second step in an operating system installation?

    A. To create a primary partition

    B. To create logical drives

    C. To format partitions

    D. To create an extended partition

13. Which file is used to log all of the devices that have been detected during a Windows 9x installation?

    A. detect.log

    B. logdetection.txt

    C. devices.log

    D. detlog.txt

14. What are the minimum RAM requirements for a Windows NT Server?

    A. 12MB

    B. 32MB

    C. 16MB

    D. 64MB

15. What type of partition should be flagged as being active?

    A. Primary

    B. Logical drives

    C. Extended

    D. The second partition

16. What does it mean when you boot off your Windows 98 startup disk and choose to enable large disk support?

    A. Any partitions you create will use FAT32 as the file system

    B. Partitions that are currently FAT will get converted to FAT32

    C. Any partitions created over 512MB will use FAT32 as the file system

    D. Any partitions that are created will use NTFS

17. What switch tells setup not to run a scandisk prior to installing Windows 9x?

    A. /IS

    B. /IH

    C. /ID

    D. /IW

18. Which of the following would be your first step in installing an operating system?

    A. Create a primary partition

    B. Create logical drives

    C. Format partitions

    D. Create an extended partition

19. What command installs Windows NT 4.0 on a previous version of Windows NT?

    A. winnt.exe

    B. winnt32.exe

    C. winnt.exe /p

    D. winnt32.exe /p

20. If you want to upgrade a Windows 3.1 machine to Windows 2000, what should you do first?

    A. Format the drive

    B. Delete partitions and re-create them

    C. Uninstall Windows 3.1 and install Windows 9x

    D. Upgrade Windows 3.1 to Windows 9x

Scenario

This chapter has presented a number of issues dealing with the installation of different Windows operating systems. The following scenario will test your ability to apply what you have learned in this area.

1. A customer wants you to upgrade their current operating systems to Windows 2000. They currently have ten Windows 3.1 systems and twenty Windows 95 systems. What are some of the issues surrounding the upgrade to Windows 2000 Professional?

Lab Exercises

Lab 21.1 Installing Windows 95

1. Use the information provided in the following table to install the Windows 95 operating system; accept any other defaults.

Directory	C:\windows
Type of Installation	Typical
Computer Name	Install 1
Workgroup	Aplus

2. If at all possible after the installation of Windows 95, install some applications, such as the Microsoft Office Suite or the Lotus Suite. This will allow you to verify whether the upgrade worked correctly.

Lab 21.2 Installing Windows 98

1. Upgrade Windows 95 to Windows 98 by running the Windows 98 setup from within Windows 95. Install the new operating system into the c:\windows folder (which will result in an upgrade). When asked to save system configuration, choose Yes.

2. After the upgrade to Windows 98, verify that the applications you installed in Lab 21.1 still work from within the Start menu.

Lab 21.3 Uninstalling Windows 98

1. Uninstall Windows 98 from within the Add/Remove Programs icon in Control Panel.

2. After Windows 98 has been uninstalled, verify that the applications you installed in Lab 21.1 still work.

Answers to Chapter Questions

Chapter Pre-Test

1. The setup switch used to run scandisk in the foreground in Windows 9x is **/IH**.

2. If the user has saved the system configuration information during the installation of Windows 98 and they wish to uninstall the operating system, they can do so **by going to Add/Remove Programs in Control Panel.**

3. A Windows 95 installation requires **4MB** of RAM.

4. You would run a **compact** setup of Windows 95 on a system with limited RAM.

5. The command to create the three Windows setup boot disks in Windows NT 4.0 is **winnt.exe /OX.**

6. You can use the **winnt.exe /u:acme.txt** to install Windows NT 4.0 using an unattend answer file named acme.txt.

7. You can upgrade a Windows NT Workstation to a **Windows 2000 Professional** computer.

8. The minimum RAM requirements for Windows NT Workstation is **12MB.**

9. The four setup boot disks for Windows 2000 can be created **by going to the Windows 2000 CD and running the makeboot.exe.**

10. Windows creates a file called **detcrash.log,** which it uses to determine the steps that has caused it to crash.

Assessment Questions

1. **B.** The command to start a Windows NT installation is winnt.exe. For more information, see the section labeled "Running the Setup Program."

2. **C.** To uninstall the Windows 9x operating system, you would run uninstal.exe off the startup disk—assuming that the system configuration from the previous operating system was saved. For more information, see the section labeled "Upgrading Windows."

3. D. To tell Windows 9x to run scandisk in the foreground, you will run setup with a /IH. For more information, see the section labeled "Running the Setup Program."

4. A. To provide Windows NT with an answer file, you will run the Windows NT installation program with a /U: and then the file that has the answers to use for the installation. For more information, see the section labeled "Running the Setup Program."

5. B. The minimum processor requirement to install Windows 95 is a 386DX processor, which is a 32-bit processor. For more information, see the section labeled "Preparing for Installation."

6. C. To install Windows on a laptop, you will run a portable setup that will install features used by mobile users, such as direct cable connect and dial-up networking. For more information, see the section labeled "Running the Setup Program."

7. D. The minimum RAM requirements for Windows 98 are 16MB of memory. Windows 95 is 4MB of RAM and Windows NT Workstation is 12MB of RAM. For more information, see the section labeled "Preparing for Installation."

8. C. To create the Windows NT setup boot disks that have a generic driver that will get loaded, you would run the winnt.exe program with an /OX. Using the /B switch will do an installation that will not use these diskettes. For more information, see the section labeled "Running the Setup Program."

9. A. You would create a Windows 95 or Windows 98 startup boot disk through the Add/Remove Programs icon in Control Panel. Use makeboot.exe to create the setup boot disk for Windows 2000. For more information, see the section labeled "Booting for Installation."

10. C. The minimum RAM requirement for Windows NT Workstation is 12MB of RAM. Windows 95 requires 4MB of RAM and Windows 98 requires 16MB of memory. For more information, see the section labeled "Preparing for Installation."

11. B. One of the files that the Windows 9x setup program creates on the root of the C: drive is setuplog.txt, which is a recording of everything that happens during the Windows installation. For more information, see the section labeled "Running the Setup Program."

12. D. The first step in an operating system installation is to create a primary partition. The second step is to create the extended partition. The third step is to create logical drives within the extended partition, and finally, the fourth step is to format the partitions. For more information, see the section labeled "Understanding Partition Issues."

13. D. The detlog.txt file that is created during the installation of the Windows 9x operating system lists all of the devices that have been detected during the installation process. For more information, see the section labeled "Running the Setup Program."

14. C. The minimum RAM requirement for Windows NT Server is 16MB of RAM, whereas the minimum RAM requirement for Windows NT Workstation is 12MB of RAM. For more information, see the section labeled "Preparing for Installation."

15. A. The primary partition is the partition that is flagged as being active. Setting a partition as being active makes that partition the partition that will be booted from. For more information, see the section labeled "Understanding Partition Issues."

16. C. When you boot off the Windows 98 startup disk, you are asked if you want to enable large disk support. This means any partitions created in that fdisk session over 512MB will be FAT32. Any partitions created in that session under 512MB will use the FAT file system. For more information, see the section labeled "Understanding Partition Issues."

17. A. When installing Windows 9x, run the /IS switch with setup.exe to tell it not to run a scandisk prior to the installation. For more information, see the section labeled "Running the Setup Program."

18. A. Of the steps that were listed, defining a primary partition should be the first action you take. Then you would build an extended partition and create the logical drives. Finally you would format the partitions. For more information, see the section labeled "Understanding Partition Issues."

19. B. If you are upgrading a previous version of Windows NT, you will run the 32-bit version of the Windows NT 4.0 setup program, winnt32.exe. For more information, see the section labeled "Running the Setup Program."

20. D. If you want to upgrade Windows 3.1 machines to Windows 2000, you have to upgrade the operating system to either Windows 95 or Windows 98 first, and then upgrade to Windows 2000. For more information, see the section labeled "Upgrading Windows."

Scenario

1. One issue regarding this upgrade is that Windows 3.1 computers need to be upgraded to Windows 95 or Windows 98 before they can be upgraded to Windows 2000.

You will also need to evaluate the hardware on all desktop computers to verify that they meet the hardware requirements of Windows 2000. Test all applications used by the employees to ensure that they function with Windows 2000 (before you roll it out).

Boot Sequences and Methods

EXAM OBJECTIVES

Exam 220-202 ✦ A+ OS Technologies

✦ **2.3** Identify the basic system boot sequences and boot methods, including the steps to create an emergency boot disk with utilities installed for Windows 9x, Windows NT, and Windows 2000. Content may include the following:

- Startup Disk
- Safe Mode
- MS-DOS mode
- ntldr (NT Loader), boot.ini
- Files required to boot
- Creating an emergency repair disk (ERD)

CHAPTER PRE-TEST

1. What file systems does Windows 2000 support?

2. What file is the boot loader for the Windows 9x OS?

3. What key is used to access the boot menu on Windows 95 computers?

4. What files are required to initiate the boot process for Windows 2000?

5. In your `boot.ini` file, each line of the [operating systems] section begins with `SIGNATURE(87AB45FF)`. Is this format a potential problem, and what are the other words that the [operating systems] section could start with?

6. How can you launch the Recovery Console?

7. What major change in the structure of Startup Disks allows Windows 98 versions to hold more files than the Windows 95 versions?

8. What files make up the core of the Windows 9x operating system?

9. In Windows 2000, do devices or services load first?

10. How do you create installation disks for Windows 2000?

✦ Answers to these questions can be found at the end of the chapter. ✦

The process of starting a computer has long been referred to as booting. Before you can use your computer, you need to be able to boot it to a point where the operating system is functional. Otherwise, your computer is like a safe without a known combination. This chapter will help you get that "safe" open by examining the boot process.

The boot process encompasses a series of steps, from the application of power to the loading of the OS shell. This section will review the hardware POST (Power On Self Test) process and will concentrate on the OS portion of the overall process. You will learn the major differences between the Windows 9x boot process and the Windows NT/2000 boot process. There are many differences between Windows 9x and Windows 2000 and the boot process is where the differences begin.

The MS-DOS boot process is very similar to the Windows 9x process, but very different from the Windows 2000 process. If you are unfamiliar with boot processes in general, focus on the entire chapter.

Standard Boot Process for Windows 95/98

2.3 Identify the basic system boot sequences and boot methods, including the steps to create an emergency boot disk with utilities installed for Windows 9x, Windows NT, and Windows 2000. Content may include the following: Files required to boot

This section will cover the boot process for Windows 9x, which has not changed much since the days of MS-DOS and Windows 3.11. It will discuss the differences in the process for Windows 95 and Windows 98, starting with the POST and continuing through to the loading of Windows 9x.

POST process

The POST process starts when power is applied to the system. Current makes its way from the power lead on the motherboard to the ROM-BIOS chips. When current is received by the BIOS chips, they immediately begin executing their programs. One of the first checks is the memory (both a count and integrity test). After the memory check, the POST process moves on to find out what ports or I/O devices exist on the system. If the system is equipped with a PNP-BIOS, as most new systems are, then the BIOS level PNP configuration takes place. The next thing that happens is a search for bootable disk devices. The order of this search is defined by the settings stored in CMOS memory, but is often: a: (floppy drive), c: (first partition on the first bootable hard drive), CD-ROM.

For each device in the list of potential bootable devices, the partition table is checked for the active partition. Floppy disks and the CD-ROM will only check the first partition. For this partition, the first sector is read and checked for a boot loader. The Windows 9x boot loader is io.sys. When this file is located, it is executed. If it was not found on the first potential bootable device, then the second and third devices are checked before reporting a boot failure.

io.sys

io.sys executes and proceeds to display the opening Windows splash screen, and launches the real-mode operating system components of Windows 9x. The Windows splash screen is the graphic with the cloud background and the animated band at the bottom of the screen that is displayed at the start of the boot processes. Real-mode is one of the operating modes of Windows 9x. It is used to process the initial boot of Windows 9x, to process boot files such as autoexec.bat, and to call win.com. When in real-mode, the memory structures and restrictions that apply to MS-DOS apply to Windows 9x.

When loading the logo for display, Windows 9x first checks to see if a file (c:\logo.sys) exists. If it does exist, it displays the file; if it does not exist, then it uses a copy of the file that is embedded in io.sys.

Tip

If you do not like your startup splash screen, you can make your own by working with a bitmapped graphic that is 320 × 400 pixels in size, with 256 colors. Just save the graphic as c:\logo.sys.

You can also create or modify c:\windows\logow.sys ("Windows is shutting down.") and c:\windows\logos.sys ("It is now safe to turn off your computer.") Both of these files have the same dimensions as logo.sys.

io.sys reads MS-DOS environment settings from msdos.sys and then config.sys before moving onto loading and passing control to command.com. command.com then calls on autoexec.bat and processes all of the commands in the batch file. At the end of processing config.sys (or if it does not exist), Windows 9x will enforce certain settings that are deemed necessary to Windows 9x. If autoexec.bat does not exist, there are also certain elements that will be processed and enforced. The following section will describe msdos.sys, config.sys, and autoexec.bat in more detail. All of these files exist on the root of your bootable drive, usually C:.

msdos.sys

The msdos.sys file is used to create the initial real-mode environment for Windows 9x. In MS-DOS 6.x and earlier, this file was a binary file, but in Windows 9x, this file is an ASCII file. If you open it with any text editor (such as Notepad), you will be able to see the current settings. You will also see a message stating that you should not delete the rows of x's. Some anti-virus and other programs check the size of msdos.sys to ensure that it has not been tampered with. Oddly enough, these programs are really only testing for a minimum file size of 1,024 bytes. There are many settings that can be changed by editing the values found in this file.

The msdos.sys file has two major sections and resembles an ini file. The two sections are [Paths] and [Options]. The Paths section contains information about where Windows 9x is installed (Table 22-1 lists these settings).

Table 22-1
Paths for msdos.sys

Value	Description
WinDir	The Windows directory where most of the operating system files are run from.
WinBootDir	Usually the same location as WinDir. This option individually denotes the location of specific startup files. If WinDir is located on a drive other than C:, then WinBootDir may point to a location on the C: drive.
HostWinBootDrv	The drive letter associated with the WinBootDir.
UninstallDir	The location of the files that should be replaced in the event of an uninstall of Windows 95. The files are stored in w95undo.dat and the original location information is stored in w95undo.ini.

The Options section contains options about the boot process (Table 22-2 lists these settings).

Table 22-2
Options for msdos.sys

Option	Description
AutoScan	Windows 95–OSR2 and Windows 98 support the automatic running of Scandisk. If this is set to 0, then Scandisk is disabled. A setting of 1 prompts the user to scan the system after an improper shutdown, while a setting of 2 will scan automatically.
BootDelay	This sets the length of time (in seconds) that you have to press one of the boot keys when you see the text "Starting Windows 95. . . " at boot.

Continued

Table 22-2 *(continued)*

Option	Description
BootSafe	A setting of 1 forces a safe mode boot of Windows 9x.
BootGUI	A setting of 0 will cause the boot process to stop after processing `autoexec.bat`. You will be able to launch Windows 9x by typing `WIN`. This is useful during troubleshooting the boot process.
BootKeys	Enables (1) or disables (0) the ability to press the boot keys during boot. The boot keys include F8, F5, F6, and the Ctrl key.
BootMenu	Automatically displays the Windows 9x boot menu if set to 1.
BootMenuDefault	Automatically pre-selects a choice in the boot menu.
BootMenuDelay	Sets the timeout value for the boot menu.
BootMulti	Enables the option in the boot to the previous version of MS-DOS when set to 1. This option should not be enabled on OEM versions of Windows 9x.
BootWarn	Enables the Safe-Mode warning message when set to 1.
BootWin	`BootWin = 0`, will cause the system to automatically boot to the previous version of MS-DOS. This option should not be enabled on OEM versions of Windows 9x.
DoubleBuffer	Enables the double-buffering driver for SCSI controllers when set to 1.
DBLSpace	Loads the Double Space driver (`dblspace.bin`) if it exists on the root of your drive, when this is set to 1.
DRVSpace	Loads the Drive Space driver (`drvspace.bin`) if it exists on the root of your drive, when this is set to 1.
LoadTop	By default, Windows 9x will load `command.com` and `drvspace.bin` to the top of the 640K memory range. A value of 0 causes these files to load at the bottom of the range. Some applications, such as the Novell Netware client, require that `command.com` be loaded low.
Logo	A value of 0 will disable the animated logo. The animated logo can cause problems with some TSR (Terminate Stay Resident) programs or memory managers.
Network	A value of 1 will load network support when entering Safe Mode.

In the Options section, `BootWin=1` and `AutoScan=1` are standard options. Other options may be necessary to enable certain features or boot methods.

config.sys

The config.sys file has been around since early versions of MS-DOS. It stores modifications to the default environment that is created through msdos.sys. If the file does not exist, then Windows 9x will apply some default settings to the environment for itself. If the config.sys file does exist, then Windows 9x ensures that the settings at least meet the default settings. If config.sys does not meet the default settings, then Windows 9x will apply the default settings. Your settings may have been changed from the default settings in order to support an application; the files value is often increased for application support. The default entries that will be enforced are found in Table 22-3. config.sys usually contains environment settings and device drivers load lines.

Table 22-3
Default config.sys Values

Entry	Description
buffers=23	Buffers are used when some older MS-DOS–based applications attempt to make file I/O calls. They are not used by Windows 9x or its applications.
dos=High, Auto	Loads some of the command.com and msdos.sys files into the High Memory Area.
files=30	Like buffers, this setting is only used by older applications. files sets the number of files that the application or command.com environment can have open simultaneously.
himem.sys	High Memory Manager. This file gives Windows 9x access to memory above 1MB. In a round about way, it also includes all memory above 640K.
ifshlp.sys	Installable File System Driver Helper. This driver is required to allow access to both network file systems and VFAT (the local file system).
Lastdrive=Z	This gives access to drive letters up to Z:. It is only required for older applications.
settver.exe	Emulates different versions of MS-DOS for compatibility with some applications.
shell=command.com /p	Sets the command shell to be permanent.
stacks=9,256	Like buffers, this is used for compatibility with some older MS-DOS–based applications.

command.com

command.com is the command interpreter for Windows 9x. The job of the command interpreter is to execute non-graphical applications for Windows 9x. It is located in several places on your hard drive: C:\command.com and C:\windows\command.com, and possibly either C:\windows\command\command.com or C:\windows\command\ebd\command.com. These additional files provide a small amount of fault tolerance to this file. Windows 9x usually uses the copy located in the Windows folder rather than the copy located on the root of the C: drive. The copy on the root of the drive is only used during the first stage of the boot process.

autoexec.bat

After command.com loads and initializes, it has been configured to look for and process autoexec.bat. autoexec.bat is a batch file. Batch files simply store a list of commands that are executed in order, and autoexec.bat is configured to be executed at boot.

autoexec.bat is used to set environment variables, such as the location of the temporary directory and the search path. Windows 9x will enforce certain variables and settings prior to executing autoexec.bat, which allows you to change, append, or replace any of these values. The default values for autoexec.bat are listed in Table 22-4. Since the temporary directory is set to the Windows directory, many people change at least this one path to point to a different location. If you want to add to the default system path, you can do so with a statement such as:

```
SET PATH = %PATH%;C:\MYAPPS;
```

This will add to the existing path (%path%), rather than overwrite it.

If win.com is not called during autoexec.bat, then command.com will process the call to win.com.

Table 22-4 Default autoexec.bat Values	
Variable	**Value**
Tmp	C:\windows
Temp	C:\windows
Path	C:\windows;C:\windows\command
Prompt	pg
Comspec	C:\windows\command.com

win.com and vmm32

win.com can be called through autoexec.bat or from the command line. When called this way, you will be able to pass switches to win.com in order to disable certain features. Table 22-5 summarizes these switches. win.com immediately turns control over to vmm32 (Virtual Memory Manager), which proceeds to load the Windows 9x Graphical User Interface (gui). vmm32 scans the system Registry and attempts to load any devices that are listed in there.

During setup, all required drivers are merged into a single file named vmm32.vxd. If additional drivers are required or loaded after setup, then they are stored in the C:\windows\system\vmm32 directory. If setup is re-executed later, then these files are merged into vmm32.vxd. Due to this handling of vmm32.vxd, it is a file that is specific to each workstation.

vmm32 then attempts to load any devices that are listed in the [386enh] section of system.ini. Once all of the hardware devices have been identified, vmm32 places the processor into Protected Mode and loads the OS Kernel (krnl386.exe and kernel32.dll), followed by gdi.exe, gdi32.dll, user.exe, and user32.dll. Then system resources and fonts are initialized. The last step is to check the win.ini file to see if there are any additional settings that should be enforced on the system, and what the shell application is supposed to be. Table 22-5 examines each of these components.

Table 22-5
Components Used When Loading Windows 9x

Component	Description
Registry	A registry is a place to record information. For example, at a university you can find out what students are attending which classes by consulting the Registrar's Office. The same is true with Windows 9x and Windows 2000. The Registry is used to store information that is used by other components on the system. In Windows 9x, the Registry is composed of two OS files: user.dat and system.dat. It is used by vmm32 to identify devices that are supposed to be loaded or initialized on the system. Settings for each device are also located in the Registry. Great care must be taken when editing the Registry
system.ini	system.ini contains loading information for all real-mode devices. In most cases, you will find that this includes your mouse and video drivers.
kernel32.dll	kernel32.dll is the core set of code that makes up the Windows 9x operating system. It takes over from vmm32 for managing the system. It schedules and manages all other processes or applications that are running on the system.

Continued

Table 22-5 *(continued)*

Option	Description
krnl386.exe	This component exists on the system for backwards compatibility with older Windows 3.x programs that want to pass calls to krnl386.exe. Any calls that are passed to krnl386.exe are redirected to kernel32.dll.
gdi.exe	This is the 16-bit component that is responsible for handling the Graphic Device Interface. If there are graphics (such as windows) that must be presented on the screen or on a printer, then this is the component that is responsible for it.
gdi32.dll	This is the 32-bit version of gdi.exe. Functionality is not duplicated in these two GDI components; rather, some features are implemented in one or the other. Both components accept all of the component calls, but may pass the request to the other component. A program is able to call on a component using a 32-bit GDI call. If that feature is actually in gdi.exe, then gdi32.dll will pass the call to gdi.exe and process the response. This allows a programmer to program to one interface, regardless of where Microsoft actually stored the components.
user.exe	This is the 16-bit component that is responsible for user input. Most of the functionality of the user interface components are located in user.exe.
user32.dll	This is the 32-bit version of user.exe. Since most of the functionality has been implemented in user.exe, user32.dll passes most of its calls over to user.exe.
Resources and fonts	System resources are reserved for most of the main system components. Fonts actually make up an integral part of the OS, so they are assigned system resources at this point, along with some other components.
win.ini values	win.ini stores information on a number of shell-related settings. Some shell settings are stored in the Registry, but for compatibility with older applications, some of these settings are also found in win.ini.

Cross-Reference For information on editing the Registry, see the regedit.exe section in Chapter 27.

Loading the shell

After the processing of all the device drivers, the user's shell loads. The application that makes up the shell is actually defined by a shell = line in system.ini, the default being explorer.exe. If the current shell ever crashes and is removed from RAM, then explorer.exe will be loaded. Explorer checks the Registry to see what desktop components are supposed to be displayed and then checks the RUN SERVICES key in the Registry to auto-start other applications. One of the services that is started up at this point is the network service. When the network service is started up, you will be presented with a logon screen.

After loading the requested services, Explorer then executes any entries that it finds in the Registry in the RUN ONCE key. Each entry under RUN ONCE is executed sequentially, waiting for each to finish before moving on to the next. When these are completed, Explorer then moves onto the run and load entries in win.ini to launch additional applications, followed by the run entries in the Registry, and finally the Startup group from the Start menu.

This process is almost identical for all versions of Windows 9x. Some versions may differ slightly, whereas the Windows NT and Windows 2000 boot processes are very different.

Standard Boot Process for Windows NT/2000

Windows NT and Windows 2000 have their roots in IBM's OS/2. It is partly due to this history that their boot processes are very different from Windows 9x. Unlike Windows 9x, there is no real-mode boot component to the OS; Windows 2000 is a pure 32-bit OS. Similar to the Windows 9x boot process, the first components are the same, up until the boot sector of the bootable disk is read.

The boot sector is created when the disk is formatted, and it contains a small program that has a mini file-system driver to read FAT, FAT32, and NTFS partitions. This program then looks for the real boot loader. In this case, the boot loader is ntldr.

Exam Tip   Due to ARC naming conventions, Microsoft refers to the drive that has the boot sector on it as the System Partition, and to the partition that has the winnt directory on it as the Boot Partition. To help keep these terms straight for the exam, remember that the OS does not really boot until ntoskrnl.exe is launched from the winnt directory.

ntldr

2.3 Identify the basic system boot sequences and boot methods, including the steps to create an emergency boot disk with utilities installed for Windows 9x, Windows NT, and Windows 2000. Content may include the following: ntldr (NT Loader)

ntldr is the boot loader for Windows 2000. Its job is to coordinate the loading of the rest of the OS. ntldr is located on the root of your system partition, and if it is corrupted, it can easily be replaced from any other working copy of Windows 2000. ntldr switches the memory model that is used on the system to a flat memory model, treating all memory on the system as one contiguous block. ntldr reads the boot.ini file if it exists and displays the list of possible OSs that can be booted.

After choosing any version of Windows NT or Windows 2000, ntdetect.com is called. ntdetect.com performs a hardware detection, scanning all hardware ports, processor make, model, and description, and the amount of RAM on the system. Once this information has been collected, it is returned to ntldr and will eventually make up the HKEY_LOCAL_MACHINE\HARDWARE key of the Registry. The last step that is performed by ntldr is to launch ntoskrnl.exe.

To launch ntoskrnl.exe, ntldr goes to the system32 subdirectory or the directory that is listed in the boot.ini file.

When formatting a floppy disk using Windows 2000, the boot sector is set to look for ntldr. If you leave a disk in your computer when it is being rebooted, you will see this message:

```
NTLDR is Missing
Press any key to restart.
```

For disks formatted with Windows 9x, this message will appear:

```
Invalid system disk
Replace the disk, and then press any key
```

boot.ini

2.3 Identify the basic system boot sequences and boot methods, including the steps to create an emergency boot disk with utilities installed for Windows 9x, Windows NT, and Windows 2000. Content may include the following: boot.ini

The boot.ini file lists the OSs that are available to boot. It is a text file on the root of your system partition. It contains the default timeout value for the boot menu to be displayed, and where to find each copy of the OS. Upon looking at the boot.ini for the first time, you may be confused by the strange notation used to donate locations (this notation is called an ARC pathname and it is discussed in the next section).

A sample boot.ini would look like:

```
[boot loader]
timeout=10
default= multi(0)disk(0)rdisk(0)partition(4)\WINNT
[operating systems]
C:\="Microsoft Windows 98"
multi(0)disk(0)rdisk(0)partition(4)\WINNT="Windows 2000"
multi(0)disk(0)rdisk(0)partition(4)\WINNT="Win 2K Error"/SOS
multi(0)disk(0)rdisk(0)partition(2)\WINNT="Windows NT 4.0"
```

The first section in the boot.ini file is the [boot loader] section. It lists both the timeout value to display the boot menu and the default OS to boot. The default OS is located in the OS listing in the file. The first OS in the list with a matching path is loaded by ntldr.

In this code listing, the [operating systems] section lists all of the OSs that boot.ini knows about on the system. This section would be built and added to as you install multiple copies of Windows NT or Windows 2000 on a system. You may have multiple versions of an OS installed if this is a testing or development system. This file also has two entries that refer to the same path (partition 4). The difference between them is the application of the SOS switch at the end of the second line. The description strings that are used in this section are the display text for the boot menu, but they have no effect on the boot process of the OS.

ARC pathnames

Advanced RISC Computing Specification is a rigid set of standards that has been presented by the ACE (Advanced Computing Environment) initiative. This initiative has been sponsored by major vendors in the industry, and one of the standards that arose was a naming convention to refer to disk partitions. To understand the parts of this name, refer to Table 22-6. In the previous code example, multi(0) referred to the first non-SCSI controller on the system; disk(0) did not refer to anything, as it would be a SCSI ID of a disk; rdisk(0) referred to the first disk on the controller; and partition(4) would be the fourth partition on the disk. Windows 2000 uses this specification since the assignment of drive letters to partitions is flexible, but partition locations are very rigid, thus preventing errors.

Table 22-6
ARC Path Components

Type	Class	Description
SCSI	Adapter	This is the ordinal number of the SCSI controller that is located in the system. The ordinal number refers to the order in which the controller was located. The hardware is scanned according to the buses that exist on the motherboard, and each bus is scanned starting with slot number 1. If controllers were located in slots 1 and 3, then the controller in slot 1 would be SCSI(0) and the controller in slot 3 would be SCSI(1). SCSI is only used in cases where the SCSI controller either does not have an on-board BIOS, or is disabled.
Multi	Adapter	The ordinal number of the Multifunction controller in the system. Multifunction is used for all devices that do not use the previous listing for SCSI. This includes IDE controllers and SCSI controllers with the BIOS enabled.
Signature	Non-Classed	This notation can be used in place of SCSI or Multi, in order to help conform to plug-and-play specifications. Each drive that is identified by the Windows 2000 OS has a Signature written to it. The signature notation looks like Signature(8765bfa4), and tells ntldr to look for a drive that has that signature and to load the OS from there, regardless of which controller it happens to be found on.
Disk	Controller	The SCSI ID number that has been assigned to the SCSI drive on the system. This is set to 0 when using the Multi (multifunction) adapter.
Rdisk	Peripheral	The rigid disk number, referring to the physical location on the controller rather than the logical ID. The SCSI ID number refers to a logical ID.
Partition	Block Device	The partition number for the partition that the OS will be found on. Partition(0) would refer to a drive with no partitions. Since Windows 2000 requires a partitioned drive to store files, the partition number will always be 1 or greater.

The next step after having Windows 2000 chosen from the boot.ini menu is to have ntdetect.com run.

`ntdetect.comntdetect.com`'s only job is to find out what hardware is present on the system. This detection process is similar to what happens during the POST process at the hardware level. `ntdetect.com` checks for the following components:

✦ Bus/adapter type

✦ Communication ports

✦ Computer ID

✦ Floating-point coprocessor

✦ Floppy disks

✦ Keyboard

✦ Mouse/pointing device

✦ Parallel ports

✦ SCSI adapters

✦ Video adapters

This information creates a hardware tree that is passed back to `ntldr` and eventually given to `ntoskrnl.exe`, which places it in the Registry.

ntoskrnl.exe

The main goal of the boot process is to get the operating system kernel loaded and functioning. The computer has already given you a choice of OSs, inventoried the hardware, and is now ready to actually start loading the OS into memory. `ntoskrnl.exe` represents the first and most important step in this process. The OS kernel for Windows 2000 is responsible for all thread level scheduling on the system. It plays a major control role, managing all of the other components on the system. Without it, there would be anarchy in the OS.

`ntldr` proceeds to the path that is specified in `boot.ini` to locate `ntoskrnl.exe` in the `system32` folder. If `ntldr` locates the kernel, it proceeds to execute it. `ntldr` will generate a missing kernel error message if it fails to locate the kernel. Startup error messages are covered in Chapter 25. Once the kernel is running, `ntldr` passes control of the system over to it. There are several steps to the kernel load, starting with loading devices, and then moving on to loading any system services. Once the services are running, it loads the default shell application and user profile.

The default user profile is used to run the user logon process. At this point, the logon screen will tell you to "Press Ctrl+Alt+Delete to begin." After providing logon credentials, that user session is discarded, and a new one is started up for the new user.

The device load process

All the devices that are to be loaded during the system startup are listed in the Registry. The Registry includes information about each device in:

HKEY_LOCAL_MACHINE\SYSTEM\CurrentControlSet\Services\<device>

In this location, you will find several values that describe how the device will start up. These values are listed in Table 22-7.

	Table 22-7	
	Device and Service Settings in the Registry	
Value	**Description**	
Display Name	This string is used to display the name in areas of Windows 2000, such as the Device Manager or the Services MMC.	
Error Control	This value configures how errors will be reported back to the OS. A value of 0 does not report any errors with the device back to the OS. A value of 1 reports errors normally. A value of 2 makes errors severe and will cause an automatic reboot of the computer to the "Last Known Good Configuration". A value of 3 makes errors critical and will also cause an automatic reboot of the computer to the "Last Known Good Configuration." If the "Last Known Good Configuration" is already being used, then severe errors will enable the computer to continue to boot, but critical errors will start the bug-check routine.	
Group	Devices can be grouped together. This is done mostly for dependencies. If any device in a group fails, then dependent devices will not start up.	
Image Path	This is the path and name of the actual driver file that is used for the device or service.	
Start	This identifies when the device will start up. There are 5 start types: 0 – boot, 1 – system, 2 – automatic, 3 – manual, and 4 – disabled. Most devices have boot or system for a start value, but you may find a few that are set to automatic. Most services are set for either automatic or manual.	
Tag	A Tag ID is assigned to the service when it is installed, but is not actually used by the OS.	
Type	Identifies that type of service or device. All devices should have a value of 1. Service types should be; 1 for Kernel device drivers, 2 for File System drivers, 4 for arguments for an adapter, 10 for single process Win32 applications that follow the Service Control Protocol, and 20 for Win32 Services that can share their process with other Win32 Services.	

The service load process

All the services that are to be loaded during the system startup are listed in the Registry. The Registry includes information about each device in the following location:

HKEY_LOCAL_MACHINE\SYSTEM\CurrentControlSet\Services\<service>

This is the same location that is used for devices. The biggest difference between devices and services is that devices map out to a physical piece of hardware; while services are only software. The values for services are listed in Table 22-7.

Booting into Safe Mode

 2.3 Identify the basic system boot sequences and boot methods, including the steps to create an emergency boot disk with utilities installed for Windows 9x, Windows NT, and Windows 2000. Content may include the following: Safe Mode

If either Windows 9x or Windows 2000 fails to boot properly and you think that the problem is related to a service or driver that is loading, then you may be able to boot the computer into Safe Mode. Windows NT 4.0 does not have a Safe Mode boot, but it does have a VGA graphic mode boot that can be selected from the main boot menu. If the computer hangs or crashes and reboots during the boot process, then it may be a device-related error.

When Windows 9x detects that it has failed to boot properly, it will automatically attempt to boot into Safe Mode during the next boot. There may be other times when you want to manually enable a safe mode boot. When using Windows 9x, you can press the F8 key when you see the words "Starting Windows 9x" on the screen. On some computers, Windows 98 will require that you press and hold the Ctrl key immediately after the POST process completes rather than using the F8 key. With Windows 2000, a message will appear at the bottom of the screen during the boot menu that tells you to press the F8 key to see the advanced boot options. Any of these methods will bring you to a boot menu, where you will be able to choose Safe Mode or Safe Mode with Networking. Windows 2000 also has a Safe Mode with Command Prompt option that loads cmd.exe as your shell application.

When booting into Safe Mode, the operating system skips config.sys and autoexec.bat, as well as any drivers that have been considered crucial to the boot process. This means that you will have a VGA driver providing video in a daring 640 x 480 resolution (16 colors), and a mouse. Initially, your screen will look like that shown in Figure 22-1. Outside of these devices, you will have very few working devices — for example, no sound cards, scanners, and CD burners. With just the basics running, you should be able to identify the driver that did not load properly and correct the problem.

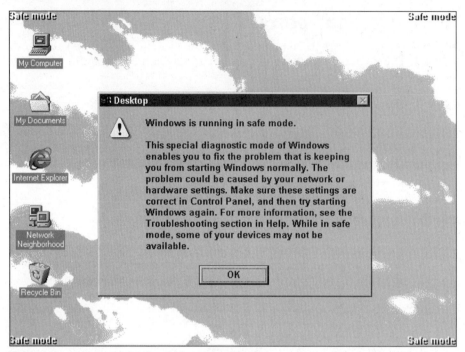

Figure 22-1: Safe Mode should be easy to spot.

The next three boots after entering Safe Mode will automatically create a `bootlog.txt` file on the root of your drive. If your next attempt at a normal boot does not succeed, then you will be able to read the `bootlog.txt` file and attempt to locate the misbehaving driver or service there.

Entering MS-DOS Mode

2.3 Identify the basic system boot sequences and boot methods, including the steps to create an emergency boot disk with utilities installed for Windows 9x, Windows NT, and Windows 2000. Content may include the following: MS-DOS Mode

Windows 9x supports a non-graphical boot. In the boot menu described in the Safe Mode section, DOS Mode is accessed by choosing Command Prompt, or Safe Mode Command Prompt. If you choose to boot to the command prompt, you will have a normal boot until the launch of `win.com`, which does not launch. In Safe Mode Command Prompt, you do not process `config.sys` and `autoexec.bat`, and the system does not load the `himem.sys` memory manager. This boot stops prior to launching `win.com` as well.

The Command Prompt is a full boot of Windows 9x, but it stops early. From the command prompt, you will be able to copy files and import or export Registry settings. Windows can be launched with or without debugging switches.

Windows 2000 also supports a Safe Mode with Command Prompt boot. In Windows 2000, the command prompt boot does a boot of Windows 2000 GUI, but opens cmd.exe as your shell. This allows you to perform many actions to correct your problem (using utilities like ScanDisk or the Registry Editor), and when you are done, exiting the command prompt will reboot your system.

Other F8 Options

When you access the F8 boot menu at system startup, there are several options available, such as:

✦ Logged

✦ Safe Mode

✦ Step-by-Step with Confirmation

✦ Command Prompt

✦ Safe Mode Command Prompt Only

✦ Previous version of MS-DOS

Booting into Safe Mode and to the command prompt have already been covered in this chapter, so this section will cover the stragglers. The options that have not been discussed are booting to the previous OS on your system (if Windows 9x upgraded an MS-DOS installation), and creating a bootlog.txt during the boot.

The bootlog.txt file is very useful when attempting to troubleshoot boot problems. It logs all drivers, services, and resources as they are loading. This file can then be referenced to locate problems with the boot, especially since the system does not give you any indication as to what is happening during the boot. If a bootlog.txt file already exists when creating a new file, then the existing one is renamed to bootlog.prv.

The bootlog.txt from Windows 98 has the following structure:

```
[00055731] Loading Device = C:\WINDOWS\COMMAND\DRVSPACE.SYS
[00055731] LoadFailed    = C:\WINDOWS\COMMAND\DRVSPACE.SYS
[00055731] Loading Device = C:\WINDOWS\HIMEM.SYS
[00055732] LoadSuccess    = C:\WINDOWS\HIMEM.SYS
<Stuff Deleted>
[0005578C] SYSCRITINIT   = VMM
[0005578C] SYSCRITINITSUCCESS  = VMM
```

```
[0005578C] SYSCRITINIT   = MTRR
[0005578C] SYSCRITINITSUCCESS   = MTRR
[0005578C] SYSCRITINIT   = VCACHE
[0005578C] SYSCRITINITSUCCESS   = VCACHE
[0005578C] SYSCRITINIT   = DFS
[0005578C] SYSCRITINITSUCCESS   = DFS
<Stuff Deleted>
[0005578D] DEVICEINIT   = VMM
[0005578D] DEVICEINITSUCCESS   = VMM
[0005578D] DEVICEINIT   = MTRR
[0005578D] DEVICEINITSUCCESS   = MTRR
[0005578D] DEVICEINIT   = VCACHE
[0005578D] DEVICEINITSUCCESS   = VCACHE
[0005578E] DEVICEINIT   = DFS
[0005578E] DEVICEINITSUCCESS   = DFS
<Stuff Deleted>
[0005578D] Dynamic load device   bios.vxd
[0005578D] Dynamic init device   BIOS
[0005578D] Dynamic init success BIOS
[0005578D] Dynamic load success bios.vxd
<Stuff Deleted>
[0005579F] Dynamic load device
C:\WINDOWS\system\IOSUBSYS\apix.vxd
[0005579F] Dynamic load success
C:\WINDOWS\system\IOSUBSYS\apix.vxd
[0005579F] Dynamic load device
C:\WINDOWS\system\IOSUBSYS\cdfs.vxd
[0005579F] Dynamic load success
C:\WINDOWS\system\IOSUBSYS\cdfs.vxd
<Stuff Deleted>
Initializing KERNEL
LoadStart = system.drv
LoadSuccess = system.drv
LoadStart = keyboard.drv
LoadSuccess = keyboard.drv
LoadStart = mouse.drv
LoadSuccess = mouse.drv
<Stuff Deleted - This portion starts a shutdown.>
Terminate = User
Terminate = Query Drivers
EndTerminate = Query Drivers
Terminate = Unload Network
EndTerminate = Unload Network
Terminate = Reset Display
EndTerminate = Reset Display
EndTerminate = User
```

This file lists the devices that were loaded and their loading order. In this case, both drvspace.sys and himem.sys loaded. They were followed by the Virtual Memory Manager, the Disk Cache, and the Distributed File System driver. Look through the list above and see what other drivers or devices you can identify. When checking the file, you should look for items that list LoadFailed.

When using the Enable Boot Logging option of the Windows 2000 boot menu, you will also create a log file. This file is found in the `winnt` directory and will be named `ntbtlog.txt`. Unlike Windows 9x, this file is appended to when performing logged boots, but has a similar structure.

Other options in the Windows 2000 advanced boot options include:

✦ Enable VGA Mode

✦ Directory Services Restore Mode (for Windows 2000 Domain Controllers)

✦ Debugging Mode

✦ Last Known Good Configuration

If your system is in a state that is not bootable, then you will want to use a Startup disk. The next two sections will discuss Startup disks for both Windows 95 and Windows 98.

Startup Disks for Windows 95

 2.3 Identify the basic system boot sequences and boot methods, including the steps to create an emergency boot disk with utilities installed for Windows 9x, Windows NT, and Windows 2000. Content may include the following: Creating an emergency repair disk (ERD)

There are several different versions of the Windows 95 startup disk, one for each version of Windows 95 (Retail/Upgrade, Plus Pack, OSR1, or OSR2). Keep in mind that when you are attempting to repair a system, some functions will require that you use the correct version of the disk.

You can create a startup disk with just a couple of steps. This procedure is the same for both Windows 95 and Windows 98.

1. Open the Control Panels folder accessing Start menu ➪ Settings ➪ Control Panel.

2. Open the Add/Remove Programs applet.

3. Select the Startup Disk tab and the Make Disk button. You will be prompted to provide a blank, unformatted disk, as shown in Figure 22-2.

The basic repair disk for Windows 95 is the same across all versions of Windows 95. This disk contains the files that are listed in Table 22-8. These files represent the minimum number of files that Microsoft feels you should need to recover or re-install a Windows 95 system.

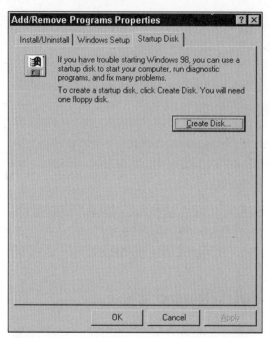

Figure 22-2: Creating a startup disk is an easy process.

Table 22-8
Common Windows 95 Startup Disk Files

File	Description
fdisk.exe	Used to modify the partition table on your drive. This is useful if you need to destroy and re-create the partitions on your disk.
format.com	Used to format existing partitions or new partitions.
edit.com	Used to edit text files on your disk. These files include batch, configuration, and Registry import files.
Scandisk.exe	Used to check the drive for bad clusters and other disk-related problems.
regedit.exe	Used to export or import Registry settings. This is the same file that is used graphically under windows, but can be used here with a series of optional switches.
sys.com	Copies the required files needed to make a disk bootable. This can be used if the boot files on your hard drive have become damaged.

File	Description
attrib.exe	Changes file attributes.
chkdsk.exe	Checks the disk for errors in directory tables. This was the precursor to scandisk.exe.
Command.com	The 16-bit real-mode OS kernel.
debug.exe	Used to kernel level debugging.
Drvspace.bin	The code to handle disk compression.
ebd.sys	This is a flag file that lets the computer know that this is an Emergency Boot Disk.
io.sys	The real-mode boot loader.
msdos.sys	Real-mode boot settings.
Uninstal.exe	The uninstaller for Windows 95. If a backup of system files was chosen during the installation of Windows 95, then this will allow you to uninstall Windows 95. This file is not on OEM versions of Windows 95, as they were not supposed to be installed over another operating system.
Scandisk.ini	Preferences for Scandisk.

The files that truly make these versions of the startup disk different are io.sys, command.com, and drvspace.bin. Each of these files is version-dependent. If you are using one version of the boot loader, then you must be using a matching version of command.com. If you are not, then you will get an error telling you that command.com is the wrong version, and your system will not boot. Since Drive Space disk compression was upgraded by applying the Windows 95 Plus Pack, the version of the boot disks include:

✦ Windows 95 Retail/Upgrade

✦ Windows 95 Plus Pack

✦ Windows 95 OSR1

✦ Windows 95 OSR2

If you are attempting to resolve boot or missing command.com problems, and you don't know the exact version of Windows 95 that is being used, then you may have to try all versions of the boot disk to resolve the problem.

Startup Disks for Windows 98

2.3 Identify the basic system boot sequences and boot methods, including the steps to create an emergency boot disk with utilities installed for Windows 9x, Windows NT, and Windows 2000. Content may include the following: Creating an emergency repair disk (ERD)

With Windows 98, there are also two versions of the startup disk: one for Windows 98 and one for Windows 98 Second Edition (SE). These disks are primarily the same, with the exception of the version of `command.com` that is used by the two operating systems. Both Windows 98 startup disks start by creating a large RAM disk and extracting a compressed file (`ebd.cab`) to the RAM disk. A RAM drive is a portion of RAM that is treated like a hard disk, and assigned a drive letter. Key files that are different from the Windows 95 startup disk are summarized in Table 22-9. One of the other main differences between the Windows 95 and Windows 98 startup disks relates to CD-ROM support. Windows 98 will attempt to load several different CD-ROM drivers, while attempting to find one that works in your computer. This makes the process of loading a CD-ROM driver much easier.

Table 22-9 Windows 98 Startup Disk Files	
File	**Description**
`aspi2dos.sys` `aspi4dos.sys` `aspi8dos.sys` `aspi8u2.sys` `aspicd.sys` `btcdrom.sys` `btdosm.sys` `flashpt.sys` `oakcdrom.sys`	Several CD-ROM drivers for the Windows 98 Command Interpreter. Windows 98 actually loads all of the drivers in an attempt to find one that works. If the device does not exist on your computer, then the driver load will fail.
`Autoexec.bat`	A file that continues the select device load that is started with the `config.sys` file.
`Command.com`	The 16-bit real-mode OS kernel.
`config.sys`	A file that loads initial device drivers and is used to build the boot menu that loads when booting from the disk.
`Drvspace.bin`	This code handles disk compression.

File	Description
ebd.cab	This is a 266K compressed file that contains most of the troubleshooting and diagnostic tools that are found on the startup disk, such as attrib.exe, chkdsk.exe, debug.exe, edit.com, ext.exe, extract.exe, format.com, help.bat, mscdex.exe, restart.com, scandisk.exe, scandisk.ini, and sys.com. This file is decompressed on to a RAM drive that is created during the boot process of the startup disk.
extract.exe	Used to decompress the ebd.sys file.
fdisk.exe	Used to modify the partition table on your drive. This is useful if you need to destroy and re-create the partitions on your disk. This version can work with FAT32 partitions and is aware of NTFS partitions.
findramd.exe	Responsible for finding the drive letter that is assigned to the RAM drive that is created by ramdrive.sys.
himem.sys	The DOS-mode high memory manager.
ramdrive.sys	The driver file for the RAM drive.
setramd.bat	Searches for the first drive letter that may be used for the RAM drive.

Since the Windows 98 startup disk is very good at locating and loading CD-ROM drivers, many people are now using it as a generic disk to load support for a local CD-ROM, even if they are not planning on installing Windows 98.

Setup Disks for Windows NT/2000

 2.3 Identify the basic system boot sequences and boot methods, including the steps to create an emergency boot disk with utilities installed for Windows 9x, Windows NT, and Windows 2000.

You can start Windows NT/2000 from a bootable CD-ROM or a floppy disk. Windows NT/2000 have special boot disks to start the installation of their OS. If you have a computer that has a bootable CD-ROM, then you will not need these Setup Boot Disks. If, however, your CD-ROM is not bootable, or you choose not to use it, then you can make a set of boot disks. These disks will allow you to start the installation of Windows NT or Windows 2000.

For Windows NT, the Setup Boot Disks are made by running either winnt /ox or winnt32 /ox from the I386 directory on the Windows NT CD. This command will make a three-disk set of disks, and the installation can be started by booting from the first disk.

To make a set of disks for Windows 2000, run either `makeboot` or `makebt32` from the `bootdisk` directory on the Windows 2000 CD. This will make a four-disk set, and the installation can be started by booting from the first disk.

The Setup Boot Disks will allow you to start an installation of Windows or start the Emergency Repair Process.

Emergency Repair

2.3 Identify the basic system boot sequences and boot methods, including the steps to create an emergency boot disk with utilities installed for Windows 9x, Windows NT, and Windows 2000. Content may include the following: Creating an emergency repair disk (ERD)

When things go wrong with the boot of Windows NT/2000, you can try a special boot (as into Safe Mode) to repair the error. However, there are times when the system will not boot at all. In this case, you can make a final attempt to resurrect the system or start the installation. If you choose to attempt this Emergency Repair Process, then you should try to be prepared by creating an emergency repair disk prior to your computer experiencing problems, and you should be familiar with the repair process.

Emergency repair disk

Windows 2000 and Windows NT both allow you to create an emergency repair disk (ERD). The ERD contains a small replacement of the system account database and a major portion of the system registry. This disk can restore the settings and list the devices or services on the system. It can also replace the account database with a copy of the account database that existed immediately after the installation completed.

With Windows NT, the emergency repair disk is created with the `rdisk` utility. This will update several of your system files and place copies of them in a special directory. The directory is `%winroot%\repair` and can be copied to a floppy disk after updating. The normal `rdisk` command will not update the SAM and SECURITY files, but these can be updated by using `rdisk /s`.

If you are using Windows 2000, the emergency repair disk is created with the backup utility. The backup utility is found in Start menu ⇨ Accessories ⇨ System Tools ⇨ Backup. Once you open it, there is an option to create an emergency repair disk on the Welcome tab.

Emergency Repair Process

The Emergency Repair Process begins with booting the system with the Setup Boot Disks that were created in the previous section. When booting, the first question you will be asked is if you would like to perform an installation of Windows 2000, or if you would like to perform an Emergency Repair.

After choosing to perform an Emergency Repair, you will be asked if you would like to launch the Recovery Console (discussed in the next section) or perform an Emergency Repair. If you choose to perform an emergency repair, you will be asked if you have an emergency repair disk. Even if you do not, the Emergency Repair Process will search your drive for a Windows 2000 installation. If it finds one, it will use the repair information found in the `%winroot%\system32\repair` directory. You will have four choices for the Emergency Repair Process:

+ Inspect boot files
+ Inspect startup environment
+ Inspect system files
+ Inspect Registry

If you choose to inspect the boot files or the startup environment, the Emergency Repair Process will fix problems that may exist with either the boot sector or start files, such as `boot.ini`.

If you choose to inspect the system files, the Emergency Repair Process will compare every file that makes up the Windows installation to the originals that are found on the Windows CD. This allows you to find corrupted files, and to uninstall Service Packs if you failed to backup prior to installing them.

If you choose to inspect the Registry, you will then have three choices:

+ Load the SYSTEM key
+ Load the SOFTWARE key
+ Load the SAM and SECURITY keys

The Inspect the Registry option does not so much inspect the sections of the Registry as replace them. The SYSTEM and SOFTWARE sections of the Registry contain settings for services, devices, and applications that are operating on the system. Most services store their settings in the SYSTEM key, but some (for Windows logo requirements) are also stored in the SOFTWARE key. The SOFTWARE key is used primarily for applications.

The SAM and SECURITY keys get replaced as a set. They contain the entire local account database. Replacing the account database on a member server will only affect that one computer. If you make the replacement on your Windows NT primary domain controller, then you will have replaced your entire domain account database. On Windows 2000 domain controllers, the local account database is not used.

Rather than choosing to perform the Emergency Repair Process, you could choose to launch the Recovery Console, which contains its own repair and troubleshooting tools.

Recovery Console

The Recovery Console is a command line base OS that can be used to help diagnose and repair problems with your installation of Windows 2000. This command line interface comes with several commands that will look familiar to MS-DOS or Windows commands, as well as some that are unique to the Recovery Console. Even the commands that are named the same as MS-DOS commands tend to perform different functions. Keep in mind that this is not MS-DOS, nor is it Windows 2000. It is the Recovery Console — a unique OS used to repair Windows 2000.

You can get to the Recovery Console through the Emergency Repair Process, or you can install it into your boot menu by re-running the Windows 2000 setup program with the `cmdcons` switch.

```
<winnt_src>\i386\winnt32.exe /cmdcons
```

To initially get into the Recovery Console, you will have to log into the Recovery Console. The Recovery Console will check for copies of Windows 2000 on your system, and let you log in to one that you choose. In order to log in, you will need the name and password of the local Windows 2000 administrator account. After providing that information, you will have access to only the files that make up that copy of Windows 2000.

You will only have access to the `winnt` directory. This directory restriction has been done to limit the amount of access you have during the Recovery Console session. By limiting your access, Microsoft increases security and restricts the amount of damage/harm you can do. If you are booting to the Recovery Console, there may not be much more that can go wrong.

There are several tools available to you in the Recovery Console that enable you to manage files. Of these, the most notable are `copy`, `del`, and `ren`. All three of these commands only work with one file and do not support wildcards like their Windows 2000 equivalents. `Format` is the other major file management command at the console. `Format` enables you to specify the file system for your partition — FAT, FAT32, or NTFS.

Several commands let you manage the disk and boot sectors on your drive: chckdsk for checking your disk for errors; diskpart for repartitioning, much like fdisk would; and fixboot and fixmbr for rewriting either the boot sector or the Master Boot Record.

In addition to these commands, there is often a need to control services and devices in the troubleshooting process. To help with this, you can use listsvc, which lists the available services and devices; disable, which disables selected services and devices at boot; and enable, which enables selected devices and services at boot.

A couple of unclassified commands include the logon and systemroot commands. logon allows you to log on to another local copy of Windows 2000 for systems that dual boot. systemroot switches you to the Windows directory that you are logged onto.

With this assortment of tools, you should be able to get an unbootable copy of Windows 2000 bootable again. Don't expect to perform much troubleshooting through the Recovery Console, but if your server is having STOP errors on boot, the Recovery Console will allow you to get around them. Once you are running a full copy of Windows 2000, you should be able to complete your troubleshooting procedures.

Key Point Summary

This chapter examined the process that is undertaken by the software on your computer during the boot process. The basic boot process for both Windows 9x and Windows 2000 was discussed, as well as the differences between them. You also took a look at the files that make up a Startup Disk, and what the files could be used for.

When examining the Windows 2000 boot process, you learned about some of the files that are required to boot a system, including boot.ini, ntbootdd.sys, and ntldr. Alternatively, you took a look at the emergency repair disk that can be used when your system does not boot.

Finally, the chapter provided an overview of the Recovery Console, a tool to repair your Windows 2000 when it is not able to boot to the GUI.

✦   ✦   ✦

STUDY GUIDE

This Study Guide presents 15 assessment questions and 3 lab exercises to test your knowledge of this exam topic area.

Assessment Questions

1. When enabling a logged boot of Windows 2000, what is the name of the log file that is created?

   A. `ntbtlog.txt`

   B. `bootlog.txt`

   C. `btlog.txt`

   D. `ntlog.txt`

2. What command would you use from the Recovery Console to attempt to repair the boot sector?

   A. `rbldbsec`

   B. `rbldmbr`

   C. `fixmbrec`

   D. `fixboot`

3. You would like to disable the automatic running of `scandisk.exe` when your computer is shut down improperly. What file should you edit?

   A. `system.dat`

   B. `system.ini`

   C. `msdos.sys`

   D. `config.sys`

4. You get a call from a user who tells you about the problems he is having with his Windows 98 laptop. He accidentally deleted `c:\command.com` from his computer. He got a copy of it from his desktop computer at home and replaced the one on his system, but it still does not boot. A friend told him to use a Startup Disk and the SYS command to correct the problem. He got a copy of a Startup Disk from his friend's desktop computer that also uses Windows 98. After issuing the command `sys.com c:` his computer still does not boot. What may be the problem that he's having? (Select the best answer)

A. Windows 98 Startup Disks are different between laptops and desktops to support the differences in hardware.

B. His friend's desktop was running Windows 98 Second Edition, and the disk is not compatible with the original Windows 98.

C. Startup Disks are unique to each computer, due to differences between disk geometry and boot sector locations.

D. `sys.com` will only repair boot sector problems, and will not replace the `command.com` file.

5. A user has a program that automatically starts up when he logs into his computer. He would like to disable it. Where should he look for possible settings?

    A. `load` = lines in `win.ini`

    B. The Startup group in the Start menu

    C. The RUN key in the Registry

    D. All of the above

    E. None of the above

6. A user bought a new video card with 128MB of RAM on it. He needs it to play the new version of his favorite video game. After installing the video card, he boots up his Windows 98 computer and is overjoyed when he sees the plug-and-play wizard detect the new hardware. When prompted, he provides the driver disk that came with his computer. After loading the driver for his new video card, his computer reboots. During the next boot, his computer halts and will not respond to any controls. What should he do next?

    A. Reboot his computer by using the power button. His computer will automatically boot to the Last Known Good Configuration.

    B. Reboot his computer by using Ctrl+Alt+Del, and choose F8 when he sees the "Starting Windows 98" text. He will then be able to choose Enable VGA Mode from the boot menu.

    C. Reboot his computer by using the power button. His computer will automatically display the boot menu and attempt to boot to Safe Mode.

    D. Reboot his computer by using Ctrl+Alt+Del and then hold down F9 to enable Safe Mode.

7. A user has attempted to boot his computer, but instead of seeing the Windows 2000 boot menu, he sees a message stating, "NTLDR is missing. Press any key to restart." What should he do first?

   A. Set the CD-ROM as bootable in the system CMOS and insert the Windows 2000 CD. This will allow him to complete an Emergency Repair.

   B. Reinstall Windows 2000.

   C. Reboot the computer and enter Safe Mode, then choose `RebuildBootSect.exe` from the `\winnt\system32` directory.

   D. Remove the floppy disk from the A: drive.

8. What is the first file that configures the basic environment settings for Windows 9x computers?

   A. `sys.com`

   B. `msdos.sys`

   C. `win9x.sys`

   D. `io.sys`

9. The search order for bootable drives is stored in which location?

   A. System BIOS

   B. PNP Configuration

   C. `io.sys`

   D. CMOS Memory

10. If the file `C:\logo.sys` is deleted, what is the impact on a Windows 9x system?

   A. The animated startup screen is not shown.

   B. You will be missing the animated logo in Internet Explorer.

   C. The default animated startup screen will be used.

   D. Non-associated files on your drive will have the default windows icon on them.

11. A user has attempted to boot his computer, but instead of seeing the Windows 2000 boot menu, he sees a message stating, "NTLDR is missing. Press any key to restart." He checked to see if there was a floppy in the A: drive, but there was not. What should he do to attempt to repair his system? (Select all that apply)

  A. Set the CD-ROM as bootable in the system CMOS and insert the Windows 2000 CD. This will allow him to complete an Emergency Repair with the Emergency Repair Process.

  B. Reinstall Windows 2000.

  C. Set the CD-ROM as bootable in the system CMOS and insert the Windows 2000 CD. This will allow him to complete an Emergency Repair with the Recovery Console.

  D. Reboot from a Windows 98 System Startup Disk, and type `sys c:`.

12. You would like to change the default behavior of Windows 98 — that of running ScanDisk when your system is improperly shutdown. What file will you have to modify?

  A. `io.sys`

  B. `msdos.sys`

  C. `system.ini`

  D. `system.dat`

13. You are running an MS-DOS program on your Windows 95 computer that requires the use of a large number of open files on your hard drive. What line must be added to what file?

  A. `files = 99` must be added to `config.sys`

  B. `filehandles=99` must be added to `autoexec.bat`

  C. `openhandles=99` must be added to `system.ini`

  D. `files = 99` must be added to `autoexec.bat`

14. The system Registry for Windows 95 is extremely important. What file or files make up the Registry?

  A. `registry.dat`

  B. `system.ini` and `registry.dat`

  C. `user.dat` and `computer.dat`

  D. `user.dat` and `system.dat`

15. How do you build a startup disk for Windows 98?

   A. From the Windows 98 CD, run `setup /ox`.

   B. Use the System Control Panel applet.

   C. Use the Add/Remove Programs Control Panel applet

   D. Run `makeboot.bat` from the Windows 98 CD.

Lab Exercises

Lab 22.1 Examining the Boot Process

This lab exercise requires a computer running Windows 95 or Windows 98. Have the computer shut down and powered off for the start of the lab.

1. Turn your computer's power on.

2. Watch for the "Starting Windows 9x" text. Then Press F8 on your keyboard. You only have about two seconds to press the F8 key.

3. On the boot menu, select Step by Step with Confirmation.

4. You will be prompted to choose Yes or No for each component of Windows 9x before it is loaded. Choose Yes for all components, but record the list of components and items that are processed. This list should contain devices and drivers in `config.sys`, as well as `himem.sys`. Does your computer have either `config.sys` or `autoexec.bat` on it?

Lab 22.2 Making a Windows 9x Startup Disk

This lab exercise requires a blank, formatted disk, and a computer running Windows 95 or Windows 98.

1. Open the Control Panel folder. This can be done through the My Computer icon on the desktop.

2. Open the Add/Remove Programs Control Panel applet.

3. Switch to the Startup Disk tab.

4. Choose the Create Disk button.

5. Place your disk in your floppy drive, and choose the OK button.

6. After the disk is built, leave it in your drive.

7. Restart your computer using the Start menu ⇨ Shutdown command.

8. If you are using Windows 98, choose "With CDROM support" from the boot menu.

9. Type `dir a:` to see a list of commands that are available to you. If you are using Windows 98, check the screen during boot to see what letter was assigned to your RAM drive, then type `dir <ram_drive_letter>` to see the additional commands.

10. Remove the floppy disk and restart your computer by typing Ctrl+Alt+Del.

Lab 22.3 Examining the Recovery Console

For this exercise, you will need a computer running Windows 2000 Professional or a version of Windows 2000 Server. In addition, you will need an installation CD for the operating system and four blank, floppy disks. Even though your computer may be able to boot directly from the CD-ROM, this lab will make installation boot disks for Windows 2000 and use them to initiate the setup routine. If you choose to boot from the CD-ROM, you may have to change the settings in your CMOS, and you can skip down to Step 5 in this lab exercise.

1. Boot your computer and log in.

2. Place the Windows 2000 CD in your CD-ROM.

3. Locate the `bootdisk` folder on the CD, and run `makebt32`. Follow the instructions for inserting and labeling the boot disks.

4. Place the first disk (the Installation Setup Disk) in the floppy drive, and the Windows 2000 CD in the CD-ROM.

5. Reboot your computer and follow the instructions for switching disks during the boot process. If you are booting directly from the CD, you will enter setup directly.

6. If you are using an evaluation copy of Windows 2000, then you will be given a Setup Notification screen that lets you know this. This is important if you are installing on a production computer, as the evaluation copy is only valid for 120 days. Press Enter to continue.

7. On the Welcome to Setup screen, you should choose "To Repair a Windows 2000 installation", press R.

8. On the Windows 2000 Repair Options screen, you will choose "To Repair a Windows 2000 installation by using the Recovery Console", press C. If you wanted to use the Emergency Repair Process, you could have chosen "To Repair a Windows 2000 installation by using the emergency repair process", press R.

9. You should now have the option of logging onto any copy of Windows 2000 that is installed on your computer. If you are not dual booting, you will log on to #1 by typing `1<enter>`. If you have a multi-boot configuration, then choose the copy that you want to log onto.

10. Provide the password that was assigned as the Recovery Console during the installation of Windows 2000.

11. You should now be logged on to your console. The current directory should be something similar to c:\winnt. To get a list of the available commands, type help. To get help on the syntax and description of any of the other commands, type help <command> or <command> /?.

12. After exploring the Recovery Console, remove any floppy disks or CDs from the system; then type EXIT to reboot your system or Logon to choose another copy of Windows 2000 to examine.

Answers to Chapter Questions

Chapter Pre-Test

1. Windows 2000 supports **FAT**, **FAT32**, and **NTFS**.

2. io.sys is the Windows 9x boot loader.

3. When "Starting Windows 95" appears on the screen, **F8** will bring you to the boot menu.

4. The files that initiate the Windows 2000 boot process are ntldr, ntdetect.com, boot.ini, and ntbootdd.sys (if it exists).

5. The lines in the operating system section of boot.ini may start with **SCSI()**, **MULTI()**, or **SIGNATURE()**. Neither of these should represent a problem, as long as the identifier in the brackets is correct.

6. The Recovery Console can be installed in the Windows 2000 boot menu **using the setup command,** winnt32 /cmdcons, **or it can be chosen as an option during the Emergency Repair Process**.

7. The Windows 98 Startup Disk uses **compressed files and a RAM disk** to allow more information to be loaded on the disk. The RAM disk is loaded, and then the startup files are uncompressed to the RAM disk.

8. The core Windows 9x operating system is made up of krnl386.exe, kernel32.dll, gdi.exe, gdi32.dll, user.exe, and user32.dll.

9. **Devices** load before services do.

10. Installation disks for Windows 2000 can be made **by running either** makeboot.cmd or makebt32.cmd, **which can be found on the Windows 2000 CD**.

Assessment Questions

1. **A.** The file is named ntbtlog.txt. For more information, see the section titled "Booting into Safe Mode."

2. **D.** fixboot is the command to repair the boot sector. For more information, see the section titled "Emergency Repair."

3. C. The automatic settings for `scandisk.exe` are found in `msdos.sys`. For more information, see the section titled "Standard Boot Process for Windows 95/98."

4. B. The startup disk was not from his version of Windows 98. Each version of Windows 98 (original and Second Edition) have their own startup disk. For more information, see the section titled "Startup Disks for Windows 98."

5. D. Automatic commands can be found in either of the listed locations (`win.ini`, Startup group, or the Registry). For more information, see the section titled "Standard Boot Process for Windows 95/98."

6. C. Safe Mode should be his next step to correct the problem. For more information, see the section titled "Booting into Safe Mode."

7. D. "`ntldr` is missing" is the error message that you will see if you attempt to boot from a Windows NT/2000 formatted disk that does not contain `ntldr`. For more information, see the section titled "Standard Boot Process for Windows NT/2000."

8. B. The first Windows 9x file that configures the system environment is `msdos.sys`. For more information, see the section titled "Standard Boot Process for Windows 95/98."

9. D. CMOS memory contains the boot device order. For more information, see the section titled "Standard Boot Process for Windows 95/98."

10. C. The default animated logo is used when `C:\logo.sys` is missing. For more information, see the section titled "Standard Boot Process for Windows 95/98."

11. A, C. Using the Emergency Repair Process or Recovery Console are ways to replace a missing boot file. For more information, see the section titled "Emergency Repair."

12. B. `msdos.sys` contains settings for running `scandisk.exe` during the Windows 9x boot. For more information, see the section titled "Standard Boot Process for Windows 95/98."

13. A. The files statement in `config.sys` configures the number of open files that will be supported by MS-DOS applications. For more information, see the section titled "Standard Boot Process for Windows 95/98."

14. D. The files that make up the Registry are `user.dat` and `system.dat`. For more information, see the section titled "Standard Boot Process for Windows 95/98."

15. C. The Add/Remove Programs Control Panel applet is used to build a startup disk for Windows 9x. For more information, see the section titled "Startup Disks for Windows 95."

Loading and Configuring Device Drivers

Exam 220-202 ✦ A+ OS Technologies

✦ **2.4** Identify procedures for loading/adding and configuring application device drivers, and the necessary software for certain devices. Content may include the following:

- Windows 9x Plug-and-Play and Windows 2000
- Procedures for set up and configuring Windows printing **subsystem:** Setting Default printer, Installing/Spool setting, Network printing (with help of LAN admin)

CHAPTER PRE-TEST

1. What are two locations in the OS that may be used to add devices to a computer?

2. What are two of the system resources that devices may require?

3. What tool allows you to see the settings of all devices on your computer, and allows you to delete selected devices?

4. What tool can be used to query information about devices, but cannot delete devices?

5. What are two components of the plug-and-play architecture?

6. What are some features that all plug-and-play devices must support?

7. What is the easiest way to add a printer to computer, if your computer supports a bi-directional printer port?

8. What is a printer pool?

9. What is one way that you can initiate a connection to a network printer?

10. What is PCL an acronym for?

✦ Answers to these questions can be found at the end of the chapter. ✦

Device drivers are responsible for establishing and maintaining communication links between the operating system and the various hardware devices that exist on the computer. Each hardware device has its own language that it uses to communicate. The job of the device driver is to translate data from the device into something that the OS can understand, and then translate the OS data into something that the device can understand. With the advent of plug-and-play, the job of identifying the correct driver and configuration settings became easier. Plug-and-play devices are supposed to be self-configuring if they are being used in an appropriate computer and OS. A printer is one of the devices that users will be working with and installing the most, so this chapter will take a close look at printer configuration.

Loading Device Drivers

2.4 Identify procedures for loading/adding and configuring application device drivers, and the necessary software for certain devices.

Since device drivers are so important, you should consider how device drivers are loaded onto your system. You will take a look at loading device drivers under Windows 9x, as well as under Windows 2000. In the previous chapters of this book you saw how to configure the hardware to be added to a system; in this chapter you will focus on the software side of configuring these devices.

Windows 9x

There are two ways to load drivers under Windows 9x: you can load them manually, or load them automatically through plug-and-play or the Add New Hardware wizard. There is no guarantee that either plug-and-play or the Add New Hardware wizard will actually perform trouble-free, so even if you choose to install your hardware using these options, you may still end up doing a manual hardware installation.

Before attempting a detection, ensure that the device is properly plugged in and powered; if not, the device will never be detected. If the device is not detected, you will have to manually load the drivers and configure the device. Manual loading of drivers is discussed in the chapter.

To load a device through the Add New Hardware wizard, open the Add New Hardware Control Panel, which opens the Add New Hardware wizard, and then click the Next button. Click the Next button again. You may be presented a list of the items that are not currently working properly, and asked if you would like to install them. If the item you want to install is not on the list, choose No, and click Next. On the next screen you will be asked if you would like Windows to scan for new hardware (see Figure 23-1). If you think the device that you have added to the system will be detected by Windows, click Yes, and then click Next. If you think Windows will not be able to detect the device, click No, and perform a manual installation.

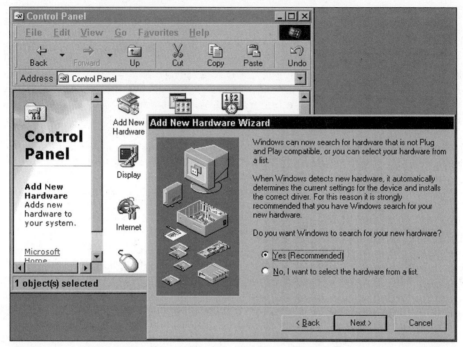

Figure 23-1: The Add New Hardware Wizard is launched through the Control Panel.

If you are letting Windows automatically detect drivers, click the Next button, and then click the Next button again. Windows then starts the detection process. This process is not supposed to hang or crash your computer, but it sometimes does. If you find that your computer is not responding to any input for what you consider to be an extended amount of time, you may have to reboot it. Should you need to reboot your computer, turn it off for ten seconds, and then turn it back on. This reboot helps reset the PCI bus on the motherboard. If you do not do this type of reboot, future detections may have problems. Now the question may be, what is an extended period of time? The definition has changed over the years. With non-plug-and-play machines, that time used to be about 30 seconds; but with many modern machines you may find that this time is substantially longer — possibly several minutes. In short, you should wait as long as you think is reasonable.

If any devices are found, they are listed in a dialog at the end of the wizard. If the device you want to install is in the list, select it, and then click Next to begin the driver installation process. The installation process may prompt you for driver disks that would be used for normally detected devices. If the device you want to install does not appear in the list, just click Next and you will start the manual installation process. The manual installation process starts by you choosing the type of device you are installing, as shown in Figure 23-2.

Figure 23-2: Even if Windows cannot locate the devices, you will still be able to add them manually.

If you are manually installing drivers, select No when the wizard asks if you want Windows to search for new devices, and then choose the Next button. You will have to choose one of the listed device categories. Select the category for the device you are adding, whether it is a display adapter or a network card, and then click Next. After Windows updates its driver database, you are presented with a list of drivers from various manufacturers. Select the manufacturer of the device you are installing, and then select the device driver for your device. If your device is not on the list, click the Have Disk button. You will have to type in the location of your driver's `.inf` file or browse for its location, as shown in Figure 23-3. The `.inf` file is usually named `oemsetup.inf` or `setup.inf`, but could have any name, and it contains the installation instructions for the driver. If the .inf file you want is in the same directory as several others, you will not be able to choose the file directly, but rather you must choose the directory.

Regardless of how you installed the drivers for the device, if Windows is not able to detect the device settings for the device, you are prompted to specify IRQ, I/O, and DMA, and memory resource settings. The prompt should only be necessary for non-plug-and-play devices. If you are not sure of the current settings for the device, confirm the settings by examining the hardware or by using the configuration utility that came with the device. A configuration utility should be included on the driver disk of any devices that support software configuration. If the device in your computer is configured for plug-and-play, you should not have to worry about this.

For many devices, you are able to add drivers in the device configuration screen. The screen is not available for all devices, but is available for network cards, display adapters, and several other devices. To change the display adapter that you are using, open the Control Panel, double-click on Display, and click the Settings tab. If you are using Windows 98, click the Advanced button, and then the Adapter tab. Click the Change button, and the Update Device Driver Wizard appears (see Figure 23-4).

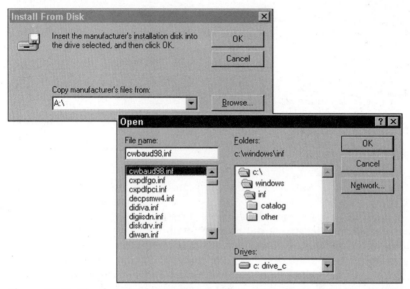

Figure 23-3: You have to locate the .inf file for the devices you want to install.

If you want to change the settings for a device that is installed on your system, you can either use the Control Panel applet for the device (such as Modems, Multimedia, Display, or Network) or the Device Manager. Since each Control Panel applet is different, you will not be looking at them here, but rather you will look at the Device Manager. To access the Device Manager, open the Control Panel, double-click System applet (which will open a window labeled System Properties), and then click the Device Manager tab in the System Properties dialog box. You can also open the System Properties dialog box by right-clicking on My Computer and choosing Properties. With the Device Manager open, expand the appropriate device tree until you see the device that you want to work with, then right-click the device and choose Properties. You will be able to use the Properties window to disable the device in the current hardware profile, change the driver, and set resources for the device (see Figure 23-5). Based on how the driver was designed, you may not have a Driver or Resources tab, and will not be able to configure the settings on those tabs.

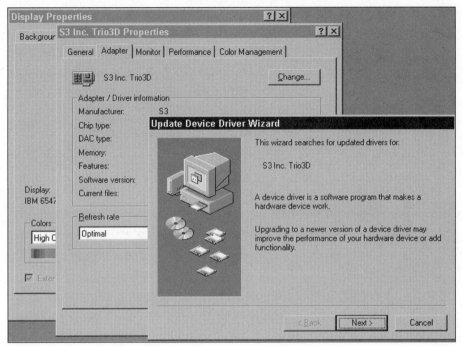

Figure 23-4: You can change the driver you are using for your video card through the Display applet in the Control Panel folder.

If you want to delete a device driver that's been installed, you can do this in the individual device's Control Panel applet, such as the Network Control Panel applet, or you can use the Device Manager. If you use the Device Manager, you will be able to delete any device that is listed in the computer. With the Device Manager open, expand the device category your driver belongs to, select the device that you want to delete, and then click the Delete button.

Windows 2000

When working with devices in Windows 2000, you also have an Add/Remove Hardware control panel. (Windows 9x has only an Add Hardware control panel.) The proper and clean removal of devices represents a large step forward in device management for the Windows operating system.

When you open the control panel, the Add/Remove Hardware Wizard starts. Click Next to proceed. The first question you will be asked is whether you want to add/troubleshoot a device or uninstall/unplug a device. Make your choice, and click the Next button.

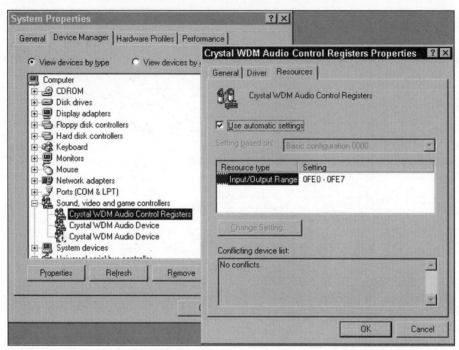

Figure 23-5: Device Manager is a very powerful tool when it comes to device management.

If you are adding a device, Windows 2000 performs a search of plug-and-play devices. The results of this search are displayed for you and include any unknown devices. Since adding includes troubleshooting, this is your opportunity to select the device already installed on the system that you would like to troubleshoot. If the device that you need to load the drivers for is not listed on this page, choose the option to add a new device, and then click Next to proceed. If you are troubleshooting a device, the next screen in the wizard informs you that when you finish the wizard, you will start the troubleshooter. The troubleshooter lets you set resource settings, such as IRQ and I/O addresses.

If you choose to add a new device, you have the option of letting Windows search for new hardware or of selecting hardware from a list. Searching for hardware with Windows 2000, as shown in Figure 23-6, is similar to searching for hardware with Windows 9x. Once again, if your computer appears to not be responding, give it some time to finish its detection process. If no devices are found, click the Next button to manually choose a driver.

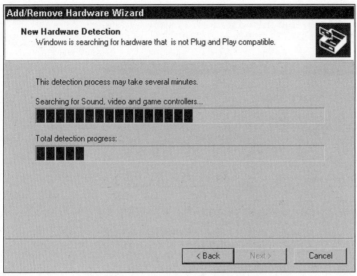

Figure 23-6: Plug-and-play detection is used to initially locate all devices on your computer.

If you are installing a device manually, you first choose the hardware type from batteries to tape drives (see Figure 23-7). Once you make your selection, click Next.

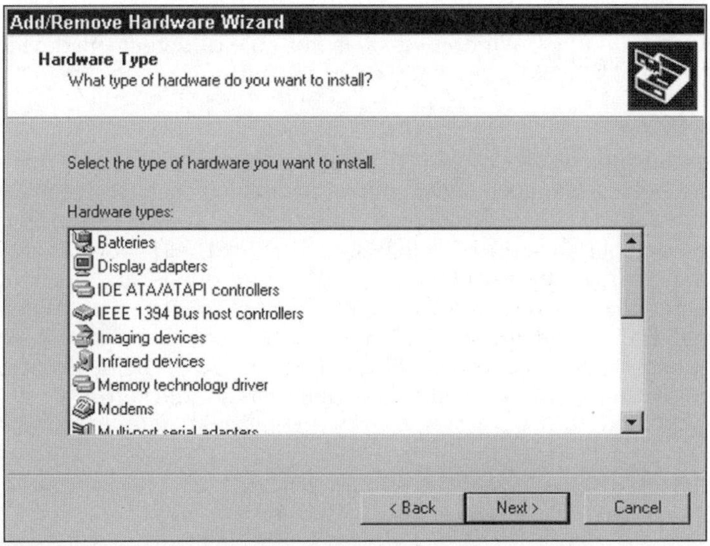

Figure 23-7: When starting manual installations, you have to choose the type of device you are installing.

A screen listing manufacturers and devices appears. Choose the manufacturer, and then choose a device from that manufacturer, as shown in Figure 23-8.

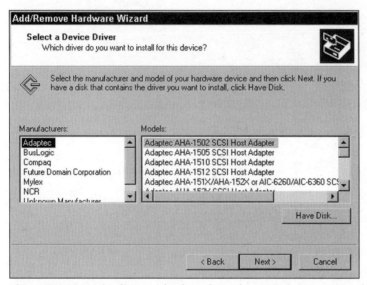

Figure 23-8: Device lists are broken down by manufacturer to make it easier to locate specific devices.

After you select your device, click the Have Disk button to browse for or type in the location of the device's .inf file. If Windows 2000 is not able to detect the device settings for your device, it asks you to manually enter the settings, as shown in Figure 23-9.

You can change the settings on one of your devices by using either the device's control panel or the Device Manager. Since control panels for each device are different, you will look only at the Device Manager in this section. To access the Device Manager, open the Control Panel, double-click System, click the Hardware tab, and then click the Device Manager button. The Device Manager opens, and you can expand the device tree and select the device that you want to work with. When you find the device, right-click it and choose Properties. The Properties window for the device lets you choose which hardware profiles will make use of the device, troubleshoot the device, examine driver details, and change resource settings.

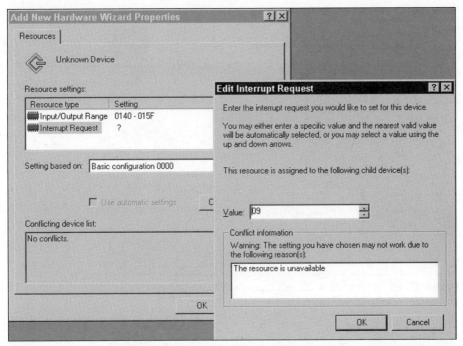

Figure 23-9: You may have to tell Windows 2000 what resources your device requires.

When you want to remove a device, you can use either the Add/Remove Hardware Wizard or the Device Manager. The Device Manager allows you to select any installed device on your system and delete it. To use the Device Manager, open it, expand the hardware tree to locate your device, right-click the device, and choose Uninstall. You are presented with one confirmation dialog box, and then the device is uninstalled. If you use the Add/Remove Hardware Wizard, you can uninstall or unplug/eject a device, as shown in Figure 23-10.

Unplug/eject a device can be used to temporarily remove a device, such as a PC card that you will be re-adding at a later date. If you are planning to permanently remove the device, choose the uninstall option, and then click the Next button. You are presented with a list of devices; select the device that you want to uninstall, and click Next. Confirm that you want to delete the device by selecting Yes (see Figure 23-11), and then clicking Next. The removal of the device is completed. The next screen tells you that the device has been uninstalled; click the Finish button.

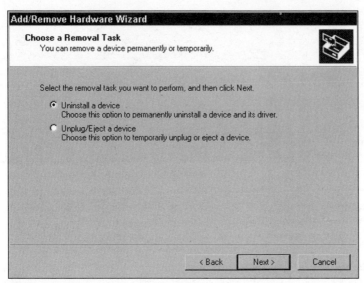

Figure 23-10: Device removal now comes with options. You can temporarily remove devices with the unplug option.

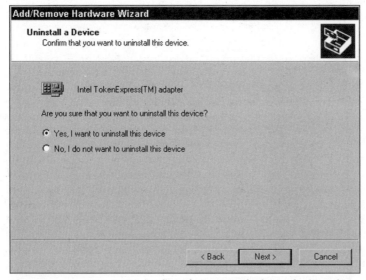

Figure 23-11: You must confirm the removal of any devices, for the sake of safety.

Working with Plug-and-Play

2.4 Identify procedures for loading/adding and configuring application device drivers, and the necessary software for certain devices. Content may include the following: Windows 9x Plug and Play and Windows 2000

When working with plug-and-play devices, there should be less work for you to do, since device identification, driver selection, and hardware configuration is handled by plug-and-play. The plug-and-play specification says that devices should:

✦ Be uniquely identified

✦ State the services that they provide and the resource that they require

✦ Identify the driver that supports it

✦ Allow software to configure them

The plug-and-play standard also requires that plug-and-play devices are backward-compatible with non-plug-and-play systems — at least that's the recommendation. All plug-and-play hardware should also be independent of operating systems that are installed on the system.

The plug-and-play process starts with the computer BIOS that supports plug-and-play. In addition, you also need an operating system that supports plug-and-play, and plug-and-play devices. Windows 9x and Windows 2000 both represent plug-and-play-aware operating systems; Windows NT 4.0 does not support plug-and-play. The plug-and-play process contains three major components:

✦ Bus Enumerator

✦ Configuration Manager

✦ Resource Arbitrator

Figure 23-12 shows how these components fit together.

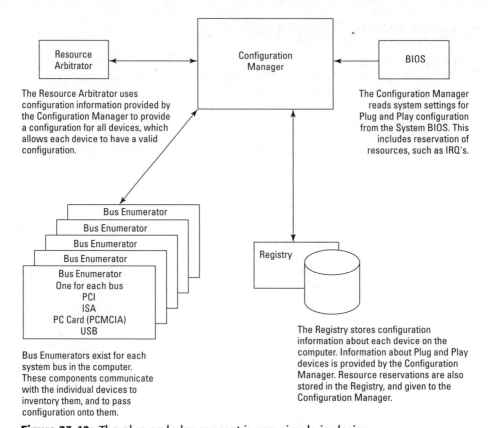

Figure 23-12: The plug-and-play concept is very simple in design.

When Windows NT 4.0 was released, it provided a shell or user interface update to make it appear like Windows 9x. There were also some architectural changes to provide additional power and stability over Windows NT 3.51. Since plug-and-play represented a major structural change in the OS, Microsoft opted not to support it in Windows NT 4.0.

One of the lowest components in the plug-and-play process is the Bus Enumerator. The job of the Bus Enumerator is to directly deal with individual devices. Each bus inside your computer has a Bus Enumerator, PCI, ISA, EISA, PCMCIA (PC Card), SCSI, and USB. When a device is added to the system, especially in the case of PCMCIA devices, it announces its presence to the Bus Enumerator. The Bus Enumerator assigns an ID to the device, interrogates the device IRQ and I/O preferences, and possibly reconfigures the device based on requests from the Configuration Manager. The Bus Enumerator is called into action when a plug-and-play computer boots, and it has work to do whenever a device is added or removed from a particular bus.

When the Bus Enumerator and the rest of the plug-and-play system are given a notification of device removal, then they can prepare for it. For example, if you wanted to remove a PC Card bus Ethernet adapter, you could notify the plug-and-play system by stopping the device using the PC Card icon in the System Tray or the PC Card Control Panel applet.

Tip   Devices that can be removed or added to a system while it is running are referred to as hot swappable. Cold swapping takes place when the machine is powered down, which is the case for most devices. PCMCIA or PC cards support hot swapping, and some of the newer computers support hot swapping on the PCI bus.

The Bus Enumerator does not decide what resources the new device is going to use — that is the job of the Configuration Manager. The Bus Enumerator passes all of the information about the device to the Configuration Manager, which takes a look at all of the resources that are required by all of the devices on the system. If there are multiple devices that require the same resources, the Configuration Manager calls on the Resource Arbitrator. The Resource Arbitrator evaluates which devices can operate at which settings and provides a solution in which all devices are able to use settings that are compatible for them.

Once the Resource Arbitrator has worked its magic, a new resource configuration is passed to the Configuration Manager. The Configuration Manager accepts the new configuration, contacts each Bus Enumerator and has the Bus Enumerator reconfigure any devices that require reconfiguration. So while the Bus Enumerator does not decide how to reconfigure devices, it does actually carry out the reconfiguration of the devices.

All of the information about devices on your computer is written into the Registry, which maintains the hardware tree. The Configuration Manager is responsible for writing the information into the registry. In a computer that supports the plug-and-play BIOS, the basic plug-and-play configuration is actually performed at the BIOS level. When the operating system loads, it goes through the plug-and-play process and modifies any configurations that require modification.

If legacy or non-plug-and-play devices exist on your system, resources are assigned to them first. This makes perfect sense, since these devices cannot be reconfigured through the plug-and-play process. In order to ensure that the proper resources are allocated to legacy devices, you can reserve those resources in a number of areas, including:

✦ The system BIOS

✦ The Device Manager

In most BIOS configurations, you have the option of reserving resources for non-plug-and-play devices. The settings in the BIOS either tell you that you are reserving resources for non-plug-and-play devices, reserving resources for legacy devices, or disabling resources. Those resources are not actually disabled, but their use by plug-and-play devices is disabled; legacy devices are still able to use these resources. The BIOS represents the best place to reserve legacy resources for this reason: it represents the first area where plug-and-play resources are actually assigned to devices.

 Caution Before changing any of your BIOS settings, consult your motherboard documentation. Incorrect modification of your BIOS can result in your computer not functioning.

If you choose to use the Device Manager to reserve resources, open the Device Manager and right-click on the computer icon at the root of the Device Manager. By choosing properties of the computer, you can view the resources that are being used across the system, and reserve resources for legacy devices. You can reserve IRQs, I/O addresses, DMA channels, and driver memory locations. To reserve a resource, select the Reserve Resources tab and then:

1. Select the radio button for the type of resource you want to reserve.

2. Select the Add button.

3. Select the resource value to reserve.

4. Select the OK button to complete the reservation.

Since legacy devices cannot be reconfigured through the plug-and-play process, they should always be allowed to use the resources that they require. In a perfect world that would be all that would be required. Since we don't live in a perfect world, you must reserve resources. It would make sense that you can reserve resources at either the BIOS or the OS level, but reserving them at the BIOS level is more consistent for achieving a working configuration.

When plug-and-play systems first entered the market, they were plagued with difficulty. Much of this difficulty came from devices that were not fully plug-and-play compliant or from non-plug-and-play–aware system BIOS. Other problems were caused by mixing plug-and-play and non-plug-and-play devices together in a computer. Over the years, everyone has learned a lot about how plug-and-play should and can work, and today plug-and-play is much closer to its ideal.

Configuring Windows Printing

 2.4 Identify procedures for loading/adding and configuring application device drivers, and the necessary software for certain devices. Content may include the following: Procedures for set up and configuring Windows printing subsystem

One of the devices that is found in most computing networks is a printer. This section takes a look at how to install and configure a printer to support printing under Windows 9x and Windows 2000. The first thing that you need in order to support printing is a printer. Before you get too far along, consider some terminology. A printer can refer to one of two things, either the object in your printer's folder or the physical printing device. This can often lead to confusion when people are referring to a printer. In most cases when working with the Windows operating system, the printer refers to the object in your Printers folder; and the actual printing device is referred to as the printing device.

Exam Tip When dealing with hardware-related questions on the exam, the term printer refers to the physical printing device.

Installing a printer

Objective

2.4 Identify procedures for loading/adding and configuring application device drivers, and the necessary software for certain devices. Content may include the following: Installing

As with everything in the Windows environment, there are several different ways to install a printer. Here are some of the ways to install a printer:

+ Plug it in, and power it up.
+ Reboot your computer.
+ Run the Add New Hardware Wizard.
+ Use the Add Printer icon in the Printers folder.

Any of these methods can be used to add a printer to your system. If your computer is currently configured with a bi-directional parallel port, then all you should have to do is attach the cables and power up the printer. If that does not work, rebooting your computer allows Windows to probe the parallel port for new devices.

Adding a printer to a Windows 9x computer

To use the Add Printer Wizard to add a printer to your system, double-click the Add Printer icon in the Printers folder. The wizard's first screen asks if the printer you are adding is a local printer or a network printer (see Figure 23-13).

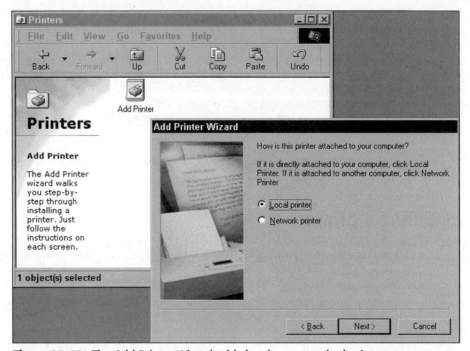

Figure 23-13: The Add Printer Wizard adds local or networked printers to your system.

If you are adding a local printer, you will be asked to choose a printer driver for the device (see Figure 23-14). The list of devices you are presented with is very comprehensive, but if the printer you are using is not included on the list, click the Have Disk button, and provide a driver disk for your printer.

Now that you have told Windows 9x what type of printer you're printing to, you just have to let the operating system know where to find the printer. When choosing the port that the printing device is connected to, you can choose from COM1, COM2, LPT1, LPT2, or File (see Figure 23-15). Printing to a file generates a file whose contents are in the printer's RAW or native format. This file can later be directed to the printer port using either the `print` or `copy` command. An example of the `copy` command looks like this:

```
copy "My Print File" LPT1
```

Printing to a file provides a useful way of outputting data to a non-shared printer on another computer without having to install specific applications on that computer. The output file still has to be copied to the remote computer in some manner, which could be done by floppy disk, email, or network server.

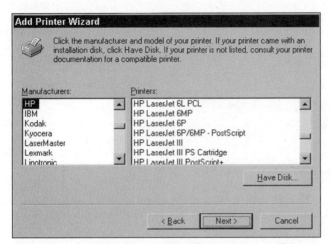

Figure 23-14: If Windows cannot detect it, you will have to choose your printer model.

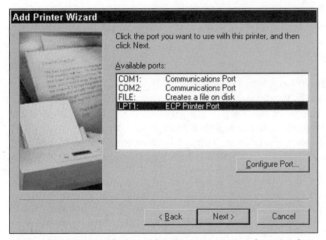

Figure 23-15: You have to let your computer know where to find your printer.

If you are adding a network printer, you are asked to identify the location on the network where you will be printing. The network location is usually specified by a server name followed by a share (\\server\printer, for example), as shown in Figure 23-16. In addition to the network location, you are asked if you print from MS-DOS-based programs. Printing from MS-DOS-based programs is an important question, since MS-DOS-based programs can only print to a local port, such as LTP1. If you answer Yes to printing from MS-DOS-based programs, the next screen has you capture a printer port. Capturing a printer port merely directs what would have been sent to LTPx to the network printer. You then are asked to choose the type of device you are printing to. After choosing the make and model of the printer you are installing, Windows 9x copies the drivers over to your system.

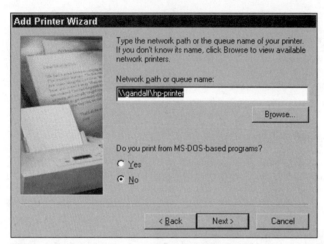

Figure 23-16: Network printers are listed on your computer, but actually reside elsewhere.

At the end of the installation process, you are asked if you would like to print a test page. If you are not certain that you set up the printer correctly, this is a great practice to confirm that everything is working. If the printer is correctly installed, it shows up in your Printers folder, as shown in Figure 23-17. You can easily spot networked printers in your folder; their icons have a wire across the bottom. Once your printer is installed, you can adjust how it functions by modifying the spool settings.

Adding a printer to Windows 2000

To add a printer to your Windows 2000 computer you can use the Add Printer Wizard. One of the first questions you are asked during the Add Printer Wizard is whether the printer you are adding is local to your computer or on the network, as shown in Figure 23-18. If the printer is local to your computer, you also have the option of letting Windows automatically detect and install a plug-and-play printer on your computer with no additional questions to answer. If the printer you are installing is not a plug-and-play printer, then you'll have to deal with the following questions:

✦ What port is your printer connected to?

✦ What is the make and model of your printer?

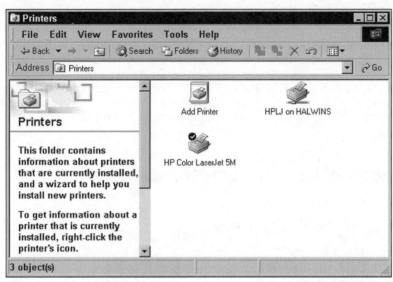

Figure 23-17: Installed printers are displayed in your Printers folder.

 Exam Tip You may get a Windows 2000 permission question on your exam. Remember that only users who belong to the Windows 2000 administrators group or power users group can install printers on a Windows 2000 computer. After the printer is installed, it is available to all users.

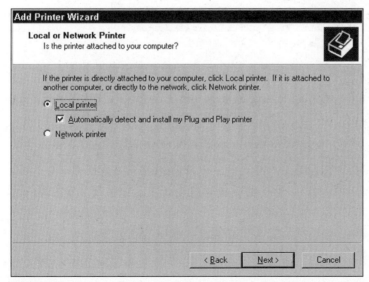

Figure 23-18: As with Windows 9x, you can install local or networked printers.

When selecting a port for your printer device to use, you can choose from among local printer ports (LTP), local communications ports (COM), Files, UNC pathnames for remotely shared printers, or standard TCP/IP printer ports. The last two actually make your local printer print to remote printing devices — what you would normally consider to be network printers — but you have local control over how printing options are handled. If you would like to use either of the last two printer ports, select the Create a new port option in the Select the Printer Port wizard page, as shown in Figure 23-19. Then select whichever type of printer port is appropriate for your system.

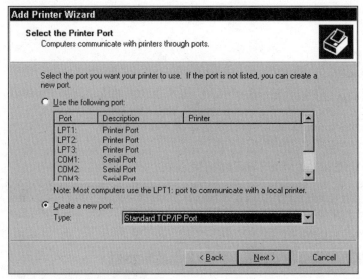

Figure 23-19: TCP/IP printer ports must be created.

If you are adding a standard TCP/IP port to your system, you have to supply the IP address of the printer that you are printing to or its registered DNS name and port name (see Figure 23-20). When using a TCP/IP port, you are actually printing directly to a device that is attached to the network, rather than attached to another computer. These printing devices will be using network cards manufactured by HP, Apple, Canon, Compaq, Epson, Lexmark, or Xerox. The information (IP address or DNS name) that you provide to Windows 2000 is used to locate this printing device on your network.

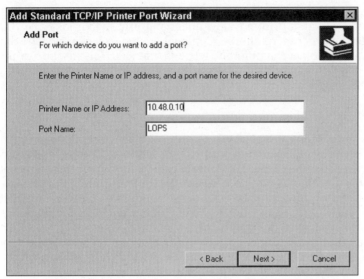

Figure 23-20: Specific information is required in order to print to TCP/IP-based printers.

After choosing where the printer is attached in your system, you have to tell Windows 2000 what type of printer it is. For that task, you are presented with a list of printers similar to the list you would see under Windows 9x. If your printer is not on the list, click the Have Disk button, and then add your printer.

In the last few screens of the Add Printer wizard, you choose a friendly name for the printer, set the printer as the default printer (or not), share the printer (or not), and print a test page (or not). You'll look at sharing the printer later in this chapter when you consider spool settings for your printer. Printing a test page confirms that your printer is properly configured.

Once again, you can easily spot network printers in your Printers folder; their icons have a horizontal wire or cable across the bottom.

Adjusting your spooler settings

2.4 Identify procedures for loading/adding and configuring application device drivers, and the necessary software for certain devices. Content may include the following: Procedures for set up and configuring Windows printing subsystems — Spool setting

The spooler settings for your printer affect the way it prints documents. Spooler settings can speed document printing, slow document printing, or just give you more control over the process. As there are many benefits to having a well-adjusted spooler, we will take a look at the different settings that exist for the spooler under both Windows 9x and Windows 2000. The spool settings for Windows 9x and Windows 2000 differ slightly.

Windows 9x

On a Windows 9x computer, right-click your printer in the Printers folder and choose Properties to closely examine your printer's settings. The General tab of a printer's Properties dialog box does not contain critical modifiable settings, but the Details tab does. On the Details tab, you are able to set the printing port, the print driver, the captured port, timeout settings, port settings, and spool settings. The Details tab (see Figure 23-21) turns out to be a useful place if you move a printer from one local port to another, change the driver that is connected to a printer port, or need to change the capture settings for your printer. Access to the spool settings is also found on this page, and since that is what we are going to focus on, let's take a look at them now. Click the Spool Settings button.

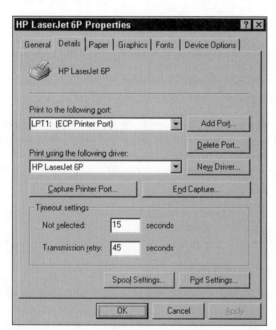

Figure 23-21: The Details tab allows you to modify how the printer is connected to your computer.

One of the big options that you have for spool settings is whether you want a spool at all. See Figure 23-22. Selecting the Print directly to the printer option disables spooling. Oddly enough, if you disable spooling, your pages come off the printer in the least amount of time. The drawback to disabling spooling is that you have to wait until the entire document is printed before you regain control of the application from which you were printing. In other words, when you tell Microsoft Word to print, it will not be able to do any more typing until all the pages you are printing are at the printer. If you spool the print job, then the application passes the entire print job to the operating system, and lets you get back to work. The operating system then takes care of printing the job as a background process (without a foreground window). Although spooling is slightly slower, it appears to be much faster to most people. It only appears to be faster printing since the time between your clicking the Print button and when your documents are available at the printer is actually longer than printing directly. Slower printing is acceptable with spooling because you regain control (use) of your application in a shorter period of time.

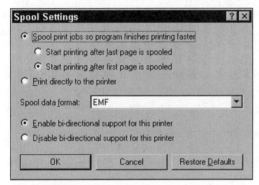

Figure 23-22: Spool settings modify how your printer manages print jobs.

When spooling, you can configure printing to start after the first page is spooled or after the last page is spooled. The benefits of either method may not appear clear at first glance. In most cases, you want to start printing after the first page is spooled. If you have shared your printer, and large slowly rendered documents are being printed, then you may want to start printing after the last page is spooled. The main consideration for printing after the last page is spooled is that applications can take a long time to fully render a document once the Print button is clicked. An application may take 10 or 15 minutes to print a four- or five-page document, during which time the printer is effectively tied up. Owners of smaller, faster-printing documents will be waiting to access the printer until the larger document finishes. Starting to print after the last page has spooled does not speed up the printing time for the document, or the spooling time, but it does cause less interference at the printer for owners of the smaller documents. Starting to print after the last page is spooled actually slows down the printing process, since a document does not even start to print until all of its pages have been spooled. On smaller documents, this makes only a very small difference in the total time it takes to print.

If you have chosen to share the printer on your Windows 9x computer, then the spool data format may make a difference to you. The spool data format can either be EMF (Enhanced Metafile) or RAW (fully rendered for printer). If the spool data format is set to RAW, then data that enters the spool has already been sent through the print processor, and converted from a Windows graphic into data that the printer understands. If the spool data format is set to EMF, then a graphic that represents the data is spooled. This actually speeds up the process of getting data into the spool (but not the printing), since now print processing has to take place. Spooling the job faster gives the user the appearance of faster printing, since they gain control of their application in a shorter period of time. If you have shared your printer, and chosen EMF spooling, then the printer output can actually be sent to your computer in this graphical format. The EMF document cannot be printed out in its current form; it still has to be sent through the print processor. If you allow spooling of EMF files, it is the print processor on your computer that does all the work. If your spool type is set to RAW, then each individual computer that is submitting print jobs to your printer does its own print processing. When using EMF as a spool format, it appears that your application prints even faster, but it actually takes even longer before the documents are printed off your printer. This is partly due to the fact that the file still has to be converted into a RAW format before it can be printed.

The last setting in the Spool Settings dialog box is to enable or disable bi-directional printer support. Bi-directional printer support requires either an ECP or EPP configured parallel port, and an IEEE 1284 compatible cable. The benefit of bi-directional support is that status information about your printer can be returned to the computer.

Options on the rest of the tabs in the printer's Properties dialog box are specific to various printers, so we won't discuss the individual options here as they will likely be different on your printer. Some general options that you will see on the various tabs include:

- ✦ Form or paper tray assignments on the Paper tab
- ✦ Graphic quality settings on the Graphics tab (dots per inch)
- ✦ Downloadable soft and TrueType fonts on the Fonts tab
- ✦ Printer memory and page protection settings on the Device Options tab

Page protection options deserve a special note. When you are printing out graphics, there is a chance that the size of individual graphics may exceed the RAM space installed on your printer. When printing, the RAM on the printer is used to buffer each page before it is output to the printer. When the page buffer becomes full, its contents are output to the printer. If you are printing text, then several pages could be in the RAM buffer at any given time. If you are printing graphics, the page buffer can become full and the page will output, even if it does not contain the entire graphic. If you have not guessed already, this is a very big problem. To solve it, you can enable page protection. Page protection buffers only one page at a time, but it guarantees that the complete page will be printed. Depending on the amount of RAM that is available on your printer, page protection will dictate the maximum dpi (dots per inch) setting that will be available. This may lower the dpi setting for your print job, lowering the quality of the output, but the lower resolution print job will then be small enough to fit in RAM and print on the printing device.

Windows 2000

As mentioned earlier, spooler settings for Windows 2000 and Windows 9x differ somewhat. In this section we'll take a look at the spooler settings for a Windows 2000 computer. To access the spooler settings, open your Printers folder, right-click on your printer, and choose Properties.

On the General tab, you can set the printer's friendly name as well as your default printing preferences, such as page orientation and page order.

On the Sharing tab, you can choose to share the printer and assign it a share name. If you expect people with other operating systems to print to your printer, you can click the Additional Drivers button to preload drivers on your computer (see Figure 23-23). Loading additional drivers on the server will mean that users on the network will not need a copy of the drivers in order to install the printer on their computer, they will be able to copy them from your computer. When you choose to install additional drivers, you are presented an extensive list of systems for which Windows 2000 can install drivers. These systems include Windows NT 3.1 through to Windows NT 4.0, as well as Windows 95 and Windows 98.

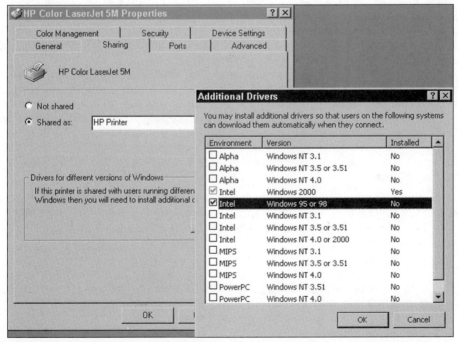

Figure 23-23: Windows 2000 allows you to store and distribute drivers for other operating systems.

The Ports tab enables you to reassign the port to which you are printing. You are given the same list of ports that you had during the installation of the printer. This is useful for temporarily or permanently redirecting the printer output when you are experiencing physical problems with the printing device, such as no toner, out of paper, or mechanical breakdown. An additional option that can be set on the Ports tab is to enable printer pooling. Printer pooling allows you to select more than one port for the printer to output to. This can be used if you have multiple printing devices of the same type attached to different LPT ports on the same physical computer. By pooling the printers, all users output to one printer, and their print jobs show up on whichever printing device is actually available at any given time. This provides one of the best ways of load balancing print jobs among multiple printing devices. It is important that all of these printing devices be physically close to one another, as users of the printer will not know which device will print their documents.

The spool options are on the Advanced tab, as shown in Figure 23-24. The settings include printer availability, which does not affect when jobs may be spooled to the printer, but only modifies when the printer will actually output to the printing device. You also can set the Priority for the printer on this tab; it can be set anywhere from 1 to 99. If multiple printers are configured to print to the same physical device, whichever printer has the highest priority always prints first. Since the Security tab can be used to assign who has print permissions, you can actually provide priority printing to specific users. The Driver setting on the Advanced tab enables you to assign a different print driver to this printer when necessary, such as when you have changed the physical printer.

The first set of spool-setting options is almost identical to the Windows 9x settings. You can choose not to spool at all or, if you choose to spool, you can start printing immediately, or after the last page has spooled. When you looked at the spool settings for Windows 9x, you examined the benefits of spooling and not spooling. In short, spooling returns control of your application more quickly while possibly taking slightly longer to print. Other Advanced tab settings that appear in Windows 2000 (and in Windows NT 4.0) include:

✦ Holding mismatched documents so that you do not end up with pages of garbled text

✦ Printing documents that have completed spooling first, in preference to jobs that are still in the middle of spooling. If the job is not finished spooling then the printer may have to wait for more data in the middle of the printing process

✦ Keeping documents after they have printed

✦ Enabling advanced printing features so that they actually show up in the print dialog box

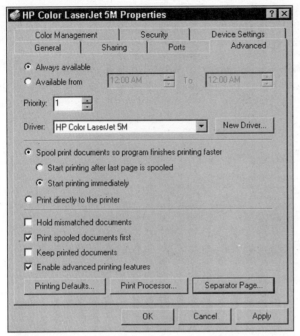

Figure 23-24: The Advanced tab contains the spooler settings.

With Windows 9x, you were able to set spool formats, with Windows 2000 you choose a spool format by clicking the Print Processor button. The only print processor that is available, without the addition of third-party software, is the WinPrint print processor, but there are a number of default datatypes. The list of datatypes should include RAW, with or without form feeds; several different versions of NT EMF formats; and text. If you allow NT EMF files to be spooled, then your print processor generates the RAW output that is sent to the printer. This reduces processor utilization on remote machines, but increases processor utilization on your machine.

The Advanced tab also has an option, as shown in Figure 23-25, for setting up separator pages, which you access by clicking the Page Separator button. Separator pages serve two functions: to provide a header page and to change printing formats. If you are using a printer that supports both PostScript and PCL (Printer Control Language) printing, then you may want to set up two printers in your Printers folder. On one printer you can set a PCL separator page (pcl.sep), and on the other you can set the PostScript separator page (pscript.sep). Then a signal is sent to the printer before each print job that sets the printer into either PostScript mode or PCL mode. Ordinarily if you mistakenly send a PCL print job to a PostScript printer or vice versa, you'll end up with several pages (or several hundred pages) of garbled text. Since this is the type of thing that most people want to avoid, the separator pages provide you with a foolproof method of providing good output. Most new printers that support dual-mode printing do not require this task to be performed because they automatically detect and switch modes as needed. The PCL separator page also prints a rudimentary cover page for your print job. If you would like a cover page for your PostScript print job, you can use sysprint.sep rather than pscript.sep as your separator page. Microsoft also provides sysprtj.sep, which is the same as sysprint.sep, except it also supports the Japanese character set.

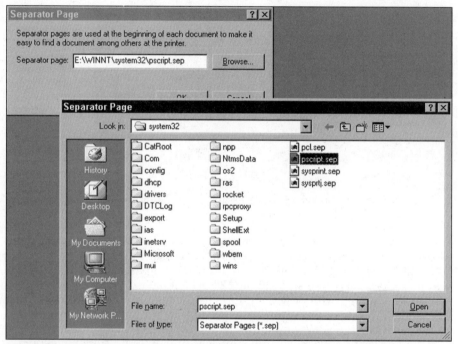

Figure 23-25: You have four pre-configured separator pages to choose from.

As with Windows 9x, the Device Settings page varies from printer to printer, based on each printer's capabilities (see Figure 23-26). Common options on the Device Settings tab include:

✦ Form and paper tray assignments

✦ Printer memory

✦ Page protection options

✦ Font substitution and downloading options

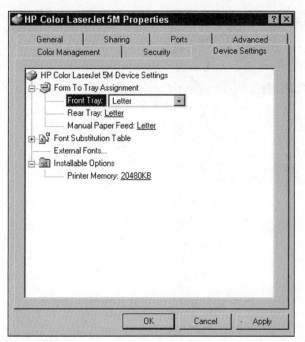

Figure 23-26: The Device Settings tab contains information that is specific to your model of printer.

Windows NT 4.0 and Windows 2000 also provide a Security tab, as shown in Figure 23-27. The Administrator can use this tab to assign Print, Manage Printers, and Manage Document permissions. Any of these three permissions can be assigned to any user on the Windows 2000 computer or in a Windows 2000 domain.

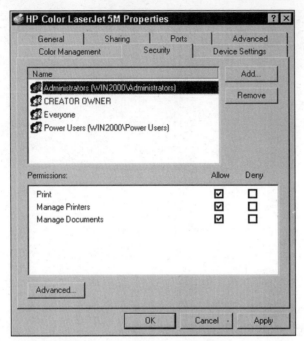

Figure 23-27: The Security tab allows you to specify who has print and/or management permissions.

The default printer

 2.4 Identify procedures for loading/adding and configuring application device drivers, and the necessary software for certain devices. Content may include the following: Procedures for set up and configuring Windows printing subsystem — Setting Default printer

Whether you are using Windows 9x or Windows 2000, you want to set a default printer. If you do not think that you have set a default printer, it is because the first printer you installed is automatically your default printer. You can identify the default printer in your Printers folder by the little checkmark in the upper-left corner of the default printer icon. If you would like to change which printer is your default printer, right-click on the printer you want and choose Set as Default Printer, as shown in Figure 23-28. Certain applications only print to your default printer, the most notable being notepad.exe. When you launch most applications, they print to the default printer. If you specify a different printer after opening an application, that printer is used for the current session, but the application switches back to the default printer when you begin your next session.

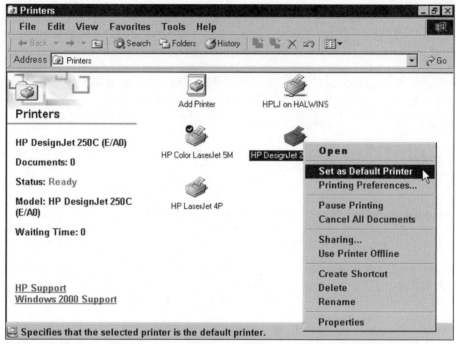

Figure 23-28: Your default printer should be the one you print to most often.

Network printing

2.4 Identify procedures for loading/adding and configuring application device drivers, and the necessary software for certain devices. Content may include the following: Procedures for set up and configuring Windows printing subsystem — Network printing (with help of LAN admin)

When dealing with printing to network locations, you have to install and configure a printer on your local machine. In the previous sections of this chapter the installation of both local and network printers were discussed. Although using the Add Printer Wizard was the only method covered in this chapter, there are a few other ways to initiate the installation of a network printer. This section will discuss those other methods.

If you know of a server on your network that has a shared printer, you can configure this printer on your computer by browsing the server through the network neighborhood. Once you have located and opened a window to that server, you should see the network printer listed in that window. Before you can print to this printer, you have to install it on your computer. There are several things that you can do to trigger the installation, including:

✦ Double-clicking on the printer

✦ Dragging a document onto the printer, which also prints a document

✦ Dragging the printer into your Printers folder

Once the installation is triggered, you may be prompted to configure capture settings, as well as selecting the printer model information.

Key Point Summary

In this chapter, you examined the differences between printer installation and configuration in Windows 9x and Windows 2000 computers, starting with a discussion of device drivers. In the installation process, you examined the selection of the printer type, as well as the printer port that it will be printing on. You also took a look at common spooler settings and other printer configuration options.

During both installation phases, you took a look at the installation of network printers. You also examined some additional options for starting the installation of network printers.

✦   ✦   ✦

STUDY GUIDE

This Study Guide presents 16 assessment questions and 2 lab exercises to test your knowledge of this exam topic area.

Assessment Questions

1. Device drivers are used to:

   A. Provide power to the device while it is operating.

   B. Act as a software interface between the operating system and the device.

   C. Provide advanced configuration options for the device.

   D. Steer the device to a new location on the computer.

2. Plug-and-play devices must be able to support all of the following except _____.

   A. Dynamic reconfiguration of resources

   B. Configuration through jumpers and dip switches

   C. Backward-compatibility with legacy systems

   D. Unique identification

3. Which of the following operating systems support plug-and-play?

   A. Windows NT 4.0

   B. Windows 2000

   C. Windows 98

   D. MS-DOS 6.22

4. Which of the following is not part of the plug-and-play procedure?

   A. Resource Arbitrator

   B. Dynamic Reconfigurator

   C. Configuration Manager

   D. Bus enumerator

5. Which of the following bus architectures support plug-and-play?

   A. PCI

   B. PCMCIA

   C. USB

   D. PCQ

6. Device settings such as IRQs can be modified through which tool?

   A. Device Manager

   B. Resource Manager

   C. Device's Control Panel, such as Network Control Panel

   D. Device Arbitrator

7. When removing devices with Windows 2000, what should you do first?

   A. Physically remove the device.

   B. Unplug the device.

   C. Shut down your computer.

   D. Remove the device through the Add/Remove Hardware Control Panel.

8. Which tool can be used to examine the status of a device?

   A. Device Manager

   B. Resource Explorer

   C. Device Explorer

   D. Status Examiner

9. You have just purchased a new printer for your Windows 2000 computer. You have attached your printer to your computer while the computer was powered off. What must you do to initiate the installation of the drivers?

   A. Insert the driver disk or the Windows 2000 CD-ROM, and restart your computer.

   B. Place a clean sheet of paper in your printer and restart your computer.

   C. Power on your printer, restart your computer, and provide necessary disks when prompted.

   D. Unplug the printer, restart your computer, and then plug your printer in again.

10. When printing to a local printer, what can you do to improve the performance of the printing process with Windows 2000?

   A. Spool in an NT EMF format.

   B. Print after the last page is spooled.

   C. Use a TCP/IP port.

   D. Disable spooling.

11. Which of the following is not a spooling option in Windows 98?

   A. Print after the last page is spooled.

   B. Print directly to a network printer.

   C. Print after the first page is spooled.

   D. Spool data format = EMF.

12. How do you set a default printer in Windows 2000?

   A. Open the Printers folder, right-click the printer, and choose Set as Default Printer.

   B. Open the Printers folder, and choose Set Default Printer from the Settings menu.

   C. Open the Printers folder and choose Promote to Default from the Printers menu.

   D. You are not able to specify a default printer.

13. You want to print to a network printer that is controlled through a Windows 2000 Advanced Server on your network. Which of the following is the correct way to refer to the printer?

   A. //<server>/<printer>

   B. \\<server>\Shares\<printer>

   C. //<server>/Printers/<printer>

   D. \\<server>\<printer>

14. Which of following spool methods restores control of your application the fastest?

   A. Start printing after the last page is spooled

   B. Spool data format = EMF

   C. Print directly to the printer

   D. Enable bi-directional support for this printer

15. Which of the following spool methods provides final printouts the fastest?

    A. Start printing after the last page is spooled

    B. Spool data format = EMF

    C. Print directly to the printer

    D. Enable bi-directional support for this printer

16. What must you do to allow other users on your network to print to your printer?

    A. Publish your printer into Active Directory.

    B. Share your printer through the File and Printer Sharing service.

    C. Open the Printers folder, right-click on your printer, and select Allow Printing.

    D. This is not possible.

Lab Exercises

Lab 23.1 Examining Driver Resource Settings with Device Manager

In this exercise, you can use either Windows 9x or Windows 2000. You will be examining the resources that are in use by your network card.

1. Open your My Computer window. Open the Control Panel folder. Then open the System control panel.

2. If you are using Windows 9x, choose the Device Manager tab. If you are using Windows 2000, choose the Hardware tab, and click the Device Manager button.

3. Expand the Network Adapters section.

4. Select your network card, and get the properties for it.

5. Select the Resources tab and record the following settings (if available):

Memory Range:

Input/Output Range:

Interrupt Request:

Direct Memory Access:

6. Close the Network Card Properties window, and the associated windows.

Lab 23.2 Installing a Printer with Windows 9x

For this lab exercise, you will install a printer on a computer with Windows 9x. If you are using Windows 2000, most of the steps are similar. You will require access to the source files, such as the Windows 9x CD-ROM.

1. Open your My Computer window. Open the Printers folder.

2. Open Add Printer.

3. Click Next to pass the welcome screen.

4. Choose Local printer, and click Next.

5. Choose Generic in the Manufacturers column, and Generic / Text Only in the Printers column. Click Next.

6. Select FILE as a port. Click Next.

7. Name the printer Text Printer, and do not make it your default printer (unless it is the only printer on your computer).

8. Choose Yes for printing a test page. Then click Finish.

9. At this point, you may be prompted to provide your CD-ROM or locate the source files. The driver files for your new printer are copied to your hard drive. After the driver is installed, the printer is listed in your Printers folder, and a Print to File dialog box appears. This is to output the test page that you asked for. In the Folder list, select c:\labfiles; type `testpage.prn` in the File Name box; and click OK. You are always prompted for a filename when you print to this printer.

10. Open your labfiles folder to locate the test page. Double-click testpage.prn to open it. The Open With dialog box appears. Clear the checkbox for the Always use this program to open this file option, and then select WordPad from the list of applications.

11. WordPad displays the text-only test page that was printed by Windows 9x. After examining the page, close WordPad.

12. If you do not want the printer any longer, select the Text Printer in the Printers folder, right-click it, and choose Delete. Confirm the deletion. Close the Printers folder.

Answers to Chapter Questions

Chapter Pre-Test

1. Locations include **Add New Hardware control panel; Add/Remove Hardware control panel; Printers folder; and individual device control panels, such as the Display control panel.**

2. The four system resources that may be used by devices are **IRQ, DMA, I/O Address, and memory address.**

3. The tool that lets you view settings and delete devices is the **Device Manager.**

4. The tool that lets you view settings on devices but does not let you delete the devices is the **System Information Tool.**

5. The components in the plug-and-play architecture are the **Bus Enumerator, Resource Arbitrator, and Configuration Manager.**

6. All plug-and-play devices **must be uniquely identified, state the services provided and the resources that are required, identify the drivers that support them, and allow software to configure them.**

7. **Plug it in, and turn it on.** You may be asked to provide the driver disks.

8. **A collection of local printing devices that all function using the same driver can be configured as a printer pool.** This is done by adding ports to one of the printers within the Printers folder.

9. You can initiate the installation or connection to a network printer **by double-clicking it in the network server, dragging it to your Printers folder, or dragging a document to the printer.** Each of these methods connects to the printer, and possibly installs a local reference to the network printer.

10. PCL is an acronym for **Printer Control Language**, which was developed by Hewlett Packard.

Assessment Questions

1. **B.** Device drivers act as an intermediary between the operating system and physical device. For more information, see the section titled "Loading Device Drivers."

2. **B.** Plug-and-play devices must be software configurable and may not be configured through jumpers or dip switches. For more information, see the section titled "Working with Plug-and-Play."

3. **B, C.** Windows NT 4.0 and MS-DOS 6.22 are not plug-and-play-aware operating systems. For more information, see the section titled "Working with Plug-and-Play."

4. B. The Bus Enumerator identifies and configures devices, the Configuration Manager coordinates devices, and the Resource Arbitrator assigns resources such as IRQs and I/O addresses. For more information, see the section titled "Working with Plug-and-Play."

5. A, B, C. All of the bus architectures mentioned support plug-and-play except PCQ, which was made up just for this question. For more information, see the section titled "Working with Plug-and-Play."

6. A, C. Most device settings can be modified through either the Device Manager or the device's control panel. Resource Manager and Device Arbitrator are made-up terms. For more information, see the section titled "Working with Plug-and-Play."

7. D. When removing a device under Windows 2000, the first thing you should do is remove the device through the Add/Remove Hardware control panel. After you've done this, you can shut down your computer and physically remove the device. For more information, see the section titled "Loading Device Drivers."

8. A. Device Manager would be used to examine the status of the device. For more information, see the section titled "Loading Device Drivers."

9. C. The computer should detect the printer if it is powered on when the computer is starting up. For more information, see the section titled "Configuring Windows Printing."

10. D. Disabling spooling generates output on the printer in the fastest time, thus providing the best performance. For more information, see the section titled "Configuring Windows Printing."

11. B. There is an option to print directly to a printer, but it does not stipulate that it must be a network printer. For more information, see the section titled "Configuring Windows Printing."

12. A. To set a default printer, open the Printers folder, right-click on the printer, and choose Set as Default. For more information, see the section titled "Configuring Windows Printing."

13. D. The correct way to refer to a network printer is \\<server>\<printer>. For more information, see the section titled "Configuring Windows Printing."

14. B. Spooling in EMF format returns control of the application to the user the fastest. For more information, see the section titled "Configuring Windows Printing."

15. C. Not spooling at all provides final printouts the fastest, but causes your application to wait for printing to complete. For more information, see the section titled "Configuring Windows Printing."

16. B. If you would like other people to be able to print to your printer, you must share it. For more information, see the section titled "Configuring Windows Printing."

Working with Applications

Exam 220-202 ✦ A+ OS Technologies

- ✦ **2.4** Identify procedures for loading/adding and configuring application device drivers, and the necessary software for certain devices. Content may include the following:
  - Identify the procedures for installing and launching typical Windows and non-Windows applications. (Note: There is no content related to Windows 3.1.)

CHAPTER PRE-TEST

1. How many 32-bit applications run from within one virtual machine?

2. What is the purpose of Windows on Windows (WOW)?

3. Running separate WOWs serves what purpose?

4. Will a 32-bit application that has decided to hang cause problems for other applications running on the system?

5. When working with Windows 2000, what is the name of the executable that provides the virtual computer for MS-DOS-based applications?

6. What type of multitasking do 32-bit Windows applications use?

7. What file maintains settings for the MS-DOS environment for MS-DOS-based applications?

✦ Answers to these questions can be found at the end of the chapter. ✦

When MS-DOS was first created, there were very few applications for it. Many people chose to use the BASIC programming language to write their own applications. In a short period of time, people developed faster applications using Assembler, and then higher-level languages, such as C and later C++. These applications served users well for several years, and when Windows first arrived on the scene, Microsoft built in as much backward compatibility for these older applications as it could. Microsoft knew that if the Windows OS did not allow older applications to work with it, then Microsoft was risking adoption of Windows by their current MS-DOS users.

When the 16-bit Windows environment, such as Windows 3.0, needed applications, they were developed and worked well. In later generations, these applications were superseded by 32-bit versions for the even newer Windows 9x operating system. The newer applications worked with data in larger chunks, and were faster. This chapter will take a look at how all of these applications run on your computer. You will examine the level of backward compatibility that is built into both Windows 9x and Windows 2000, but you will start by exploring multitasking.

Installing and Removing Applications

 Objective

2.4 Identify procedures for loading/adding and configuring application device drivers, and the necessary software for certain devices. Content may include the following: Identify the procedures for installing and launching typical Windows and non-Windows applications. (Note: there is no content related to Windows 3.1)

Before you are able to work with applications on your computer, you will need to get them installed. With the ever-increasing rate of change that affects the computer industry, you will certainly want to upgrade or remove one of the applications that you have installed on your computer.

 Tip

The term *application* and *program* are synonymous—each represents programming code that performs a function. In this section, I will be using the term *application* to describe the programming code that represents the functions you want installed on your computer, such as a word processing application or a game. I will use the term *program* to describe the programming code that represents the utility that allows you to install the application.

Most applications come with an installation program that must be run in order to install the application. There are some applications that are actually standalone applications that do not require several files and settings to be created on your computer, but these are rare. Most applications require several files to be installed and often require Registry entries to be created that will hold the settings for the application. Due to the complexity involved in copying the files and creating the settings, the installation program is used to ensure that the application is installed properly. The developer of the application decides the name of the setup program, which in many cases will be `setup.exe` or `install.exe`.

Most application installation programs (such as `setup.exe` or `install.exe`) run slightly or completely different from other installation programs. In general, you will be asked to provide the location where you want the application installed, but most other options are application-specific, such as whether you want a shortcut to the application created on your desktop or whether you want to enable the *xyz* option.

Microsoft has provided a Control Panel applet named Add/Remove Programs to manage the installation and removal of applications on your computer running Windows 9x or Windows NT 4.0. On the Install/Uninstall tab, there is a large Install button to help you with your installation. By clicking the Install button and then the Next button, you will open a window that will allow the Control Panel applet to scan your floppy disk drive and CD-ROM drive for a program named `install.exe` or `setup.exe`. If either of these programs is found, they will be launched, otherwise you will be asked to provide the command line for the installation application. After providing the path to the installation application, you can start the installation by clicking on the Finish button.

When installing applications with Windows 2000, the Add/Remove Programs Control Panel applet has a tool bar on the left side of the screen. On this tool bar you will have to click on the button named Add New Programs and then click on the CD or Floppy button. This will open the same window as the Install button in the previous paragraph. Clicking on the Next button will have Windows 2000 scan your floppy disk drive and your CD-ROM drive for a program named `install.exe` or `setup.exe`. If either program is present it will be executed, otherwise you will be asked to provide the path to the setup program for the application you want to install, and then click the Finish button.

Many applications today are distributed on CD-ROM. When you insert a CD-ROM into your CD-ROM drive, Windows searches for an `autorun.inf` file and launches the program that is specified by the `autorun.inf` file. In most cases the specified program will start the setup of the application if the program is not already installed. This "AutoPlay" feature of Windows makes installing applications even easier.

Caution   Always use care when working with the Registry, as improper changes can leave you in a position where you will be required to re-install the operating system.

Most applications also provide a program to uninstall the application when you no longer want it on your hard drive. The path to the program and any switches that are required for it to function are usually stored in the Registry during the installation of the application.

Tip   If an application uninstalls incorrectly or you would like to know what program is used to uninstall a program, the settings are stored in the Registry under the Uninstall key, which is found at:

```
HKLM\Software\Microsoft\Windows\CurrentVersion\Uninstall
\<Application_Key>\UninstallString
```

> If the application was uninstalled, but still shows up in the Add/Remove Programs Control Panel applet, then you can delete the entire `<Application_Key>` from the Registry.

To uninstall or remove a program from your computer running Windows 9x or Windows NT 4.0, you should use the uninstall program (if one was provided with your application). The easy way to uninstall a program is to open the Add/Remove Programs Control Panel applet, select the application you want to remove from the list of applications, and click the Add/Remove button. Windows will then lookup the name of the program to run from the Registry and execute it.

To uninstall or remove a program from your computer running Windows 2000, the procedure is slightly different. This difference is apparent immediately after opening the Add/Remove Programs Control Panel applet. When you choose an installed application, you are provided more details about that application, like its size and the last time you used it. There will also be one or more buttons beside the application, either Change, Remove, or Change/Remove. To remove the application, select the application you want to remove from the list of applications, and click the appropriate button. Windows will then lookup the name of the program to run from the Registry and execute it.

Like the installation procedure, there is no set uninstall procedure, and it is left up to the software developer to design the uninstall routine. Some developers do an excellent job, while others do not. In the case of applications that do not uninstall properly, you may find the icons, files, or registry entries are still present after the uninstall has completed. If that is the case, you will have to manually remove the leftover components.

Tip
In many cases applications are removed by using special options with the setup program that originally installed them. One nice feature of using the setup program is that many developers allow you to not only remove the application, but also change the components that are installed.

Getting the Most Out of Multitasking

There are two basic types of multitasking: cooperative and preemptive. In this section, we look at the differences between the two types.

Cooperative

Just from its name, you would think cooperative multitasking is the better form of multitasking. This is probably because cooperation has always been thought of as a good thing. If you needed a job done (like building a house) and you had five people who were able to help you, through teamwork and cooperation you will probably get the house raised quickly. This is a good illustration of when cooperation works. However, if a couple of those people do not work with the rest of the team (they go to get more nails and never come back), their lack of cooperation could actually slow the entire process down.

With cooperative multitasking in the computer environment, a few programs that do not cooperate well with others can slow the entire process down. If you launch Microsoft Excel, for example, and start a large recalculation of the entire spreadsheet, Excel occupies 100 percent of the processor's time. At periodic intervals, Excel checks to see if any other programs require processing time, at which time Excel turns control of the processor over to the other applications. Each of these applications follows the same process as Excel: they occupy 100 percent of the processor's time if needed, and only give up control when they reach their periodic interval for checking with the rest of the operating system. If a program does not check with the other applications often enough, it is thought of as a non-cooperative program. The big problem with non-cooperative programs is that they can hog 100 percent of the processor's time.

Cooperative multitasking was created to allow multitasking in a 16-bit Windows environment. Most of that environment was single threaded, and as such, all applications had to work well sharing a single execution thread. Now it may seem that cooperative multitasking is inefficient, but cooperative multitasking is better than no multitasking.

Preemptive

Preemptive multitasking takes a different approach to multitasking in the Windows environment. With preemptive multitasking the operating system decides which processes get execution time. Preemptive multitasking is designed to work in a 32-bit multithreaded environment.

Each application is given a certain percentage of execution time to use during each second. The operating system then manages each of the processes that access the processor. With the operating system acting as the conductor, sharing of the processor is more equal with fewer conflicts. This does not mean that certain tasks do not attempt to run away with all of the processor's computing time, it is just less likely to happen. Preemptive multitasking entered the Windows operating system with the development of Windows 95 and Windows NT, and has been improving ever since.

Running 32-Bit Windows Applications

2.4 Identify procedures for loading/adding and configuring application device drivers, and the necessary software for certain devices. Content may include the following: Identify the procedures for installing and launching typical Windows and non-Windows applications. (Note: there is no content related to Windows 3.1)

Thirty-two-bit Windows applications represent the ideal type of application to run under a Windows 32-bit environment. Windows 9x, Windows NT, and Windows 2000 all represent Windows 32-bit environments. Since all of these operating systems are 32-bit in nature it only makes sense that the applications that are run in these environments are also 32-bit. With that said, we'll take a look at the benefits of running 32-bit applications and how those applications are executed in a Windows 9x environment and a Windows 2000 environment.

Benefits of 32-bit applications

There are several benefits to running Windows 32-bit programs, such as:

✦ Multithreading

✦ 32-bit data transfers

✦ Process isolation

One of the greatest benefits is the ability of 32-bit Windows applications to be multi-threaded. Multithreaded applications run several threads of code concurrently. Each one of these threads usually is assigned to a specific task. In the case of Microsoft Word, different threads can process typed characters, check spelling, or check grammar in your document all at the same time. If your computer only has one processor, then only one task is actually performed at any given instance, but the scheduling of all of these different tasks is optimized. If you are lucky enough to have a multiprocessor computer, then each of these threads can be assigned to execute on a different processor. This not only optimizes the execution of the program, but also evenly utilizes the processors.

32-bit Windows applications work with data in 32-bit blocks, and 16-bit applications work with data in 16-bit blocks. In any given clock cycle, a 32-bit application should be able to process more information than a similarly written 16-bit Windows application. In a perfect world, the speed factor of a 32-bit application would be twice that of a 16-bit application, but we do not live in a perfect world, so this multiplier is not actually realized. Other factors that affect the performance of the application include how the logic in the code was optimized to allow these 32-bit blocks to provide better performance.

32-bit Windows applications also run with some level of isolation from other applications that are executing on the system. This is done to provide better stability for the applications that are executing. There are some differences between how this is actually accomplished in Windows 9x and Windows 2000 computers. These differences will be examined in the next two sections of this chapter.

Windows 9x

Review Chapter 16's Windows 9x architectural diagram, which is shown in Figure 24-1, and take note that each 32-bit Windows application runs in its own area, but still under the system virtual machine. Each of the 32-bit Windows applications has its own memory space, message queue, and potentially multiple threads. Having its own memory space provides a couple of basic functions: one, it reduces the risk of conflict; and two, it is easier to terminate all resources in the event the application hangs or crashes. The application memory space contains the executable as well as any DLLs (Dynamic Link Libraries) or other code that the executable may have loaded into memory.

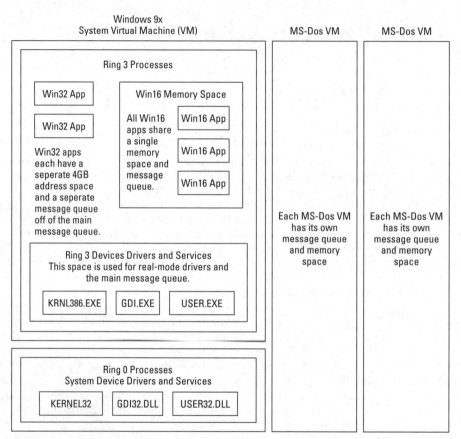

Figure 24-1: Thirty-two-bit applications run in a virtual machine that is shared with 16-bit applications.

When running 32-bit Windows applications under Windows 9x, you are provided with a very stable environment for executing your code. The only problem with this environment is that it still relies on an OS that shares some of its code with the 16-bit computing environment. This basically hampers the Windows 9x OS with some inherent system instability. Although system instability is the result, the OS was set up this way to increase backward compatibility.

Windows 2000

Review Chapter 16's architectural diagram of Windows 2000, shown in Figure 24-2, and note that 32-bit Windows applications are executed as separate processes in the user mode portion of the operating system.

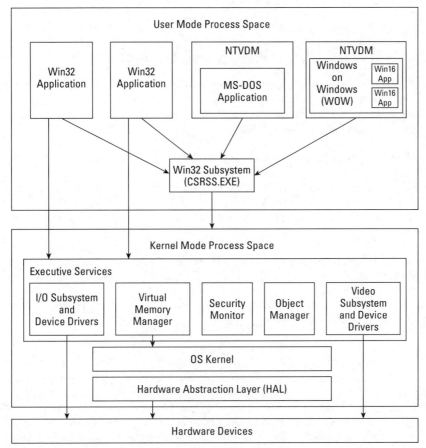

Figure 24-2: 32-bit applications run in their own execution area in Windows 2000.

In Windows 2000, 32-bit Windows applications are executed in an area that is completely separate from where the operating system executes. Unlike the Windows 9x operating system, the Windows 2000 OS does not actually contain any 16-bit code. This provides the best stability for both the operating system and the applications that are running in it, but does hinder some of the backward compatibility of the product. This does not mean that Windows 2000 is not backward compatible, but rather that it is less backward compatible than Windows 9x.

Each 32-bit Windows application is given its own address space to work with, a separate message queue, and the ability to own several threads that are preemptively multitasked by the operating system. In the event that an application hangs or crashes; the separate memory space makes it easy to destroy or flush the entire memory that deals with that application; and separate message queues means that the halted application does not block messages that are destined for other computers.

Running 16-Bit Windows Applications

 2.4 Identify procedures for loading/adding and configuring application device drivers, and the necessary software for certain devices. Content may include the following: Identify the procedures for installing and launching typical Windows and non-Windows applications. (Note: there is no content related to Windows 3.1)

Sixteen-bit Windows applications were originally designed to run under Windows 3.x. Some of these applications look for specific components in the operating system in order to function properly. Both Windows 9x and Windows 2000 emulate the 16-bit Windows environment to support 16-bit Windows applications. The actual way in which this emulation is performed represents one of the big differences between Windows 9x and Windows 2000.

Sixteen-bit Windows applications are single threaded applications that actually share a single unit of execution with the 16-bit Windows environments. This is what was referred to earlier in the chapter as cooperative multitasking. The entire 16-bit Windows environment executes using a single processor thread. This thread is then shared among all 16-bit Windows applications that are running in the 16-bit Windows environment.

Sixteen-bit Windows programming code is non-reentrant, which means that each section of code can only be executed once (or by one application) at any given time. When one application starts executing a section of code, it sets a flag (called the Win16Mutex) on that code. While the flag is set on the code, no other application is able to execute or enter that code. This is done to prevent multiple applications from executing the same section of code and thereby causing systemwide problems. One of the problems caused by the Win16Mutex flag is that any other program that wants to execute that section of code must wait until the current program has completed and the flag is removed. If the current application freezes, hangs, or crashes, it never removes its flag, thus the code is not released.

All 16-bit Windows applications suffer from these problems. Whenever possible, 16-bit applications should be replaced with equivalent 32-bit Windows applications to create an environment that is more stable and offers greater performance.

Windows 9x

In this section we'll examine the specifics of how 16-bit Windows applications are supported in the Windows 9x operating system. You'll take a look at where the application executes, how resources are shared, and stability issues.

All 16-bit Windows applications run within a common memory space in the Windows 9x environment to reduce the load on system resources, and to improve backward compatibility with applications that communicate with other applications through a shared memory address. This method of sharing data would only have been done in applications that were written prior to OLE (object linking and embedding) and DDE (dynamic data exchange).

Having these applications run within one memory space causes issues when one application must be terminated from memory. Windows 9x is able to terminate only the application proper (the executable itself) from memory, but is not able to remove any other components that were loaded into memory by the application. There was never a facility in the 16-bit Windows environment that allowed you to track these lost resources. It could actually be some of these "leftover" components that cause the application to hang or crash, so re-launching in the application in the same 16-bit environment often results in the application being unstable. The best practice is to completely reload the 16-bit Windows environment, which, in Windows 9x, means rebooting the computer. Rebooting is not necessary when a 32-bit Windows application crashes or hangs.

All 16-bit Windows applications running under Windows 9x share a common message queue. The message queue contains keyboard input and mouse input that has been directed toward the applications. If an application crashes or hangs while it has data in the message queue, it does not remove its data from the queue. This causes the queue to become jammed and prevents other 16-bit Windows applications from getting their messages. When this happens, all data input to 16-bit Windows applications appears to be suspended. You notice this when you move your mouse over the top of any 16-bit Windows application — the mouse pointer remains an hourglass. To free up the message queue, you have to terminate the application that is having a problem.

Caution

When working with Windows 9x, you can get a list of running tasks by pressing Ctrl+Alt+Delete. If you press this keystroke twice, you will cause an immediate reboot of your computer. No questions or confirmations are asked! Be careful not to press this key combination twice and don't be impatient.

To terminate an application running under Windows 9x, press Ctrl+Alt+Delete once. A dialog box that lists all the running tasks appears. You can select one of the running tasks, and then click the End Task button. If Windows 9x has attempted to contact the application but has not received a reply, the application has the text "not responding" written next to it. "Not responding" usually signifies that the application is hung, but that message may also show up next to applications that are very busy performing a specific task, too busy to respond to the operating system.

If the stalled application has set the Win16Mutex flag on sections of code that the operating system requires when running its own 16-bit code, then the operating system may actually be prevented from running its own tasks. This can affect various parts of the GDI (Graphic Device Interface) and user interface, as you can tell by looking at the Windows 9x architectural diagram in Figure 24-1. The GDI is responsible for screen redraws and window movement, and the user interface is responsible for managing mouse and keyboard input. If the Win16Mutex flag is blocking these two operating system components, you may find that your keyboard and screen have frozen. In this situation, the only thing you can really do is reboot your computer.

Windows 2000

Running 16-bit Windows applications under Windows 2000 is very similar to running them under Windows 9x, but "very similar" does not mean the same. This section will take a look at the differences between running these applications under Windows 9x and running them under Windows 2000.

The areas of similarity include the following:

✦ 16-bit Windows applications run in a common memory space

✦ 16-bit Windows applications share a common message queue

✦ 16-bit Windows applications cooperatively multitask

Even with these similarities, there are a number of differences with Windows 9x. These differences start with where the application code is actually run. Within Windows 2000, all 16-bit Windows applications are executed from within a 32-bit Windows NTVDM (virtual DOS machine). This NTVDM is a complete emulated DOS environment on to which is loaded a complete emulated 16-bit Windows environment. It is within this environment that 16-bit Windows applications are executed. Although this seems like a small point, it means that the entire 16-bit Windows environment that is implemented within Windows 2000 is contained within a 32-bit environment. That makes the entire environment as safe and stable as any other 32-bit Windows application running on the system. Within the 16-bit Windows environment, all of the normal rules that apply to 16-bit Windows still apply. Applications are still cooperatively multitasked. There is still a Win16Mutex flag, and code is still non-reentrant; but the reentrant code and other processes that can be halted are limited to this one environment. When you consider the separation of 16-bit applications, and the fact that Windows 2000 does not contain any 16-bit code at the OS level, Windows 2000 has a major stability advantage over Windows 9x.

Another advantage is that 16-bit Windows applications can be run in separate memory spaces. When a 16-bit Windows application runs in separate memory space, a new NTVDM is loaded along with a new Windows on Windows environment (WOW) as shown in Figure 24-3. The benefits of running applications in separate memory space are preemptive multitasking between applications and process isolation.

Although the application still cooperatively multitasks within this Windows environment, there are no other applications for the clock to share cycles with. Since the entire 16-bit Windows environment is run within a 32-bit Windows process, the 32-bit Windows process is preemptively multitasked with other 32-bit Windows processes running on the system. With process isolation, each application can be run within its own 32-bit Windows process; thereby isolated from the other applications. The benefit of separate processes is that when one 16-bit Windows application hangs or crashes, it does not affect any of the other applications running within other processes on the system. Any other 16-bit Windows applications that are running in the same process as the hung application are halted. Windows 2000 uses the default memory space to run all 16-bit Windows applications, with the exception of those that are run in separate memory spaces. A process running in a separate memory space is the only process that may run in that memory space.

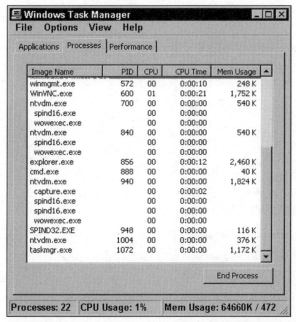

Figure 24-3: Task Manager shows that 16-bit applications are loaded within a Windows on Windows (WOW) environment.

Since you have taken a look at the benefits of running applications in separate memory spaces, you should also consider the drawbacks. There are two drawbacks to running applications in separate memory spaces. The lesser of these is that applications that communicate through a shared memory address will not be able to communicate. This has been listed as a minor problem, since very few applications that you will be running well actually perform this type of communication. This has never been an issue with any of the applications I've worked with. The other drawback, which is more substantial, is that you will use additional system resources for every NTVDM and every WOW that is loaded into memory. The overhead is associated with loading these resources in about half a megabyte for each NTVDM/WOW combination. This may not seem like a lot, but if you are running a large number of applications, it does add up.

There are several ways to start a 16-bit Windows application in a separate memory space:

✦ Add a command prompt, uses `start /separate <application name>`.

✦ Create a shortcut to modify the properties on the Shortcut tab to run in a separate memory space, as shown in Figure 24-4.

✦ Modify the open command for an associate file using My Computer ➪ Tools ➪ Folder Options.

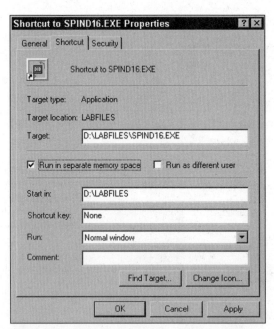

Figure 24-4: Shortcuts represent one of the ways to open 16-bit applications in a separate memory space.

Any of these methods allow you to launch a 16-bit Windows application in a separate memory space, where it can run in isolation from other 16-bit Windows applications.

Terminating an application that is running under Windows 2000 can be accomplished through the Task Manager. Access the Task Manager by pressing Ctrl+Alt+Delete, and clicking the Task Manager button, or by right-clicking on the taskbar and selecting Task Manager. The Task Manager has three tabs: Applications, which lists all the running foreground applications; Processes; which lists all running applications (foreground and background); and Performance, which provides performance statistics about your computer. You can terminate an application from either the Applications tab or the Processes tab by selecting the application and clicking the End Task button. To terminate the entire 16-bit Windows environment, select the NTVDM that contains the application, and terminate it.

Incompatibilities

When running 16-bit Windows applications within Windows 9x or Windows 2000, there is a chance that you will find incompatibilities with your operating system. Some developers want to make their applications available to you as quickly as possible. This could mean that they follow nonstandard programming practices, which may actually cause problems when you attempt to run these applications under Windows 9x or Windows 2000. For example, if you have developed a fax application, you may use all standard Windows COM driver system calls in order to communicate with the modem. Upon investigating how the COM calls are actually made, you may decide that you can achieve more speed through your application by making direct hardware calls. Direct hardware calls represent nonstandard communication with that COM device. This will not affect your application when running within the 16-bit Windows environment, but when running within a simulated 16-bit Windows environment, such as Windows 2000, then these nonstandard calls may not be properly processed. Part of the problem arises from the fact that in an attempt to provide better system stability, Windows 9x and Windows 2000 restrict direct access to some hardware components. Windows 9x restricts access to COM devices, and Windows 2000 restricts access to most hardware components. If an application requires direct hardware access to these components, it simply will not function under Windows 9x or Windows 2000.

Running MS-DOS-Based Applications

 2.4 Identify procedures for loading/adding and configuring application device drivers, and the necessary software for certain devices. Content may include the following: Identify the procedures for installing and launching typical Windows and non-Windows applications. (Note: there is no content related to Windows 3.1)

MS-DOS-based applications represent the oldest type of applications you are likely to run on your computer. MS-DOS applications are supported by both Windows 9x and Windows NT/2000. MS-DOS-based applications were only ever designed to run alone on a computer. They expect to be the only application ever running on that PC, and as such expect to see certain things, like no Windows presence. Microsoft uses virtual machines to provide a unique environment for these applications. It designed a virtual machine for Windows 9x and a different type of virtual machine for Windows NT 4.0 and Windows 2000. These virtual machines virtualize all the hardware that would normally be found in a computer, including the:

✦ Keyboard

✦ Mouse

✦ Monitor

✦ COM ports

✦ RAM

✦ Disk drives

With all of these components being virtualized, an MS-DOS-based application believes that it is running alone in a computer. The virtual computer's settings can be modified through a program information file (PIF), as shown in Figure 24-5.

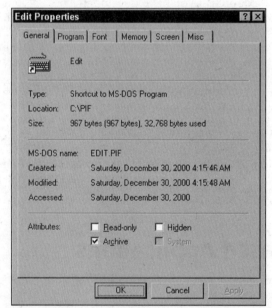

Figure 24-5: PIF files have several tabs that contain settings for a simulated MS-DOS environment.

PIF settings

Every MS-DOS-based application that executes on your computer configures a working environment from settings found in a `.pif` file. This is the case even if you are not aware that a `.pif` file is being used because there is a `_default.pif` file on your hard drive that is used if no other PIF file exists. If you want to create a `.pif` for a specific application, and make it the default `.pif` for that application, then create a file named <application>.pif in the same directory as the application executable. This `.pif` then becomes the default for that application. The easiest way to create a default `.pif` for an application is to right-click the application and choose Properties. You'll notice there are additional tabs at the top of the Properties window. If you make any changes to these tabs and apply them, then a new file is created in the application's directory. The new file has the same name as the application, but has a `.pif` extension instead an `.exe` extension. Unlike most files, the `.pif` extension stays hidden even if displaying file extensions is enabled. You can tell that it is a `.pif` file if you get the properties of the file, as shown in Figure 24-5. You may also be confused by the fact that a `.pif` for an application looks exactly like a shortcut for a `.lnk` file. Figure 24-6 shows a series of `.pifs` that have been created for three MS-DOS-based applications. Notice that the three icons in the left column are MS-DOS application icons, the icons in the middle column are the default `.pif`'s for the applications, but edit.com has three additional `.pifs` that have been created for it in the right-hand column. Each of these `.pifs` can have its own unique settings. Now let's take a look at the settings for a `.pif`. To access the settings for the `.pif`, right-click on it and select Properties. The properties of a `.pif` contain six tabs, which are:

- ✦ General
- ✦ Program
- ✦ Font
- ✦ Memory
- ✦ Screen
- ✦ Misc

General tab

The first tab that exists inside the `.pif` is the General tab, and it is the same as the General tab for any other file on your hard drive. Note that this is one of the locations where you will actually see the `.pif` file extension. You should also note the size of the `.pif` file — `.pifs` are very small (usually 1K in size).

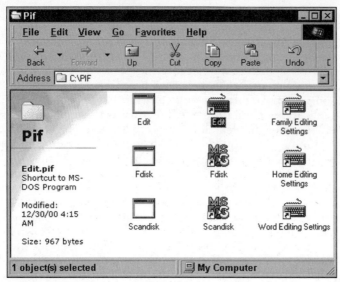

Figure 24-6: Each `.pif` for a common application can contain unique settings.

Program tab

The Program tab enables you to configure the following settings (shown in Figure 24-7):

+ **Cmd line:** The path to the executable.

+ **Working:** Specifies the working directory for the program; this is often used as the default save directory.

+ **Batch file:** Specifies the name of a batch file or program that you would like to execute prior to launching the executable, but after establishing the MS-DOS environment.

+ **Shortcut key:** Specifies a keystroke that can be executed at any time to either launch or switch to this program.

+ **Run:** Specifies whether the program is supposed to run in a normal window, maximized, or minimized.

+ **Close on exit:** Specifies whether the application should close its window when it completes execution. Note that having the program close on completion sometimes hides error messages that could be useful when troubleshooting.

Figure 24-7: Each `.pif` for a common application can contain unique settings.

With much trying, this author very rarely has seen the shortcut key in a `.pif` work the way it is supposed to. Rather than working, it does nothing.

There are two buttons at the bottom of the Program tab; one is Change Icon that allows you to change the icon that is used by the path, and the other is Advanced, which allows you to modify some additional settings.

Changing the icon is purely cosmetic, but you can specify an icon from any Windows-based executable or from a few of the system DLLs. Every Windows-based executable contains an icon list that includes the executable's icon (icon No. 0), and icons for its documents or files. Icons can also be found in several system DLLs, such as `moricons.dll`, `pifmgr.dll`, and `shell32.dll`. `shell32.dll` contains many of the default system icons that you would see used in Windows.

Clicking the Advanced button presents different options, depending on whether you are using Windows 9x or Windows 2000. In Windows 9x, the Advanced button will show options that enable you to tell Windows to do a better job of hiding itself from the MS-DOS-based program. Windows does this by substituting MS-DOS-based routines for some of the Windows-based routines that it uses to perform tasks within the MS-DOS environment. Windows 9x uses Windows-based routines in order to improve performance, so replacing them with MS-DOS-based routines will slow the application down, but at least it will execute. Windows 9x has a list of programs that require it to startup in MS-DOS mode, and when one of these is launched, Windows 9x normally suggests entering DOS mode.

You also have an option to force a program into MS-DOS mode, and when doing so you can specify that new config.sys and autoexec.bat files be created, as shown in Figure 24-8. If you use the currently running MS-DOS configuration, your computer will exit Windows and run the program within the MS-DOS version 7.0 command prompt. When you exit the MS-DOS program, Windows re-launches, as if you had typed win. If you have to specify a new MS-DOS configuration, your current autoexec.bat and config.sys files are temporarily renamed and your computer reboots. When your computer reboots it will use the temporary autoexec.bat and config.sys files that were created with the information in the .pif. When you exit this application, the temporary files are deleted, your original files are put back, and then your computer is rebooted. Microsoft gives you this option so that you can run programs that require specific settings in config.sys or autoexec.bat. Since having custom autoexec.bat and config.sys files requires your computer to reboot when launching the application, most people find it advantageous to add the specialized settings into their default autoexec.bat and config.sys files when possible.

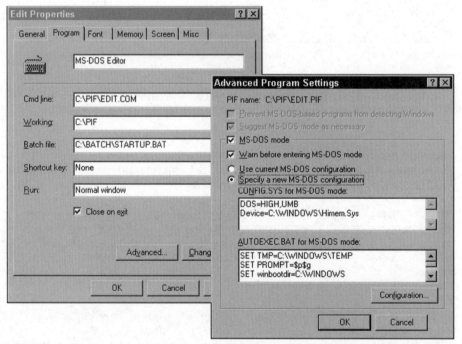

Figure 24-8: Custom configuration files can be used for your MS-DOS-based application.

If you are using Windows 2000, clicking the Advanced button brings up the Windows PIF Settings dialog box, which enables you to override the default autoexec.bat and config.sys files. The default files (autoexec.nt and config.nt) are found in the %SystemRoot%\system32 directory. These two files are used to create the default MS-DOS environment for Windows 2000. You can create new files with any names and specify the files here. There is also a check box to enable compatible timer hardware emulation. This is used to reduce the rate at which the computer sends timing signals to the application. In short, it makes the application think that it is running on a slower computer.

Font tab

The Font tab is used to specify the type of screen font that can be used by the window that contains the running MS-DOS application. These fonts can either be TrueType fonts or bitmap fonts. By default, Windows uses both and chooses the best font based on the window size. The Font tab can be seen in Figure 24-9.

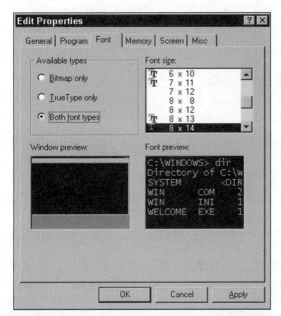

Figure 24-9: Fonts are chosen for readability of output.

Memory tab

The Memory tab enables you to specify limits for application memory. There are four types of memory that you can configure (see Figure 24-10):

- ✦ Conventional memory
- ✦ Expanded memory
- ✦ Extended memory
- ✦ MS-DOS protected mode memory

Cross-Reference   For more information about the different types of memory and how to configure them, consult Chapter 18.

The default settings for each of these types of memory are either auto or none.

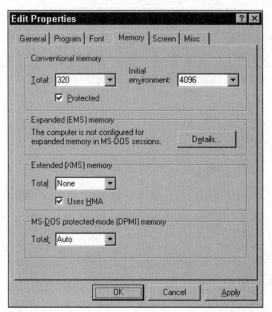

Figure 24-10: Memory that is available to the application is simulated through system memory.

Conventional memory is where the application actually runs. When the application is run from within Windows, it does not actually execute between 0K and 640K in memory, but rather from wherever the Virtual Memory Manager allocates memory. When Total memory dropdown menu is set to auto or automatic, the application is provided with as much conventional memory as it requests. It seems odd that more conscientious applications actually have problems with this setting. The conscientious application queries in the operating system before launching to inquire about the amount of free memory that is available, but rather then returning a value, Windows asks the question, "How much memory do you want?" This merely confuses the application, which then generates an error message stating that an insufficient amount of memory exists to run this application. If that happens to you, you can adjust the amount of conventional memory that is available to the application. You can allocate up to 640K of conventional memory to the application, but you should only allocate what the application truly requires. If your application requires the entire 640K and you are still having problems, you can allocate up to an additional 4K of memory to hold environment variables. There is also an option to protect this memory, which prevents the memory space from being swapped out to the Windows swap or paging file. Some applications crash when they are swapped out to the swap or paging file. Protecting memory should be avoided unless absolutely necessary because it locks the application into physical RAM, reducing the amount that is available for other applications.

> **Tip**   When dealing with the virtual memory file that is found on your hard drive, Windows 9x refers to this file as the Swap File, while Windows NT/2000 refer to it as the Paging File.

In order to use expanded memory under Windows 9x, you have to load `emm386.exe` in your `config.sys` file. Once the Expanded Memory Manager is loaded, you can specify up to 16MB of expanded memory to be available to the application.

Most MS-DOS applications do not make use of extended memory, but you are able to allocate up to 16MB of extended memory to be available to the application. The MS-DOS environment can make use of the high memory area that is provided by this extended memory.

Very few applications make use of MS-DOS protected mode interface (DPMI) memory these days, and most of those are games like DOOM and Descent by Interplay. This is a memory management technique that allows MS-DOS-based applications to make use of Extended memory (sometime referred to as Protected Mode Memory) through special MS-DOS and BIOS calls. The big advantage that is provided by DPMI memory use is that it allows MS-DOS applications direct memory access above 1MB, which provides better performance than using extended memory which uses swapping to move information between extended memory and conventional memory areas. If your application does, you can specify up to 16MB of DPMI memory.

Screen tab

The Screen tab enables you to specify whether the application is to run full-screen or in a window. You are also able to set the number of lines that will appear on a screen; the default is 25 lines but you can specify up to 50 lines. The benefit of adjusting the number of lines on the screen is that you can work with more data visible to you at any given time, but many applications do not accept this setting. If you are running the application within a window, then you can specify whether the toolbar is visible, or if Windows should automatically restore your last settings upon the next startup of the application. Figure 24-11 shows these settings, and the other display settings that can be modified on the Screen tab.

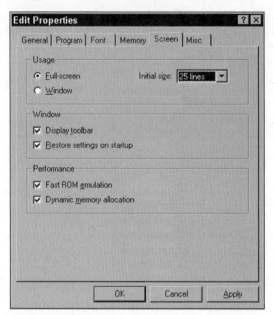

Figure 24-11: Screen settings hold several screen and video-related settings.

There are also two check boxes that play a big role with video performance. The first of these is Fast ROM emulation, which copies the video ROMs into RAM to optimize performance. Fast ROM emulation is incompatible with some applications. The second check box enables Dynamic memory allocation, which only allocates a text mode video buffer for the application. What this means is that some applications work in graphics mode from time to time, and when they do, Windows dynamically changes the size of the buffer to support graphics mode. Once again, this may cause some applications to crash. When you are troubleshooting problems with your MS-DOS-based application, it is worth checking these settings. You do not necessarily have to disable the settings, but if the problems you are having with the application are video related, there is a good chance that the settings should be disabled.

Misc tab

The Misc (miscellaneous) tab is a grab bag of settings that affect how the MS-DOS application will behave. These settings are shown in Figure 24-12. The settings affect how the program operates in the foreground or background, how it terminates, the number of clock cycles it receives, and the shortcut keys that it makes use of.

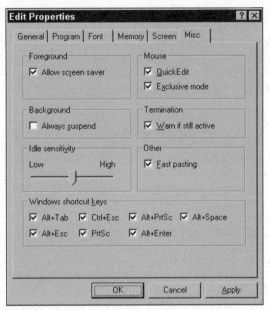

Figure 24-12: The leftover settings are all stored on the Misc tab.

The first of these settings enables you to choose whether the Windows screen saver is allowed to function when the application is active. If your application is running in full-screen mode, it has to be minimized in order for the Windows screen saver to be active. If your application does not like running from within a window, or while minimized, then this setting could cause problems. Not allowing the Windows screen saver to be active leaves your screen running 100 percent of the time when the application is active in the foreground. This may not be such a big deal since many of the monitors now have an energy-saving standby feature.

The background settings specify whether the application is suspended when it is the background task, which means it receives clock cycles only when it is the foreground application. If the application requires clock cycles at all times, having it suspended in the background may cause it to crash. Most applications do not like being suspended when in the background, although if you have an application that utilizes a large number of clock cycles, you may want to try this option.

The Warning still active Termination setting applies to MS-DOS Windows that are closed by using the Close box in the top right-hand corner of the window. This has been designed to help prevent data loss when the application is improperly closed, by displaying a confirmation dialog box, which allows you to cancel the closing of the application. Windows applications usually ask you if you want to save your changes when they are being closed, but closing an MS-DOS-based application through the Close box bypasses the normal close functions and promptly terminates the MS-DOS session and therefore the application. You should always exit your MS-DOS application from within the program, using whatever command or options are required. Unlike Windows programs that have a standard Exit in the File menu, MS-DOS applications usually have their own special commands for exiting or closing the application.

The Mouse settings of Quick edit and Exclusive mode affect the way the mouse functions for the MS-DOS-based application. Quick edit allows you to use Windows-like mouse movements to select, delete, and insert text. Quick edit only applies to Windows 9x computers, and does not apply to Windows 2000 computers. Exclusive mode may seem a little odd; when enabled, it locks your mouse into the confines of the MS-DOS-based application. This is an option because some MS-DOS-based applications have nonstandard mouse routines. Normally when your application is running in a window, you can move your mouse out of the window at any position around the window and bring it back in at any other position. However, in some applications you find that the application thinks the mouse is still in the exit location, while Windows thinks the mouse is in the re-entry location, which leaves your application mouse pointer and your Windows mouse pointer in different locations. This is an example of an application that makes use of nonstandard mouse routines. In most cases when your mouse is brought back into the application, the location of your pointers is resynchronized which is an example of standardized mouse routines. If this is not the case for you, set your mouse in exclusive mode. You can still move your mouse outside of the window using any of the standard Windows shortcut keys, such as Alt+Tab. When you click on the application to make it active again, Windows synchronizes the mouse pointers for you.

The Fast pasting option uses Windows-based routines for inserting text into your application, rather than standard MS-DOS routines. This works with most MS-DOS-based applications, but will cause problems for some. You will know that you have a problem, since pasting operations will cause errors or will not function, so disable Fast pasting in these cases.

Idle sensitivity specifies how your application responds to having its clock cycles reduced. When multiple applications are running on your system, Windows splits clock cycles among all applications that are actively requesting CPU time. When it comes to the MS-DOS-based applications, Windows only provides clock cycles to applications that appear to require them. The problem is that some applications requiring CPU time do not appear to need CPU time. If you have an application that seems to stall or crash for no apparent reason, then you may want to lower its sensitivity to being idle. Selecting this option means that the application receives additional clock cycles even when Windows does not perceive that it needs them.

The last section on the Misc tab provides a list of standard Windows shortcut keys. If your application makes use of any of the shortcut keys, you must clear the appropriate check boxes here to prevent the standard Windows-based responses to the shortcut keys. For example, if your application makes use of the Alt+Tab shortcut and you have not disabled the Alt+Tab check box on this tab, every time you press Alt+Tab you will be switched to another application. Unless disabled here, the Windows shortcut keys always take precedence.

As mentioned earlier, these options make up a bit of a grab bag of settings. Since they are all small options, it really did not make sense to place them on separate tabs.

Incompatibilities

When you examined 16-bit Windows-based applications earlier in this chapter, you looked at potential incompatibilities that could arise from direct hardware access. The same incompatibilities apply to MS-DOS-based applications. If your application attempts to make direct hardware calls instead of standard MS-DOS-based system calls, it will not function under Windows 9x or Windows 2000. In an effort to be more backward compatible, Windows 9x places restrictions on fewer hardware devices; but Windows 2000 is far less forgiving. Basically, if you have an application that makes direct hardware calls, it will not work under Windows 9x or Windows 2000.

Key Point Summary

In this chapter, you took a look at how 16-bit, 32-bit, and DOS-based applications function under Windows 9x and Windows 2000. You examined the architectural differences between Windows 9x and Windows 2000, and how support for these types of applications differ based on the architectural differences. You also examined how system stability and application support seem to go hand-in-hand for these operating systems, and the fact that Windows 2000 provides more stability, but a lower level of application support.

✦   ✦   ✦

STUDY GUIDE

This Study Guide presents 15 assessment questions and 3 lab exercises to test your knowledge of this exam topic area.

Assessment Questions

1. Windows 95 is capable of running which of the following types of applications?

    A. 16-bit Windows applications

    B. OS/2-based applications

    C. Linux applications

    D. MS-DOS-based applications

2. Which of the following types of multitasking are supported by Windows 9x?

    A. Share-based multitasking

    B. Equality multitasking

    C. Co-operative multitasking

    D. Preemptive multitasking

3. Which of the following types of multitasking provides better sharing of CPU time between processes?

    A. Share-based multitasking

    B. Equality multitasking

    C. Co-operative multitasking

    D. Preemptive multitasking

4. Which operating system(s) allows for 16-bit Windows applications to be pre-emptively multitasked?

    A. Windows 2000

    B. Windows 98

    C. Windows 95

    D. MS-DOS

5. Which of the following are benefits of 32-bit Windows applications?

    A. They share a common message queue.

    B. They run in separate memory spaces.

    C. They are preemptively multitasked.

    D. They support running multiple applications in one virtual machine.

6. How large is the memory space that each 32-bit Windows application has to work with?

    A. 16MB

    B. 1GB

    C. 2GB

    D. 4GB

7. Which of the following operating systems support 16-bit Windows applications? (Select all that apply)

    A. Windows 2000

    B. Windows 98

    C. Windows 3.1

    D. MS-DOS

8. How can you preemptively multitask 16-bit Windows applications when using Windows 2000?

    A. Right-click the application icon, and choose Launch in Separate Memory Space.

    B. Use Start menu ➪ Run then use the Browse button to locate the application, and then select the Start in Separate Memory Space check box.

    C. Type `start /separate <application>`

    D. This cannot be done.

9. What effect does a 32-bit Windows application have on the rest of a Windows 2000 system when it hangs or crashes?

    A. It halts 32-bit Windows applications that are running on the system.

    B. It halts 16-bit Windows applications that are running on the system.

    C. It halts MS-DOS-based applications running on the system.

    D. It has no affect on other applications.

10. What effect does a 16-bit Windows application have on the rest of a Windows 2000 system when it hangs or crashes?

    A. It halts 32-bit Windows applications that are running on the system.

    B. It halts 16-bit Windows applications that are running on the system.

    C. It halts MS-DOS-based applications running on the system.

    D. It has no affect on other applications.

11. What is the extension that is assigned to shortcuts to MS-DOS applications?

    A. .pif

    B. .lnk

    C. .dos

    D. .bin

12. What is the name of the default config.sys file that is processed by Windows 2000 when launching an MS-DOS-based application?

    A. config.sys

    B. config.nt

    C. ntconfig.sys

    D. ntconfig.sys

13. Bill has modified the settings for his application c:\customapp\custom.exe by editing c:\customapp\custom.pif. When he launches the application using the shortcut that is on his desktop, he does not get the changes that he made. Why?

    A. By using the .pif on his desktop, he has requested the settings stored in that .pif, rather than those in c:\customapp\custom.pif.

    B. He probably clicked the Cancel button rather than the OK button when leaving the Settings window for the .exe.

    C. Application setting changes for .pif files requires you to reboot before they are in effect.

    D. .pif files do not affect the execution of programs.

14. Which of the following file extensions are usually associated with MS-DOS-based executables within Windows 2000?

    A. .prg

    B. .bin

    C. .cme

    D. .com

15. How many applications can be assigned to an NTVDM when using separate memory spaces to launch the applications?

   A. 1

   B. 2

   C. 4

   D. 8

Lab Exercises

Lab 24-1 Modifying PIF Settings

In this lab exercise, you will create a .pif that is used to launch the MS-DOS edit command. You can perform this lab using either Windows 9x or Windows 2000. The path to edit.com in Windows 9x is c:\windows\command, and in Windows 2000, it's c:\winnt\system32.

1. Open the directory that contains edit.com.

2. Locate the edit.pif and delete it. (If it exists, it is in the same directory as edit.com.)

3. Right-click on edit.com and choose Properties.

4. Select the Program tab, and change the working directory to c:\.

5. To test this new setting, use Start ⇨ Run, and type edit.com to launch the editor. Press Esc to clear the Welcome dialog, type at least one letter or space and then press Alt+F, and press S to save the file. Note that the default directory that you are saving to is c:\.

6. Close the editor by pressing Esc, Alt+F, and then press X.

7. To create a new .pif for edit.com on your desktop, right-click on edit.com and choose Copy. Minimize all active windows, right-click on the desktop and select Paste Shortcut.

8. Examine the settings found in the shortcut by right-clicking on the shortcut and choosing Properties. Change the working directory to another location that exists on your computer, such as c:\temp.

9. Test your new shortcut by double-clicking on it to launch the editor. Press Esc to clear the Welcome dialog, type at least one letter, then press Alt + F to open the File menu, and press S to Save the file. You should note that the default directory that you are saving to is c:\temp (or whatever the default directory you were using). Close the editor by pressing Esc, Alt+F, and then press X.

10. Re-open the editor using the Run command that was used in Step 5.

11. The default save directories will be different, depending on which PIF (or shortcut) is used to launch the file. The default PIF for the application is used when the application is launched from the Run command.

Lab 24-2 Examining Resources that are Used by Windows on Windows

This lab requires that you obtain copies of 16-bit Windows applications from a copy of Windows 9x. These applications will be copied into `c:\labfiles` folder on the lab computer. For this lab, you will have to use either Windows NT 4.0 or Windows 2000.

To locate the file required for this lab, use a computer running Windows 9x, and then follow these steps:

1. Place a blank floppy disk in the floppy drive.

2. Select Start menu ➪ Find ➪ File or Folders.

3. In the Named text box type `*.exe`.

4. In the Look In text box type `c:\windows` or the path to your Windows directory. Make sure there is a check mark in the check box "Include Subfolders".

5. Press the Find Now button and wait for the search to complete.

6. Click on the column heading Name to sort that column in alphabetical order.

7. Locate each of the following files and then right-click on them and select Send to ➪ 3 1/2 Floppy (A), to copy the files to the floppy disk. The required files are: `dialer.exe`, `mshearts.exe`, `sol.exe`, `sysedit.exe`, and `winmine.exe`. Your files may not have the `.exe` at the end of the name if your computer has been set to hide the file extensions.

8. Remove the floppy disk, and close the Find window.

To copy the files onto the computer running Windows NT 4.0 or Windows 2000, use the following steps.

1. Right-click on My Computer and choose Explore.

2. In the left-hand pane, select the C: drive.

3. If the `labfiles` folder is not listed in the right-hand pane, then choose File menu ➪ New ➪ Folder, and then type `labfiles` for its name.

4. Insert the floppy disk you created in the previous set of steps into the floppy drive. In the left-hand pane, select the floppy drive icon. You should see a list of the files on the disk. Select one of the files, and then select Edit menu ➪ Select All. Then select Edit menu ➪ Copy.

5. Select the C: drive in the left-hand pane, locate the `labfiles` folder, right-click on the `labfiles` folder, and choose Paste. This will copy the files from the A: drive to `C:\labfiles`. When it has completed, you can close Explorer and remove the floppy disk from the floppy drive.

This lab exercise will now have you use the 16-bit applications that you copied into the `C:\labfiles` folder, and examine how they operate on your Windows NT 4.0 or Windows 2000 computer.

1. Open the `C:\labfiles` folder by using Start menu ➪ Run, and then typing `C:\labfiles`.

2. Open `dialer.exe` by double-clicking on it. A window with a number pad opens.

3. Open Task Manager by pressing Ctrl+Alt+Delete once, and clicking the Task Manager button.

4. Select the Processes tab and scan down the items in the Image Name column. You should notice that the NTVDM is running `wowexec.exe` and `dialer.exe`. The amount of memory that the NTVDM is using is close to the amount of memory that every application that runs in separate NTVDM will use.

5. Close Task Manager and Phone Dialer (`dialer.exe`).

Lab 24-3 Running Applications

The lab assumes that the required lab files have been installed to your disk, using the default installation path of c:\labfiles. If you have not completed Lab 24-2, then follow the steps at the beginning of that lab exercise to get the proper files in your labfiles directory. You can use either Windows NT 4.0 or Windows 2000 for this lab exercise.

1. Open the labfiles folder: `C:\labfiles`.

2. Create a shortcut to `sol.exe` by right-clicking it and choosing Copy. Right-click in the current folder and choose Paste Shortcut. Right-click on the new shortcut and select rename it to `Separate Sol`. Then right-click on the `Separate Sol` shortcut and select Properties. On the Shortcut tab, choose Run in Separate Memory Space. Click OK to close the properties window.

3. Open the following applications from the `labfiles` folder: `dialer.exe`, `winmine.exe`, `sol.exe`, `Separate Sol`, and `mshearts.exe`. When you open `mshearts.exe` there will be an error message telling you that `cards.dll` is missing and the program is exiting. Press OK to continue.

4. Open Task Manager by pressing Ctrl+Alt+Delete once, and clicking the Task Manager button. Minimize Task Manager.

5. Switch to the Processes tab and locate mshearts.exe in the Image Name column. Notice that it is still running, even though the earlier message said that it was going to exit. This application has hung on exit and could not complete its task. Although it did not in this case, mshearts.exe could have caused problems for other applications running on the system, but only those running in the same NTVDM. Examine the other applications that are running in the same NTVDM. You should see dialer.exe, sol.exe, and winmine.exe in the same NTVDM.

6. Close the mshearts.exe program by selecting it and clicking the End Process button.

7. Notice that sol.exe is also running in its own copy of NTVDM. This was the copy that was launched using the Separate Sol shortcut. It is running in its own NTVDM rather than the default NTVDM.

8. Close the other applications that were running on the system, but leave the Task Manager window open.

9. Notice in the Task Manager window that you still have a listing for NTVDM and wowexec.exe. This is the default copy that is left running after you open your first 16-bit application. You can select ntvdm.exe and click the End Process button to free up this memory.

10. Close the Task Manager window.

Answers to Chapter Questions

Chapter Pre-Test

1. **None** — Win32 or 32-bit Windows applications run in their own memory space and not in a virtual machine.

2. **WOW is used to emulate a 16-bit Windows environment within an MS-DOS virtual machine.**

3. Applications running in separate WOWs **will not affect other applications in the event that one of them crashes**, and they are **preemptively multitasked.**

4. **No** — 32-bit Windows applications that crash or hang should not cause problems for other applications that are running on the system.

5. **NTVDM (NT Virtual DOS Machine)** provides the working space for MS-DOS-based applications.

6. 32-bit Windows applications use **preemptive** multitasking. 16-bit Windows applications use cooperative multitasking.

7. **PIF, or Program Information Files**, maintain settings for the MS-DOS environment for MS-DOS-based applications.

Assessment Questions

1. **A, D.** Windows 9x is capable of running MS-DOS-based, 16-bit Windows, and 32-bit Windows applications. This information is covered across the entire chapter.

2. **C, D.** Windows 9x supports preemptive and co-operative multitasking. For more information, see the section titled "Getting the Most Out of Multitasking."

3. **D.** Preemptive multitasking provides more even distribution of CPU time between applications. For more information, see the section titled "Getting the Most Out of Multitasking."

4. **A.** 16-bit applications can be preemptively multitasked within Windows 2000 by running each application in a separate memory space. For more information, see the section titled "Getting the Most Out of Multitasking."

5. **B, C.** 32-bit applications use separate message queues so that when one application hangs, it does not affect the others. Only 16-bit Windows applications may be run in a common VM. Running applications in separate memory spaces and preemptive multitasking are benefits of running 32-bit applications. For more information, see the section titled "Running 32-Bit Windows Applications."

6. **D.** Each application or VM runs in a 4GB memory space. For more information, see the section titled "Running 32-Bit Windows Applications."

7. **A, B, C.** Only MS-DOS does not support 16-bit Windows applications. For more information, see the section titled "Running 16-Bit Windows Applications."

8. **C.** Using the `start` command allows you to run applications in separate memory spaces. For more information, see the section titled "Running 16-Bit Windows Applications."

9. **D.** When a 32-bit Windows application crashes, it has no affect on other applications running on the system. For more information, see the section titled "Running 32-Bit Windows Applications."

10. **B.** When a 16-bit Windows application crashes, it halts other 16-bit Windows applications on the computer. MS-DOS-based applications and 32-bit Windows applications should continue to operate. For more information, see the section titled "Running 16-Bit Windows Applications."

11. **A.** .pif is used as the extension for shortcuts to MS-DOS-based applications. For more information, see the section titled "Running MS-DOS-Based Applications."

12. **B.** config.nt is the default config.sys file that is processed by MS-DOS PIF files. For more information, see the section titled "Running MS-DOS-Based Applications."

13. **A.** Application settings are used from the launching PIF. If the application is launched directly, the PIF in the application's directory is used; if there is none in the directory, the default system PIF is used. For more information, see the section titled "Running MS-DOS-Based Applications."

14. **D.** COM is the only extension that is used as an executable file. For more information, see the section titled "Running MS-DOS-Based Applications."

15. **A.** When starting applications in separate memory spaces, you can only assign one application to each NTVDM. For more information, see the section titled "Running 16-Bit Windows Applications."

Troubleshooting Operating Systems

One of the main difficulties with servicing a system is trying to narrow down the cause of a problem. Part VI shows you how to troubleshoot common system problems encountered on a day-to-day basis.

This part will first explore common errors when different configuration files are missing or set incorrectly. It will then introduce you to a troubleshooting methodology, which outlines the steps you should take to identify the source of the problem.

Finally, this part will discuss some of the popular troubleshooting utilities found in the Windows environment to aid in fixing common issues with your system.

Managing Error Codes and Startup Messages

CHAPTER PRE-TEST

1. You boot your computer and it attempts to enter Safe Mode. Why does Windows 9x usually attempt to enter Safe Mode?

2. Will Windows 9x load if `himem.sys` is missing?

3. What command is commonly used to transfer OS files to a drive to make it bootable?

4. What program can be used to make changes to `config.sys`?

5. Where is `command.com` found on a drive?

6. What is the purpose of a swap file?

7. Can the event log size be adjusted?

8. What program can quickly edit `system.ini` and `win.ini`?

✦ Answers to these questions can be found at the end of the chapter. ✦

This chapter examines problems that are common to the Windows environment. Many of these problems occur during the boot process, but a few can occur at any time. You will examine Windows 9x boot errors first, then Windows 2000 boot errors, and finally other errors that occur within the operating system. Some of these errors can be directly resolved, while others you may have to live with.

Windows 9x Boot Files

There are many types of errors that you can encounter during the boot process of Windows 9x. Windows 9x follows its own boot process steps, but also incorporates steps from MS-DOS. It is because of this behavior that troubleshooting the boot process of Windows 9x is rather complex. Most of the problems surrounding the boot process involve the five main startup files: `io.sys`, `msdos.sys`, `config.sys`, `autoexec.bat`, and `command.com`.

Error in CONFIG.SYS line XX

3.1 Recognize and interpret the meaning of common error codes and startup messages from the boot sequence, and identify steps to correct the problems. Content may include the following: Error in CONFIG.SYS line XX

When working with Windows 9x, your `config.sys` and `autoexec.bat` files are still processed, if they exist. The purpose of the Windows 9x animated logo is to hide the processing of these two files. When processing the `config.sys` file, any errors in the file are reported to the screen to notify the user of the error, and the animated logo is suspended.

Cross-Reference

`config.sys` and `autoexec.bat` are required startup files for MS-DOS, but are used by Windows 9x to override default settings that Windows 9x already uses, or the startup files are used to allow backward compatibility with MS-DOS based applications. If you do not need to override settings or provide backward compatibility, your system does not require these two files. For more information about these files and the Windows 9x boot process consult Chapter 22.

If you want to see all of the lines in the `config.sys` process, press the Esc key when you see the text `Starting Windows 9x...` or anytime after the animated logo is on the screen. If you press the Esc key after the animated logo is displayed, it will show up again when the monitor's refresh rate is adjusted, so you will have to press the Esc key a second time to remove it again.

As the error message suggests, there is an error in line xx of your `config.sys` file. `config.sys` is a text file on the root of your C drive. Since it is a text file, you can open it with any text editor. Count down the number of lines, starting with one, to get to the offending line. It is likely that this line has some type of syntax error. Check to make sure the drive or file that is referenced is in the directory that `config.sys` is attempting to use it from. This error can also result from passing the wrong parameters to a program or driver.

HIMEM.SYS not loaded

3.1 Recognize and interpret the meaning of common error codes and startup messages from the boot sequence, and identify steps to correct the problems. Content may include the following: HIMEM.SYS not loaded

MS-DOS did not really care if it had access to the High Memory Area or Extended memory. If these components were not available, then it lived within the 640KB memory limits. Windows 9x is not willing to do this. `himem.sys` is supposed to be loaded from the `config.sys` file; if it has not been loaded by the time Windows 9x finishes processing the file, then it will attempt to load it again. If the file is corrupted or missing, it cannot be loaded. Without access to the additional memory resources that `himem.sys` provides, Windows 9x refuses to load, because it does not have enough memory.

In normal circumstances, this error can be traced back to a missing `himem.sys` file. If you place a working copy of `himem.sys` in the `c:\windows` directory, this error should go away.

To get a copy of `himem.sys` you can `extract.exe` a copy from your Windows 9x source files. For information about this procedure consult Chapter 27.

Missing or corrupt HIMEM.SYS

3.1 Recognize and interpret the meaning of common error codes and startup messages from the boot sequence, and identify steps to correct the problems. Content may include the following: Missing or corrupt HIMEM.SYS

A missing `himem.sys` yields much the same result as `HIMEM.SYS not loaded`. In either case, this file is required to load the Windows GUI. If you do not have a copy of the file available, you can use the extract command to retrieve a copy of the file from the Windows 9x CD-ROM. This file belongs in the Windows directory.

Bad or missing COMMAND.COM

3.1 Recognize and interpret the meaning of common error codes and startup messages from the boot sequence, and identify steps to correct the problems. Content may include the following: Bad or missing COMMAND.COM

`command.com` represents the 16-bit real-mode component of the Windows 9x OS. It is called extremely early in the boot process — immediately after the boot loader `io.sys` configures the environment using `msdos.sys` and `config.sys`. Since the real-mode environment actually loads the 32-bit graphical environment, a missing or corrupt `command.com` means you do not have a working system. In order to replace or repair `command.com`, you need a working copy of `command.com`. This can be found on your emergency disk. If you don't have one, you can create one by using the Startup disk tab of the Add/Remove Programs control panel.

Remember from Chapter 22 that each different version of Windows 9x has a different version of the Startup disk. When replacing system files, you must use the correct version of the disk for your version of Windows.

If you have a valid, current Startup disk, you can boot your computer using it, and then type

```
sys c:
```

This copies a fresh set of boot files over to Drive C:. These files include `io.sys`, `msdos.sys`, and `command.com`. If you do not have a valid Startup disk, then you must create one on another computer. You may also make a bootable disk on another computer by formatting a disk and including the system files. You also want to include `c:\windows\command\sys.com`.

No operating system found

3.1 Recognize and interpret the meaning of common error codes and startup messages from the boot sequence, and identify steps to correct the problems. Content may include the following: No operating system found

Although the `No operating system found` error problem can affect both Windows 9x and Windows 2000, this section deals with solutions for Windows 9x. For solutions from a Windows 2000 perspective, read the next section, "Windows 2000 Boot Files."

When dealing with Windows 9x, this error message means that there is actually a problem with the boot loader program in the boot sector of your drive. Running `sys.com` on your boot drive should solve the problem.

Windows 2000 Boot Files

Just as Windows 9x suffers from boot problems, so does Windows 2000. This section takes a look at some Windows 2000 boot problems.

Windows NT and Windows 2000 boot issues

 3.1 Recognize and interpret the meaning of common error codes and startup messages from the boot sequence, and identify steps to correct the problems. Content may include the following: NT boot issues

Windows 2000 and Windows NT 4.0 follow identical boot procedures, so this section and objective covers both operating systems. Windows 2000 suffers from boot sector corruption, boot loader problems, and drive identification problems within boot.ini. For most problems, the emergency repair process or the Recovery Console are reasonable troubleshooting steps.

SCSI

 3.1 Recognize and interpret the meaning of common error codes and startup messages from the boot sequence, and identify steps to correct the problems. Content may include the following: SCSI

The boot.ini file on your hard drive identifies the controller bus that contains the hard drives in your computer. This controller bus will be identified as either SCSI or multi. If your drives are connected to a SCSI controller with the BIOS disabled, the controller is identified as SCSI. In all other circumstances the controller is identified as multi. This identification is recorded in your boot.ini file. If your system is not able to initiate the boot process or you receive an error regarding a missing ntoskrnl.exe, then the problem could be a misidentified SCSI controller. Chapter 22 has more information about the boot.ini file.

No operating system found

 3.1 Recognize and interpret the meaning of common error codes and startup messages from the boot sequence, and identify steps to correct the problems. Content may include the following: No operating system found

Just as with Windows 9x, this error in Windows 2000 is tied to severe corruption of the boot sector on your hard drive. To restore your drive to working condition, you should perform an emergency repair of your hard drive to restore the boot sector. Minor corruption of the boot files would report missing files, such as ntldr or ntdetect.com. Chapter 22 has more information about the emergency repair process.

Missing boot files

With Windows NT 4.0 or Windows 2000, there are four core files that are required to boot, and a fifth file that is optional. The required files are `ntldr`, `ntdetect.com`, `boot.ini`, and `ntoskrnl.exe`. The optional file is `ntbootdd.sys` — the SCSI adapter driver that Windows 2000 or Windows NT 4.0 is booting off of (if the SCSI adapter does not have an active BIOS). This section will take a look at what can be done if any of these files are missing or appear to be missing on your computer.

 Cross-Reference For more information about the Windows 2000 or Windows NT 4.0 boot processes, consult Chapter 22.

ntldr

If `ntldr` is missing, you will receive the following error message when you are booting:

```
NTLDR is missing
Press any key to restart
```

This message often means that there was a formatted floppy left in the drive. If this file is actually missing, it can be replaced with a working copy from any Windows 2000 or Windows NT 4.0 computer; although you should try to replace the Windows 2000 version with another Windows 2000 version to maintain full compatibility. To replace this file, you may have to make a boot disk to get your computer booted. This can be done with the following steps:

1. Format a disk on a working Windows 2000 or Windows NT 4.0 computer.

2. Copy the files `ntldr`, `ntdetect.com`, and `boot.ini` form the root of the C: drive. These files are hidden, system, and read-only, so you will have to modify their attributes to copy them.

3. Edit the `boot.ini` file to reflect the boot configuration of your target computer (the one that will not boot).

boot.ini

If the `boot.ini` file is missing and you have installed Windows 2000 or Windows NT 4.0 in its default location (`C:\winnt`) then the system will boot, but will not display a boot menu. If you have not installed Windows 2000 or Windows NT 4.0 in its default location, you will receive a message stating that `ntoskrnl.exe` is corrupted or missing, and that you should replace the file. The message will look like this:

```
Windows 2000 could not start because the following file is missing or corrupt:
<Windows 2000 root drive>\system32\ntoskrnl.exe
```

This message is misleading since the problem is with the `boot.ini` file. The reason for the message is that the boot loader (`ntldr`) has gone to the default location, and `ntoskrnl.exe` was not there. If the `boot.ini` file is replaced and the boot path specified in the `boot.ini` file is correct, then the boot process will continue as normal. `boot.ini` is a text file and can be edited with any text editor. To replace the `boot.ini` file you may need to create a boot disk as you did to replace the missing `ntldr` file, but you may have to edit the `boot.ini` file to reflect the boot configuration of the target computer.

ntdetect.com

If `ntdetect.com` is missing, you will receive the following error message:

```
NTDETECT failed
```

This file is generic like the `ntldr` file was and can be replaced following the exact same method.

ntoskrnl.exe

The `ntoskrnl.exe` file is found in the `<Windows 2000 root drive>\winnt\system32\` directory and if it is missing you receive a message like this one:

```
Windows 2000 could not start because the following file is missing or corrupt:
<Windows 2000 root>\system32\ntoskrnl.exe
```

This message may look familiar since it is the same message that you would receive if your `boot.ini` is mis-configured. After checking the `boot.ini` file, if the `ntoskrnl.exe` is actually missing, you will have to perform an Emergency Repair of Windows NT 4.0 or Windows 2000, restore a backup of your system, or re-install the operating system.

Tip   Ninety-nine out of a hundred times, the missing `ntoskrnl.exe` error message is informing you of an error with the `boot.ini` file, and the `ntoskrnl.exe` file is fine.

ntbootdd.sys

Most systems either boot from IDE/ATA hard drives or from SCSI drives that are attached to a SCSI controller or adapter that has a working BIOS. In either of these cases you will not find a `ntbootdd.sys` file on your drive. If you are booting from a SCSI drive that is attached to a SCSI controller that has its BIOS disabled, then you will find a `ntbootdd.sys` file on the root of your bootable drive along with `ntldr`, `ntdetect.com`, and `boot.ini`. This file is computer specific, as it is the SCSI driver for your SCSI controller. It can be replaced with a copy of the file found on any other computer that is booting from the same SCSI controller. If you do not have another system that has the same configuration, you can get a copy of the SCSI driver from either the driver disk for the SCSI controller or possibly from your Windows 2000 or Windows NT 4.0 CD-ROM. This driver will have to be renamed to `ntbootdd.sys` and copied to the boot drive, you may need to make a boot disk like the one described earlier in the `ntldr` section.

Drivers

It is unfortunate that the devices and their drivers that allow us to accomplish so much of our day-to-day work with computers are also one of the biggest factors in not being able to do work on our computers. Ideally, once all the devices are configured on your computer, you should be able to work with no problems from your drivers. Most people's computers do not remain in a static mode, but rather are in a constant state of flux. Even though devices are working fine, many people feel the need to attempt to improve performance by changing settings, upgrading drivers, or installing service packs. Although upgrading drivers and installing items such as service packs are common practice, they should be done carefully. A service pack, for instance, can change the way all of the drivers on your computer function. In the rare case where something does go wrong, you may find that the fix is difficult.

Safe Mode

3.1 Recognize and interpret the meaning of common error codes and startup messages from the boot sequence, and identify steps to correct the problems. Content may include the following: Safe Mode

In order to let you repair the operating system from within the operating system, Microsoft has provided Safe Mode. Safe Mode is available with both Windows 9x and Windows 2000, and is a minimal driver boot of Windows. The only drivers that are loaded are the ones that are required to get the operating system running. Instead of loading the normal video driver, Safe Mode loads a 16-color VGA graphics driver. The `config.sys` and `autoexec.bat` files are skipped completely. You can enter Safe Mode by pressing the F8 key when the operating system is booting up. When booting in to Safe Mode the words "Safe Mode" are written on your desktop in each corner of your display. If Windows 9x fails to boot properly then it will suggest, and attempt to boot into Safe Mode on the next boot. Windows 9x does this Safe Mode boot by displaying the F8 boot menu for thirty seconds with the Safe Mode option already selected. If your computer boots into Safe Mode automatically, it is likely that the last boot process was interrupted (usually by the user).

For more information about Safe Mode and other boot methods, consult Chapter 22.

A device referenced in SYSTEM.INI, WIN.INI, Registry is not found

3.1 Recognize and interpret the meaning of common error codes and startup messages from the boot sequence, and identify steps to correct the problems. Content may include the following: A device referenced in SYSTEM.INI, WIN.INI, Registry is not found

From time to time, you will find that one of your startup files still references a device that you thought had been removed from your system. The files that reference devices, include `system.ini`, `win.ini`, and the Registry. If this happens, you may have to edit these files manually in order to fix the problem. If `win.ini` or `system.ini` are referencing devices that do not exist, Windows 9x generates a message that is displayed on the screen prior to switching to graphical mode. Take note of the device that is being referenced, because you will have to search for it in your startup files. Most devices are found within your `system.ini` file, so this is the first file that should be checked. Both `ini` files can be opened and edited with `notepad.exe`.

If the device is listed in the Registry, then it should be listed in Device Manager (System Control Panel applet, Device Manager tab). Locate the device in Device Manager, and delete it. If the device is still physically present in the computer, it will be re-added to Device Manager when your computer is rebooted. If you keep removing the device, and it keeps coming back, that is because it is still physically present. Physically remove the device first, and then remove it from Device Manager.

Other Errors

As with all things in life, some things cannot easily be categorized, so this section discusses errors that do not fit in the other categories.

Swap file

3.1 Recognize and interpret the meaning of common error codes and startup messages from the boot sequence, and identify steps to correct the problems. Content may include the following: Swap file

The Windows swap file is used as additional virtual memory. The location of the swap file is recorded in the Registry. If the drive that contains the swap file becomes too full, you may encounter errors informing you of this fact. If this happens, create some additional space for the swap file by deleting files, or move the swap file to a new location. The default location for the swap file is the same drive as your Windows directory. Both Windows 9x and Windows 2000 allow you to move the swap file to an alternate drive. If you have done so, and that drive has been removed from your system, you encounter errors telling you that the swap file could not be created. If this happens, configure Windows to use another drive for the swap file.

Dr. Watson

 3.1 Recognize and interpret the meaning of common error codes and startup messages from the boot sequence, and identify steps to correct the problems. Content may include the following: Dr. Watson

Dr. Watson has been designed to help troubleshoot problems on your system. It was first included with the Windows 3.x operating system. Dr. Watson helps troubleshoot problems after they have occurred by generating log files and system snapshots.

Figure 25-1 shows Dr. Watson in action on a Windows 9x computer. For this operating system, Dr. Watson records extremely detailed information about what processes are currently running. This information is stored on the tabs that are across the top of the Dr. Watson window. It breaks these processes into categories such as MS-DOS, 16-bit Windows, and 32-bit Windows. The Diagnosis tab allows the user to record additional information about what they were doing when the error occurred, since the information may be useful during the troubleshooting process. When loading Dr. Watson for Windows 9x, use the Run command, and type `drwatson.exe`. Dr. Watson then shows up in your system tray.

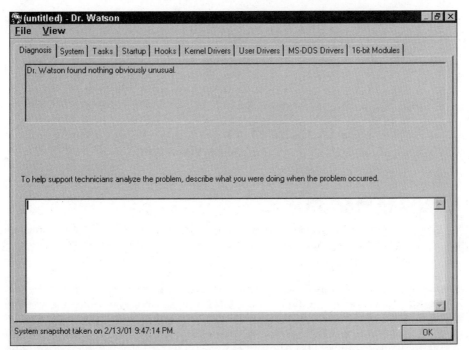

Figure 25-1: Dr. Watson provides the Diagnosis tab for you to describe what you were doing when the error occurred.

Figure 25-2 shows Dr. Watson's configuration screen for a Windows 2000 computer. Configure Dr. Watson in Windows 2000 by running `drwtsn32.exe` from the Run command. Dr. Watson is capable of dumping application memory to a memory dump file. This may be useful for the application developer to troubleshoot the error. Dr. Watson also logs any errors that fall into its scope of authority. With Windows 2000, Dr. Watson is always ready to generate these log and memory dump files.

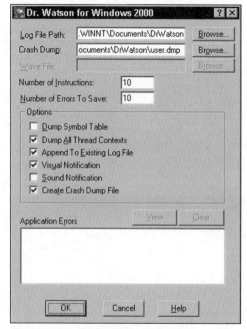

Figure 25-2: Dr. Watson deals with applications that crash.

Failure to start GUI

 3.1 Recognize and interpret the meaning of common error codes and startup messages from the boot sequence, and identify steps to correct the problems. Content may include the following: Failure to start GUI

With Windows, there may be times that the operating system is not able to boot into graphical mode. Depending on the operating system you are using, you may have different choices available to you.

If you are using Windows 9x, your only choice is to perform a logged boot. When your computer is booting and you see the text Starting Windows... appear on your screen, press F8 to display the boot menu, which allows you to choose the bootlog option.

If you are using Windows 2000, you have a couple of choices. You can perform a launch boot, in a fashion that is similar to Windows 9x. You could also use the Recovery Console to potentially fix any service-related problems.

For more information about the Recovery Console and its use, consult Chapter 22.

Windows Protection Error

3.1 Recognize and interpret the meaning of common error codes and startup messages from the boot sequence, and identify steps to correct the problems. Content may include the following: Windows Protection Error

You may receive a Windows Protection Error when you are starting up or shutting down your Windows 9x computer. This error is usually caused as a result of a driver that is being loaded, but may also be the result of a device conflict, damaged hardware, corrupt Registry, or damaged `win.com` file. If it is the result of a driver, you should create a bootlog, and check to see what driver was being loaded last. It is usually the driver that is causing the problem.

To learn how to create a bootlog for your operating system, consult Chapter 22.

Event Viewer — Event log is full

3.1 Recognize and interpret the meaning of common error codes and startup messages from the boot sequence, and identify steps to correct the problems. Content may include the following: Event Viewer — Event log is full

Windows 2000 offers various logging capabilities that are not available to Windows 9x, the greatest of which uses the Event Log service. The Event Log service logs errors and events into several different log files. Windows 2000 always has at least three default logs: Application, Security, and System. These log files have a default size of 512KB each and automatically overwrite events after seven days. These settings can be adjusted through the Properties dialog for each log file, as shown in Figure 25-3. In the event any log fills up, you receive a pop-up message on your screen. When this happens, open the Event Viewer from the Administrative Tools program group. Before clearing the filled log, examine the most recent events to see if there is an error that caused the log to fill quickly. To clear the log, right-click on the log and choose Clear All Events. When you clear the log, you have the opportunity to save the events to a file.

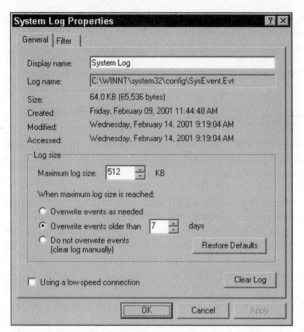

Figure 25-3: The default settings for the log files should be enough to prevent filling.

Key Point Summary

This chapter examined a number of common errors that you are likely to encounter with Windows 9x or Windows 2000. These errors range from configuration settings and files, to boot files and driver problems. You also saw some common resolution methods, such as Safe Mode.

✦   ✦   ✦

STUDY GUIDE

This Study Guide presents 15 assessment questions to test your knowledge of the exam topic area.

Assessment Questions

1. When using Windows 9x, how can you see what drivers and statements are being loaded in `config.sys` and `autoexec.bat`?

    A. Press Esc when the animated logo is onscreen.

    B. Edit `boot.ini` and include the line `Show Startup=1`.

    C. Press Enter when the animated logo is on the screen.

    D. Edit `msdos.sys` and include the line `Show driver load=1`.

2. Your `himem.sys` file is corrupted. What is the result for the boot process of Windows 9x?

    A. Windows continues to load normally, but many system processes are slower.

    B. Windows continues to load, but there is no access to extended memory.

    C. Windows 9x is not able to load any further than the command prompt, and will not be able to enter the graphical mode.

    D. The boot process does not proceed beyond the `Starting Windows 9x...` text on the screen.

3. You have just discovered that your `emm386.exe` file is corrupted. What result will this have on loading Windows 9x?

    A. Your computer continues to boot normally, but access to extended memory is denied.

    B. Your computer does not boot.

    C. `emm386.exe` is not a system file.

    D. There is no direct result.

4. You were having problems with your boot files on your Windows 98 computer. In order to fix the problem, you borrow a startup disk from a friend who is running Windows 98 Second Edition. If you use the `sys.com` command from his disk, what effect will it have on your computer?

   A. Your computer is not bootable until you run the `sys.com` command from a normal Windows 98 Startup Disk.

   B. Your computer can now boot normally.

   C. You can boot as far as the command prompt.

   D. You have to install Windows 98 Second Edition.

5. Which of the following options are valid procedures for trying to resolve corrupted boot files with Windows 2000? Choose two.

   A. Recovery Console

   B. `sys.com`

   C. `fidisk.exe`

   D. Emergency Repair Process

6. Which of the following are loaded when you boot into Safe Mode? Choose all that apply.

   A. Your normal video driver.

   B. Your mouse driver.

   C. `config.sys`

   D. `himem.sys`

7. The Windows swap file is used to _____.

   A. Prepare files to be copied to other disks

   B. Act as additional memory for the system

   C. Act as an extension to the hard drive

   D. Prepare files that are saved to disk

8. You have just had an application crash, and you would like to know what else was running on your computer. You think that this may be helpful in diagnosing the problem. Which program should you run?

   A. `whatsup.exe`

   B. `sysrun.exe`

   C. Device Manager

   D. `drwatson.exe`

9. Windows Protection Errors are usually related to which of the following?

    A. Applications

    B. Disk access

    C. Drivers

    D. Solar flares

10. Where do you go to read and clear the Windows 2000 event log?

    A. Event Log

    B. Event Viewer

    C. Log Reader

    D. Disk Cleanup

11. You need to replace a corrupted `himem.sys` file. What is the name of the command that you will use to retrieve the file from the `.cab` files that are found on the Windows 9x CD-ROM?

    A. `getcab.exe`

    B. `decab.exe`

    C. `extract.exe`

    D. `expand.exe`

12. You have installed Windows 2000 in the default location of `C:\winnt`. What will be the effect of deleting your `boot.ini` file?

    A. Your system will boot as normal, but will not display a boot menu.

    B. Your system will not boot and will display a missing `boot.ini` error message.

    C. Your system will not boot and will display a missing `ntoskrnl32.exe` error message.

    D. Your system will not boot and will display a missing `ntdetect.com` error message.

13. You are missing your copy of `ntldr` and your Windows 2000 computer will not boot. From where can you get a replacement copy?

    A. Using the `retrieve.exe` command to get a copy from the Windows 2000 CD-ROM.

    B. The only method by which this file can be replaced is through the Recovery Console.

    C. This file is not required and does not have to be replaced.

    D. Any other computer that is running Windows 2000.

14. You have just noticed that your `ntbootdd.sys` file is missing from your computer. What is the `ntbootdd.sys` file?

   A. Text configuration information for your Windows 2000 system.

   B. The boot loader.

   C. The SCSI driver for you SCSI adapter if the BIOS is disabled on the adapter.

   D. Nothing of importance.

15. When should you boot into Safe Mode?

   A. Every boot up.

   B. When your system will not boot normally.

   C. If you are not configured to a network interface card.

   D. Only to play `freecell.exe`.

Answers to Chapter Questions

Chapter Pre-Test

1. Windows 9x automatically attempts to enter Safe Mode **if the last boot of Windows 9x was unsuccessful.**

2. **No.** Windows 9x requires `himem.sys` to enter the GUI. If you stop the boot at the command prompt, then you can still perform some tasks.

3. `sys.com` is used to copy the files that are required to initiate a system boot.

4. `edit.com`, `notepad.exe`, **or any text editor** can be used to make changes to `config.sys`.

5. `command.com` is found **on the root of your hard drive**, and is also found in the Windows directory.

6. A swap file is **used to provide additional memory for your computer.** Space is allocated on the hard drive to simulate actual memory, but it is much slower than actual RAM.

7. **Yes,** it can be adjusted through the Event Viewer application.

8. To edit `system.ini`, `win.ini`, `protocol.ini`, `config.sys`, and `autoexec.bat`, you can use `sysedit.exe`, **the System Editor.**

Assessment Questions

1. **A.** Pressing Esc when the animated logo is on the screen gets rid of it. For more information, see the section titled "Windows 9x Boot Files."

2. **C.** Windows 9x requires `himem.sys` in order to load the Windows GUI and the `vfat` disk driver. For more information, see the section titled "Windows 9x Boot Files."

3. **D.** The one result that would be most evident is that you would not be able to access expanded memory. You do have access to extended memory as that is provided through `himem.sys`. For more information, see the section titled "Windows 9x Boot Files."

4. **A.** Each version of Windows has a different Startup Disk. You will have to rerun `sys.com` for the hard drive with the appropriate Startup Disk. For more information, see the section titled "Windows 9x Boot Files."

5. **A, D.** Both the Recovery Console and the Emergency Repair Process allow you to repair problems with the boot files. For more information, see the section titled "Windows 2000 Boot Files."

6. **B, D.** Your mouse driver and `himem.sys` are two things that load when you enter Save Mode. It also loads a VGA-compatible video driver and a minimal set of device drivers. For more information, see the section titled "Windows 9x Boot Files" and "Drivers."

7. **B.** The Windows swap file acts as additional memory for the OS. For more information, see the section titled "Other Errors."

8. **D.** Dr Watson will provide detailed information regarding what was running on the computer. For more information, see the section titled "Other Errors."

9. **C.** Windows Protection Errors are usually related to drivers and their access of memory. For more information, see the section titled "Other Errors."

10. **B.** Event Viewer is used to read, back up, and clear your event logs. For more information, see the section titled "Other Errors."

11. **C.** `extract.exe` is the name of the file that retrieves files from the source `.cab` files. For more information, see the section titled "Windows 9x Boot Files."

12. **A.** Your system will boot as normal, when `boot.ini` is missing Windows 2000 attempts to boot from the default installation location. For more information, see the section titled "Windows 2000 Boot Files."

13. **D.** `ntldr` is identical across all copies of Windows 2000 so it can be copied from any working installation of Windows 2000. For more information, see the section titled "Windows 2000 Boot Files."

14. **C.** The `ntbootdd.sys` file contains the SCSI driver for your SCSI adapter if the BIOS on the adapter has been disabled. For more information, see the section titled "Windows 2000 Boot Files."

15. **B.** You should enter Safe Mode to correct problems when your computer will not boot normally. For more information, see the section titled "Drivers."

Managing Common Problems

EXAM OBJECTIVES

Exam 220-202 ✦ **A+ OS Technologies**

✦ **3.2** Recognize common problems and determine how to resolve them. Content may include the following:

- Eliciting problem symptoms from customers

- Having customer reproduce error as part of the diagnostic process

- Identifying recent changes to the computer environment from the user

- **Troubleshooting Windows-specific problems:** Print spool is stalled, Incorrect/incompatible driver for print, Incorrect parameter

- **Other common problems:** General protection faults; Illegal operation; Invalid working directory; System lock up; Option (sound card, modem, input device) will not function; Application will not start or load; Cannot log on to network (option — NIC not functioning); TSR (Terminate Stay Resident) programs and virus; Applications don't install; Network connection

CHAPTER PRE-TEST

1. Does Dr. Watson for Windows 2000 create crash dump files?

2. What tool would you use to restart a stalled print spooler?

3. You just tried to but could not access the network. What are two possible problems?

4. You are using MS-DOS, and attempting to install Windows 98. Immediately after starting the setup, you are told that you do not have enough free memory. What can you do to make more conventional memory available?

5. You have just sent a document to the printer. When you arrive at the printer, you find several pages that are totally unreadable and resemble gibberish. What is the most likely cause of the problem?

6. What happens when a program commits an illegal operation?

7. What file stores configuration settings for MS-DOS-based applications?

8. With Windows 9x computers, how do you know at the logon screen if you are logging into the computer or the network?

✦ Answers to these questions can be found at the end of the chapter. ✦

This chapter examines some of the common errors that you will encounter when performing service on computers. It covers how to gather the information that you will require to properly diagnose and deal with the problem. You will also look at several common errors or problems that you are likely to encounter when dealing with Windows-based systems.

Solving Common Problems

 3.2 Recognize common problems and determine how to resolve them.

One of the first steps in diagnosing a problem is dealing with the person who has the problem. Your goal is to get a firm grasp and understanding of exactly what the problem is. This is sometimes harder than you would expect.

Eliciting information

 3.2 Recognize common problems and determine how to resolve them. Content may include the following: Eliciting problem symptoms from customers

The first step in the troubleshooting process is to get a complete list of the symptoms and the problems. In many cases, the person (customer) who is having the problem does not fully understand what the problem is, and the description he provides can be very vague. An example of a description would be, "My computer does not work." This description sums up what the customer sees as a problem with his system, but it does nothing to aid you in solving or resolving the problem.

When presented with a vague problem, you have to request additional information so that you can understand exactly what the problem is. This process takes the form of a series of questions that you ask the customer. The answers should prompt other questions that will probe deeper into the problem details provided by the customer. "What part of the computer seems to be not working?" or "What are you not able to do with it?" are examples of questions that you might ask. The answers to these questions should lead you in the direction of the actual problem. Usually, you will use this information to either test the boundaries of the existing error, or to reproduce a periodic error as part of the troubleshooting process.

Reproducing the error

 3.2 Recognize common problems and determine how to resolve them. Content may include the following: Having customer reproduce error as part of the diagnostic process

Some errors that occur are one-time errors. If an error occurs only once, there is not a lot you can do to troubleshoot it. Most errors occur at periodic intervals. In order to easily troubleshoot a problem like that, you must be able to reproduce the problem. To do this, you have to try to find out what the customer was doing when the problem occurred. If you can gather enough information about what the user was doing when the error occurred, you have a greater chance of diagnosing the problem.

Once you have gathered enough information about what the customer was doing, you should be able to reproduce the problem. One of the benefits of reproducing the problem is that you can see firsthand what the complaint is. Sometimes an actual problem doesn't really exist. The user might have a mistaken belief about how certain hardware or software should function. In such a case, the technician's job is to explain how the hardware/software works without making the user feel like a time-wasting fool.

Identifying any changes

3.2 Recognize common problems and determine how to resolve them. Content may include the following: Identifying recent changes to the computer environment from the user

One question that should be asked fairly early on is if there have recently been any changes in the computer's configuration or environment. This would include the changing of settings, as well as the loading of drivers for the installation software. The answer to these questions is often a resounding "no." This "no" does not necessarily mean that there have not been changes, only that the customer has not realized that there were changes. It is only through additional questioning and some physical investigation that the truth can be discovered. For example, questions such as the following can often retrieve additional information:

✦ What is this software box on top of your computer?

✦ Why is there an icon for Electronic Arts "Quake III Revolution" sitting on your Desktop?

✦ What have you been doing with this QuickCam?

✦ Why is there coffee leaking out of your keyboard?

These questions can often get a customer to change their answer from "no" to a "no, but. . ." If that does not work, you can always interrogate the person in a dark room with a bright light.

Solving Windows-Specific Printing Problems

 3.2 Recognize common problems and determine how to resolve them. Content may include the following: Troubleshooting Windows-specific printing problems

One of the areas in which you will encounter problems is printing. Everybody has some sort of issue with printing. Be it a printer that is not printing, or a driver compatibility problem, there are problems. This section examines stalled spoolers, wrong drivers, and incorrect parameters.

Stalled print spool

 3.2 Recognize common problems and determine how to resolve them. Content may include the following: Troubleshooting Windows-specific printing problems — Print spool is stalled

From time to time, when dealing with Windows 2000 and Windows NT 4.0 servers, you encounter a stalled print spooler. This is a feature of the print spooler. After a period of printing, and printing well, the print spooler decides to stop responding to commands. This has been a long-running issue for Microsoft, and does seem to happen less and less with newer versions of the software.

 Tip   Windows 9x does not give detailed control over the spooler, and with that OS, your first choice for printing problems is to reboot.

You can usually identify a stalled spooler from the following symptoms:

✦ Users are not able to add new jobs to the print queue.

✦ Nobody is able to remove jobs from the print queue.

✦ Existing jobs do not print.

✦ The print queue appears empty, even though you have sent print jobs.

If the print queue exhibits these symptoms, you should be able to remedy them by restarting the print queue. This can be done using either of the following methods:

✦ Restart the spooler service using the Services MMC snap-in.

✦ Restart the spooler service using the Net command.

To restart the spooler using the Services MMC snap-in, you will find a pre-saved console in your Administrative tools folder. Open My Computer ➪ Control Panel ➪ Administrative Tools ➪ Services. Locate the spooler service in the list of services, and right-click it; choose All Tasks, and Restart (as shown in Figure 26-1). Restart is a new command in Windows 2000; in Windows NT 4.0, you have to choose Stop, wait for that action to complete, and then choose Start.

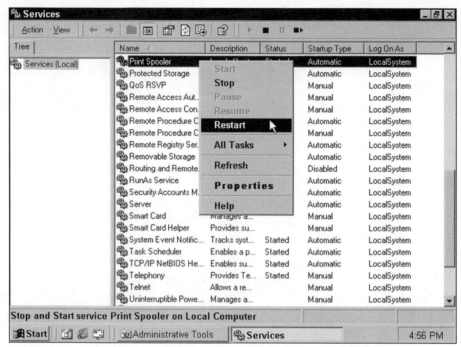

Figure 26-1: Restarting services is easy from the Services Administrative Tool.

To use the Command Prompt to restart the spooler, open a command prompt, and type

```
net.exe stop spooler
net.exe start spooler
```

or

```
net.exe stop "print spooler"
net.exe start "print spooler"
```

Tip   If you don't know the name of the service you want to start or stop, type `net.exe start` and Windows 2000 or Windows NT 4.0 will list the registered services.

Once the spooler has restarted, the problems should be gone, assuming you have configured the client to use the correct driver.

Tip   When stopping some services, you will be told that other services have to be stopped as well. These are "dependent services" that require or depend on the service that you are stopping. When you start the service backup, you will find that these dependent services do not automatically restart. You will have to manually start them. The Spooler service does not have any dependencies or dependents.

Incorrect/incompatible driver

3.2 Recognize common problems and determine how to resolve them. Content may include the following: Troubleshooting Windows-specific printing problems — Incorrect/incompatible driver for print

Drivers are often one of the big problems for administrators. You notice that the printer is being heavily used, spitting out page after page of data, and you are happy that this tool is being put to such a good use. But your happiness is shattered when you examine one of the printed pages, and notice that up at the top of the page there is small band of text that looks like it was typed over about 100 times. This should not greatly concern you, because obviously one of the users on the network is using the wrong printer driver, and this is something that can be easily fixed.

The print driver for your computer acts as a translation tool between your computer's OS and the printer. If you install the incorrect driver, you have a poor translation taking place. The level of poor translation shows up in the printout. Sometimes the incorrect driver just causes some special characters to not print, but other times it will cause a much larger problem.

The solution to the problem is easy: just install the correct driver. This involves checking the model of the printer, getting the disks for it, and installing the correct driver for the OS. If you do not have the driver disks, you may be able to download them from the printer manufactures web site, the Internet, or get the manufacture to mail the drivers to you.

Incorrect parameter

3.2 Recognize common problems and determine how to resolve them. Content may include the following: Troubleshooting Windows-specific printing problems — Incorrect parameter

There are several settings that can be configured for a printer that are specific to the individual printer. These settings are found on the Device Options tab of the printer's Properties sheet. Since the settings are specific to the device, this book does not discuss them, but we will look at generic settings that would apply to all printers. Of these, the one that is most likely to cause problems is the port setting.

Port settings are found on the Details tab. When choosing a port, you can pick from a local port like `LPT1`, a network port such as `\\<server>\<printer>`, or a file to be redirected to a printer later. If you have specified an incorrect network location, you are not able to print; and if you print to a file, you may not know where the file is. These can cause problems for people who are trying to print.

The timeout setting on the Details tab could also cause problems. If the value is set too low, you can have communication problems with your printer, such as your computer not waiting long enough for your printer to answer any queries.

Solving Other Problems

 3.2 Recognize common problems and determine how to resolve them. Content may include the following: Other common problems—General protection faults, Illegal operation, Invalid working directory, System lock ups, Option (sound card, modem, input device) will not function, Application will not start or load, Cannot log on to network (option: NIC not functioning), TSR (Terminate Stay Resident) programs and virus, Applications don't install, Network connection.

In addition to printing problems, there are a number of other things that may go wrong. This section examines some of those problems.

General protection faults

 3.2 Recognize common problems and determine how to resolve them. Content may include the following: Other common problems—General protection faults

General protection faults (GPFs) are operating system-level errors. When applications are running, Windows prevents them from interfering with each other by running them in their own memory spaces. There are, however, some applications (and OS components) that share a memory space; these are mostly 16-bit applications. When one of these components attempts to reference memory that does not belong to it, then Windows generates a general protection fault and attempts to prevent the improper reference by terminating the offending application.

Since this problem may have affected some of the 16-bit OS components on the system, you should reboot after a GPF to ensure system stability. To reduce the occurrence of GPFs, reduce the number of open applications that are running.

Illegal operation

 3.2 Recognize common problems and determine how to resolve them. Content may include the following: Other common problems—Illegal operations

The illegal operation error is similar to the GPF. In most cases, but not necessarily all, the illegal operation is a memory reference problem. When one 32-bit application attempts to reference an area of memory that belongs to another application, or a memory location that it is using has somehow become corrupted, it generates an illegal operation. The memory could have been corrupted by the application, due to a read or write error swapping, or because of damaged RAM. When these memory problems happen, Windows treats application as a rogue or damaged application and terminates it before it can cause damage outside of its own memory space.

The big difference between illegal operations and GPFs is what components are in use and affected at the time. Illegal operations are caused by 32-bit applications while GPF's are caused by 16-bit applications and can cause damage outside of the application memory space. In most cases, you can recover from an illegal operation by re-launching the application. Reducing the number of open applications reduces the chance of illegal operations happening, as there will be less space that can be considered out of bounds.

Invalid working directory

 3.2 Recognize common problems and determine how to resolve them. Content may include the following: Other common problems — Invalid working directory

When creating shortcuts of MS-DOS-based applications, you configure a working directory. This directory is used to create any associated files that the application requires, and to locate sub-applications that it requires to be able to perform its functions. If, after installing and configuring the application, this directory is removed or renamed, you get an error message regarding the working directory (see Figure 26-2). As part of the error message, you are given a chance to launch the application. If you choose to launch the application, you should do so knowing that some functions in it may not work.

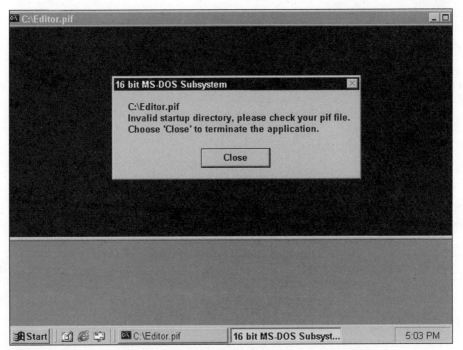

Figure 26-2: You are notified if the working directory does not exist.

This error can be resolved by changing the working directory path in the .pif (Program Information File) for the MS-DOS-based application. Do this by right-clicking the shortcut to the application, or the application itself, and changing the Working Directory setting on the Program tab, as shown in Figure 26-3. If there were required support files for the application, they may need to be restored. For more information about configuring .pifs, see Chapter 24.

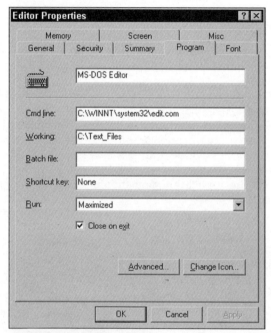

Figure 26-3: The Working Directory setting is part of the .pif settings.

System lock up

3.2 Recognize common problems and determine how to resolve them. Content may include the following: Other common problems — System lock up

It's rare to have a system lock up in Windows 2000 or Windows NT 4.0; more likely you will have a period of slow responsiveness. If you are using Windows 9x, though, you are likely to have complete system lock ups. This has to do with how the operating systems work, and you may want to review Chapter 24.

If you are using Windows 2000 or Windows NT 4.0, you may experience a runaway application that can cause the system to be unresponsive. This unresponsiveness may lead you to believe that your computer is locked up, but actually it does not have enough clock cycles to pay attention to you. Press Ctrl+Alt+Delete once, and the Security dialog box (shown in Figure 26-4) appears, from which you can launch the Task Manager.

Figure 26-4: The Security dialog box for Windows 2000 allows you to launch Task Manager.

Look at the Task Manger's Processes tab and you can see which application is the runaway—it is the one with the highest CPU value, which indicates that the application is hogging the time. You may want to switch to the application and close it normally, but there is a good chance that this will not work. If it doesn't work, return to Task Manager, select the task, and click the End Task button. This should return your system to its previous level of responsiveness, if not, open the Task Manager and look for another application that is using up the processor time—sometimes there is more than one. In rare cases, you may have to reboot to correct the problem.

If you are using Windows 9x, you are in for a different experience. Chapter 24 examines how the system architecture leads to a lack of system stability. This is mainly due to OS components running in the same area of the system in which 16-bit applications execute. When any 16-bit application crashes, it has the potential to lock the 16-bit OS components as well, including `user.exe`. `user.exe` is responsible for user input; if it locks, so do your keyboard and mouse. When that happens, you have no choice but to reboot.

Optional device will not function

3.2 Recognize common problems and determine how to resolve them. Content may include the following: Other common problems—Option (sound card, modem, input device) will not function

There are many devices that may be attached to your computer from time to time, but three devices that most people almost always have are a sound card, modem, and mouse of some sort. Each of these devices requires an IRQ and I/O address. You may have other devices on your computer that are using resources that you require for these devices. If all of the devices on your computer are plug-and-play, and you have a plug-and-play BIOS, this is not an issue. But if you are using legacy devices, you have to configure IRQ and I/O settings for them. Sound cards usually use IRQ 5, and your COM ports (for your modem) are IRQ 3 and IRQ 4. If you are using a serial mouse, you want to make sure that it is not sharing its IRQ with an active modem on COM 3 or COM 4, as only one device will be able to use the IRQ at a time. In other words, you will have mouse problems when you are using the modem! Chapters 10 and 15 discuss the topic of configuring resources in more detail.

In addition to configuring the hardware support for the devices, you have to load the appropriate drivers. This can be done through Add New Hardware in the Control Panel. Chapter 23 has more information about installing devices on your computer.

Application will not start

3.2 Recognize common problems and determine how to resolve them. Content may include the following: Other common problems — Application will not start or load

From time to time, you will have applications that won't start. A few reasons for this problem include corrupted or damaged shortcuts, damaged PIF settings, or corrupted memory space.

Corrupted shortcuts

When you create a shortcut to a program, the shortcut records information about the target file, such as its size and creation date. If something happens to the original file, such as its being moved to another directory, the shortcut searches the hard drive for the program and attempts to repair the shortcut. If you are using Windows 95, you are prompted to verify that the shortcut chose the right file to link to, as shown in Figure 26-5, while Windows 98, Windows NT 4.0, and Windows 2000 will link the file without prompting. If this is not possible, you have to re-create the shortcut by hand.

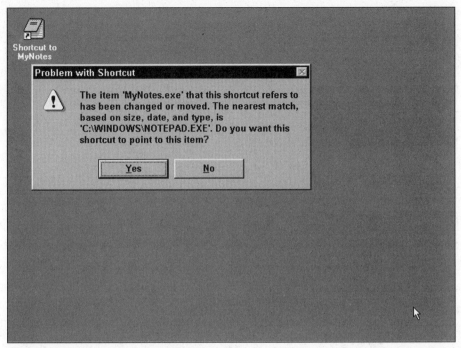

Figure 26-5: When using Windows 95, shortcuts prompt you to confirm corrections for broken links.

Damaged PIF

In addition to improper locations, MS-DOS PIFs could also have inappropriate information in them. The PIF or shortcut to an MS-DOS application has information about the memory environment and reserved keystrokes. If this information has changed, you have to update the PIF. This can be done by right-clicking the PIF and choosing Properties. The settings that must be changed depend on your application. Chapter 24 deals with what those settings should be.

Corrupted memory space

This problem occurs mostly with 16-bit Windows applications. Occasionally, you have 16-bit Windows applications that crash completely or partially when they are closed. The crashing application has a chance to corrupt the 16-bit Windows operating environment. If this happens, you will find that you are not able to open or launch 16-bit Windows applications, even though 32-bit Windows applications run fine.

If you are using Windows 9x, you have to reboot to allow for a new 16-bit Windows environment to load. If you are using Windows 2000 or Windows NT 4.0, you can terminate the 16-bit Windows environment through the Task Manager. To open Task Manager, press Ctrl+Alt+Delete, and click the Task Manager button. In Task Manager, choose the Processes tab. Locate the NTVDM that contains an empty wow.exe, right-click on it, and choose End Task. The next time you load a 16-bit Windows application, it reloads the default 16-bit Windows environment.

Network logon problems

3.2 Recognize common problems and determine how to resolve them. Content may include the following: Other common problems — Cannot log on to the network (option: NIC not functioning) and network connection

If you find yourself in a position where you are not able to log on to the network, you may find that it is related to your logon credentials, poor NIC configuration, or an unplugged cable.

Logon credentials

If you see a dialog box titled "Enter Network Password" in Windows 9x, then Windows does see that you have a network card, and it appears to be plugged into a network. If the network is missing, you see a dialog box titled "Welcome to Windows." If the network is missing, check to see that the cables are correctly plugged in and that a network interface card (NIC) is present in the Network Control Panel applet. When you are logging into the network, your network credentials are tested against a server. If they fail, then you have typed your username or password incorrectly, or your account has been locked out due to multiple failed logins. You may have to contact your network administrator to provide you with valid network credentials or unlock your account. The exact procedure will vary depending on what network operating system you are using.

Windows NT 4.0 and Windows 2000 will always display the same logon dialog box whether or not they detect a network card. If the network card is not present, you will receive an error stating a Domain Controller was not available for logon. If you have provided the wrong logon credentials for your logon, you will receive a message suggesting you check the use of shift and caps lock keys. If your account has been locked out, you will receive a message stating that was the problem. If you are not able to log on you will have to contact your network administrator to verify your logon credentials or unlock your account.

Tip   When working with a Windows NT 4.0 or Windows 2000 server, Windows 9x does not know how to implement case-sensitive passwords. Regardless of the case you use, the password is always passed to the server as uppercase. Windows NT 4.0 and Windows 2000 do have case-sensitive passwords when authenticating against a server.

NIC configuration

If the login dialog box you see on your Windows 9x computer is titled "Welcome to Windows," then there is likely a problem with your network interface card (NIC). Once these things are working, they tend to continue to work as long as you leave them alone. Some of the reasons that a network card may not be working include:

✦ Wrong drivers

✦ Wrong or conflicting hardware resources for non-plug-and-play cards

✦ Corrupted driver files

Each of these problems requires you to replace installed drivers or correct another configuration error.

If you are using Windows NT 4.0 or Windows 2000, an improperly configured NIC will generate an error message telling you to check the event log for more details. When you check the event log using the Event Viewer, you will see some red x's in the left column that denote items that did not work. One of those red x's will be associated with your network interface card and will describe what the problem is. If a network interface card is not present and you attempt to logon to a domain rather than the local computer, then you will receive an error message telling you that the domain is not available. To solve this problem you will have to install a network interface card.

Cable problems

In many cases, this is the first thing that should be examined. If you are unplugged from the network, then you cannot log on to it. In addition to simply being unplugged, there could be a short or break in the cable, as well. Since shorts and breaks can be internal to the cable, a cable tester is useful for troubleshooting problems. These cable problems can exist between your computer and the wall, between the wall and your wiring room, between the patch panel in the wiring room and the hub or switch that you are using, or with the hub or switch that you are using. In any of these cases, you will have to replace the cable or device that is not functioning properly.

TSR programs and viruses

 Objective

3.2 Recognize common problems and determine how to resolve them. Content may include the following: Other common problems — TSR (Terminate Stay Resident) programs and virus

Terminate Stay Resident programs (TSRs) are usually small useful programs that were designed when MS-DOS only allowed you to run one program at a time. TSRs load into memory, and then tell the OS that they're done, while remaining in memory, performing their tasks. One of the ways that viruses spread is by loading into memory as a TSR, and then they are able to set about infecting other files on your system. Chapter 27 discusses viruses, and some of the ways that they attempt to hide from detection.

This is not to say the TSRs are to be avoided, but any program that runs without a user interface may be running without your being aware of it. With Windows 9x and Windows 2000, you can see which applications are running in the background (as services) by bringing up the Task List or Task Manager. To do this with Windows 9x, press Ctrl+Alt+Delete once to bring up the Task List (which is a dialog labeled "Close Program") and scan through the list of what is running on your computer. The items in Task List may be the names of the executables — which may not be name that you commonly use to refer to the application. For example, MSN Messenger Service shows up in the task list as msmsgs. To view running tasks on Windows 2000 or Windows NT 4.0, press Ctrl+Alt+Delete once and click on the Task Manager button. The Applications tab will list all of the foreground applications and the Processes tab will list all applications that are running on the system, including system services that are running on the computer such as winlogon.exe and lsass.exe.

Your virus scanner has a list of known viruses that it does not permit to run. There is a chance that it can prevent other unknown viruses from running if they are doing things that are suspicious. If you are sure that the file is not a virus, then you can temporarily disable your virus protection. Many virus programs have an agent that is running all of the time as a background service, looking for suspicious activity.

Caution   To prevent viruses, you should keep your list of known viruses up to date by downloading updated virus definitions from your anti-virus manufacturer regularly.

Application will not install

3.2 Recognize common problems and determine how to resolve them. Content may include the following: Other common problems — Applications don't install

In some cases, you find that applications will not install. There are a number of reasons for this. It could be because the application performs a compatibility test, which your computer failed. If this is the case, you should be notified by the application's setup program of the compliance failure. If your computer is less powerful than recommended, it should be upgraded to support the application.

In addition to compliance failure, there may be a problem with how the setup program was written. Very often, the setup program itself is a 16-bit Windows-based application. If you recently had a 16-bit Windows application crash on your system, and you have not corrected the corruption of the 16-bit memory space by rebooting Windows 9x or by terminating the NTVDM in Windows 2000, the setup program may fail.

Key Point Summary

This chapter examined some problems that support personnel typically encounter when working with systems. We started by discussing the types of questions you can ask the user of the computer to get a clear picture of the problem. We also looked at some OS-related printing problems, and then moved into other areas, such as GPFs, illegal operations, and system lockups. Finally, we looked at application problems, such as what can cause installation and network connection problems.

✦   ✦   ✦

STUDY GUIDE

This Study Guide presents 15 assessment questions and 4 lab exercises to test your knowledge of the exam topic area.

Assessment Questions

1. Problems with computers are often caused by which of the following?

    A. Poorly planned configuration changes

    B. Untested software updates

    C. Hard drive fragmentation cyclical errors

    D. Solar flares

2. When the print queue is unresponsive, what should you do?

    A. Reboot the server

    B. Reinstall the printer

    C. Restart the spooler service

    D. Redirect the printer to a remote print device

3. What command is used to restart a service from the command prompt?

    A. service.exe

    B. services.exe

    C. cmdrun.exe

    D. net.exe

4. You get a call from a user who is complaining that his document has bullets in it, but when he prints the document he gets check boxes instead. What is the problem?

    A. He is using the incorrect print driver.

    B. The application that he is using does not support bullets.

    C. His computer has a problem with the serial cable connecting his printer.

    D. He is using the wrong parallel cable.

5. Your MS-DOS based application will start up, but does display an error message stating the working directory is invalid. What should you do?

    A. Delete the application directory and re-install the application.

    B. Edit the associated `.pif` file.

    C. Modify the settings found in the `.cmd` file.

    D. Create a directory named `c:\<application>`.

6. To set a working directory for an MS-DOS application, you should modify which file?

    A. <application>.ini

    B. <application>.wdr

    C. <application>.pif

    D. <application>.set

7. When troubleshooting optional devices on non plug-and-play systems, what is a common problem that you will encounter?

    A. The operating system configures legacy cards with invalid resources.

    B. ICQ conflicts.

    C. Devices are incorrectly identified by the OS.

    D. IRQ conflicts.

8. You have found that your serial mouse and your modem have problems when they are used at the same time. What is a potential cause of the problem?

    A. Your mouse and your modem are using the serial connector on the back of your computer.

    B. They both happen to be malfunctioning at the same time.

    C. Your modem and mouse are using COM3 and COM1, respectively.

    D. They are both using the same PCI slot.

9. You are attempting to log in to your network using a Windows 9x computer, when you type your username and password at the "Welcome to Windows" logon dialog, you are told that your password was not authenticated by a network server. You are not able to access files on the server. What is the causing the problem?

    A. You server is down.

    B. You are using the wrong network protocol.

    C. You provided the wrong password.

    D. Your network interface card is not functioning.

10. How can you find out what background applications are running on your Windows 9x computer?

    A. Press Ctrl+Alt+Delete once and choose the Task Manager button.

    B. Press Ctrl+Alt+Delete once and use the Task List

    C. Press Ctrl+Alt+Delete to open the Task List

    D. This cannot be done.

11. You are installing a plug-and-play sound card into your Windows 2000 computer that has a plug-and-play BIOS. What IRQ should you configure it for?

    A. Configure the sound card for IRQ 5

    B. Disable LPT1 and configure the sound card to use IRQ 7

    C. Configure the sound card for IRQ 9

    D. You should not configure it all.

12. What is the most likely cause of a total system lockup when using Windows 9x?

    A. A conflict between 32-bit applications code and 32-bit OS code running on the computer.

    B. A conflict between 32-bit applications code and 16-bit OS code running on the computer.

    C. A conflict between 16-bit application code and 16-bit OS code running on the computer.

    D. A conflict between 16-bit applications code and 32-bit OS code running on the computer.

13. You get a call from a user who has tried repeatedly to log onto the network. You get him to walk you through the log on process. He tells you in detail about the entire process, including typing his correct name and password in the Welcome to Windows dialog box. Why is he having a problem?

    A. He is wrong about using the correct password.

    B. The network is not present or functioning.

    C. He is attempting to log onto the wrong server or domain.

    D. He should be typing his password in uppercase.

14. You get a call from a user who has tried repeatedly to log onto the network. You get him to walk you through the logon process. He tells you in detail about the entire process, including typing his correct name and password in the Enter Network Password dialog box. Why is he having a problem? (Select all that apply)

    A. He is wrong about using the correct password.

    B. The network is not present or functioning.

    C. He is attempting to log onto the wrong server or domain.

    D. He should be typing his password in lowercase.

15. You need to stop the spooler service that is running on a Windows 2000 computer. What can you type on the Windows 2000 command line to stop this service?

    A. `net.exe stop spooler`

    B. `service.exe stop spooler`

    C. `net.exe service stop spooler`

    D. `service.exe halt spooler`

Lab Exercises

Lab 26-1 Restarting the Print Spooler from the Command Prompt

This lab requires a Windows 2000 Professional or Windows 2000 Server computer. Each of the lines that you are asked to type in this lab are complete commands within the Command Prompt, so you will have to press the Enter key on your keyboard at the end of each command.

1. Start up Windows 2000 and log in.

2. Open a new command prompt by using Start menu ➪ Programs ➪ Accessories ➪ Command Prompt.

3. Check the name of the Print Spooler service by typing

   `net.exe start`

4. Check the syntax of the net command by typing

   `net.exe stop /?`

5. Stop the Print Spooler by typing

   `net.exe stop "print spooler"`

After a few seconds, the print spooler should stop.

6. Restart the print spooler by typing

```
net.exe start "print spooler"
```

After a few seconds, the print spooler should be running. Follow the same process when the spooler stalls.

Lab 26-2 Printing with the Wrong Drivers

This lab can be performed with either Windows 9x or Windows 2000. It has been written for Windows 9x, but can be followed by Windows 2000 users. If you are using Windows 2000 or Windows NT 4.0, then some of the dialogs may have different information in them or may have a different layout to them. If you get stuck with one of the dialogs, consult the printing information in Chapter 23.

In this exercise, you will install two new printer drivers on your computer, configure them to print to a file, and examine the output of two print jobs.

This exercise assumes you have created your lab files directory and that it is on the root of Drive C.

1. Start up your Windows 9x computer and log in.

2. Open the Printers folder using Start menu ⇨ Settings ⇨ Printers.

3. Double-click on Add Printer.

4. Click Next, and select Local Printer.

5. Select Apple from the Manufacturers pane and Apple LaserWriter from the Printers pane. This is a Postscript printer and the output that you eventually see will be text with a lot of formatting codes. Click Next.

6. Choose File as a printer port. This sends the output to a file that you will be able to examine. Click Next.

7. Leave the default name, and click Next.

8. Leave Yes selected for the Test Page, and click Next.

9. Windows 9x now copies files to your computer; you may be prompted to provide either the Windows 9x CD-ROM or the location of your source files.

10. You are prompted to provide a location to save your test page. Type in the Filename box, or browse to:

```
c:\labfiles\apple.prn
```

11. When asked if the test page printed correctly, choose Yes.

12. Repeat Steps 1-11 to create a second printer. This time, add an HP Deskjet. Name the test page

```
c:\labfiles\deskjet.prn
```

13. Open WordPad and then open both c:\labfiles\apple.prn and c:\labfiles\deskjet.prn. The Apple printer is printing in Adobe Postscript, which means that all of the commands that are passed to the printer are in text with the commands embedded in the file. The HP printer is printing in HP PCL, which is a binary file with its own formatting embedded into it.

14. Open your Printers folder (if it is not already open), select your Apple LaserWriter printer, and press the Delete key. Confirm the deletion, and the deletion of its files. Repeat this action for the HP Deskjet printer.

Lab 26-3 Terminating the Default Memory Space with Windows 2000

The lab assumes that the required lab files have been installed to your disk, using the default installation path of c:\labfiles. If you have not completed Lab 26-2, then follow the steps at the beginning of that lab exercise to get the proper files in your labfiles directory. This lab requires a Windows NT 4.0 or Windows 2000 computer.

1. Open the Task Manager by right-clicking in an empty gray area of the Taskbar, and choosing Task Manager.

2. Switch to the Processes tab.

3. Attempt to locate a copy of NTVDM running that contains wowexec.exe. You may not find one, and that is fine. If you see a copy running, select the NTVDM, and click the End Process button. Keep the Task Manager open, but minimized.

4. Now open the labfiles folder (c:\labfiles) and launch dialer.exe.

5. Restore Task Manager and locate the running copy of dialer.exe. It should be running within an NTVDM with wowexec.exe.

6. Switch back to Phone Dialer and close the application.

7. Switch back to Task Manager and locate the copy of NTVDM that now has a copy of wowexec.exe in it. This should close down automatically if your computer is short of RAM or if you terminated the 16-bit Windows application. If it still exists, select the NTVDM and click the End Process button.

Lab 26-4 Testing Link Tracking

The lab assumes that the required lab files have been installed to your disk, using the default installation path of c:\labfiles. If you have not completed Lab 26-2, then follow the steps at the beginning of that lab exercise to get the proper files in your labfiles directory. This lab can be performed with either a Windows NT 4.0, Windows 2000, or Windows 9x computer.

1. Open the labfiles folder, which should be c:\labfiles.

2. Change the name of `sysedit.exe` (or `sysedit` if your extensions are hidden) to `myedit.exe`.

3. Create a shortcut to `myedit.exe` on your desktop. Do this by right-clicking and dragging the icon to your desktop. When you release the mouse button, you are asked what you would like to do. Choose Create Shortcut.

4. After creating the shortcut, go back to the labfiles folder and rename `myedit.exe` back to its original name: `sysedit.exe`.

5. Now double-click the shortcut on the desktop. If you are using the retail version of Windows 95, it asks you if its choice for the shortcut is correct. Windows 98, Windows NT 4.0, and Windows 2000 automatically correct the problem with the shortcut.

6. Delete the shortcut.

Answers to Chapter Questions

Chapter Pre-Test

1. **Yes**—Dr. Watson for Windows 2000 does create crash dump files for application memory. Windows 9x only creates log.

2. To restart the print spooler, you can use **the `net.exe` command or the Services Administrative tool.**

3. Some reasons for not being able to log on include **having the wrong credentials, an incorrectly configured network card, and a physical cable problem.**

4. To make more memory available for MS-DOS, you can **load `himem.sys` and `emm386.exe`, and load some drivers into extended memory. You can also not load some of your current TSRs.**

5. When you get gibberish in your printer output, it is usually due to **an incorrect driver.**

6. The program committed the illegal operation **by accessing the memory space of another application.**

7. The **Program Information File (PIF).**

8. When logging into a network, the **login dialog box is titled "Enter Network Password." When logging in without a network, it is titled "Welcome to Windows."**

Assessment Questions

1. **A, B.** Poorly planned configuration changes and untested updates are very common reasons for problems on your systems. For more information, see the section titled, "Solving Common Problems."

2. C. Restarting the print spooler service should fix problems with the print queue. If it does not, you may have to restart the server. For more information, see the section titled "Solving Windows-Specific Printing Problems."

3. D. `net.exe` is the command that can be used to stop and start services from the command prompt. For more information, see the section titled "Solving Windows-Specific Printing Problems."

4. A. He is probably using the incorrect print driver. The problem should go away when the driver is updated. For more information, see the section titled "Solving Windows-Specific Printing Problems."

5. B. Edit the associated `.pif` file and modify the working directory settings. For more information, see the section titled "Solving Other Problems."

6. C. The `.pif` file is the file that contains settings for the working directory. For more information, see the section titled "Solving Other Problems."

7. D. IRQ conflicts are a common problem. For more information, see the section titled "Solving Other Problems."

8. C. They are using COM3 and COM1, which share an IRQ. Changing the mouse to COM2 will fix this problem. For more information, see the section titled "Solving Other Problems."

9. D. When your network is not functioning, your logon dialog reads "Welcome to Windows" rather than "Enter Network Password." For more information, see the section titled "Solving Other Problems."

10. B. Pressing Ctrl+Alt+Delete will open the Task List for Windows 9x. For more information, see the section titled "Solving Other Problems."

11. D You should not configure it all and let plug-and-play do its job. For more information, see the section titled "Solving Other Problems."

12. C. Most system lockups occur when 16-bit application code conflicts with 16-bit OS code on the system. For more information, see the section titled "Solving Other Problems."

13. B. The Welcome to Windows dialog tells you the network interface card is not detecting that it is on the network or that you do not have a network interface card. For more information, see the section titled "Solving Other Problems."

14. A, C. The Enter Network Password dialog informs you that the network interface card seems to be functioning and that it thinks that it is on the network. Since the network is functioning, the user is either wrong about his username or password, or he is attempting to log onto the incorrect domain (one where his user account does not exist). For more information, see the section titled "Solving Other Problems."

15. A. `net.exe stop spooler` is the correct command to stop the spooler service from the command prompt. For more information, see the section titled "Solving Windows-Specific Printing Problems."

Using Windows-Based Utilities

EXAM OBJECTIVES

Exam 220-202 ✦ A+ OS Technologies

✦ **1.2** Identify basic concepts and procedures for creating, viewing and managing files, directories and disks. This includes procedures for changing file attributes and the ramifications of those changes (for example, security issues). Content may include the following:

- **Windows-based utilities:** ScanDisk, Device manager, System Manager, Computer Manager, MSCONFIG.EXE, REGEDIT.EXE (View information/Backup registry), REGEDT32.EXE, ATTRIB.EXE, EXTRACT.EXE, DEFRAG.EXE, EDIT.COM, FDISK.EXE, SYSEDIT.EXE, SCANREG, WSCRIPT.EXE, HWINFO.EXE, ASD.EXE (Automatic Skip Driver), Cvt1.EXE (Drive Converter FAT16 to FAT32)

✦ **3.2 Recognize common problems and determine how to resolve them.** Content may include the following:

- **Viruses and virus types:** What they are, Sources (floppy, e-mails, etc.), How to determine presence

CHAPTER PRE-TEST

1. If you need to convert your drive from FAT32 to FAT16, what operating system utility can you use?

2. You just installed a new hard drive in your computer. What is the first operating system utility you should use to configure this drive?

3. You think some of the files on your hard drive have invalid file dates; what utility can be used to repair this error?

4. You need to edit `autoexec.bat`, `config.sys`, and `system ini`; what utility can you run to help you quickly edit all of these files?

5. You need to back up a portion of the Registry, and you need to be able to edit this backup with a text editor. Should you use `regedit.exe` or `regedt32.exe`?

6. You believe that the network card on your Windows 9x computer is not starting up correctly; what is the first utility you should check for problems?

7. You need to create a new disk partition on your Windows 2000 computer; what utility should you use?

8. You need to create user accounts on your Windows 2000 computer; what utility should you use?

9. You have found a file on your hard drive that has a `.vbs` a file extension; what type of file is this?

10. One of the driver files for your Windows 9x installation is corrupted; you know which driver it is and would like to replace it from the original CD. What command can you use to retrieve the file from the compressed CAB file?

11. You overheard a conversation in your office today that revolved around a Trojan horse and Melissa. What was this conversation about?

✦ Answers to these questions can be found at the end of the chapter. ✦

This chapter looks at Windows-based utilities. These utilities fall into categories such as *disk maintenance, configuration,* and the ever-popular *miscellaneous* category. One major utility topic that we cover in this chapter is Registry-editing utilities. We examine this component thoroughly because this topic is often neglected. The content that we will examine will be more detailed than what you will require for the exam so that when you finish this book, you will have a great grasp of what this tool is capable of. There will be questions about these topics on the exam.

You also take a detailed look at the important category of antivirus utilities, and we give you some insights about exactly what viruses are. These pesky bits of code often wreak havoc on large and small organizations alike.

Operating System Utilities for Disk Maintenance

1.2 Identify basic concepts and procedures for creating, viewing and managing files, directories and disks. This includes procedures for changing file attributes and the ramifications of those changes (for example, security issues). Content may include the following: Windows-based utilities — ScanDisk, System Manager, DEFRAG.EXE, FDISK.EXE, Cvt1.EXE (Drive Converter FAT16 to FAT32)

In this section, you examine different utilities that you can use to perform disk maintenance on your system. These utilities include the FAT32 Drive converter utility, fdisk, defrag, and ScanDisk. Each of these utilities serves a specific purpose for your operating system.

Drive converter FAT16 to FAT32

1.2 Identify basic concepts and procedures for creating, viewing and managing files, directories and disks. This includes procedures for changing file attributes and the ramifications of those changes (for example, security issues). Content may include the following: Windows-based utilities — Cvt1.EXE (Drive Converter FAT16 to FAT32)

The drive converter utility is found in the Start menu by choosing Programs ➪ Accessories ➪ System Tools (see Figure 27-1). The utility is only available on Windows 95 OSR2 and later versions of Windows. The purpose of this utility is to convert FAT16 partitions into FAT32 partitions without repartitioning your hard drive. When you open this utility, you are presented with the Drive Converter wizard that guides you through converting your hard drive to FAT32. The main benefit of FAT32 over FAT16 is that FAT32 utilizes smaller cluster sizes, which allows you to store more data on your disk.

Caution FAT32 conversion is a one-way process and after conversion you will not be able to use previous versions of a Windows 95 or Windows NT 4.0 on that computer.

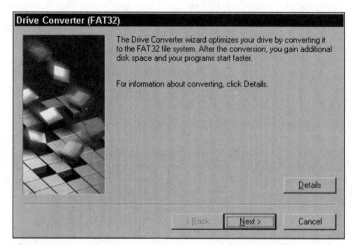

Figure 27-1: Drive Converter allows for a one-way conversion to FAT32.

The first stage of the Drive Converter wizard has you choose the drive that you would like to convert to FAT32. Upon selecting the drive to convert, Windows displays a warning that tells you that you will not be able to use previous versions of a Windows 95 or Windows NT 4.0 on this computer, because they do not support FAT32 (see Figure 27-2).

The FAT32 converter then checks your system for utilities that are incompatible with FAT32 (see Figure 27-3). After checking the Drive converter utility, the wizard lists the incompatible utilities on a page, and you will be able to view details of each of these utilities.

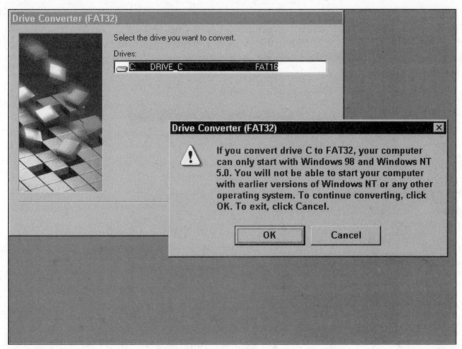

Figure 27-2: Most operating systems are not able to read FAT32, so be careful when converting.

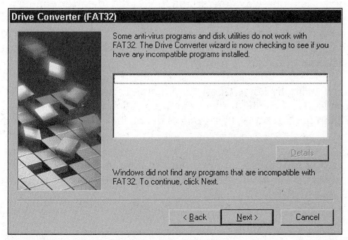

Figure 27-3: If you have known applications that are incompatible with FAT32, you will be warned.

After confirming that you want to convert your disk into FAT32, Windows reboots your computer to perform the conversion (see Figure 27-4). The biggest reason for the reboot is to prevent other utilities from attempting to access the drive during the conversion process. Depending on your computer hardware, the conversion process can be lengthy.

Figure 27-4: Drive Converter reboots your computer to gain exclusive access to the drive.

One of the main things to remember before attempting to convert your drive into FAT32 is that this process is a one-way conversion. If you decide after converting your drive that you would like to revert back to FAT16, you will have to delete the partition from your hard drive, and create a new partition, which can then be formatted as FAT16. Because there is no easy way to reverse this conversion, great care should be taken before converting your drive.

Currently there is a utility by PowerQuest Corp. named Partition Magic that can convert to or from FAT32. If you find yourself in the position where you must convert a FAT32 partition back to FAT16, this is one of the utilities that can perform this action for you.

When using any utility that modifies a large amount of data on your hard drive, you should back up your data before attempting drive conversion.

fdisk.exe

1.2 Identify basic concepts and procedures for creating, viewing and managing files, directories and disks. This includes procedures for changing file attributes and the ramifications of those changes (for example, security issues). Content may include the following: Windows-based utilities — FDISK.EXE

Prior to storing any data on your disk, you need to prepare the disk for use. You can use the fdisk.exe utility to prepare your disk to hold data. The fdisk.exe utility dates back to the earliest versions of MS-DOS, in which it was used to create partitions on your disk. The fdisk.exe utility was modified with the release of Windows 95 OSR2 to allow it to support FAT32 partitions. Windows NT and Windows 2000 do not use fdisk.exe, as Windows NT uses a program named disk administrator and Windows 2000 uses the Disk Management snap-in for the Microsoft Management Console. The fdisk.exe utility supports many command line switches, as well as an interactive interface. It is the interactive interface that most people are familiar with, so we will cover that first and the command line switches later in this section.

If you are using fdisk.exe from either Windows 95 OSR2 or Windows 98, then you will be prompted on whether to enable large disk support, as shown in Figure 27-5. If you enable this support, then any new partitions that you create in excess of 512MB will be formatted as FAT32. As noted in Figure 27-5, this can leave this partition unreadable by operating systems that are not able to read FAT32 partitions, like Windows NT and most versions of Windows 95.

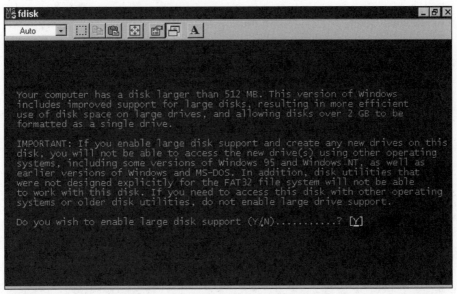

Figure 27-5: The Large Disk support warning should not be ignored, as it enables you to create FAT32 partitions.

After deciding whether you would like to support FAT32 or not, you'll be presented with the normal list of options for the fdisk.exe utility. These options include:

✦ Create DOS partition or logical DOS drive

✦ Set the active partition—your drive will not be bootable without one

✦ Delete partition or logical DOS drive

✦ Display partition information

Each drive can have only one primary partition. You can also create one extended partition on each drive, which can contain multiple logical drives. Primary partitions are represented on your computer with an associated drive letter, while extended partitions require logical drives to maintain a drive letter representation. Each of the drive letters that appears on your computer is still limited to the size that is specified by the file system. This means that FAT16 drives are limited to 2GB and FAT32 drives are limited to 2TB.

Tip　　You can only boot from an active partition, so if you fail to set up an active partition on a new drive, then you will be unable to boot from that drive. If you select no in response to the prompt to create a partition of the maximum size and make it active, then you will have to create the partition and set it active yourself.

Figure 27-6 shows the partition table of the typical hard drive. The drive that is shown is 6GB in size. It contains a 2GB partition, as well as a 4GB partition. The 4GB partition will likely contain two or more logical drives. If the extended partition contains logical drives, `fdisk.exe` inquires whether you would like to see them.

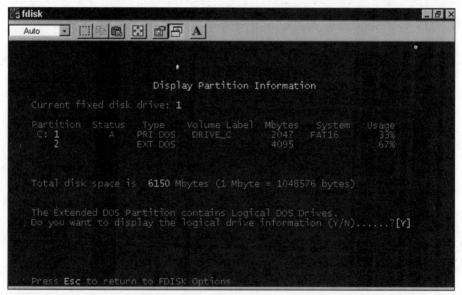

Figure 27-6: Primary partitions and logical drivers are associated with drive letters.

The `fdisk.exe` utility supports several switches. Of the switches that it supports, only a few are actually documented. One of the more useful and heavily documented of the switches is `/status`. This command returns a one-screen listing of your drive's partition tables and then exits the `fdisk.exe` program.

The /mbr switch is one of the undocumented fdisk.exe switches. This command rewrites the Master Boot Record (MBR) for your hard drive. The MBR is read by your computer's POST (Power On Self Test) process when it is looking for a bootable drive. If your drive should be bootable, but is not being detected as bootable by your computer, you can try rewriting the MBR. This may give you a bootable drive. This process may also help to remove some viruses that store themselves in the MBR, but a good anti-virus program provides better protection and removal.

Caution Take care when using the /mbr switch with fdisk.exe, as a number of programs may have problems if the Master Boot Record is rewritten. Rewriting the Master Boot Record can also cause problems if your computer is currently configured to dual boot with another operating system that has modified the boot sector, such as Windows NT or Windows 2000.

The last of the undocumented options allows you to partition your hard drive without loading the interactive version of fdisk.exe. The correct syntax for this command is:

```
FDISK.EXE <drive_number>/<Pri|Ext|Log>:<Size in MB>
```

If you want to partition a new drive into two partitions, you could use the following commands:

```
FDISK.EXE 1/Pri:2048
FDISK.EXE 1/Ext:2048
FDISK.EXE 1/Log:2048
```

The interactive version of fdisk.exe will be required if you need to delete or change the partition table on your hard drive.

defrag.exe

1.2 Identify basic concepts and procedures for creating, viewing and managing files, directories and disks. This includes procedures for changing file attributes and the ramifications of those changes (for example, security issues). Content may include the following: Windows-based utilities — DEFRAG.EXE

The defrag.exe utility can be used to improve the performance of your hard drive. As you write data to your hard drive, it is always written into that largest area of free space that is available, but when you delete files, areas of free space become broken up and scattered around your drive. There will be instances when the largest area of free space will not be large enough to hold the data that is being written — when this happens, the file will be broken up into pieces to the areas of free space. When files are broken into pieces, they are fragmented. You can use defrag.exe to repair the disk fragmentation. When using defrag.exe, you'll be able to enable two different settings, as shown in Figure 27-7. The settings are:

✦ Rearrange program files so my programs start faster

✦ Check drive for errors

You have the option to use the settings for this session only, or to save the settings for future executions.

If you choose to rearrange your files so that the programs start faster, the disk defragmenter program not only consolidates free space on the disk, but it also rearranges files. When the files are rearranged, programs that do not change frequently are placed near the beginning of the drive, and files that you change frequently are placed near the end of the drive next to the largest area of free space. Rewriting a file effectively creates a new file and deletes the old one — in that order. The process of rewriting files generates additional small areas of free space. Files that are rewritten frequently should be left near the free area of the drive. This is so that when you defragment the drive again, all of the files that have to be moved to consolidate the free space will be close to each other and the defragmentation process will take less time.

If you choose to check the drive for errors, then the ScanDisk utility checks the integrity of the directory structures before starting the defragmentation process.

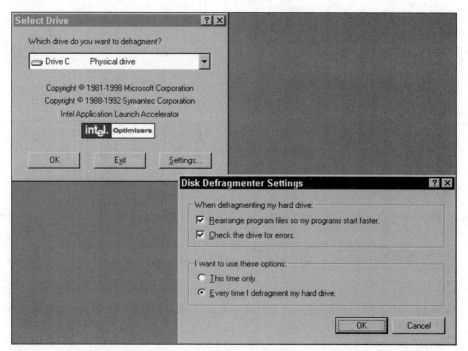

Figure 27-7: There are only a few settings to go along with the disk defragmenter.

The defrag.exe utility runs with minimal user interface by default. To achieve the fastest defragmentation, you should always use the minimal user interface, as seen in Figure 27-8, rather than the detailed interface.

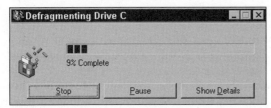

Figure 27-8: The operating system has the least overhead when not viewing details.

If you are dying to know what is really going on behind the scenes, you can click the Show Details button to get a picture of what is happening on your drive, as shown in Figure 27-9. This view shows you the reads and writes that are taking place on your disk, and you can see what the individual blocks refer to by looking at the legend. Even though this is nice to watch and you can see a bit of what is actually happening, you should avoid it in practice because a large number of additional clock cycles are necessary to display the animations.

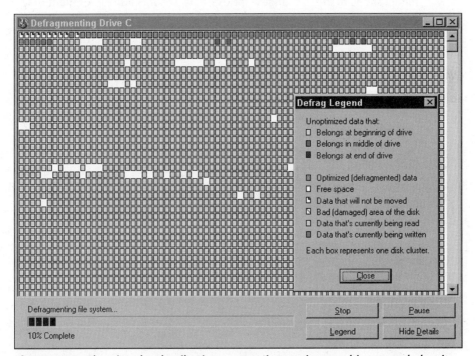

Figure 27-9: Showing the details gives you an interesting graphic to watch, but it provides little else (and slows down the process).

Because the disk fragmentation utility rearranges the data on your drive and can therefore improve performance, it should be run periodically to ensure maximum performance of your computer. The exact amount of time that the word *periodically* refers to varies. If your hard drive is extremely full (containing perhaps only a few hundred megabytes of free space), then you should run defrag.exe as often as every few days. If you have a large amount of free space on your drive, files will take longer to become fragmented on your disk, and you may only need to defragment your drive once every month or two. When you open defrag.exe it will make a recommendation if your drives really need to be defragmented, if defrag.exe recommends that you defragment, then you are likely experiencing noticeable performance degradation. There is no harm in defragmenting your drive, even if the recommendation is not made, as you may still gain a performance increase.

The important thing to remember is that free space and disk performance should be monitored in order to achieve an optimal level of performance.

ScanDisk

1.2 Identify basic concepts and procedures for creating, viewing and managing files, directories and disks. This includes procedures for changing file attributes and the ramifications of those changes (for example, security issues). Content may include the following: Windows-based utilities — ScanDisk

The ScanDisk utility is used to identify potential problems with either your file system's allocation or with the physical hard drive.

When you choose to run the ScanDisk utility you will have a few initial options, which include performing a standard scan or a thorough scan of your hard drive, as well as automatically fixing errors (see Figure 27-10).

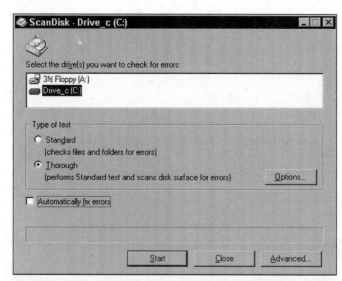

Figure 27-10: Standard scans will check the structure of the file tables, whereas a thorough scan will check disk integrity.

The major difference between a standard scan and a thorough scan lies in what is actually checked, as the following list illustrates.

✦ **Standard:** This option examines the structure of the file allocation table, including information about each individual file that is found in the table.

✦ **Thorough:** This option performs a standard scan and then proceeds to check each physical cluster on the disk to ensure that it is not damaged.

You can set options for performing a thorough scan of your hard drive by clicking the Options button to display the Surface Scan Options dialog box, as shown in Figure 27-11. You can determine which areas of the disk to scan, whether to perform write testing, and whether to repair damage to hidden and system files.

In most cases, you will be able to scan your entire hard drive without worrying about hidden or system files — the option to skip these have to do with disk-based copy protection of software, and manufacturers no longer use this method of copy protection. The system area of your hard drive includes the area that contains the file allocation table for your disk. Because this is a key area of your drive, ScanDisk gives you the option of bypassing it in order to prevent you from causing additional damage. This option has been included to satisfy some users' fear of damaging their drives, as scanning this area is always safe.

Figure 27-11: In most cases, the default scan options are sufficient for use.

You can also skip the write-testing phase if you're in a hurry. Write testing reads data from each cluster on your drive, writes the data to back to the cluster, and then checks whether the correct data was actually written. If you skip write testing, then the data is only read from the disk. If the data looks consistent, then it is considered to be a good cluster. Going without write testing is somewhat faster, but it is also less accurate in determining weak clusters on your drive.

You should select the option to avoid repairing bad sectors on hidden and system files if your computer uses older software. In the past, some software manufacturers used disk-based copy protection schemes. This copy protection placed certain files in unique locations on your hard drive, which were marked as being either hidden or system and prevented users from modifying the files. If ScanDisk reads one of these files and finds that it is stored on a weak cluster, it will move the data to new clusters elsewhere on the disk. If the file were part of a copy protection procedure, then the software that it is protecting would cease to work. This type of copy protection was used when the IBM PC was introduced in the 1980s, but it is not used by vendors today.

Whether you perform a thorough scan or a standard scan, you can set advanced options, as shown in Figure 27-12. These options include: displaying a summary, logging the scan, checking for cross-link files, looking for lost file fragments, checking for files with invalid, names, dates, or duplicates, and reporting errors in MS-DOS file lengths.

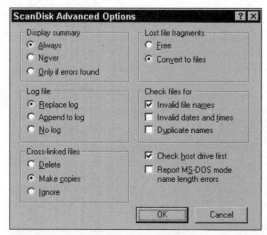

Figure 27-12: Most of the default Advanced options are sufficient for scanning your drive.

Most of the advanced ScanDisk options are self-explanatory, but one that may not be is cross-link files. The file allocation table contains a pointer to the starting cluster for each file. As the file is read, a pointer at the end of each cluster is used to identify where the next cluster of the file can be found, with the last cluster of the file not containing a further pointer. From time to time, the pointer at the end of a cluster becomes corrupted and starts pointing to the wrong location for the next bit of data. If the new location already contains file data (which contains a pointer to the next bit of data for the second file), you end up with two files that are using the same set of clusters.

When two files point to the same cluster (and clusters that follow), the situation is known as a cross-linked file. Depending on your outlook, you may choose to make copies of these files or to ignore them altogether. If you are a pessimist, then you probably believe that both of these files are corrupt and probably garbage. If you are an optimist, then you probably believe that one or both of these files are still readable and usable.

File fragments or lost chains, on the other hand, tend to be the leftover portions of cross-linked files (the portions of a file that would have belonged to a file had its clusters not been corrupted or lost). You have the option of either deleting these file fragments or converting them to files. If you choose to convert them to files, then a new folder is created on the root of your drive, and the files are incrementally named.

In the Real World Although you have the option to convert lost file fragments to files, I have yet to see useful data recovered from file fragments, so you might as well delete them and free the space.

Depending on the settings for your advanced options, you may see a results window when the scan process is complete (see Figure 27-13). This summary provides useful information about the usage of disk space in the drive that was being scanned. For more details about allocation units, refer to Chapter 20.

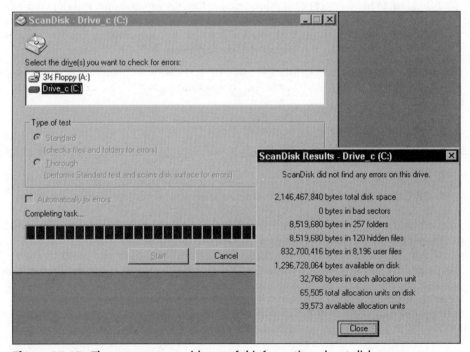

Figure 27-13: The summary provides useful information about disk usage.

ScanDisk serves an important purpose on your system for ensuring data integrity of the files on your disk.

Configuration Utilities

1.2 Identify basic concepts and procedures for creating, viewing and managing files, directories and disks. This includes procedures for changing file attributes and the ramifications of those changes (for example, security issues). Content may include the following: Windows-based utilities — Device manager, System Manager, Computer Manager, MSCONFIG.EXE, REGEDIT.EXE (View information/Backup registry), REGEDT32.EXE, SYSEDIT.EXE, SCANREG

This section discusses many of the configuration utilities that ship with the Windows operating system. These utilities provide easy ways to modify configuration files and the Registry.

System Configuration Utility

1.2 Identify basic concepts and procedures for creating, viewing and managing files, directories and disks. This includes procedures for changing file attributes and the ramifications of those changes (for example, security issues). Content may include the following: Windows-based utilities — MSCONFIG.EXE

The System Configuration Utility (`msconfig.exe`) is one of the newer utilities for maintaining settings on your Windows 9*x* computer (see Figure 27-14). This application is capable of:

✦ Creating custom startup configurations (for troubleshooting)

✦ Performing a selective startup which only processes some of the system files

✦ Editing `config.sys`, `autoexec.bat`, `system.ini`, and `win.ini`

✦ Disabling programs that have been added to the Run key of the Registry

All the changes in the preceding bullet list can be accomplished from within a simple Windows user interface, making this an extremely easy configuration tool to work with. If you choose to set additional options, the Advanced settings (see Figure 27-15), allows you to enable troubleshooting settings, such as the exclusion of adapter memory, 16-bit disk access, VGA video, Startup Menu, and maximum memory settings. These settings will only be used when trying to identify the source of boot or file-corruption problems.

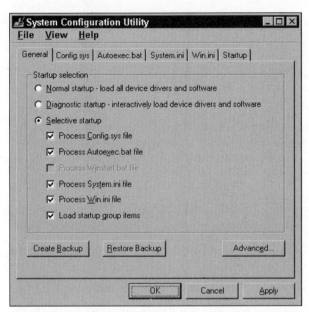

Figure 27-14: The initial window for the System Configuration Utility allows you to modify the basic system files.

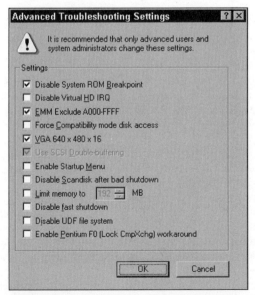

Figure 27-15: Advanced settings allows for the configuration of extreme troubleshooting settings.

regedit.exe

1.2 Identify basic concepts and procedures for creating, viewing and managing files, directories and disks. This includes procedures for changing file attributes and the ramifications of those changes (for example, security issues). Content may include the following: Windows-based utilities — REGEDIT.EXE (View information/Backup registry)

If you have ever talked to anybody about the system Registry, then you have probably been given a stern warning that this is not a place where the timid should go. The reason for this warning is that the Registry stores system-wide configuration information for almost all services on your computer. If you experience major problems with the Registry, then it is very likely that you will be experiencing major problems with your entire computer.

With Windows 3.1, the Registry held information about file associations. With Windows 9*x*, Windows NT, and Windows 2000, the Registry now stores key information about all system services.

The Windows 9*x* Registry has six major subtrees. These subtrees are:

✦ HKEY_Classes_Root

✦ HKEY_Current_User

✦ HKEY_Local_Machine

✦ HKEY_Users

✦ HKEY_Current_Config

✦ HKEY_Dyn_Data

Of these subtrees, there are only two that you really should worry about. These are HKEY_Current_User and HKEY_Local_Machine, as shown in Figure 27-16. The information in the other subtrees is either duplicated within these keys, or the data cannot be modified.

HKEY_Classes_Root contains information about all the file associations and registered file types that exist in your computer. This information is actually a copy of the information stored in the HKEY_Local_Machine\software\classes key. HKEY_Users contains information for the currently logged on user, as well as information for the default user. The information that is found in HKEY_Current_User is a duplicate of the information that is found in HKEY_Users within a key for the user. HKEY_Dyn_Data contains dynamic information that is actually used by the system monitor utility. The two keys that you need to be most familiar with are:

✦ **HKEY_Current_User:** This key contains configuration information for the currently logged on user. This information includes items like control panel settings (such as mouse acceleration or screensaver preferences) and user-related software settings for installed applications.

✦ **HKEY_Local_Machine:** This key contains information about your computer. This information includes configuration information about hardware components and system settings for all software on the computer.

Figure 27-16: The two subtrees that most configuration changes are made in are HKEY_Local_Machine and HKEY_Current_User.

All the entries in the Registry are stored in a hierarchical tree. This tree contains several subfolders that are called *keys*. If you want to create a new key within the Registry, you can do so by using the Edit ➪ New ➪ Key command. Every key within the Registry is capable of storing values. The Windows 9*x* Registry contains three different types of values: string value, binary value, and DWORD value (see Figure 27-17).

Some hardware components or software components that you may install on your computer may create entries inside of both HKEY_Local_Machine and HKEY_Current_User. This makes sense if you think about an application such as Microsoft Office. Microsoft Office is going to create entries into HKEY_Local_Machine that relate to the location of Office components on this particular computer, such as the spell checker, which can be found within `C:\program files\microsoft office\tools`. At the same time, Microsoft Office will install entries into HKEY_Current_User that relate to the user configuration on the system, such as what the default save as file type is going to be.

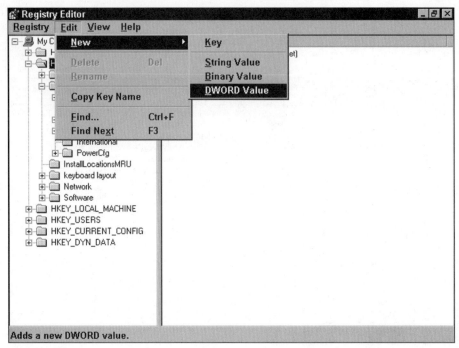

Figure 27-17: There are three basic data types for the Windows 9x Registry.

The Registry is an important part of your computer, and great care should be taken not to corrupt this database. Before you start doing any procedure that involves the Registry, you should ensure that you have a clean backup of the Registry. This backup can be achieved through a variety of methods, such as the scanreg utility that will be discussed later in this chapter, or by physically copying the files that make up the Registry.

To copy the files that make up the Registry, you need to know where the files actually are. HKEY_Current_User in the Windows 9x Registry can be found in your Windows directory in a read-only hidden file named user.dat. If you are using Windows NT, or Windows 2000, then you will find the user portion of the Registry in your user profile directory, and it will be named NTuser.dat. HKEY_Local_Machine can also be found on Windows 9x computers in the Windows directory, but it will be named system.dat. For Windows 2000 computers, HKEY_Local_Machine is actually composed of several files that are found in the Winnt directory. These files should be backed up and restored by using the Windows 2000 backup program. The Windows 2000 backup utility is capable of creating an Emergency Repair Disk, which will be able to restore your Registry.

Cross-Reference   For more information about the Emergency Repair Disk and the Emergency Repair Process, consult Chapter 22.

If you would like to be a little more selective in your procedure for backing up the Registry, then you can actually back up and restore individual keys within the Registry.

STEP BY STEP: Backing Up Individual Keys

1. Choose Start ⇨ Run and type `regedit` in the Run dialog box that appears.

2. Select the key that you want to back up by clicking on it.

3. Choose Registry ⇨ Export Registry File. Doing so displays the Export Registry File dialog box, as shown in Figure 27-18. This dialog box looks similar to a standard Save As dialog box—with the addition of the Export Range panel at the bottom. The Export Range panel contains your selected branch within the Registry by default.

4. Type a name for the file and choose a location for `regedit` to save it. The file will be given the default `.reg` extension.

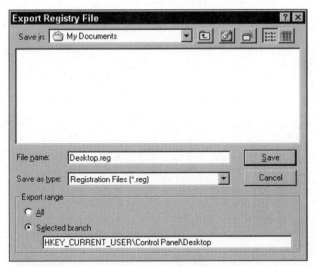

Figure 27-18: Exporting sections of the Registry is a great way to back up settings in the portion of the Registry that you are editing.

Tip   You can use `regedt32.exe` to save Registry keys to be restored at a later date, but these files are in a binary format, and cannot be edited with a text editor.

Files that end in the .reg extension are Registry export files that you can edit with a text editor (as shown in Figure 27-19) and import into the Registry by double-clicking on the file. With Windows 9*x* systems, double-clicking on the .reg file causes the file to be immediately merged into your Registry. Windows 2000 has added a safety feature where Windows prompts you to confirm that you would like to import the settings into your Registry, as shown in Figure 27-20.

```
Desktop - Notepad                                          _ □ x
 File  Edit  Search  Help
REGEDIT4

[HKEY_CURRENT_USER\Control Panel\Desktop]
"DragFullWindows"="0"
"FontSmoothing"="0"
"Wallpaper"=""
"TileWallpaper"="0"
"ScreenSaveTimeOut"="600"
"UserPreferencemask"=hex:be,00,00,00
"WallpaperStyle"="2"
"ScreenSaveActive"="1"
"ScreenSaveUsePassword"=dword:00000000

[HKEY_CURRENT_USER\Control Panel\Desktop\WindowMetrics]
"Shell Icon BPP"="16"
"IconSpacingFactor"="100"
"BorderWidth"="-15"
"ScrollWidth"="-240"
"ScrollHeight"="-240"
"CaptionWidth"="-270"
"CaptionHeight"="-270"
"SmCaptionWidth"="-270"
"SmCaptionHeight"="-270"
"MenuWidth"="-270"
"MenuHeight"="-270"
"CaptionFont"=hex:0a,00,00,00,00,00,00,00,bc,02,00,00,00,00,00,00,00,41,72
    69,61,6c,00,73,20,53,65,72,69,66,00,00,00,70,2a,00,00,5f,02,57,01,97,00,00,
    00,60,5e,5e,cc
```

Figure 27-19: All Registry export files share a structure that resembles .ini files.

 In the Real World When working with Windows 9*x* computers, .reg files are automatically imported into your Registry if you double-click on them. Rather than using the .reg extension on your files, you may choose to use .txt files. Files with the .txt extension can also be imported into your Registry by typing regedit.exe <import_file> at the command line.

After a file has been successfully merged with your Registry, a dialog will be displayed confirming the merge, as shown in Figure 27-21. Periodically, .reg files may become corrupted due to editing them with certain text editors, such as notepad.exe. This corruption is because some text editors may add extended (non-visible) characters into the text file that are not compatible with regedit.exe. The only editor that does not exhibit this behavior is edit.com. If you have a file that has been corrupted, you can fix it by opening the file using edit.com, resaving the file, and closing. Even if the file is corrupt, you still receive a dialog stating that the information has been successfully entered into your Registry.

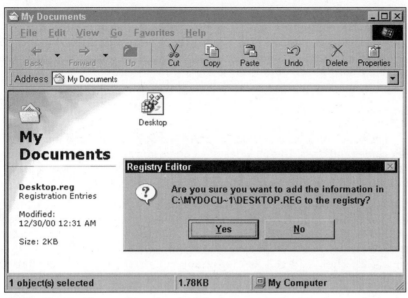

Figure 27-20: The confirmation for Windows 2000 Registry import helps to limit accidental imports.

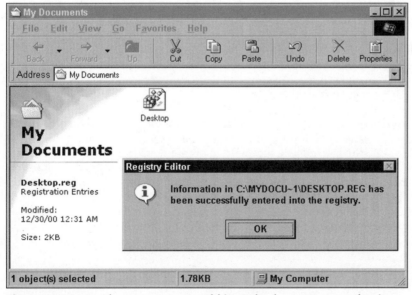

Figure 27-21: Just because you are told it works does not mean that it really did. The import process does not always report errors.

The `regedit.exe` program is capable of editing the Registry for Windows 9*x* computers, Windows NT computers, and Windows 2000 computers. One of the few differences between the different Registry editing programs is that the Windows 2000 version has added a Favorites menu, which allows you to quickly return to common Registry keys for editing.

regedt32.exe

1.2 Identify basic concepts and procedures for creating, viewing and managing files, directories and disks. This includes procedures for changing file attributes and the ramifications of those changes (for example, security issues). Content may include the following: Windows-based utilities — REGEDT32.EXE

The `regedt32.exe` program is the Registry Editor for Windows NT and Windows 2000. You cannot use `regedt32.exe` on a Windows 9*x* computer. Most of the user interface for `regedt32.exe` is still based on the Windows NT 3.51 user interface. That means that many of the Windows have a Windows 3.0 look and feel to them (see Figure 27-22). The `regedt32.exe` program supports many features that are not available in `regedit.exe`. These features include:

✦ Viewing and setting permissions on Registry keys

✦ Loading and unloading Registry hives (which are registry files on your hard drive)

When working with Windows NT 4.0, `regedt32.exe` allowed you to connect to remote Registries, while `regedit.exe` did not. When you work with Windows 2000, you can use either program to connect to a remote Registry. Connecting to a remote Registry allows you to change the Registry settings on a remote computer without having to leave your own computer. To connect to a remote Registry from across the network, choose Registry ➪ Select Computer in `regedt32.exe` or Registry ➪ Connect Network Registry in `regedit.exe`.

One big advantage of `regedt32.exe` is that you can load Registry hives. This ability becomes useful when you want to modify the entries for the default `ntuser.dat`. The default `ntuser.dat` is used as a template to create new user profiles for users who do not yet have a profile. You can find the `ntuser.dat` file for this default template account in `c:\documents and settings\default user\ntuser.dat`, and you can load this subtree or hive into `regedt32.exe` and edit the settings for this default template. This default user template should not be confused with the default user that is in use prior to a user logging on to your computer. The Registry settings for the pre-logon default user are actually found in the Registry under `users\.DEFAULT`.

The other large advantage of `regedt32.exe` is that you are able to manage the security on Registry keys. In order to view or modify the security settings on a Registry key, first select the key, and then choose Security ➪ Permissions. You can work with permissions on Registry keys only — not Registry values.

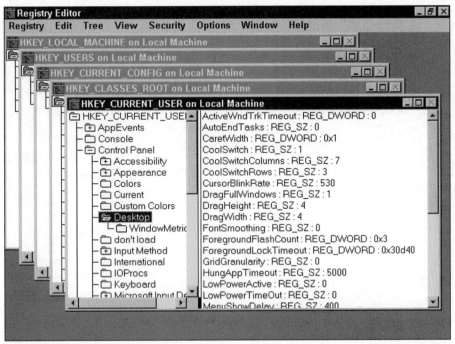

Figure 27-22: The `regedt32.exe` program sports the Windows 3.0 user interface that was used with Windows NT 3.51.

The System Configuration Editor

1.2 Identify basic concepts and procedures for creating, viewing and managing files, directories and disks. This includes procedures for changing file attributes and the ramifications of those changes (for example, security issues). Content may include the following: Windows-based utilities — SYSEDIT.EXE

The System Configuration Editor (`sysedit.exe`) provides a quick way to edit several core operating system files. The operating system files that it is able to edit include:

- `autoexec.bat`
- `config.sys`
- `win.ini`
- `system.ini`
- `protocol.ini` (only when working with Windows 9*x*)

The `sysedit.exe` program is available in Windows 9*x*, Windows NT, and Windows 2000. The program provides a user interface similar to Windows Notepad with an enhancement that allows for multiple files to be open at the same time, as shown in Figure 27-23.

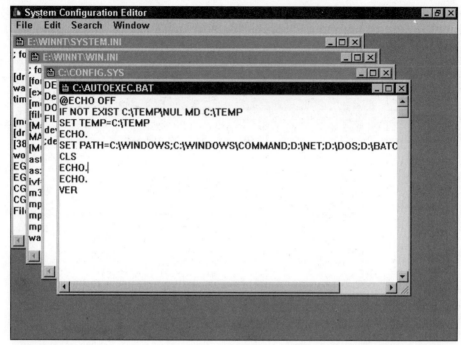

Figure 27-23: The System Configuration Editor is similar to a multi-window version of Notepad.

The Registry Checker

1.2 Identify basic concepts and procedures for creating, viewing and managing files, directories and disks. This includes procedures for changing file attributes and the ramifications of those changes (for example, security issues). Content may include the following: Windows-based utilities — SCANREG

The Registry Checker (`scanreg.exe`), shown in Figure 27-4, is a Windows 9x utility that you can use to scan, back up, and restore your Registry. The scanning process examines the Registry for potential corruption.

Tip   `scanreg.exe` must be run from the MS-DOS mode of Windows 9x. If you run `scanreg.exe` from the graphical user interface, then `scanreg.exe` launches `scanregw.exe`. `scanregw.exe` is discussed in more detail in the next section.

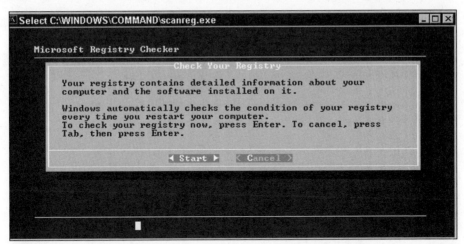

Figure 27-24: The Registry Checker will scan your Registry for errors.

If your Registry appears to be intact, then the Registry Checker prompts you to decide whether to create a backup of your current Registry, as shown in Figure 27-25.

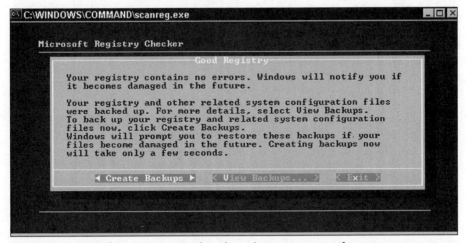

Figure 27-25: Backing up your Registry is an important part of `scanreg.exe`.

If your Registry ever becomes corrupt, you will be able to restore one of the backups that `scanreg.exe` has made. In order to restore a backup, you can either run `scanreg.exe` and then follow the prompt to view the backups, or run `scanreg.exe /restore`. In order to run `scanreg.exe` (shown in Figure 27-26) to restore your Registry, you will have to boot into MS-DOS mode.

Cross-Reference   For more information about MS-DOS mode and other boot methods for Windows 9x, consult Chapter 22.

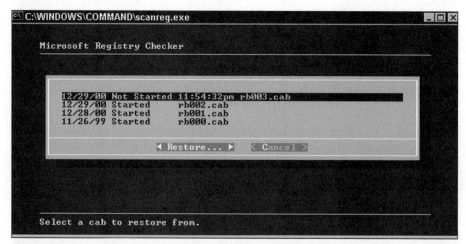

Figure 27-26: The restore process allows you to choose a backup that you want to restore.

Because your Registry represents an important part of your operating system, you should back it up on a regular basis.

The Windows Registry Checker

The Windows Registry Checker (`scanregw.exe`) is a Windows-based version of `scanreg.exe`. If you attempt to launch `scanreg.exe` from the Windows graphical user interface, then `scanreg.exe` calls `scanregw.exe`, which allows you to back up your Registry, as shown in Figure 27-27. This Windows-based version of `scanreg.exe` is only capable of backing up your Registry, but not of restoring it. If you try to restore a backup version of your Registry, then you will have to exit Windows, enter MS-DOS mode, and then launch `scanreg.exe`.

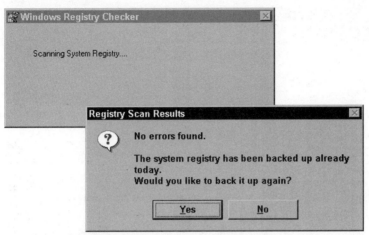

Figure 27-27: The Windows version of the Registry Checker is capable only of backing up the Registry, not restoring it.

Device Manager

1.2 Identify basic concepts and procedures for creating, viewing and managing files, directories and disks. This includes procedures for changing file attributes and the ramifications of those changes (for example, security issues). Content may include the following: Windows-based utilities such as — Device Manager

Device Manager is available to both Windows 9*x* and Windows 2000. You access it through the system control panel in both programs:

✦ On Windows 9*x* systems, Device Manager is a tab in the System properties window.

✦ On Windows 2000 systems, you can access Device Manager by clicking the Device Manager button on the Hardware tab of the System properties window.

On either system, devices that have hardware problems on your system are easily visible with a red x in the device tree, as shown in Figure 27-28. The red x identifies devices that are in conflict or are disabled, while a yellow exclamation identifies devices that are not properly configured. You can use Device Manager to identify problems with your hardware, configure the drivers for the devices, and configure hardware resources, such as IRQs and I/O addresses.

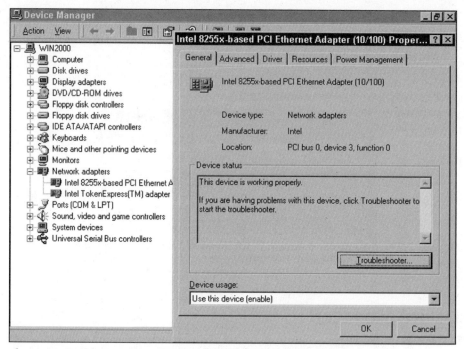

Figure 27-28: If you are looking for malfunctioning devices, look for the red x on the device.

Computer Management

1.2 Identify basic concepts and procedures for creating, viewing and managing files, directories and disks. This includes procedures for changing file attributes and the ramifications of those changes (for example, security issues). Content may include the following: Windows-based utilities—Computer Manager

Windows 2000 includes a utility called Computer Management. Computer Management is actually more of a user interface to a number of other utilities than a utility itself. Computer Management is a Microsoft Management Console (MMC) settings file that contains the following utilities or snap-ins:

✦ **Event Viewer:** Viewer for system logs.

✦ **System Information:** Displays information about your OS and its hardware. This is covered later in this chapter.

✦ **Performance Logs and Alerts:** Records system status and health based on measurable counters and generates alerts when the counters exceed threshold values.

✦ **Shared Folders:** Status of shared or published folders on the computer.

✦ **Device Manager:** Hardware status and configuration information in a format that can be edited, unlike the System Information Tool.

✦ **Local Users and Groups:** Management of the local account database.

✦ **Disk Management:** Management of disk partitions. The Windows 2000 version of `fdisk.exe`.

✦ **Disk Defragmenter:** Optimizes disk performance by defragmenting files.

✦ **Removable Storage Management:** Manages and tracks removable media on your computer, such as CD-ROMs and magnetic tapes.

✦ **Services:** Manages system services (like the Server and Workstation services) on the local computer.

✦ **Other administration utilities:** Other tools are included with this tool, like Telephony, WMI Control, Indexing Service, DNS, Internet Information Services, and Routing and Remote Access.

Tip

Computer Management is a Microsoft Management Console (MMC) snap-in that acts as a container for other MMC snap-ins. Its only offering or benefit over the individual snap-ins, is that you only have to add one snap-in to the MMC, rather than a whole series of snap-ins. For practice with the use of the MMC, try Lab 27.3.

By putting all these utilities together in one location, as shown in Figure 27-29, system management is made substantially easier for most users.

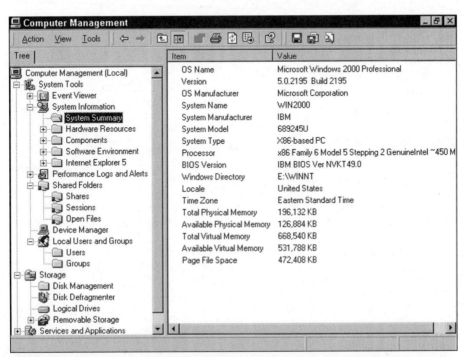

Figure 27-29: By using Computer Management, it is likely that you will not need other utilities, as they have been consolidated here.

The System Information Tool

The System Information Tool (`msinfo32.exe`) is available in both the Windows 9*x* and Windows 2000 operating systems. This tool has been designed to provide information about as many components in the operating system as possible. Figure 27-30 should give you a good feel for the type of information that is available within this tool. If it is part of the operating system, then the System Information Tool will provide you with information about it.

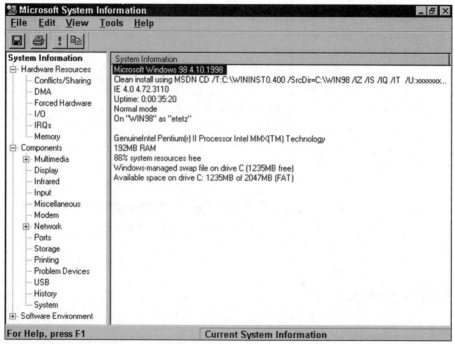

Figure 27-30: The Windows 98 System Information Tool provides information about your installation and hardware configuration.

The Windows 2000 version provides a greater level of detail about most of the settings and components within the computer than does the Windows 9*x* version. This high level of detail can be seen in Figure 27-31 by examining the amount of memory that is available on the computer. The specific information available is a function of a mature tool, and future versions will provide even more detail.

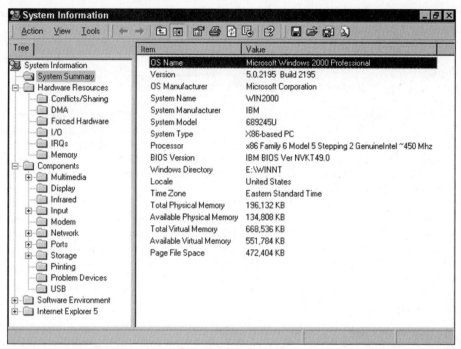

Figure 27-31: The Windows 2000 System Information Tool provides similar information as the Windows 9x version, but in greater detail.

Miscellaneous Utilities

1.2 Identify basic concepts and procedures for creating, viewing and managing files, directories and disks. This includes procedures for changing file attributes and the ramifications of those changes (for example, security issues). Content may include the following: Windows-based utilities — ATTRIB.EXE, EXTRACT.EXE, EDIT.COM, WSCRIPT.EXE, HWINFO.EXE, ASD.EXE (Automatic Skip Driver)

A number of miscellaneous utilities are also available within Windows 9x and Windows 2000. This section takes a look at some of these utilities.

Windows Script Host

1.2 Identify basic concepts and procedures for creating, viewing and managing files, directories and disks. This includes procedures for changing file attributes and the ramifications of those changes (for example, security issues). Content may include the following: Windows-based utilities — WSCRIPT.EXE

Windows Script Host (`wscript.exe`) is one of those miscellaneous utilities that doesn't fit easily into other categories. Windows Script Host is used to execute Visual Basic Script (VBScript) or JavaScript. The tasks that you are able to accomplish by using VBScript are numerous and almost unlimited. Most Windows-based applications support ActiveX automation, and so can be controlled through VBScript. You can use Windows Script Host to execute such scripts.

Windows Script Host has two components that can execute script. These are `wscript.exe` and `cscript.exe`. The `wscript.exe` program executes VBScript from within the Windows environment; `cscript.exe` executes scripts from the command prompt. Both these utilities are interpreters for VBScript; if the scripts were converted into true Visual Basic and compiled into executables, you would achieve much better performance.

Windows Script Host is included with Windows 2000 and Windows 98, and it can be added to Windows 95 or Windows NT 4.0, by installing Internet Explorer 4.0 or greater. To get the latest version of Windows Script Host, you can download it separately from `http://msdn.microsoft.com/scripting`.

System Manager

1.2 Identify basic concepts and procedures for creating, viewing and managing files, directories and disks. This includes procedures for changing file attributes and the ramifications of those changes (for example, security issues). Content may include the following: Windows-based utilities — System Manager

The CompTIA exam objective regarding System Manager refers to a product that does not exist in the Microsoft family of products. I believe that they meant to refer to System Monitor, which is the Windows 9x tool for taking readings of key system counters and thereby viewing the health and responsiveness of the operating system. Performance Monitor is a similar tool that is used by Windows NT 4.0 and Windows 2000.

For more information about both Performance Monitor and System Monitor, consult Chapter 16.

attrib.exe

1.2 Identify basic concepts and procedures for creating, viewing and managing files, directories and disks. This includes procedures for changing file attributes and the ramifications of those changes (for example, security issues). Content may include the following: Windows-based utilities — ATTRIB.EXE

The `attrib.exe` program is used to view or change the attributes of files. This utility is covered at depth in Chapter 17.

edit.com

1.2 Identify basic concepts and procedures for creating, viewing and managing files, directories and disks. This includes procedures for changing file attributes and the ramifications of those changes (for example, security issues). Content may include the following: Windows-based utilities — EDIT.COM

The edit.com program, shown in Figure 27-32, allows you to modify the contents of text files. We cover edit.com in detail in Chapter 17. The version of edit.com that ships with Windows 9x and Windows 2000 includes some enhancements over the original version that ships with MS-DOS. The two largest enhancements are:

✦ The ability to open multiple files

✦ The use of Windows shortcut keystrokes for Cut, Copy, and Paste operations

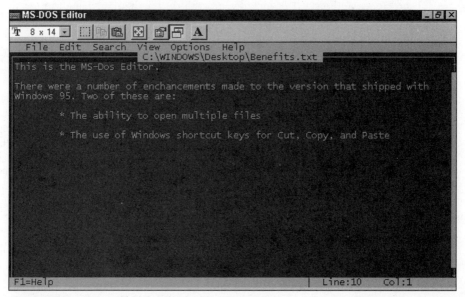

Figure 27-32: Even though it looks like MS-DOS 6.x, edit.com offers some nice new features.

extract.exe

1.2 Identify basic concepts and procedures for creating, viewing and managing files, directories and disks. This includes procedures for changing file attributes and the ramifications of those changes (for example, security issues). Content may include the following: Windows-based utilities — EXTRACT.EXE

The `extract.exe` utility can be used in Windows 9*x* (only) to extract operating system files from the original source .cab files. Use this utility to replace corrupt files that the operating system needs.

expand.exe

The `expand.exe` utility is a Windows NT and Windows 2000 utility that you can use to expand individual source files that are shipped in a compressed format. This utility can be used to replace corrupt files that are being used by the operating system in these operating systems.

Hardware Info

 1.2 Identify basic concepts and procedures for creating, viewing and managing files, directories and disks. This includes procedures for changing file attributes and the ramifications of those changes (for example, security issues). Content may include the following: Windows-based utilities — HWINFO.EXE

The Hardware Info utility (`hwinfo.exe`) is part of Windows 98 and can be launched with the following command line:

```
hwinfo.exe /ui
```

Hardware Info can be used to generate a report that tells you how Windows 98 is currently configured on your system — including historical information about the installation and information about programs that have been configured to automatically start when the operating system loads. If Hardware Info is executed without any switches, it will generate a text file in the Windows directory named `hwinfo.dat`, which will contain the same information that you could view on-screen.

Automatic Skip Driver

 1.2 Identify basic concepts and procedures for creating, viewing and managing files, directories and disks. This includes procedures for changing file attributes and the ramifications of those changes (for example, security issues). Content may include the following: Windows-based utilities — ASD.EXE (Automatic Skip Driver)

Automatic Skip Driver (`asd.exe`), shown in Figure 27-33, takes a look at your current processes and any that are not responding or appear to be frozen. The `asd.exe` program determines which process has been blocked by which other process and allows you to continue running a process that Windows has suspended due to a blocking error.

Figure 27-33: Any processes or driver calls that prevent Windows 98 from operating will be suspended so that Windows can continue to function.

Viruses and Virus Types

3.2 Recognize common problems and determine how to resolve them. Content may include the following: Viruses and virus types — What they are, Sources (floppy, e-mails, etc.), How to determine presence

Computers do not get colds or flues, so when discussing viruses on computers, you do not need to worry about your computer having a runny mouse. A virus is a small program or piece of programming code that is unwanted. This section will take a look at what they are and some of the things that you can do to avoid viruses and get rid of them.

What are viruses?

Viruses are small pieces of programming code that are embedded into other programs. They usually distribute themselves by attaching to other programs and *replicating*, or copying their code and hiding it in another program. The ability to replicate or spread is one of the features of a virus.

Viruses are often benign and will do little more than display pop-up messages or affect the performance of your computer. Malignant viruses, on the other hand, tend to leave a wake of destruction by deleting or corrupting files. Often malignant viruses will wait for a predetermined time or event before launching, and in the meantime only replicate themselves.

Viruses tend to fall into several categories that are based on how they spread. These categories are:

✦ Macro viruses

✦ File level viruses

✦ Boot sector level viruses

Macro viruses are written using any of the macro languages that exist within different applications. Many applications now use a form of Visual Basic to provide a robust macro development environment; but this robust environment can also be used for mischief. Visual Basic provides a truly powerful environment that can be used to control or access other applications. Some of the first macro viruses that came out used this environment to infect Microsoft Word documents. When an infected document was opened, it used an autoexec type action to run the initial code that copied itself into `normal.dot` (the template for most new documents), which is automatically loaded every time you run Microsoft Word. From there, every document that is opened will be infected and become a carrier. Infected documents sent to other people will quickly infect other documents on the destination computers.

Microsoft quickly responded by building macro virus protection into their applications. If you open a document that contains a macro, you will be prompted as to whether you would like to allow it to run.

File level viruses attach themselves to, or replace normal executables on your computer, and then infect other files when the program is run. For instance, if `xcopy.exe` is infected, it can infect other files that it copies, or it can scan the entire hard drive to look for files to infect when it executes next. Often these viruses load into memory and stay resident (like TSRs), infecting other files they find. These viruses are spread by exchanging program files with other computers.

Boot sector level viruses infect the boot sector of computers. The boot sector of your disks contains a program that is used to load the operating system that may be found on the disk. If you take an infected floppy disk and boot your computer with it, then the boot sector virus is executed and copied into memory, where it then copies itself to your hard drive. This may happen even if the floppy disk does not have an operating system on it, and you will see the "Missing Operating System" error message. When you reboot from your hard drive, the virus again loads itself into memory and starts to infect all floppy disks that are placed into your computer and read. These new infected floppies will then infect other computers when they are used to attempt to boot the target computers, or when the disk is accidentally left in during a reboot.

What are not viruses?

There are programs that are scanned for by virus scanning software, but are not actually viruses. These programs include:

✦ Trojan Horses or Trojans

✦ Worms

Trojans are actually malicious software (MalWare) that cause damage when they are executed. These programs are distributed under a false pretense, such as update to a common program like WinZip, or a game. They entice you to run the program so that they can perform their task of destroying your files. Unlike viruses, Trojans do not replicate themselves.

Worms do replicate themselves, but they copy themselves from one computer to another in order to carry out their task. They travel from computer to computer either by using the underlying network protocol (such as TCP/IP), or by using e-mail. Worms often use scripting languages such as Visual Basic to carry out the job of replicating themselves. Two of the most notable worms are Melissa and LoveBug. Both of these viruses arrive through e-mail, and when run, will use your mail system to send themselves to people in your address book before continuing with their malicious intent.

Where do they come from?

All viruses initially start with a developer or programmer. Viruses are programs that have been written for a purpose. Often the goal is to get a message to appear on the target (infected) computers. Sometimes they are destructive only due to poor programming.

This virus developer decides to program a method of infection and replication to transport his or her program between computers. Once a method of delivery has been established, then it is started in action. Online services (since their inception) have always been a great place to start this delivery. Because the Internet is so widely used now, it has become one of the main delivery methods for most viruses, especially since it offers the programmer a high level of anonymity. However, the current state of the Internet — and computer crimes — have been changing over time, and some of these viruses are now able to be traced back to their source. If the source can be traced, legal action can follow.

In short, viruses are written by people.

How to determine presence

In order to protect your computer from viruses, you must know that they are present. There are many different virus scanners available from a variety of manufacturers. If you do a quick search on the Internet, you will find dozens to choose from.

Some virus scanners will search for specific types of viruses, while others are considered general-purpose. Also, some scanners will scan existing files on your hard drive, remain in memory to scan files as they are accessed, and scan e-mail files as they are downloaded to your computer. The scanning programs from the major vendors all support updatable databases of viruses, so as new viruses emerge, you only have to update the database, rather than the entire program.

Many viruses are identified by a fingerprint. The actual programming code, that constitutes the virus, is identified as being attached to a program, or (in the case of Trojans) within executable files. To make themselves less visible, virus developers started to encrypt their virus code and include a decryption engine. These viruses can still often be identified by scanning for the decryption engine. Polymorphic and stealth viruses take additional steps to hide from detection. Polymorphic viruses continually modify code segments in both the decryption engine and virus code as they infect new files, making it harder to locate them in files; and stealth viruses continually move from one memory location to another when in memory, to reduce the chance of being detected by memory scans. As new methods of hiding viruses are detected, anti-virus programs are updated to detect them.

Tip   Retro viruses have been designed to actively attack anti-viral programs by deleting or corrupting files, rendering them useless. This technique can accompany other virus attacks.

Since virus programmers are constantly coming up with new viruses, fingerprint detection alone is not sufficient to catch viruses early. Major virus scanners now support Heuristic-based scanning. Heuristic scanning looks for general patterns and behaviors when files are executing. This allows them to detect and prevent viruses from operating.

What about hoaxes?

There are several virus hoaxes that are regularly sent around in e-mails, and most follow a format:

"I received this notice from Bob who works for xyz corp., a major vendor in the computing industry, and he has told me that pqr virus has just been discovered. It is spread through e-mail. If you get a message with a subject of x or an attachment of y, then delete it immediately as it will cause bad things to happen to you or your data."

Although e-mail aids in the delivery and spread of viruses, these mail messages are generally hoaxes. The following section provides some links to hoax info Web sites. Remember that you are not in danger of being affected by viruses if you are not reading Web content in your e-mail. Viruses that are attached to e-mail have to be opened or executed to cause damage. If you don't know where the file attachments came from, it may be wisest to not open them.

Where can I get more info? Many of the major anti-virus software manufacturers post excellent information about viruses on their Web sites. Vendor-neutral Web sites are also a good source of information. Here's a short list of three vendor-neutral sites:

✦ http://www.eicar.org/. The official site of the European Institute for Computer Anti-Virus Research contains the test virus that is used in Lab 27.6, as well as links to other major anti-virus sites.

✦ http://agn-www.informatik.uni-hamburg.de/vtc/naveng.htm. The official site of the Virus Test Center at the University of Hamburg's Computer Science Department contains the testing results of several products against viruses.

✦ http://www.virusbtn.com/. The Virus Bulletin contains general announcements and a hoax list.

Key Point Summary

This chapter examined several Windows-based utilities. You learned about disk maintenance programs, such as Drive Converter, Fdisk, Defrag, and Scandisk. These utilities are used to improve performance and reliability of the disk subsystem. You also learned about configuration utilities, such as the System Configuration Utility, System Information Tool, Registry editors, System Editor, Registry scanners, Device Manager, and the Computer Management console. A number of miscellaneous tools—ASD, Windows Script Host, and so on—were discussed. The chapter finished up with a description of viruses and what you can do to avoid them.

✦   ✦   ✦

STUDY GUIDE

This Study Guide presents 24 assessment questions and 6 lab exercises to test your knowledge of the exam topic area.

Assessment Questions

1. Early in the morning one day, you convert your drive from FAT16 to FAT32. You realize that sometime the following day, you will have to boot your computer into MS-DOS by using a boot disk. What is the name of the utility that will convert your drive back to FAT16?

    A. `cvt1.exe`

    B. `cvt2.exe`

    C. `cvtfat.exe`

    D. This cannot be done

2. Which of the following is a benefit of FAT32?

    A. Smaller cluster sizes

    B. Larger access blocks

    C. More directory entries

    D. Dynamic allocation of sector granularity

3. `Defrag.exe` does what for your computer?

    A. Rearranges memory, so that access to it is improved

    B. Removes dust and fragments from your computer

    C. Rearranges data on your disk drive, so that access to it is improved

    D. Recovers files that have been corrupted

4. Scandisk can do which of the following?

    A. Rearrange data on your drive so that disk access is faster

    B. Consolidate free space on your hard drive

    C. Correct problems with the storage of files on your hard drive

    D. Change the partition table of the drive from FAT16 to FAT32

5. You have to edit several of the configuration files on your computer. Which of the following utilities might you choose to use?

    A. `systmedt.exe`

    B. `editcnfg.exe`

    C. `msconfig.exe`

    D. `setfile.bat`

6. What programs can be used to edit the Registry on a Windows 9x computer?

    A. `registry.exe`

    B. `cfgedit.exe`

    C. `regedt32.exe`

    D. `regedit.exe`

7. What command is used to export a section of your Registry while using `regedit.exe`?

    A. Export Registry File from the Registry menu

    B. Extract to Recovery File from the Registry menu

    C. Set Restore Options from the Export menu

    D. Backup Key from the Registry menu

8. What tool should you use to change an exported Registry file?

    A. `sysedit.exe`

    B. `regedit.exe`

    C. `edit.com`

    D. Microsoft Word

9. Which files on your hard drive make up the Windows 9x Registry?

    A. `system.dat` and `registry.dat`

    B. `user.dat` and `system.dat`

    C. `user.dat` and `hardware.dat`

    D. `system.dat`, `sam.dat`, `security.dat`, and `user.dat`

10. Which operating system makes use of `regedt32.exe`?

    A. MS-DOS

    B. Windows 95

    C. Windows 2000

    D. Windows 98

11. Which of the following programs can be used to edit your `system.ini` file?

    A. `sysconfig.exe`

    B. `notepad.exe`

    C. `regedit.exe`

    D. `scanreg.exe`

12. `scanreg.exe` can do which of the following?

    A. Delete specific Registry entries

    B. Edit specific Registry entries

    C. Back up and restore specific Registry entries

    D. Back up and restore the entire Registry

13. You need to find what memory addresses are being used by a driver. What tool will tell you what you need to know?

    A. `memedit.exe`

    B. System Resource Meter

    C. Device Manager

    D. System Driver Checker

14. You have a non-Plug and Play card that is in conflict with other plug and play cards on your computer. What tool would you use to reserve the resources used by your non-Plug and Play card?

    A. Resource Arbitrator

    B. System Resource Meter

    C. PNP Configurator

    D. Device Manager

15. You need to automate a procedure on your computer. What tools could you use?

    A. Wscript.exe

    B. Scriptlt.exe

    C. Config.sys

    D. Local ASP

16. You need to automate the process of copying information from a Microsoft Excel spreadsheet into a Microsoft Word document. What tools could you use?

    A. Wscript.exe

    B. ScriptIt.exe

    C. Config.sys

    D. Local ASP

17. What is the name of the command-line version of Windows Script Host?

    A. ComScript.exe

    B. Wscript.exe

    C. Cmscript.exe

    D. Cscript.exe

18. You need to create a new Visual Basic Script for Windows Script Host. What tool will you use?

    A. Script Developer

    B. Script Editor

    C. Notepad

    D. Visual Basic Script IDE

19. You would like to use the command prompt to make a series of files read-only. What tool would you use?

    A. Readonly.exe

    B. Attrib.exe

    C. Perms.exe

    D. Cacls.exe

20. You need to replace `notepad.exe`, which was accidentally deleted from your Windows 9x computer. What command can you use to retrieve a copy from the original CAB files?

    A. `extract.exe`

    B. `expand.exe`

    C. `filerepl.exe`

    D. `cabget.exe`

21. What command is used to create or modify text files?

    A. `textedit.com`

    B. `notepad.com`

    C. `edit.com`

    D. `fileedit.com`

22. What command is used to change the partitioning on your hard drive?

    A. `format.com`

    B. `fdisk.exe`

    C. `diskpart.exe`

    D. `repart.exe`

23. Which of the following statements are true about viruses? (Select all that apply)

    A. Viruses are not destructive.

    B. Viruses can affect the performance of your computer.

    C. Viruses are computer code.

    D. Viruses can make you sneeze.

24. What are the best steps to take to avoid viruses? (Choose two)

    A. Scan your files regularly with an Anti-virus program.

    B. Get a flu shot every year.

    C. Execute every program that is currently on your hard drive to ensure that they do not have viruses.

    D. Practice safe computing. Do not use programs if you do not know where they came from.

Lab Exercises

Lab 27.1 Exporting your Desktop Settings to a File

This lab exercise can be completed with either Windows 9x or Windows 2000. In this lab, you will use the Registry Editor to export a section of your Registry.

Caution

Care must always be used when working with the Registry Editor. This lab will only perform an export of the Registry information. Do not change any of the values in the Registry.

1. Use the Run command to open `regedit.exe`.

2. Expand the following path, using the (+) plus signs in front of the key names: `HKEY_CURRENT_USER\Control Panel\Desktop`. Then select the Desktop key.

3. In the right pane of the Registry Editor, you should see your current desktop settings, including Wallpaper, Tile Wallpaper, ScreenSaver (if one is configured), and PaintDesktopVersion (if using Windows 2000).

4. Select Export Registry File for the Registry menu. Ensure that Selected Branch is selected, and type the filename of `c:\labfiles\desktop_reg.txt`.

5. Close the Registry Editor by selecting Exit from the Registry menu.

6. Open the folder `c:\labfiles` and locate the files `desktop_reg.txt`. This should look like a text file. If it does, double-click on it to open it. The contents should look something like:

```
REGEDIT4

[HKEY_CURRENT_USER\Control Panel\Desktop]
"DragFullWindows"="0"
"FontSmoothing"="0"
"wallpaper"=""
"TileWallpaper"="0"
"ScreenSaveTimeOut"="900"
"UserPreferencemask"=hex:ae,00,00,00
"WallpaperStyle"="0"
"ScreenSaveLowPowerActive"="0"
"ScreenSave_Data"=hex:31,42,41,32,33,39,34,41,33,37,32,36,45,
41,35,45,00
"ScreenSaveActive"="0"
"ScreenSaveUsePassword"=dword:00000001

[HKEY_CURRENT_USER\Control Panel\Desktop\WindowMetrics]
<content not displayed>
```

If you are using Windows 2000, then the first line will identify this as a Windows Registry Editor Version 5.00 file. The `WindowsMetrics` section deals with sizing and spacing of various Window components, such as icons and menus.

The values in this file represent your current desktop settings. If you edit this file and change the Wallpaper entries to:

```
"Wallpaper"="c:\\labfiles\\NewDesk.bmp"
"TileWallpaper"="1"
```

you will be able to import these modified settings into your Registry.

Caution

When specifying file paths in the Registry Editor, you will type paths normally; but when using Registry export files, you must double the backslashes that are used in the path. This is because the backslash is used as a control character in the key names.

If you only wanted to modify these settings in a target Registry, then you could delete all of the lines except for:

```
REGEDIT4
[HKEY_CURRENT_USER\Control Panel\Desktop]
"Wallpaper"="c:\\labfiles\\NewDesk.bmp"
"TileWallpaper"="1"
```

This new file could be used to import just the wallpaper settings. If you import these settings, you will not see the change until you log out and log in again. If the settings do not appear, then you will have to open and resave the file using `edit.com`.

Lab 27.2 Customizing the Pre-User Login Desktop with Windows 2000

There are times when you may want to modify user profile settings for the desktop environment that is used prior to user log on. If you are using Windows NT 4.0, Windows 2000, or Windows 9x (with User Profiles enabled), the following steps will show you how to do this.

Caution   Care must always be used when working with the Registry Editor. This lab will only edit certain values in the Registry. Do not change any of the values in the Registry other than the ones listed in the lab.

1. Open `regedit.exe` by using the Run command in the Start menu.

2. Expand `HKEY_USERS\DEFAULT\Control Panel\Desktop`.

3. Select the Desktop key. Record your current settings for:

    Wallpaper:

    TileWallpaper:

4. Right-click on Wallpaper and choose Modify.

5. Change the data to:

    `c:\labfiles\profiledesk.bmp`

6. Press OK to save your change.

7. Right-click on TileWallpaper and choose Modify.

8. Change the data to:

    1.

9. Press OK to save your change.

10. Close the Registry Editor by choosing Exit from the Registry menu.

11. To test your settings, log out of your current session. You should see a new wallpaper behind the Login dialog box.

12. Log in, reopen the Registry Editor, and follow the steps in this lab to restore your original settings.

Lab 27.3 Creating a Computer Manager MMC file

This lab exercise will help you create a customized Computer Management console. You will have to use a Windows 2000 computer to perform this lab.

1. Open the Microsoft Management Console by typing mmc at the Run command.

2. Choose Add/Remove Snap-in from the Console menu.

3. Choose the Add button to see a list of available snap-ins.

4. Select and Add the following snap-ins (yes — it is the Folder snap-in three times):

Folder

Folder

Folder

Choose the Close button, then the OK button.

5. Right-click on each item, starting with Console Root, and choose rename. Change Console Root to Computer Management, New Folder to System Tools, New Folder to Storage, and New Folder to Services and Applications.

6. Choose Console menu ⇨ Add/Remove Snap-in, and then change the drop-down menu "Snap-ins added to:" to System Tools. Choose the Add button, and add the following snap-ins:

Event Viewer (Local Computer then Finished)

System Information (Local Computer then Finished)

Performance Logs and Alerts

Device Manager (Local Computer then Finished)

Local Users and Groups (Local Computer then Finished)

7. Choose the Close button and change the Snap-ins added to: menu to Storage. Choose the Add button, and add the following snap-ins:

Disk Management (Local Computer then Finished)

Disk Defragmenter

8. Choose the Close button and change the Snap-ins added to: menu to Services and Applications. Choose the Add button, and add the Services (Local Computer then Finished) snap-in.

9. Choose the Close button and the OK button. You will now be looking at your new management console. Expand the tree structure on the left pane to see the elements that were added.

10. To save, select Save As from the Console menu, name your console My Computer Management, and change the save directory to `c:\labfiles`. If you open the labfiles directory, you will be able to launch your custom console by double-clicking on the icon.

Lab 27.4 Working with Windows Script Host

In this exercise, you will be building a script that will create a shortcut on your desktop. You will need Windows Script Host installed on your computer. If you are using Windows 98 or Windows 2000, then you will already have it installed. If you are using Windows 95 or Windows NT 4.0, you can download it from `http://msdn.micrsoft.com/scripting` or `http://www.microsoft.com/msdownload/vbscript/scripting.asp`.

In the script that you will be creating, blank lines have been left between each actual line in the script. For example, the code that is typed in Step 5 is only one line of text, but due to the constraints of this book, it is displayed as two lines, and Step 7 actually contains five lines of code.

1. Open Notepad.

2. Type the following:

```
MsgBox "Hello World"
```

3. Save the file as c:\labfiles\shortcut.vbs, but leave it open.

4. Open the c:\labfiles folder and double-click on the shortcut file. If you have Windows Script Host installed on your computer, then a message box labeled VBScript will appear containing the text "Hello World". Press OK to dismiss the window, but leave the Labfiles folder open.

5. Switch back to Notepad, and give your dialog box a Title by changing the line to:

```
MsgBox "This script will create a shortcut on your desktop.",
, "Shortcut Creation Script"
```

6. Save and run this script. It should now have a title. The two commas exist since you are supposed to identify the type of buttons in your dialog. Type:

```
MsgBox "This script will create a shortcut on your desktop.",
vbOKCancel + vbInformation, "Shortcut Creation Script".
```

7. Save and run this script. It should now be Information dialog (with a Blue Information mark). It currently does not matter which button you press. To put the appropriate controls in, type:

```
Dim RunProg

RunProg =  MsgBox("This script will create a shortcut on your
desktop.", vbOKCancel + vbInformation, "Shortcut Creation
Script" )
```

```
If RunProg = vbCancel Then

WScript.Quit

End If
```

8. You should take note of the changes in the MsgBox command. You will take the input from the MsgBox command (the button that was pushed) and place it in a variable named in RunProg. This is also the reason that there is a pair of brackets, since you are getting input. Run the script and test the buttons.

9. Now add the following lines to the end of your script file, to create a shell level object that will be called upon to make the shortcut:

```
Dim WSH

Set WSH = WScript.CreateObject("WScript.Shell")
```

10. Declare your variables using:

```
Dim NewShortcut, ShortcutName, DesktopLocation
```

11. Find out where the current Desktop folder is:

```
DesktopPath = WSH.SpecialFolders("Desktop")
```

12. Prompt the user for a name to be given to their new Shortcut to Notepad. The InputBox command is similar to MsgBox in that the parameters are body text and title. The result of what is typed in is stored in a variable named ShortcutName. If no name is typed, then the name will be "Shortcut to Notepad".

```
ShortcutName = InputBox("What would you like to name the
Shortcut to Notepad?","Need Info")

if ShortcutName = "" then ShortcutName = "Shortcut to Notepad"
```

13. Finally, create the shortcut on the desktop with the .lnk extension:

```
Set NewShortcut = WSH.CreateShortcut(DesktopLocation & "\" &
ShortcutName & ".lnk")

NewShortcut.TargetPath =
WSH.ExpandEnvironmentStrings("%windir%\notepad.exe")

NewShortcut.WorkingDirectory =
WSH.ExpandEnvironmentStrings("%windir%")

NewShortcut.WindowStyle = 4

NewShortcut.IconLocation =
WSH.ExpandEnvironmentStrings("%windir%\notepad.exe, 0")

NewShortcut.Save
```

14. Save your shortcut and try it. You should be prompted for a name, and it will use that name for the shortcut. If you do not provide a name, then "Shortcut to Notepad" will be used.

This exercise is just the tip of the iceberg when dealing with the programming of Windows Script Host. For complete details, download Microsoft's self study course at http://msdn.microsoft.com/scripting and follow the links for Windows Script Host ⇨ Documentation.

Lab 27.5 Extracting and Expanding Damaged Drivers from the Source Media

This lab will have you extract a file (freecell.exe) from your Windows 9x CD. The scenario is based on results of troubleshooting, which have identified freecell.exe as the corrupted or problem file. You will then repeat the process to expand the same file from the Windows 2000 source files.

Extracting files for use with Windows 9x

1. Place the Windows 9x CD into your CD-ROM drive.

2. Open a command prompt (Start menu ⇨ Programs ⇨ MS-DOS Prompt), and type the following:

```
<CD_Rom drive letter>:
```

Your CD-ROM should now be the active drive. Then type:

```
cd win9x
```

You should now have the source files for Windows 9x as your current directory. If your source files are in an alternate location, make that your current directory.

3. Type the following line and review the output to become familiar with the options:

```
extract /?
```

4. To find out which cabinet has freecell.exe, find out which cabinet file comes first. Type:

```
dir /w /on *.cab
```

For my copy of Windows 98, the first cabinet in the list is base4.cab.

5. Using the filename from Step 4, locate the cabinet that has the file by typing in one statement:

```
extract /a /d <first cabinet filename> freecell.exe >
c:\labfiles\freecell.txt
```

6. The previous command should have created a text file in your labfiles directory. To open the file with Notepad, type:

```
notepad.exe c:\labfiles\freecell.txt
```

Examine this file to locate the cabinet that has the required file. This is useful if you are planning to distribute the cabinet files to users that require them (rather than distributing the extracted files).

7. Since you have the name of the cabinet file, you can now type in the following command to extract `freecell.exe` to the labfiles directory:

```
extract /a /l c:\labfiles <located cabinet filename>
freecell.exe
```

8. (Optional) If you did not originally have `freecell.exe` installed on your computer, you will also require `cards.dll`. To extract this file, use:

```
extract /a /l c:\labfiles <first cabinet filename> cards.dll
```

If you need help on playing Freecell, you will need to install the help files using this command:

```
extract /a /l c:\labfiles <first cabinet filename> freecell.*
```

You will be prompted to overwrite the existing `freecell.exe` that was extracted in Step 7, and either of the choices will work.

9. Test Freecell by typing the following commands:

```
c:
cd labfiles
freecell.exe
```

Expanding files for use with Windows 2000

1. In the same manner as Steps 1 and 2 for extracting files with Windows 9x, place your Windows 2000 CD in your CD-ROM drive, open a command prompt, and switch to the drive letter. Then type `cd i386` to enter the source directory.

2. Create a directory to hold the Windows 2000 version of Freecell using the following command:

```
mkdir c:\labfiles\win2000
```

3. Type the following line and review the output to become familiar with the options:

```
expand /?
```

When you examine the options that are available, you will notice that the expand command will work to extract files from within cabinet files as well.

4. Search the source directory for files that are used by Freecell by typing:

```
dir /w /on freecell.*
```

This should provide a list of three files: `freecell.ex_`, `freecell.ch_`, and `freecell.hl_`. These files are actually `freecell.exe`, `freecell.chm`, and `freecell.hlp`. The .hlp file is the help file, the .chm file is a compiled help file (that has the Explorer interface), and the .exe file is the executable itself.

5. Expand the executable into your new destination directory using the following command:

```
expand freecell.ex_ c:\labfiles\win2000\freecell.exe
```

You should note that if you do not know what the destination filenames are supposed to be, you could use the -r option and only specify the destination directory, as in the following example:

```
expand -r freecell.ex_ c:\labfiles\win2000
```

6. Test Freecell by typing:

```
c:\labfiles\win2000\freecell.exe
```

Lab 27.6 Scanning for Viruses

If you have anti-virus software installed on your computer, then you can attempt this lab exercise. This exercise will create a file that is not a virus as such, but will be identified as one.

 Caution

This is a standard industry test file, and should not cause any problems for your computer. If you are hesitant, skip this lab exercise.

1. Open Notepad and type the following string as a single line:

```
X5O!P%@AP[4\PZX54(P^)7CC)7}$EICAR-STANDARD-ANTIVIRUS-TEST-
FILE!$H+H*
```

2. Save the file as `"c:\labfiles\testvirus.com"`. Include the quotation marks when saving your file, and it will have the .com extension rather than the .txt extension.

3. Now you are on your own. Open your installed anti-virus program, and instruct it to scan the `c:\labfiles` directory. It should detect the `testvirus.com` file as having a virus, and provide you with choices such as isolate, repair, or delete. If you have an option to delete the file, go ahead. If your software does not allow you to delete the file, manually delete `c:\labfiles\testvirus.com` after you exit your anti-virus software.

Answers to Chapter Questions

Chapter Pre-Test

1. This cannot be done with an operating system utility. Cvt1.exe or Drive Converter is used to convert from FAT16 to FAT32. Windows 98 does not provide a tool to perform the reverse conversion.

2. **Fdisk** is the first tool you should use. This utility allows you to create the partition(s) that the OS requires for disk access.

3. **Scandisk** can be used to check and repair a series of small errors dealing with file storage, such as invalid dates.

4. **Sysedit** opens all of these files at the same time, which makes it an extremely easy way to edit the listed files.

5. **Regedit** makes backups of the Registry that can be edited with a text editor. Regedt32 backups are in binary format or text output of the registry structure that cannot be re-imported.

6. **Device Manager** will quickly identify hardware-related problems with devices.

7. You should use **Disk Management or Computer Management** to create a new disk partition. The Disk Management snap-in is actually found within Computer Management.

8. **Computer Management** allows for the creation of users and groups.

9. **Visual Basic Script (VBS)**, which can be executed with either `wscript.exe` or `cscript.exe`.

10. `Extract.exe` can be used to retrieve files from CAB archives.

11. **Trojan horse** and **Melissa** are different types of files that are considered by most people to be viruses.

Assessment questions

1. **A.** `cvt1.exe` is the executable for Drive Converter. For more information, see the section labeled "Operating System Utilities for Disk Maintenance."

2. **A, C.** Smaller cluster sizes waste less space on a disk as files are stored, and more directory entries allow for a larger number of files to be stored on the disk. For more information, see the section labeled "Operating System Utilities for Disk Maintenance."

3. **C.** `defrag.exe` rearranges data on your disk so that access to files is faster. By allowing your disk to perform reads of data in contiguous blocks, it takes less time to read files. For more information, see the section labeled "Operating System Utilities for Disk Maintenance."

4. **C.** Scandisk is used to fix minor problems with files that are stored on your hard drive, and can also test and verify the clusters on your drive. For more information, see the section labeled "Operating System Utilities for Disk Maintenance."

5. **C.** `msconfig.exe` allows you to edit several configuration files at the same time. These files include `config.sys`, `autoexec.bat`, `win.ini`, and `system.ini`. For more information, see the section labeled "Configuration Utilities."

6. **D.** `regedit.exe` is the editor for Windows 9x computers. If you are using Windows 2000, then you can use either `regedit.exe` or `regedt32.exe`. For more information, see the section labeled "Configuration Utilities."

7. **A.** Export Registry File from the Registry menu will export a section of your Registry. For more information, see the section labeled "Configuration Utilities."

8. **C.** Registry import files must be straight text. Notepad and many other programs that edit text files add different characters to handle carriage returns and line feeds. This can create files that will not be imported through `regedit.exe`. For more information, see the section labeled "Configuration Utilities."

9. **B.** `user.dat` and `system.dat` are both found in your `c:\windows` directory. For more information, see the section labeled "Configuration Utilities."

10. **C.** Only Windows 2000 and Windows NT make use of `regedt32.exe`. For more information, see the section labeled "Configuration Utilities."

11. **B.** `system.ini` is a text file and can be edited by Notepad, or any text editor. For more information, see the section labeled "Configuration Utilities."

12. **D.** `scanreg.exe` is able to scan the Registry for structural errors, and back up or restore the Registry for Windows 9x computers. For more information, see the section labeled "Configuration Utilities."

13. **C.** Device Manger will tell you what resources are being used by which devices. For more information, see the section labeled "Configuration Utilities."

14. **D.** Device Manger will tell you what resources are being used by which devices. For more information, see the section labeled "Configuration Utilities."

15. **A.** `Wscript.exe` or Windows Script Host can be used to automate processes. For more information, see the section labeled "Miscellaneous Utilities."

16. **A.** `Wscript.exe` can control applications that support ActiveX automation, such as Microsoft Word and Microsoft Excel. For more information, see the section labeled "Miscellaneous Utilities."

17. **D.** `Cscript.exe` is the command-line script interpreter. For more information, see the section labeled "Miscellaneous Utilities."

18. C. Notepad or another text editor can be used to create or edit your Visual Basic scripts. For more information, see the section labeled "Miscellaneous Utilities."

19. B. Attrib.exe is the program that would be used to change the Read-only attribute. For more information, see the section labeled "Miscellaneous Utilities."

20. A. Extract.exe is used to extract files from the source CAB files, while expand.exe is used to uncompress the individual source files for Windows 2000. For more information, see the section labeled "Miscellaneous Utilities."

21. C. Edit.com can be used to create or modify text files. For more information, see the section labeled "Miscellaneous Utilities."

22. B. Fdisk.exe is used to change the partition table on your hard drive. For more information, see the section labeled "Operating System Utilities for Disk Maintenance."

23. B, C. Viruses can affect the performance of your computer, and are human-generated programming code. Many viruses are destructive. For more information, see the section labeled "Viruses and Virus Types."

24. A, D. Using a protective program such as an anti-virus scanner will help to protect your computer, but is not a replacement for following safe computing habits. For more information, see the section labeled "Viruses and Virus Types."

Networking

Because many companies today have some form of network running, a corporate computer technician is not only responsible for hardware and software troubleshooting, but for troubleshooting the connection to the network or the Internet.

Part VII starts by discussing some basic networking concepts, then introduces you to common networking terms and the hardware components that make up a network. You will learn to configure the Windows operating system to provide resources and connect to resources on the network.

The last chapter in this part will discuss Internet-related concepts and the utilities you can use to help troubleshoot day-to-day issues when connecting to the Internet.

Basic Networking Concepts

EXAM OBJECTIVES

Exam 220-201 ✦ A+ Core Hardware

✦ **6.1** Identify basic networking concepts, including how a network works and the ramifications of repairs on the network. Content may include the following:

- Installing and configuring network cards

- Network access

- Full-duplex, half-duplex

- Cabling — Twisted Pair, Coaxial, Fiber Optic, RS-232

- Ways to network a PC

- Physical network topographies

- Increasing bandwidth

- Loss of data

- Network slowdown

- Infrared

- Hardware protocols

CHAPTER PRE-TEST

1. What is the speed of Category 5 cabling?

2. What topology is used in Token Ring architectures?

3. UTP cabling has a maximum distance of _____ meters.

4. What is the purpose of an access method?

5. What is the speed of Category 3 cabling?

6. Which network device sends information from one network to another?

7. Which access method uses a single packet that is used to send information out on the wire?

8. Which network device is responsible for converting data from one format to another?

9. Which topology has a central hub device with all hosts connected to it?

10. Which network device amplifies the signal so that it can go a greater distance?

✦ Answers to these questions can be found at the end of the chapter. ✦

The A+ exams cover two areas of networking: networking theory/networking hardware, and networking at the operating system level. This chapter focuses on the networking theory/networking hardware area of the A+ exams, which encompasses many of the terms you will find yourself running into when supporting workstations on a network.

Types of Networks

6.1 Identify basic networking concepts, including how a network works and the ramifications of repairs on the network. Content may include the following: Ways to network a PC

This section provides an overview of the two major types of networks: peer-to-peer and client-server. The advantages and disadvantages of each type will be discussed — as well as how to implement them.

Peer-to-peer

A *peer-to-peer* network is one in which you connect all of the user's computers together without purchasing a central machine that will act as a server. This type of network usually involves only a small number of users — ten or less. All computers take part in the networking services, which usually involves the sharing of files. In other words, each computer stores files that the other computers in the peer-to-peer network require, as shown in Figure 28-1.

Because a central machine is not storing files in a peer-to-peer network, your system is no longer based on "centralized administration." Centralized administration means that you go to just one location to complete your entire network administration or configuration. In Figure 28-1, because all three computers act as "peer servers," you need to do the administration on all three computers — a major disadvantage of peer-to-peer networking.

Another major disadvantage is the fact that you have compromised your security or have no security at all. In Figure 28-1, you notice that each computer is a Windows 95 computer — a limiting security model, because there is no central server where usernames and passwords are stored and verified. You will probably have to put passwords on shares so that users are prompted for that password as they connect to the share.

For more information about shares, consult Chapter 29.

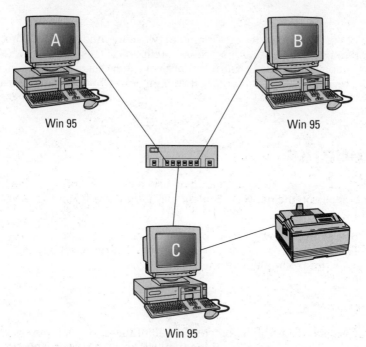

Win 95   Win 95

Win 95

Figure 28-1: Peer-to-peer networking environments

The major advantage of peer-to-peer networking is that you don't spend any money on a central server, which may sometimes cost the company thousands and thousands of dollars. Not only do you save in the hardware area of this server, but you also don't need to purchase the "network operating system" that runs on this server. The *network operating system* is the operating system that runs on the server and has been designed for the purpose of networking services, such as sharing files.

Client-server

Client-server networking is the networking model that companies usually choose when there are ten or more workstations on the network. Unlike a peer-to-peer network, there is a central machine that delivers network services to the workstations. Once again, these network services could be file and print sharing.

The benefit of a client-server configuration is that you now have centralized administration. As the administrator of this network, you will create all of the shared directories on the server. Everyone will connect to this server and store their files on it.

Tighter security is also a benefit of client-server networking. The server usually has an account (a username and password) that is used to control who can get access to what files stored on the server. When users turn their workstations on in the morning, they are responsible for logging on (providing their username and password) to the server, which then uses the information to determine what files the user has access to. Figure 28-2 illustrates a client-server network.

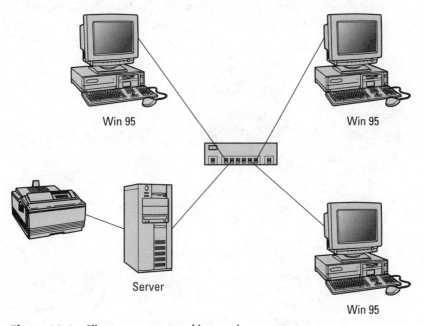

Figure 28-2: Client-server networking environments

The disadvantage of a client-server environment is the cost involved in purchasing the server hardware, as well as the cost of the server operating system.

Network Topologies

6.1 Identify basic networking concepts, including how a network works and the ramifications of repairs on the network. Content may include the following: Physical networking topographies

When building a network, it is important to understand some of the decisions that need to be made as far as setup is concerned. Building a network is like building a database. You have to understand the theory before you start the hands-on work.

In this section, we will discuss the different network topologies and their characteristics. Topology refers in a general sense to "layout," so a network topology defines the "layout" of the network.

Bus

A bus topology uses a main wire, or *trunk*, that all network devices connect to. The installation of this main trunk is fairly cheap to install, but expensive to maintain. Figure 28-3 shows a diagram of a bus topology. You can see that if a new workstation needed to be added to the trunk, it would involve cutting the cable and adding the appropriate connector.

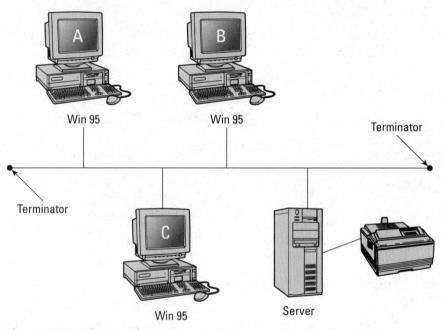

Figure 28-3: A bus topology

When a workstation sends data to another workstation on the trunk, the data (sometimes called the *signal*) is delivered across the full length of the trunk. Each workstation looks at all data that is running along the trunk, and if the data is destined for a particular workstation, that workstation will copy the data to the memory on its network adapter. For example, Figure 28-3 can be used to demonstrate what happens when Computer A sends information to Computer B. The information will run along the trunk, and when it passes by Computer C, Computer C will check to see if it is also a destination for the information; if not, Computer C ignores the data. The information will continue down the wire and make its way to Computer B. Computer B looks at the data to determine if the data is destined for him; if so, Computer B makes a copy of the data and stores it in the memory on the network card. Note that because Computer B has made a copy of the data, there is still data on the wire. The data continues on the wire past the server and hits the terminator at the end of the trunk segment.

A *terminator* is a device that absorbs any signals that are running on the wire. If there were no terminator at the end of the cable, the signal would bounce back in the other direction and collide with any new data being placed on the wire. So, to prevent this, the terminator grabs any signals that hit it and throws them away.

In a bus topology, any break in the wire (creating a non-terminated end, and thus, signal bounce) will result in the collapse of the entire network

Star

One of the most popular types of network topologies is the star topology. A star topology, shown in Figure 28-4, involves a central component that all network devices connect to. This central component is called a *hub*. Another term for a hub is a *concentrator*, which is a device that connects all other devices together.

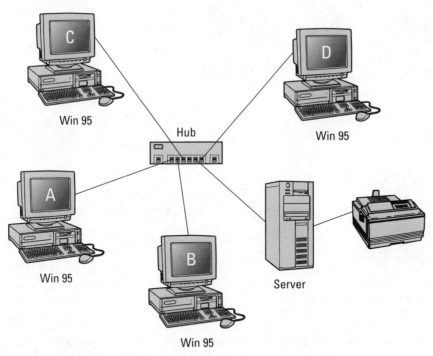

Figure 28-4: A star topology

Thus, if Computer A sends information to Computer D, the information would first travel from Computer A to the hub. The hub would send the information to each workstation so that they could determine if the data is destined for it or not. When Computer D receives the data, Computer D checks the address, identifies itself as the recipient of the data, and then copies the data to the network adapter's memory.

One of the major benefits of the star topology is that if a cable breaks, it doesn't take down the entire network. Only the workstation connected to the cable is affected. If the hub device breaks, however, the entire network will fail. Note that the cost of implementing a star topology may be a little more than a bus topology due to the high price of the hub device.

Ring

In a ring topology, each computer is connected to the next computer, creating a physical ring. Although ring topologies are not common today, you still see them in IBM's token ring architecture (architectures are discussed in the network architecture section found later in this chapter). Figure 28-5 shows a ring topology.

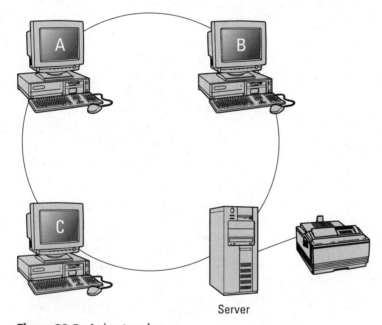

Server

Figure 28-5: A ring topology

In environments that use the ring topology, data is usually passed from workstation to workstation. Because data becomes distorted when it travels great distances, each workstation is responsible for reading the data, then regenerating the data and passing the information on to the next workstation. As with a bus topology, any break in the ring will cause the entire network to fail.

Hybrid

A hybrid topology is a mixture of two or more of the three basic topologies. For example, you could use a bus topology as a main trunk and connect hubs to the main bus. A number of network devices would be connected to each hub. Figure 28-6 shows an example of a hybrid topology.

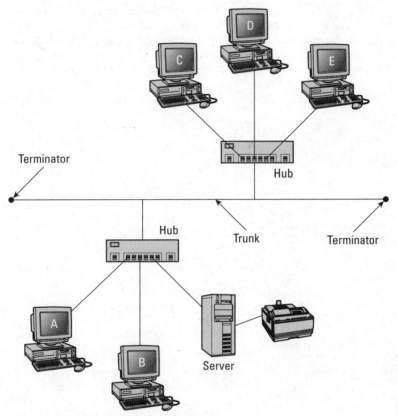

Figure 28-6: A hybrid network topology

To be more accurate, the configuration shown in Figure 28-6 could be called a star-bus topology—a star topology mixed with a bus. Today, the most popular topology in use is the star topology—or maybe even a hybrid topology using a star-bus layout.

Network Cabling

6.1 Identify basic networking concepts, including how a network works and the ramifications of repairs on the network. Content may include the following: Cabling— Twisted Pair, Coaxial, Fiber Optic

Now that the different types of network layouts have been evaluated, it's time to connect all the network devices together, which means making a decision about the type of cabling you will use. The following section will discuss and evaluate the different types of cabling available to standard networks.

Twisted pair

Twisted pair cabling, which is inexpensive and easy to use, is probably one of the most popular types of cabling. It gets its name from the fact that there are four pairs of wires twisted around each other inside the cable's jacket. In addition, twisted pair cabling comes in two different flavors — *unshielded twisted pair* (UTP) and *shielded twisted pair* (STP) — shown in Figure 28-7 and Figure 28-8.

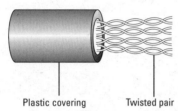

Plastic covering   Twisted pair

Figure 28-7: Identifying unshielded twisted pair cabling

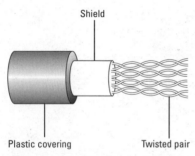

Shield

Plastic covering   Twisted pair

Figure 28-8: Identifying shielded twisted pair cabling

The two types of twisted pair cabling are fairly similar, the only difference being that STP cabling has an extra layer of insulation. The extra layer helps prevent interference from outside devices or cabling — interference that can distort the data traveling along the cable length.

Unshielded twisted pair cabling comes in five different flavors, called grades or categories. Table 28-1 lists the five categories of UTP cabling, as well as their purpose and speed.

	Table 28-1 UTP Category	
Category	*Purpose*	*Speed*
Category 1	Voice only	
Category 2	Data	4 Mbps
Category 3	Data	10 Mbps
Category 4	Data	16 Mbps
Category 5	Data	100 Mbps

Exam Tip   For the exam, you will be expected to know the speeds of the different categories of UTP cabling. I suggest memorizing them.

Because of the lack of shielding found in twisted pair cables, it has been found that the data is pretty much unreadable — or the integrity of the data is questionable — after 100 meters. For this reason, twisted pair cabling has a maximum length of 100 meters.

Exam Tip   For the exam, it may be useful to remember that twisted pair cabling has a maximum distance of 100 meters.

Twisted pair cabling uses a special type of connector to connect the cable to the network devices. This connector is similar to the one used to connect a telephone to a telephone jack. Network devices that use twisted pair cabling use the RJ-45 connector, while telephones use the RJ-11 connector. Figure 28-9 shows an example of an RJ-45 connector.

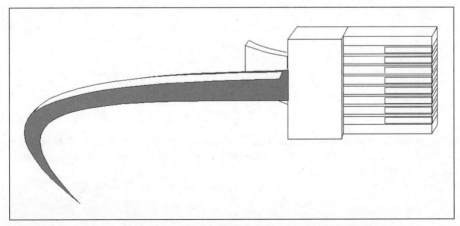

Figure 28-9: RJ-45 connector to connect TP cables to network device

Coaxial

Coaxial cabling is the same type as that which is used for cable television. There is a copper wire in the center of coaxial cable that is responsible for transmitting information. Furthermore, the copper wire is protected by two levels of insulation and an exterior plastic covering, as shown in Figure 28-10.

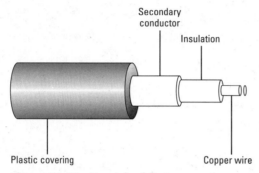

Figure 28-10: Coaxial cabling

Like UTP, coaxial cabling comes in different flavors — two to be exact. The first type of coax, called *thinnet*, is only .25 inches in diameter. The second type of coax, *thicknet*, is .50 inches in diameter. Table 28-2 shows the difference between thinnet and thicknet.

Table 28-2 **Types of Coax Cabling**			
Type	*Maximum Cable Length*	*Diameter*	*Speed*
Thinnet	185 meters	.25 inches	10 Mbps
Thicknet	500 meters	.50 inches	10 Mbps

Exam Tip   For the exam, know the differences between thinnet and thicknet cabling. I would suggest memorizing them.

Coaxial cable that is connected to a workstation requires the use of the BNC connector, as shown in Figure 28-11. The BNC connector connects to a metal barrel on the back of the network card.

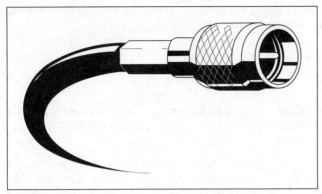

Figure 28-11: BNC connector on a coaxial cable

Fiber optic

Fiber optic cabling is one of the fastest types of network medium available today. Fiber optic cabling is made up of a glass fiber core, surrounded by a layer of insulation that is then covered with a plastic jacket. There are two fiber channels in fiber optic cable: one for sending information and the other for receiving information. Figure 28-12 illustrates a fiber optic cable.

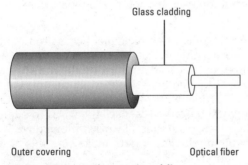

Glass cladding

Outer covering

Optical fiber

Figure 28-12: Fiber optic cabling

Fiber optic cabling has a maximum distance of about 2 km and transmits information at speeds of 100 Mbps to 1 Gbps. Because fiber carries data in pulses of light instead of electronic signals, it is impossible for the data to be corrupted by outside electronic interference.

Exam Tip You will be expected to know details regarding fiber optic cabling for the exam. Fiber carries data through pulses of light along its glass core and can reach distances up to 2 km. Fiber optic cable transmits information at speeds that range from 100 Mbps to 1 Gbps.

The primary disadvantage of fiber optic cabling is the cost of the implementation and the expertise that is required for the wiring.

Network Access

 6.1 Identify basic networking concepts, including how a network works and the ramifications of repairs on the network. Content may include the following: Network Access

Now that you are comfortable with the different types of network topologies and the different types of cabling, it is important to talk about network access (or access methods). Network access refers to the different methods that computers use to place data on the network. This section will discuss these methods and identify the advantages and disadvantages of each.

CSMA/CD

One of the most popular types of access methods is CSMA/CD, which stands for *Carrier Sense Multiple Access/Collision Detection*. You may have a better understanding of this term if I break it down into its individual parts, and examine each part in detail:

✦ **Carrier sense.** All computers on the network are watching, or sensing, the network for network traffic. Computers are watching the network to see whether it has data on it or not.

✦ **Multiple access.** All computers on the network have equal access to the network at any given time. In other words, anyone can place data on the network whenever they choose. Note, however, that workstations on the network will try not to place data on the wire at the same time the wire is transmitting other data, because the two pieces of data will collide, destroying the data. That is why it's so important for workstations to "sense" the wire. To summarize, "carrier sense multiple access" suggests that all workstations have access to the network and are watching the network to make sure it is clear of data before they send their information out.

✦ **Collision detection.** When two workstations send information out at the same time and the data collides, the workstations will see that collision and resend their data. When two workstations have data that has been involved in a collision, they will resend the information out on the network again at variable intervals. This will prevent the data from colliding again.

The nice thing about CSMA/CD is that the workstations are making decisions on when to send data, trying to prevent collisions. However, there is always the possibility that multiple workstations will send data out at the exact same moment the network is clear, resulting in data collision.

CSMA/CA

CSMA/CA, or *Carrier Sense Multiple Access/Collision Avoidance*, is similar to CSMA/CD except for one main difference: when a workstation senses that the wire is free, it sends out dummy data instead of real data. If the dummy data collides with other information on the wire, then the workstation has avoided a collision with the real data; if the dummy data does not collide, then the workstation will send the real data.

CSMA/CA is not a popular access method, but it has been used in AppleTalk networks.

Token passing

You may have attended meetings where a ball was passed around to indicate who had the authority to speak: in order to speak, you had to be holding the ball. If you didn't have the ball, you had to wait your turn.

Token passing is based on the same principle. A token, which is an empty piece of information running around the network from computer to computer, must be in a computer's possession before the computer can put data out on the wire.

Once the token has reached the computer, or workstation, the workstation puts data out on the wire by filling the token with information and marking the token as used. The token (with the information) is then released out onto the network and travels towards its destination. Each workstation will check to see if the token is destined for them when the token passes by. Each workstation regenerates the data and passes it to the next workstation.

Network Architectures

6.1 Identify basic networking concepts, including how a network works and the ramifications of repairs on the network. Content may include the following: Hardware protocols

A *network architecture* describes a network technology that uses a specific topology, cable type, and access method. This section will describe the major types of architectures and their characteristics.

Many people take the term "architecture" to mean topology; stating that there are three main types of architectures: bus, star, and ring. However, bus, star, and ring are properly defined as types of topologies, not architectures. Be careful not to confuse the two terms.

Tip It is important to identify the difference between a topology and an architecture. A topology defines the network layout, while an architecture is made up of a topology, cable type, and access method.

Ethernet

Ethernet is probably the most popular type of network architecture in use today. Ethernet is an example of a network architecture that comes in multiple flavors. Thus, if someone says to you, "I have an Ethernet network," you will probably ask, "What type of Ethernet?"

There are four major types of Ethernet: 10BaseT, 10Base2, 10Base5, and 100BaseT. The following section will describe the differences between these Ethernet architectures.

10BaseT

10BaseT Ethernet is a network architecture that typically uses a star topology, but may, in some cases, use a hybrid topology of star-bus. 10BaseT networks primarily use category 3 UTP cabling, which transfers information at 10 Mbps. 10BaseT uses the CSMA/CD access method for putting information on the network.

10Base2

10Base2 Ethernet is a network architecture that uses a bus topology, but may sometimes use a hybrid topology of star-bus. 10Base2 networks typically use thinnet coaxial cabling, which transfers information at 10 Mbps. 10Base2 uses CSMA/CD as its access method.

10Base5

10Base5 Ethernet is a network architecture that uses a bus topology. 10Base5 networks primarily use thicknet coaxial cabling, which transfers information at 10 Mbps. Like 10Base2, 10Base5 uses CSMA/CD as its access method.

100BaseT

100BaseT Ethernet is a one of the faster network architectures that uses a star topology, but can be found using a hybrid topology of star-bus. 100BaseT networks primarily use Category 5 UTP cabling, which transfers information at 100 Mbps. 100BaseT also uses CSMA/CD as its access method.

Tip Nowadays, you will probably purchase network cards that are marketed as 10/100 cards. This means that the network card can be used with 10BaseT or 100BaseT, transferring information at either 10 Mbps or 100 Mbps.

Exam Tip It may be useful to remember for the exam that all Ethernet architectures use CSMA/CD as their access method.

Token Ring

Token Ring is a unique network architecture, because it is completely different in design from Ethernet. As its name implies, Token Ring uses a ring topology with token passing as the access method. Although a Token Ring network can use almost any type of cabling, it typically uses UTP.

Note   The Token Ring architecture was developed by IBM.

Token Ring comes in two flavors: 4 Mbps or 16 Mbps. Token Ring also has a special name for the "hub" that connects all of the workstations together — *MAU (MultistationAccess Unit)*. Because of this MAU, a Token Ring network appears to use a star topology, but internally the MAU is connected as a ring — making a complete circle.

Exam Tip   For the exam, remember that Token Ring architectures use token passing as their access method.

Hardware protocols

The Institute of Electrical and Electronics Engineers (IEEE) has developed a number of LAN standards that define the physical components of networking technologies. In these standards, IEEE has defined such things as the way that network cards place data on the wire and the type of cabling used in different types of LANs. The LAN standards are defined by Project 802, which was launched in February 1980; these standards define different networking architectures. Table 28-3 displays the twelve 802 LAN standards.

Table 28-3 Project 802 LAN Standards	
Project	**Description**
802.1	Internetworking
802.2	Logical Link Control (LLC)
802.3	Ethernet (CSMA/CD)
802.4	Token Bus LAN
802.5	Token Ring LAN
802.6	Metropolitan Area Network
802.7	Broadband Technical Advisory Group

Continued

Table 28-3 *(continued)*	
Project	**Description**
802.8	Fiber Optic Technical Advisory Group
802.9	Integrated Voice/Data Network
802.10	Network Security
802.11	Wireless Networks
802.12	Demand Priority Access LAN

Exam Tip   For the exam, you will not be required to memorize the entire list of standards, but it is important to know that Ethernet is defined in project 802.3, and Token Ring is defined in project 802.5.

Network Performance

Objective   **6.1** Identify basic networking concepts, including how a network works and the ramifications of repairs on the network. Content may include the following: Increasing bandwidth; Loss of data; Network slowdown; Full-duplex, half-duplex

In this section, we will identify different types of network devices that are used to solve issues with network performance. It is important to understand the different types of network devices and their purpose.

Network devices

Before looking at an example of optimizing network performance, you should become familiar with the characteristics and function of repeaters, bridges, and routers—all types of network devices.

Repeater

One major concern with cabling is the maximum distance of the cable length. For example, UTP cabling has a maximum of 100m, while thinnet has a maximum length of 185m. The reason for putting a maximum distance on cable lengths is that it was found that the signal traveling along the cable was too weak when the maximum length was reached. This would cause the information to be resubmitted and thus generating more network traffic.

One way to increase the distance of a cable length is to use a repeater. A repeater regenerates a signal so it can travel the extra distance. For example, the repeater shown in Figure 28-13 joins two lengths of thinnet coaxial cable. It joins the two cable lengths so that the signal can travel the distance from Computer A to Computer B. Note that this distance exceeds 185m, which is the maximum distance of thinnet. When the signal hits the repeater, the repeater rebuilds the signal so that it can travel another 185m.

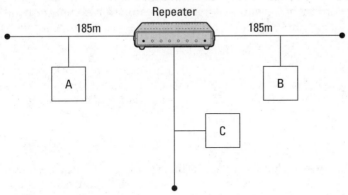

Figure 28-13: A repeater

Bridge

Because all the data passing through the repeater is regenerated and sent to all parts of the network, a great deal of network traffic is generated that will affect the overall performance of the network.

To prevent this buildup of network traffic, you can use a bridge, shown in Figure 28-14. A *bridge* is a device that connects network segments together and also regenerates the signal (as with a repeater). A bridge will also filter the data so that it is only sent to the proper portion of the network, cutting down on network traffic and increasing overall performance.

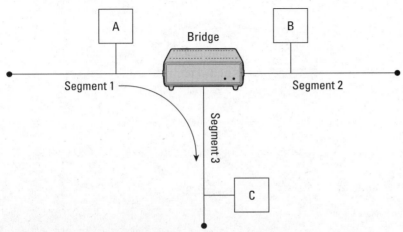

Figure 28-14: A network bridge

Figure 28-14 illustrates that when Computer A sends information to Computer C, the information travels along Segment 1 and eventually reaches the bridge. The bridge will look at its bridging table (which runs in memory) to see which network segment Computer C exists on; in this example, it is Segment 3. At this point, the bridge will only forward the information where the destination computer resides and not send the information to any other segment. This has the effect of filtering traffic.

Bridges increase performance on the network by filtering the network traffic, which as a result will give the network and all of its devices and applications more bandwidth to work with. The less network traffic, the less chance of collision and retransmission.

Router

A router, which is responsible for sending information from one network to another, is an important network device because nowadays, most companies are connected to the Internet. When a computer on your network wants to send information to a computer on another network, your computer will pass the information to your router. Figure 28-15 shows three different networks, each connected to the Internet by a router. All computers on Network A know that any information with an outside-network destination must be passed to the router, because the router is the only device with a physical connection to the outside world.

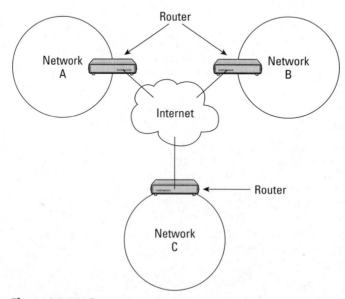

Figure 28-15: Routers

Gateway

A gateway is a very unique network device, responsible for converting information from one format to another. Think of a gateway as a translator between two different languages — as information passes from one side to another, the gateway "translates" the information to a format that can be understood on the other side.

A gateway might be used in a situation where personal computers need to access information on a mainframe system. Typically, dumb terminals are used to connect to mainframes, but with the popularity of desktop PCs these days, companies are now substituting the dumb terminal with a personal computer. Somewhere between the personal computer and the mainframe is a gateway that will translate the data from the mainframe language to something that the PC can understand.

Exam Tip   You may encounter questions on the exam where a description is given to you and you must identify the device based on that description. For the exam, know that a gateway is a device or piece of software that translates data from one format to another.

Simplex

Another issue surrounding network performance is the communication method that you are using. There are three major types of communication methods in the computer world: simplex, half-duplex, and full-duplex.

A *simplex* device is a device that can only deliver information in one direction. Typically, it can send information but not receive it.

Half-duplex

A *half-duplex* device is a device that can deliver information in two directions, but not at the same time. A typical example of a half-duplex device is a walkie-talkie or CB radio, which enables you to send and receive information, but not at the same time. When you use a CB radio, you use the term "over," letting the person on the other end know that you are done talking and it is their turn to send information.

Full-duplex

A *full-duplex* device is one that can send and receive information at the same time. Full-duplex is similar to talking on the phone with an individual — you are free to speak and listen at the same time.

When purchasing networking or other types of devices for your computer, it is important to know whether you are buying a device that is using simplex, half-duplex, or full-duplex. I have a few musician friends who enjoy recording their own material on the computer using four-track software. One friend had a problem when trying to record a second track because his sound card was only a half-duplex device. He could record the first track, but when he tried to record the second track he wanted to listen to the first track and play along with it. In this example, the goal of the sound card is to send and receive information at the same time, something that a half-duplex device cannot do. The solution — get a new sound card that is full-duplexed.

Ways To Network A Computer

 6.1 Identify basic networking concepts, including how a network works and the ramifications of repairs on the network. Content may include the following: Installing and configuring network cards, Ways to network a PC, Cabling (RS232), Infrared

Now that you have been introduced to the wonderful world of networking technologies, you should be aware of the different and varied methods used to network two computers, including:

✦ Installing network cards

✦ Using serial ports

✦ Using parallel ports

✦ Using USB ports

Installing network cards

The first task when using network cards to network two computers is to find out what type of network card will be required for each system. You will have to find out if the network card will be an ISA, EISA, or PCI device; you can do this by opening up the system and looking at the different expansion slots that exist, or you can look at the documentation for the system.

 For more information on ISA, EISA and PCI, see Chapter 3.

After you have purchased the network card and installed it into your system, you will have to load the driver for the network card. If you are lucky and the network card is a plug-and-play device, then the driver may load automatically for you, or you may be prompted by the operating system to provide a manufacturer diskette that contains the driver for the device.

After you install the driver, you may have to spend some time troubleshooting the device because of resource conflicts with other existing devices. Once again, if you have a plug-and-play device, this step will probably not happen because the resources will be assigned dynamically by the operating system.

 For more information on troubleshooting system resources, see Chapter 8.

Serial/Parallel ports

You may also network two computers by using the serial or parallel ports of both systems. Using standard parallel ports or serial ports for the purpose of networking two devices can be a lot slower than networking two computers by a network card. You will connect the parallel ports by what is called a *laplink cable*, and you will use a null modem cable for RS-232 ports (serial ports).

There are actually two methods to networking using your serial ports. You can connect a modem to each computer's serial port and have the modems use the phone lines as the cabling. You can also connect two computers directly together by connecting the serial ports using a special serial cable. If you try to connect two computers together using a normal serial cable, you will have the TD (transmit data) wire on one computer connected to the TD wire on the other computer. This also means that the RD (receive data) wire on one computer will be connected to the RD wire on the other computer. No communication will occur in this situation. What we need is the TD wire on one computer connected to the RD wire on the other computer. A null modem cable is designed to do this, crossing the sending and receiving wires along with some general handshaking wires.

Infrared

Many systems today, especially laptop computers, have built-in infrared ports that can be used to connect to other devices on the network. For example, you could print to a printer without the use of a parallel cable between the computer and a printer, using infrared technology.

Infrared technology uses an infrared light beam to carry data between devices. It typically uses clear line of sight where there must be a clear path between the two devices. Infrared is limited in distance to about 100 feet and can transfer information up to 10 Mbps.

Key Point Summary

This chapter has introduced you to a number of key concepts in network terminology. You learned the three major components that make up network architecture: topology, cabling, and access methods.

You learned about some of the major network devices, such as routers, bridges and repeaters. You also learned the three types of communication methods used in computer devices — simplex, half-duplex, and full-duplex — and the importance of purchasing the correct type of device.

✦   ✦   ✦

STUDY GUIDE

This Study Guide presents 20 assessment questions, 2 scenarios, and 1 lab exercise to test your knowledge of the exam topic area.

Assessment Questions

1. What category of UTP cabling transmits data at 16 Mbps?

    A. Category 5

    B. Category 2

    C. Category 3

    D. Category 4

2. Which of the following defines simplex communication?

    A. Allows information to be sent and received, but not at the same time

    B. Allows information to only be sent

    C. Allows information to be sent and received at the same time

    D. Allows information to be sent, but only after dependent information is received

3. What is the transfer rate of Category 3 cabling?

    A. 2 Mbps

    B. 10 Mbps

    C. 16 Mbps

    D. 100 Mbps

4. What is the maximum distance of a thinnet segment?

    A. 100m

    B. 500m

    C. 250m

    D. 185m

5. What is the recommended number of users for a peer-to-peer network?

    A. Less than 100

    B. More than 100

    C. Less than 10

    D. More than 10

6. What access method is used in Ethernet?

    A. Token passing

    B. CSMA/CA

    C. Twisted pair

    D. CSMA/CD

7. Which of the following defines half-duplex communication?

    A. Allows information to both be sent and received, but not at the same time

    B. Allows information to only be sent

    C. Allows information to be sent and received at the same time

    D. Allows information to be sent, but only after dependent information is received

8. What category of UTP allows for data transfer at 4 Mbps?

    A. Category 5

    B. Category 2

    C. Category 3

    D. Category 4

9. Which topology must be terminated at either end to prevent signal bounce?

    A. Ring

    B. Star

    C. Bus

    D. Coaxial

10. What access method best describes CSMA/CA?

    A. Data is placed out on the wire; the sending workstation detects if there is an error and retransmits if there is.

    B. A token is running around the network; when you wish to send data out on the network, you fill the token with information.

    C. Dummy data is placed on the wire; if the dummy data collides with other information, then the real information is not transmitted. If the dummy data does not collide, then the real data is delivered.

    D. Dummy data is placed on the wire; if the dummy data collides with other information, then the real information is transmitted the next second. If the dummy data does not collide, then the real data is withheld.

11. Which of the following best describes a client-server environment?

    A. All users on the network connect to one another for the purpose of file sharing.

    B. All users on the network connect to a central server and access resources on that central server.

    C. All users on the network connect to one another for the purpose of printer sharing.

    D. Each user only accesses one other user's computer.

12. What is the maximum distance of UTP cable?

    A. 100m

    B. 500m

    C. 250m

    D. 185m

13. Which of the following best describes token passing?

    A. Data is placed out on the wire; the sending workstation detects if there is an error and retransmits if there is.

    B. A token is running around the network; when you wish to send data out on the network, you fill the token with information.

    C. Dummy data is placed on the wire; if the data collides with other information, then the real information is not transmitted. If the dummy data does not collide, then the real data is delivered.

    D. Dummy data is placed on the wire; if the data collides with other information, then the real information is transmitted the next second. If the dummy data does not collide, then the real data is withheld.

14. Which of the following sends data in the format of pulses of light?

    A. Fiber

    B. 100BaseT

    C. 10BaseT

    D. Coaxial

15. What is the maximum length of 10Base5 cabling?

    A. 100m

    B. 500m

    C. 250m

    D. 185m

16. Which of the following best describes full duplex communication?

    A. Allows information to both be sent and received, but not at the same time

    B. Allows information to only be sent

    C. Allows information to be sent and received at the same time

    D. Allows information to be sent, but only after dependent information is received

17. What Ethernet architecture transfers information at 100 Mbps and uses Category 5 cabling?

    A. 10BaseT

    B. 10Base2

    C. 10Base5

    D. 100BaseT

18. What is the name of the connector that connects a Category 5 cable to a network card?

    A. BNC Barrel

    B. RJ-45

    C. RJ-11

    D. BNC

19. What is the maximum distance of fiber optic cabling?

    A. 100m

    B. 185m

    C. 2km

    D. 500m

20. What is the name of the connector that connects 10Base2 to a network card?

   A. BNC Barrel

   B. RJ-45

   C. RJ-11

   D. BNC

Scenarios

This chapter has introduced you to a number of networking terms and technologies. The following scenarios will test your ability to apply what you have learned.

1. You have a network with five network segments and 50 computers on each segment. The network has grown drastically over the last couple of months, and you are noticing a dramatic decrease in performance. What can you do to help increase network performance?

2. Your manager would like to know if there is some way your PC users can access information on the company mainframe. You know that the two environments are normally incompatible, so what could you offer as a solution?

Answers to Chapter Questions

Chapter Pre-Test

1. Category 5 cabling delivers data at **100 Mbps.**

2. The Token Ring architecture uses the **ring** topology.

3. UTP cabling has a maximum distance of **100** meters.

4. An access method **determines how a host puts information out on the network.**

5. Category 3 cabling delivers information at **10** Mbps.

6. A **router** is responsible for delivering information from one network to another.

7. The **token passing** access method uses a single packet that is used to send information out on the wire. Users fill the token with data and send the token out onto the network.

8. A **gateway** is responsible for converting data from one format to another.

9. A **star** topology has a central hub with all hosts connected to it.

10. A **repeater** is responsible for regenerating a signal so that the signal can travel a greater distance.

Assessment Questions

1. **D.** Category 4 UTP cabling transfers data at 16 Mbps. For more information, see the section titled "Network Cabling."

2. **B.** Simplex devices only deliver information in one direction. For more information, see the section titled "Simplex."

3. **B.** Category 3 cabling transfers information at 10 Mbps. For more information, see the section titled "Network Cabling."

4. **D.** The maximum distance of a thinnet segment is 185m. For more information, see the section titled "Coaxial."

5. **C.** The recommended number of computers in a peer-to-peer network is 10 or less. For more information, see the section titled "Peer-to-peer."

6. **D.** CSMA/CD is the access method that is used in all Ethernet environments. Token passing is used in Token Ring architectures, and CSMA/CA has been used in AppleTalk networks. For more information, see the section titled "CSMA/CD."

7. **A.** Half-duplex devices allow you to send and receive information, but not at the same time. For more information, see the section titled "Half-duplex."

8. **B.** Category 2 UTP cabling transfers data at 4 Mbps. For more information, see the section titled "Network Cabling."

9. **C.** A bus topology must have all loose ends terminated to prevent signal bounce. For more information, see the section titled "Bus."

10. **C.** With CSMA/CA, you are avoiding a collision with the real data by placing dummy data on the wire first. If the dummy data collides, you know that it is not safe to send the real information; if it doesn't collide, then the real data is sent. For more information, see the section titled "CSMA/CA."

11. **B.** Client-server environments are implemented for the purpose of centralized administration and security. It is much easier for an Administrator to control resources if they are sitting on one computer and all users connect to that one computer. For more information, see the section titled "Client-server."

12. **A.** The maximum distance of UTP cable is 100m. For more information, see the section titled "Network Cabling."

13. **B.** With token passing, there is an empty token running around on the network and when you want to submit information on the wire, you fill the token with the information and release the token onto the network. For more information, see the section titled "Token passing."

14. **A.** Fiber optics sends information in pulses of light on cabling with a glass core. For more information, see the section titled "Fiber optic."

15. **B.** 10Base5 is thicknet that has a maximum distance of 500m. UTP cabling has a maximum distance of 100m, while thinnet has a maximum cable distance of 185m. For more information, see the section titled "Network Cabling."

16. **C.** Full duplex devices can send and receive information at the same time. For more information, see the section titled "Full duplex."

17. **D.** 100BaseT Ethernet architectures can transfer information at 100 Mbps. For more information, see the section titled "Ethernet."

18. **B.** RJ-45 connectors connect UTP cabling to the network card. For more information, see the section titled "Twisted pair."

19. **C.** Fiber optic cabling has a maximum distance of about 2km. For more information, see the section titled "Fiber optic."

20. **D.** A BNC connector connects a 10Base2 cable to a network card. For more information, see the section titled "Network Cabling."

Scenarios

1. You could use a bridge to connect the network segments, which would help filter traffic so that information is only being passed to the network segments that need it.

2. This is the type of situation where you would try to find software that could translate the mainframe information into a format that the PC could understand. This is the typical implementation of a gateway (translating information from one format to another so it can be understood on the other side).

Understanding Networking at the Operating System Level

Exam 220-202 ✦ A+ OS Technologies

✦ **4.1** Identify the networking capabilities of Windows, including procedures for connecting to the network. Content may include the following:

- Protocols
- IPCONFIG.EXE
- WINIPCFG.EXE
- Sharing disk drives
- Sharing print and file services
- Network type and network card
- Installing and configuring browsers
- Configuring OS for network connection

CHAPTER PRE-TEST

1. What utility is run on a Windows NT operating system to view TCP/IP configuration?

2. What is the syntax for connecting to a shared resource using a UNC path?

3. When connecting to \\myserver\data across a TCP/IP Windows NT network, which Windows NT service is responsible for converting the computer name to an IP address?

4. What three settings of TCP/IP must be configured on a Windows operating system to be able to access resources on another network?

5. When connecting to ftp://ftpserver.glensworld.com, which name resolution technique typically resolves the fully qualified domain name to an IP address?

6. When troubleshooting connectivity to a Novell server from your Windows desktop, what characteristic of IPX should be checked on the Windows client?

7. How can a hidden share be created?

8. What must be installed and configured on a Windows 95 desktop to allow someone access to files on that computer?

9. What is the purpose of a network browser?

10. What networking components must be installed to allow the Windows desktop to connect to a Novell network?

✦ Answers to these questions can be found at the end of the chapter. ✦

Today, one of the most important troubleshooting skills support personnel could adopt is the troubleshooting of networking connectivity. *Network connectivity* is the term used for two computers establishing a connection to one another. There are a number of components that allow this communication to happen, and a lot of times it is these components that a support person ends up troubleshooting.

This chapter discusses the software components that make up a network, and the troubleshooting issues that could arise while configuring the network. Some of the tools that are used to troubleshoot the network also are addressed in this chapter.

Networking Components

4.1 Identify the networking capabilities of Windows, including procedures for connecting to the network. Content may include the following: Protocols, Network type and network card, Configure OS for network connection

When setting up a network, you must have the appropriate hardware and software in place. Since this chapter focuses on the software components that are needed to allow Windows to network, you can assume that you have all of the necessary hardware in place. You have purchased a hub, at least two computers and network cards to go in the computers, and the appropriate cabling to connect the network cards to the hub. Once all the hardware is in place, what do you have to do at the operating system level to get these two computers talking?

When building your network, it is important to identify the four major software components that allow a Windows operating system to function in a networking environment. These components are

 ✦ Network adapter

 ✦ Network client

 ✦ Protocol

 ✦ Service

The following sections discuss each of these components.

Network adapter

The network adapter is the physical network card that is inserted into one of the computer's expansion bus slots. It is responsible for sending information out onto the network, and receiving information from the network.

Before purchasing this network card, you have to ensure that you get the right type of card. To do this, you need to open up the computer (for more information on safety procedures, refer to Chapter 12) and look at the expansion buses that are supported in your system, and then identify which bus architecture has an empty slot. For example, you may open your computer and see that you have three ISA slots and three PCI slots, but only one PCI slot is free, while two ISA slots are free. So you have a choice of purchasing a PCI or an ISA network adapter. Typically, you would purchase the PCI network adapter because of the performance benefits of PCI devices over ISA devices (see Chapter 3 for more information about the different bus architectures).

Once you have inserted the network card into the empty expansion slot, you need to install the driver for that card at the operating system level. Installing the network card driver is the first major step to networking your two computers. The *driver* is software that allows the operating system to communicate with the physical device, which in this case is the network card. Figure 29-1 shows the relationship between the operating system and the hardware device.

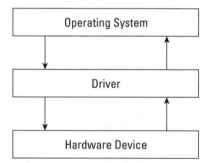

Figure 29-1: Viewing the relationship between the operating system and hardware devices

The following Step By Step walks you through the process of installing a network adapter in Windows 95/98.

STEP BY STEP: Installing a Network Adapter

1. Select Start menu ⇨ Settings ⇨ Control Panel.

2. Double-click the network icon.

3. On the Configuration page, click the Add button. A dialog box appears asking you to select the type of network component you wish to install (see Figure 29-2).

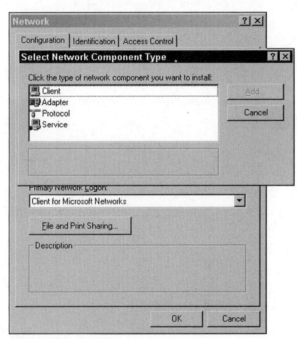

Figure 29-2: Adding a network adapter

4. On the Network Component dialog box, select adapter, and then click the Add button.

5. The Select Network Adapter dialog box appears (see Figure 29-3). Within this dialog box, select the manufacturer of your network card on the left side, and then choose your network card model on the right side.

If your network card is not in the list, you may click the Have Disk button and specify the path to the diskette or network location of the driver files you have obtained from the network card manufacturer. If you do not see your network card in the driver list or you do not have the driver diskette for the network card, you can go to the manufacturer's Web site and download an updated driver.

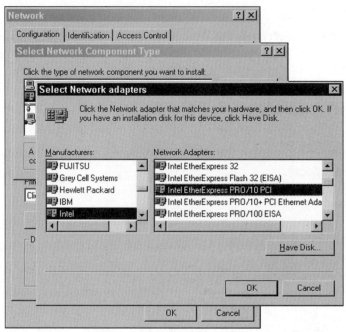

Figure 29-3: Selecting a network adapter during installation

6. Once you select the model of your network card on the right side of the Select Network Adapter dialog box, click OK.

7. Click the OK button on the Configuration page.

8. Click Yes to reboot the system.

Once you have installed the network card, you may have to configure its resources, such as the IRQ and IO address. If you are running a computer with a plug-and-play BIOS and a plug-and-play network card, then the IRQ and IO address should be assigned to the network card appropriately by the operating system. You may want to change the IRQ and the IO address if you do not like the resources the operating system has assigned.

If you are in a non-plug-and-play environment, you may also have to change the resources of the network card. You have to configure the resources for the device at the operating system level to match the settings that were actually assigned to the device with the manufacturer's setup program.

In order to change the resources that were assigned to the device in Windows 95/98, do the following:

STEP BY STEP: Changing Network Card Resources

1. Select Start ➪ Settings ➪ Control Panel.

2. Double-click the system icon, and then choose the Device Manager tab.

3. Expand the network adapters icon (see Figure 29-4).

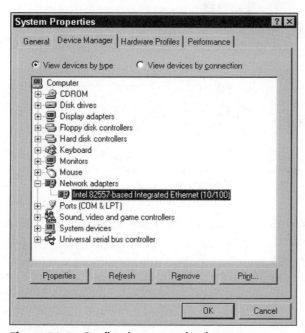

Figure 29-4: Configuring network adapters

4. Select your network adapter, and click the Properties button.

5. In the Properties dialog box of the network card, you will see the device status of the network card, which should say that the device is working properly. If the device status states that the device is not working properly you may have installed an incorrect driver, this means that you will need to install the appropriate driver for your network card. Another reason why the device may not be working properly is the fact that you may have resource conflicts with other devices. For information on resolving resource conflicts, consult Chapter 8.

6. Select the Resources tab (see Figure 29-5).

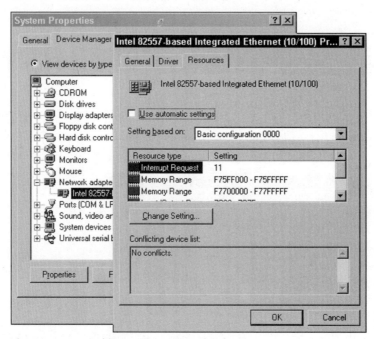

Figure 29-5: Looking at resources of a device

7. To change the IRQ of the device, select Interrupt Request from the Resource Settings list.

8. In the Resource Settings dialog box, you will see a check box labeled Use automatic settings. Disable this check box. Disabling this check box allows you to change the IRQ by not using the operating system assigned (automatic setting) IRQ.

9. Click the Change Setting button, and use the spinner to change the value of the resource. Notice the Conflict information below the spinner. It shows you if the resource value you are going to choose will conflict with another device. Once you have changed the resource to a value that does not conflict, click OK.

Tip   To change the IO address that is used by the device, use the same steps as you did for changing the IRQ, but change the IO Address resource setting instead of the Interrupt Request.

Once you have ensured that the correct hardware settings are applied to the network adapter, your next step is to attempt to connect to a network resource. Unfortunately, you can't connect to a network resource until you have the appropriate network client running. The following section describes the purpose of the network client.

Network client

A network client is no different than a client or customer in the real world. A client in the real world is visiting your company because you are providing some sort of service. For example, you might be running a tailor shop, which provides a particular service to customers who come into your store to drop off pants or dresses that need tailoring. In a sense, the customer is a client of tailoring.

Computer networks work the same way. On your Windows desktop, you must be running a client for the type of service you are requesting. For example, if you are working for a medium-sized company that is running Novell's NetWare as the server operating system, then you must load a client that will connect your Windows desktop computer to the Novell server. Another example would be if you want to connect to a Windows NT server; you would have to load a Microsoft client on your Windows desktop to do so.

Two major clients come with the Windows operating systems: Client for Microsoft Networks and Client for NetWare Networks. When you want to connect to a Microsoft server, you load the Client for Microsoft Networks, and when you are connecting to a Novell server, you load the Client for NetWare Networks.

In the Real World   If you are running Windows operating systems in a Novell environment, you will probably decide not to load the Client for NetWare Networks, which is the client to connect to Novell networks that Microsoft has built in to its operating system. Microsoft has built that client with limited capabilities, so most networks that are running Novell actually load Novell's Client 32 on the Windows desktops.

To return to our tailor shop example, remember that your client has asked for your service by getting some tailoring done on their pants. When the client finally receives the mended pants, they are very pleased — however, the pants have to be dry-cleaned before they are used. Unfortunately, your business does not offer dry-cleaning services, so your client will have to request the service from a third-party. The point is that your client can be a client of tailoring and a client of dry cleaning at the same time. There is no rule that says you can only be a client of one particular service at a time.

This applies to the network as well. A lot of companies are running both Windows NT server and Novell's NetWare on the same network, at the same time. Maybe they are using the Novell server for the sharing of files and the Windows NT server for e-mail services. In this instance, the Windows desktops would have to run two clients, Client for NetWare Networks and Client for Microsoft Networks.

In order to install a client, follow these steps:

STEP BY STEP: Installing Client for Microsoft Networks

1. Select Start ➪ Settings ➪ Control Panel.

2. Double-click the network icon.

3. On the Configuration page, click the Add button.

4. Select Client, and then click Add.

5. In the Select Network Client dialog box, select Microsoft from the Manufacturer list on the left side (shown in Figure 29-6).

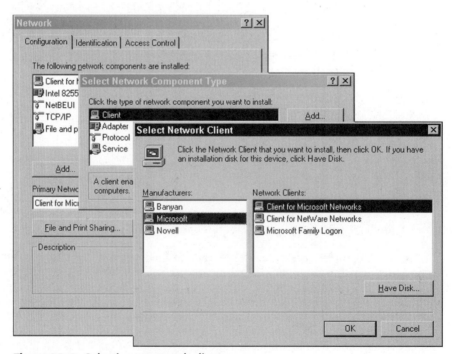

Figure 29-6: Selecting a network client

6. Select Client for Microsoft Networks from the Network Client list on the right side.

7. Click OK.

8. Click OK to exit.

Tip   To install Client for NetWare Networks, follow the same steps but instead of choosing Client for Microsoft Networks, select Client for NetWare Networks.

At this point you have your network card and its driver installed, and you also have installed the appropriate client. Unfortunately, you are still unable to communicate with someone on the network, because you still have to install the appropriate protocol. The following section talks about the purpose of protocols and what common protocols are running on networks today.

Protocols

Protocols are languages that are used to hold a conversation on the network. Your system can have a network card installed and have the proper client running, but if it is not speaking the same language (protocol) as the remote system, then the two systems are not going to hold a conversation. To go back to the tailor shop example — you are now ready to service your clients. There is only one problem. When your first client walks into your store and requests service, your client speaks French, while you only know English. To solve this problem, you and your client must speak a common language. It doesn't matter what that language is, as long as you both can speak it.

There are a few things to look for when choosing which protocol to install, but the bottom line is that all computers on the network install the same protocol — much like choosing a common denominator to allow all individuals to participate in a conversation.

NetBEUI

NetBEUI (NetBIOS Extended User Interface) was originally developed by IBM to be used on small networks. Today, Microsoft has implemented NetBEUI in the different Windows operating systems for the same purpose, small networks. NetBEUI is intended for small networks because it is a non-routable protocol, meaning that it cannot leave the network. Since many companies have large networks spanning some form of WAN (wide area network) link, this protocol is impractical in those environments.

You will find yourself using NetBEUI if you have a small number of computers that need to be networked in a workgroup-type environment. You want to get this network up and running without the hassle of having to configure all kinds of settings. This is the benefit of NetBEUI: there is no configuration — it just works!

IPX

IPX (Internetwork Packet Exchange) is Novell's native protocol and has been used on large networks since its design. IPX is a routable protocol, so data that it is delivering can move from one network to another.

Microsoft has its own implementation of IPX in its operating systems, and you will want to install it if you are communicating with Novell servers on the network. Like NetBEUI, there is not a lot of configuration to IPX, but one very important property of IPX is the frame type.

The *frame type* is the type of envelope that is being used to deliver the information from one computer to another computer on the network. Different envelopes have different characteristics, and you need to make sure that everyone is using the same type of envelope on the network.

Windows operating systems like Windows 95 and Windows 98 can auto-detect the frame type that is running on the network, usually first set by the Novell server. Although this generally works out fine, it is important that you know how to install IPX and configure the frame type. The big question is, what frame type do you use? The answer is probably whatever is set on the Novell server, but you should ask the network administrator. Popular frame types are 802.2, 802.3, and Ethernet II.

The following steps walk you through installing IPX and configuring the frame type.

STEP BY STEP: Installing and Configuring IPX

1. Select Start ⇨ Settings ⇨ Control Panel.

2. Double-click the network icon.

3. On the Configuration page, click the Add button.

4. On the Components dialog box, select Protocol, and click the Add button.

5. From the Manufacturer list, choose Microsoft; and from the Protocol list, select IPX/SPX compatible protocol. Click OK.

6. On the Configuration page, select the IPX/SPX protocol, and click the Properties button.

7. On the Advanced page, select the Frame Type property.

8. Notice that the value on the right defaults to Auto, meaning auto detect. Click on the drop-down list to change it to the desired frame type (shown in Figure 29-7).

9. Once you have changed the frame type, choose OK.

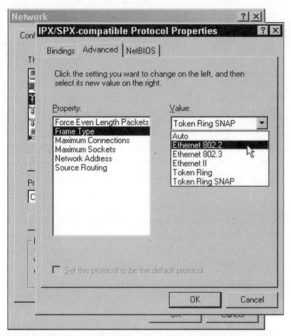

Figure 29-7: Configuring the frame type property

TCP/IP

Transmission Control Protocol/Internet Protocol (TCP/IP) is the hot protocol on the market these days because it is the protocol of the Internet and Internet-based technologies. TCP/IP has become the protocol of choice for Windows NT, Windows 2000, and Novell networks because of its capabilities to communicate in heterogeneous environments. The bottom line is this: it doesn't matter what kind of operating system you are running, if you are running TCP/IP you have the capabilities to communicate at a global level.

TCP/IP is known as a protocol suite. Protocol suites are like application suites in the sense that there is more than one in the group. For example, if you purchase the Microsoft Office suite, you have purchased an entire group of applications, or an entire suite of applications. TCP/IP has a group of protocols that make up the protocol suite, and some of these protocols are used day in and day out. For example, adding the TCP/IP protocol to your computer means that you have a telnet application for running applications from another computer, and you have an FTP application for downloading files from another computer.

Since configuring TCP/IP is such a big topic, there has been an entire section dedicated to it later in the chapter.

Services

One of the most forgotten networking components is the service. Going back to our tailor shop example, before you can have clients you must have first made the decision to offer the service. If you don't offer the service then there would be no reason for customers to want to communicate with you.

On the network, someone has to be offering the service, but not everyone needs to. For example, a small company with five Windows 98 machines may only have the machine with the printer on it providing the service — it provides the printer sharing service. The other four Windows 98 computers connect to it by installing Client for Microsoft Networks and the same protocol.

Windows NT servers and Novell servers usually run at least two services by default once they are installed: file-sharing services and print-sharing services. This was their original purpose in life, to provide file and print services, but the number of services that can be added to these system has grown over the years to include services such as mail services and name resolution services.

To install a service on Windows operating systems, follow these steps:

STEP BY STEP: Installing File and Print Sharing Services

1. Select Start ⇨ Settings ⇨ Control Panel.

2. Double-click the network icon.

3. On the Configuration page, click the Add button.

4. From the Network Component Type dialog box, select Service, and click the Add button.

5. From the Network Service dialog box, select File and Print Sharing for Microsoft Networks (shown in Figure 29-8).

6. Click the OK button.

7. Click the OK button to exit.

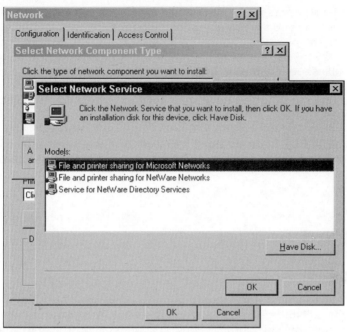

Figure 29-8: Looking at installing File and Print Services

Be aware that File and Print Sharing for Microsoft Networks allows only computers running Client for Microsoft Networks to connect to your machine. If you want to share files or printers with Novell clients, you should install File and Print Sharing for NetWare Networks. You cannot run both types of file and print sharing at the same time, only one file and print sharing service can be installed at any given time.

Configuring TCP/IP

4.1 Identify the networking capabilities of Windows, including procedures for connecting to the network. Content may include the following: Protocols, IPCONFIG.EXE, WINIPCFG.EXE

Since the drastic growth of the Internet, TCP/IP has become the preferred protocol on networks today. The reason for this is that TCP/IP is the common protocol on all desktops, including DOS, Windows, Windows NT, and Windows 2000, as well as other operating systems, such as Macintosh and Unix. All of these operating systems running a similar protocol means that we can have global communication.

It does not matter what operating system you are running or what kind of network you have—as long as you are running a common protocol, you can access resources across any platform.

In order to troubleshoot communication across TCP/IP, it is important that you understand the types of settings that need to be configured. In this section, you'll look at how to configure TCP/IP and at some utilities to help you troubleshoot the protocol.

When you install TCP/IP, there are three major settings that need to be configured to allow the computer to communicate with other computers on different networks:

✦ IP address

✦ Subnet mask

✦ Default gateway

IP address

The IP address is a 32-bit number that is unique to your computer. No two systems can have the same IP address. An IP address is similar to the address of your home, which is the method by which other people send messages or mail to you. An IP address works the same way on a TCP/IP network—the number is assigned to your computer, and it is the method other computers use to send your computer information.

An IP address is made up of four numbers or sets of numbers separated by periods. This is called the dotted decimal notation format of the IP address. 131.107.2.200 is an example of an IP address in the dotted decimal notation format. Each set of numbers that is being separated by a decimal is referred to as an *octet*, which means there are four octets in an IP address.

The IP address is made up of a network ID and a host ID. The *Network ID* is a unique number used only by your network, while the *Host ID* portion uniquely identifies a computer on your network. The network ID is the same for all computers on the same network. For example, in the IP address 131.107.2.200, the first two octets make up the network ID, and the last two octets make up the host ID. So if computer A with an IP address of 131.107.2.200 talks to computer B, which has the IP address of 131.107.3.5, you can assume that the two computers are on the same network because 131.107.x.y is the network ID for both computers. Since it is the same number, they must reside on the same network.

The big question is, how do you know which octets make up the network ID and which octets make up the host ID portion of the IP address? Is it always the first two octets? The answer is no, it is not always the first two octets of the IP address that will make up the network ID—it depends on what class IP address you have.

There are three major classes of IP addresses: Class A, Class B, and Class C. The different IP address classes support a different total number of workstations on the network. For example, a Class A network (a network using Class A addresses) supports up to 16,777,214 network devices, while a Class B network supports 65,534 network devices, and a Class C network supports only 254 network devices.

Class A networks use the first octet as their network ID and the remaining three octets as the host ID. A Class B network uses the first two octets for the network ID and the last two octets as the host ID. A Class C network uses the first three octets as the network ID and the last octet for the host ID.

How do you know what class IP address you have? Look at the first octet; if it has a value between 1 and 126, the IP address is a Class A address; if it has a value between 128 and 191, the IP address is a Class B address; and if it has a value between 192 and 223, the address is a Class C address. Table 29-1 summarizes IP address classes.

Table 29-1
IP Address Classes

Network Class	Number of Hosts	Octet Summary	First Octet Value
Class A	16,777,214	n.h.h.h	1-126
Class B	65,534	n.n.h.h	128-191
Class C	254	n.n.n.h	192-223

Let's take a look at an example. Computer A has an IP Address of 194.12.11.10, and it initiates communication with Computer B whose IP address is 194.13.11.9. Are the two workstations on the same network? Looking at the first octet, you can see that the number 194 is a Class C address, which means that the first three octets make up the network ID, and the last octet is the host ID. Since there is a difference in the first three octets (which is the network ID), these two computers are on different networks.

Tip

Identifying whether the computer you are trying to communicate with is on your network could be important when troubleshooting communications. If the computer that you are trying to communicate with is not on your network, then the problem could be with your computer, the remote computer, or the router. This means you have more places to look for the cause of the problem.

Subnet mask

Another way to tell whether your computer is on the same network as the computer you are trying to communicate with is to look at the subnet mask. The *subnet mask* is what your computer uses to determine whether the network device it is trying to communicate with is on the same network.

There are default subnet masks associated with the different classes of IP addresses. For example, a Class A address has a default subnet mask of 255.0.0.0, while a Class B address has a default subnet mask of 255.255.0.0, and a Class C address has a default subnet mask of 255.255.255.0. Looking at the subnet mask, any octet that has the value of 255 means that the corresponding octet in the IP address is part of the network ID. Let's put this all together; Table 29-2 shows an example of two computers and their IP address configurations.

Table 29-2 Comparing IP Addresses with Subnet Mask	
Item	*Address*
Computer A - IP Address	13.10.12.120
Computer A - Subnet Mask	255.0.0.0
Computer B - IP Address	18.23.48.119

Using this example, computer A tries to connect to computer B. The first thing that computer A does is compare its IP address with its own subnet mask to determine what octets make up the network ID. Here it sees that the first octet is the network ID, because the subset mask has the number 255 only in the first octet. Then computer A compares its subnet mask with the IP address of computer B, the remote computer it is trying to communicate with, and identifies that the network IDs of computer A and computer B are different — the two computers are on different networks.

Once computer A realizes that the remote computer it is trying to communicate with (computer B) is on a different network, it starts to panic because it does not have the capabilities to send the information over to the other computer. Computers can only pass information directly to other computers if both systems are on the same network. So what happens? This is where the default gateway fits into the story.

Default gateway

When information has to be forwarded from a computer on one network to a computer on another network, a special network device, called a *router*, must be used. The router has a table that lists all the networks it knows about and the network ID associated with each of those networks. When the router receives information destined for a particular IP address, it checks its table of network IDs for a match. If a match is found, it delivers the information to the appropriate network.

How does the information get to the router so that it can be forwarded? Looking back to the example in Table 29-2, computer A has information for computer B, and computer A realizes that computer B sits on a different network. At this point computer A looks at its default gateway, which is the address of the router that will forward the information on to computer B's network. The default gateway is a TCP/IP option configured on each workstation. Typically, all computers on the same network point to the same router.

Now that you are comfortable with the concepts of an IP address, subnet mask, and default gateway, let's walk through how to configure these options on a Windows 98 operating system.

STEP BY STEP: Configuring TCP/IP

1. Select Start ⇨ Settings ⇨ Control Panel.

2. Double-click the network icon.

3. On the Configuration page, select TCP/IP, and then click the Properties button.

4. On the IP Address page, select the Specify an IP address option (shown in Figure 29-9).

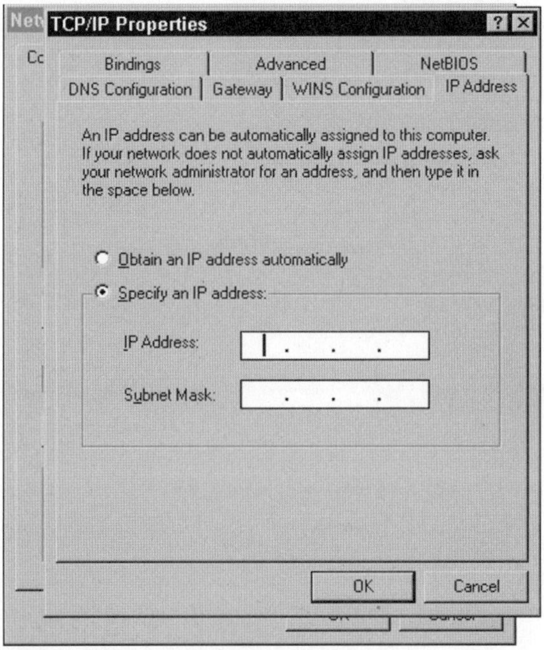

Figure 29-9: Configuring TCP/IP

5. Type in the IP address and subnet mask.

6. On the Gateway page, type in the IP address of the new gateway, and then click the Add button. The address of the newly added gateway appears in the Installed Gateways list (shown in Figure 29-10).

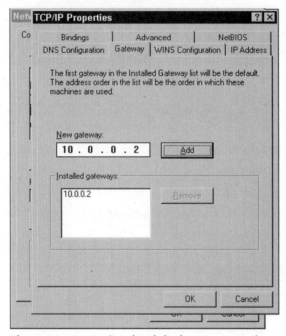

Figure 29-10: Setting the default gateway option

7. Click OK to exit the TCP/IP Properties dialog box.

8. Click OK.

9. If you are asked to reboot, click Yes.

DHCP

If you are the network administrator of a large network you are not going to want to run around to 400 workstations and configure an IP address, subnet mask, and default gateway on each computer. Not only is this time consuming to initially set up, but it also becomes a nightmare to manage because of all the potential for human error. I have spent my days running around to each computer on the network with a sheet of paper in my hands making sure that each computer was configured properly, and I can tell you that it is not fun!

Today's network operating systems support a feature called DHCP, Dynamic Host Configuration Protocol. *DHCP* is a standard that allows the network administrator to tell the server a range of IP addresses that it is allowed to give out, along with the other TCP/IP options, such as a subnet mask and default gateway. Once the DHCP server has been configured to give out the addresses, the Windows desktop computers automatically request an IP address from the server on startup, and the server hands them all the IP address information. This means that the network administrator does not have to run around to each computer individually to configure TCP/IP *and* in the long run, that saves time and money.

To configure the Windows 98 operating system to be assigned an IP address from DHCP, follow these steps:

STEP BY STEP: Configuring a DHCP Client

1. Select Start ➪ Settings ➪ Control Panel.

2. Double-click the network icon.

3. Select the TCP/IP protocol and click the Properties button.

4. On the IP Address page, select the Obtain an IP address automatically option (shown in Figure 29-11).

5. Click the OK button to exit the TCP/IP Properties dialog box.

6. Click OK.

7. If you are asked to restart the system, click Yes.

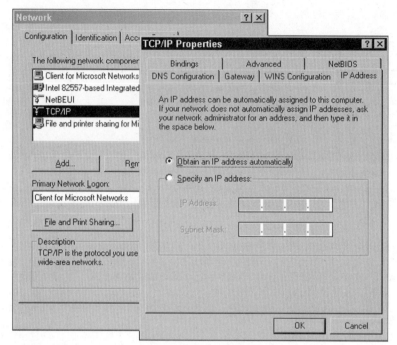

Figure 29-11: Configuring a client for DHCP

Utilities

Once you have TCP/IP installed and configured, you are running a TCP/IP network, and it is important to be able to troubleshoot this network. When problems arise on the network with Windows desktops, there are a few commands that you can use to do your troubleshooting, including the following:

✦ IPCONFIG

✦ WINIPCFG

✦ PING

✦ TRACERT

This section discusses these popular TCP/IP utilities that are used to troubleshoot TCP/IP connectivity.

IPCONFIG

If you are running Windows NT or Windows 2000 desktops, you can run the IPCON-FIG utility, which shows you the current TCP/IP configuration of the Windows desktop, such as the IP address, the subnet mask, and the default gateway. If the computer is a DHCP client, IPCONFIG identifies the server that has given the IP address and also shows how long the IP address will be used by the client. Table 29-3 shows some of the switches supported by the utility ipconfig.exe.

<table>
<tr><td colspan="2" align="center">Table 29-3
ipconfig.exe Switches</td></tr>
<tr><td>*Switch*</td><td>*Description*</td></tr>
<tr><td>/?</td><td>Shows a list of switches supported by ipconfig.exe, and a brief description of each switch.</td></tr>
<tr><td>/all</td><td>Shows all TCP/IP information; for example, DHCP lease period and the DNS server.</td></tr>
<tr><td>/release</td><td>Releases the current IP address information assigned by the DHCP server.</td></tr>
<tr><td>/renew</td><td>Requests new IP address information from the DHCP server.</td></tr>
</table>

WINIPCFG

The ipconfig.exe utility is used to view IP address information on Windows NT/2000 operating systems. If you want to see the same information on Windows 95 or Windows 98 operating systems, use the winipcfg.exe utility. To run this utility, click the Start button, select Run, and when the Run dialog box appears, type in `winipcfg.exe`, then choose OK.

The winipcfg.exe shows the same IP address information as ipconfig.exe, except that you have gone from a command utility to a Windows utility. In winipcfg.exe there are options to view all IP address information and also options to release and renew your IP address from the DHCP server. Figure 29-12 shows the winipcfg.exe utility.

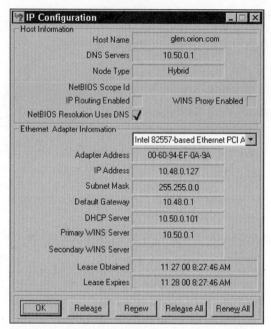

Figure 29-12: Looking at TCP/IP configuration with the winipcfg.exe utility

PING

One of the most popular TCP/IP utilities is the Ping.exe utility. Ping is used to test whether your computer can communicate with a remote network device. If the ping test is successful, you get a ping response from the remote device; if it is not successful, the response will time out. The general syntax for using the ping utility is `ping <IP address>`, the IP address being the IP address of the network device you are testing.

When troubleshooting TCP/IP communication problems, it is important to understand the steps to find exactly where the problem is occurring. Is the problem in the computer you are using, in the computer you are trying to connect to, or in the default gateway?

Table 29-4 lists the order of each network device to ping when trying to figure out at what stage the TCP/IP communication is failing.

Table 29-4
Troubleshooting Network Connectivity

Address to Ping	Description
127.0.0.1	This IP address is referred to as the *loopback* address. It always tests your own workstation's TCP/IP software to ensure that it has loaded.
IP address of your computer	Once you get a response from loopback, ping the IP address that has been physically assigned to your network card. To find out what IP address is assigned to your network card, use either ipconfig.exe or winipcfg.exe.
IP address of default gateway	Once you get a response from your network card's IP address, ping the IP address of the default gateway. If you don't know the IP address of your default gateway, then run winipcfg.exe (Windows 9x) or ipconfig.exe (Windows NT/2000). Remember that the default gateway is the router, which is responsible for passing information to other networks. If you are having trouble communicating with the router, you can't communicate with any devices off the network.
IP address of remote computer	After verifying that the default gateway is not the problem, if you know the IP address of the computer you wish to talk to (and chances are you don't because you are not the person who assigns the address to that computer) you can try pinging it. If you get a timeout at this step, you know that the computer you are trying to communicate with is the problem.

TRACERT

The ping utility is probably the most overused TCP/IP utility, and rightfully so. It is a very useful utility for troubleshooting communication problems. But the ping utility only tells you whether you have communicated with the remote hosts; it does not tell you what path the information took. This is where the Trace Route (tracert.exe) utility is useful. It is similar to the ping utility in the sense that responses are sent back to you if communication is established. The difference is that it sends a response from every network it hits on the way, not just a response from the final destination. So tracert.exe shows you the path the information takes and also the number of networks between your computer and the computer you are talking to.

The Trace Route utility uses the following syntax: `tracert <IP address or DNS name>`.

Name resolution

To communicate with another computer across a TCP/IP network, you have to know the IP address of the computer you are trying to communicate with. This is unrealistic, considering that you are probably not too interested in trying to memorize all the IP addresses of the different Web sites you visit every day.

When running a TCP/IP network, you assign a friendly name to each computer, and reference each computer by the friendly name, instead of using the IP address. This means that instead of using an address like 204.56.78.6 to connect to Bob's computer, you would use a friendly name, like Bob.

There are two types of names to understand when troubleshooting TCP/IP networks: computer names and fully qualified domain names. Let us take a look at computer names first.

Current Windows operating systems have the capability to function in a networking environment, but in order to network you have to be able to connect to each computer. How do you connect to Bob's computer? As an administrator, you assign a computer name to Bob's computer. The *computer name* is a friendly 15-character name that is assigned to each computer. The following steps show you how to assign the computer name.

STEP BY STEP: Changing the Computer Name

1. Select Start ➪ Settings ➪ Control Panel.

2. Double-click the network icon.

3. On the Identification page, type in the desired computer name in the Computer Name text box (shown in Figure 29-13).

   You may also change the value of the workgroup on this page. A workgroup is a way to group similar computers in a network neighborhood. For example, you may want to group the computers in the accounting department in a group called accounting, so you would type that workgroup name into all the computers in accounting.

   There is also a description that can be set in this dialog box. Usually the computer name is kept short, and a more descriptive term is entered in the description text box. If you look at Network Neighborhood in detail view, you see the description along with the computer name.

4. Click the OK button to exit the network dialog box.

5. Restart the computer if asked to do so.

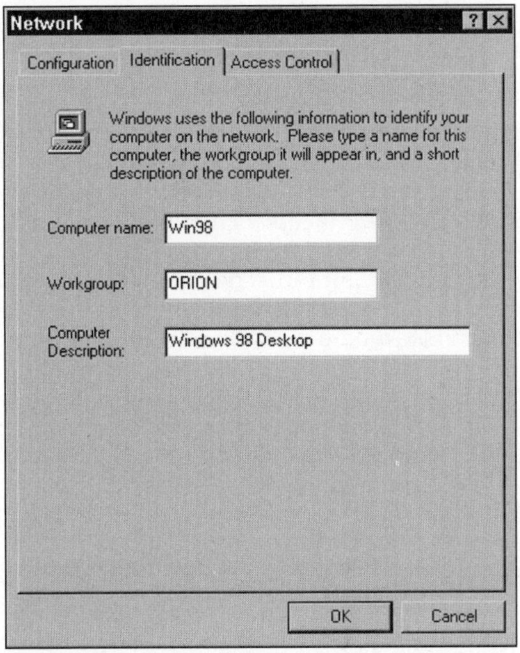

Figure 29-13: Setting identification properties

The other type of name that can be assigned to the computer when you are running a TCP/IP network is a domain name or a fully qualified domain name. *Fully qualified domain names (FQDN)* are being used when you run a TCP/IP- (or Internet-) based application like FTP, Email, or Web browser applications. For example, to see what is new with Hungry Minds, Inc. start up your Web browser and type in `www.hungryminds.com`—this is an example of an FQDN.

The point is that when you use a computer name or an FQDN on a TCP/IP-based network, the names always need to be converted to the actual IP address. The converting of names (either computer names or FQDNs) to IP addresses is the process referred to as *name resolution*.

There are a number of techniques used for name resolution, some techniques being more popular than others. The following section describes the name resolution techniques and their purposes.

DNS

DNS stands for Domain Name System and is the desired name resolution technique for resolving (converting) fully qualified domain names to IP addresses. Remember that fully qualified domain names are the names that are used with Internet-based applications, such as e-mail and Web browsers. DNS is like a big database of fully qualified domain names and their matching IP addresses. Think of this database as having two columns — one for the FQDN and the other for the IP address.

When you are running Internet or TCP/IP applications and you type in a fully qualified domain name, your computer sends a query, which is just a question, to the DNS database asking something like: "I am trying to connect to www.hungryminds.com, do you have an IP address?" The IP address is returned to your computer, and your computer then connects using that IP address.

The big question is, where is the database stored? The database is stored on what is called DNS servers, or Domain Name System servers. These servers are where the actual records are located and also where each client computer on your network sends its question.

When configuring TCP/IP on Windows client computers, you also have to point the client to the DNS server that it is supposed to send its queries to. To point your Windows client computer to a DNS server, follow these steps:

STEP BY STEP: Configuring a Client for DNS

1. Select Start ➪ Settings ➪ Control Panel.

2. Double-click the network icon.

3. Select the TCP/IP protocol, and click the Properties button.

4. On the DNS Configuration page, select Enable DNS (shown in Figure 29-14).

5. Enter a host name in the Host Name text box. If you also want to supply a domain name, you may. The combination of the host name and the domain name makes up the fully qualified domain name for the computer.

6. In the DNS Server Search Order, type in the IP address of your DNS server, and then click the Add button. This is the address of the server to which your DNS queries will be sent.

7. If you want to, you may enter a Domain Suffix Search Order, and DNS will search for the name of the host in the domain order specified. For example, if you add microsoft.com and then novell.com, and try to ping bob, DNS tries to resolve bob+<your domain name> first, then tries bob.microsoft.com, and finally bob.novell.com.

8. Click OK.

9. Restart if prompted.

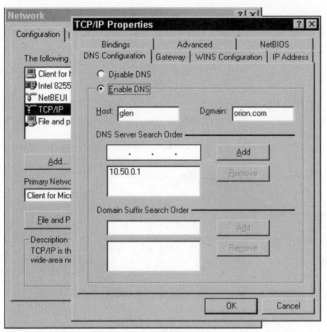

Figure 29-14: Configuring a Windows client for DNS

WINS

When networking in Microsoft environments, you will use the computer name to connect to other systems. This computer name must be converted to an IP address when running a TCP/IP network for communication to happen. For example, you may want to connect to Bob's computer, so you connect to \\bob through the Run command off the Start button. When you try to connect, \\bob is an example of a computer name that also has to be converted to an IP address. This is a different type of name, so DNS cannot be used; instead, your computer sends a query to a Windows Internet Naming System (WINS) database. The WINS database has the same structure as the DNS database but is used for computer names instead of fully qualified domain names. Think of this database as having two columns: one for the computer name and one for the matching IP address.

Windows client computers that connect to other computers on the network by using computer names query the WINS server with a question like: "Hi there, Mr. WINS server, I am trying to connect to a computer named Bob — do you have an IP address for this computer?" At this point the WINS server looks in the database for a computer named Bob and returns the IP address to the client.

The following steps show you how to configure TCP/IP on the Windows client to query the WINS server.

STEP BY STEP:Configuring a Client for WINS

1. Select Start ⇨ Settings ⇨ Control Panel.

2. Double-click the network icon.

3. Select TCP/IP, and click Properties.

4. On the WINS Configuration page, select the Enable WINS resolution option (shown in Figure 29-15).

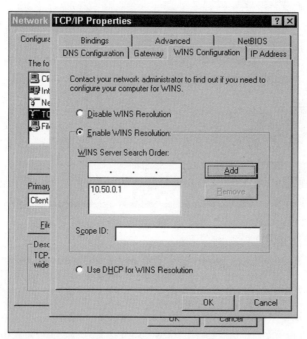

Figure 29-15: Configuring a Windows client for WINS

5. Type in the IP address of your WINS server, and click the Add button. This is the IP address of the server that your Windows client will query for resolving computer names to IP addresses.

6. Click OK to exit the TCP/IP Properties dialog box.

7. Click OK.

8. Restart the computer if prompted.

ARP

When computer A tries to connect to computer B using the fully qualified domain name or the computer name, those names must be converted to IP addresses. You know that there is a different database for each of these types of names — the DNS database that stores fully qualified domain names and the IP addresses, and the WINS database that stores computer names and associated IP addresses. But when computer A wants to talk to computer B, computer A must know the network card address, not the IP address, of computer B. So there is another address resolution (conversion) that takes place after the name is converted to an IP address. This address resolution is called the Address Resolution Protocol (ARP). ARP is the conversion of an IP address to the network card address, which is also known as the Media Access Control address, or MAC address for short.

ARP is a broadcast or a yell out on the wire for a particular address. In the example of computer A trying to establish communication with computer B, once computer A has the IP address of computer B (say it is 204.56.78.3), A yells at the top of his lungs: "Hey, 204.56.78.3! What is your network card's MAC address?" This yell runs along the network and eventually reaches computer B, which responds with its MAC address, and then the two can communicate.

Sharing File System Resources

4.1 Identify the networking capabilities of Windows, including procedures for connecting to the network. Content may include the following: Sharing disk drives, Sharing print and file services

In this section we discuss how to setup the Windows operating system for sharing of network resources. The topic begins with a discussion of some of the core options that must be set in order to network in a Windows operating system.

Every Windows computer must have a computer name set in order to participate in a Windows network, and each computer name must be unique on the network in order to properly address a specific computer. To review the steps to change your computer name, take a look at the "Changing the Computer Name" steps shown earlier in the chapter.

Another important networking option to talk about before we take a look at sharing resources is the level of access control that is set on the computer. *Access control* determines what level of security you want to place on your Windows desktop. Figure 29-16 shows the Access Control dialog box found in the network icon of Control Panel.

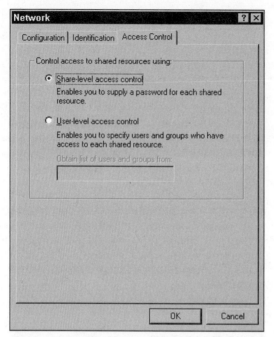

Figure 29-16: Looking at access control options

There are two levels of access control to enable on a Windows 95 or Windows 98 desktop, the first being share level. *Share-level access control* means that the security is placed on the share. A *share* is the concept of publishing a resource like a folder or printer out on the network so that others can connect to it. When you share a resource and share-level access is enabled, you have the opportunity to place a password on the share.

This is limited security because you are basing the security model on the fact that if someone knows the password, he can get into the share. It is limited because a user on the network could find out the password by accident and then be able to connect to the share without anyone knowing. Wouldn't it be better to assign a specific user the right to the share, so that only that particular user could get to the resource, increasing the security?

The second type of access control is user level. *User-level access control* means that when you share a resource out onto the network, you actually assign permissions to a particular user. If someone wants access to the share, he has to have been given permissions and then log in as that user. When you enable user-level access control, you are required to supply a security provider. The security provider is where the actual user accounts exist; this could be a Windows NT server or a Novell server. To set the security provider, choose the user-level access control option, and then type the Windows NT domain or the Novell server name in the Obtain list of users and group from: textbox.

Tip   Windows NT and Windows 2000 products always have File and Printer Sharing enabled with user-level access control enabled. There is not an option to switch to share-level access control in the network properties with these operating systems.

Now that you understand the two levels of access control, you are ready to allow your Windows machines to share resources out on the network. First you must enable sharing and then physically share each folder or printer that you want other users on the network to be able to access. The following steps lead you through the process for enabling file and print sharing.

STEP BY STEP: Enabling File and Print Sharing

1. Select Start ➪ Settings ➪ Control Panel.

2. Double-click the network icon.

3. On the Configuration page, click the File and Print Sharing button.

4. Enable both check boxes to be able to share folders and printers, or just enable one or the other (shown in Figure 29-17).

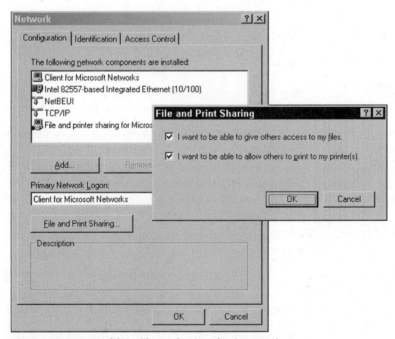

Figure 29-17: Enabling file and print sharing services

5. Click the OK button.

6. Click the OK button to exit the network Properties dialog box.

7. Restart the system if prompted.

Once the system has restarted, you are ready to start sharing resources out to the network.

Creating shares

Shares are what other users on the network connect to your computer for. If you have not shared any resources, then there is no reason for anyone to want to connect to your computer — it would be like giving someone the key to an empty room that is locked.

Know that you can only share folders or printers; you cannot actually share a file specifically. To share only one file, you have to put the file in a folder all by itself, and then share that folder. The following steps show how to share a folder.

STEP BY STEP: Sharing a Folder

1. Select Start ➪ Programs ➪ Windows Explorer.

2. Right-click on the folder that you want to share.

3. Choose the Sharing command from the context menu

4. In the Sharing dialog box, select the option Share as (shown in Figure 29-18).

5. Type a share name in the Share Name text box. This is the name that users will use to connect to this folder through Network Neighborhood. If you have any Windows 3.1 clients or DOS clients, you want to keep this name to eight characters without spaces. Otherwise, you may use up to 12 characters, and you are allowed to have spaces.

You may type in a description if you like; it is displayed to users when they are viewing the window in detail view.

6. Select the type of access that users will have on the share. There are three different options:

- **Read Only:** Users have only the right to read the contents of the folder and the contents of files. They are not able to add new items to the folder or make changes to a file. (The third option is to specify the password that the user has to supply when connecting to the share for read-only purposes.)

- **Full Control:** Users have full capabilities in the share, including creating and deleting files from the share. They also can change the contents of existing files. (The third option is to specify the full control password that a user has to supply to connect to the share for full-control purposes.)

- **Depends On Password:** Depends on password means that you make up two different passwords for the share, one for read-only access and one for full-control access. The type of access a user gets when he connects to the share depends on the password he supplies.

7. Click the OK button.

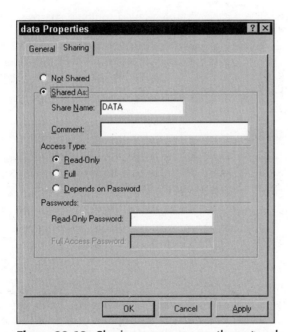

Figure 29-18: Sharing a resource on the network

 Tip You share a hard drive or CD-ROM the exact same way that you share a folder. To share the hard drive or CD-ROM, open My Computer, right-click on the drive, and then choose the Sharing command.

Hidden shares

In the Windows world, we also have the capability to create hidden shares. Hidden shares are like normal shares in the sense that users on the network can connect to them; the difference is that hidden shares are not advertised through Network Neighborhood.

To create a hidden share, use the steps for creating a normal share, but at step 5, where you type a share name in the Share Name text box, you create the hidden share by appending a dollar sign ($) to the end of the share name. For example, if the share name is data, and you want it to be a hidden share, you would type data$ in the Share Name text box; the share is automatically hidden from Network Neighborhood and users on the network.

Multiple shares

In Windows NT you have the capability to create multiple shares for the same folder. This gives flexibility to the network administrator so that a user could have different permissions in a folder, depending on what share that user connects to.

In the Real World

On our network in the office we have implemented multiple shares per shared folder so that under day-to-day activities not even an administrator can make changes to files on the server. If an administrator wants to make changes to a folder he/she has to connect to the secondary share for that particular folder where he/she has full-control access. This helps prevent a lot of unfortunate mistakes in modifying or deleting files by accident.

Connecting to shares

Once you have created the shared resource, you may connect to the shared resource from anywhere on the network. There are a number of ways to connect to shared folders; here are a few of the most common:

- ✦ Browsing Network Neighborhood
- ✦ Using a UNC path through the Run command
- ✦ Mapping a drive

To browse Network Neighborhood, double-click the Network Neighborhood icon on the desktop. Double-click the computer you want to connect to, and a list of shares on that computer appears. This is referred to as *network browsing*. At this point, you may open any of the shares by double-clicking it.

Tip

Remember that you can't see any hidden shares through Network Neighborhood. For this reason it is important to know additional ways to connect to shares.

You may also connect to a share using the Universal Naming Convention (UNC) path. The UNC path is made up of two backslashes (\\), the computer name you want to connect to, one more backslash, and the share name of the folder you want to connect to. The entire syntax looks like this: \\computername\sharename. You would type this into the Run command, found by clicking the Start button.

Using UNC paths means that you have to be aware of the exact names used for resources on the network, including hidden shares. Once you get used to the computer names and share names on the network, you'll find that the Run command is quicker than waiting to see the list of computers in Network Neighborhood.

You may also connect to shares by mapping drives. If you find that you are constantly connecting to the same resource, you may want to map a drive for simplicity sake. The idea of mapping a drive is that in the end you have a new drive letter in the My Computer icon that points to the UNC path of the resource.

To map a drive, right-click on Network Neighborhood, and choose Map Network Drive. In the Map Network Drive dialog box, select the letter for the drive you want to create, and then type the UNC path to the shared resource into the Path text box. You may also choose the option to re-create this drive mapping the next time you log on so that you do not have to do this again. Figure 29-19 shows the Map Network Drive dialog box.

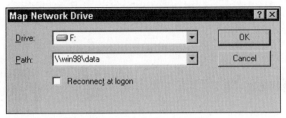

Figure 29-19: Mapping a network drive

Sharing Printer Resources

4.1 Identify the networking capabilities of Windows, including procedures for connecting to the network. Content may include the following: Sharing print and file services

You share printers much the same way as you share folders on the hard drive. Once you have installed the printer and configured the settings so that the printer is functioning properly, it is time to share it. To share a printer, follow these steps:

STEP BY STEP: Sharing a Printer

1. Select Start ➪ Settings ➪ Printers.

2. Right-click the printer that you want to share, and choose the Sharing command.

3. In the Sharing dialog box, fill in the share name of the printer, along with a description and password.

4. Click the OK button to exit the Sharing dialog box.

Tip   In order to share a printer, you must have installed the File and Print Sharing service

When sharing printers, all the same rules apply as far as the share name goes and how to create hidden shares.

To print to a shared printer out on the network, you have to install a printer locally that points to the network printer. You can do this a number of different ways; the two most popular methods are through the Add Printer Wizard, or through the Run command, depending on the network setup.

To install a printer that points to a network location, double-click the Add Printer icon in the Printers folder. The wizard starts up and walks you through connecting to a shared printer. The following steps walk you through the installation of a printer that points to a network location.

STEP BY STEP: Installing a Network Printer

1. Select Start ⇨ Settings ⇨ Printers.

2. Double-click the Add Printer icon.

3. Read the welcome message, and click Next.

4. Select Network Printer, and click Next.

5. Type the UNC path to the printer, or click the Browse button to browse the network for it. You may also choose whether or not you want to print to DOS-based applications (shown in Figure 29-20).

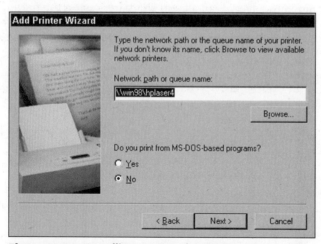

Figure 29-20: Installing a network printer

6. Click Next.

7. Type a friendly name for the printer, and then click Next.

8. If you would like to print a test page, select Yes, and then click Finish.

Configuring Browsers

 4.1 Identify the networking capabilities of Windows, including procedures for connecting to the network. Content may include the following: Installing and configuring browsers

When connecting to network resources on the network, clients need to know who is out there providing the resources. They can find this out by contacting the computer browser for their workgroup. The *computer browser,* or *browse master,* is a computer that is maintaining a list of servers that have either the file and print sharing service running or a server service running (on Windows NT products).

The first computer in the workgroup that is started with file and print sharing enabled becomes the computer browser for that workgroup. All other computers that start up and have file and print sharing enabled advertise themselves to the computer browser so that the computer browser can update the lists of computers that are sharing resources on the network.

When Windows clients browse Network Neighborhood, they contact the computer browser and ask for a list of servers on the network. The computer browser returns the lists to the client, and then the client connects to the appropriate server to see a list of shares.

It is important to understand how to designate a computer browser because there will be certain machines on the network that you want to be a browser and other computers you do not want to be a browser. Being the computer browser takes up resources on the system, so if you have a low-end computer, you may not want it to ever be a computer browser. To configure whether a computer will be a computer browser, go to the Network Properties, select the file and print sharing service on the Configurations page, and then click Properties. Figure 29-21 shows the properties of file and print sharing services.

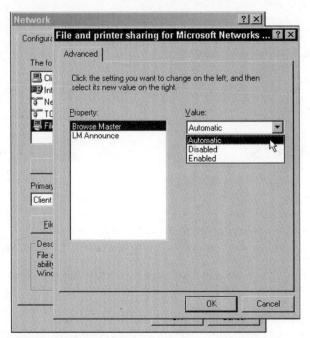

Figure 29-21: Changing the browse master options

Change the Browse master property to one of the following:

✦ **Automatic:** When selected, the computer has the potential to become a browse master. Any computer with Enabled chosen takes precedence over this system's Automatic option and becomes the browse master.

✦ **Enabled:** When selected, this means that this computer should be the browse master for the workgroup.

✦ **Disabled:** When selected, this computer will never become the browse master for the workgroup.

Key Point Summary

This chapter discussed the different networking components that allow a Windows operating system to function in a networking environment.

✦ There are four major networking components that are required in Windows networks:

- A network client

- A network adapter

- A common protocol

- A service

✦ TCP/IP is the most popular networking protocol used today. When installing TCP/IP, you need to configure the following:

- An IP address

- A Subnet mask

- A default gateway

✦ The NetBEUI protocol is a non-routable protocol used on small networks.

✦ The IPX protocol is primarily used on Novell networks.

✦ In Microsoft networking environments, to allow users to connect to your hard drive or printer, you must install the File and Print Sharing Service.

✦ You may use the IPCONFIG (Windows NT/2000) or the WINIPCFG (Windows 95/98) utilities to view TCP/IP configuration.

✦   ✦   ✦

STUDY GUIDE

This Study Guide presents 20 assessment questions, 2 scenarios, and 3 lab exercises to test your knowledge of this exam topic area.

Assessment Questions

1. What networking component allows you to log on to a Windows NT server?

    A. File and Print Sharing services

    B. Client for Netware Networks

    C. TCP/IP configured

    D. Client for Microsoft Networks

2. There is a folder named public, which is shared as data on a computer named Server1. What is the syntax to connect to the shared resource using the UNC path?

    A. \\server1\public

    B. \\server1\data

    C. \\data\server1

    D. \server1\\data

3. Which of the following IP addresses has a default subnet mask of 255.255.255.0?

    A. 10.45.65.78

    B. 132.107.2.34

    C. 48.123.45.67

    D. 216.83.24.56

4. You have installed a new Windows 98 computer in a Novell environment, and you are having trouble connecting to the Novell server. You have verified that you have the Client for Netware Networks installed. What other networking component should you make sure is installed?

    A. Client for Microsoft Networks

    B. File and Print Sharing

    C. The TCP/IP protocol

    D. The IPX protocol

5. You would like other people in the office to be able to access your printer that is attached to your Windows 98 computer on your small network. Which networking component must you install?

   A. Client for Microsoft Networks

   B. Client for Netware Networks

   C. File and Print Sharing

   D. NetBEUI

6. Which of the following is an example of a Class B IP address?

   A. 164.34.56.8

   B. 12.45.76.2

   C. 202.34.65.32

   D. 125.67.6.7

7. What are the two properties of TCP/IP that must be configured to communicate with other hosts on your local network? (Choose two.)

   A. IP Address

   B. DNS Server

   C. Default Gateway

   D. Subnet Mask

8. A user tries to connect to a shared resource called data on server1 using the UNC path \\server1\data, but is unsuccessful. The user knows the IP address of server1 and can successfully ping it. What is the problem?

   A. The user should be typing in \\data\server1.

   B. The client computer is not configured to query the WINS server.

   C. The client computer is not configured to query the DNS server.

   D. The user needs to install TCP/IP.

9. Which utility allows you to see the path that information may take when communicating with a remote system?

   A. ipconfig.exe

   B. tracert.exe

   C. winipcfg.exe

   D. arp.exe

10. Which of the following TCP/IP settings are required to connect to the Internet?

    A. IP address

    B. WINS

    C. Subnet mask

    D. Default GATEWAY

11. Which resolution technique is used to resolve the IP address to a MAC address?

    A. DNS

    B. WINS

    C. ARP

    D. ipconfig.exe

12. Which utility allows you to see the IP address information on a Windows NT computer?

    A. winipcfg.exe

    B. ipconfig.exe

    C. tracert.exe

    D. arp.exe

13. Which service is responsible for automatically assigning IP address information to each computer on the network?

    A. DNS

    B. WINS

    C. winipcfg.exe

    D. DHCP

14. You have verified that you have a network adapter installed and an appropriate client, but you cannot connect to computer B across NetBEUI. What could be the problem?

    A. You have the wrong IP address assigned to the computer.

    B. Computer B is not running NetBEUI.

    C. You should check the frame type on your computer.

    D. You need to install File and Print Sharing to connect to another computer.

15. When you type in `ipconfig.exe`, you do not see the IP address of the DHCP that has given you the IP address. What should you do?

    A. Type `ipconfig /renew` at the command prompt.

    B. Type `ipconfig /all` at the command prompt.

    C. Ping the IP address of the DHCP server.

    D. Type `ipconfig /release` at the command prompt.

16. You have installed a printer and want to share it out to the network. How can you do this?

    A. Type `"net print"` at the command prompt.

    B. Install the Client for Microsoft Networks.

    C. Install the IPX/SPX protocol.

    D. Right-click the printer in the Printers folder, and choose the Sharing command.

17. Which service is responsible for converting `www.hungryminds.com` to an IP address?

    A. DHCP

    B. DNS

    C. WINS

    D. ARP

18. You want to share the data folder as a resource to be used only by network administrators. How should you do this?

    A. Hide the share by naming it data$, and set up the permissions so that only administrators have access. Tell the administrators the UNC path.

    B. Don't share the folder; tell the administrators to go to the local computer to access the resource.

    C. Set up the share permissions so that only administrators have access to the share.

    D. Share the resource and don't set any permissions.

19. You need to install software on all five computers on your small network. What should you do?

    A. Place the software in a CD-ROM on one computer, and share it out to the network.

    B. You must go to each computer to install the software because CD-ROMs cannot be accessed from across the network.

    C. Use DHCP to automatically install the software.

    D. Type `"net install"` at a command prompt.

20. Which of the following services is responsible for keeping track of the computers on the network that are sharing resources?

    A. DNS

    B. WINS

    C. Computer browser

    D. DHCP

Scenarios

This chapter has presented you with a number of networking terms and concepts, and many issues that surround the implementation of Windows clients on a network. For these two critical-thinking exercises, identify the protocols and services that are required to meet the needs of the organization.

1. You are in charge of implementing the network infrastructure for your organization. There are two Windows NT servers and three Novell servers servicing 200 Windows 98 Clients. There is one Windows 98 computer in the manager's office that the word processing department will be sending print jobs to. What networking components would you load to allow the clients to access both the Novell servers and the Windows NT servers?

2. You are responsible for implementing a TCP/IP-based network across all of the office locations in your region. What TCP/IP options will you set and which additional TCP/IP-based services would you implement?

Lab Exercises

Lab 29-1 Configuring TCP/IP

1. Select Start ➪ Settings ➪ Control Panel.

2. Double-click the network icon.

3. On the Configuration page, select TCP/IP, and click the Properties button.

4. Select the Specify an IP address option.

5. Type in an IP address of 10.0.0.1 and a subnet mask of 255.0.0.0.

6. Click the OK button.

7. Click the OK button to exit the network Properties dialog box.

8. Restart the computer if prompted.

Lab 29-2 Testing TCP/IP

1. After the computer has restarted, select Start ⇨ Programs ⇨ MSDOS Prompt.

2. In the DOS prompt, type `Ping 10.0.0.1`. You should get a reply, if not verify that TCP/IP is installed.

3. Close the command prompt.

4. Select Start ⇨ Run.

5. Type `winipcfg`. and click the OK button. You should see the IP address assigned and the subnet mask information in the winipcfg dialog box. If you don't see the IP address and subnet mask, verify that TCP/IP has been installed and configured.

6. Close the winipcfg dialog box.

Lab 29-3 Sharing Resources

1. Right-click Network Neighborhood, and choose Properties.

2. On the Configuration page, click the File and Print Sharing button.

3. Select both check boxes to enable file sharing and print sharing.

4. Click the OK button.

5. Click the OK button to exit network Properties.

6. Restart the computer when prompted.

7. After the computer has restarted, start up Windows Explorer by choosing Start ⇨ Programs ⇨ Windows Explorer.

8. Select drive C, and choose the File ⇨ New ⇨ Folder command from the menu bar.

9. Type `data` as the name of the newly added folder, and press Enter.

10. Select the data folder.

11. Right-click the data folder, and choose Sharing.

12. In the Sharing dialog box, choose the option Share as. Notice that the default share name is data.

13. In the Sharing dialog box, make sure that read only is the type of access users will have to the share, and then click OK.

14. To test the shared folder, go to the Run command in the Start menu, type `\\<yourcomputername>\data`, and press Enter. The folder contents will appear.

Answers to Chapter Questions

Chapter Pre-Test

1. **Ipconfig.exe** is run in a command prompt to view TCP/IP configuration.

2. The syntax to connect to a shared resource using a UNC path is **\\server-name\sharename.**

3. **WINS** is responsible for converting computer names to IP addresses.

4. To access resources on another network, you must have the **IP address, subnet mask, and default gateway** configured.

5. **DNS** is responsible for converting the fully qualified domain name to an IP address.

6. You should always make sure **that the Windows client is running the same frame type as the Novell server.**

7. You may create a hidden share **by sharing a resource and adding a dollar sign ($) to the end of the share name.**

8. **File and print sharing** must be installed to allow someone to access files on the computer.

9. The network browser **keeps a list of all the computers that are sharing resources on the network.** Clients connect to the network browser to retrieve the list of computers sharing resources.

10. You must install **Client for Netware Networks** to connect to a Novell network.

Assessment Questions

1. **D.** In order to connect to a resource, you must have the appropriate client running. In this example, you are logging into a Windows NT server, so you must load the Client for Microsoft Networks. For more information, see the section labeled "Networking Components."

2. **B.** Although the folder name is public, the share name is what you connect to when connecting to network resources. The proper syntax for a UNC path is \\servername\sharename. For more information, see the section labeled "Sharing File System Resources."

3. **D.** 216.83.24.56 is an example of a Class C address, whose default subnet mask is 255.255.255.0. The other addresses are Class A or Class B, which have different default subnet masks. For more information, see the section labeled "Configuring TCP/IP."

4. **D.** Once you have Client for Netware Networks installed, you have to ensure that IPX is installed and configured for the same frame type as the server you are trying to communicate with. For more information, see the section labeled "Networking Components."

5. C. File and Print Sharing must be installed to allow someone to connect to your resources. For more information, see the section labeled "Networking Components."

6. A. The number in Class B addresses' first octet ranges from 128 to 191. The number in Class A addresses' first octet ranges from 1 to 126, and the number in Class C IP addresses' first octet ranges from 192 to 223. For more information, see the section labeled "Configuring TCP/IP."

7. A, D. Since the computer is functioning on a small local area network where there is not a router, all you need to configure the functionality of TCP/IP is the IP addresses and subnet mask. Since there is no information leaving the network, you do not have to configure a default gateway. For more information, see the section labeled "Configuring TCP/IP."

8. B. The computer name, server1, must be converted to an IP address. WINS is the service that maintains a database holding computer names and matching IP addresses. For more information, see the section labeled "Configuring TCP/IP."

9. B. Tracert.exe is the utility used to see the number of networks between you and the remote host. Ipconfig.exe and winipcfg.exe display the TCP/IP configuration. For more information, see the section labeled "Configuring TCP/IP."

10. A, C, D. To participate on the Internet, you need an IP address, subnet mask, and a default gateway. The default gateway is the IP address of the router that is sending information off the network. For more information, see the section labeled "Configuring TCP/IP."

11. C. Address Resolution Protocol (ARP) converts the IP address to the network card address (MAC address). DNS and WINS convert different types of names to an IP address. For more information, see the section labeled "Configuring TCP/IP."

12. B. Ipconfig.exe is the utility run on Windows NT products to view TCP/IP configuration. Winipcfg.exe is the utility on Windows 95 and Windows 98. For more information, see the section labeled "Configuring TCP/IP."

13. D. Dynamic Host Configuration Protocol (DHCP) is a service on a server that automatically assigns IP address information to each computer on the network, saving the network administrator from having to manually configure each computer. For more information, see the section labeled "Configuring TCP/IP."

14. B. If you have a client and a network adapter installed, and they are working correctly, then the reason you can't connect across NetBEUI would be because the person on the other end is using a different protocol. For more information, see the section labeled "Networking Components."

15. B. Without switches, ipconfig.exe only displays the IP address, subnet mask, and default gateway. Use the ipconfig /all switch to view all TCP/IP configurations, including who the DHCP server is that has assigned you an IP address. For more information, see the section labeled "Configuring TCP/IP."

16. D. Once you have installed file and print sharing, all you need to do to share is to right-click on the printer and choose the Sharing command. For more information, see the section labeled "Sharing Printer Resources."

17. B. DNS is responsible for converting fully qualified domain names to IP addresses. WINS converts the computer name to an IP address, and DHCP is responsible for automatic configuration of TCP/IP. For more information, see the section labeled "Configuring TCP/IP."

18. A. The best way to be sure that no one except network administrators can access a shared resource is to share the resource and set the proper permissions. When you share the resource, though, it may be best to hide it from Network Neighborhood so that no one tries to sneak into it. For more information, see the section labeled "Sharing File System Resources."

19. A. One of the most efficient ways of installing software these days is to share the CD-ROM on one computer and have the other computers connect to the CD-ROM to install. This is one of the purposes of having a networked environment. For more information, see the section labeled "Sharing File System Resources."

20. C. The computer browser is maintaining a browse list, which is a list of computers that have file and print sharing enabled. For more information, see the section labeled "Configuring Browsers."

Scenarios

1. The Windows 98 computer that is in the manager's office will have File and Print Sharing for Microsoft Networks loaded so that the Windows 98 client in the word processing department may connect to it.

You would have to load Client for Netware Networks so that the Windows 98 clients could connect to the Novell servers. You would also have to make sure that the IPX/SPX protocol is loaded and the proper frame type is configured.

To allow the Windows 98 client to connect to the Windows NT servers, you have to load the Client for Microsoft Networks if it's not already loaded. You may get away with just running IPX if the Windows NT servers are running IPX as well; otherwise, you will have to install an additional protocol.

2. You may want to set a DNS server to store the FQDN and IP addresses of the different servers on your network. You may also want to run a WINS server for computer name resolution since it is a WAN environment.

Once you have setup the DNS and WINS server, you could install a DHCP for each network segment so that you can hand out IP address, subnet mask, and default gateway information to the clients on the network. You can also hand out the IP address of the DNS server and the WINS server through DHCP, so that the clients are fully configured.

Configuring Internet Access

EXAM OBJECTIVES

Exam 220-202 ✦ **A+ OS Technologies**

> ✦ **4.2** Identify concepts and capabilities relating to the Internet and basic procedures for setting up a system for Internet access. Content may include the following: Concepts and terminology:
>
> - ISP
> - TCP/IP
> - IPX/SPX
> - NetBEUI
> - E-mail
> - ping.exe
> - HTML
> - HTTP
> - FTP
> - Domain Names (Web sites)
> - Dial-up networking
> - tracert.exe
> - nslookup.exe

CHAPTER PRE-TEST

1. What is the core networking protocol that is used by the Internet?

2. What does the acronym HTML represent?

3. What utility can test the speed of your connection to other computers?

4. What protocol enables you to read your e-mail?

5. What is required to be unique for every computer on the Internet?

✦ Answers to these questions can be found at the end of the chapter. ✦

This chapter will examine how you can become connected to the Internet. It will discuss the terminology that you need to be familiar with, as well as different methods that are available to access the Internet.

The Internet

4.2 Identify concepts and capabilities relating to the Internet and basic procedures for setting up a system for Internet access. Content may include the following: Concepts and terminology

The Internet was originally created and implemented by DARPA (Defense Advanced Research Projects Agency)—often referred to as just ARPA—in response to a U.S. Department of Defense request. At the time, the U.S. Department of Defense was concerned about their centralized communications network. Most communications were relayed through a central computing system, and damage to that system could stop computer communication. To avoid this, the U.S. Department of Defense tasked another government agency (ARPA) with the responsibility of devising a new system.

The information in the history listing was condensed from the *Hobbes' Internet Timeline*, (c)1993-2001 by Robert H. Zakon, with the author's permission. You can find the complete *Hobbes' Internet Timeline* at `http://www.zakon.org/robert/internet/timeline/`.

The following section will take you through a quick timeline of events starting in the 1960s. This section is just meant to signpost some of the major events and to let you see that the Internet evolved from something small, developing in steps to become what we now know it as. Even today, the Internet is constantly evolving—it will be interesting to see what it looks like in the year 2010. Many of the terms in the following list will be discussed at further length in the chapter.

To find out more about the name confusion between ARPA and DARPA and their name changes since they were established in 1958, read the page titled "ARPA—DARPA, the history of the name" on the ARPA Web site at `http://www.arpa.gov/body/arpa_darpa.html`.

Throughout the 1960s, the following events took place:

✦ ARPA theorized about traffic flow on computer networks and investigated packet-switching—networking that provides no single point of outage.

✦ In the late 1960s, ARPA created their first communication protocols, as well as ARPANET, connecting four hosts (computer systems) together.

Tip
The first four hosts on the ARPANET (in the order they were added) came from the following networks: University of California Los Angeles (UCLA), Stanford Research Institute (SRI), University of California Santa Barbara (UCSB), and University of Utah.

During the 1970s, the following events took place:

✦ Several different communications protocols were established and tested on the ARPANET, with Network Control Protocol (NCP) becoming an early favorite.

✦ The number of networks on the ARPANET grew quickly to fifteen, supporting 2000 users.

✦ Telnet was implemented as a remote terminal protocol that enabled remote users to run commands on many of the servers.

✦ The @ sign was chosen as a separator between user names and server names in e-mail addresses because of its "at" meaning.

✦ TCP (Transmission Control Protocol) was implemented as a communication protocol.

✦ TCP was split into two components: TCP and IP (Internet Protocol).

✦ Emotion-icons, or emoticons, were suggested as a method for putting emotion back into communication — they were widely criticized and then accepted.

✦ At the end of the 1970s, the National Science Foundation (NSF) joined the project to further their plans to develop a Computer Science Department research computer network.

During the 1980s, the following events took place:

✦ BITNET (Because It's Time NETwork) started by providing e-mail and listserv (mailing lists) services as a method of distributing information.

✦ TCP/IP was chosen as the protocol suite for the ARPANET

✦ The term "internet" was defined as a connected set networks and "Internet" was defined as many connected TCP/IP internets.

Tip
Due to confusion between internet and Internet, the term "Intranet" replaces "internet" in normal use. Intranet actually refers to the use of Internet technologies (such as Web servers) on an internal TCP/IP internet or network.

✦ NCP was dropped as a protocol in favor of TCP/IP.

✦ In 1983, as desktop computers entered the market, many joined the ARPANET running Berkley UNIX (BSD), which includes as a standard feature the TCP/IP suite of protocols.

✦ Domain Name System (DNS) is introduced as a way of resolving the name and addresses of the 1,000 hosts on the ARPANET.

✦ USENET newsgroups are created and allow people another type of group discussion.

✦ Canada joins the network when the University-oriented NetNorth Network is connected to BITNET.

✦ NSF establishes NSFNET by joining their five super-computing centers together.

✦ A new body is formed as the Internet Architecture Board (IAB) with major divisions of:

- Internet Research Task Force (IRTF), which is responsible for researching technologies that may be used on the Internet. The IRTF is controlled by the Internet Research Steering Group (IRSG).

- Internet Engineering Task Force (IETF), which is responsible for planning the application of technologies and the smooth operation of the Internet. The IETF is controlled by the Internet Engineering Steering Group (IESG).

- Internet Assigned Numbers Authority (IANA), which is responsible for the management of IP address allocation and DNS (Domain Name System) management. IANA formed ICAAN, the Internet Corporation for Assigned Names and Numbers, to assume the actual management of these services. Actual DNS name registration was then contracted to Network Solutions Inc., which worked under the name InterNIC.

Tip   The IAB was originally named the Internet Activities Board, but changed their name because they thought "Architecture" better represented their focus.

✦ Network News Transfer Protocol (NNTP) developed to improve USENET news capabilities.

✦ First Internet Worm (Morris Worm) virus affects 10% of the 60,000 hosts on the Internet.

✦ Computer Emergency Response Team (CERT) is formed by ARPA to deal with issues such as the Morris Worm.

✦ The first Freenet is formed to provide public access to the Internet.

✦ Internet Relay Chat (IRC) is created to allow real-time (typed) conversations over the Internet.

✦ Canada (CA), Denmark (DK), Finland (FI), France (FR), Iceland (IS), Norway (NO), Sweden (SE), and later Australia (AU) join the NSFNET.

✦ The Internet breaks 100,000 hosts.

✦ ARPANET is dissolved and NSFNET takes over the role as Internet backbone.

During the 1990s, the following events took place:

✦ The World (world.std.com) joins the Internet as the first public Internet Service Provider (ISP).

✦ Ten Canadian regional networks join to form the CA*net — Canada's Internet backbone — with a direct connection to NSFNET.

✦ Gopher protocol released by University of Minnesota.

✦ World Wide Web (WWW) released by CERN.

✦ More countries joined the Internet, including South Africa (ZA), Taiwan (TW), Antarctica (AQ), Luxembourg (LU), Russian Federation (RU), Egypt (EG), and US Virgin Islands (VI).

✦ In 1992, the number of hosts broke the one million mark.

✦ InterNIC created by NSF to manage the DNS.

✦ The White House (www.whitehouse.gov) gets connected under Bill Clinton.

✦ Shopping starts on the Internet.

✦ WWW becomes the most popular service on the Internet.

✦ In the mid-1990s, the first banner advertisement appears.

✦ The Vatican (www.vatican.va) gets connected.

✦ Online banking starts on the Internet.

✦ MP3 standard is created and starts to catch on.

The Internet is defined by a series of standards that are currently being put forth by Internet Architecture Board (IAB), which represents the governing body of the Internet. These Internet standards are defined by IAB, but discussed in RFC (Request for Comments) documents. The first RFC defined how the host at UCLA and the host at SRI would send and receive data with each other. All of the RFCs are available from www.rfc.net — over 3,100 of them.

TCP/IP is the protocol suite that is used by the Internet, but it is composed of many different protocols that function at different levels of the network model. There are network protocols, transport protocols, and application protocols. In fact, the number of protocols is limitless. Many key protocols have already been discussed (for example, in Chapter 29), but this chapter will cover some of the others, such as:

✦ SMTP (Simple Mail Transport Protocol)

✦ POP3 (Post Office Protocol version 3)

✦ HTTP (Hyper Text Transfer Protocol)

✦ FTP (File Transfer Protocol)

✦ IMAP (Internet Message Access Protocol)

✦ NNTP (Network News Transport Protocol)

What is an ISP?

 4.2 Identify concepts and capabilities relating to the Internet and basic procedures for setting up a system for Internet access. Content may include the following: Concepts and terminology — ISP

ISP is short for Internet Service Provider. Essentially, the Internet is a large routed network, with technology similar to the networks that would be found in a large corporation. The main difference between the Internet and a corporate network, however, is that all the small networks that make up the Internet are joined together, while corporate networks are kept private. To gain access to the Internet, you must gain access to one of the networks connected to the Internet. These networks are run by Internet Service Providers, which are in place simply to allow you to access the Internet. Figure 30-1 illustrates how a connection to the Internet works.

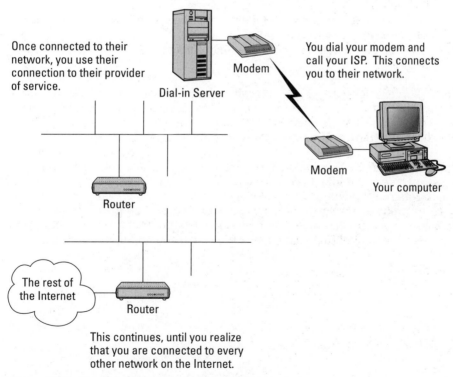

How you get your connection to the Internet

Once connected to their network, you use their connection to their provider of service.

Dial-in Server

Modem

You dial your modem and call your ISP. This connects you to their network.

Modem

Your computer

Router

The rest of the Internet

Router

This continues, until you realize that you are connected to every other network on the Internet.

Figure 30-1: How you get connected to the Internet

In addition to connection services, most ISPs provide other services, such as:

✦ E-mail addresses and message space on servers.

✦ Local news servers that replicate USENET news groups. These are discussion groups on various topics in a bulletin board format.

✦ Web page storage space.

In the past, most Internet access service was provided over standard modems or through a dedicated link, such as 56K-frame relay. Currently, dial-up access to the Internet is giving way to permanent connections like cable and ADSL (Asynchronous Digital Subscriber Line), which offer a great improvement in access speed.

What is an ASP?

The acronym ASP is often used for two different technologies: Active Server Pages and Application Service Providers.

 Exam Tip   You will not be tested on ASP for the exam. This information has been included since Application Service Providers are sometimes considered to be a type of ISP, although they usually just offer data and content services, and not connection services.

Active Server Pages are a form of HTML document that contains Visual Basic or Java script that is rendered into straight HTML by the server before passing data to the Web client. They are used to limit the amount of work that has to be done by the client and to protect your code, since only the results are sent to the client.

Application Service Providers (ASPs) are companies that provide a service by hosting servers for their clients. These servers may be database or mail servers. They may be shared or dedicated to a single customer. In either case, the server's hardware and software are maintained by someone other than the customer. This is a useful setup for smaller organizations, since they do not have to invest in large servers or personnel to manage them; they basically rent space on them.

Protocols

When many people think of protocols and computers, they think specifically of network and transport protocols, since these two types of protocols seem to get all of the credit. Network and transport protocols are the components of network communications that connect your computer to a network and send and receive bundles of data between hosts, and include protocols such as TCP/IP, IPX/SPX, and NetBEUI. In actuality, a protocol is a set of standards or conventions that are followed when formatting data to be used for electronic communications, and data transfer is just one level in the electronic communications model. Since this definition of protocol is not limited to data transfer, there are a number of protocols that work at other layers, most notably the application layer. Application-layer protocols establish a standard or format for data that is to be communicated. They are referred to as application layer protocols since they are the first layer to which programs or applications on a computer will communicate; this is also true for the server components.

After the creation of TCP/IP, the International Standards Association (ISO) proposed a new standard for people to follow. This new standard represented utopia in data communiations and was called the Open Systems Interconnection, or OSI. It was a utopia since many networking standards were already in place and were not about to change. Instead of being a standard that is followed, it has become more of a yard stick for comparison. The OSI model contained seven layers from application down to network, and components at each layer only need to be able to communicate with those components that are immediately above or below themselves. This provides a certain degree of flexibility if someone wanted to replace components somewhere in the network model, as the new components would only need to communicate with the level above and below itself.

The TCP/IP protocols operate at different layers of the network model, from the application layer down to IP. Figure 30-2 compares the TCP/IP network model against the OSI model. Within TCP/IP, the protocols that operate at the transport and network layers are TCP (Transmission Control Protocol), UDP (User Datagram Protocol), and IP (Internet Protocol). There are many other protocols that are used at those levels, such as ARP (Address Resolution Protocol), ICMP (Internet Control Message Protocol), and IGMP (Internet Group Message Protocol). In addition to the transport and network protocols, there are also Application layer protocols, such as SMTP (Simple Mail Transport Protocol), HTTP (Hyper Text Transfer Protocol), and FTP (File Transfer Protocol), which define the way data will be formatted but rely on the lower-level protocols, such as IP, to actually transfer the data. Application layer protocols establish the format in which you will place the data. If TCP/IP is the language that will be spoken, then FTP dictates the sentence structures and slang that will be allowed.

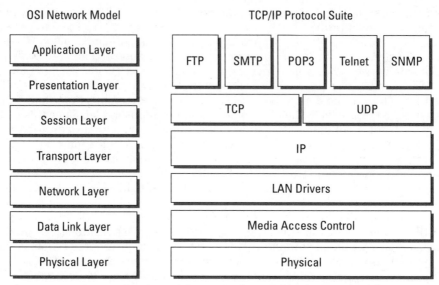

Comparing the TCP/IP protocol to the OSI model

Figure 30-2: Comparing the TCP/IP network model to the OSI model

TCP/IP

4.2 Identify concepts and capabilities relating to the Internet and basic procedures for setting up a system for Internet access. Content may include the following: Concepts and terminology – TCP/IP

TCP/IP (Transmission Control Protocol/Internet Protocol) is not a protocol in and of itself; rather, it is a suite of industry standard protocols. It is a routable wide area network protocol that shares many similarities with Novell's IPX/SPX. One main difference, however, between IPX/SPX and TCP/IP is that TCP/IP is an open, or free, protocol, while IPX/SPX is owned specifically by one company. TCP/IP standards are developed, established, and used by the computing community itself, while Novell is responsible for the development and standards for the IPX/SPX protocol.

Figure 30-3 shows some of the protocols that are used as part of the TCP/IP protocol suite, and what each protocol is responsible for. At the lowest level, IP offers best effort delivery services. This means that it will attempt to deliver all network packets to the best of its ability. It will process any errors that are reported back from routers. At the next level, TCP offers guaranteed delivery services, and UDP offers best effort delivery services. Session services for TCP/IP are offered by either NetBIOS over TCP/IP (NetBT), or Window Sockets. The Microsoft network clients for Windows 9x and Windows NT 4.0 are NetBIOS clients and make use of that interface, while most IP-based utilities and the Windows 2000 network client are socket-based. The Windows 2000 client supports NetBIOS, as well for backward-compatibility. IP-based utilities include applications such as Web browsers, e-mail clients, and FTP programs. The session layer is above the application layer, where all of the application protocols reside, such as HTTP, FTP, SMTP, and POP3.

A Breakdown of the TCP/IP Protocol Suite

FTP	SMTP	POP3	Telnet	SNMP		MS Netowrk Client	Other NetBios Application
Sockets						NetBios	
UDP				TCP			

ARP	IGMP				
ICMP		IP			

Physical

Figure 30-3: TCP/IP uses many protocols at different layers to accomplish its task.

IPX/SPX

4.2 Identify concepts and capabilities relating to the Internet and basic procedures for setting up a system for Internet access. Content may include the following: Concepts and terminology—IPX/SPX

IPX/SPX is a protocol of comparable features to TCP/IP with a couple of major differences. It is a proprietary protocol which is owned by Novell Corporation—although Novell has now moved their server software entirely to TCP/IP with the release of NetWare 5.0—and it is not capable of being used on the Internet. Since this chapter is devoted to Internet connectivity, this is the total coverage we will give to IPX/SPX in this chapter.

Cross-Reference IPX/SPX is covered in greater detail in the previous networking chapter, Chapter 29.

NetBEUI

4.2 Identify concepts and capabilities relating to the Internet and basic procedures for setting up a system for Internet access. Content may include the following: Concepts and terminology — NetBEUI

The NetBEUI is the result of a joint venture between Microsoft and IBM. The server OS (LAN Manager) that they jointly developed required a networking protocol, and Microsoft and IBM felt that TCP/IP was more network protocol than they required. NetBEUI is a lightweight non-routable protocol, which is ideally suited to small networks. After Microsoft and IBM stopped their joint venture, Microsoft went on to release Windows NT 3.1, and IBM went on to release IBM Warp Server. Both of these server OSs were heavily NetBIOS-based. Since NetBIOS is non-routable, it is not capable of being used on the Internet, and since this chapter is devoted to Internet connectivity this is the total of the coverage of NetBEUI in this chapter.

Cross-Reference
NetBEUI is covered in greater detail in the previous networking chapter, Chapter 29.

E-mail

4.2 Identify concepts and capabilities relating to the Internet and basic procedures for setting up a system for Internet access. Content may include the following: Concepts and terminology — E-mail

E-mail is one of the applications that made the Internet indispensable to most people. E-mail was an early tool for ARPANET that enabled users to communicate ideas and concepts. E-mail allows for individually addressed text messages to be transferred over the Internet and delivered directly to the targeted recipients. Compared to conventional land-based mail, these transfers were instantaneous.

Tip
Land-based mail is often referred to as "snail-mail" because of its slow speed compared to e-mail.

Attachments that accompany e-mail messages are converted to a text stream by means of encoding. MIME (Multipurpose Internet Mail Extensions) is currently one of the most popular encoding methods on the Internet. Other popular encoding formats include BinHex and Uuencode. Encoding, which takes 8-bit per byte binary data and converts it to 7-bit per byte ASCII or text data, enables binary attachments to be sent over the text-based e-mail network. When you receive attachments, they must be decoded by your e-mail program. If your e-mail program cannot do this, however, you will have to use a third-party application to decode the files.

When it comes to e-mail, you can choose from a wide variety of applications that will be used to read your mail. In fact, the list of clients is extensive, including command line clients, Windows-based clients, and Web-based clients. Figure 30-4 shows examples of several different clients.

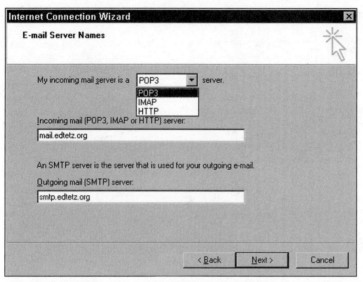

Figure 30-4: With so many available e-mail clients, you should be able to find one that suits you.

Three basic protocols are used with e-mail: POP3, SMTP, and IMAP. Figure 30-5 illustrates the fact that some e-mail clients may support more that one access protocol. SMTP and POP3 are the most commonly used protocols, although IMAP is increasing in popularity on private networks.

SMTP

The Simple Mail Transport Protocol (SMTP) is a mail delivery protocol. It is used to transfer mail messages from your mail client to a mail server. Once the mail message is in the queue on the server, SMTP is also used to transfer the message to the mail server that is responsible for the target domain, such as @mailtarget.loc. The primary goal of SMTP is to get the mail messages to the targeted server.

POP3

The Post Office Protocol Version 3 (POP3) is a client access protocol. POP3 is used to access or retrieve mail from a server. POP3 is not a protocol that is capable of sending mail – that's the responsibility of the SMTP protocol. When you configure your e-mail client, you will configure it with the pair of servers, POP3 for downloading or reading, and SMTP for sending. POP3 clients will usually download all mail messages for their server and delete the mail from the server. This action then leaves the mail only on the client computer.

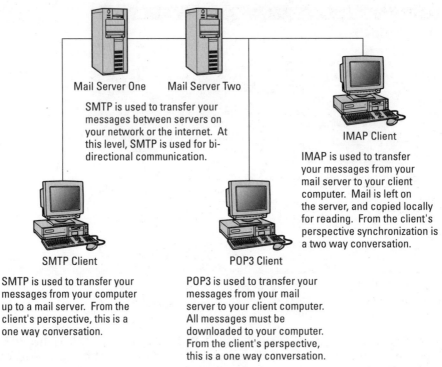

Figure 30-5: Where the mail protocols are used

The following text appears within the figure:

Mail Server One   Mail Server Two

SMTP is used to transfer your messages between servers on your network or the internet. At this level, SMTP is used for bi-directional communication.

IMAP Client

IMAP is used to transfer your messages from your mail server to your client computer. Mail is left on the server, and copied locally for reading. From the client's perspective synchronization is a two way conversation.

SMTP Client

POP3 Client

SMTP is used to transfer your messages from your computer up to a mail server. From the client's perspective, this is a one way conversation.

POP3 is used to transfer your messages from your mail server to your client computer. All messages must be downloaded to your computer. From the client's perspective, this is a one way conversation.

IMAP

The Internet Message Access Protocol (IMAP) is also a client access protocol for mail. IMAP clients retrieve a list of messages that exist on the mail server and download only messages that you want to read. Any messages that are downloaded are also left on the server. Changes to your mail files locally can also be replicated to the server. Since you can download all messages, you can work entirely offline. If you delete messages while working offline, those deletions will be replicated to the server the next time you connect, which will in turn delete the messages that are on the server.

In the Real World HTTP mail accounts like hotmail are also becoming increasingly popular. These accounts leave their mail messages on the server in a manner that is similar to IMAP. HTTP mail accounts usually require you to use less than 2MB of storage.

HyperText Transport Protocol

4.2 Identify concepts and capabilities relating to the Internet and basic procedures for setting up a system for Internet access. Content may include the following: Concepts and terminology — HTTP

In the early days of the Internet, you could transfer data between computers as files. After being uploaded to the server by the data owner, these files were available for download from those servers, which meant you had to know what files you needed and what servers they came from. Your text files, formatted documents, and graphics could be transferred between computers. Once you had downloaded the files, they could be opened and viewed, but there was no way to view them in an attractively formatted style in the online environment, especially a format that was viewable by anybody who wanted to see the files. Most formatted documents had been made so by using programs like Microsoft Word or Aldus Pagemaker, which are only readable by people that have those programs.

In order to address the problem of knowing which servers you were accessing data from, Paul Lindner and Mark McCahill from the University of Minnesota came up with an idea that became the Gopher protocol. Gopher allowed you to place a pointer on your server that would connect people to specific directories on other servers elsewhere on the Internet. This made browsing information that was scattered across servers very easy, since switching between servers became completely transparent. Gopher became the most popular tool for downloading files and data from the Internet.

At the same time Gopher was being developed, the researchers at CERN (European Organization for Nuclear Research) were working on a protocol called HTTP, which allowed for transparent linking between servers and offered something the Gopher lacked — the capability to view text and graphics mixed together in a single frame. This was capable in thanks to the Hypertext Markup Language (HTML). HTML was the component that allowed for the text and graphics to be blended together on a single page. Users of the Internet flocked to this new technology, which gave their data the same appearance as their paper-bound copies.

The tool used to access HTTP servers and HTML files is known as a Web browser. The job of the browser is to retrieve the files from the server, display the formatted document, and link to the other servers as required. Figure 30-6 shows a formatted document in a Web browser.

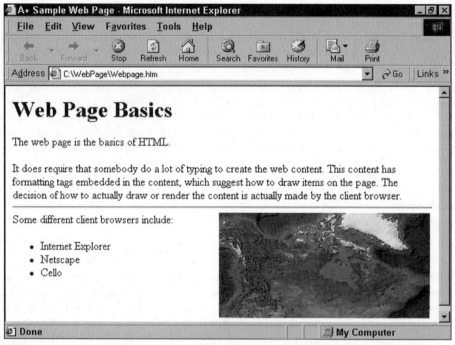

Figure 30-6: Web browsers enable you to retrieve data from a server using HTTP.

HyperText Markup Language

4.2 Identify concepts and capabilities relating to the Internet and basic procedures for setting up a system for Internet access. Content may include the following: Concepts and terminology — HTML

Hyper Text Markup Language (HTML) is a form of SGML (Standard Generalized Markup Language) that offers a universal way to format documents. HTML files themselves are text files, but they contain formatting codes that are embedded in the text. Most HTML files will be saved in the operating system with an extension of either .html or .htm (for MS-DOS 8.3 character compatibility). The Web, or HTML, page that was displayed in Figure 30-6 was generated with the following script:

```
<html>
<head><title>A+ Sample Web Page</title><head>
<body>
<h1>Web Page Basics</h1>
<p>The web page is the basics of HTML.</p>
It does require that somebody do a lot of typing to create the
web content. This content has formatting tags embedded in the
content, which suggest how to draw items on the page. The
decision of how to actually draw or render the content is
actually made by the client browser.
```

```
<br>
<img src="photo.gif" width="400" height="50">
<hr>
Some different client browsers include:
<ul>
<li>Internet Explorer
<li>Netscape
<li>Cello
</ul>
</body>
</html>
```

HTML has gone through many revisions (the current revision is four). New changes are being made to HTML that are referred to as XML (Extensible Markup Language). XML adds functionality to support database data exchange. XML is designed to not only transfer sections of data from a database, but also its structure. XML has become very popular and is the new Internet buzzword. XML has been rolled into the HTML standard, forming the new XHTML standard. For more information about XML, HTML, and XHTML standards, visit the Web site where the standards are kept at www.w3.org.

SGML

The standards for Standard Generalized Markup Language (SGML) make it a more complex language than HTML. SGML is actually a method of creating interchangeable structured documents, using data from a variety of sources like word processors and graphic applications, structure the document with Document Type Definitions (DTD), and show divisions with the aid of markup. HTML is actually just a DTD that plays a small part of SGML. With the simple initial requirements for formatting of documents, it was decided that keeping the formatting language simple was the best course of action for the Web, so HTML was adopted in favor of SGML, which was perceived to be overkill.

File Transfer Protocol

4.2 Identify concepts and capabilities relating to the Internet and basic procedures for setting up a system for Internet access. Content may include the following: Concepts and terminology — FTP

It was established early on during the evolution of the Internet that there would have to be some format to allow for the transfer of data (as opposed to text messages) across the Internet. The solution was File Transfer Protocol (FTP). FTP allows files to be uploaded and downloaded from servers. FTP requires a directory structure that is going to be shared, a server-side service or daemon, and a client. There are a large number of FTP clients to choose from, ranging from command line to graphical. Figure 30-7 shows some different clients that are available on the Windows platform.

Tip   A Windows 2000 or Windows NT 4.0 "service" is an application that runs without a user interface and without anybody being logged onto the computer. This background application provides functions to the local computer or to remote users. These functions include items such as: File and Printer Sharing, Messaging, and Web serving. Linux and Unix calls these background services "daemons".

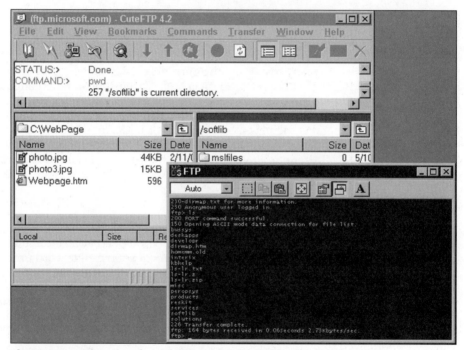

Figure 30-7: Choosing the right client for the job is important.

Other access methods

Table 30-1 summarizes some of the access methods for resources on the Internet that are available to you from time to time. These access methods can be specified from the command line, or from within a Web browser. A typical URL (Uniform Resource Locator) resembles the following:

```
http://www.edtetz.org/sample-files/default.htm
```

where `http:` represents the access method, `//www.edtetz.org` represents the name of the server that is being contacted, `/sample-files` represents the directories that are being navigated, and `/default.htm` represents the file that is being requested. All URLs follow the same basic structure, but if you leave out a part of it, like the document name, you will be given the default document for that directory or server.

Table 30-1
Access Methods

Access Method	Description
`http:`	http is used to access Web content on servers.
`ftp:`	ftp is used to copy files to or from remote servers.
`telnet:`	telnet is used to access remote terminal services with a remote server.
`gopher:`	gopher is a hyperlink protocol similar to http, but with less flexible display options.
`mailto:`	mailto activates the local e-mail client to send a message to the address specified in the server portion of the URL.
`news:`	news is used to access files on a NNTP (Network News Transport Protocol) server or USENET newsgroup.

Troubleshooting TCP/IP

Objective

4.2 Identify concepts and capabilities relating to the Internet and basic procedures for setting up a system for Internet access. Content may include the following: Concepts and terminology — Ping, Tracert, and Nslookup

Various utilities provided with the different operating systems enable you to troubleshoot problems with the TCP/IP protocol. This section will discuss some of these utilities, which include ping, tracert, netstat, and pathping and nslookup.

Exam Tip

`pathping.exe` is a new utility with Windows 2000 and has not made it onto Comptia's exam objectives. It will not be on the exam, but has been included here to provide more complete coverage of tools that may help you with troubleshooting the TCP/IP suite of protocols on your computer. `netstat.exe` is another utility that was not on the Comptia exam objectives, so will not be on the exam. It was also included here to complete the coverage of troubleshooting tools.

ping.exe

`ping.exe` is one of the basic utilities that is used to test network connectivity. It sends out packets of a set size and waits for them to be returned by the target computer. The default size for the packets is 32 bytes. The packets are sent to the target computer using the ICMP (Internet Control Message Protocol) echo request format. The receiving computer takes the 32 bytes of data and returns them to the original computer using an echo response packet. If the packet is not answered, you will be notified. As part of the information that is displayed for returned packets, you will see the time that was taken and a value called TTL (Time to Live). The TTL will let you know approximately how many routers had to handle the packet on the return. The TTL value starts its return trip at a preset value, usually 64, 128, or 255. Each router that handles the packet lowers the number by one, and the router will subtract an additional one for each second that it had to delay the response packet. A sample of the output of the ping statement follows.

```
ping.exe www.edtetz.org

Pinging www.edtetz.org [24.222.16.98] with 32 bytes of data:

Reply from 24.222.16.98: bytes=32 time=60ms TTL=249
Reply from 24.222.16.98: bytes=32 time=30ms TTL=249
Reply from 24.222.16.98: bytes=32 time=30ms TTL=249
Reply from 24.222.16.98: bytes=32 time=30ms TTL=249

Ping statistics for 24.222.16.98:
    Packets: Sent = 4, Received = 4, Lost = 0 (0% loss),
Approximate round trip times in milli-seconds:
    Minimum = 30ms, Maximum =  60ms, Average =  37ms
```

tracert.exe

`tracert.exe` (Trace Route) can be used to display the path that was taken by packets from your computer to a remote computer. The output of the command will show the time results of three pings to each router on the path. If possible, it will also resolve the names of the servers along the way. A sample of the output follows. The * represents "request timed out" packets.

```
tracert.exe www.edtetz.org

Tracing route to www.edtetz.org [24.222.16.98]
over a maximum of 30 hops:

  1    <10 ms    <10 ms    <10 ms   homegate.home.loc [192.168.1.254]
  2     20 ms     30 ms     31 ms   gw-23.accesscable.net [24.138.23.1]
  3     20 ms     30 ms     30 ms   cdr7-3.accesscable.net [24.138.7.3]
  4     20 ms       *         *     cdr7-153.accesscable.net [24.138.7.153]
  5     30 ms     20 ms     20 ms   cdr7-149.accesscable.net [24.138.7.149]
  6     30 ms     30 ms     50 ms   access-peer.andara.com [24.222.16.101]
  7     40 ms     30 ms     30 ms   www.edtetz.org [24.222.16.98]

Trace complete.
```

In the event that ping yields results that have slower than expected times, or a high number of "Request Timed Out" responses, `tracert.exe` can be used to isolate at exactly which location along the path the problem exists.

pathping.exe

`pathping.exe` is a new utility with the Windows 2000 operating system. It performs comprehensive testing and displays the number of packets that were lost by each router along the path to the target host. A sample of the results are provided here:

```
pathping www.etetz.org

Tracing route to www.edtetz.org [24.222.16.98]
over a maximum of 30 hops:

  0  SQL.nwtraders.msft [192.168.1.5]
  1  homegate.home.loc [192.168.1.254]
  2  gw-23.accesscable.net [24.138.23.1]
  3  cdr7-3.accesscable.net [24.138.7.3]
  4  cdr7-153.accesscable.net [24.138.7.153]
  5  cdr7-149.accesscable.net [24.138.7.149]
  6  access-peer.andara.com [24.222.16.101]
  7  www.edtetz.org [24.222.16.98]

Computing statistics for 175 seconds...

                 Source to Here   This Node/Link
Hop  RTT     Lost/Sent = Pct   Lost/Sent = Pct   Address
  0                                               SQL.nwtraders.msft [192.168.1.5]
                                 0/ 100 =  0%       |
  1   0ms    0/ 100 =  0%       0/ 100 =  0%     homegate.home.loc [192.168.1.254]
                                 0/ 100 =  0%       |
  2  21ms    0/ 100 =  0%       0/ 100 =  0%     gw-23.accesscable.net [24.138.23.1]
                                 0/ 100 =  0%       |
  3  27ms    0/ 100 =  0%       0/ 100 =  0%     cdr7-3.accescable.net [24.138.7.3]
                                 0/ 100 =  0%       |
  4  25ms    0/ 100 =  0%       0/ 100 =  0%     cdr7-153.accble.net [24.138.7.153]
                                 0/ 100 =  0%       |
  5  56ms    5/ 100 =  5%       5/ 100 =  5%     cdr7-149.accble.net [24.138.7.149]
                                 0/ 100 =  0%       |
  6  32ms    0/ 100 =  0%       0/ 100 =  0%     access.andara.com [24.222.16.101]
                                 0/ 100 =  0%       |
  7  38ms    0/ 100 =  0%       0/ 100 =  0%     www.edtetz.org [24.222.16.98]

Trace complete.
```

netstat.exe

netstat.exe, or network statistics, displays the list of connections that are made to or from your computer running Windows. It is useful for identifying the ports that are used by services, or problems with establishing connections. Typical output from the netstat.exe command would look like the following:

```
netstat -n

Active Connections

   Proto  Local Address          Foreign Address       State
   TCP    192.168.1.5:1142       192.168.1.2:139       TIME_WAIT
   TCP    192.168.1.5:1143       64.4.13.40:1863       ESTABLISHED
   TCP    192.168.1.5:1167       64.4.30.24:80         TIME_WAIT
   TCP    192.168.1.5:1168       207.46.188.251:80     ESTABLISHED
   TCP    192.168.1.5:1174       207.46.176.108:80     ESTABLISHED
   TCP    192.168.1.5:1184       64.4.30.24:80         TIME_WAIT
   TCP    192.168.1.5:1185       64.4.30.24:80         TIME_WAIT
```

nslookup.exe

nslookup.exe is short for Name Server Lookup and it is a Windows 2000 and Windows NT 4.0 DNS query utility and can be used for troubleshooting DNS related problems. It offers two user interfaces, command line or interactive. This section will examine three command line options and show you how to enter and exit the interactive mode.

Exam Tip   For the exam, be aware of what this tool is capable of doing, but do not expect to be given questions dealing with specific options or commands.

To enter interactive mode, open a command prompt window and type nslookup.exe. This will tell you the name and IP address of your primary DNS server and leave you at a meaningless > prompt. This is the server that will attempt to resolve your DNS queries. If you want to test DNS queries by using a different DNS server then type the following: server <server_name_or_IP_address>. To get a list of all of the commands that are available to you, type help or ?, and to exit the interactive mode type exit. Interactive mode is a convenient way to type in a series of DNS queries.

If you only have a single query for nslookup.exe, then you may find the command line options easier to use. If you have a DNS name and you would like to get a list of IP addresses that are assigned to it, then just type nslookup.exe <DNS_name>, like the following query for Hungry Minds:

```
C:\>nslookup www.hungryminds.com
Server:  mercury.accesscable.net
Address:  10.1.0.9
```

```
Non-authoritative answer:
Name:    hungryminds.com
Address: 168.215.86.100
Aliases: www.hungryminds.com
```

The results of this query let you see that there is one server — based on the single IP address — that acts as the Web server for Hungry Minds, but it will answer to the name `http://hungryminds.com` or the alias of `http://www.hungryminds.com`. This is different from the lookup for `www.msn.com`, which yields very different results:

```
C:\>nslookup www.msn.com
Server:  mercury.accesscable.net
Address: 10.1.0.9

Non-authoritative answer:
Name:    www.msn.com
Addresses:  207.46.185.140, 207.46.209.218, 207.46.209.243, 207.46.176.121
     207.46.179.143, 207.46.179.71, 207.46.185.138
```

The results for `www.msn.com` shows you that there are seven servers that answer to the name of `http://www.msn.com`, but they do not have an alias for the server. The servers allow them to load balance between servers using something called "DNS Round Robin" where the next address in the list is returned for each request. If you use `ping.exe` to successively ping the name `www.msn.com`, then you should get results in sequence from each of the IP addresses in the list.

Another major component to `nslookup.exe` is its ability to resolve the names of servers when you provide an IP address. This is useful when looking at things like Web server log files and you want to know who has been connecting to your server. Here is a command, looking for the name of the server at one of the IP addresses that you were given for the MSN Web server earlier.

```
C:\>nslookup 207.46.179.71
Server:  mercury.accesscable.net
Address: 10.1.0.9

Name:    msn.net
Address: 207.46.179.71
```

You should notice that the name that you got through this process tells you that the name of the server is actually msn.net — not www.msn.com like the name that started this resolution circle. You started with the name (`www.msn.com`), got the IP address (`207.46.179.71`), and went back to the official name (`msn.net`), which is different than the one we started with. Basically you should image two phone directories (one listing names and providing phone numbers and the other listing phone numbers and providing names). Now most people are listed in both books, but often one name was given in one directory and another is given in the other.

The last option you will see with `nslookup.exe` is actually passing `nslookup.exe` command line options. When displaying help (in interactive mode) you will see a large list of options. For this example you will attempt to find out the IP address of the server that will be receiving e-mail for Hungry Minds. This option is very useful when trying to find out why traffic may not be going through. The reason it may not be going through is it may be going to the wrong server. This type of DNS lookup is useful to find out where things are really going. In this case, you are looking for MX (Mail Exchange) records that are used to list SMTP servers in DNS, and this is specified with the `type` option in the following command:

```
C:\nslookup -type=MX hungryminds.com
Server:  mercury.accesscable.net
Address:  10.1.0.9

Non-authoritative answer:
hungryminds.com MX preference = 20, mail exchanger = ny-bridge.hungryminds.com
hungryminds.com MX preference = 20, mail exchanger = in-exchange.hungryminds.com

hungryminds.com      nameserver = NS2.hungryminds.com
hungryminds.com      nameserver = NS1.hungryminds.com
ny-bridge.hungryminds.com      internet address = 64.244.103.6
in-exchange.hungryminds.com    internet address = 168.215.86.23
NS2.hungryminds.com            internet address = 64.244.103.10
NS1.hungryminds.com            internet address = 168.215.86.10
```

The results of the command let you know that Hungry Minds has two SMTP servers (one in `ny` (New York) and one in `in` (Indianapolis). Both servers have the same preference (20), so mail could go to either server when you send it to `hungryminds.com`.

`nslookup.exe` serves its job as DNS lookup agent well, and proves to be a useful tool when attempting to resolve DNS name resolution problems.

Domain Names and Web Sites

4.2 Identify concepts and capabilities relating to the Internet and basic procedures for setting up a system for Internet access. Content may include the following: Concepts and terminology — Domain Names (Web sites)

Every computer on the Internet has a unique IP address. This address enables a computer to find and establish communication sessions with any other computer — as long as you know the IP address of the computer you want to connect to. Because every IP address is a 12-digit number (and most people do not remember hundreds of 12-digit numbers), the Domain Name System (DNS) was established in 1984. With this system, you can specify a name, and a DNS server will look up the required address for you.

Because each server would never be able to hold the names of all the computers that exist on the Internet, DNS servers split up the job. Each server is responsible for knowing only a small number of computers, but the servers know how to find other servers. Figure 30-8 illustrates how the DNS is structured. At the top of the structure is the root (.) domain, which knows about all of the servers that manage the top-level domains. Top-level domains include com (commercial), org (organization), mil (military), edu (education), gov (government), and net (network), as well as a two-letter domain for every country in the world, such as au (Australia), us (United States), ca (Canada), uk (United Kingdom), de (Germany), fi (Finland), and nz (New Zealand). The servers at the top level know about the servers that are responsible for the next level down, and so on.

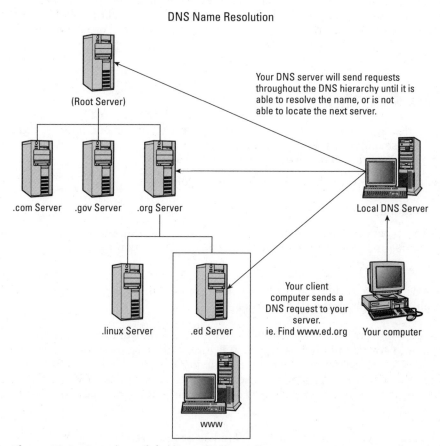

Figure 30-8: Overview of the Domain Name System

If you had to connect to a server such as `www.edtetz.org`, you would check against your local server to see if it knows the answer. Even if your server is not the owner of those records, it may have looked them up before and have them cached. If they are not cached on the local server, your server will forward the request to one of the root level servers, which will direct it to the com server, which will direct it to the edtetz server, which will then look up the www record.

This system enables you to find any computer on the Internet, as long as it has a name that was registered in DNS. Many people register their servers by the type of service that they offer, such as `ftp.edtetz.org`, `smtp.edtetz.org`, `pop3.edtetz.org`, or `mail.edtetz.org`. HTTP allows you to place links on any server to any other server on the Internet, which allows you to have a very complex path configured to lead people through the Internet. This path is web-like, and as such, the interconnection of HTTP servers is referred to as the World Wide Web (`www`). `www` is the standard name that is given to the HTTP or Web servers on the Internet.

Dial-Up Access

4.2 Identify concepts and capabilities relating to the Internet and basic procedures for setting up a system for Internet access. Content may include the following: Concepts and terminology – Dial-up networking

To get connected to the Internet, you need the following:

+ A computer
+ A connection to a network through a network interface card or modem. The connection can be direct (such as a cable or ADSL connection) or dial-up
+ The TCP/IP protocol
+ A service provider that enables you to connect to their network, which is already connected to the Internet

If you are connecting through a dial-up connection, you will have to install a modem into your computer, as shown in Figure 30-9. 56 Kbps is a standard connection speed for getting your connection to the Internet. You can install a modem through the modem control panel. The standard dialing and hardware configuration should be fine, if not, you will have to contact your ISP to set up the proper dialing configuration.

Once installed, your modem will be treated as a slow network card. You will also require the TCP/IP protocol for network access, as shown in Figure 30-10. TCP is installed through the Network control panel. Select Add ➪ Protocol ➪ Microsoft ➪ TCP/IP. The network card (modem) and TCP/IP are the only components that are required, and the Microsoft network client is optional.

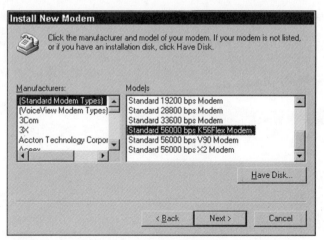

Figure 30-9: Configuring your modem

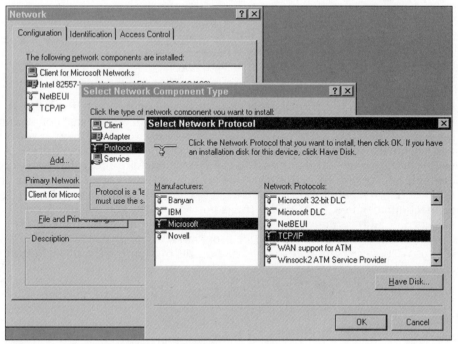

Figure 30-10: Adding the TCP/IP protocol

Now that the infrastructure is in place, you will also need to create a connection document to connect to your ISP. This is done through the Dial-up Networking program that is found in My Computer. Choose Make New Connection to launch the Wizard, and provide a name, dialing device, and phone number for the connection. Figure 30-11 shows the information that is required for your connection to an ISP.

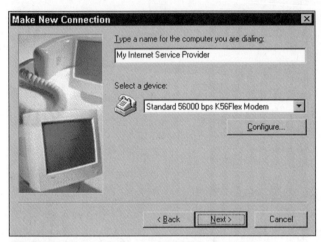

Figure 30-11: Adding a new dial-in connection

Figure 30-12 shows the normal network settings for connection to the Internet. These settings are found in the Properties of the Dial-Up Networking connection on the Server Types tab. Usually to authenticate your user credentials with your ISP, you will have to authenticate using clear text passwords. Clear text passwords are enabled clearing the checkbox next to the setting "Require encrypted password." The only network protocol that you have to support is TCP/IP, so you will be able to deselect IPX/SPX and NetBEUI. If you need to change IP Address settings for the connection, then use the TCP/IP Settings button. Usually you will use Server Assigned IP Address and Server Assigned Name Server Addresses to accept dynamic IP addressing. If your service provider does not provide the addresses of DNS or WINS servers, or if you would like to specify your own, you will be able to specify them here.

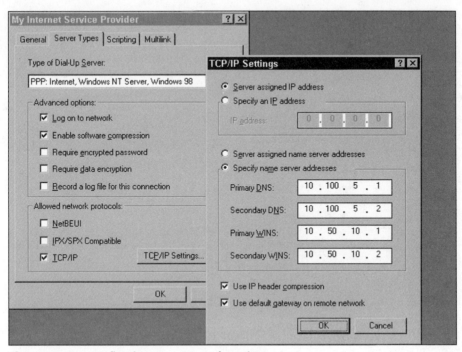

Figure 30-12: Configuring your network settings

To establish your connection to the Internet, you will need to dial the connection and authenticate your username and password. This will also get your assigned IP address and IP configuration from your ISP. To verify this configuration, you can use `ipconfig.exe /all` from a command prompt on your Windows 2000 or Windows NT 4.0 computer, or `winipcfg.exe` on your computer running Windows 9x. Figure 30-13 shows a typical IP configuration, including the IP address and DNS addresses through `winipcfg.exe`.

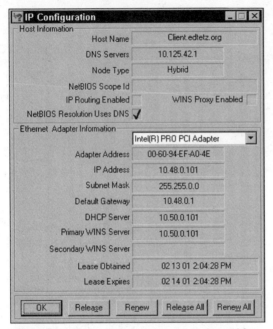

Figure 30-13: Verifying your connection with winipcfg.exe

Other Ways to Access the Internet

In addition to dial-up connections, there are many other types of connections that can be made to the Internet, some of which may be available in your area from local Internet providers. Some of these are used for home connections, and others are used for connecting LANs to the Internet. These methods include:

✦ Cable

✦ ADSL

✦ ISDN

✦ T1/T3

Cable

Cable connections implement a cable modem in your house that takes a digital network signal from your network card and translates it into an analog broadband signal. This signal is then passed onto the cable network. Cable companies usually offer transmission speeds of about 4 Mbps to their customers, while actual speeds may vary.

ADSL

The Asynchronous Digital Subscriber Line (ADSL) implementation looks similar to that of cable, except the device that you will have in your home will take the digital signal from your network card and pass it on to a digital phone line that is in your house. ADSL companies usually offer transmission speeds of about 4 Mbps to their customers, while actual speeds may vary. Although cable offers the same transmission speeds going to and from the Internet, ADSL only uploads to the Internet at a speed of 64 Kbps (in most cases).

ISDN

The Integrated Services Digital Network (ISDN) service comes in two basic forms: basic rate and primary rate. Basic rate ISDN uses three channels; two 64 Kbps lines for data, and one 16 Kbps line as a control channel. The data channels are referred to as B channels, and the control channel is referred to as a D channel. Primary rate ISDN uses twenty-three 64 Kbps B channels and one 64 Kbps D channel.

T1/T3

T1 connections offer transmission speeds of 1.544 Mbps over 24 pairs of wires. Each pair of wires can carry a 64 Kbps signal called a channel. T1 connections can be implemented over copper wire.

T3 connections, on the other hand, require a better medium than copper, such as microwave or fiber optic. They are capable of speeds ranging from 6 Mbps to 45 Mbps.

T1 and T3 standards are North American, while E1 and E3 are similar standards for the European community.

Key Point Summary

This chapter provided a brief history of the Internet and identified Internic as its managing body. Other concepts that were covered include:

✦ The mechanics of getting connected to an ISP

✦ The TCP/IP protocol, as well as some of the protocols that make up TCP/IP, such as FTP and SMTP

✦ POP3, SMTP, and IMAP

✦ HyperText Markup Language files, and how to browse them using a Web browser

✦ Tools used to test your Internet connection and different ways you can access the Internet

✦　　✦　　✦

STUDY GUIDE

This Study Guide presents 20 assessment questions to test your knowledge of the exam topic area.

Assessment Questions

1. What is the name of the governing body of the Internet?

   A. W3.org

   B. DodNet

   C. IAB

   D. IABnet

2. What is the networking protocol used by the Internet?

   A. TCP/IP

   B. IPX/SPX

   C. Banyan/Vines IP

   D. HTTP

3. What does the acronym ISP stand for?

   A. Internet Security Porthole

   B. Individually Serviced Person

   C. Internet Solution Provider

   D. Internet Service Provider

4. What does the acronym ASP stand for? (Choose all that apply.)

   A. Active Server Pages

   B. Action System Performance

   C. Additives for System Providers

   D. Application Service Provider

5. The TCP/IP networking protocol is composed of how many subprotocols?

    A. 2

    B. 5

    C. 10

    D. Many, too numerous to list

6. TCP/IP shares many similarities to what other protocol?

    A. IPX/SPX

    B. NetBEUI

    C. Streams

    D. Banyan Vines

7. What purpose does MIME serve?

    A. It is used as an encryption method on e-mails.

    B. It encodes binary data into ASCII data so that it may be sent through e-mail.

    C. It is used to convert HTML data into an e-mail format.

    D. It is entertaining.

8. What protocol is used to send e-mail?

    A. POP3

    B. SNTP

    C. IMAIL

    D. SMTP

9. What protocols are used to read e-mail? (Choose two.)

    A. IMAL

    B. POP3

    C. IMAP

    D. PPP

10. What does the acronym HTML stand for?

    A. Hardcore Traversing Marking Language

    B. Hyperlinked Text Marking Language

    C. Hip Totally Modern Living

    D. Hypertext Markup Language

11. What does the acronym FTP stand for?

     A. Folder Transport Protocol

     B. File Transport Protocol

     C. File Transfer Protocol

     D. Folder Traversing Protocol

12. What is the first part of an Internet URL (`http://`) called?

     A. Pointer

     B. Access method

     C. Control source

     D. Activation header

13. What utility is used to test basic connectivity to the Internet?

     A. Ping

     B. Poke

     C. Grepper

     D. Pong

14. What utility will show you your IP address configuration?

     A. ipcfg.exe

     B. showip.exe

     C. ifconfig.exe

     D. winipcfg.exe

15. What utility is used to show the path of routers that you have to pass through to get to a remote computer?

     A. showpath.exe

     B. routehops.exe

     C. tracert.exe

     D. routers.exe

16. What utility will show a list of current connections made between your computer and remote computers?

     A. ping.exe

     B. netstat.exe

     C. tracert.exe

     D. whatsup.exe

17. What system converts names you type in URLs to IP addresses?

    A. Dual Naming Standards

    B. Name Resolution Servers

    C. Name Recognition System

    D. Domain Name System

18. Which of the following are types of connections that you can use to get to the Internet? (Choose all that apply.)

    A. HSINet

    B. Cable

    C. Digital Phone Link

    D. ISDN

    E. Wire

    F. T1

    G. Subscriber lines

19. What does the acronym POP stand for?

    A. Post Office Protocol

    B. Private Outside Postal Service

    C. Portable Office Protocol

    D. Peoples Office Protocol

20. HTML files are what type of files?

    A. Text/ASCII

    B. Run Length Encoded

    C. Binary

    D. Hyperlinked

Answers to Chapter Questions

Chapter Pre-Test

1. **TCP/IP** is the core protocol used by the Internet.

2. **Hyper Text Markup Language** is what **HTML** represents.

3. **Ping** can test the speed of your connection to another computer over a TCP/IP-based network.

4. **POP3** is the protocol that is used to retrieve and read your e-mail. SMTP is used only for sending new mail to your mail server.

5. Every computer on the Internet requires a unique **IP address**.

Assessment Questions

1. **C.** Internet Architecture Board (IAB) is the managing body of the Internet. For more information, see the section titled "The Internet."

2. **A.** TCP/IP is the networking protocol that is used. For more information, see the section titled "Protocols."

3. **D.** Internet Service Provider is the correct answer. For more information, see the section titled "The Internet."

4. **A, D.** The acronym ASP is usually short for Active Server Pages, but the term Application Service Provider is becoming very popular. For more information, see the section titled "The Internet."

5. **D.** Some of the subprotocols that make up TCP/IP include SMTP, POP3, SNMP, FTP, TFTP, and 500 to 1,000 other protocols. For more information, see the section titled "Protocols."

6. **A.** TCP/IP and IPX/SPX share many similarities with each other. For more information, see the section titled "Protocols."

7. **B.** MIME (Multipurpose Internet Mail Extensions) is used to convert binary files into something that can traverse the text-only e-mail system. For more information, see the section titled "Protocols."

8. **D.** SMTP is used to send mail messages over the Internet. For more information, see the section titled "Protocols."

9. **B, C.** POP3 and IMAP are used to read mail that is on a mail server. For more information, see the section titled "Protocols."

10. **D.** The acronym HTML stands for Hypertext Markup Language. For more information, see the section titled "Protocols."

11. **C.** The acronym FTP stands for File Transfer Protocol. For more information, see the section titled "Protocols."

12. **B.** The first part of a URL represents the access method that is being used to connect to the server. For more information, see the section titled "Protocols."

13. **A.** Ping is used to test basic network or Internet connectivity. For more information, see the section titled "Troubleshooting TCP/IP."

14. **D.** Winipcfg is used to see your TCP/IP configuration, including your IP address. For more information, see the section titled "Troubleshooting TCP/IP."

15. **C.** Trace Route (`tracrt.exe`) is used to show the path the data takes to a remote computer. The path is identified the IP addresses or names of the routers that forward your data. For more information, see the section titled "Troubleshooting TCP/IP."

16. **B.** Network Statistics (`netstat.exe`)will show you what computers you have open connections with. For more information, see the section titled "Troubleshooting TCP/IP."

17. **D.** Domain Name System resolves requested names into IP addresses to allow you to make a connection to the named computer. For more information, see the section titled "Domain Names and Web Sites."

18. **B, D, F.** Cable, ISDN, and T1 are methods of connecting to the Internet. For more information, see the section titled "Other Ways to Access the Internet."

19. **A.** The acronym POP stands for Post Office Protocol. For more information, see the section titled "Protocols."

20. **A.** HTML files are text or ASCII files. For more information, see the section titled "Protocols."

What's on the CD-ROM

This *A+ Certification Bible* contains a CD-ROM with several useful features to help you study for the A+ Certification exams. The CD-ROM will run under any Windows operating system (95 and above). The following sections give you a brief overview of the CD-ROM's contents.

CD-ROM Contents

The CD-ROM that accompanies this book provides the following to enhance your preparation for the A+ Certification exam:

✦ Adobe Acrobat Reader

✦ An electronic version of this book, *A+ Certification Bible,* in PDF format

✦ A custom-designed exam-simulation test engine

✦ A+ Test Bundle from Self Test Software

✦ Prep! for A+ 2000 from Dali Design

✦ A+ Certify Exam 8.0 from Super Software

✦ Lab files in a self-extracting executable file and expanded version

Installing and Using the Software

This section will cover how to install the software that is on the accompanying CD-ROM. The software that has been provided on the CD-ROM includes Adobe Acrobat Reader and an exam test engine to provide sample exams. The first piece of software you will look at is Adobe Acrobat Reader.

To install the items from the CD to your hard drive, follow these steps:

1. Insert the CD into your computer's CD-ROM drive.

2. A window appears with the following options: Install, Explore, and Exit.

   - **Install:** Installs the test engine and gives you the option to install the software supplied on the CD-ROM.

   - **Explore:** Allows you to bypass the interface and view the contents of the CD-ROM.

   - **Exit:** Closes the AutoRun window.

If you do not have AutoRun enabled, or if the AutoRun screen doesn't appear, follow these steps to access the CD:

1. Click Start ⇨ Run.

2. In the dialog box that appears, type `d:\setup.exe`, where *d* is the letter of your CD-ROM drive. This brings up the menu screen described above.

3. Choose the option from the menu: Install, Explore, or Exit. (See Step 2 that precedes this set of steps for a description of these options.)

Adobe Acrobat Reader

Adobe Acrobat Reader has been included on the CD-ROM to enable you to read this book in its electronic form. Acrobat Reader can be installed through the main software installation screen on the CD-ROM.

Custom-designed exam test engine

Included on the CD-ROM is a testing engine. This is a program that resembles the testing engine that will be used by the testing center where you will be taking your exam. The goal of the testing engine is to make you comfortable with the testing interface so that taking your exam will not be the first time you see that style of exam.

The questions that will be used in the testing engine will cover all aspects of the exam, will be similar to the assessment questions that you will see in each chapter of this book, and will be similar to the questions that will be on your exam.

Since the A+ Certification exams will be released as standard and then changed to adaptive (scheduled for the 3rd quarter of 2001), the test engine on the accompanying CD-ROM can be configured to provide exams in the standard or adaptive formats.

A+ Test Bundle from Self Test Software

Make sure when you go to Self Test's Web site (www.selftest.co.uk) that you use the co.uk on the end of the URL. The com URL will take you to another company with a completely different type of self-test. Self Test Software practice tests are very good, and the test software simulates the test very well.

Prep! for A+ 2000 from Dali Design

Jeff Thorssell and the Dali Design team have consistently produced the very best practice tests available for the money. Typically, the Prep! tests are the first available and are usually right on target regarding what you need to study for the exams. Check out these tests at www.dalidesign.com/prepap/.

A+ Certify Exam 8.0 from Super Software

The Super Software (www.aplusexam.com) people produce some of the best practice exams available. Their reasonably priced CD-ROM contains sample tests (usually more than one), specific to each domain of the exam objectives, and tips and cram notes for the actual test.

Lab files

Many of the chapters in this book provide lab exercises that enable you to get hands-on experience dealing with the concepts covered in the various chapters. Some of these lab exercises require you to access files from the accompanying CD-ROM. The lab files are provided on the CD-ROM in a self-extracting archive in the `Labfiles` folder on the CD-ROM. The lab exercises that use lab files will expect the contents of the `Labfiles` folder to be copied to `c:\labfiles`. You can copy them by hand, or extract the files from `labfiles.exe`. The lab files for this book consist of only two files `newdesk.bmp` and `profiledesk.bmp`.

✦   ✦   ✦

Objective Mapping Table

In this appendix, you'll find two tables listing the exam objectives for the A+ Hardware and A+ Technologies certification exams. Each table is an exhaustive cross-reference chart that links every exam objective to the corresponding materials in this book where the subject matter is covered.

The tables you'll find in this appendix are the following:

◆ Table B-1: Exam 220-201
◆ Table B-2: Exam 220-202

Table B-1
A+ Core Hardware Exam (220-201)

Exam Topic	Related Chapter

Domain 1.0 Installation, Configuration, and Upgrading

1.1 Identify basic terms, concepts, and functions of system modules, including how each module should work during normal operation and during the boot process.

Examples of concepts and modules are: 1

- System board
- Power supply
- Processor/CPU
- Memory
- Storage devices
- Monitor
- Modem
- Firmware
- BIOS
- CMOS
- LCD (portable systems)
- Ports
- PDA (Personal Digital Assistant)

1.2 Identify basic procedures for adding and removing field replaceable modules for both desktop and portable systems.

Examples of modules: 11, 13

- System board
- Storage device
- Power supply
- Processor/CPU
- Memory
- Input devices
- Hard drive
- Keyboard
- Video board
- Mouse
- Network Interface Card (NIC)

Exam Topic	Related Chapter
Portable system components:	11, 13

- AC adapter
- Digital Camera
- DC controller
- LCD panel
- PC Card
- Pointing Devices

1.3 Identify available IRQs, DMAs, and I/O addresses and procedures for device installation and configuration.

Content may include the following: 8

- Standard IRQ settings
- Modems
- Floppy drive controllers
- Hard drive controllers
- USB ports
- Infrared ports
- Hexadecimal/Addresses

1.4 Identify common peripheral ports, associated cabling, and their connectors.

Content may include the following: 6

- Cable types
- Cable orientation
- Serial versus parallel
- Pin connections

Examples of types of connectors:

- DB-9
- DB-25
- RJ-11
- RJ-45
- BNC
- PS2/MINI-DIN
- USB
- IEEE 1394

Continued

Table B-1 *(continued)*

Exam Topic	Related Chapter
1.5 Identify proper procedures for installing and configuring IDE/EIDE devices.	
Content may include the following:	9

- Master/Slave
- Devices per channel
- Primary/Secondary

1.6 Identify proper procedures for installing and configuring SCSI devices.	
Content may include the following:	9

- Address/Termination conflicts
- Cabling
- Types (example: regular, wide, ultra-wide)
- Internal versus external
- Expansion slots (EISA, ISA, PCI)
- Jumper block settings (binary equivalents)

1.7 Identify proper procedures for installing and configuring peripheral devices.	
Content may include the following:	10

- Monitor/Video Card
- Modem
- USB peripherals and hubs
- IEEE 1284
- IEEE 1394
- External storage

Portables

- Docking stations
- PC cards
- Port replicators
- Infrared devices

1.8 Identify hardware methods of upgrading system performance, procedures for replacing basic subsystem components, unique components and when to use them.	
Content may include the following:	11, 13

- Memory
- Hard Drives

Exam Topic	*Related Chapter*
• CPU	
• Upgrading BIOS	
• When to upgrade BIOS	
Portable Systems	
• Battery	
• Hard Drive	
• Types I, II, III cards	
• Memory	

Domain 2.0 Diagnosing and Troubleshooting

2.1 Identify common symptoms and problems associated with each module and how to troubleshoot and isolate the problems.

Content may include the following: 15

- Processor/Memory symptoms
- Mouse
- Floppy drive
- Parallel ports
- Hard Drives
- CD-ROM
- DVD
- Sound Card/Audio
- Monitor/Video
- Motherboards
- Modems
- BIOS
- USB
- NIC
- CMOS
- Power supply
- Slot covers
- POST audible/visual error codes
- Troubleshooting tools, e.g., multimeter

Continued

Table B-1 *(continued)*

Exam Topic	Related Chapter

- Large LBA, LBA
- Cables
- Keyboard
- Peripherals

2.2 Identify basic troubleshooting procedures and how to elicit problem symptoms from customers.

Content may include the following: 15

- Troubleshooting/isolation/problem determination procedures
- Determine whether hardware or software problem
- Gather information from user regarding:
  - Customer Environment
  - Symptoms/Error Codes
  - Situation when the problem occurred

Domain 3.0 Preventive Maintenance

3.1 Identify the purpose of various types of preventive maintenance products and procedures and when to use them.

Content may include the following: 12

- Liquid cleaning compounds
- Types of materials to clean contacts and connections
- Non-static vacuums (chassis, power supplies, fans)

3.2 Identify issues, procedures and devices for protection within the computing environment, including people, hardware and the surrounding workspace.

Content may include the following: 12

- UPS (Uninterruptible Power Supply) and suppressors
- Determining the signs of power issues
- Proper methods of storage of components for future use

Potential hazards and proper safety procedures relating Lasers:

- High-voltage equipment
- Power supply
- CRT

Exam Topic	*Related Chapter*

Special disposal procedures that comply with environmental guidelines:

- Batteries
- CRTs
- Toner kits/cartridges
- Chemical solvents and cans
- MSDS (Material Safety Data Sheet)

ESD (Electrostatic Discharge) precautions and procedures:

- What ESD can do, how it may be apparent, or hidden
- Common ESD protection devices
- Situations that could present a danger or hazard

Domain 4.0 Motherboard/Processors/Memory

4.1 Distinguish between the popular CPU chips in terms of their basic characteristics.

Content may include the following: 2

- Popular CPU chips (Intel, AMD, Cyrix)
- Characteristics
- Physical size
- Voltage
- Speeds
- On board cache or not
- Sockets
- SEC (Single Edge Contact)

4.2 Identify the categories of RAM (Random Access Memory) terminology, their locations, and physical characteristics.

Content may include the following: 4

Terminology:

- EDO RAM (Extended Data Output RAM)
- DRAM (Dynamic Random Access Memory)
- SRAM (Static RAM)
- RIMM (Rambus Inline Memory Module 184 Pin)
- VRAM (Video RAM)
- SDRAM (Synchronous Dynamic RAM)
- WRAM (Windows Accelerator Card RAM)

Continued

Table B-1 *(continued)*

Exam Topic	*Related Chapter*
Locations and physical characteristics:	

- Memory bank
- Memory chips (8-bit, 16-bit, and 32-bit)
- SIMMS (Single In-line Memory Module)
- DIMMS (Dual In-line Memory Module)
- Parity chips versus non-parity chips

4.3 Identify the most popular type of motherboards, their components, and their architecture (bus structures and power supplies).

Content may include the following: 3

Types of motherboards:

- AT (Full and Baby)
- ATX

Components:

- Communication ports
- SIMM and DIMM
- Processor sockets
- External cache memory (Level 2)
- Bus Architecture
- ISA
- PCI
- AGP
- USB (Universal Serial Bus)
- VESA local bus (VL-Bus)
- Basic compatibility guidelines
- IDE (ATA, ATAPI, ULTRA-DMA, EIDE)
- SCSI (Wide, Fast, Ultra, LVD (Low Voltage Differential))

4.4 Identify the purpose of CMOS (Complementary Metal-Oxide Semiconductor), what it contains and how to change its basic parameters.

Example Basic CMOS Settings: 5

- Printer parallel port — uni-directional, bi-directional, disable/enable, ECP, EPP
- COM/serial port — memory address, interrupt request, disable

Exam Topic	Related Chapter

- Floppy drive — enable/disable drive or boot, speed, density
- Hard drive — size and drive type
- Memory — parity, non-parity
- Boot sequence
- Date/Time
- Passwords
- Plug and Play BIOS

Domain 5.0 Printers

5.1 Identify basic concepts, printer operations and printer components.

Content may include the following: 7

Paper feeder mechanisms

Types of Printers:

- Laser
- Inkjet
- Dot matrix

Types of printer connections and configurations:

- Parallel
- Network
- USB
- Infrared
- Serial

5.2 Identify care and service techniques and common problems with primary printer types.

Content may include the following: 14

- Feed and output
- Errors (printed or displayed)
- Paper jam
- Print quality
- Safety precautions
- Preventive maintenance

Continued

Table B-1 *(continued)*

Exam Topic	Related Chapter

Domain 6.0 Basic Networking

6.1 Identify basic networking concepts, including how a network works and the ramifications of repairs on the network.

Content may include the following: 28

- Installing and configuring network cards
- Network access
- Full-duplex, half-duplex
- Cabling — Twisted Pair, Coaxial, Fiber Optic, RS-232
- Ways to network a PC
- Physical Network topographies
- Increasing bandwidth
- Loss of data
- Network slowdown
- Infrared
- Hardware protocols

Table B-2
A+ OS Technologies Exam (220-202)

Exam Topic	Related Chapter

Domain 1.0 Operating System Fundamentals

1.1 Identify the operating system's functions, structure, and major system files to navigate the operating system and how to get to needed technical information.

Content may include the following: 16, 17, 18

- Major operating system functions
- Create folders
- Checking OS version
- Major operating system components
- Explorer
- My Computer
- Control Panel

Exam Topic	*Related Chapter*

- Contrasts between Windows 9x and Windows 2000
- Major system files: what they are, where they are located, how they are used and what they contain

System, Configuration, and User Interface files

- IO.SYS
- BOOT.INI
- WIN.COM
- MSDOS.SYS
- AUTOEXEC.BAT
- CONFIG.SYS
- COMMAND LINE PROMPT

Memory management

- Conventional
- Extended/upper memory
- High memory
- Virtual memory
- HIMEM.SYS
- EMM386.exe

Windows 9x

- IO.SYS
- WIN.INI
- USER.DAT
- SYSEDIT
- SYSTEM.INI
- SETVER.EXE
- SMARTDRV.EXE
- MSCONFIG (98)
- COMMAND.COM
- DOSSTART.BAT
- REGEDIT.EXE
- SYSTEM.DAT
- RUN COMMAND
- DriveSpace

Continued

Table B-2 *(continued)*	
Exam Topic	*Related Chapter*
Windows 2000	
• Computer Management	
• BOOT.INI	
• REGEDT32	
• REGEDIT	
• RUN CMD	
• NTLDR	
• NTDETECT.COM	
• NTBOOTDD.SYS	
Command Prompt Procedures (Command syntax)	
• DIR	
• ATTRIB	
• VER	
• MEM	
• SCANDISK	
• DEFRAG	
• EDIT	
• XCOPY	
• COPY	
• FORMAT	
• FDISK	
• MSCDEX	
• SETVER	
• SCANREG	

1.2 Identify basic concepts and procedures for creating, viewing and managing files, directories and disks. This includes procedures for changing file attributes and the ramifications of those changes (for example, security issues).

Content may include the following:

- File attributes — Read Only, Hidden, System, and Archive attributes
- File naming conventions (most common extensions)
- Windows 2000 COMPRESS, ENCRYPT

Exam Topic	Related Chapter
• IDE/SCSI	
• Internal/External	
• Backup/Restore	
• Partitioning/Formatting/File System	
• FAT	
• FAT16	
• FAT32	
• NTFS4	
• NTFS5	
• HPFS	
• Windows-based utilities	
• ScanDisk	
• Device Manager	
• System Manager	
• Computer Manager	
• MSCONFIG.EXE	
• REGEDIT.EXE (View information/Backup registry)	
• REGEDT32.EXE	
• ATTRIB.EXE	
• EXTRACT.EXE	
• DEFRAG.EXE	
• EDIT.COM	
• FDISK.EXE	
• SYSEDIT.EXE	
• SCANREG	
• WSCRIPT.EXE	
• HWINFO.EXE	
• ASD.EXE (Automatic Skip Driver)	
• Cvt1.EXE (Drive Converter FAT16 to FAT32)	19, 20, 27

Continued

Table B-2 *(continued)*	
Exam Topic	*Related Chapter*

Domain 2.0 Installation, Configuration and Upgrading

2.1 Identify the procedures for installing Windows 9x, and Windows 2000 for bringing the software to a basic operational level.

Content may include the following: 21

- Start Up
- Partition
- Format drive
- Loading drivers
- Run appropriate set up utility

2.2 Identify steps to perform an operating system upgrade.

Content may include the following: 21

- Upgrading Windows 95 to Windows 98
- Upgrading from Windows NT Workstation 4.0 to Windows 2000
- Replacing Windows 9x with Windows 2000
- Dual boot Windows 9x/Windows NT 4.0/2000

2.3 Identify the basic system boot sequences and boot methods, including the steps to create an emergency boot disk with utilities installed for Windows 9x, Windows NT, and Windows 2000.

Content may include the following: 22

- Startup disk
- Safe mode
- MS-DOS mode
- NTLDR (NT Loader), BOOT.INI
- Files required to boot
- Creating emergency repair disk (ERD)

2.4 Identify procedures for loading/adding and configuring application device drivers, and the necessary software for certain devices.

Content may include the following: 23, 24

- Windows 9x Plug and Play and Windows 2000
- Identify the procedures for installing and launching typical Windows and non-Windows applications. (Note: There is no content related to Windows 3.1.)

Exam Topic	*Related Chapter*
• Procedures for setup and configuring Windows printing subsystem	
• Setting Default printer	
• Installing/Spool setting	
• Network printing (with help of LAN admin)	

Domain 3.0 Diagnosing and Troubleshooting

3.1 Recognize and interpret the meaning of common error codes and startup messages from the boot sequence, and identify steps to correct the problems.

Content may include the following: 25

- • Safe mode
- • No operating system found
- • Error in CONFIG.SYS line XX
- • Bad or missing COMMAND.COM
- • HIMEM.SYS not loaded
- • Missing or corrupt HIMEM.SYS
- • SCSI
- • Swap file
- • NT boot issues
- • Dr. Watson
- • Failure to start GUI
- • Windows Protection Error
- • Event Viewer — Event log is full
- • A device referenced in SYSTEM.INI, WIN.INI, Registry is not found

3.2 Recognize common problems and determine how to resolve them.

Content may include the following: 26, 27

- • Eliciting problem symptoms from customers
- • Having customers reproduce errors as part of the diagnostic process
- • Identifying recent changes to the computer environment from the user
- • Troubleshooting Windows-specific printing problems
- • Print spool is stalled
- • Incorrect/Incompatible driver for print
- • Incorrect parameter

Continued

Table B-2 *(continued)*	
Exam Topic	*Related Chapter*

- Other common problems
- General Protection Faults
- Illegal operation
- Invalid working directory
- System lock up
- Option (Sound card, modem, input device) or will not function
- Application will not start or load
- Cannot log on to network (option – NIC not functioning)
- TSR (Terminate Stay Resident) programs and virus
- Applications don't install
- Network connection
- Viruses and virus types
- What they are
- Sources (floppy, e-mails, and so on)
- How to determine presence

Domain 4.0 Networks

4.1 Identify the networking capabilities of Windows, including procedures for connecting to the network.

Content may include the following: 29

- Protocols
- IPCONFIG.EXE
- WINIPCFG.EXE
- Sharing disk drives
- Sharing print and file services
- Network type and network card
- Installing and configuring browsers
- Configure OS for network connection

Exam Topic	*Related Chapter*
4.2 Identify concepts and capabilities relating to the Internet, and basic procedures for setting up a system for Internet access.	
Content may include the following:	30

Concepts and terminology:

- ISP
- TCP/IP
- IPX/SPX
- NetBEUI
- E-mail
- PING.EXE
- HTML
- HTTP://
- FTP
- Domain Names (Web sites)
- Dial-up networking
- TRACERT.EXE
- NSLOOKUP.EXE

✦   ✦   ✦

Sample Exams

The practice exams in this Appendix will test your knowledge using exams similar to the real ones. Use these exams after you finish your studies to see where your weak areas are.

Exam A

1. How many EIDE drives can be in a computer at one time?

    A. 2

    B. 4

    C. 6

    D. 8

    E. 16

2. A technician wants to install a sound card into a PC. The sound card is not plug-and-play–compliant. What two settings will the technician need to configure?

    A. MIDI

    B. IRQ

    C. IP address

    D. MAC address

    E. I/O address

3. What is an IRQ?

    A. A number assigned to a device so the operating system can identify it

    B. A number assigned to every device so the devices can communicate with one another

    C. A number representing a device that is failing

    D. A number assigned to a device that represent the device when the device requires attention from the motherboard

4. What is cache?

    A. Memory that is not erasable

    B. Faster memory that holds recently used images

    C. Faster memory that holds recently used code

    D. Slower memory that holds the BIOS

5. What is a MAC address used for?

    A. It is the same as an IP address.

    B. It identifies the NIC to the processor.

    C. It is the true identity of the network node.

    D. It represents the protocols used on the particular network card.

    E. It represents the operating system used by the PC.

6. How many USB devices can be daisy chained?

    A. 127

    B. 63

    C. 31

    D. 15

    E. 4

7. Which of the following devices can input OCR?

    A. Sound card

    B. Network card

    C. Scanner

    D. Digital camera

    E. DVD

8. A parity error is most likely related to_____.

    A. Hard drives

    B. Network cards

    C. Controller cards

    D. Memory chips

    E. Processor failures

9. A technician powers on a computer but there is no beep at startup. What is the most likely problem?

   A. Power supply is bad

   B. Floppy drive is bad

   C. Controller card is bad

   D. System board failure

   E. There is no problem; no beep should happen at startup

10. A terminator does what in a SCSI chain?

   A. Allows each device to have a unique ID

   B. Allows each device to have its own channel

   C. Allows each device to speak independently of the other devices

   D. Allows the signal to stay on the SCSI bus

11. Low humidity can generate ideal situations for _____.

   A. Power failures

   B. Electrostatic discharge

   C. Chip creep

   D. Crosstalk

   E. Electromagnetic interference

12. What component should probably be replaced rather than serviced?

   A. Monitor

   B. Network card

   C. Hard drive

   D. SCSI card

   E. Speaker

13. What component allows data to be written and appended to the disk?

   A. DVD

   B. CD

   C. CDR

   D. CDRW

14. A technician is configuring a mouse for a left-handed user. How will the technician configure this mouse?

    A. Simply place the mouse on the left side of the keyboard

    B. Reverse the mouse clicks in the System BIOS

    C. Reverse the mouse clicks in the Device Manager

    D. Reverse the mouse clicks in the Mouse applet within Control Panel

    E. A left-handed mouse must be purchased.

15. The best way to clean a keyboard is to _____.

    A. Use a small amount of isopropyl alcohol and clean each key a with a cotton swab

    B. Disassemble the keyboard and wash it with window cleaner

    C. Submerge the keyboard in water and allow it to dry overnight

    D. Use a small amount of isopropyl alcohol to clean each key with a cotton swab, then clean the crevices with compressed air

    E. Use warm soapy water and dry the keyboard completely with a hair dryer

16. A technician should store spare computer parts in _____.

    A. A cardboard box

    B. An airtight container

    C. An anti-static bag

    D. A central box with all other spare parts

17. A technician is upgrading a motherboard. What is the first step the technician must take when replacing the motherboard?

    A. Remove the expansion cards

    B. Remove the processor

    C. Remove the power supply

    D. Remove the power cord

    E. Remove the hard drives

18. What is a ZIF?

    A. A tool used to test DRAM

    B. A tool used to test voltage

    C. A tool built onto the motherboard that helps a technician add or remove a processor

    D. A tool built onto the motherboard that helps a technician add or remove a power supply

19. A technician is upgrading DRAM in a PC. The sockets for the DRAM are gold. The memory connectors should be _____.

   A. Tin

   B. Gold

   C. Doesn't matter

   D. Silver

20. What is required to install a printer in Windows 98?

   A. A parallel port

   B. A print driver

   C. A physical printing device

   D. Permissions

21. What component within a printer charges the paper so that the toner will be attracted to the printing area?

   A. Laser

   B. Print drum

   C. Transfer corona wire

   D. Fuser

   E. Feed rollers

22. What type of connection does CAT5 UTP cable use?

   A. RJ-11

   B. RJ-24

   C. RJ-45

   D. RJ-AU

23. If an entire network goes down, a technician should first check _____.

   A. The power at the server

   B. The functionality of the router

   C. The cable to the server

   D. The power at the hub

   E. Each cable to the hub

24. What is significant about token ring networks?

    A. No hub is required.

    B. There is an unlimited number of clients per ring.

    C. Each client speaks only when the token is passed to them.

    D. A client passes its messages through a token.

    E. The network isn't really a ring, but a square.

25. Plenum-grade cable is used in drop ceiling because _____.

    A. Standard cable contains PVC

    B. UTP cables are more prone to EMI

    C. Plenums cause attenuation

    D. UTP cables are prone to ESD

Exam A Answers

1. B. EIDE (Enhanced Integrated Drive Electronics) allows up to four drives in a computer at one time. IDE allows only two drives. For more drives, a technology such as SCSI must be implemented. Chapter 9.

2. B, E. A legacy sound card requires its resources to be set manually. This includes the IRQ, the I/O address, the DMA, and most likely the MIDI port address. Chapter 8.

3. D. An IRQ (interrupt request) is a number assigned to a device. The number represents the device that needs attention by the processor. Chapter 8.

4. C. Cache is typically a very fast memory that contains recently accessed code for applications. This memory can be a reserved part of memory or its own separate unit. Chapter 1.

5. C. A MAC address, or Media Access Control address, is the true identity of the network node. The manufacturer of the network card sets the MAC address. No two network cards are supposed to have the same MAC address. Chapter 29.

6. A. 127 USB devices can be connected together, in theory. The true amount depends on the specific devices being connected. Some devices will require more or less bandwidth than others, so the actual number may vary. Chapter 10.

7. C. Scanners can input OCR, or Optical Character Recognition. The scanner can be physically connected to the PC in any number of different ways. Chapter 10.

8. D. A parity error typically refers to a memory chip that has gone bad. To repair the problem, the memory needs to be replaced. The bad memory can be found by replacing the memory one DIMM at a time until the error goes away. Chapters 11, 13.

9. A. When a computer powers on, the system will beep and — depending on the BIOS of the computer — the beeps will reveal any dangers the system may be having. No beeps can mean that the power supply is bad and no power is reaching the motherboard. The lack of startup beeps could also be as simple as confirming that power is available and connected to the PC. Chapter 25.

10. D. A SCSI chain is terminated so that the signal will end down the SCSI chain. This allows the PC to communicate with each device by sending a signal through the SCSI chain for a device with a specific SCSI ID. Chapter 9.

11. B. ESD, or Electrostatic Discharge, occurs more often in low humidity environments, such as the winter months. ESD, a small spark, can damage computer peripherals, but can be avoided with the use of an ESD wrist wrap. Chapter 12.

12. A. Monitors contain large amounts of power in their capacitors, even when they are unplugged. This voltage can harm or even kill a technician. Unless the technician is certified in monitor repair, it's best to simply replace the unit. Chapter 12.

13. D. CDRW allows data to be written to the disk and added later. CDs and DVDs do not allow data to be written to the disk after the disk has been created. The CDR allows the data to be written once, but it is read-only thereafter. Sometimes the CDR is called a WORM — Write Once, Read Many. Chapter 10.

14. D. A mouse can be configured for left- or right-handed users through the Mouse applet within Control Panel. A left-handed mouse or mouse pad is not required. Chapter 15.

15. D. The best, and easiest, method to clean a keyboard is to use a small amount of isopropyl alcohol and a cotton swab. The crevices between the keys can be cleaned with compressed air. Older, mechanical keyboards could allegedly be submerged in water or even cleaned in the dishwasher — newer keyboards shouldn't be subjected to such abuse. Chapter 12.

16. C. Anti-static bags, which are used to ship computer parts, are the best storage method. While it is a good idea to keep all parts centrally located, the parts should be kept in an anti-static bag and sealed to keep out any dust. Chapter 12.

17. D. When doing any work on a PC, a technician must remember the "safety first" rule. The technician should always power off the PC and remove the power cord. Chapter 3.

18. C. A ZIF, or Zero Insertion Force, is a tool that acts as a lever to seat or remove a processor from the motherboard. Chapters 3, 9.

19. B. When adding memory to a PC, the sockets and the DRAM should be made of the same type of metal. The mixture of metals — gold and tin — can cause a chemical reaction on the surface of the memory chip and cause a failure in the connection between the DRAM and the connectors. Chapter 13.

20. B. To install a printer in Windows 98, all that is required is the print driver. A parallel port is not required, because the printer could be on the network. A physical printing device does not have to be present at the time of the install, as the device can be added later. Finally, permissions to install a printer are required in Windows 2000, but not Windows 98. Chapter 7.

21. C. The transfer corona wire charges the paper with a positive charge. The toner on the print drum has been charged with a negative charge. The toner is then attracted to the positive paper in the shape of the images being printed. As the paper moves through the printer, it passes over the static eliminator strip, which removes the charges from the paper and toner. This step prevents the paper from being attracted to the print drum and thus jamming in the printer. Chapter 7.

22. C. CAT5, or Category 5, uses the RJ-45 connector. UTP, or Unshielded Twisted Pair, is one of the most common cable types used in LANs today. Chapter 28.

23. D. If a hub loses power, the entire network will stop functioning. Chapter 28.

24. C. A token ring network is a network in a logical ring. Each client speaks only when the token is passed to it. Each client has an equal amount of time to speak on the network. Chapter 28.

25. A. Plenum-grade cable does not contain PVC, or Polyvinyl Chloride. The PVC can emit poisonous fumes in the event of a fire. Chapter 28.

Exam B

1. What type of security level does Windows 98 use? (Choose two)

    A. File level

    B. User level

    C. Share level

    D. Directory level

    E. NT Domains

2. A technician has deleted a shortcut on the desktop. Is the application also removed?

    A. Yes

    B. No

3. A user reports that his colors and settings do not follow him as he logs onto other computers throughout the network. The user requires a
_____.

   A. Local profile

   B. Hardware profile

   C. Roaming profile

   D. System policy

   E. Identical monitor and adapter on each machine the user logs onto

4. A technician wants to configure a laptop to only load network card drivers when the laptop is being used on the network. What must be configured?

   A. Local profile

   B. Hardware profile

   C. Roaming profile

   D. System policy

5. A system policy controls a user's _____.

   A. Access to files

   B. Access to printers

   C. Logon hours

   D. Activities on the system

6. Where can users change their passwords in Windows 2000? (Choose two)

   A. Security dialog box

   B. Users and Passwords applet in Control Panel

   C. Server Manager

   D. Passwords applet in Control Panel

7. In Windows 98, what is a WOW?

   A. An environment that controls processes

   B. An environment that allows access to the processor

   C. An environment that simulates a DOS machine

   D. An environment that simulates a 16-bit operating system

8. What does Dr. Watson do?

   A. Checks for viruses

   B. Updates operating systems

   C. Scans the disk for errors

   D. Collects information about application faults

   E. Controls virtual memory

9. What is the minimum processor required for a Windows 98 installation?

   A. 486DX/66

   B. Pentium 100

   C. Pentium 133

   D. Pentium 233

   E. Pentium 733

10. What operating systems allow an upgrade to Windows 98? (Choose three)

   A. Windows 95

   B. Windows 3.1

   C. Windows NT 3.51

   D. Windows for Workgroup 3.1.1

   E. OS/2

11. A technician is dual-booting between Windows 98 and Windows NT 4.0. What file system must be used?

   A. NTFS

   B. FAT32

   C. FAT16

   D. HPFS

   E. CDFS

12. What are two advantages of the FAT32 file system for Windows 98?

   A. FAT32 supports partitions up to 2GB.

   B. FAT32 supports partitions up to 2TB.

   C. FAT32 uses a larger cluster size.

   D. FAT32 uses a smaller cluster size.

   E. FAT32 allows for file-level security.

13. What is the minimum requirement for a processor when installing Windows 2000?

    A. 486DX/66

    B. Pentium 100

    C. Pentium 133

    D. Pentium 166

    E. Pentium 200

14. What file system allows security to the file level?

    A. CDFS

    B. HPFS

    C. FAT16

    D. FAT32

    E. NTFS

15. How many concurrent network connections can a Windows 2000 Professional have?

    A. 10

    B. 20

    C. 30

    D. 50

    E. Depends on the access licenses

16. What is per server licensing in Windows 2000 Server?

    A. This licensing plan requires that every connecting user has a connection license.

    B. This licensing plan requires that every connecting PC has a connection license.

    C. This licensing plan allows a pre-determined amount of concurrent connections to the specified server.

    D. This licensing plan allows a pre-determined amount of concurrent connections on all Windows 2000 Servers.

17. What file builds the OS selection menu during the boot phase of Windows 2000?

    A. OSLOADER

    B. OSKRNL

    C. Boot.ini

    D. NTLDR

    E. Pagefile.sys

18. What TCP/IP utility can trace the route a packet takes from host to host?

    A. PING

    B. Tracert

    C. Route

    D. Routetrace

    E. Tracer

19. What address is the loopback host?

    A. 127.0.0.0

    B. 127.0.0.1

    C. 192.168.127.1

    D. 255.255.255.255

    E. 255.0.0.1

20. What elements are required for a Windows 98 client to pass packets from the local subnet to a remote network?

    A. NetBEUI

    B. A subnet mask

    C. An IP address of the router

    D. Network permissions

    E. SAP

21. When combining shared permissions with NTFS permissions, what security method will be enforced when accessing the resource on the network?

    A. The share permission only

    B. The NTFS permission only

    C. The more restrictive of the two

    D. The less restrictive of the two

22. Windows 98 allows for how many concurrent connections?

    A. 10

    B. 20

    C. 30

    D. 40

    E. An unlimited number

23. What level of security must be used in Windows 98 when Novell Netware is the security provider?

    A. Share-level security

    B. User-level security

    C. Client32 permissions

    D. It doesn't matter

24. What are two weaknesses of share-level security?

    A. Windows 2000 Server is required.

    B. Novell Netware is required.

    C. Passwords can be compromised.

    D. Shares and passwords can become cumbersome.

    E. Passwords are limited to six characters.

25. What protocol is not routable?

    A. TCP/IP

    B. IPX/SPX

    C. NetBEUI

    D. UDP

Exam B Answers

    1. B, C. Windows 98 uses share-level and user-level security to secure access to resources. Share-level requires users on the network to enter a password to access each resource on a Windows 98 computer. User-level requires the user attempting to access a resource to have been validated by a security provider, such as Windows NT Server or Novell Netware Server. Chapter 28.

    2. B. No, a shortcut simply points to the application it refers to. A shortcut can refer to an application, printer, location, or files. Chapters 16, 17, 18.

3. C. A roaming profile is a server-based profile. Each time the user logs onto a computer, the profile is downloaded to the local machine. When the user logs off the PC, any changes to the profile are saved back onto the server. Chapter 16.

4. B. A hardware profile is a configuration of the system's hardware for each environment the laptop is being booted in. When starting the PC, the user would be prompted to choose a profile matching the environment he or she is working in. A technician can use whatever names are appropriate for the profiles. Chapters 16, 17, 18.

5. D. A system policy controls a user's activities on a system. Access to files and printers are controlled through permissions, not policies. Chapters 16, 17, 18.

6. A, B. Users can change their passwords through the Security dialog box and through the Users and Passwords applet in Control Panel. Chapters 16, 17, 18.

7. D. WOW stands for Windows on Windows. It is an environment within Windows 98 that simulates the Windows 3.x operating system. It is used to allow 16-bit applications to interact with 98's 32-bit environment. Chapters 16, 17, 18.

8. D. Dr. Watson is a utility used to evaluate information it collects from an application failure. Dr. Watson must be running in order to collect the information. If an application consistently fails during a task, open Dr. Watson and then test the application. Chapter 25.

9. A. Windows 98 only requires a 486DX/66 to install. However, a Pentium class processor is highly recommended. Chapter 21.

10. A, B, D. Windows 98 allows an upgrade from Windows 3.1, Windows for Workgroups 3.1.1, and Windows 95. An upgrade is not allowed from OS/2 or Windows NT 3.51. A technician would need to format the drives with FAT and then complete a new install from NT or OS/2. Chapter 21.

11. C. Windows 98 and Windows NT 4.0 can be installed on the same computer, but require a common file system—FAT16. NTFS can only be accessed through NT or Windows 2000. Windows 2000 can, however, access FAT32 partitions. Chapter 21.

12. B, D. FAT32 is a very robust file system. It allows for partitions up to 2TB. This is an important feature, since drive sizes are commonly beyond 2GB, the limit of FAT16. In addition, FAT32 uses a smaller cluster size. The smaller cluster size allows for a more efficient use of drive space. Chapters 19, 20, 27.

13. C. Windows 2000 hardware requirements are more stringent than those of Windows 98. A Pentium 133Mhz or higher is required at a minimum—a higher speed processor is more desirable, however. Chapter 21.

14. E. NTFS allows for security to the file level. File-level security allows a technician to set differing levels of security for files within the same directory. For example, a file called Sales can be assigned the read permission, while the file called Commission can have No Access permissions. Chapters 19, 20, 27.

15. A. Windows 2000 Professional allows up to 10 concurrent connections. For shares that require more than 10 connections, a Windows 2000 server is required. Chapter 16, 17, 18.

16. C. When installing Windows 2000 Server, a technician must consider the licensing type for the server. The per server licensing mode requires a pre-determined amount of concurrent connections. The per seat licensing requires that each connection to the server has its own license. Chapter 21.

17. C. The boot.ini contains the path to each operating system installed on a Windows 2000 computer. When the PC is powered on, the NTLDR loads the mini-file systems and then loads the boot.ini. The user then selects the operating system to load from the OS Loader menu. Chapter 22.

18. B. Tracert is the command used to trace the route that packets take from host to host. The command is useful when troubleshooting unusual connection times from local to remote hosts. It will display all routers the packets are passed through to the destination. Chapter 30.

19. B. The special address 127.0.0.1 is used for loopback testing of the local host. Chapter 30.

20. C. A Windows 98 client must be configured with the IP address of the gateway (also known as the router) to pass packets from the local network to the remote network. Chapter 30.

21. C. When combining NTFS permissions and share permissions, the more restrictive permission is the effective permission. Chapter 29.

22. E. Windows 98 is not limited to the number of concurrent connections. Although it may seem advantageous to use Windows 98 as a file server, it does lack the robust security and file sharing mechanisms that Windows 2000 Server offers. Chapter 29.

23. B. When using Novell Netware as the security provider, the Windows 98 machine must use user-level security. Share-level security allows for password-protected shares, while user-level security requires users to be authenticated by a security provider to access the shares. Chapter 29.

24. C, D. Share-level security is a very weak security system. Passwords can be guessed, lost, shared, or stolen, which in turn can allow unauthorized users access to resources and create other types of problems. If a user creates several shares on a Windows 98 computer, then there are several passwords to remember and share with the appropriate users. Chapter 29.

25. C. NetBEUI, or the Net Basic End User Interface protocol, is not a routable protocol. It is ideal for small networks that are not connecting to any remote networks, including the Internet. Chapter 30.

✦　　✦　　✦

Exam-Taking Tips

Exams are stressful events for most people, but if you are well prepared, you can face the challenge with the knowledge that you did your best. If you read and understood the material in this book, you should have no problem with the exam. The review questions, sample exams, and exam test engine on the companion CD were all designed to make you well prepared.

Hopefully, this appendix will remove some of that normal "fear of the unknown" you may be experiencing by giving you information about the actual test-taking process; it will also tell you how to develop good test-taking skills.

The Exam

CompTIA uses a scale score to determine the total number of points that the exam is calculated out of. This scale score is between 100 and 900. The passing score (not a percentage due to the scale score) is 683, or 76 percent, for the A+ Core Hardware Exam and 614, or 68 percent, for the A+ OS Technologies Exam. The scale score system allows the number of points assigned to questions to vary between each copy of the exam, which makes it harder for test candidates to compare scores across exams.

The revised exams for A+ were released January 31, 2001. Each exam contains 70 questions, and you have 90 minutes to complete each exam. In the third quarter of 2001, the exams will be made adaptive. Adaptive exams are described in the "Taking the Exam" section of this appendix.

Arrival

Get to the exam location early on the day of the exam. You should arrive at least 15 minutes early from the time of your exam. This will keep you from being rushed and will accommodate any delays.

Take a few minutes to get accustomed to the testing center and to get a drink and use the restroom if you need to.

Now relax. Getting to the exam site early gives you this privilege — just don't arrive so early that you are stewing and making yourself nervous.

If you are prepared and ready, you may want to see if you can start the test early.

Taking the Exam

The exam consists of multiple-choice questions. Read the entire question and try to decide what the answer should be before looking at the answer choices. Follow this method:

1. First, discard choices that are obviously wrong. There should be at least one choice that can be eliminated — perhaps two. Now the odds of choosing the right answer are 50 percent, rather than 25 percent.

2. If you don't have a clue which of the remaining choices is correct, choose C. Statistically speaking, C is the most popular answer, since it is buried in the middle of the choices.

3. Once you have made your choice, leave it. Unless you have information that proves your choice is wrong, your first instinct is usually correct.

If you are taking the adaptive exam, answer every question before proceeding to the next. You are not able to review and change your answers on the adaptive exams. The adaptive exam will deliver a series of questions to you. If you answer a question wrong, you will get additional questions in that category. There are a maximum number of questions that will be asked. Once you exceed the number of wrong answers that would allow you to pass, the exam will end and you will fail.

If you get all of the initial category questions correct, you can pass the exam in relatively few questions, but if you get an initial category question wrong, in a category in which you are weak, then you will find the adaptive format very difficult. You will not know exactly how many questions you have to answer until the exam tells you that it is complete.

If you are taking the non-adaptive exam, you are allowed to mark questions and come back to them later. However, it is good to select an answer for every question even if you are unsure, as you may run out of time before you can do your review. Remember that your first choice is usually correct — refrain from changing your first choice unless you have complete confidence in what you are doing.

Regardless of which type of exam you are taking (adaptive or non-adaptive), you will be given a Pass/Fail mark right on the spot.

Good luck!

✦   ✦   ✦

Glossary

80286 A 16-bit processor released by Intel in 1982.

80386 See *80386DX*.

80386DX A 32-bit processor released by Intel in 1985.

80386SX A 16-bit processor released by Intel in 1988. This processor is a cut-price 80386DX to help lower the cost of computers.

80387 The math coprocessor chip for an 80386 processor.

80486DX A processor designed by Intel that was released in 1989. The 80486DX was a 32-bit processor that included a built-in math coprocessor.

80486SX A cut-price processor designed by Intel that was released in 1991. The 80486SX was a 32-bit processor with the built-in math coprocessor disabled.

80487 The math coprocessor chip that could be added to a system to work with an 80486SX processor.

8086 A 16-bit processor designed by Intel in 1978.

8087 The math coprocessor chip for an 8086 or an 8088.

8088 An 8-bit processor designed by Intel in 1979.

A+ Certification A vendor neutral certification program put out by CompTIA, which is designed for IT professionals wanting to learn how to install, configure, and troubleshoot both hardware and operating system components.

AC (Alternating Current) Electrical current that reverses its direction based on a frequency measured in Hertz.

Acknowledge (ACK) A type of signal used by the receiver of information to send verification back to the sender that the receiver has received the data.

Add New Hardware A wizard used in Windows 95, Windows 98, and Windows 2000 to install a new device in the system.

Add/Remove Programs A wizard used in Windows 95, Windows 98, and Windows 2000 to install and remove applications in the operating system.

Advanced Technology (AT) The term AT is applied to any computer that uses an 80286 processor or above.

Alternating Current (AC) See *AC*.

ALU An acronym standing for Arithmetic Logic Unit, which is the part of the processor that takes care of mathematical and logic functions.

AMD K6 A processor designed by AMD to compete with Intel's Pentium Pro chip.

Analog A type of signal that has a range of values or frequencies. Examples of analog data are speech and music.

Anode A positively charged terminal that attracts electrons.

ANSI An acronym for American National Standards Institute, which is an institute that has developed and supported communication standards.

Application A program, such as a word processor or spreadsheet, that performs a specific function.

Arithmetic Logic Unit (ALU) See *ALU*.

ASCII An acronym for American Standard Code for Information Exchange, which is a 7-bit or 8-bit coding scheme that represents each letter of the alphabet, numbers, and punctuation.

ASPI An acronym that stands for Advanced SCSI Programming Interface; a specification developed by Adaptec to send commands to SCSI host adapters.

Asynchronous A communication method where data is sent one byte at a time using start and stop bits for data validation.

AT See *Advanced Technology*.

ATA An acronym that stands for Advanced Technology Attachment, which is also known as Integrated Drive Electronics (IDE); a common disk interface used by computers.

ATX A motherboard form factor popular with newer systems.

Autoexec.bat A special file used primarily on DOS systems that would control the startup environment. This file is still supported by the Windows operating system but is de-emphasized.

Band Printer A printer that uses a band to print data onto paper. This printer is typically used in high-volume environments.

Binary A number system based on the power of two. Digits based on the binary numbering system are limited in value to either one or zero.

BIOS Acronym for Basic Input Output System; the low-level instructions controlling how components in the computer communicate.

BIT An acronym for Binary Digit; a piece of information that has a value of either one or zero.

Boot The process of powering on the computer and having the operating system load.

Buffer An area of memory that is used to temporarily store information. Typically used in cases where there is an adapter that needs to process incoming information; when the information reaches the adapter, it is stored in the buffer until it can be processed.

Bus A collection of hardware lines that are used to carry information from one location to another.

Bus Controller A device that manages the flow of information on the bus system.

Bus Mastering A technology that allows devices in the bus to communicate directly with one another instead of going through the processor.

Byte Eight bits of information, which is a combination of eight ones and zeros. A byte is a piece of information that is equivalent to one character in size — for example, the letter A.

Cache High-speed memory that is used to store frequently used data.

Capacitor An electrical component that stores a small electrical charge.

Card A general term for any adapter or circuit board that is inserted into the computer. A card comes in different flavors, such as a network card, sound card, or video card.

Case The covering on the computer.

Cathode Ray Tube Also referred to as a *CRT*. The primary component that is used in a monitor to produce the display image.

CDFS An acronym for CD File System; the file system used in Windows operating systems by the CD-ROM.

CD-R An acronym for CD-ROM Recordable, which allows information to be written to the CD once.

CD-ROM An acronym for Compact Disk Read-Only Memory; CD-ROMs are read-only storage devices that use laser optic technology.

CD-RW A type of CD-ROM that can be written to and erased many times by using a CD-RW recording device.

CPU An acronym that stands for Central Processing Unit; the CPU performs all of the mathematical and logic functions for the computer and is considered the brain of the computer.

CGA An acronym for Color Graphics Adapter; An early color standard that displayed up to 80 columns of information and 25 lines of information.

CMOS An acronym that stands for Complementary Metal-Oxide Semiconductor; it stores all of the computer's configuration information, such as the size of the hard disk and the amount of memory installed. This information is stored in memory that is charged by a small battery so the information is not lost.

CMOS Setup A program that enables you to enter CMOS and change its configuration.

Coaxial Cable Also known as Coax. A type of cabling used in either 10Base2 networks or 10Base 5 networks. It transmits data at 10 Mbps and has a maximum distance of 185m or 500m.

COM1 An acronym for Communication Port 1, which is the serial port on the system that uses IRQ 4. Serial ports transmit data one bit at a time and are usually used for communication devices such as modems or mice.

COM2 An acronym for Communication Port 2, which is the serial port on the system that uses IRQ 3. Serial ports transmit data one bit at a time and are usually used for communication devices such as modems or mice.

Config.sys A configuration file that was used to load memory managers and device drivers in the DOS and Windows environment.

Control Panel A tool found in Windows where you can go to configure most characteristics of the system. In Control Panel, you can add/remove hardware, add/remove programs, configure date and time, configure your display settings, and so on.

Conventional Memory The first 640K of memory.

Corona Wire A device used in laser printers to generate electrostatic charges.

CPU See *Central Processing Unit.*

CRT See *Cathode Ray Tube*.

Cylinder The same track on all platters. (Many people use the terms "track" and "cylinder" interchangeably.)

Daisy Wheel A print element that has a central hub with print type bars attached to it. Each print type bar has a character at the end of it.

Daisy Wheel Printer A printer that uses the daisy wheel to print. Each bar on the daisy wheel prints a separate character. This printer is considered an impact type printer because a separate impact is needed to print each character.

DB-9 A standard 9-pin connector used for serial communication.

DB-25 A standard 25-pin connector used for serial communication.

Defragmentation or Defrag The process of joining all parts of one file together. When files are moved, copied, deleted and created on the hard disk, they end up spread out in different areas on the drive, slowing overall performance of the system.

Desktop The initial screen in Windows. The desktop is where My Computer and the Recycle Bin are located.

Device A computer component, such as a network card, sound card, or modem. The device usually comes in the form of a circuit board card and gets placed in an empty expansion slot.

Device Driver The software portion of the device that enables the operating system to communicate with the device.

Device Manager A utility in Windows that enables the configuration of devices once they have been installed.

DIMM An acronym for Dual Inline Memory Module; a two-sided edge connector card of memory chips that sends information in 64-bit chunks, typically used in Pentium systems. This memory package has 168 pins.

DIN Connector A type of connector used to connect mice and keyboards to computers.

Direct Memory Access (DMA) A channel given to a device that allows it to read and write to memory directly without going through the processor.

Disk The primary device for storage on systems today. The disk, or hard disk, is the place where the operating system and applications are permanently stored and then loaded into memory when activated.

Disk Controller The component that is responsible for sending and receiving signals to and from the disk. For example, the disk controller receives a signal from the processor and then converts it to an instruction that the hard disk can understand.

Display A term that refers to the visual output of the computer.

DMA See *Direct Memory Access*.

DOS An acronym for Disk Operating System. DOS is a command-based operating system in which the user types commands to communicate with the computer. The Windows operating system has replaced the DOS operating system.

Dot-Matrix Printer A printer that produces characters by using a wire-pin print head.

Dot Pitch The distance between the dots in a dot-matrix printer, which measures the clarity of the image. Generally, the smaller the number, the better the quality of the output.

DRAM See *Dynamic RAM*.

Driver A software component that is responsible for allowing the operating system to communicate with the device that is associated with the driver. The driver is responsible for allowing the device to work with the operating system.

Duplex Duplex technology enables a device to communicate in both directions, meaning that it can both send and receive information. If the device is able to send and receive information at the same time, it is said to be a *full duplex* device; if it can communicate in only one direction at one time, it is said to be *half-duplexed*.

DVD Acronym for Digital Versatile Disk, a type of optical disk technology that allows for storage of around 5GB of information to a device that looks like a CD-ROM.

Dynamic RAM Memory that needs constant refreshing from its supporting circuitry. Dynamic RAM (also known as DRAM) is the most common type of memory in computers today.

ECP See *Extended Capabilities Port*.

EDO RAM See *Extended Data Output RAM*.

EEPROM Acronym for Electronic Erasable Programmable Read-Only Memory; a type of read-only memory that can be updated by using electronic signals.

EGA See *Enhanced Graphics Adapter*.

EISA See *Extended Industry Standard Architecture*.

Extended Capabilities Port A parallel port mode that allows devices attached to the port to transfer information at 2 Mbps and support bi-directional devices.

Extended Data Output RAM A type of DRAM memory that can read memory from one memory block while preparing for the next block of memory to be read.

Extended Industry Standard Architecture Also known as EISA; a bus architecture that extends on the original ISA bus architecture while maintaining compatibility. The EISA architecture is a 32-bit technology that runs at 8 MHz.

Electrostatic Discharge Also known as ESD; the transfer of static electricity that has been built up on a person. The static electric discharge can cause permanent damage to computer components.

Emergency Recovery Disk Also known as an ERD; a floppy disk or CD-ROM that is used to recover the system in the event of data loss or any hardware failure.

EMM386 A file used in the DOS operating system to emulate expanded memory.

Enhanced Graphics Adapter A video display adapter with color support and resolution of 640×400.

Enhanced Parallel Port A parallel port mode that supports bi-directional devices and daisy chaining of the devices.

EPP See *Enhanced Parallel Port*.

EPROM See *Erasable Read-Only Memory*.

Erasable Read-Only Memory A type of read only memory that allows for reprogramming of the information stored in memory after manufacturing.

ERD See *Emergency Recovery Disk*.

ESD See *Electrostatic Discharge*.

Expanded Memory A type of memory typically used by DOS applications. A memory manager manages access to this area of memory and organizes it by pages.

Expansion Board A circuit board or card that is added to the system by being plugged into the expansion slots. Expansion boards usually increase the computer's capabilities by adding sound or network support.

Extended Memory All memory above 1MB.

FAT See *File Allocation Table*.

Fiber Optics A technology that allows transmission rates of up to 1 GHz of data by means of pulses of light across glass core cabling.

File Allocation Table A table used by the operating system to manage information about the disk, such as which clusters are free and which are bad.

File System The structure in which files are stored on a disk, then accessed by the operating system.

Flash Memory A type of ROM that can be rewritten by using an electrical device.

Floppy Disk A small storage area used to carry information from one location to another. The typical size of a floppy diskette is 1.44MB.

Floppy Disk Controller The device that manages the signals going to and from the floppy disk drive.

Formatting Preparing a disk for use by creating the root directory and building the FAT table.

Full Duplex A type of communication that allows a device to both send and receive information at the same time.

GDI See *Graphical Device Interface*.

General Protection Fault Also known as a GPF. In Windows, a computer crash that is caused when a program attempts to access memory outside of its own address space.

Gigabyte One billion bytes, or 1,000 megabytes.

GPF See *General Protection Fault*.

Graphical Device Interface The portion of the operating system that is responsible for screen updates. The file that manages the graphics display in Windows is GDI.EXE.

Graphical User Interface An environment that uses dialog boxes, icons, and other visual features to communicate with the user of the computer. Windows 98 is an example of a graphical user interface.

GUI See *Graphical User Interface*.

Half Duplex A type of communication that allows a device to both send and receive information, but not at the same time.

Hard Disk Drive Also known as a hard disk, or disk; the primary storage device in computers today. The operating system and applications are stored on the hard disk and loaded into memory when they are initialized.

HDD See *Hard Disk Drive*.

Head Also known as the read/write head; the mechanism that performs the read/write operations on a disk.

Heat Sink A cooling device for processors. Keeping a component cool provides for a longer lifetime of the component.

Hub A central device used to connect or network other devices.

IEEE An acronym for Institute of Electrical and Electronics Engineers, which is a non-profit organization composed of engineering and electronics professionals that are developing standards.

IEEE 1284 A parallel interface specification. The 1284 parallel standard supports a parallel port that can run in different modes: Enhanced Parallel Port (EPP) and Extended Capabilities Port (ECP).

Impact Printer A printer that operates by having the print wires take impact with the ribbon, which presses against the paper to create a character. A dot-matrix printer is an example of an impact printer.

Ink Jet Printer A type of printer that heats ink and sprays it onto the paper.

Input/Output Address See *I/O address*.

Interleaving A way of organizing the sectors on a disk to optimize performance of the disk.

Interrupt Request Also known as IRQ; a line that a device is given which allows it to interrupt the CPU.

I/O Address An address that a device is given which is unique to that device. The processor uses this address to send signals to the device.

IRQ See *Interrupt Request*.

ISA An acronym for Industry Standard Architecture; a 16-bit expansion bus architecture that runs at 8 MHz and is used to add expansion cards to the system.

L1 Cache Cache memory that is located on the processor and is used to store frequently used information.

L2 Cache Cache memory that is located outside the processor and is used to store frequently accessed information.

Local Bus A high-speed bus between devices and the processors. An example of a local bus is the PCI bus.

MB An acronym for megabyte; one million bytes of information.

MCA An acronym for Micro Channel Architecture, which is IBM's 32-bit expansion bus architecture.

Megahertz One million hertz, or cycles. Megahertz is a standard measurement of frequency for computer components.

Memory A component used to store information. Although the computer uses different types of memory, the term *memory* typically refers to RAM.

Microprocessor Also known as the processor; the focus of the computer and ultimately responsible for the computer's capabilities.

MMX An acronym for Multimedia Extensions. A processor with MMX contains 57 new instructions built into the chip that will enhance performance when dealing with multimedia data.

Modem A shortened version of Modulator/Demodulator; a communication device that converts a digital signal to analog when sending information over a phone line. On the receiving side, the modem converts the analog information to digital so that the computer can understand it.

Motherboard Also known as the system board; the main board that connects all computer components.

Multi-meter A testing device that can be used to measure voltage or resistance in electrical circuits.

Multitasking The ability to perform more than one task at a time.

NetBEUI A network protocol that allows computers to communicate with one another.

NetWare The network operating system manufactured by Novell that provides and manages resources to other computers on the network.

NTFS An acronym for New Technology File System; Windows NT and Windows 2000's native file system.

Ohm Meter An instrument that is used to measure resistance on a circuit.

OLE An acronym for Object Linking and Embedding; the standard for sharing of information between Windows applications.

Operating System The software that enables a user to communicate with hardware devices and computer resources, such as files.

Paging The process of taking information that has been temporarily stored on the hard disk in a swap file (pretend RAM) and moving it to true RAM.

Parallel Bi-directional communication that transmits data 8 bits at a time.

Partition A logical division or barrier built within a hard disk. Partitions are useful for organizing or segmenting data stored on the disk.

PC Card A general term used for an expansion card.

PCI An acronym for Peripheral Component Interconnect; local bus used on Pentium systems that runs at 33 MHz.

PCMCIA An acronym for Personal Computer Memory Card Industry Association; the expansion bus architecture used on laptop computers.

Pixel A small dot on a computer screen. Many pixels work together to make the image on the screen. The closer the pixels are, the finer the image.

Platter The actual media surface of a disk. The hard disk is made up of multiple platters that are used to store the data.

Plug-and-Play A technology that enables devices to be recognized automatically by the system and configures them with no user intervention.

PNP See *Plug-and-Play*.

POST An acronym for Power On Self Test; a built-in diagnostic that allows the system to check itself each time it is turned on.

Power Supply A device in the computer that supplies power to all other devices.

PROM An acronym for Programmable Read Only Memory; a type of memory that has been written to by the manufacturer.

Protected Mode A mode of operation that was introduced with the 80286 processor, which allows the operating system to run in its own protected area of memory from the rest of the applications. Protected mode processors also support virtual memory and multitasking environments.

Protocol A language that two computers use to communicate. Examples of protocols are NetBEUI and TCP/IP.

QIC An acronym for Quarter Inch Cartridge; a term associated with tape backup cartridges and devices.

RAID An acronym for Redundant Array of Inexpensive Disk; the standard for fault tolerance or duplication of data that is stored on hard drives used to prevent data loss.

RAM An acronym for Random Access Memory; a type of memory that needs constant refreshing. RAM is the most popular type of memory found in computers.

Real Mode A mode that older processors ran in that did not support multitasking, or running each application in its own address space. With real mode, there is no division of memory — it is treated as one entity.

Redirector A software component that redirects or sends a request out to an appropriate server on the network.

Registry The storage area in Windows for all of the computer configuration settings for hardware devices, applications, and user settings.

RISC An acronym for Reduced Instruction Set Chip; a term used for an integrated circuit in which the number of supported instructions is reduced. This allows for faster execution of the instructions because there are fewer of them to deal with.

ROM An acronym for Read-Only Memory; memory that can be read from but not written to.

Safe Mode A special mode in Windows that loads minimal device drivers to help restore the system to a working state.

Safe Recovery The option that you select when you continue a failed installation in Windows 9x.

SCSI An acronym for Small Computer System Interface; a technology that has a host adapter that manages devices connected to the host adapter.

SCSI Chain A series of SCSI devices connected to a SCSI controller.

SDRAM An acronym for Synchronous Dynamic RAM; a type of DRAM that synchronizes its transfer rate with the system's bus speed.

Sector An area on the disk that is 512 bytes in size. A sector is where data is written.

Serial A communication method that delivers one bit of information at a time.

SIMM An acronym for Single Inline Memory Module; a memory package that delivers data in 32-bit chunks and has 30 pins or 72 pins on the connector edge.

SmartDrive A disk caching application provided with DOS to allow faster access to data stored on disk.

SRAM An acronym for Static Random Access Memory; a type of memory that requires less refreshing than DRAM and is much quicker than DRAM. SRAM is typically used for cache memory.

SVGA An acronym for Super Video Graphics Adapter; a video adapter that supports higher resolution and colors than VGA.

Swap File A file on the hard disk that is used as pretend RAM, or virtual RAM.

Switch A special instruction on how a command should be executed.

Synchronous A communication method that involves clock pulses for timing of the conversation between two devices.

TCP/IP An acronym for Transmission Control Protocol/Internet Protocol; a suite of protocols that enables devices to communicate in dissimilar environments. It has become the protocol of the Internet.

Terminator A device that tells the SCSI controller that it has reached the end of a SCSI bus and that there are no more devices.

Thermal Printer A printer that uses heat to apply ink or wax to paper.

Toner Cartridge A cartridge found in laser printers and photocopiers that holds the toner that is used to create the image on paper.

Upper Memory The area of memory between 640K and 1MB.

USB An acronym for Universal Serial Bus; a serial bus that typically delivers information at 12 Mbps.

VESA An acronym for Video Electronics Standard Association; an association that developed a 32-bit bus architecture that was to be used for video cards.

VFAT An acronym for Virtual File Allocation Table; a copy of the FAT that is kept in memory so that applications can find files quickly and efficiently.

VGA An acronym for Video Graphics Adapter; video standard displaying a resolution of 640 × 480 and 256 colors.

Video Accelerator Card A video adapter with its own coprocessor to improve video display performance.

Virtual Memory The term used for pretend memory that is stored in the swap file on the hard disk.

Windows 9x The term used to represent both Windows 95 and Windows 98.

Windows 2000 The new secure network operating system and desktop operating system from Microsoft.

Windows NT Microsoft's original operating system that represented security and advanced technology such as RAID. Windows NT came in two flavors: Windows NT Server and Windows NT Workstation. Windows NT Server was the server operating system, while Windows NT Workstation was the secure desktop operating system.

Wizard A user-friendly method of performing a system task. The wizard is a screen that asks you questions on how you would like to perform a specific task and then performs the task for you.

Word Processor An application that is used to type documents such as letters or faxes.

Write Protect Tab A small sliding tab on a diskette that prevents changes from being made on the diskette.

ZIF Socket Short for Zero Insertion Force Socket; a type of socket used to hold the processor. The term ZIF comes from the fact that there is very little effort needed to remove the processor and insert a new one.

Index

Continued

Continued

Hungry Minds, Inc.
End-User License Agreement

READ THIS. You should carefully read these terms and conditions before opening the software packet(s) included with this book ("Book"). This is a license agreement ("Agreement") between you and Hungry Minds, Inc. ("HMI"). By opening the accompanying software packet(s), you acknowledge that you have read and accept the following terms and conditions. If you do not agree and do not want to be bound by such terms and conditions, promptly return the Book and the unopened software packet(s) to the place you obtained them for a full refund.

1. **License Grant.** HMI grants to you (either an individual or entity) a nonexclusive license to use one copy of the enclosed software program(s) (collectively, the "Software") solely for your own personal or business purposes on a single computer (whether a standard computer or a workstation component of a multi-user network). The Software is in use on a computer when it is loaded into temporary memory (RAM) or installed into permanent memory (hard disk, CD-ROM, or other storage device). HMI reserves all rights not expressly granted herein.

2. **Ownership.** HMI is the owner of all right, title, and interest, including copyright, in and to the compilation of the Software recorded on the disk(s) or CD-ROM ("Software Media"). Copyright to the individual programs recorded on the Software Media is owned by the author or other authorized copyright owner of each program. Ownership of the Software and all proprietary rights relating thereto remain with HMI and its licensers.

3. **Restrictions On Use and Transfer.**

   (a) You may only (i) make one copy of the Software for backup or archival purposes, or (ii) transfer the Software to a single hard disk, provided that you keep the original for backup or archival purposes. You may not (i) rent or lease the Software, (ii) copy or reproduce the Software through a LAN or other network system or through any computer subscriber system or bulletin-board system, or (iii) modify, adapt, or create derivative works based on the Software.

   (b) You may not reverse engineer, decompile, or disassemble the Software. You may transfer the Software and user documentation on a permanent basis, provided that the transferee agrees to accept the terms and conditions of this Agreement and you retain no copies. If the Software is an update or has been updated, any transfer must include the most recent update and all prior versions.

4. Restrictions on Use of Individual Programs. You must follow the individual requirements and restrictions detailed for each individual program in Appendix A of this Book. These limitations are also contained in the individual license agreements recorded on the Software Media. These limitations may include a requirement that after using the program for a specified period of time, the user must pay a registration fee or discontinue use. By opening the Software packet(s), you will be agreeing to abide by the licenses and restrictions for these individual programs that are detailed in Appendix A and on the Software Media. None of the material on this Software Media or listed in this Book may ever be redistributed, in original or modified form, for commercial purposes.

5. Limited Warranty.

(a) HMI warrants that the Software and Software Media are free from defects in materials and workmanship under normal use for a period of sixty (60) days from the date of purchase of this Book. If HMI receives notification within the warranty period of defects in materials or workmanship, HMI will replace the defective Software Media.

(b) **HMI AND THE AUTHOR OF THE BOOK DISCLAIM ALL OTHER WARRANTIES, EXPRESS OR IMPLIED, INCLUDING WITHOUT LIMITATION IMPLIED WARRANTIES OF MERCHANTABILITY AND FITNESS FOR A PARTICULAR PURPOSE, WITH RESPECT TO THE SOFTWARE, THE PROGRAMS, THE SOURCE CODE CONTAINED THEREIN, AND/OR THE TECHNIQUES DESCRIBED IN THIS BOOK. HMI DOES NOT WARRANT THAT THE FUNCTIONS CONTAINED IN THE SOFTWARE WILL MEET YOUR REQUIREMENTS OR THAT THE OPERATION OF THE SOFTWARE WILL BE ERROR FREE.**

(c) This limited warranty gives you specific legal rights, and you may have other rights that vary from jurisdiction to jurisdiction.

6. Remedies.

(a) HMI's entire liability and your exclusive remedy for defects in materials and workmanship shall be limited to replacement of the Software Media, which may be returned to HMI with a copy of your receipt at the following address: Software Media Fulfillment Department, Attn.: *A+ Certification Bible*, Hungry Minds, Inc., 10475 Crosspoint Blvd., Indianapolis, IN 46256, or call 1-800-762-2974. Please allow four to six weeks for delivery. This Limited Warranty is void if failure of the Software Media has resulted from accident, abuse, or misapplication. Any replacement Software Media will be warranted for the remainder of the original warranty period or thirty (30) days, whichever is longer.

(b) In no event shall HMI or the author be liable for any damages whatso-ever (including without limitation damages for loss of business profits, business interruption, loss of business information, or any other pecu-niary loss) arising from the use of or inability to use the Book or the Software, even if HMI has been advised of the possibility of such damages.

(c) Because some jurisdictions do not allow the exclusion or limitation of liability for consequential or incidental damages, the above limitation or exclusion may not apply to you.

7. **U.S. Government Restricted Rights.** Use, duplication, or disclosure of the Software for or on behalf of the United States of America, its agencies and/or instrumentalities (the "U.S. Government") is subject to restrictions as stated in paragraph (c)(1)(ii) of the Rights in Technical Data and Computer Software clause of DFARS 252.227-7013, or subparagraphs (c) (1) and (2) of the Commercial Computer Software - Restricted Rights clause at FAR 52.227-19, and in similar clauses in the NASA FAR supplement, as applicable.

8. **General.** This Agreement constitutes the entire understanding of the parties and revokes and supersedes all prior agreements, oral or written, between them and may not be modified or amended except in a writing signed by both parties hereto that specifically refers to this Agreement. This Agreement shall take precedence over any other documents that may be in conflict herewith. If any one or more provisions contained in this Agreement are held by any court or tribunal to be invalid, illegal, or otherwise unenforceable, each and every other provision shall remain in full force and effect.

CD-ROM Installation Instructions

Each software item on the *A+ Certification Bible* CD-ROM is located in its own folder. To install a particular piece of software, open its folder with My Computer or Internet Explorer. What you do next depends on what you find in the software's folder:

1. First, look for a `ReadMe.txt` file or a `.doc` or `.htm` document. If this is present, it should contain installation instructions and other useful information.

2. If the folder contains an executable (`.exe`) file, this is usually an installation program. Often it will be called `Setup.exe` or `Install.exe`, but in some cases the filename reflects an abbreviated version of the software's name and version number. Run the `.exe` file to start the installation process.

The `ReadMe.txt` file in the CD-ROM's root directory may contain additional installation information, so be sure to check it.

For a listing of the software on the CD-ROM, see Appendix A.